Great Britain
Northern Ireland
AZ Road Atlas

Motorway Junctions

Details of motorway junctions with limited interchange.......VII

Junction	M67	
1	Eastbound	Access from A57 eastbound only
	Westbound	Exit to A57 westbound only
1a	Eastbound	No access, exit to A6017 only
	Westbound	No exit, access from A6017 only
2	Eastbound	No exit, access from A57 only
	Westbound	No access, exit to A57 only

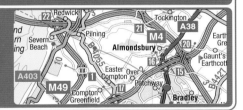

Over 32,000 Index References

A	
	Abingdon-on-Thames. *Oxon* ....
Abbas Combe. *Som* 3F 8	Abinger Common. *Surr* ....
Abberley. *Worc* 5F 26	Abinger Hammer. *Surr* ....
Abberley Common.	Abington. *S Lan* ....
Worc 5F 26	Abington Pigotts. *Cambs* ..
Abberton. *Essx* 2G 23	Ab Kettleby. *Leics* ......
Abberton. *Worc* 6H 27	Ab Lench. *Worc* ....
Abberwick. *Nmbd* 8J 61	Ablington. *Glos* ....
Abbess Roding. *Essx* ..2B 22	Ablington. *Wilts* ....
Abbey. *Devn* 4L 7	Abney. *Derbs* ....
	Aboyne. *Abers* ....

Including cities, towns, villages, hamlets and locations.......120-143

EDITION 35 2021

Copyright © Geographers' A-Z Map Company Ltd.

www./az.co.uk

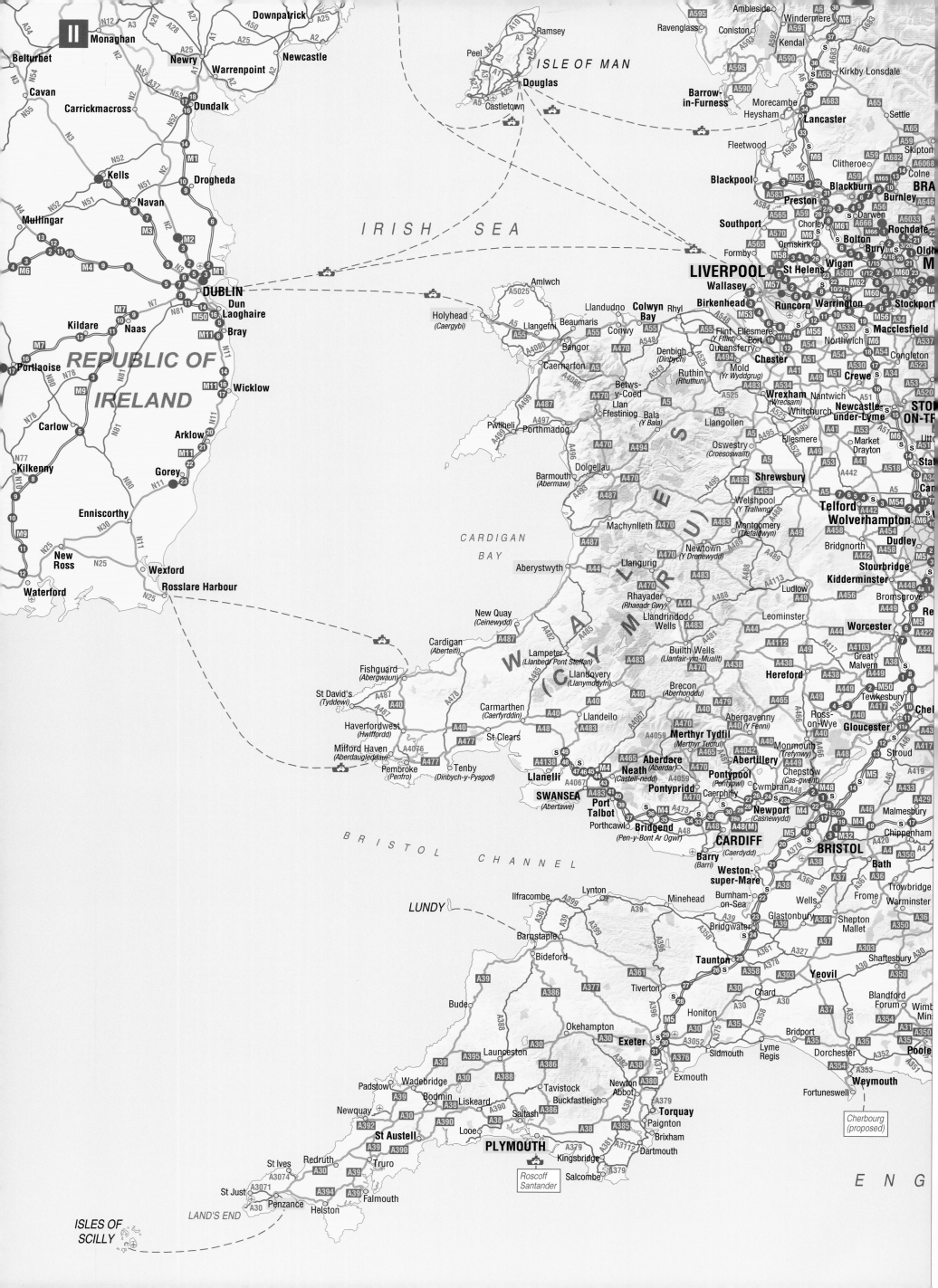

REFERENCE

MOTORWAY WITH NUMBER	M4 S Service Area
MOTORWAY (Under Construction / Proposed)	
MOTORWAY JUNCTIONS	5 7 Limited
PRIMARY ROUTE	A5
A ROAD	A272
NATIONAL BOUNDARY	
TOWNS SHOWN IN THE MILEAGE CHART	NORWICH

SCALE

0   10   20   30 Miles
0   10   20   30   40 Kilometres

NORTH SEA

ENGLAND

THE WASH

ENGLISH CHANNEL

FRANCE

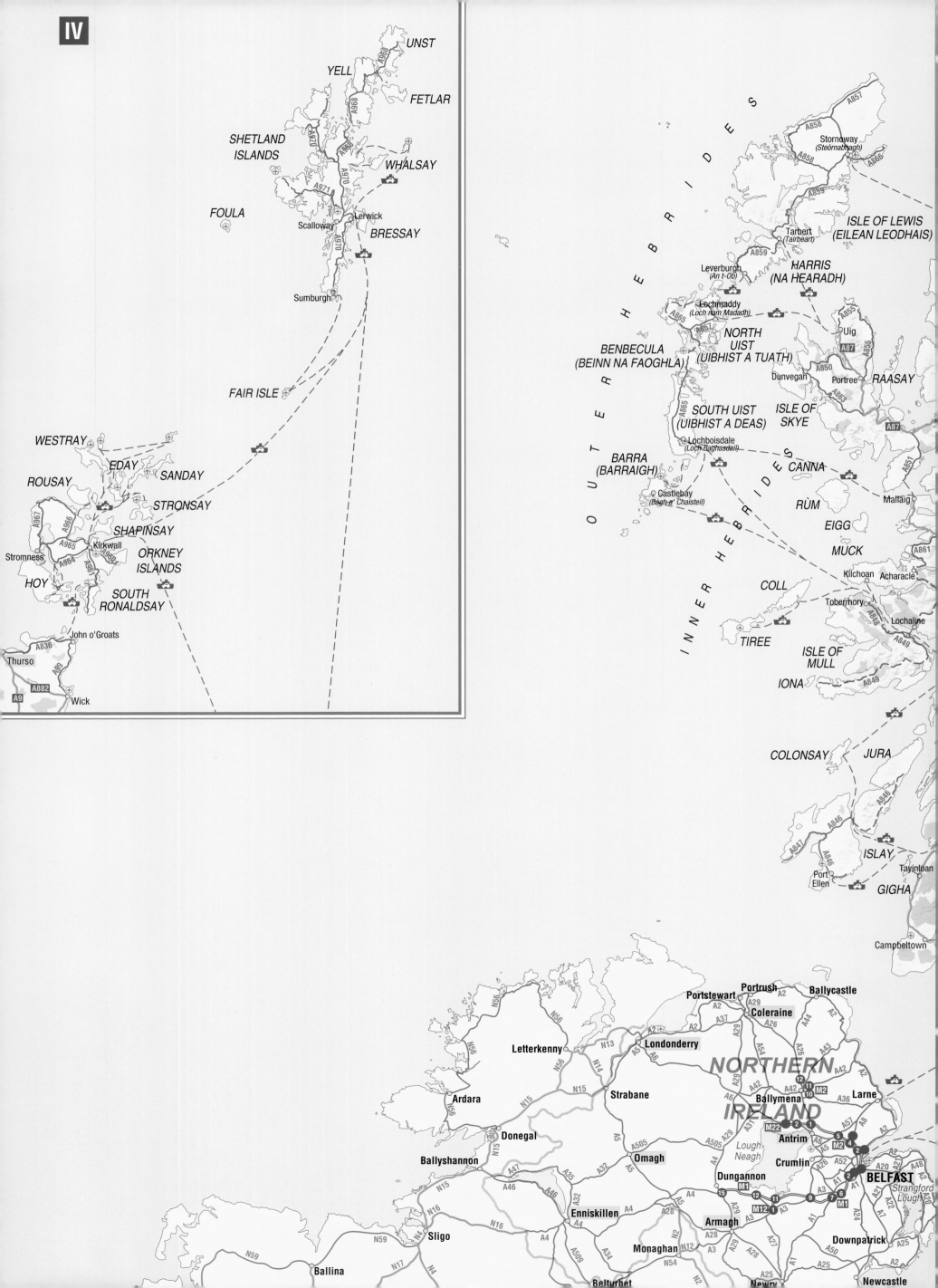

NORTH SEA

SCOTLAND

Stromness
John o'Groats
Scrabster
Thurso
Wick
Tongue
Scourie
Lochinver
Helmsdale
Lairg
Bonar Bridge
Tain
Ullapool
Poolewe
Cromarty
Lossiemouth
Fraserburgh
Banff
Kinlochewe
Dingwall
Nairn
Elgin
Keith
Peterhead
Shieldaig
Achnasheen
Inverness
Strathcarron
Dufftown
Huntly
Kyle of Lochalsh
(Caol Loch Ailse)
Grantown-on-Spey
Oldmeldrum
Inverurie
Invermoriston
Loch Ness
Aviemore
Peterculter
ABERDEEN
Invergarry
Newtonmore
Spean Bridge
Braemar
Ballater
Banchory
Stonehaven
Fort William
Glencoe
Pitlochry
Brechin
Montrose
Blairgowrie
Forfar
Dunkeld
Oban
Crianlarich
Crieff
Dundee
Arbroath
Carnoustie
Perth
St Andrews
Loch Lomond
Doune
Dunblane
Kinross
Glenrothes
Pittenweem
Inveraray
Stirling
Dunfermline
Cowdenbeath
Kirkcaldy
Firth of Forth
North Berwick
Lochgilphead
GLASGOW
Falkirk
EDINBURGH
Dunbar
Dunoon
Clydebank
Airdrie
Livingston
Musselburgh
Eyemouth
Greenock
Paisley
Dalkeith
Hamilton
Motherwell
Penicuik
Duns
Berwick-upon-Tweed
Rothesay
East Kilbride
Lauder
Kennacraig
ISLE OF BUTE
Largs
Peebles
Galashiels
Coldstream
Ardrossan
Irvine
Biggar
Selkirk
Kelso
Wooler
Brodick
Troon
Kilmarnock
Hawick
Jedburgh
ISLE OF ARRAN
Prestwick
Ayr
Cumnock
Alnwick
Girvan
Sanquhar
Moffat
Amble
New Galloway
Ashington
Newton Stewart
Lockerbie
Langholm
Morpeth
Blyth
Stranraer
Dumfries
Annan
Brampton
NEWCASTLE UPON TYNE
Whitley Bay
Amsterdam
Tynemouth
Castle Douglas
Dalbeattie
South Shields
Whithorn
Carlisle
Corbridge
Gateshead
Washington
Kirkcudbright
Hexham
Consett
SUNDERLAND
Seaham
Durham
Peterlee
Alston
HARTLEPOOL
Workington
Cockermouth
Penrith
Bishop Auckland
STOCKTON-ON-TEES
Whitehaven
Keswick
Brough
Barnard Castle
MIDDLESBROUGH
Whitby
Egremont
Darlington
Richmond
Ravenglass
Ambleside
Coniston
Windermere
Kendal
Catterick
Northallerton
Thirsk
Peel
Ramsey
ISLE OF MAN
Leyburn
Scarborough

NORTH SEA

Moray Firth
Solway Firth

Mileage Chart and Journey Times

This chart shows the distance in miles and journey time between two cities or towns in Great Britain. Each route has been calculated using a combination of motorways, primary routes and other major roads. This is normally the quickest, though not always the shortest route.

Average journey times are calculated whilst driving at the maximum speed limit. These times are approximate and do not include traffic congestion or convenience breaks.

To find the distance and journey time between two cities or towns, follow a horizontal line and vertical column until they meet each other.

For example, the 285 mile journey from London to Penzance is approximately 4 hours and 59 minutes.

Northern Ireland

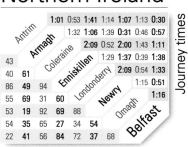

Journey times

	Armagh	Coleraine	Enniskillen	Londonderry	Newry	Omagh	Belfast
Antrim	1:01	0:53	1:41	1:14	1:07	1:13	0:30
Armagh		1:32	1:06	1:39	0:31	0:46	0:57
Coleraine			2:09	0:52	2:00	1:43	1:11
Enniskillen				1:29	1:37	0:39	1:38
Londonderry					2:09	0:54	1:33
Newry						1:15	0:51
Omagh							1:16

Distance in miles

	Antrim	Armagh	Coleraine	Enniskillen	Londonderry	Newry	Omagh
Armagh	43						
Coleraine	40	61					
Enniskillen	86	49	94				
Londonderry	55	69	31	60			
Newry	53	19	92	69	88		
Omagh	54	35	65	27	34	54	
Belfast	22	41	56	84	72	37	68

Belfast to London = 440m / 9:46h (excluding ferry)
Belfast to Glasgow = 104m / 4:46h (excluding ferry)

Great Britain

Journey times

	Aberystwyth	Ayr	Birmingham	Bradford	Brighton	Bristol	Cambridge	Cardiff	Carlisle	Coventry	Derby	Doncaster	Dover	Edinburgh	Exeter	Fort William	Glasgow	Gloucester	Harwich	Holyhead	Inverness	Ipswich	Kendal	Kingston upon Hull	Leeds	Leicester	Lincoln	Liverpool	Manchester	Middlesbrough	Newcastle upon Tyne	Norwich	Nottingham	Oxford	Penzance	Perth	Plymouth	Portsmouth	Reading	Salisbury	Sheffield	Shrewsbury	Southampton	Southend-on-Sea	Stoke-on-Trent	Swansea	Thurso	Worcester	York	London
Aberdeen	8:21	3:31	7:13	6:28	9:56	8:26	8:15	8:55	4:08	7:27	7:09	6:25	10:16	2:39	9:38	3:38	2:50	7:55	9:32	7:41	2:30	9:08	4:55	6:51	6:16	7:40	7:07	6:13	6:01	5:16	4:39	9:18	7:14	8:18	11:22	1:48	10:16	9:33	8:57	9:21	6:42	7:07	9:25	9:22	6:28	9:31	4:52	7:35	6:07	9:03
Aberystwyth		6:34	2:34	3:27	5:21	2:44	4:00	2:29	4:24	2:52	2:56	3:45	5:41	6:20	3:51	8:13	5:53	2:34	5:17	2:29	8:39	4:53	3:40	4:20	3:29	3:18	4:11	2:39	2:54	4:34	5:07	5:03	3:17	3:43	5:35	6:41	4:29	4:27	3:50	4:01	3:41	1:47	4:18	4:56	2:48	1:48	11:00	2:19	4:00	4:28
Ayr			5:28	4:28	8:11	6:42	6:31	7:10	2:24	5:43	5:25	4:41	8:32	1:48	7:54	3:03	0:48	6:11	7:48	5:56	3:51	7:24	3:10	5:06	4:32	5:55	5:22	4:29	4:16	3:56	3:28	7:34	5:29	6:34	9:37	1:53	8:31	7:49	7:13	7:37	4:57	5:23	7:40	7:37	4:43	7:46	6:12	5:50	4:22	7:16
Birmingham				2:15	3:04	1:41	1:43	2:09	3:16	0:36	1:01	1:40	3:25	5:12	2:53	7:05	4:45	1:10	3:01	2:59	7:31	2:37	2:32	2:21	2:05	1:01	1:55	1:49	1:46	2:55	3:28	2:46	1:08	1:27	4:36	5:33	3:30	2:42	2:06	2:39	1:36	0:59	2:33	2:39	1:02	2:44	9:52	0:49	2:21	2:11
Bradford					4:30	3:34	2:43	4:03	2:17	2:19	1:34	0:53	4:37	4:17	4:46	6:06	3:46	3:03	4:01	2:49	6:31	3:37	1:32	1:18	0:28	2:02	1:35	1:22	0:57	1:32	2:06	3:46	1:37	3:05	6:29	4:33	5:24	4:20	3:44	4:18	1:00	2:15	4:12	3:50	1:36	4:38	8:52	2:42	0:59	3:32
Brighton						2:49	2:09	3:26	6:00	2:42	3:15	3:53	1:53	7:53	3:41	9:49	7:29	2:47	2:19	5:39	10:14	2:20	5:15	4:35	4:19	2:57	3:43	4:32	4:29	5:08	5:42	3:05	3:21	1:58	5:24	8:16	4:18	1:14	1:39	1:54	3:49	3:45	1:35	1:41	3:45	4:01	12:35	3:07	4:35	1:27
Bristol							3:02	0:56	4:31	1:44	2:21	2:59	3:18	6:27	1:37	8:20	6:00	0:47	3:27	4:13	8:45	3:28	3:46	3:41	3:25	2:17	3:11	3:03	3:01	4:15	4:48	3:58	2:28	1:30	3:20	6:48	2:14	2:03	1:26	1:37	2:56	2:14	1:54	2:58	2:17	1:30	11:07	1:07	3:41	2:07
Cambridge								3:28	4:20	1:30	1:52	2:03	2:06	6:04	4:11	8:09	5:49	2:29	1:28	4:20	8:35	1:04	3:56	2:37	2:34	1:25	1:47	3:12	3:10	3:19	3:52	1:13	1:41	1:55	5:54	6:37	4:49	2:34	1:51	2:47	2:15	2:26	2:35	1:19	2:26	4:03	10:56	2:08	2:45	1:17
Cardiff									4:58	2:15	2:48	3:27	3:54	6:54	2:02	8:47	6:27	1:16	4:03	4:23	9:13	4:03	4:14	4:09	3:53	2:46	3:39	3:31	3:28	4:42	5:16	4:31	2:55	2:05	3:46	7:15	2:40	2:38	2:01	2:12	3:23	2:24	2:29	3:33	2:44	0:53	11:34	1:35	4:09	2:43
Carlisle										3:30	3:12	2:28	6:19	2:08	5:41	4:01	1:41	3:58	5:35	3:44	4:27	5:11	0:58	2:54	2:19	3:43	3:10	2:16	2:04	1:44	1:15	5:21	3:17	4:21	7:25	2:29	6:19	5:36	5:00	5:24	2:45	3:10	5:28	5:25	2:31	5:34	6:48	3:38	2:10	5:07
Coventry											1:03	1:41	3:05	5:29	2:55	7:22	5:02	1:12	2:49	3:13	7:48	2:21	2:49	2:23	2:06	0:45	1:39	2:06	2:03	2:56	3:30	2:31	1:09	1:04	4:38	5:50	3:32	2:19	1:43	2:17	1:37	1:18	2:11	2:20	1:19	2:49	10:09	0:56	2:22	1:53
Derby												0:57	3:33	4:58	3:31	7:02	4:42	1:48	3:09	2:52	7:27	2:45	2:28	1:39	1:23	0:49	1:24	1:45	1:42	2:13	2:46	2:55	0:33	1:51	5:14	5:29	4:08	3:06	2:30	3:04	0:54	1:21	2:58	2:48	0:53	3:22	9:49	1:27	1:39	2:19
Doncaster													3:58	4:13	4:12	6:19	3:59	2:30	3:21	3:17	6:44	2:57	2:16	0:56	0:43	1:27	0:55	1:48	1:25	1:28	2:02	3:07	1:02	2:30	5:56	4:46	4:50	3:45	3:09	3:43	0:30	2:13	3:36	3:11	1:44	4:04	9:05	2:09	0:54	2:57
Dover														7:56	4:14	10:08	7:48	3:16	2:16	5:59	10:34	2:17	5:35	4:29	4:26	3:14	3:40	4:52	4:49	5:11	5:45	3:02	3:34	2:27	5:57	8:36	4:51	2:23	2:08	2:50	4:06	4:05	2:38	1:37	4:05	4:29	12:55	3:36	4:38	1:34
Edinburgh															7:38	3:01	1:05	5:55	7:20	5:41	3:02	6:56	2:55	4:38	4:04	5:26	4:54	4:13	4:00	3:00	2:23	7:06	5:01	6:18	9:21	1:02	8:16	7:33	6:57	7:21	4:29	5:07	7:25	7:09	4:28	7:30	5:24	5:34	3:54	6:57
Exeter																9:31	7:11	1:58	4:36	5:24	9:56	4:37	4:57	4:52	4:36	3:28	4:22	4:14	4:12	5:26	5:59	5:07	3:39	2:46	1:54	7:59	0:53	2:38	2:43	1:55	4:07	3:25	2:27	4:02	3:28	2:37	12:18	2:18	4:52	3:16
Fort William																	2:26	7:49	9:26	7:35	1:32	9:02	4:49	6:44	6:10	7:34	7:00	6:07	5:54	5:34	5:06	9:12	7:07	8:12	11:15	2:09	10:10	9:27	8:51	9:15	6:35	7:01	9:19	9:16	6:22	9:24	4:04	7:28	6:01	8:56
Glasgow																		5:28	7:05	5:13	3:08	6:41	2:28	4:23	3:49	5:12	4:39	3:46	3:33	3:13	2:45	6:51	4:46	5:51	8:54	1:10	7:48	7:06	6:30	6:54	4:14	4:40	6:57	6:55	4:01	7:03	5:29	5:07	3:40	6:36
Gloucester																			3:25	3:42	8:14	3:22	3:15	3:10	2:54	1:46	2:39	2:32	2:29	3:43	4:17	3:31	1:56	1:11	3:39	6:16	2:33	2:00	1:24	1:42	2:24	1:42	1:52	2:56	1:45	1:49	10:35	0:36	3:10	2:05
Harwich																				5:38	9:53	0:42	5:13	3:55	3:52	2:43	3:05	4:30	4:28	4:37	5:10	1:32	2:59	2:26	6:20	7:55	5:14	2:49	2:17	3:12	3:33	3:44	3:01	1:09	3:44	4:38	12:14	3:26	4:03	1:42
Holyhead																					7:58	5:16	2:59	3:39	2:49	3:23	3:52	1:53	2:13	3:53	4:26	5:25	3:15	4:06	7:06	6:00	6:00	5:21	4:45	5:05	3:06	2:10	5:12	5:18	2:11	4:33	10:19	3:19	3:19	4:47
Inverness																						9:27	5:14	7:10	6:35	7:59	7:26	6:32	6:20	5:41	5:04	9:37	7:33	8:37	11:41	2:10	10:35	9:52	9:16	9:40	7:01	7:26	9:44	9:41	6:47	9:50	2:31	7:54	6:26	9:21
Ipswich																							4:50	3:31	3:28	2:20	2:41	4:06	4:04	4:13	4:46	1:08	2:35	2:27	6:21	7:31	5:15	2:50	2:18	3:13	3:09	3:20	3:02	1:10	3:20	4:39	11:50	3:02	3:39	1:43
Kendal																								2:44	1:53	3:02	3:00	1:36	1:23	1:38	1:59	5:00	2:54	3:41	6:44	3:13	5:38	4:56	4:20	4:44	2:22	2:30	4:47	4:53	1:50	4:53	7:32	2:57	2:04	4:22
Kingston upon Hull																									1:08	2:08	0:58	2:13	1:49	1:54	2:27	3:18	1:43	3:10	6:36	5:12	5:30	4:25	3:49	4:23	1:11	2:53	4:17	3:43	2:25	4:44	9:31	2:49	1:02	3:39
Leeds																										1:53	1:25	1:23	0:58	1:20	1:53	3:37	1:27	2:55	6:21	4:38	5:15	4:10	3:34	4:08	0:50	2:16	4:02	3:40	1:37	4:29	8:57	2:34	0:46	3:23
Leicester																											1:16	2:17	2:14	2:42	3:15	2:27	0:46	1:32	5:11	6:01	4:05	2:47	2:11	2:45	1:23	1:43	2:39	2:29	1:24	3:20	10:20	1:25	2:08	2:01
Lincoln																												2:31	2:02	2:11	2:44	2:20	0:59	2:28	6:07	5:29	5:01	3:43	3:07	3:41	1:07	2:33	3:34	2:54	2:10	4:16	9:48	2:21	1:35	2:51
Liverpool																													0:48	2:28	3:01	4:16	2:10	2:56	6:00	4:33	4:54	4:11	3:35	3:59	1:52	1:25	4:03	4:09	1:06	3:48	8:53	2:13	1:54	3:39
Manchester																														2:03	2:36	4:12	1:51	2:52	5:55	4:22	4:49	4:07	3:30	3:55	1:14	1:41	3:58	4:04	1:01	4:04	8:41	2:08	1:29	3:37
Middlesbrough																															0:55	4:20	2:15	3:43	7:09	3:40	6:03	4:58	4:22	4:56	1:43	3:20	4:50	4:24	2:40	5:17	8:02	3:22	1:05	4:12
Newcastle upon Tyne																																4:54	2:49	4:17	7:43	3:03	6:37	5:32	4:56	5:30	2:17	3:54	5:24	4:58	3:14	5:51	7:25	3:56	1:43	4:46
Norwich																																	2:44	2:58	6:51	7:40	5:45	3:31	2:48	3:43	3:18	3:29	3:32	2:00	3:28	5:06	11:59	3:10	3:48	2:13
Nottingham																																		1:57	5:23	5:34	4:17	3:12	2:36	3:10	0:57	1:44	3:04	2:49	1:18	3:31	9:53	1:36	1:42	2:25
Oxford																																			4:30	6:40	3:24	1:28	0:45	1:25	2:25	2:08	1:19	1:56	2:09	2:40	10:59	1:31	3:10	1:15
Penzance																																				9:43	1:41	4:22	4:27	3:39	5:51	5:09	4:11	5:46	5:12	4:20	14:02	4:02	6:36	4:59
Perth																																					8:37	7:54	7:18	7:42	5:03	5:28	7:46	7:43	4:49	7:52	4:30	5:55	4:28	7:24
Plymouth																																						3:16	3:20	2:32	4:44	4:02	3:04	4:39	4:05	3:14	12:55	2:55	5:29	3:54
Portsmouth																																							1:18	0:52	3:39	3:23	0:32	2:11	3:23	3:13	12:13	2:20	4:25	1:39
Reading																																								1:22	3:01	2:45	1:09	1:46	2:45	2:37	11:35	1:44	3:47	0:56
Salisbury																																									3:37	3:09	0:40	2:37	3:12	2:47	12:02	2:02	4:22	1:52
Sheffield																																										2:08	3:32	3:22	1:40	3:59	9:22	2:04	1:11	2:53
Shrewsbury																																											3:16	3:22	1:04	2:45	9:46	1:23	2:46	2:53
Southampton																																												2:26	3:15	3:05	12:05	2:12	4:16	1:40
Southend-on-Sea																																													3:21	4:09	12:02	3:03	3:51	1:07
Stoke-on-Trent																																														3:18	9:08	1:23	2:09	2:53
Swansea																																															12:11	2:10	4:44	3:18
Thurso																																																10:15	8:47	11:43
Worcester																																																	2:49	2:24
York																																																		3:39

Distance in miles

	Aberdeen	Aberystwyth	Ayr	Birmingham	Bradford	Brighton	Bristol	Cambridge	Cardiff	Carlisle	Coventry	Derby	Doncaster	Dover	Edinburgh	Exeter	Fort William	Glasgow	Gloucester	Harwich	Holyhead	Inverness	Ipswich	Kendal	Kingston upon Hull	Leeds	Leicester	Lincoln	Liverpool	Manchester	Middlesbrough	Newcastle upon Tyne	Norwich	Nottingham	Oxford	Penzance	Perth	Plymouth	Portsmouth	Reading	Salisbury	Sheffield	Shrewsbury	Southampton	Southend-on-Sea	Stoke-on-Trent	Swansea	Thurso	Worcester	York
Aberystwyth	471
Ayr	181	324
Birmingham	423	114	272
Bradford	377	159	196	124
Brighton	596	258	441	169	263
Bristol	505	122	375	88	215	129
Cambridge	487	198	366	102	156	117	167
Cardiff	525	106	377	106	233	168	42	201
Carlisle	229	232	89	183	107	345	286	256	288
Coventry	442	134	297	18	124	157	102	84	129	200
Derby	418	137	269	41	88	188	134	99	159	180	43
Doncaster	371	192	239	95	40	232	184	117	210	150	94	57
Dover	620	315	477	195	284	81	194	118	233	393	180	208	244
Edinburgh	126	340	75	284	198	466	377	326	379	91	303	266	212	444
Exeter	581	199	425	161	282	170	75	323	107	336	166	213	257	244	439
Fort William	159	430	136	391	305	568	478	456	486	198	415	387	345	591	131	549
Glasgow	146	322	36	291	203	468	378	355	384	96	313	282	245	491	46	449	100
Gloucester	473	109	317	53	171	152	35	132	53	228	59	93	149	189	331	107	435	324
Harwich	568	258	411	170	224	130	203	64	234	323	152	167	185	129	397	262	524	419	171
Holyhead	452	96	315	151	158	330	204	252	209	226	167	156	169	358	316	279	423	323	189	331
Inverness	105	492	198	449	353	620	536	490	558	260	458	421	369	601	157	607	63	162	496	554	481
Ipswich	538	268	420	156	210	125	206	54	240	311	138	155	171	127	381	264	510	409	177	21	307	538
Kendal	280	182	139	151	62	324	235	215	232	50	170	136	99	344	141	307	248	146	200	279	180	310	268
Kingston upon Hull	398	235	255	139	68	243	228	134	239	165	123	94	37	254	230	290	367	255	195	204	218	387	189	127
Leeds	359	171	198	119	9	256	209	144	226	111	117	74	32	275	190	279	309	208	167	217	162	345	197	72	60
Leicester	445	155	294	43	99	163	118	70	140	214	24	30	73	183	282	189	412	312	83	146	182	431	125	166	98	97
Lincoln	411	208	249	87	80	207	170	88	192	178	76	53	41	206	247	241	376	274	135	152	204	402	124	140	46	72	52
Liverpool	354	120	199	99	67	267	180	179	169	110	113	90	89	294	201	240	308	213	142	265	95	370	236	75	126	73	110	118
Manchester	349	128	204	87	37	252	167	159	188	117	99	58	51	273	208	239	315	215	132	230	120	363	211	72	96	42	95	87	34
Middlesbrough	289	233	181	174	69	316	265	196	287	92	175	130	84	316	147	337	279	192	230	266	226	306	253	77	88	64	154	127	134	106
Newcastle upon Tyne	252	266	146	209	98	345	300	232	312	58	209	165	115	350	104	369	237	153	263	297	257	263	287	88	130	96	188	153	167	136	40
Norwich	536	270	348	163	185	174	234	62	256	280	142	146	142	169	351	284	478	378	193	72	289	505	44	249	145	178	112	103	222	177	221	252
Nottingham	416	155	267	54	78	191	140	84	165	188	52	15	48	210	256	218	386	286	108	165	177	410	140	141	92	72	27	37	107	68	128	159	118
Oxford	497	151	335	68	167	106	73	92	106	267	57	101	138	142	358	151	465	365	47	134	208	515	128	223	175	162	76	123	168	157	218	253	159	104
Penzance	688	301	552	269	394	279	184	343	218	463	278	316	369	355	551	109	663	561	217	374	388	715	375	419	412	391	310	359	353	344	449	481	393	323	261
Perth	86	366	85	336	245	509	412	370	422	134	346	309	254	485	43	487	103	59	362	439	360	113	424	184	273	233	326	290	244	254	191	148	394	299	404	598
Plymouth	619	232	461	203	325	206	111	274	159	372	209	254	300	286	485	43	592	490	150	305	322	648	305	348	326	323	231	284	299	281	379	412	327	255	193	75	529
Portsmouth	579	231	440	147	274	50	95	132	138	357	132	184	231	137	448	127	555	455	114	161	303	603	158	308	268	245	166	209	254	237	315	360	200	191	83	235	486	170
Reading	538	180	399	103	213	79	77	90	112	309	90	138	184	115	402	141	506	406	75	129	264	554	126	263	209	207	113	168	193	197	264	295	152	129	25	251	445	184	60
Salisbury	538	178	383	121	245	82	53	140	101	312	113	159	207	158	400	91	510	408	73	177	262	569	177	265	251	230	132	187	213	208	287	318	200	162	65	201	443	132	43	57
Sheffield	390	173	235	79	40	225	163	121	193	154	75	35	21	268	230	245	352	250	139	185	164	387	176	102	66	33	68	46	74	40	102	133	144	37	137	361	273	293	228	160	203
Shrewsbury	419	73	260	47	100	216	116	140	107	171	64	67	114	249	262	175	369	267	77	215	104	424	195	125	163	102	79	123	59	67	166	203	196	86	105	286	309	218	195	147	150	85
Southampton	564	213	401	128	235	64	75	129	122	330	114	167	201	150	433	106	528	426	98	157	287	590	162	276	249	230	136	189	235	215	288	320	190	162	66	217	476	149	20	47	23	206	175
Southend-on-Sea	549	258	431	152	220	85	177	64	211	342	129	168	185	89	395	226	548	438	152	57	303	549	57	283	200	213	139	156	255	225	262	299	99	160	105	337	439	269	117	98	132	197	173	126
Stoke-on-Trent	381	108	243	47	75	217	127	137	140	150	64	36	74	236	241	202	348	248	95	201	122	410	179	121	117	78	55	87	56	36	142	173	171	55	118	311	287	241	201	147	168	50	35	183	199
Swansea	529	76	368	124	220	209	80	236	41	279	150	184	244	264	370	154	477	375	91	279	172	578	279	249	262	229	174	226	168	187	293	323	286	178	144	266	446	196	175	147	136	202	124	159	245	159
Thurso	212	584	304	557	461	728	644	589	640	352	552	529	475	706	262	715	169	268	604	657	589	108	654	402	492	453	544	510	463	471	410	367	613	519	621	823	220	758	709	662	664	506	523	682	659	502	631
Worcester	448	96	309	29	135	162	62	119	73	220	46	68	124	197	306	136	418	311	28	168	151	480	174	169	166	146	72	118	108	101	203	229	180	85	57	244	350	177	146	95	101	103	49	124	150	65	97	572
York	345	193	201	129	34	269	227	151	237	116	129	84	33	269	187	289	314	214	181	232	185	344	200	81	38	24	108	76	96	65	48	83	176	84	174	400	230	331	257	217	244	54	132	244	214	114	268	450	164
London	537	228	440	118	203	53	118	61	151	309	97	129	171	76	403	179	511	404	116	86	277	562	82	263	214	195	103	155	211	209	251	283	117	128	59	285	451	216	84	41	92	166	161	82	43	161	187	669	136	211

Scales to Map Pages

BRITAIN
1:221,760 = 3.5 miles to 1 inch (2.54 cm)
2.2 km to 1 cm

0 1 2 3 4 5 10 15 20 25 Miles
0 1 2 3 4 5 10 15 20 25 30 35 40 Kilometres

NORTHERN IRELAND
1:380,160 = 6 miles to 1 inch (2.54 cm)
3.8 km to 1 cm

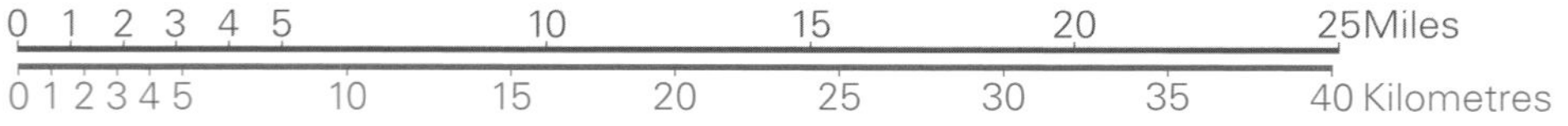

0 1 2 3 4 5 10 15 20 25Miles
0 1 2 3 4 5 10 15 20 25 30 35 40 Kilometres

Limited Interchange Motorway Junctions are shown on the mapping pages by red junction indicators 2

M1

Junction		
2	Northbound Southbound	No exit, access from A1 only No access, exit to A1 only
4	Northbound Southbound	No exit, access from A41 only No access, exit to A41 only
6a	Northbound Southbound	No exit, access from M25 only No access, exit to M25 only
17	Northbound Southbound	No access, exit to M45 only No exit, access from M45 only
19	Northbound Southbound	Exit to M6 only, access from A14 only Access from M6 only, exit to A14 only
21a	Northbound Southbound	No access, exit to A46 only No exit, access from A46 only
24a	Northbound Southbound	No exit Access from A50 only
35a	Northbound Southbound	No access, exit to A616 only No exit, access from A616 only
43	Northbound Southbound	Exit to M621 only Access from M621 only
48	Eastbound Westbound	Exit to A1(M) northbound only Access from A1(M) southbound only

M2

Junction		
1	Eastbound Westbound	Access from A2 eastbound only Exit to A2 westbound only

M3

Junction		
8	Eastbound Westbound	No exit, access from A303 only No access, exit to A303 only
10	Northbound Southbound	No access from A31 No exit to A31
13	Southbound	No access from A335 to M3 leading to M27 Eastbound

M4

Junction		
1	Eastbound Westbound	Exit to A4 eastbound only Access from A4 westbound only
21	Eastbound Westbound	No exit to M48 No access from M48
23	Eastbound Westbound	No access from M48 No exit to M48
25	Eastbound Westbound	No exit No access
25a	Eastbound Westbound	No exit No access
29	Eastbound Westbound	No exit, access from A48(M) only No access, exit to A48(M) only
38	Westbound	No access, exit to A48 only
39	Eastbound Westbound	No access or exit No exit, access from A48 only
42	Eastbound Westbound	No access from A48 No exit to A48

M5

Junction		
10	Northbound Southbound	No exit, access from A4019 only No access, exit to A4019 only
11a	Southbound	No exit to A417 westbound
18a	Northbound Southbound	No access from M49 No exit to M49

M6

Junction		
3a	Eastbound Westbound	No exit to M6 Toll No access from M6 Toll
4	Northbound Southbound	No exit to M42 northbound No access from M42 southbound No exit to M42 No access from M42 southbound
4a	Northbound Southbound	No exit, access from M42 southbound only No access, exit to M42 only
5	Northbound Southbound	No access, exit to A452 only No exit, access from A452 only
10a	Northbound Southbound	No access, exit to M54 only No exit, access from M54 only
11a	Northbound Southbound	No exit to M6 Toll No access from M6 Toll
20	Northbound Southbound	No exit to M56 eastbound No access from M56 westbound
24	Northbound Southbound	No exit, access from A58 only No access, exit to A58 only
25	Northbound Southbound	No access, exit to A49 only No exit, access from A49 only
30	Northbound Southbound	No exit, access from M61 northbound only No access, exit to M61 southbound only
31a	Northbound Southbound	No access, exit to B6242 only No exit, access from B6242 only
45	Northbound Southbound	No access onto A74(M) No exit from A74(M)

M6 Toll

Junction		
T1	Northbound Southbound	No exit No access
T2	Northbound Southbound	No access or exit No access
T5	Northbound Southbound	No exit No access
T7	Northbound Southbound	No access from A5 No exit
T8	Northbound Southbound	No exit to A460 northbound No exit

M8

Junction		
6	Eastbound Westbound	No exit, access only No access, exit only
6a	Eastbound Westbound	No access, exit only No exit, access only
7	Eastbound Westbound	No access, exit only No exit, access only
7a	Eastbound Westbound	No exit, access from A725 Northbound only No access, exit to A725 Southbound only
8	Eastbound Westbound	No exit to M73 northbound No access from M73 southbound
9	Eastbound Westbound	No access, exit only No exit, access only
13	Eastbound Westbound	No access from M80 southbound No exit to M80 northbound
14	Eastbound Westbound	No exit, access only No access, exit only
16	Eastbound Westbound	No exit, access only No access, exit only
17	Eastbound Westbound	No exit, access from A82 only No access, exit to A82 only
18	Westbound	No exit, access only
19	Eastbound Westbound	No exit to A814 eastbound No access from A814 westbound
20	Eastbound Westbound	No exit, access only No access, exit only
21	Eastbound Westbound	No access, exit only No exit, access only
22	Eastbound Westbound	No exit, access from M77 only No access, exit to M77 only
23	Eastbound Westbound	No exit, access from B768 only No access, exit to B768 only
25	Eastbound & Westbound	Access from A739 southbound only Exit to A739 northbound only
25a	Eastbound Westbound	Access only Exit only
28	Eastbound Westbound	No exit, access from airport only No access, exit to airport only
29a	Eastbound Westbound	No exit, access only No access, exit only

M9

Junction		
2	Northbound Southbound	No exit, access from B8046 only No access, exit to B8046 only
3	Northbound Southbound	No access, exit to A803 only No exit, access from A803 only
6	Northbound Southbound	No exit, access only No access, exit to A905 only
8	Northbound Southbound	No access, exit to M876 only No exit, access from M876 only

M11

Junction		
4	Northbound Southbound	No exit, access from A406 eastbound only No access, exit to A406 westbound only
5	Northbound Southbound	No access, exit to A1168 only No exit, access from A1168 only
8a	Northbound Southbound	No access, exit only No exit, access only
9	Northbound Southbound	No access, exit only No exit, access only
13	Northbound Southbound	No access, exit only No exit, access only
14	Northbound Southbound	No access from A428 eastbound No exit to A428 westbound No exit, access from A428 eastbound only

M20

Junction		
2	Eastbound Westbound	No access, exit to A20 only (access via M26 Junction 2a) No exit, access only (exit via M26 Jun.2a)
3	Eastbound Westbound	No exit, access from M26 eastbound only No access, exit to M26 westbound only
10	Eastbound Westbound	No access, exit only No exit, access only
11a	Eastbound Westbound	No access from Channel Tunnel No exit to Channel Tunnel

M23

Junction		
7	Northbound Southbound	No exit to A23 southbound No access from A23 northbound

M25

Junction		
5	Clockwise Anti-clockwise	No exit to M26 eastbound No access from M26 westbound
Spur to A21	Northbound Southbound	No exit to M26 eastbound No access from M26 westbound
19	Clockwise Anti-clockwise	No access, exit only No exit, access only
21	Clockwise & Anti-clockwise	No exit to M1 southbound No access from M1 northbound
31	Northbound Southbound	No access, exit only (access via Jun.30) No exit, access only (exit via Jun.30)

M26

Junction with M25 (M25 Jun.5)

Eastbound	No access from M25 clockwise or spur from A21 northbound
Westbound	No exit to M25 anti-clockwise or spur to A21 southbound

Junction with M20 (M20 Jun.3)

Eastbound	No exit to M20 westbound
Westbound	No access from M20 eastbound

M27

Junction		
4	Eastbound & Westbound	No exit to A33 southbound (Southampton) No access from A33 northbound
10	Eastbound Westbound	No exit, access from A32 only No access, exit to A32 only

M40

Junction		
3	North-Westbound South-Eastbound	No access, exit to A40 only No exit, access from A40 only
7	N.W bound S.E bound	No access, exit only No exit, access only
13	N.W bound S.E bound	No access, exit only No exit, access only
14	N.W bound S.E bound	No exit, access only No access, exit only
16	N.W bound S.E bound	No exit, access only No access, exit only

M42

Junction		
1	Eastbound Westbound	No exit No access
7	Northbound Southbound	No access, exit to M6 only No exit, access from M6 northbound only
8	Northbound Southbound	No exit, access from M6 southbound only Exit to M6 nothbound only Access from M6 southbound only

M45

Junction with M1 (M1 Jun.17)

Eastbound	No exit to M1 northbound
Westbound	No access from M1 southbound

Junction with A45 east of Dunchurch

Eastbound	No access, exit to A45 only
Westbound	No exit, access from A45 northbound only

M48

Junction with M4 (M4 Jun.21)

Eastbound	No exit to M4 westbound
Westbound	No access from M4 eastbound

Junction with M4 (M4 Jun.23)

Eastbound	No access from M4 westbound
Westbound	No exit to M4 eastbound

M53

Junction		
11	Northbound & Southbound	No access from M56 eastbound, no exit to M56 westbound

M56

Junction		
1	Eastbound S.E bound Westbound	No exit to M60 N.W bound No exit to A34 southbound No access from A34 northbound No access from M60
2	Eastbound Westbound	No exit, access from A560 only No access, exit to A560 only
3	Eastbound Westbound	No access, exit only No exit, access only
4	Eastbound Westbound	No exit, access only No access, exit only
7	Westbound	No access, exit only
8	Eastbound Westbound	No access or exit No exit, access from A556 only
9	Eastbound Westbound	No access from M6 northbound No exit to M60 southbound
10a	Northbound Southbound	No exit, access only No access, exit only
15	Eastbound Westbound	No exit to M53 No access from M53

M57

Junction		
3	Northbound Southbound	No exit, access only No access, exit only
5	Northbound Southbound	No exit, access from A580 westbound only No access, exit to A580 eastbound only

M60

Junction		
2	N.E bound S.W bound	No access, exit to A560 only No exit, access from A560 only
3	Eastbound Westbound	No access from A34 southbound No exit to A34 northbound
4	Eastbound Westbound	No exit to M56 S.W bound No exit to A34 northbound No access from A34 southbound No access from M56 eastbound
5	N.W bound S.E bound	No access from or exit to A5103 southbound No access from or exit to A5103 northbound
14	Eastbound Westbound	No exit to A580 No access from A580 westbound No exit to A580 eastbound No access from A580
16	Eastbound Westbound	No exit, access from A666 only No access, exit to A666 only
20	Eastbound Westbound	No access from A664 No exit to A664
22	Westbound	No access from A62
25	S.W bound	No access from A560 / A6017
26	N.E bound	No access or exit
27	N.E bound S.W bound	No access, exit only No exit, access only

M61

Junction		
2&3	N.W bound S.E bound	No access from A580 eastbound No exit to A580 westbound

Junction with M6 (M6 Jun.30)

N.W bound	No exit to M6 southbound
S.E bound	No access from M6 northbound

M62

Junction		
23	Eastbound Westbound	No access, exit to A640 only No exit, access from A640 only

M65

Junction		
9	N.E bound S.W bound	No access, exit to A679 only No exit, access from A679 only
11	N.E bound S.W bound	No exit, access only No access, exit only

M66

Junction		
1	Northbound Southbound	No access, exit to A56 only No exit, access from A56 only

M67

Junction		
1	Eastbound Westbound	Access from A57 eastbound only Exit to A57 westbound only
1a	Eastbound Westbound	No access, exit to A6017 only No exit, access from A6017 only
2	Eastbound Westbound	No exit, access from A57 only No access, exit to A57 only

M69

Junction		
2	N.E bound S.W bound	No exit, access from B4669 only No access, exit to B4669 only

M73

Junction		
1	Southbound	No exit to A721 eastbound
2	Northbound Southbound	No access from M8 eastbound No exit to A89 eastbound No exit to M8 westbound No access from A89 westbound
3	Northbound Southbound	No exit to A80 S.W bound No access from A80 N.E bound

M74

Junction		
1	Eastbound Westbound	No access from M8 Westbound No exit to M8 Westbound
3	Eastbound Westbound	No exit No access
7	Northbound Southbound	No exit, access from A72 only No access, exit to A72 only
9	Northbound Southbound	No access or exit No access, exit to B7078 only
10	Southbound	No exit, access from B7078 only
11	Northbound Southbound	No exit, access from B7078 only No access, exit to B7078 only
12	Northbound Southbound	No access, exit to A70 only No exit, access from A70 only

M77

Junction with M8 (M8 Jun.22)

Northbound	No exit to M8 westbound
Southbound	No access from M8 eastbound

Junction		
4	Northbound Southbound	No exit No access
6	Northbound Southbound	No exit to A77 No access from A77
7	Northbound	No access from A77 No exit to A77

M80

Junction		
1	Northbound Southbound	No access from M8 westbound No exit to M8 eastbound
4a	Northbound Southbound	No access No exit
6a	Northbound Southbound	No exit No access
8	Northbound Southbound	No access from M876 No exit to M876

M90

Junction		
1	Northbound Southbound	No exit No Access from A90
2a	Northbound Southbound	No access, exit to A92 only No exit, access from A92 only
7	Northbound Southbound	No exit, access from A91 only No access, exit to A91 only
8	Northbound Southbound	No access, exit to A91 only No exit, access from A91 only
10	Northbound Southbound	No access from A912 Exit to A912 northbound only No exit to A912 Access from A912 southbound only

M180

Junction		
1	Eastbound Westbound	No access, exit only No exit, access from A18 only

M606

Junction		
2	Northbound	No access, exit only

M621

Junction		
2a	Eastbound Westbound	No exit, access only No access, exit only
4	Southbound	No exit
5	Northbound Southbound	No access, exit to A61 only No exit, access from A61 only
6	Northbound Southbound	No exit, access only No access, exit only
7	Eastbound Westbound	No access, exit only No exit, access only
8	Northbound Southbound	No access, exit only No exit, access only

M876

Junction with M80 (M80 Jun.5)

N.E bound	No access from M80 southbound
S.W bound	No exit to M80 northbound

Junction with M9 (M9 Jun.8)

N.E bound	No exit to M9 northbound
S.W bound	No access from M9 southbound

A1(M)

Hertfordshire Section

Junction		
2	Northbound Southbound	No access, exit only No exit, access from A1001 only
3	Southbound	No access, exit only
5	Northbound Southbound	No exit, access only No access or exit

Cambridgeshire Section

Junction		
14	Northbound Southbound	No exit, access only No access, exit only

Leeds Section

Junction		
40	Southbound	Exit to A1 southbound only
43	Northbound Southbound	Access from M1 eastbound only Exit to M1 westbound only

Durham Section

Junction		
57	Northbound Southbound	No access, exit to A66(M) only No exit, access from A66(M)
65	Northbound Southbound	Exit to A1 N.W bound and to A194(M) only Access from A1 S.E bound and from A194(M) only

A3(M)

Junction		
4	Northbound Southbound	No access, exit only No exit, access only

Aston Expressway A38(M)

Junction with Victoria Road, Aston

Northbound	No exit, access only
Southbound	No access, exit only

A48(M)

Junction with M4 (M4 Jun.29)

N.E bound	Exit to M4 eastbound only
S.W bound	Access from M4 westbound only

Junction		
29a	N.E bound S.W bound	Access from A48 eastbound only Exit to A48 westbound only

Mancunian Way A57(M)

Junction with A34 Brook Street, Manchester

Eastbound	No access, exit to A34 Brook Street, southbound only
Westbound	No exit, access only

Leeds Inner Ring Road A58(M)

Junction with Park Lane / Westgate

Southbound	No access, exit only

Leeds Inner Ring Road A64(M) (continuation of A58(M))

Junction with A58 Clay Pit Lane

Eastbound	No access
Westbound	No exit

A66(M)

Junction with A1(M) (A1(M) Jun.57)

N.E bound	Access from A1(M) northbound only
S.W bound	Exit to A1(M) southbound only

A74(M)

Junction		
18	Northbound Southbound	No access No exit

Newcastle Central Motorway A167(M)

Junction with Camden Street

Northbound	No exit, access only
Southbound	No access or exit

A194(M)

Junction with A1(M) (A1(M) Jun.65) **and A1 Gateshead Western By-Pass**

Northbound	Access from A1(M) only
Southbound	Exit to A1(M) only

Northern Ireland

M1

Junction		
3	Northbound Southbound	No exit, access only No access, exit only
7	Westbound	No access, exit only

M2

Junction		
2	Eastbound Westbound	No access to M5 northbound No exit to M5 southbound

M5

Junction		
2	Northbound Southbound	No access from M2 eastbound No exit to M2 westbound

Reference / Légende / Zeichenerklärung

Motorway
Autoroute
Autobahn
`M1`

Motorway Under Construction
Autoroute en construction
Autobahn im Bau

Motorway Proposed
Autoroute prévue
Geplante Autobahn

Motorway Junctions with Numbers
Unlimited Interchange `4`
Limited Interchange `5`
Autoroute échangeur numéroté
Echangeur complet
Echangeur partiel
Autobahnanschlußstelle mit Nummer
Unbeschränkter Fahrtrichtungswechsel
Beschränkter Fahrtrichtungswechsel

Motorway Service Area (with fuel station)
with access from one carriageway only
Aire de services d'autoroute (avec station service)
accessible d'un seul côté
Rastplatz oder Raststätte (mit tankstelle)
Einbahn

Major Road Service Area (with fuel station) with 24 hour facilities
Primary Route
Class A Road
Aire de services sur route prioritaire (avec station service) Ouverte 24h sur 24
Route à grande circulation
Route de type A
Raststätte (mit tankstelle) Durchgehend geöffnet
Hauptverkehrsstraße
A- Straße

Major Road Junctions
Detailed `4`
Jonctions grands routiers
Détaillé
Hauptverkehrsstraße Kreuzungen
Ausführlich
Other Autre Andere

Truckstop (selection of)
Sélection d'aire pour poids lourds
Auswahl von Fernfahrerrastplatz
`T`

Primary Route
Route à grande circulation
Hauptverkehrsstraße
`A41`

Primary Route Junction with Number `5`
Echangeur numéroté
Hauptverkehrsstraßenkreuzung mit Nummer

Primary Route Destination
Route prioritaire, direction
Hauptverkehrsstraße Richtung
DOVER

Dual Carriageways (A & B roads)
Route à double chaussées séparées (route A & B)
Zweispurige Schnellstraße (A- und B- Straßen)

Class A Road
Route de type A
A-Straße
`A129`

Class B Road
Route de type B
B-Straße
`B177`

Narrow Major Road (passing places)
Route prioritaire étroite (possibilité de dépassement)
Schmale Hauptverkehrsstraße (mit Überholmöglichkeit)

Major Roads Under Construction
Route prioritaire en construction
Hauptverkehrsstraße im Bau

Major Roads Proposed
Route prioritaire prévue
Geplante Hauptverkehrsstraße

Gradient 1:7 (14%) **& steeper**
(descent in direction of arrow)
Pente égale ou supérieure à 14% (dans le sens de la descente)
14% Steigung und steiler (in Pfeilrichtung)
»»

Toll
Barrière de péage
Gebührenpflichtig
Toll

Dart Charge
www.gov.uk/pay-dartford-crossing-charge
Ⓒ

Park & Ride
Parking avec Service Navette
Parken und Reisen
`P+R`

Mileage between markers
Distance en miles entre les flèches
Strecke zwischen Markierungen in Meilen
8

Airport
Aéroport
Flughafen
✈

Airfield
Terrain d'aviation
Flugplatz
✛

Heliport
Héliport
Hubschraulberlandeplatz
Ⓗ

Ferry
(vehicular, sea) / Bac (véhicules, mer) / Fähre (auto, meer)
(vehicular, river) / (véhicules, rivière) / (auto, fluß)
(foot only) / (piétons) / (nur für Personen)

Railway and Station
Voie ferrée et gare
Eisenbahnlinie und Bahnhof

Level Crossing and Tunnel
Passage à niveau et tunnel
Bahnübergang und Tunnel

River or Canal
Rivière ou canal
Fluß oder Kanal

County or Unitary Authority Boundary
Limite de comté ou de division administrative
Grafschafts- oder Verwaltungsbezirksgrenze

National Boundary
Frontière nationale
Landesgrenze

Built-up Area
Agglomération
Geschloßene Ortschaft

Town, Village or Hamlet
Ville, Village ou hameau
Stadt, Dorf oder Weiler

Wooded Area
Zone boisée
Waldgebiet

Spot Height in Feet
Altitude (en pieds)
Höhe in Fuß
· 813

Relief above 400' (122m)
Relief par estompage au-dessus de 400' (122m)
Reliefschattierung über 400' (122m)

National Grid Reference (kilometres)
Coordonnées géographiques nationales (Kilomètres)
Nationale geographische Koordinaten (Kilometer)
¹00

Page Continuation
Suite à la page indiquée
Seitenfortsetzung
`48`

Area covered by Main Route map
Repartition des cartes des principaux axes routiers
Von Karten mit Hauptverkehrsstrecken
`MAIN ROUTE 94`

Area covered by Town Plan
Ville ayant un plan à la page indiquée
Von Karten mit Stadtplänen erfaßter Bereich
`PAGE 109`

Tourist Information / Information / Touristeninformationen

Abbey, Church, Friary, Priory ✝
Abbaye, église, monastère, prieuré
Abtei, Kirche, Mönchskloster, Kloster

Animal Collection 🐾
Ménagerie
Tiersammlung

Aquarium 🐟
Aquarium
Aquarium

Arboretum, Botanical Garden 🌳
Jardin Botanique
Botanischer Garten

Aviary, Bird Garden
Volière
Voliere

Battle Site and Date ⚔ *1066*
Champ de bataille et date
Schlachtfeld und Datum

Blue Flag Beach
Plage Pavillon Bleu
Blaue Flagge Strand

Bridge
Pont
Brücke

Butterfly Farm 🦋
Ferme aux Papillons
Schmetterlingsfarm

Castle (open to public)
Château (ouvert au public)
Schloß / Burg (für die Öffentlichkeit zugänglich)

Castle with Garden (open to public)
Château avec parc (ouvert au public)
Schloß mit Garten (für die Öffentlichkeit zugänglich)

Cathedral ✝
Cathédrale
Kathedrale

Cidermaker
Cidrerie (fabrication)
Apfelwein Hersteller

Country Park
Parc régional
Landschaftspark

Distillery
Distillerie
Brennerei

Farm Park, Open Farm
Park Animalier
Bauernhof Park

Fortress, Hill Fort ✳
Château Fort
Festung

Garden (open to public) ✿
Jardin (ouvert au public)
Garten (für die Öffentlichkeit zugänglich)

Golf Course ⚑
Terrain de golf
Golfplatz

Historic Building (open to public) 🏛
Monument historique (ouvert au public)
Historisches Gebäude (für die Öffentlichkeit zugänglich)

Historic Building with Garden (open to public) 🏛
Monument historique avec jardin (ouvert au public)
Historisches Gebäude mit Garten (für die Öffentlichkeit zugänglich)

Horse Racecourse 🏇
Hippodrome
Pferderennbahn

Industrial Monument ✷
Monument Industrielle
Industriedenkmal

Leisure Park, Leisure Pool
Parc d'Attraction, Loisirs Piscine
Freizeitpark, Freizeit pool

Lighthouse 🗼
Phare
Leuchtturm

Mine, Cave
Mine, Grotte
Bergwerk, Höhle

Monument
Monument
Denkmal

Motor Racing Circuit
Circuit Automobile
Automobilrennbahn

Museum, Art Gallery `M`
Musée
Museum, Galerie

National Park
Parc national
Nationalpark

National Trail
Sentier national
Nationaler Weg

National Trust Property
National Trust Property
National Trust- Eigentum

Natural Attraction ★
Attraction Naturelle
Natürliche Anziehung

Nature Reserve or Bird Sanctuary
Réserve naturelle botanique ou ornithologique
Natur- oder Vogelschutzgebiet

Nature Trail or Forest Walk
Chemin forestier, piste verte
Naturpfad oder Waldweg

Picnic Site 🎋
Lieu pour pique-nique
Picknickplatz

Place of Interest *Craft Centre* •
Site, curiosité
Sehenswürdigkeit

Prehistoric Monument 🗿
Monument Préhistorique
Prähistorische Denkmal

Railway, Steam or Narrow Gauge
Chemin de fer, à vapeur ou à voie étroite
Eisenbahn, Dampf- oder Schmalspurbahn

Roman Remains
Vestiges Romains
Römischen Ruinen

Theme Park
Centre de loisirs
Vergnügungspark

Tourist Information Centre `i`
Office de Tourisme
Touristeninformationen

Viewpoint (360 degrees) ☀ (180 degrees) ☼
Vue panoramique (360 degrés) (180 degrés)
Aussichtspunkt (360 Grade) (180 Grade)

Vineyard 🍇
Vignoble
Weinberg

Visitor Information Centre `V`
Centre d'information touristique
Besucherzentrum

Wildlife Park
Réserve de faune
Wildpark

Windmill
Moulin à vent
Windmühle

Zoo or Safari Park
Parc ou réserve zoologique
Zoo oder Safari-Park

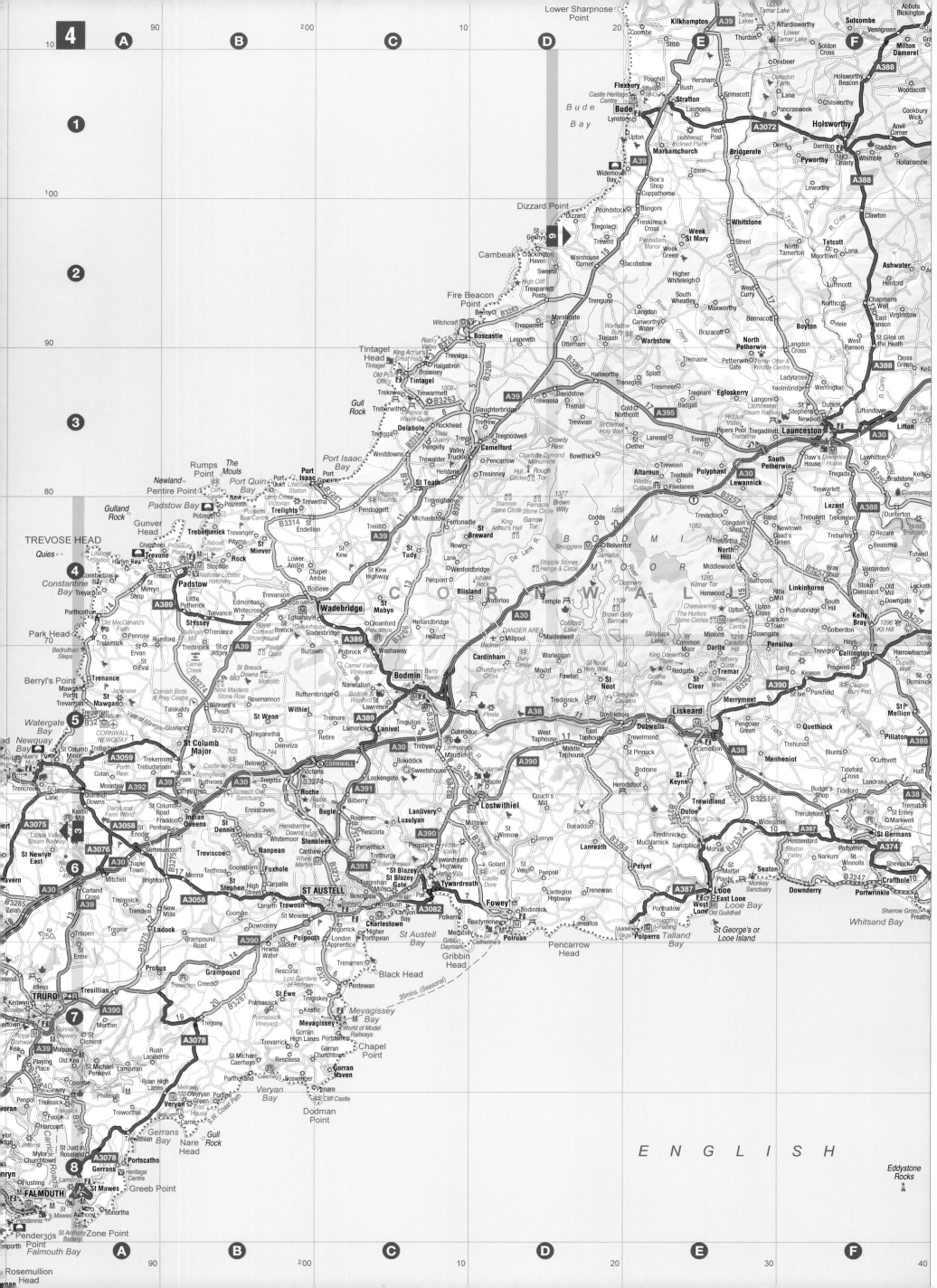

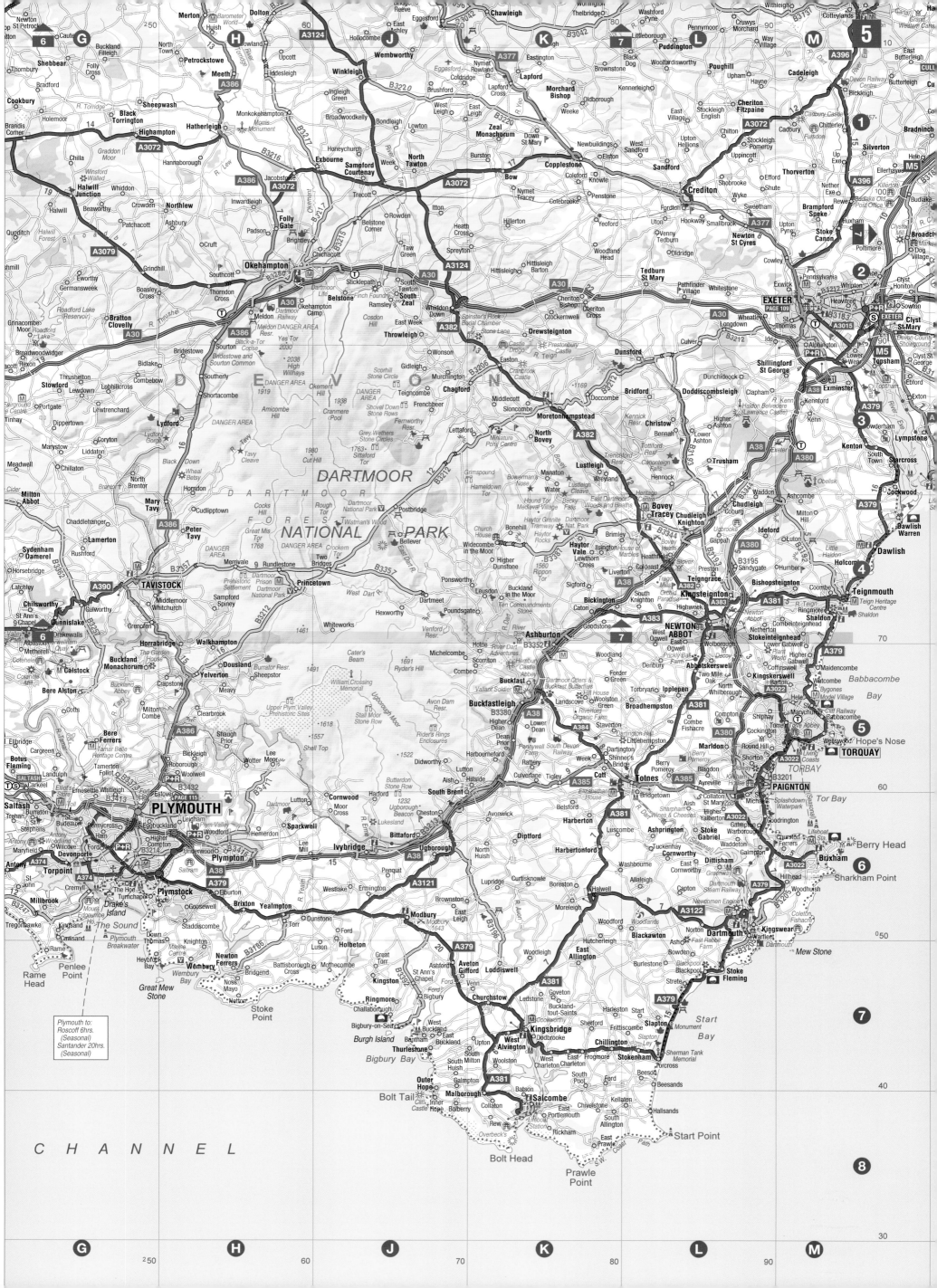

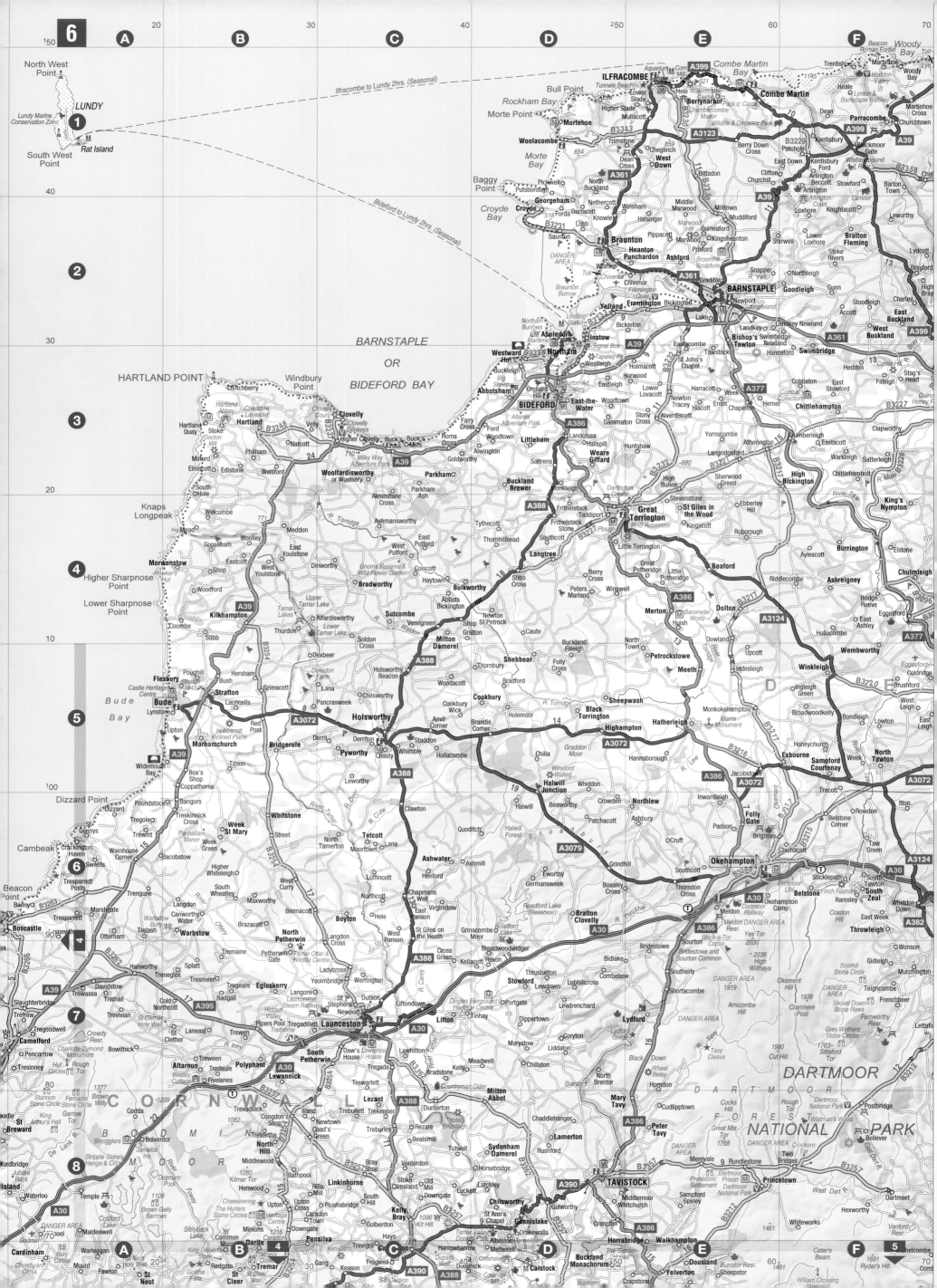

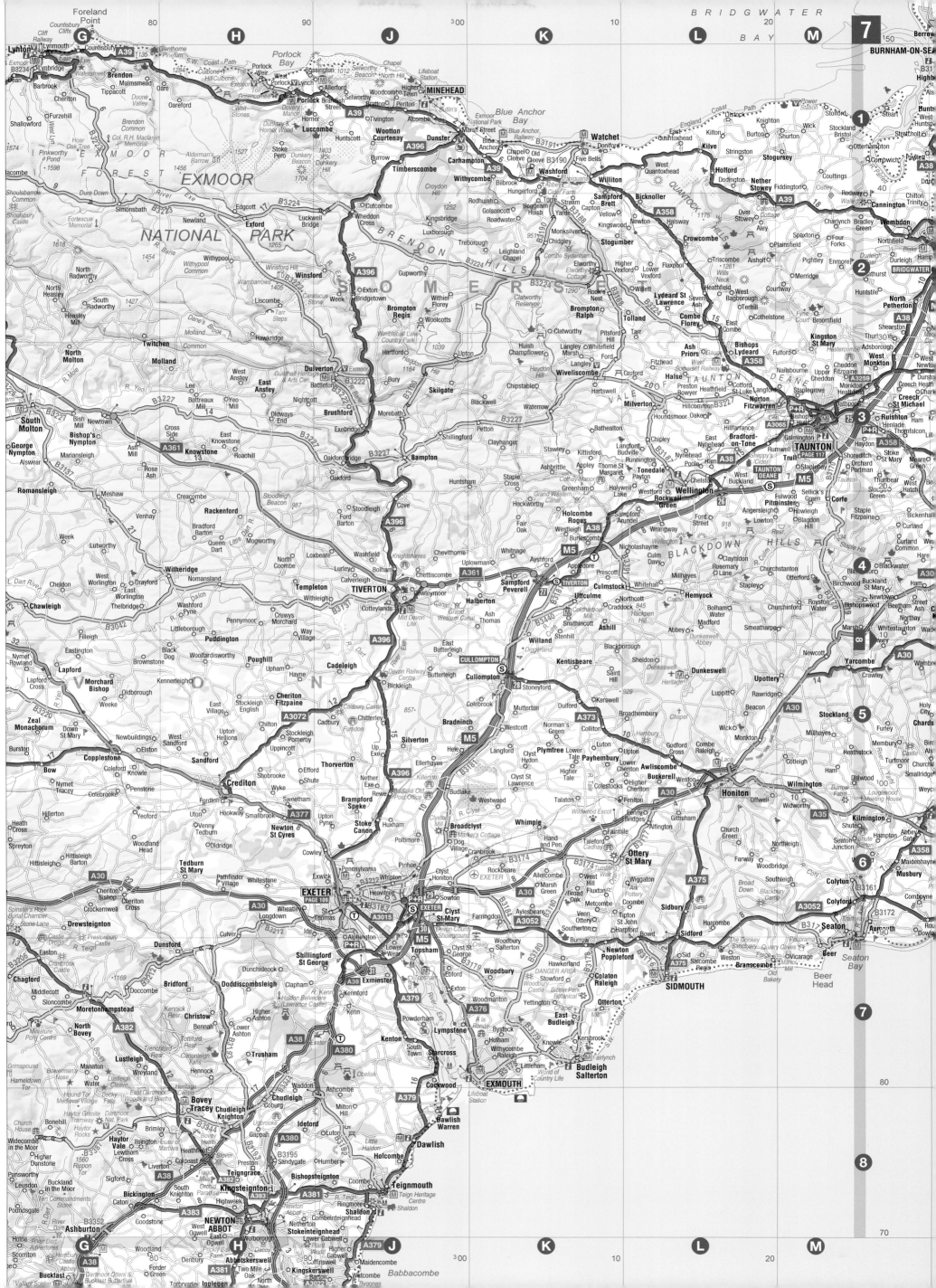

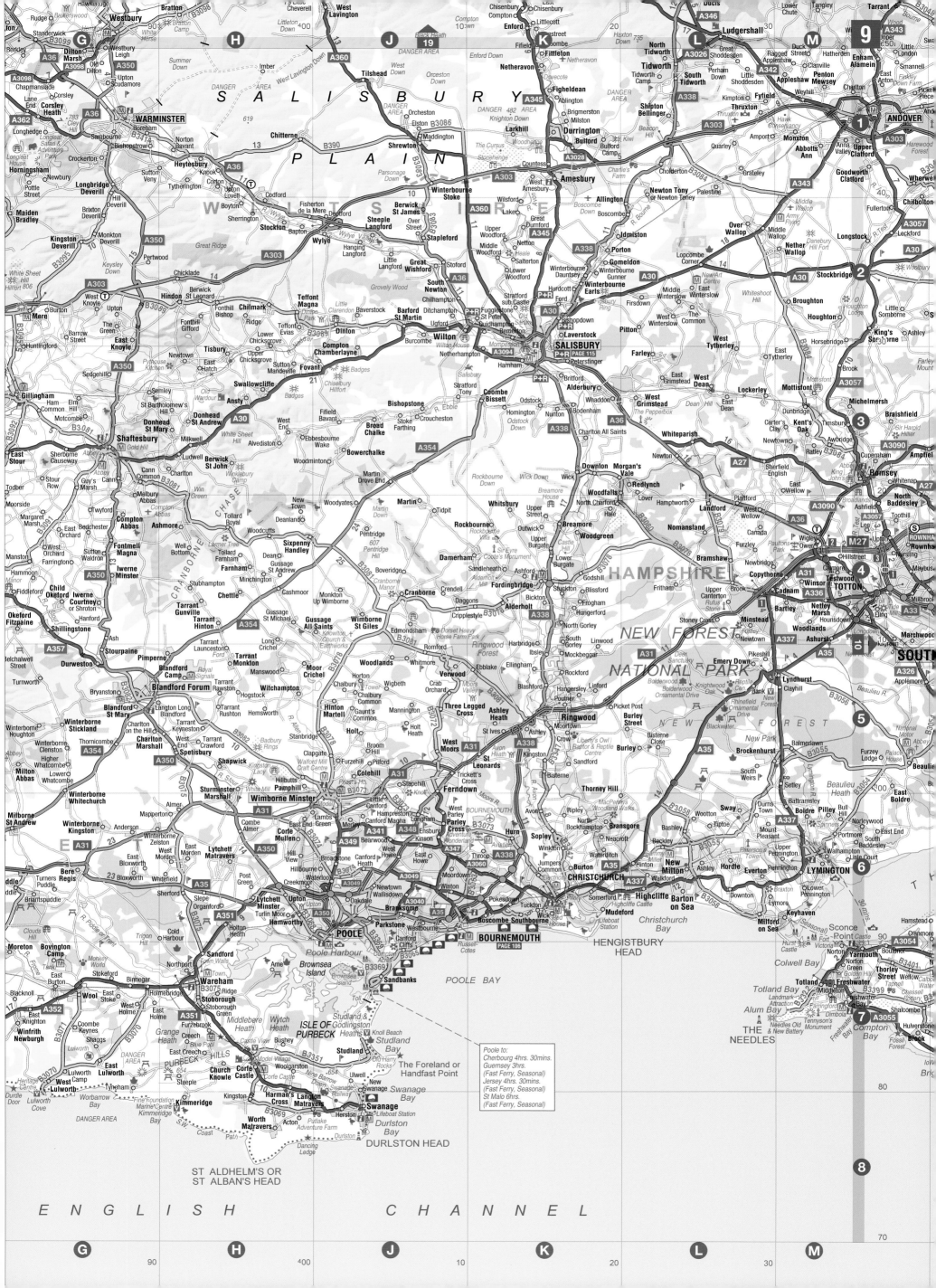

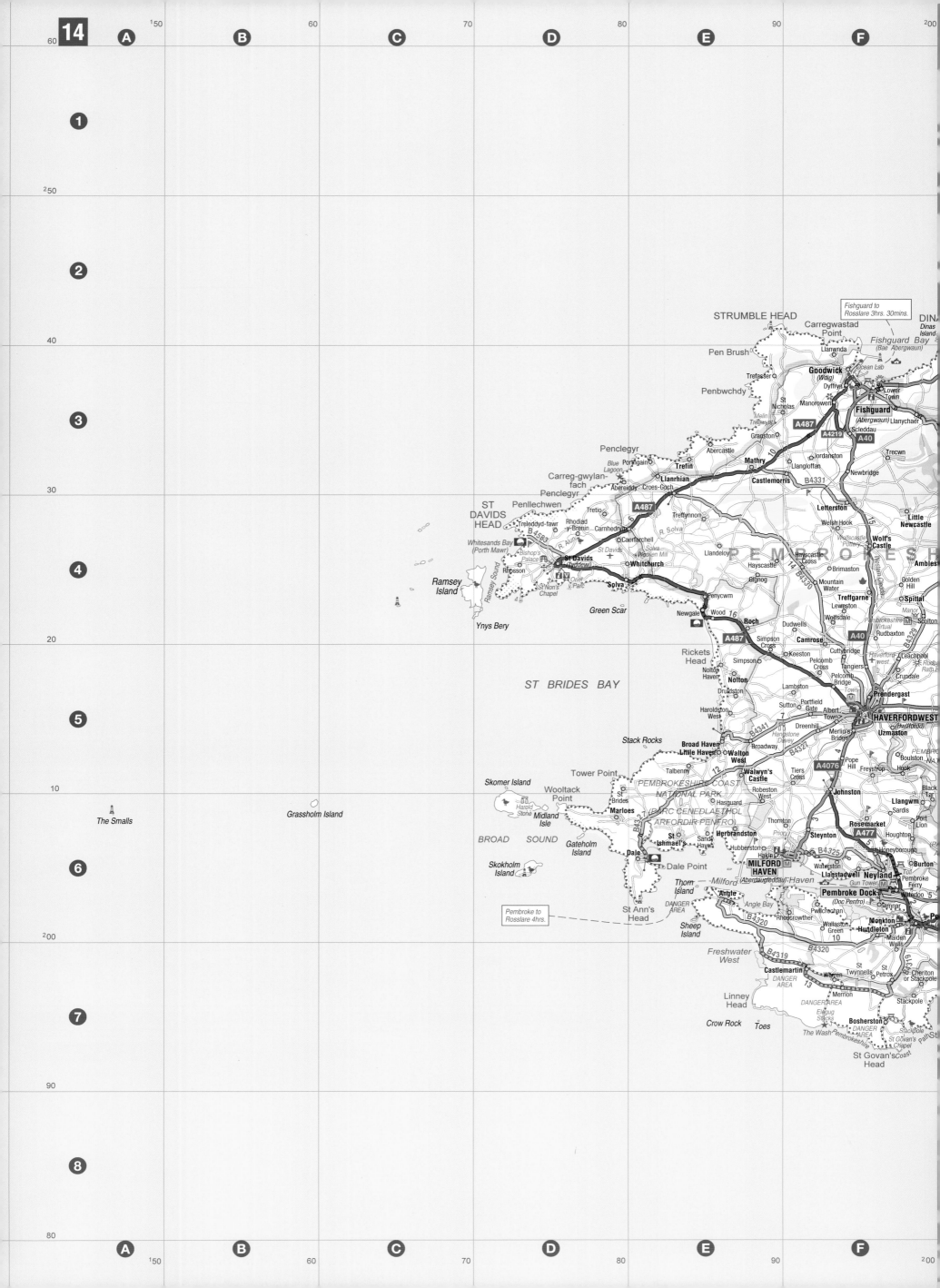

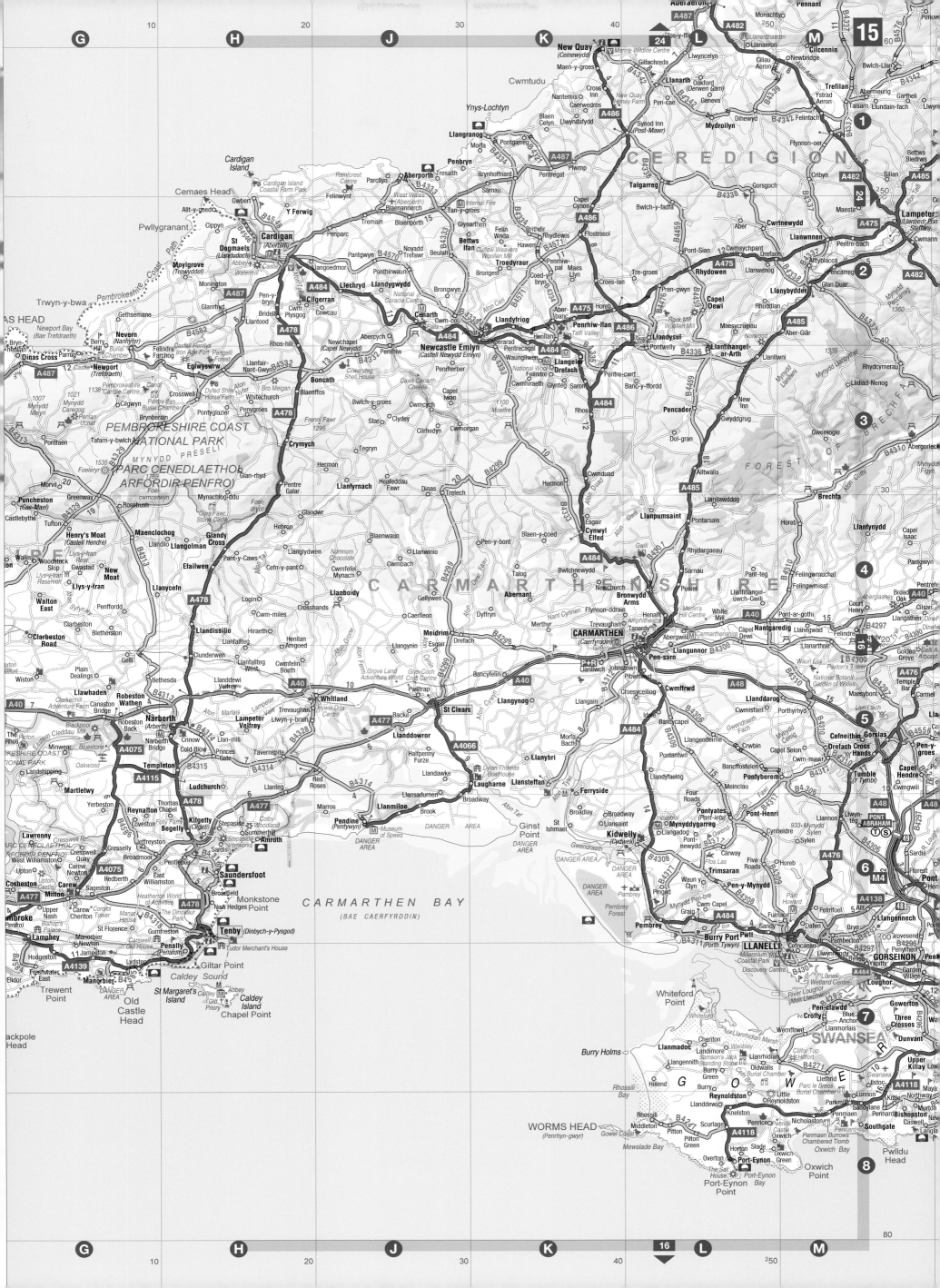

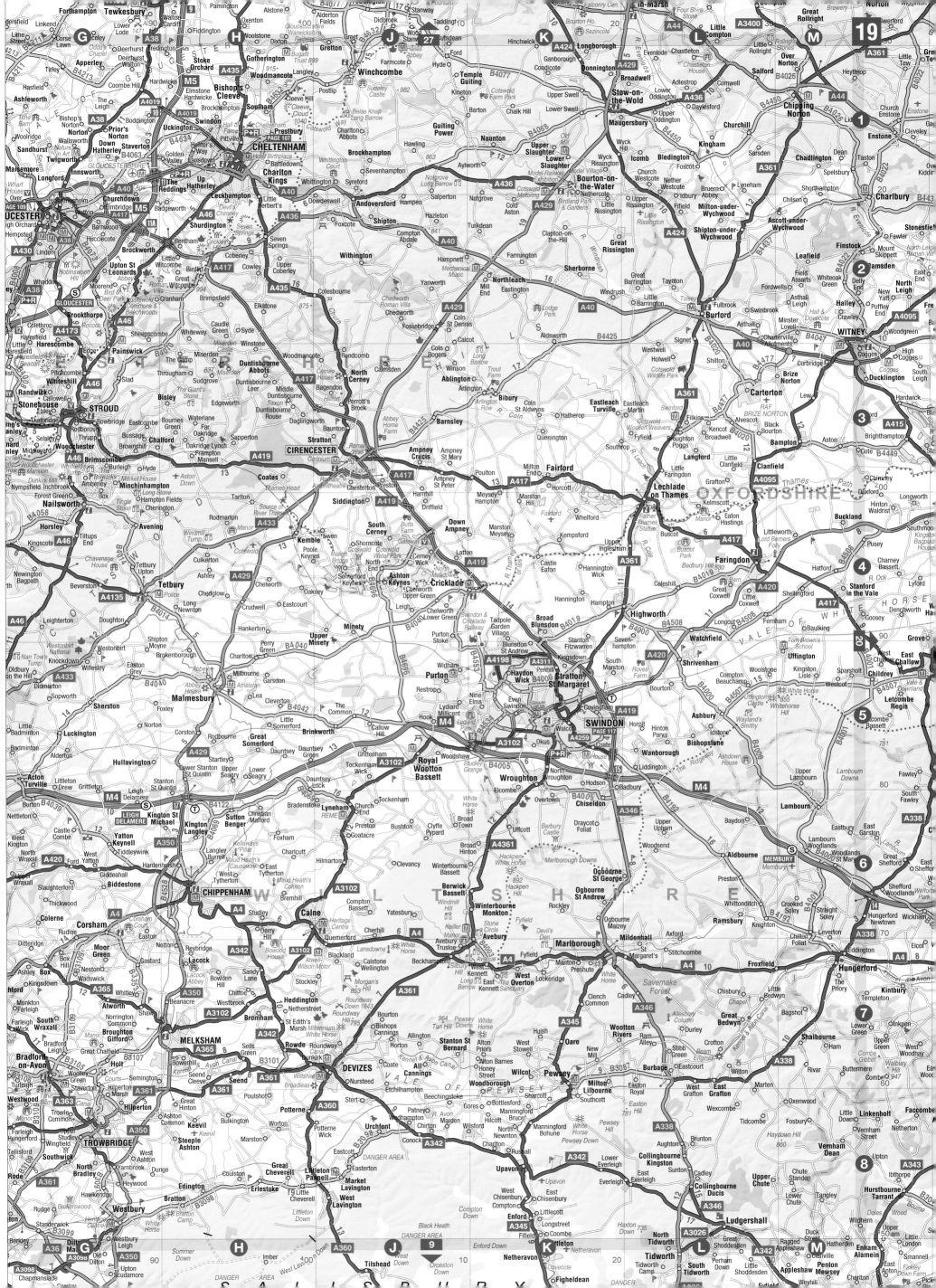

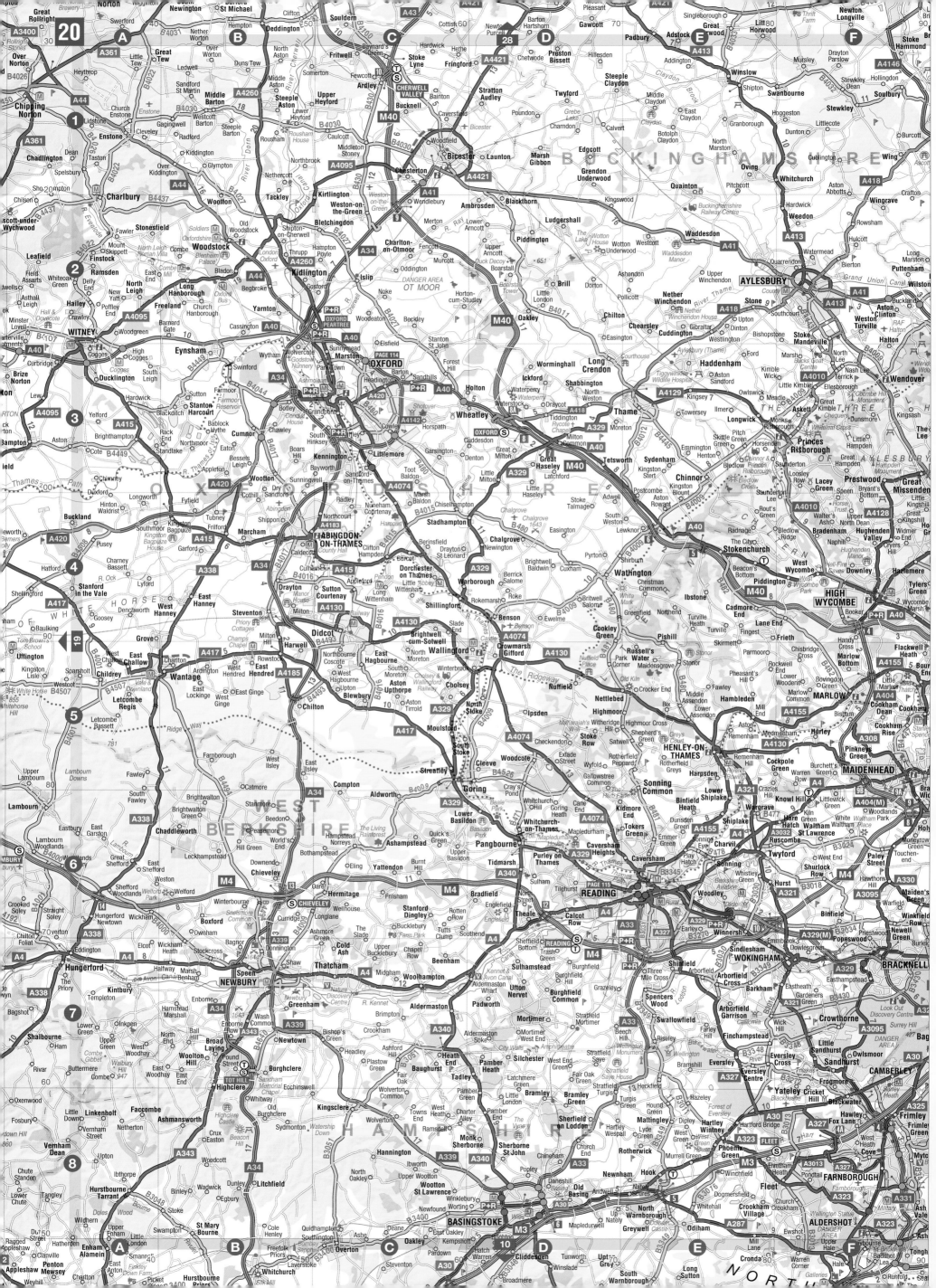

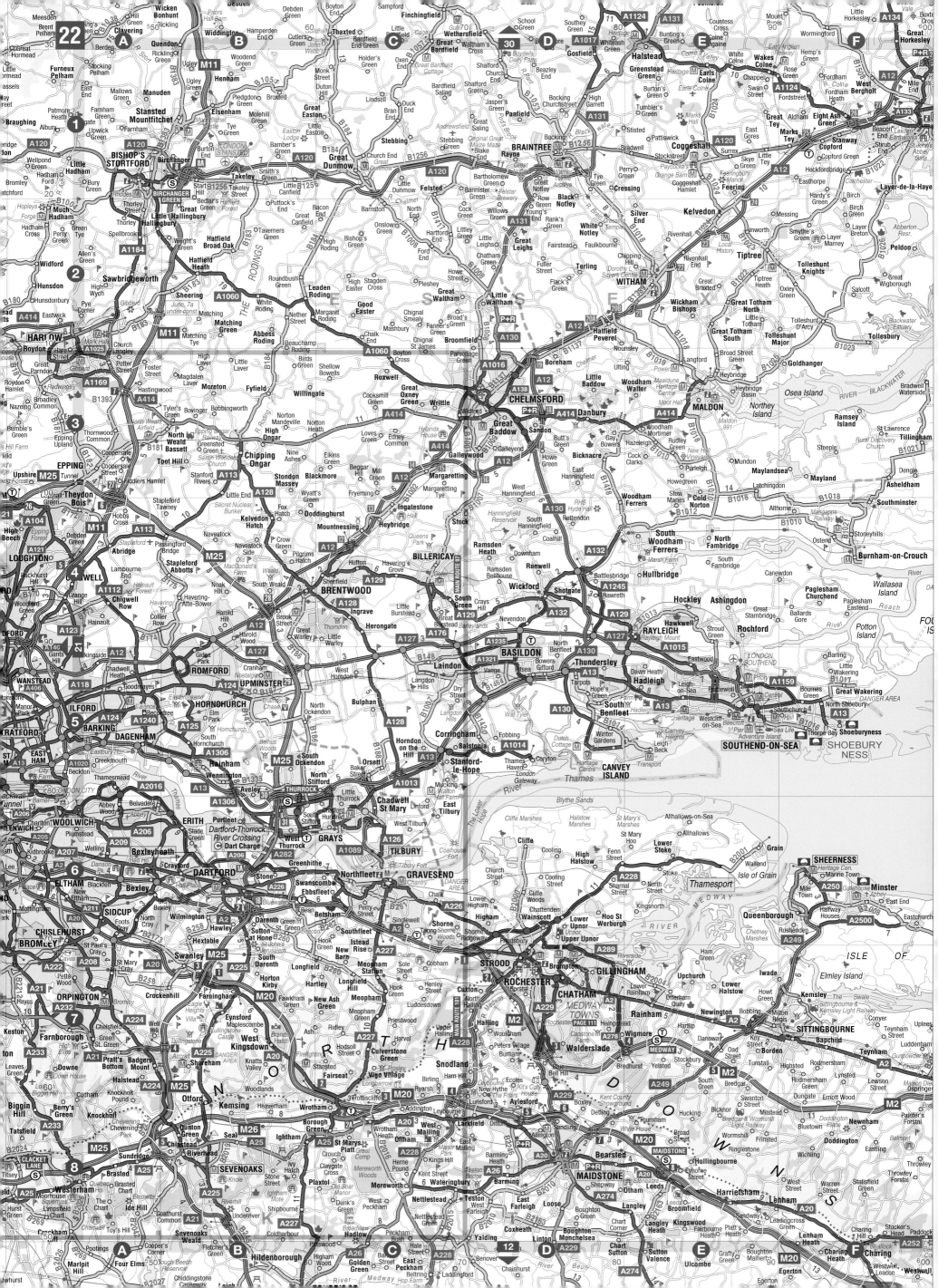

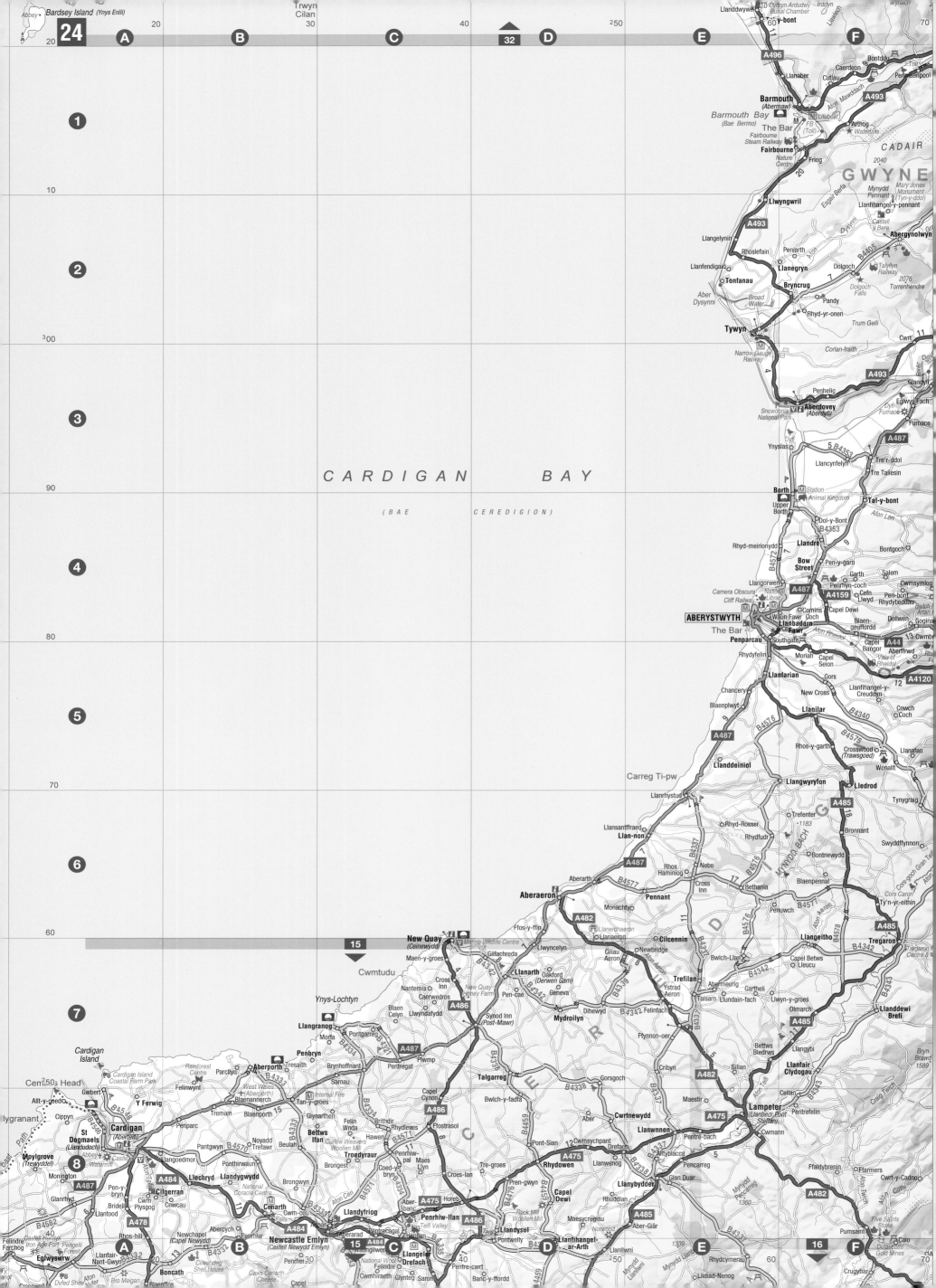

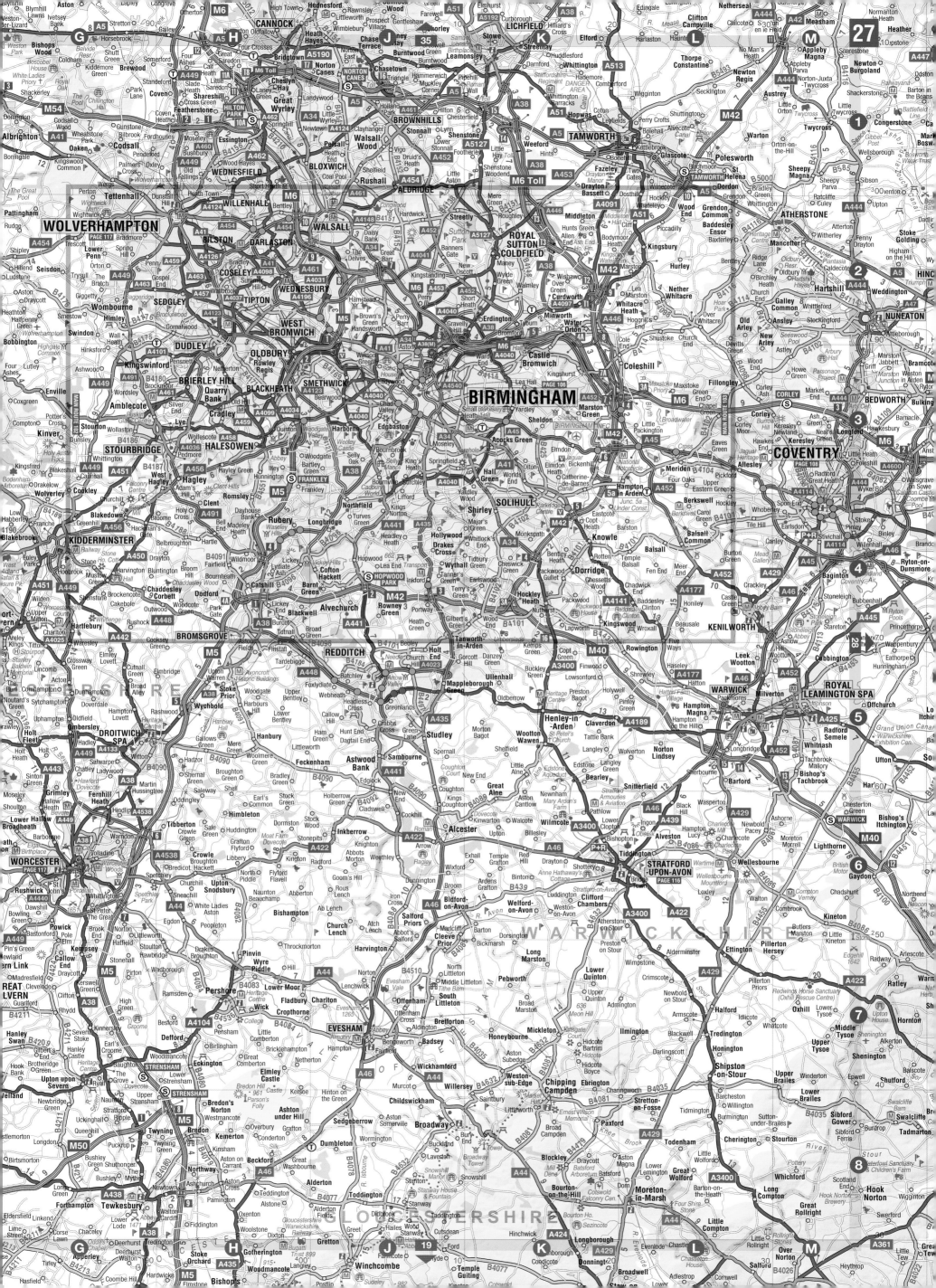

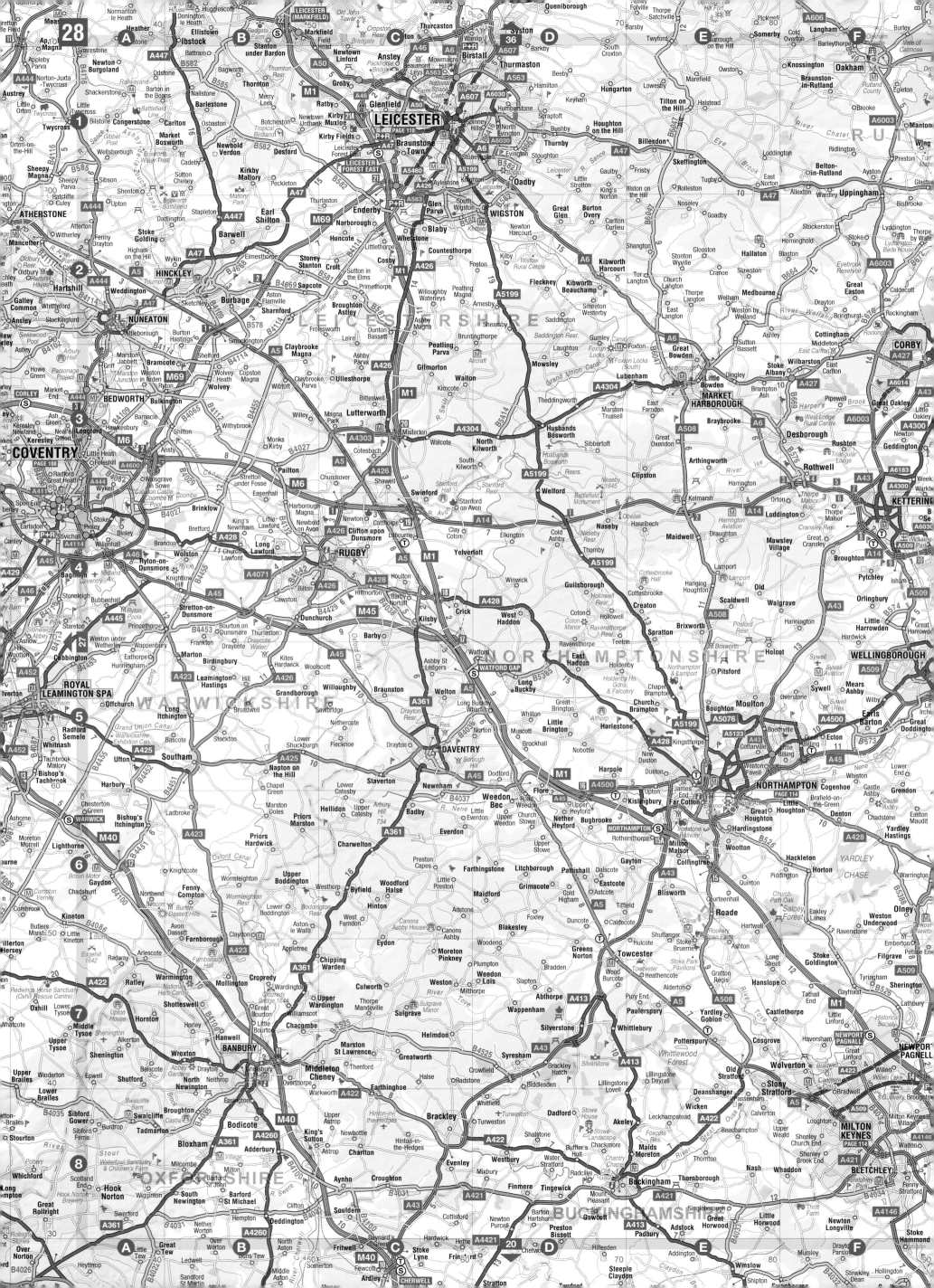

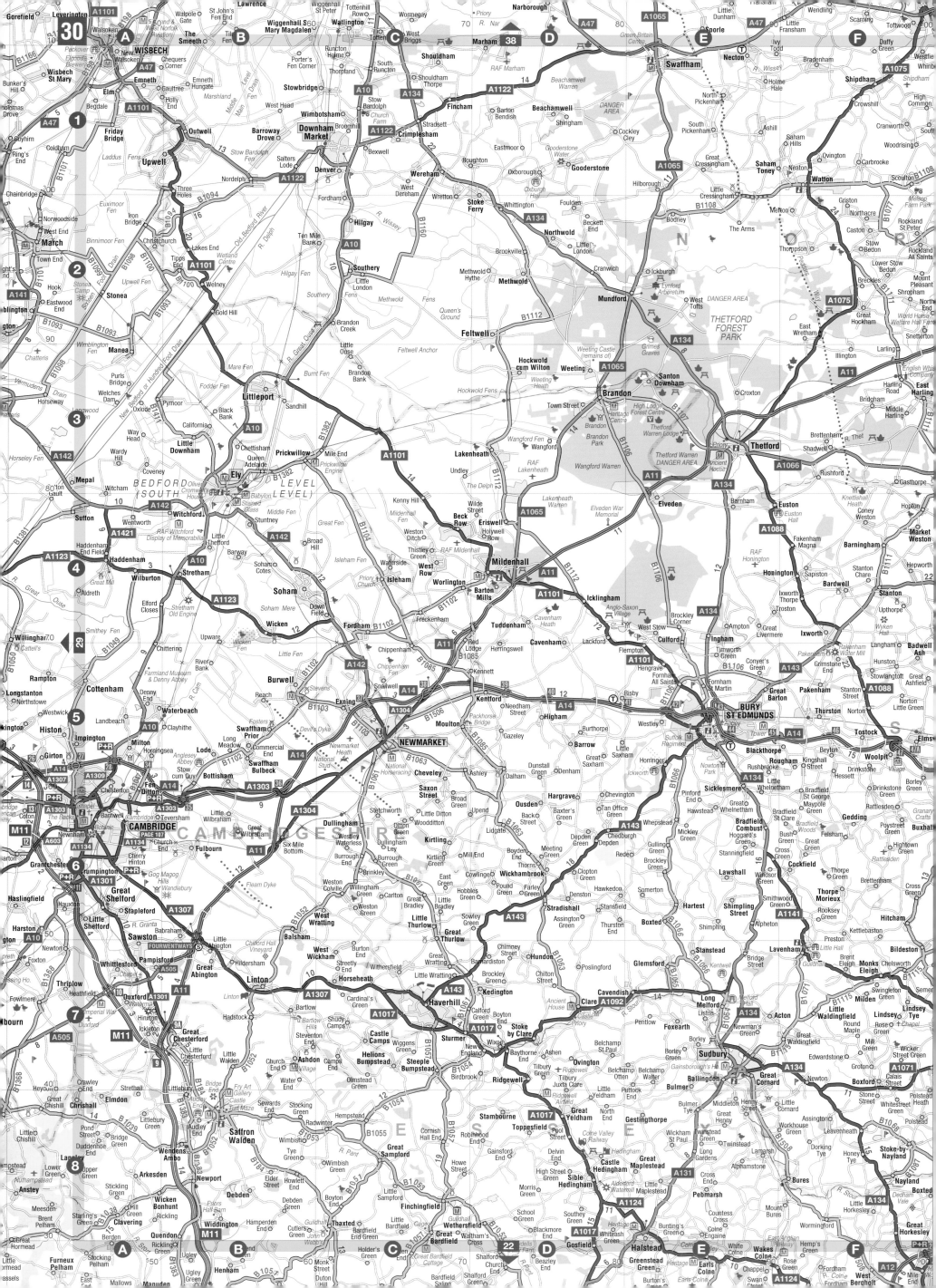

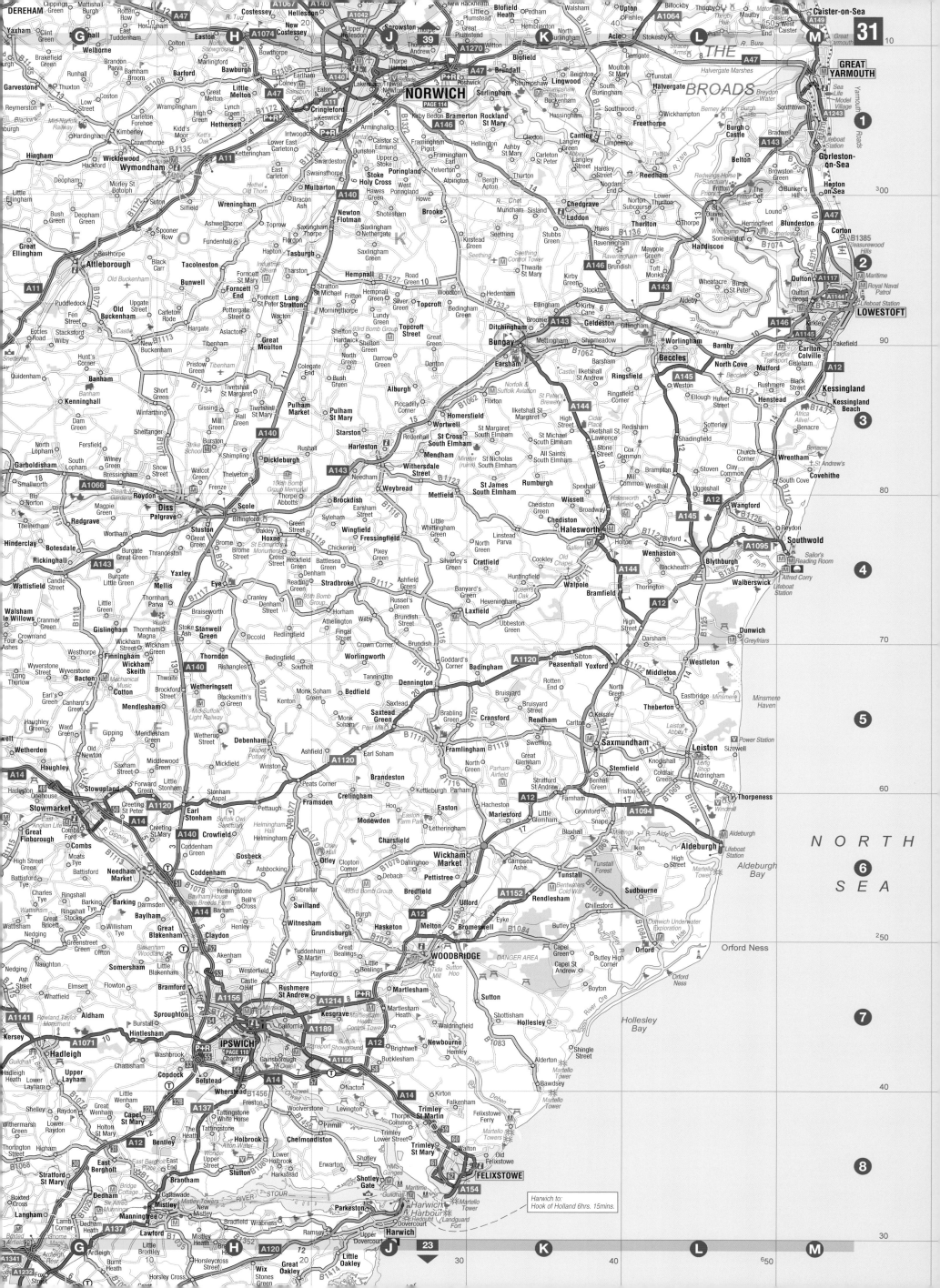

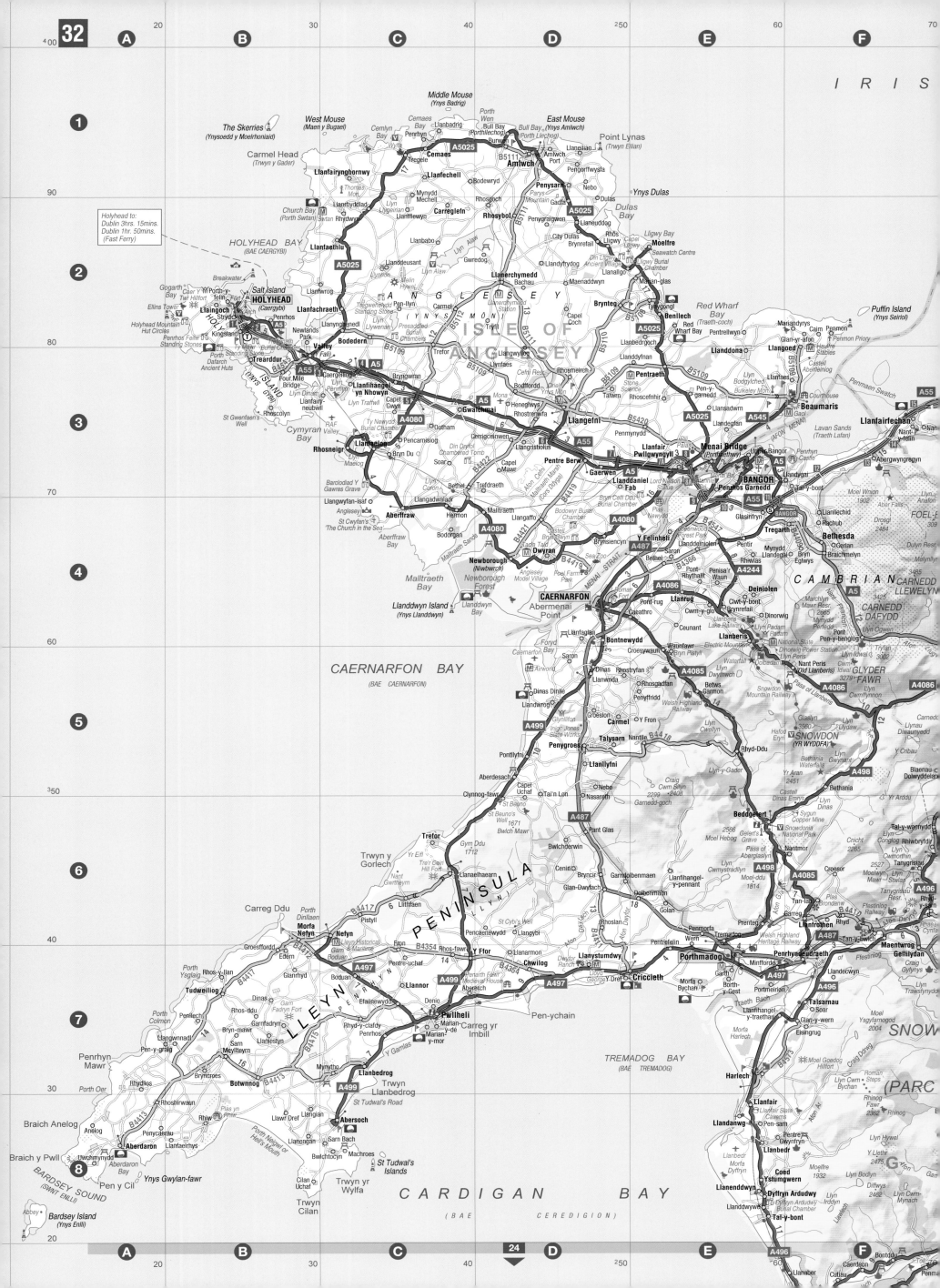

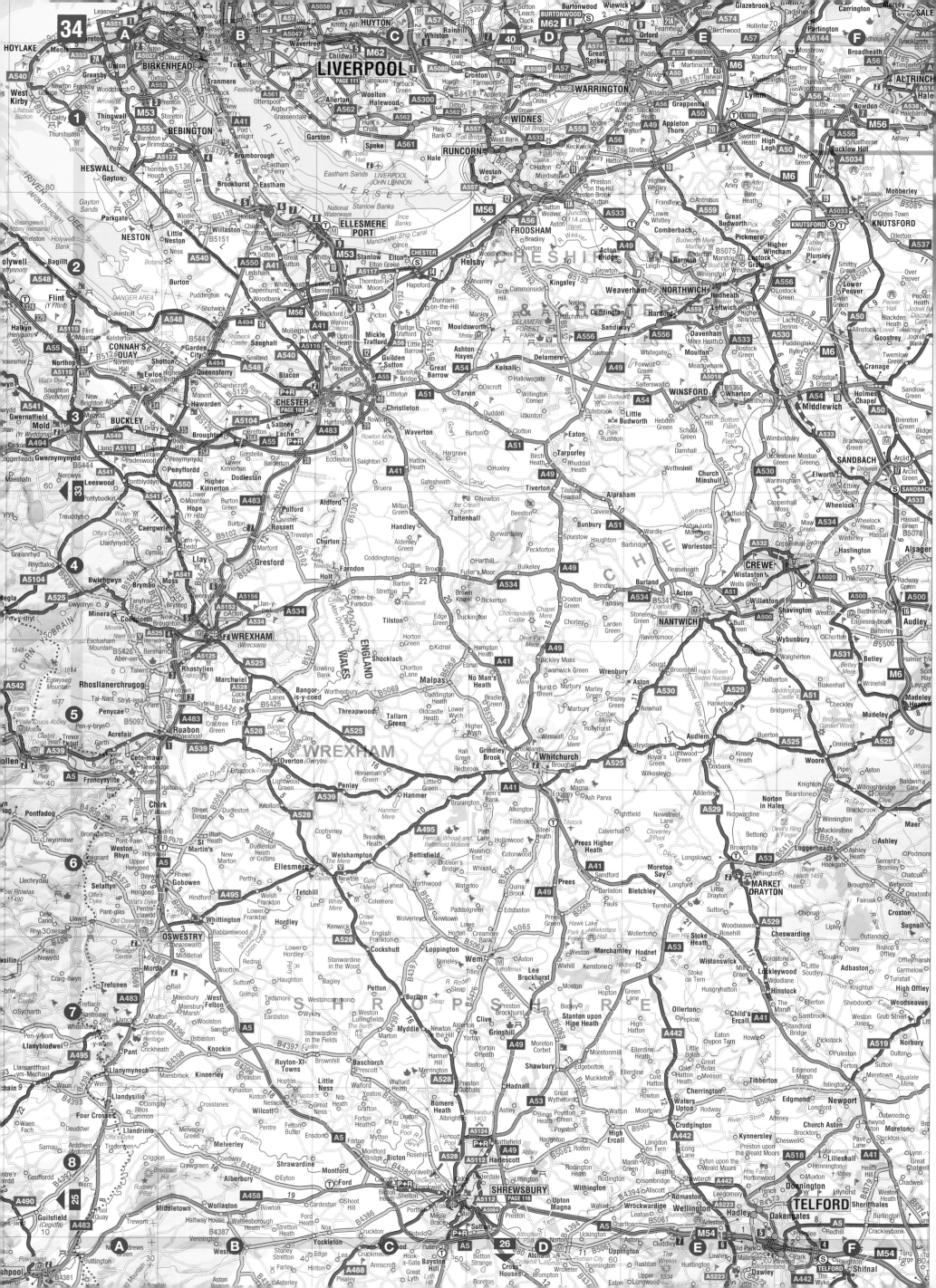

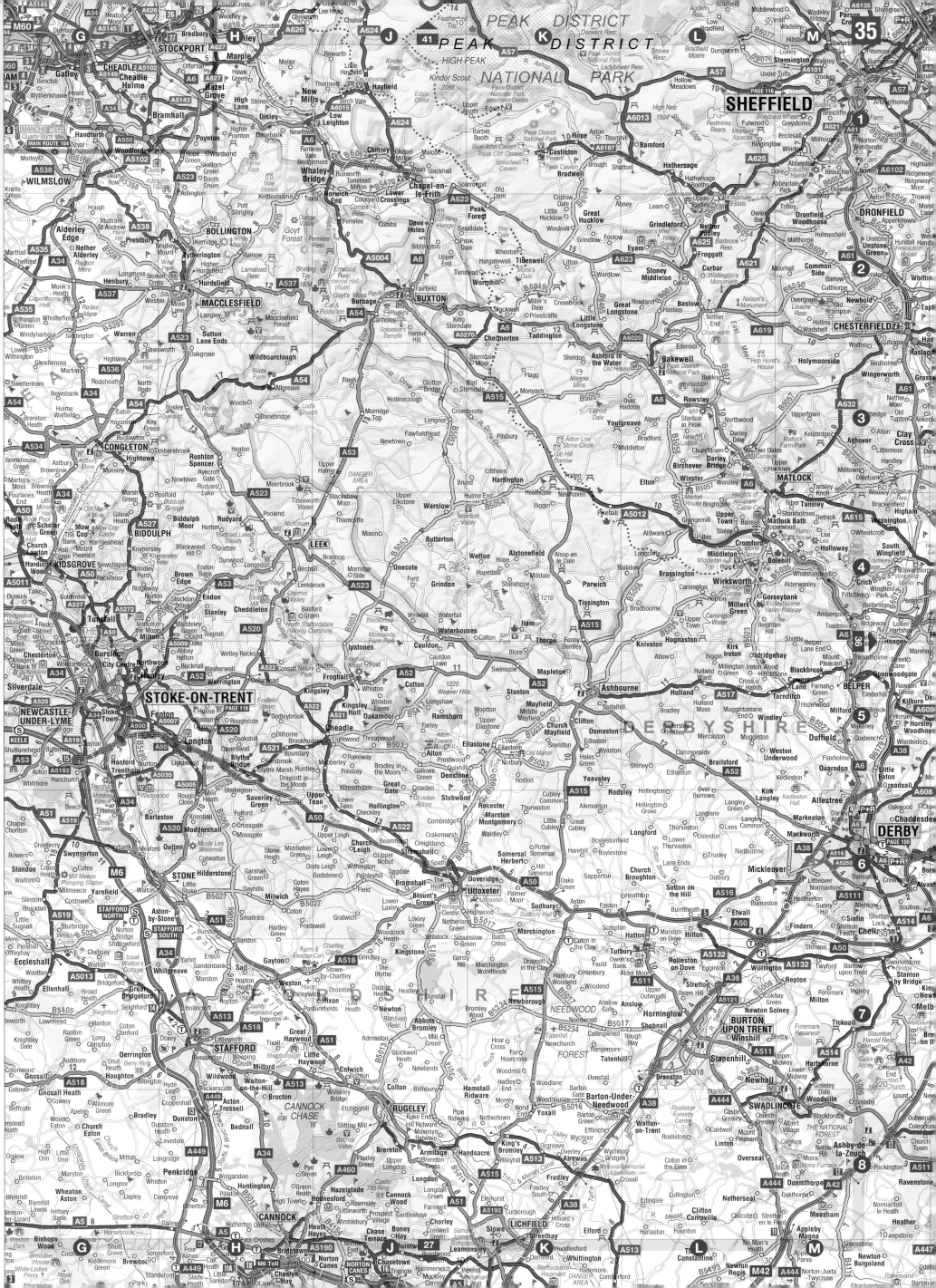

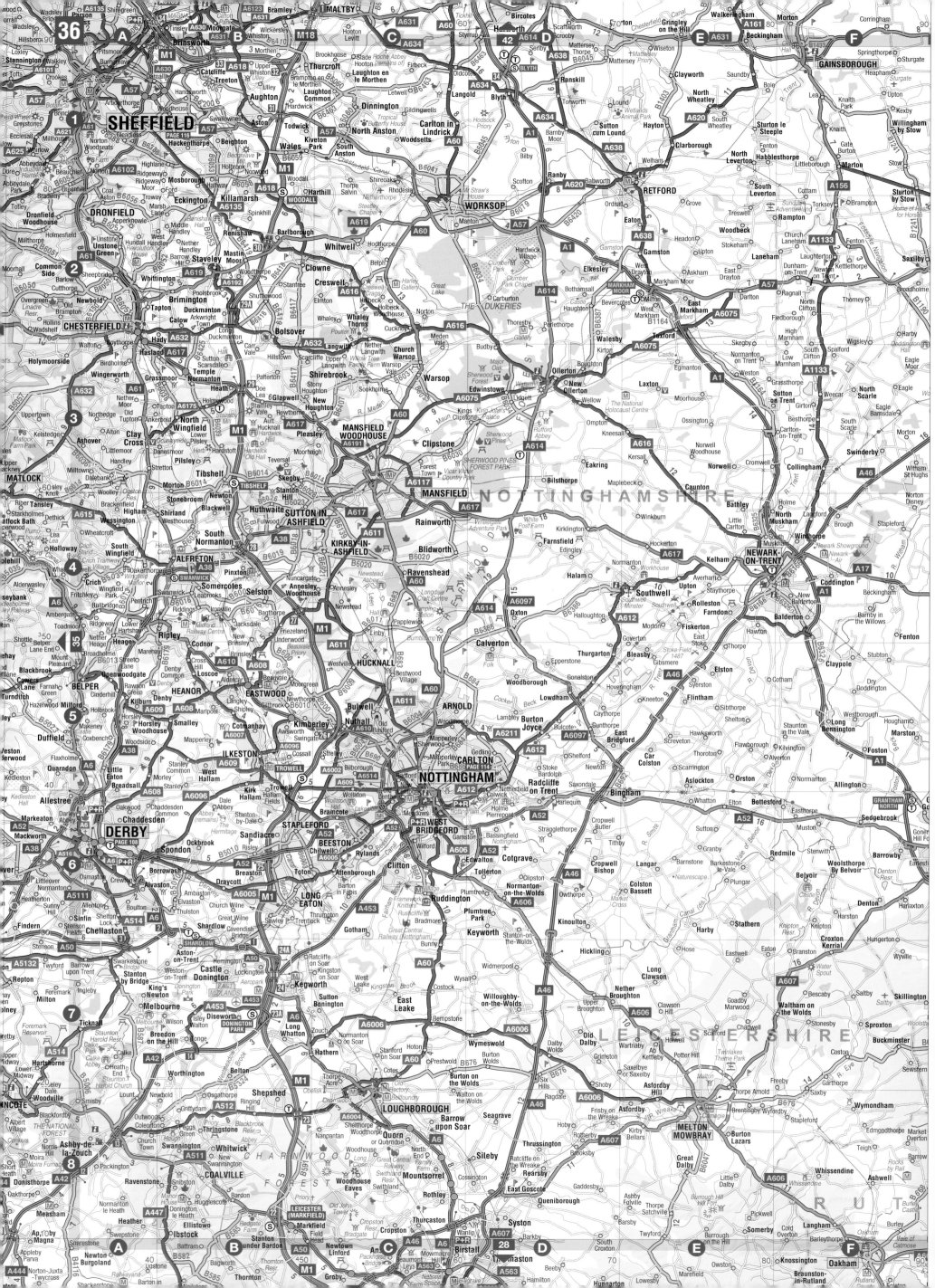

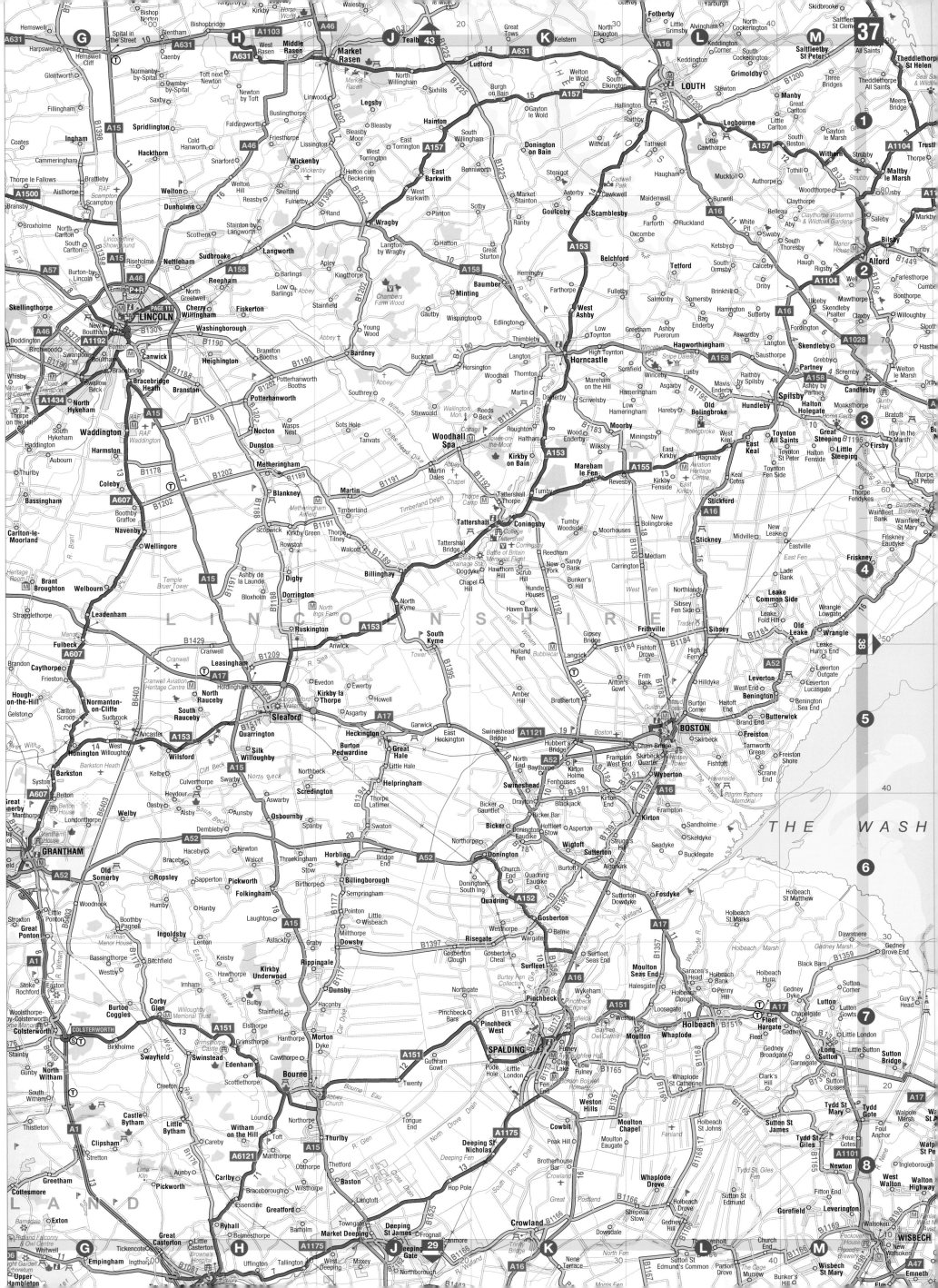

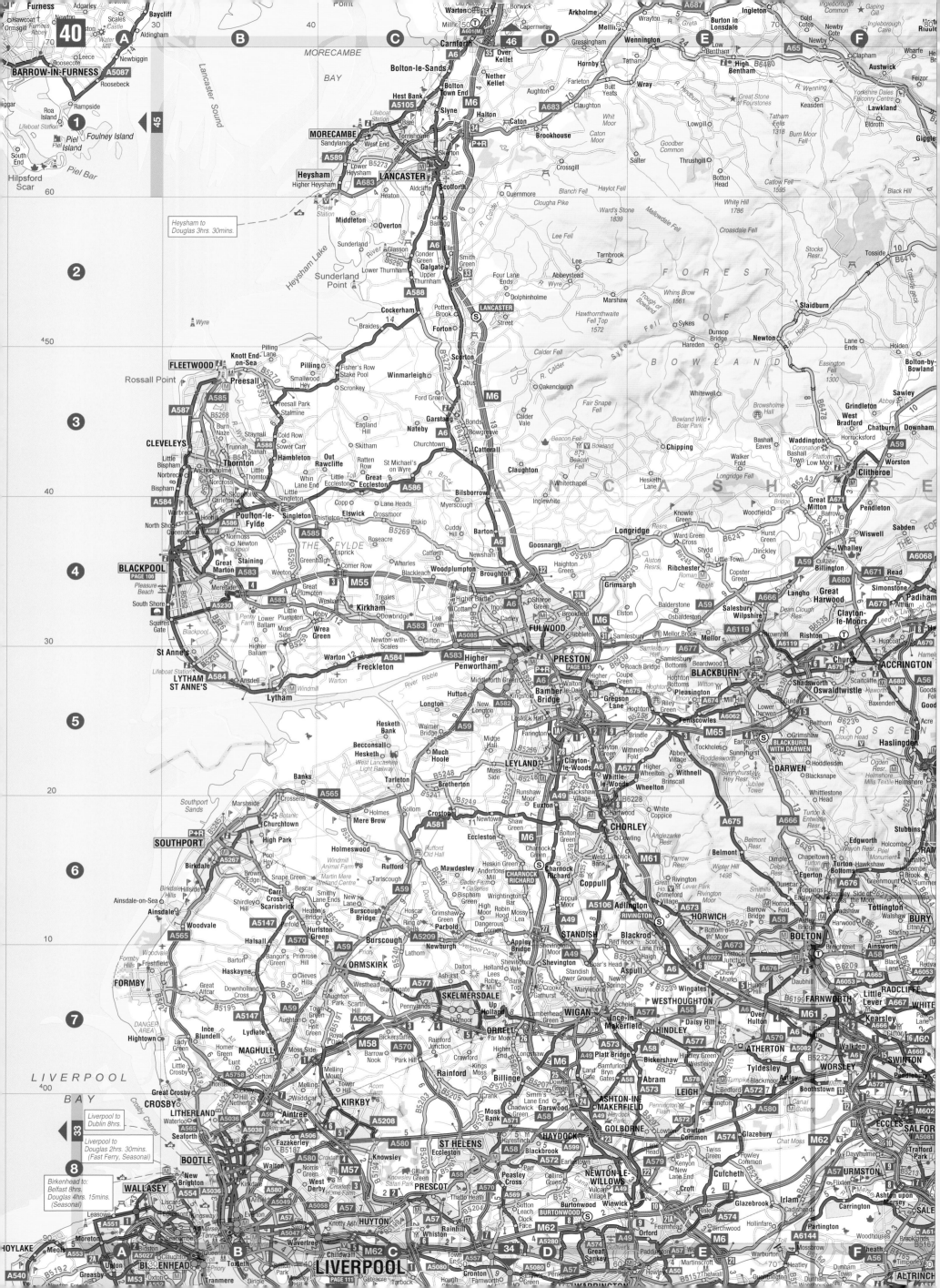

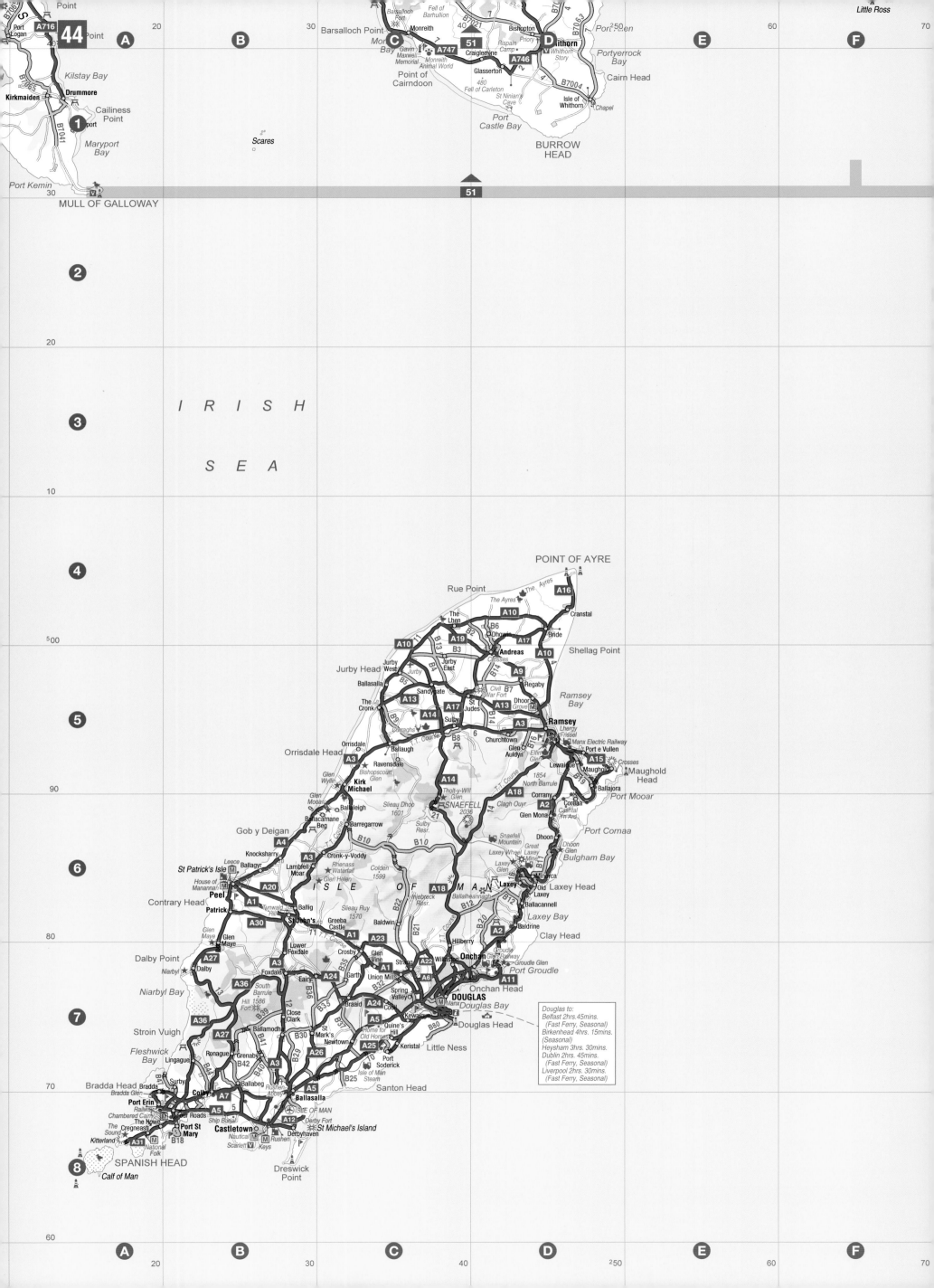

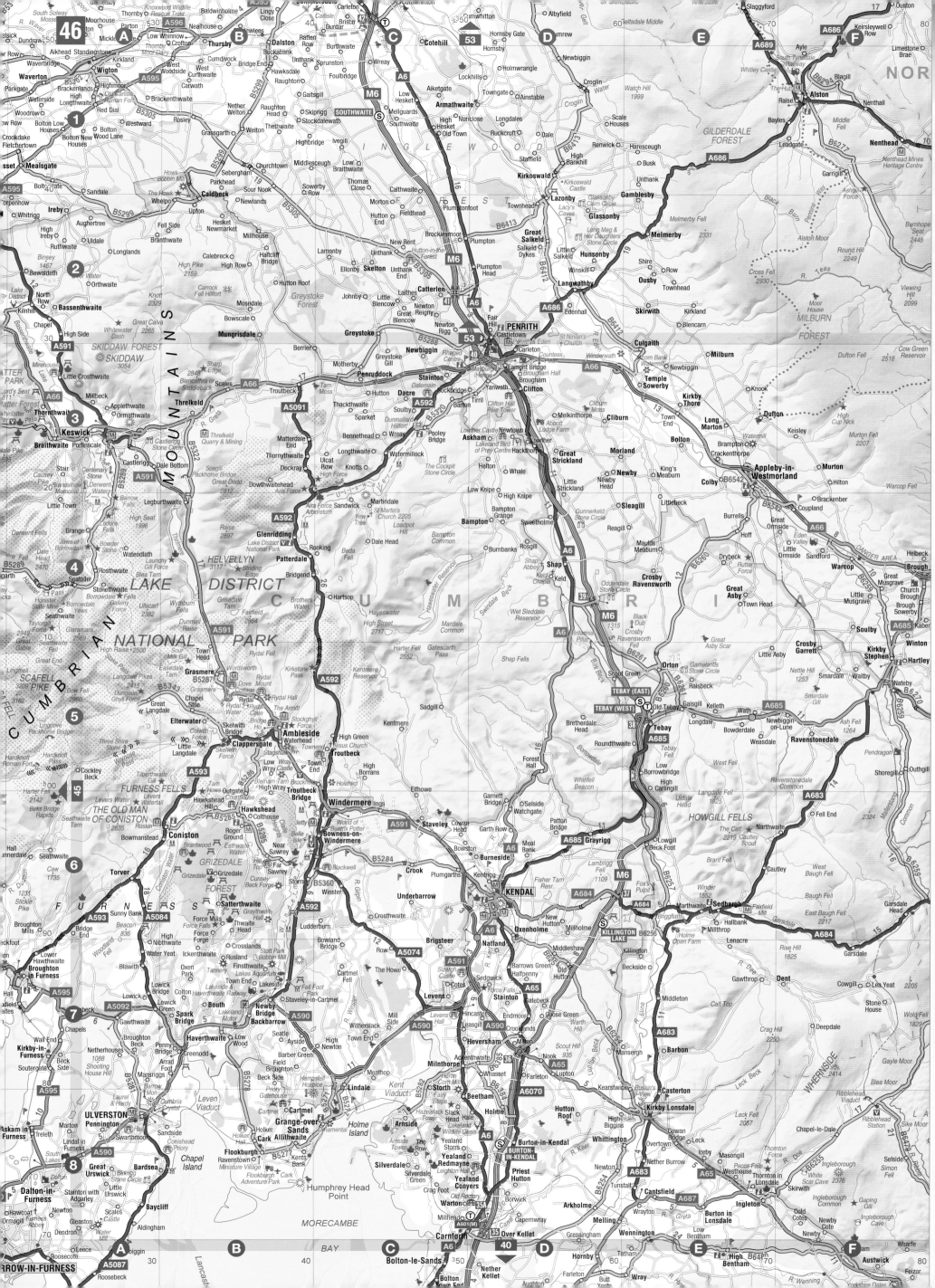

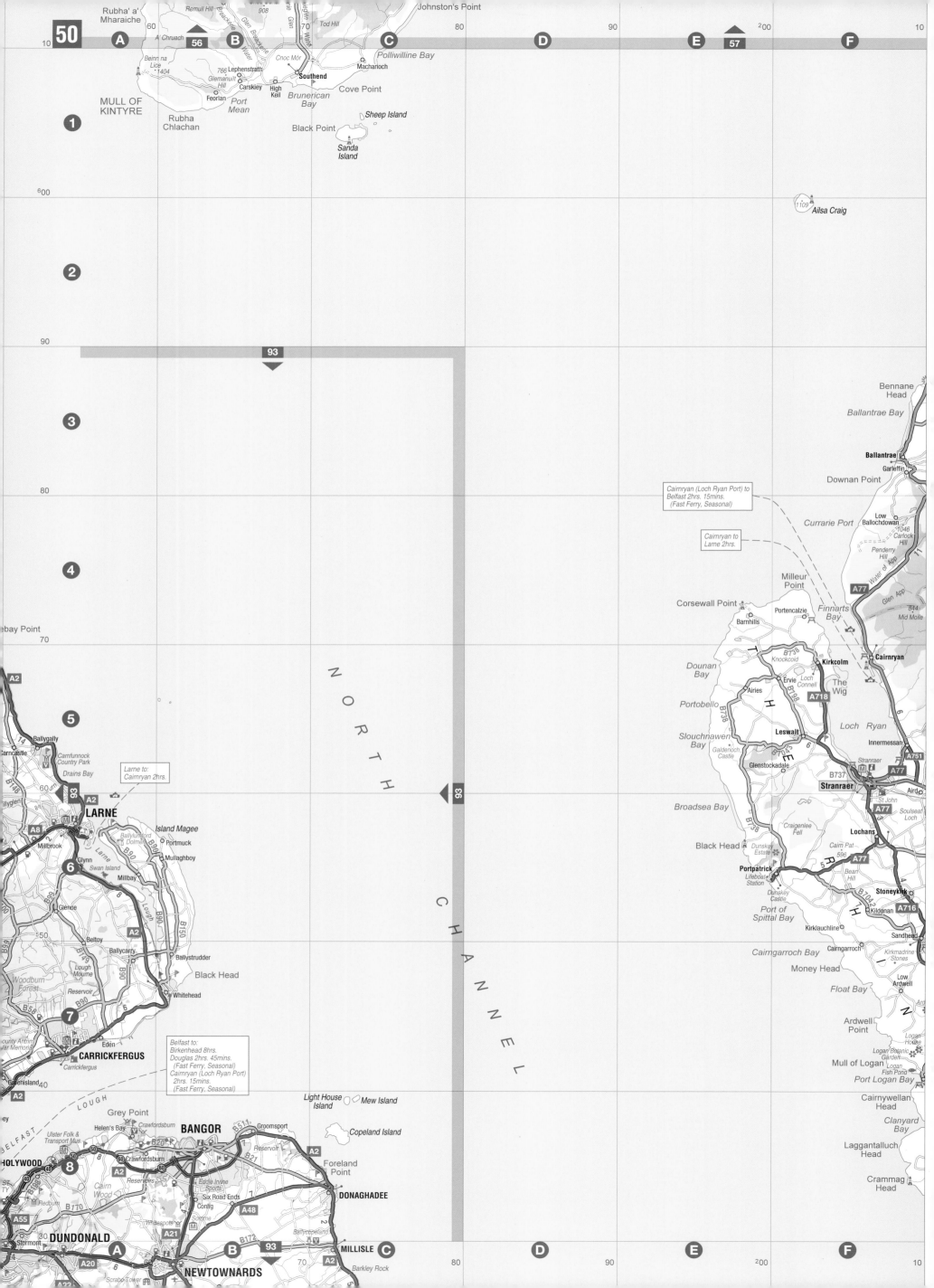

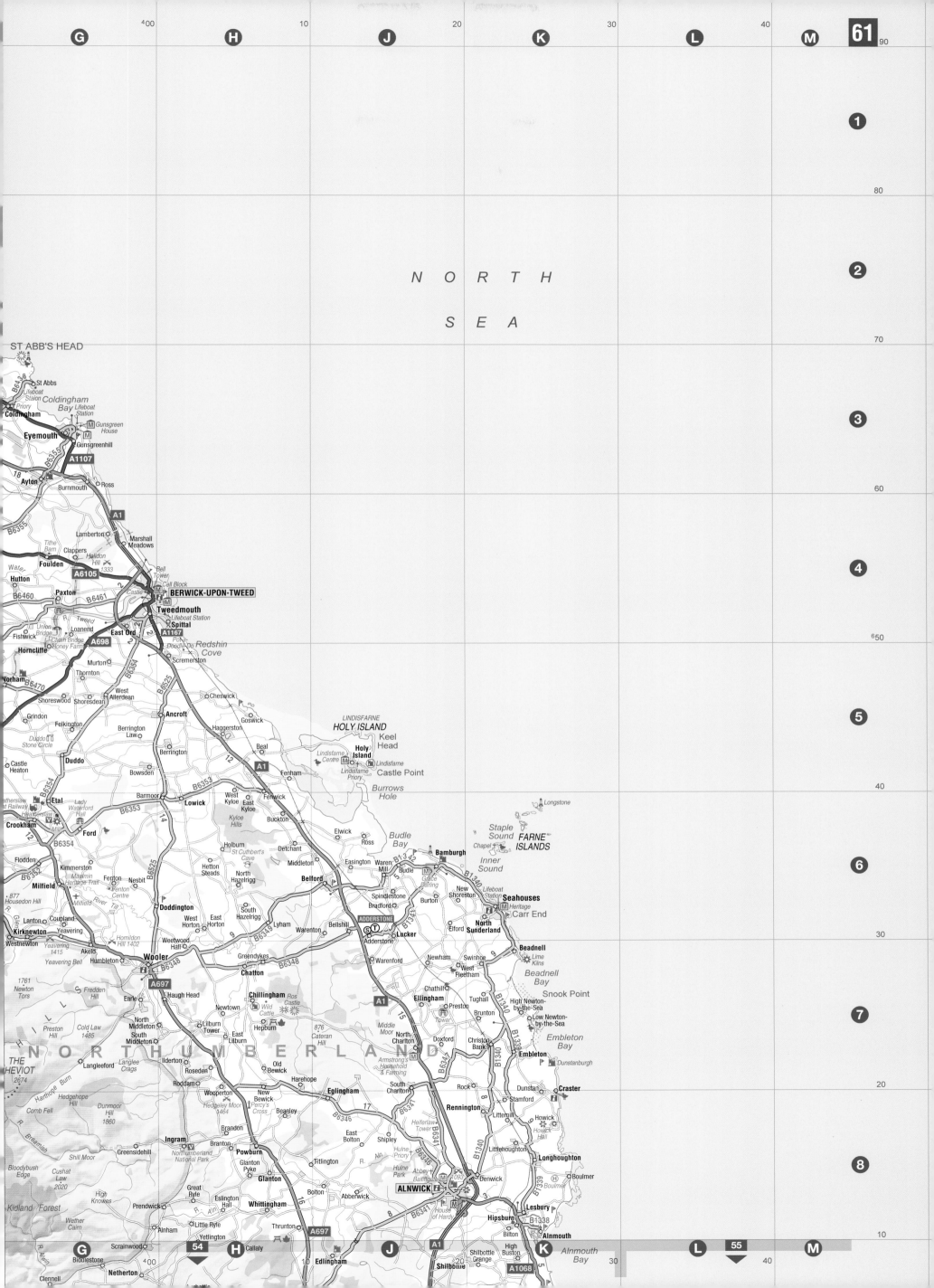

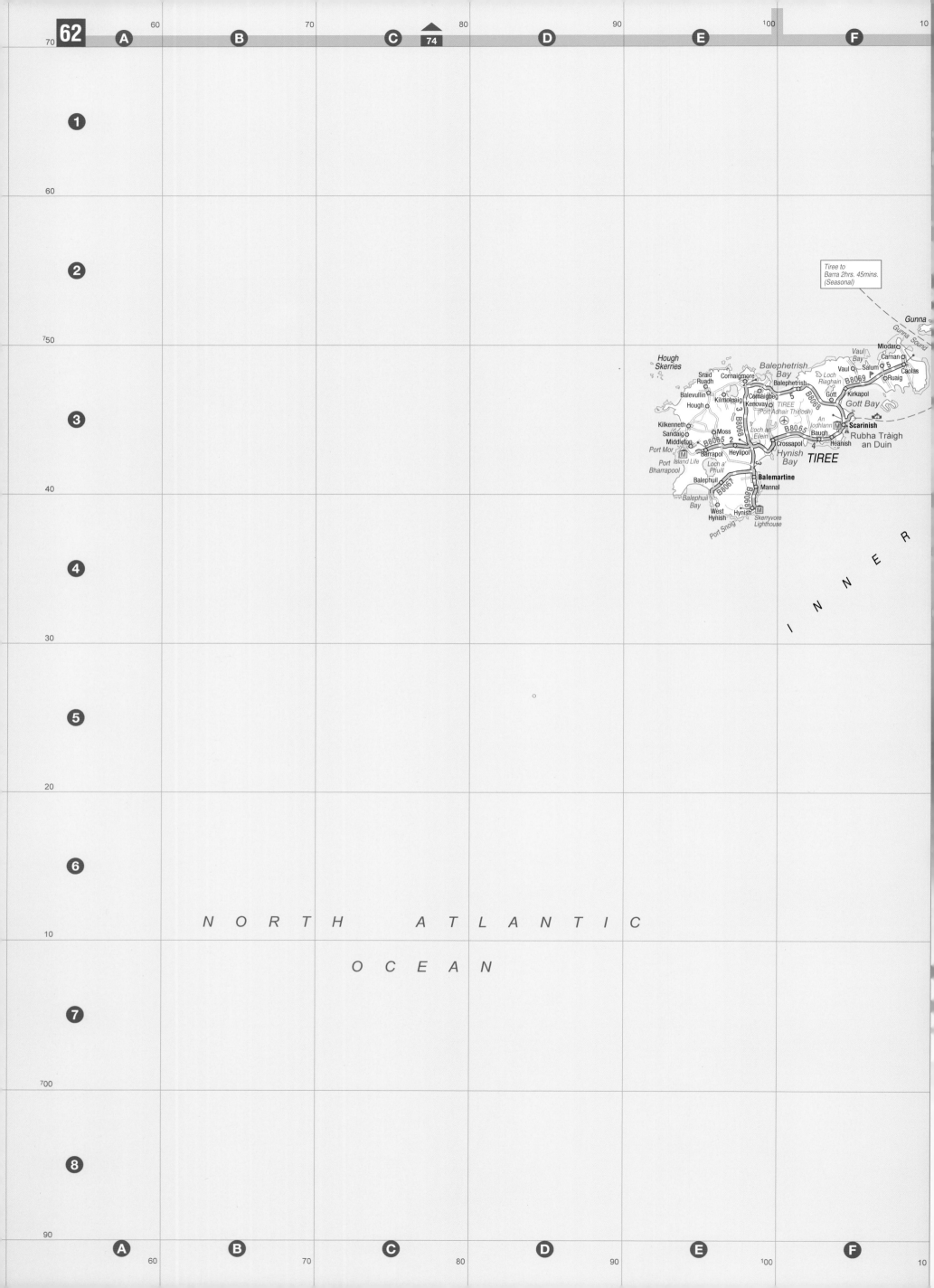

Tiree to
Barra 2hrs. 45mins.
(Seasonal)

Gunna

Gunna Sound

**Hough
Skerries**

Sraid
Ruadh
Cornaigmore
*Balephetrish
Bay*
Balevullin
Kilmoluaig
Cornaigbeg
*Loch
Riaghain*
Vaul
Bay
Miodar
Carnan
Vaul
Salum
Caolas
Ruaig
Balephetrish
B8069
Hough
Kenovay
*TIREE
(Port Adhair Thiridh)*
Gott
Kirkapol
Gott Bay
Kilkenneth
An
lodhlann
Sandaig
Moss
*Loch an
Eilein*
Scarinish
Middleton
Baugh
*Rubha Tràigh
an Duin*
Port Mor
Barrapol
Heylipol
Crossapol
Heanish
*Port
Bharrapool*
Island Life
*Loch a'
Phuill*
*Hynish
Bay*
TIREE
Balephuil
Balemartine
*Balephuil
Bay*
Mannal
West
Hynish
Hynish
*Skerryvore
Lighthouse*
Port Snoig

I N N E R

N O R T H   A T L A N T I C

O C E A N

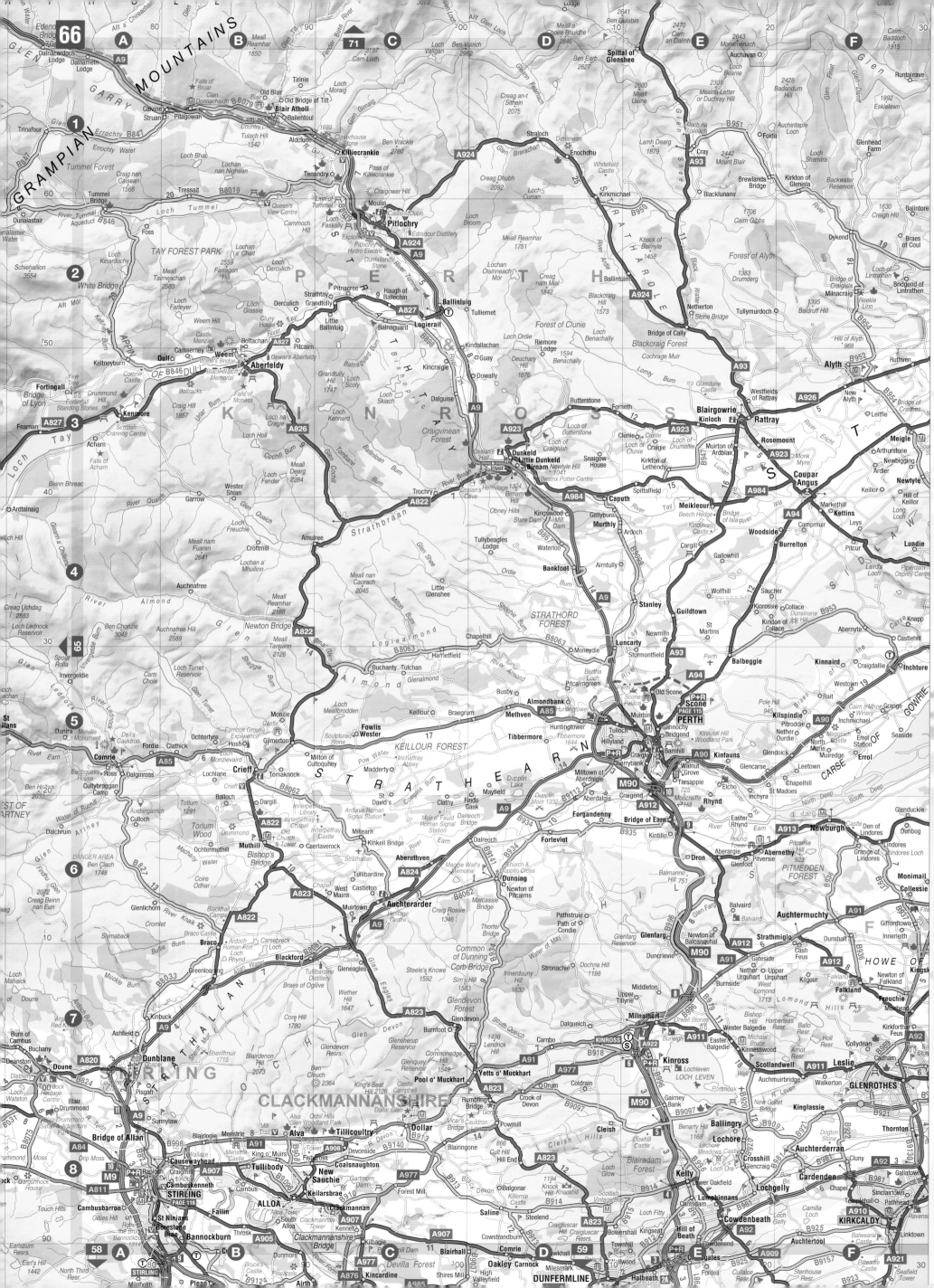

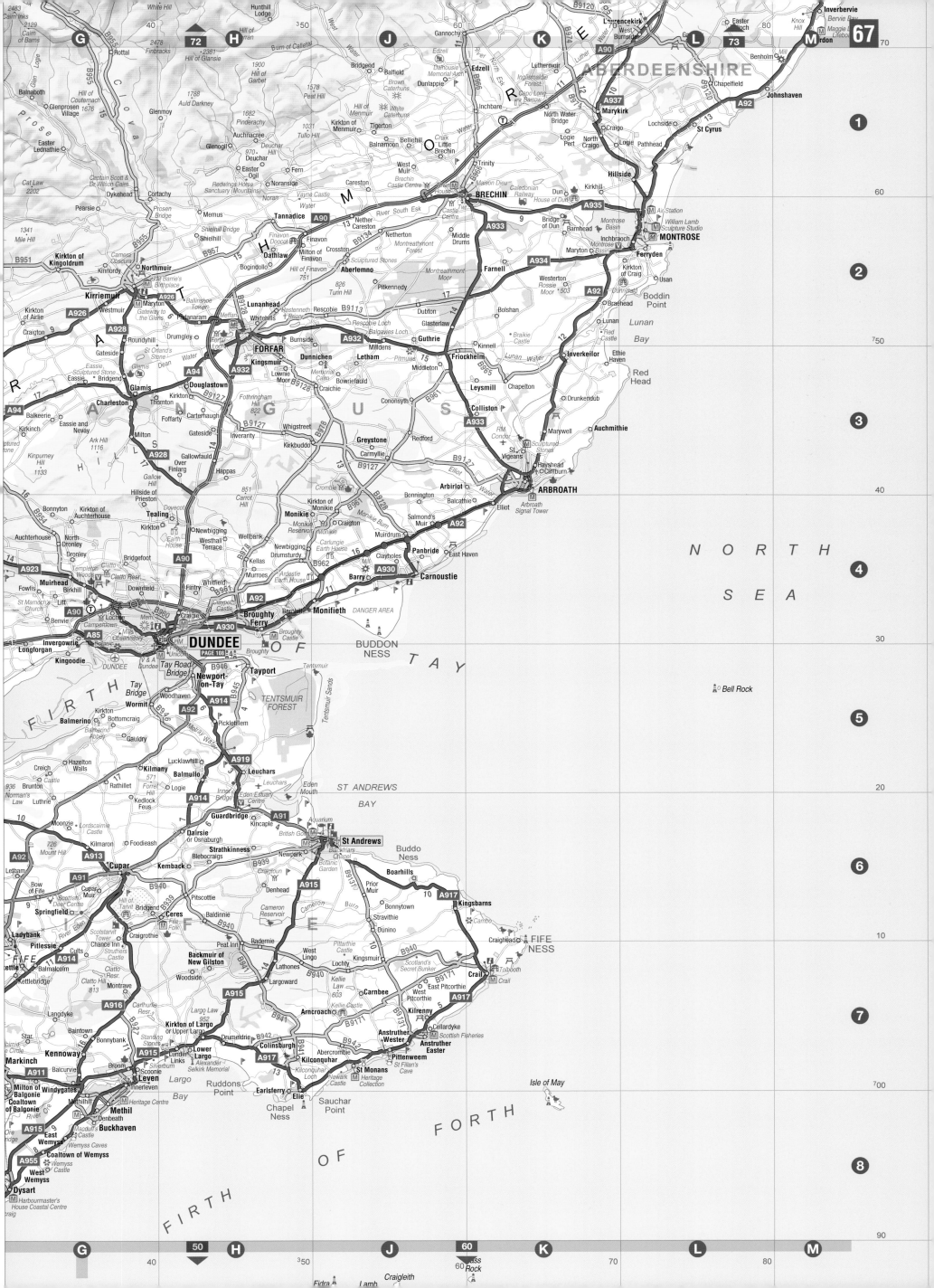

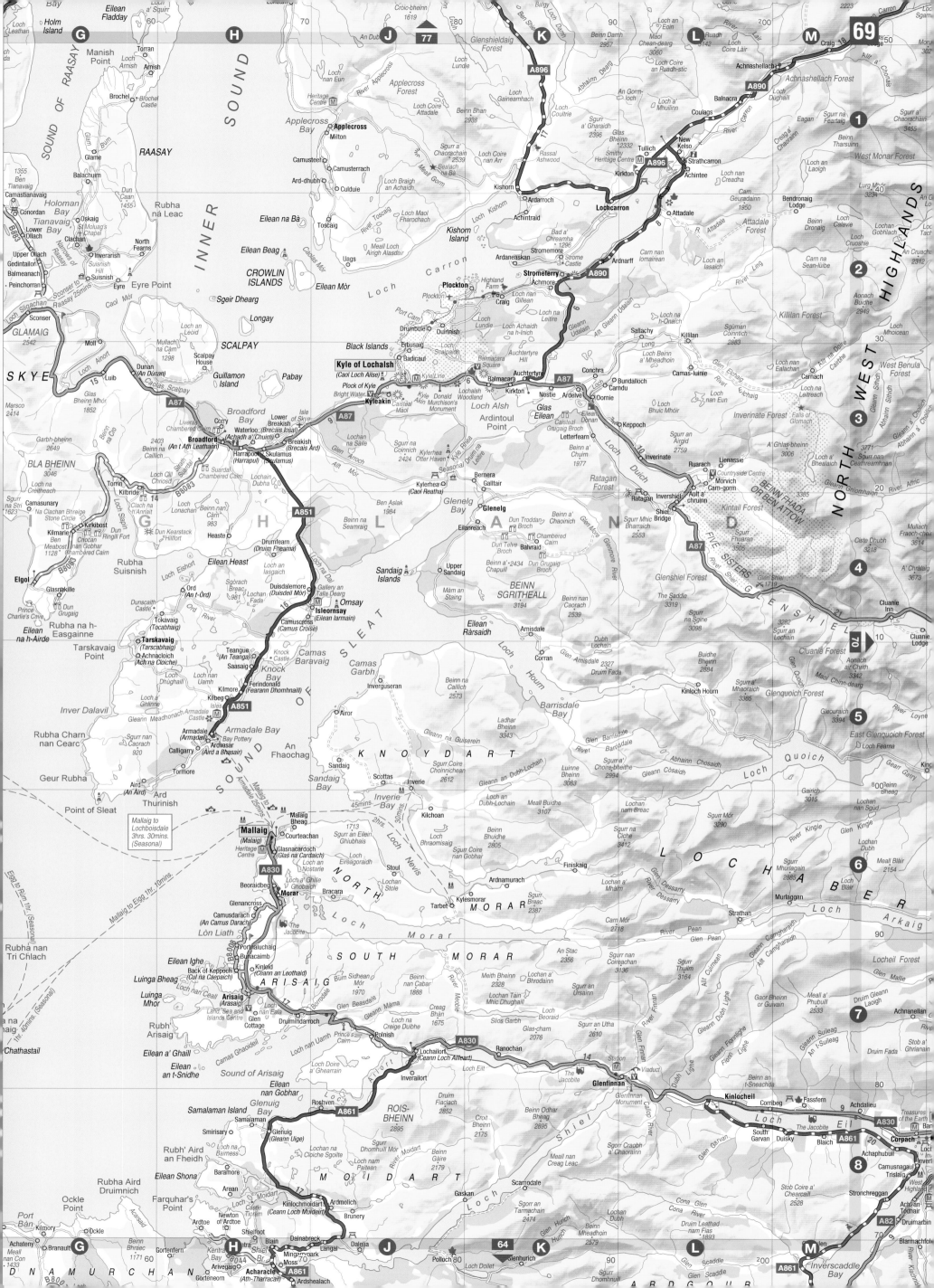

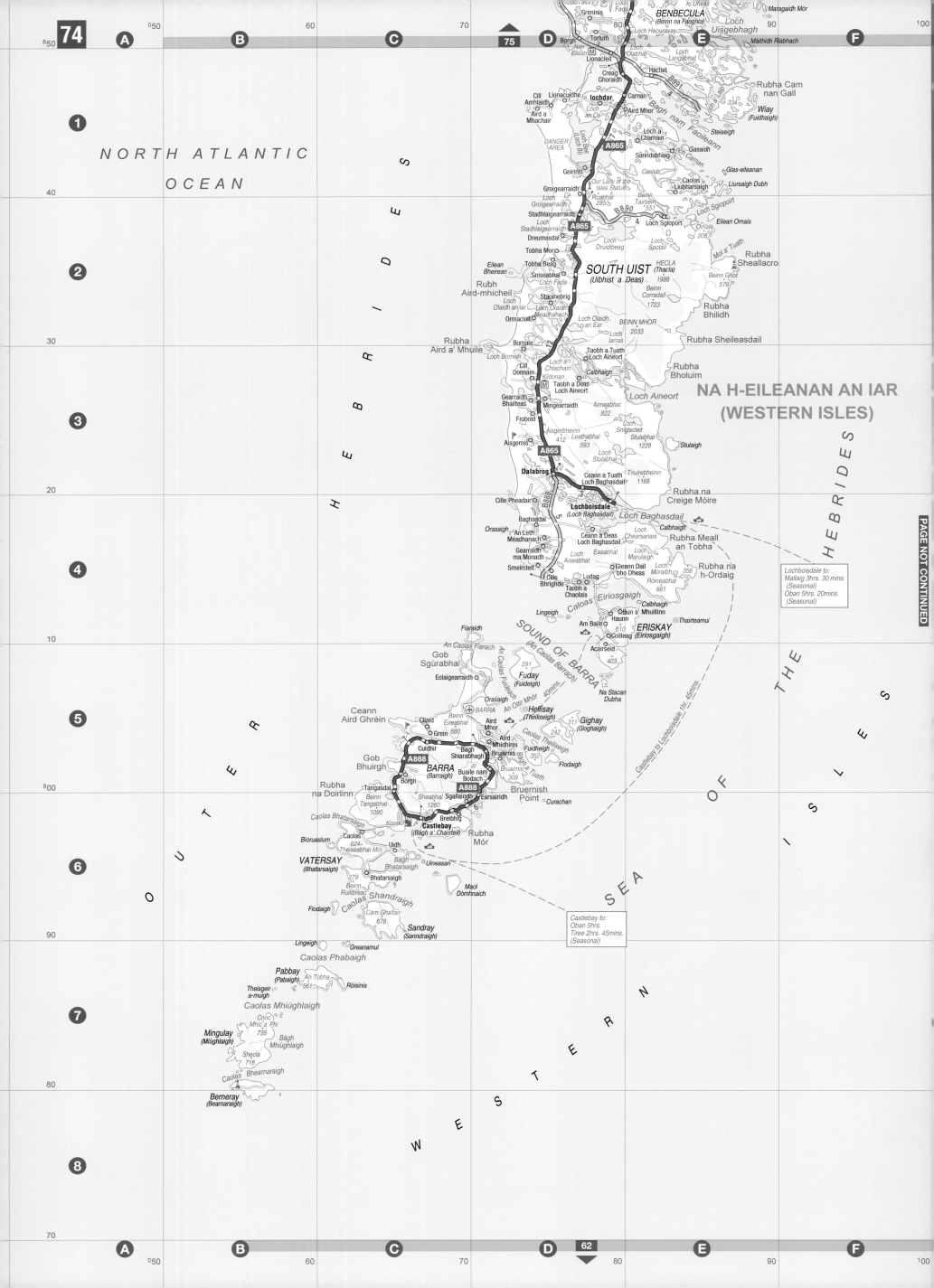

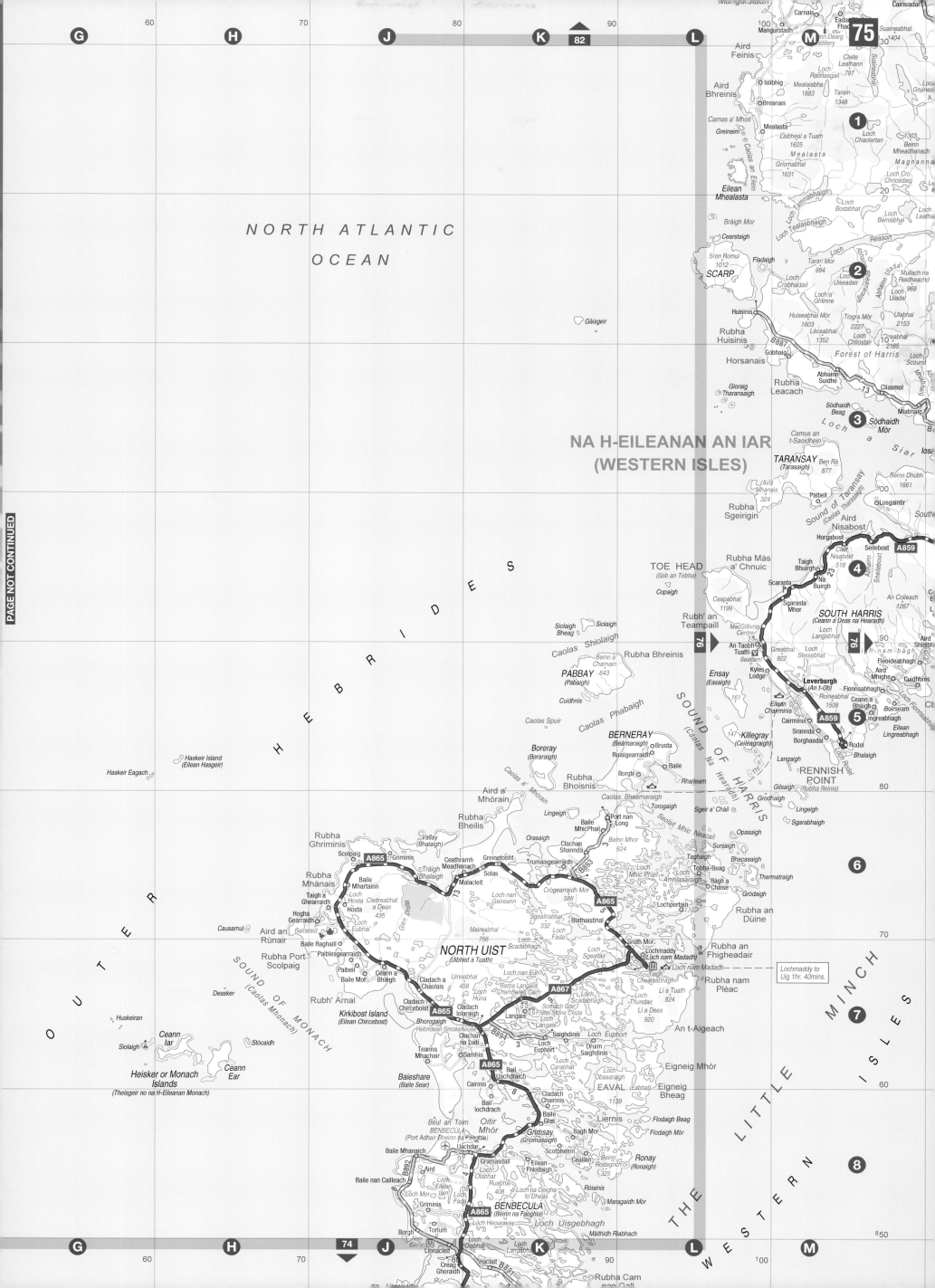

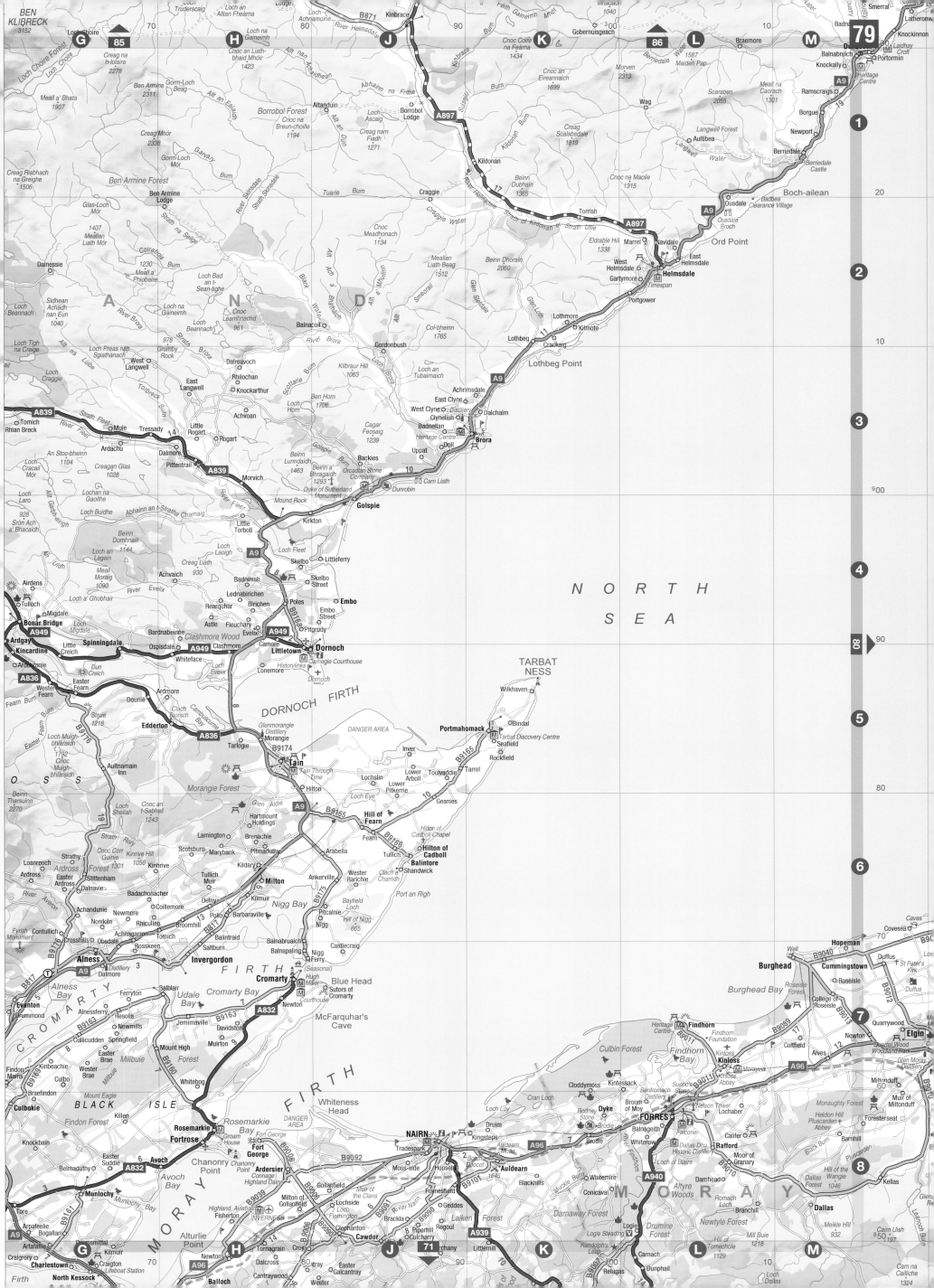

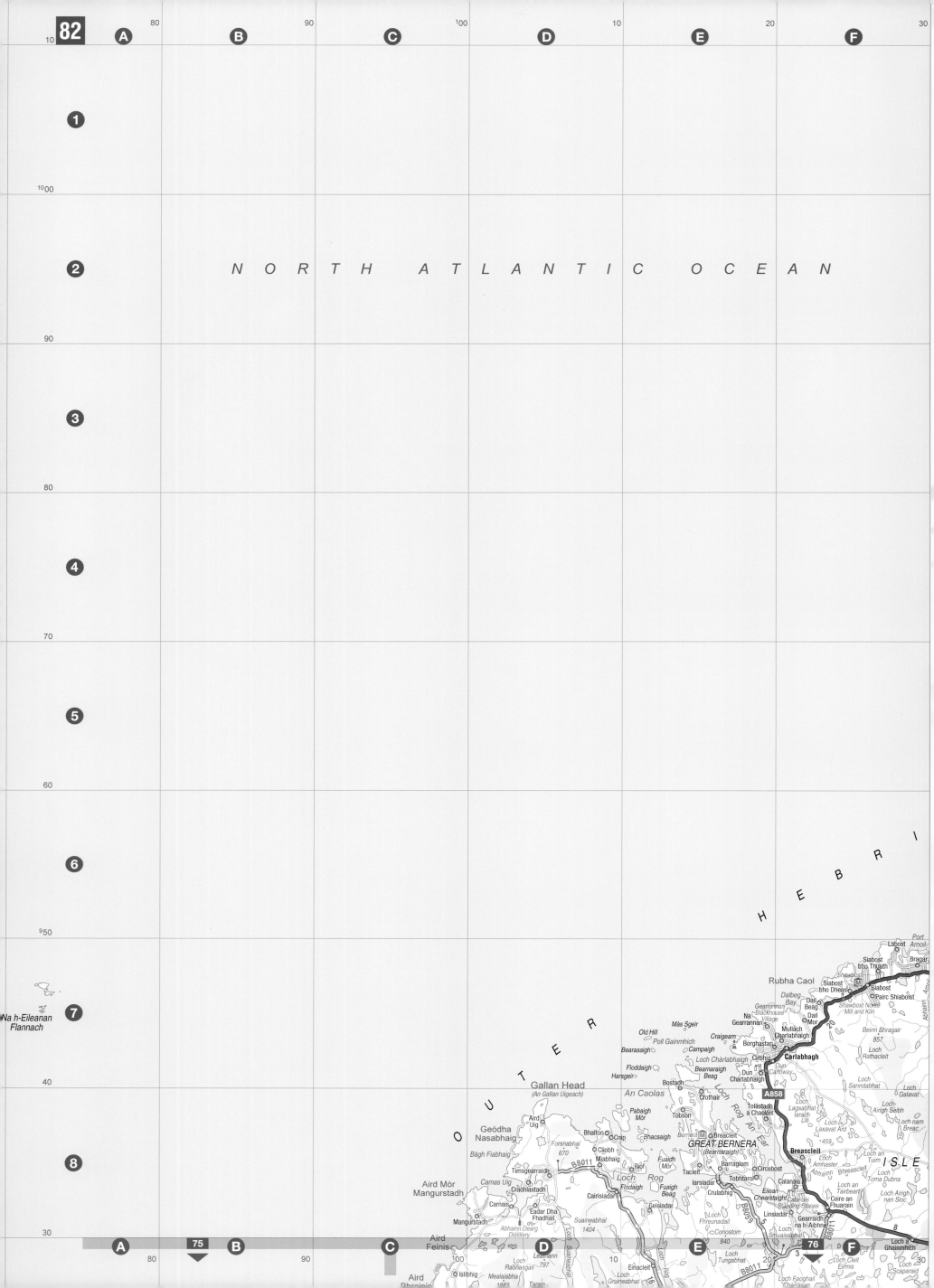

N O R T H   A T L A N T I C   O C E A N

Na h-Eileanan Flannach

O U T E R

H E B R I

I S L E

Gallan Head
(An Gallan Uigeach)

Geòdha Nasabhaig

Bàgh Fiabhaig

Aird Mòr Mangurstadh

Camas Uig

Cradhlastadh

Carnais

Eadar Dha Fhadhail

Mangurstadh

Abhainn Dearg Distillery

Suaineabhal
1404

Aird Feinis

Aird Bhroinis

Islibhig

Mealaisbha
1882

Aird
Uig

Bhalton

Cliobh

Cnip

Forsnabhal
670

Miabhaig

Riòf

Pabaigh Mòr

Bhacsaigh

Fuaidh Mòr

Tacleit

Barraglom

Fuaigh Beag

Iarsiadar

Tobhtarol

Circebost

Crulabhig

Calanais

Eilean Chearstaigh

Càlanais Standing Stones

Coire an Fhuarain

Linsiadar

Gearraidh na h-Aibhne

Loch Faoghail Charrasan

Geisiadar

Cairisiadar

GREAT BERNERA
(Bearnaraigh)

Breascleit

Bostadh

Crothair

An Caolas

Bearnaraigh Beag

Bearasaigh

Floddaigh

Harsgeiro

Loch Chàrlabhaigh

Campaigh

Craigeam

Mullach Chàrlabhaigh

Borghastan

Cirbhig

Dun Charlabhaigh

Dun Carloway

Carlabhagh

Mas Sgeir

Poll Gainmhich

Old Hill

Na Gearrannan

Gearrannan Blackhouse Village

Dalbeg

Dail Beag

Dail Mòr

Shawbost Norse Mill and Kiln

Mullàch

Siabost bho Dheas

Shawbost

Siabost

Pairc Shiabost

Rubha Caol

Siabost bho Thuath

Labost

Bragar

Port Arnoil

Dalbeg Bay

Beinn Bhragair
857

Loch Rathacleit

Loch Sanndabhat

Loch Langabhat Iarach

Loch Lagsabhat Iarach

Loch Laxavat Ard

Loch Airigh Seibh

Loch nam Breac

Loch Galavat

Loch an Tairbeart

Loch Toma Dubna

Loch Airigh nan Sloc

Loch an Amhaster

Loch Smuaisebhal

Loch Tungabhat

Loch Cleit Eirmis

Loch a' Ghainmhich

Loch Raonasgail

Loch Gruineabhal

Taraïn

Leathann
797

Einacleit

Conostom

840

459

Pabaigh Mòr

A858

B8011

B8011

B8059

B8011

Abhainn Aniol

Loch Rog

Loch Rog An Ear

Loch Flodaigh

Loch Suaineabhal

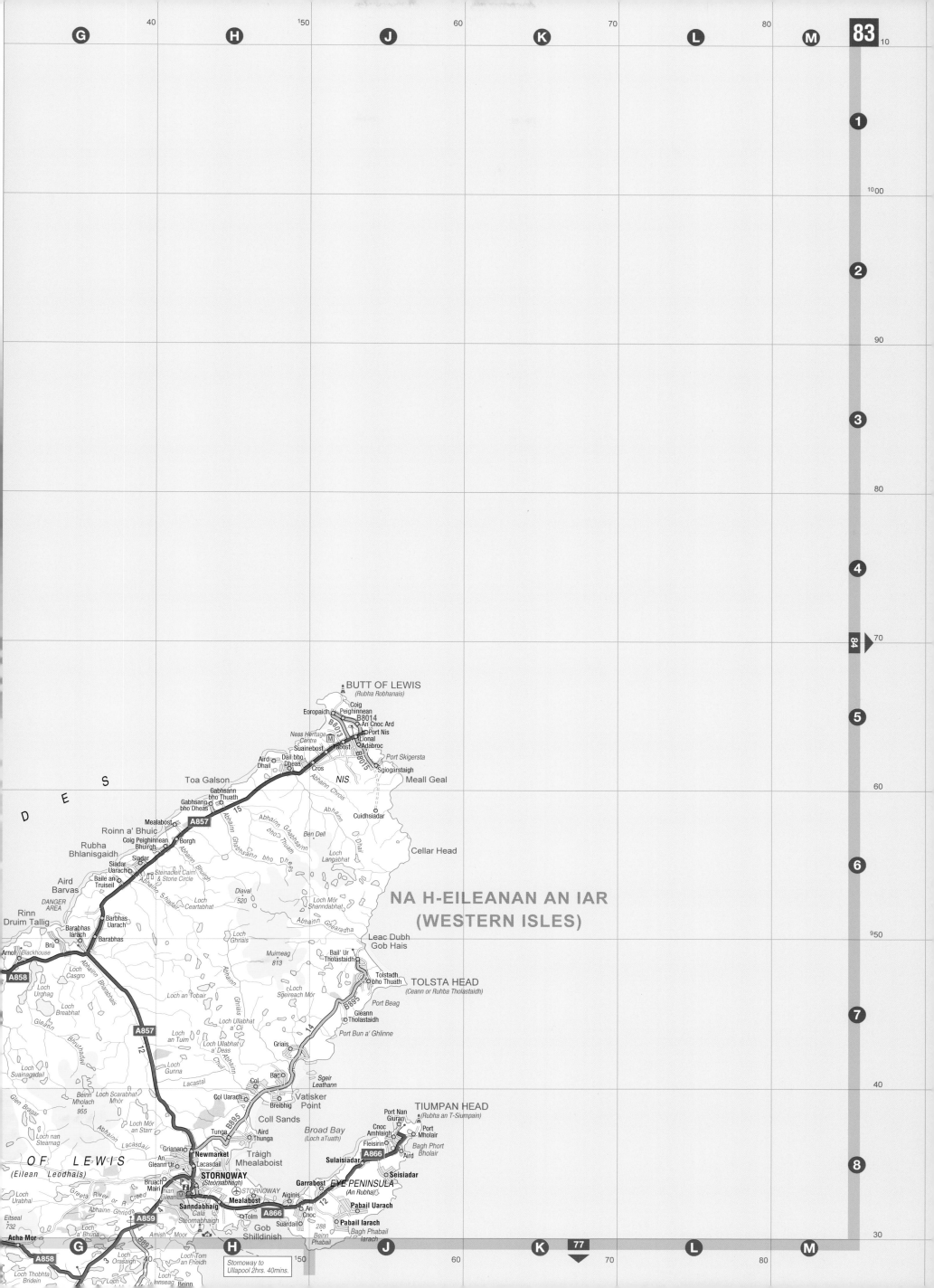

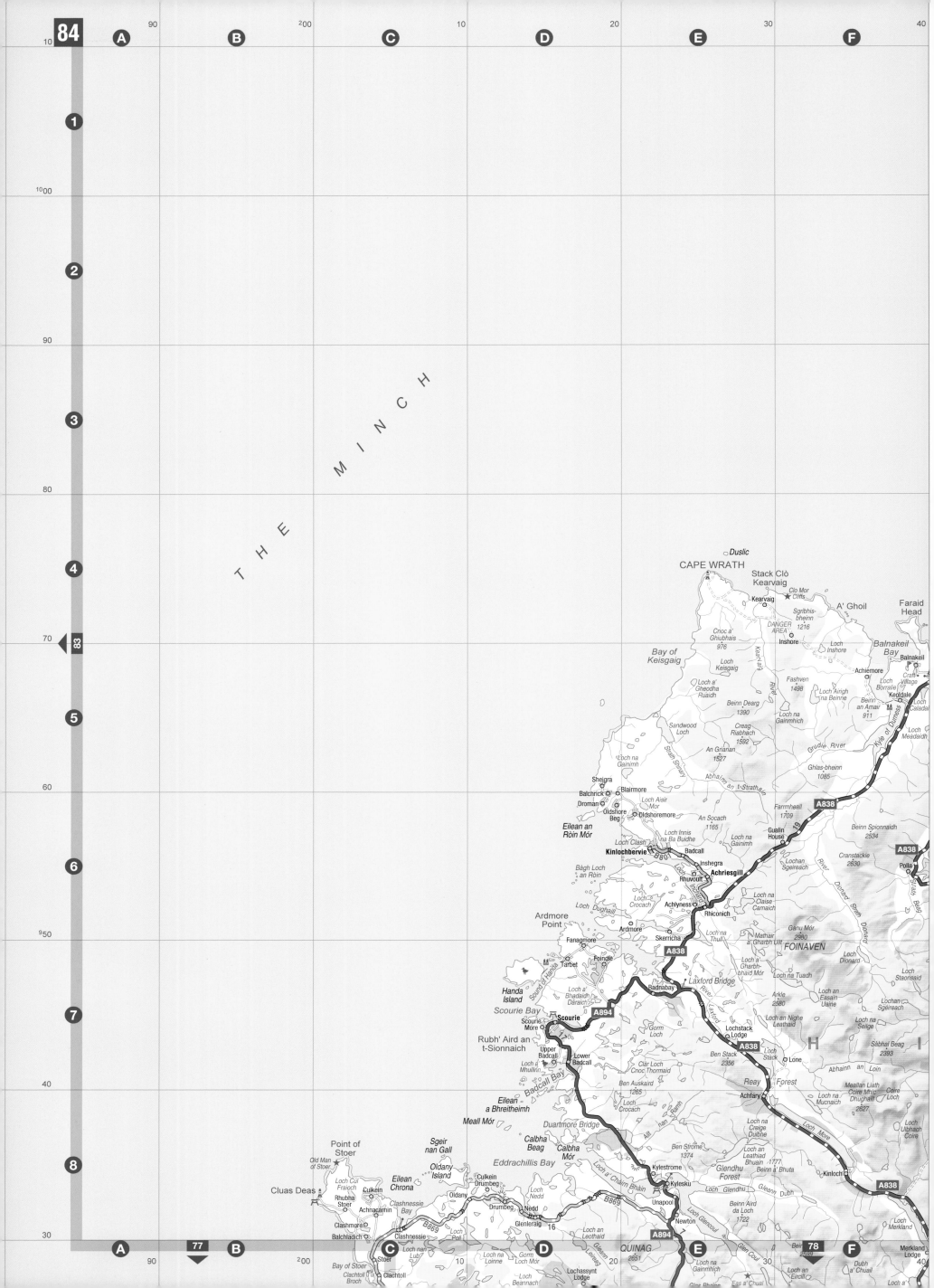

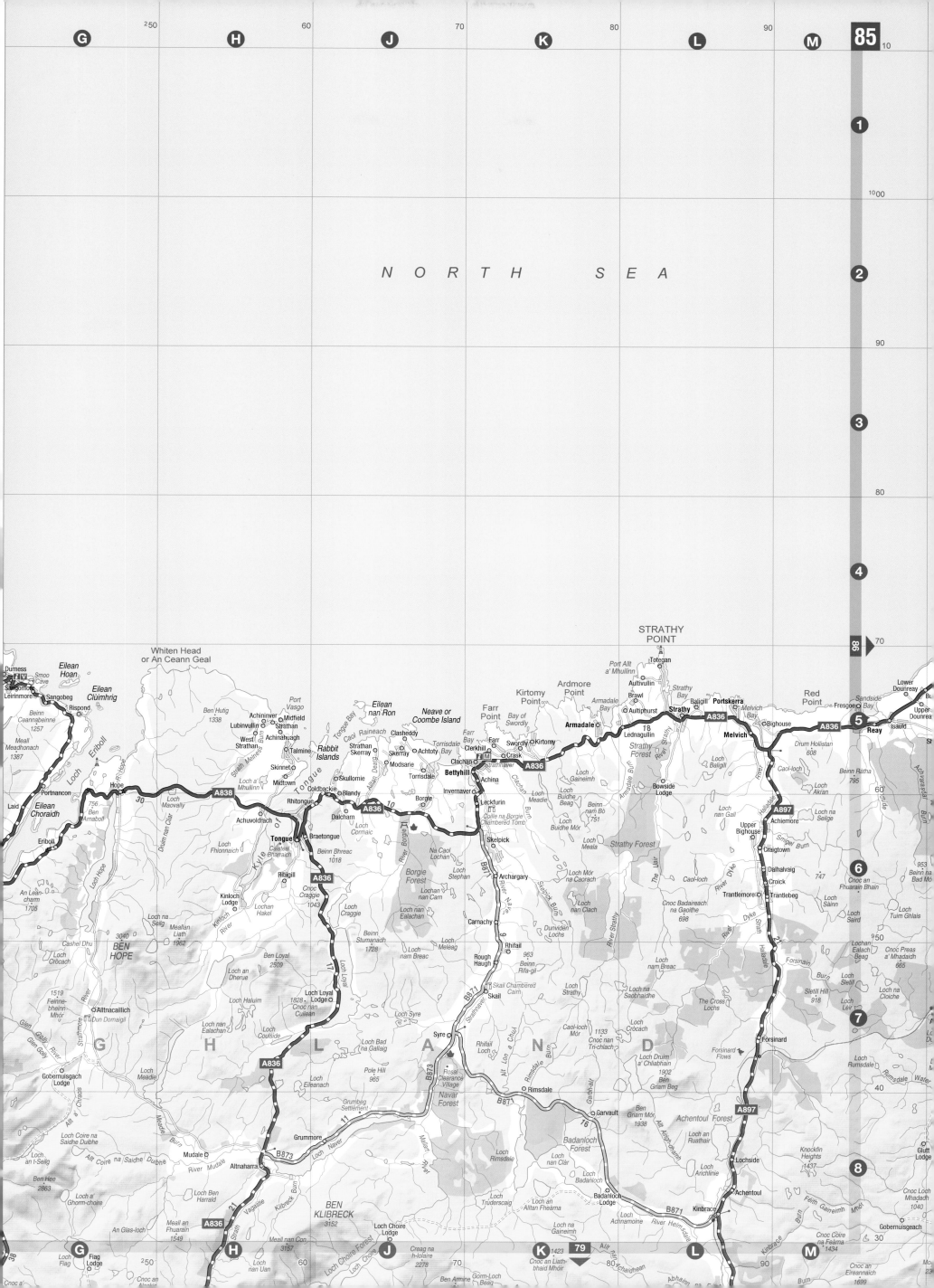

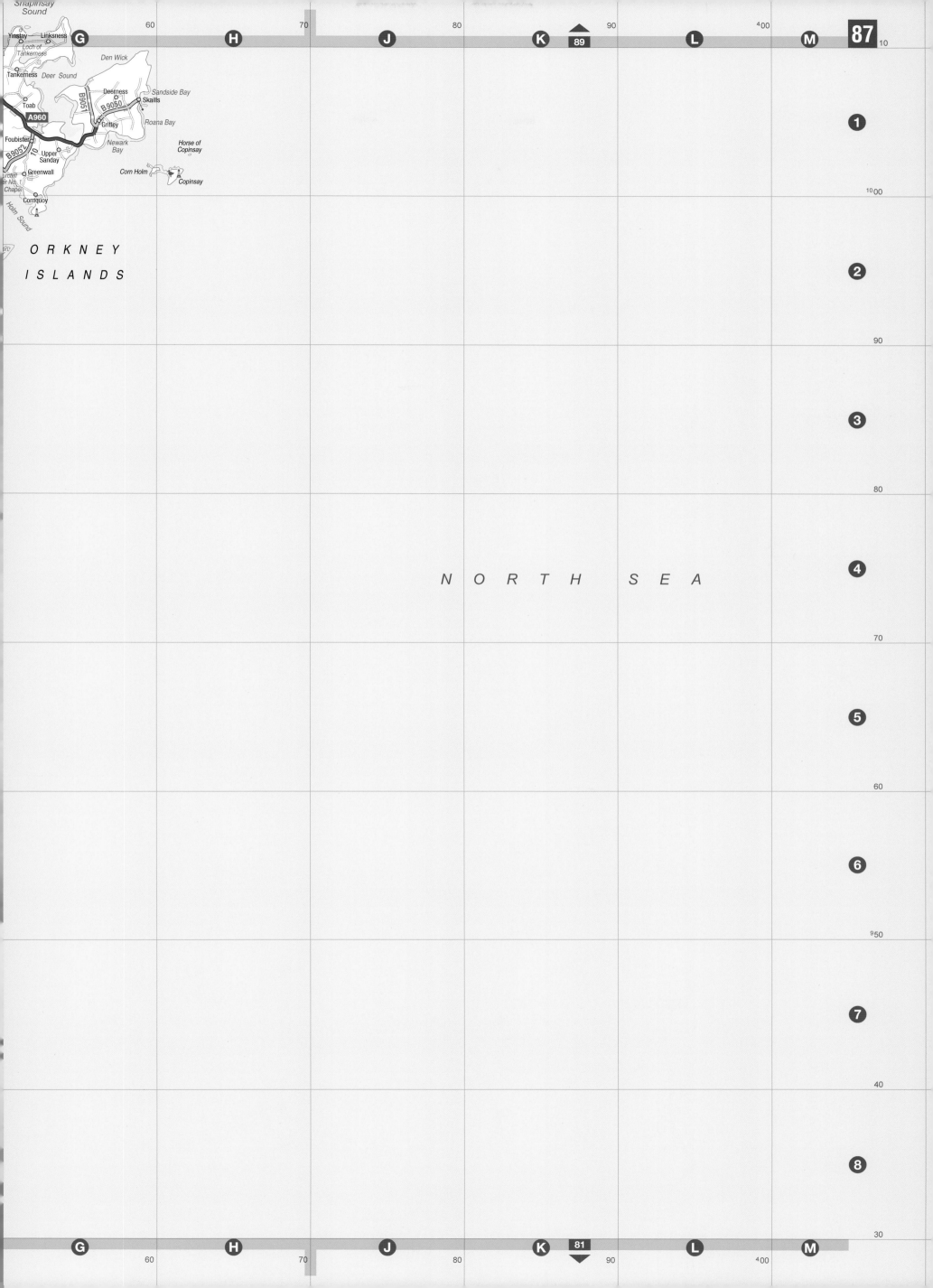

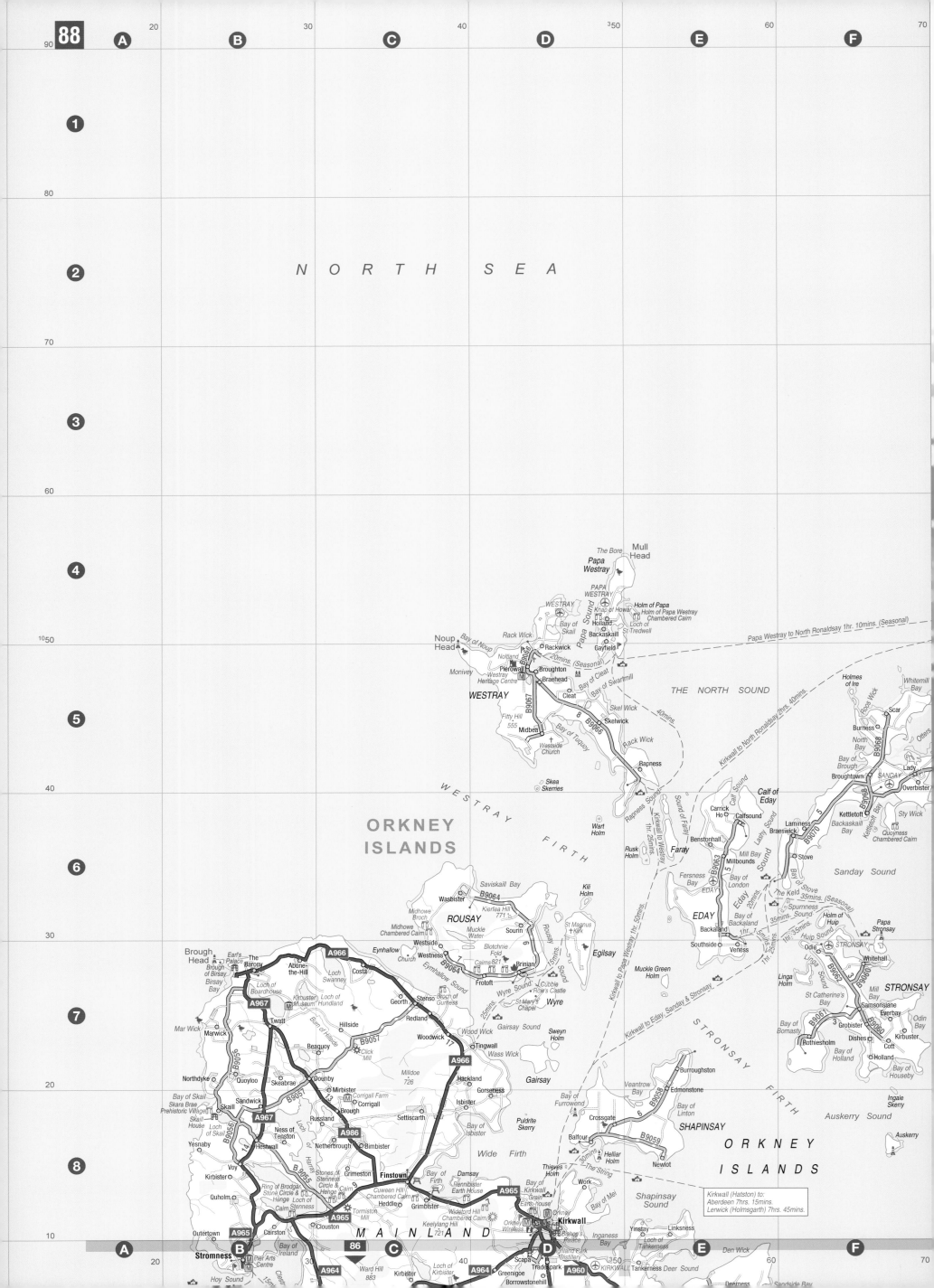

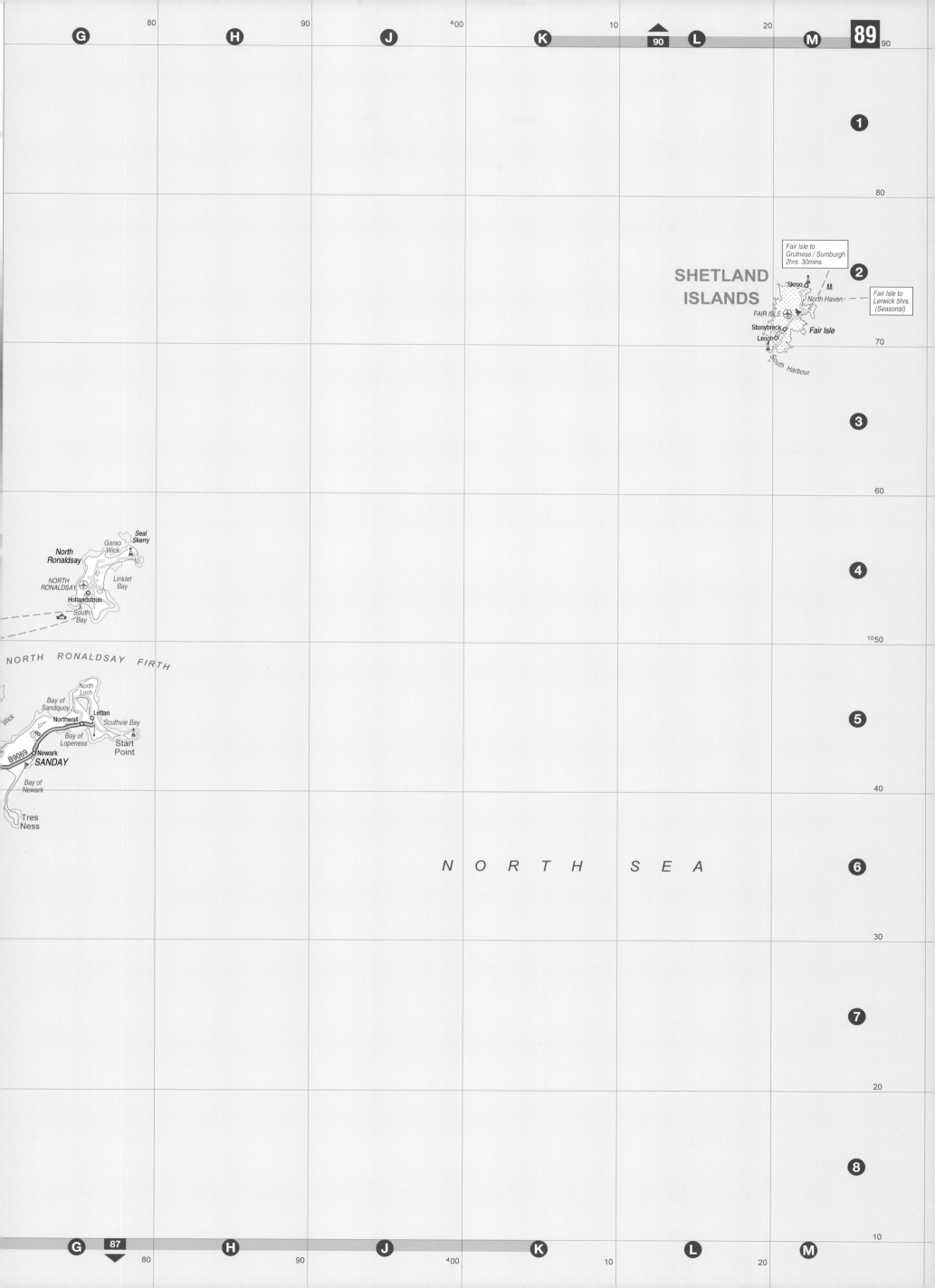

1

80

Fair Isle to Grutness / Sumburgh 2hrs. 30mins

SHETLAND ISLANDS

2

Skroo

North Haven

Fair Isle to Lerwick 5hrs. (Seasonal)

FAIR ISLE

Stonybreck

Leogh

Fair Isle

70

South Harbour

3

60

Seal Skerry

Garso Wick

North Ronaldsay

NORTH RONALDSAY

Linklet Bay

Hollandstoun

South Bay

4

1050

NORTH RONALDSAY FIRTH

North Loch

Bay of Sandquoy

Lettan

Northwall

Scuthvie Bay

Bay of Lopeness

Wick

B9069

Newark

SANDAY

Start Point

5

Bay of Newark

40

Tres Ness

N O R T H   S E A

6

30

7

20

8

10

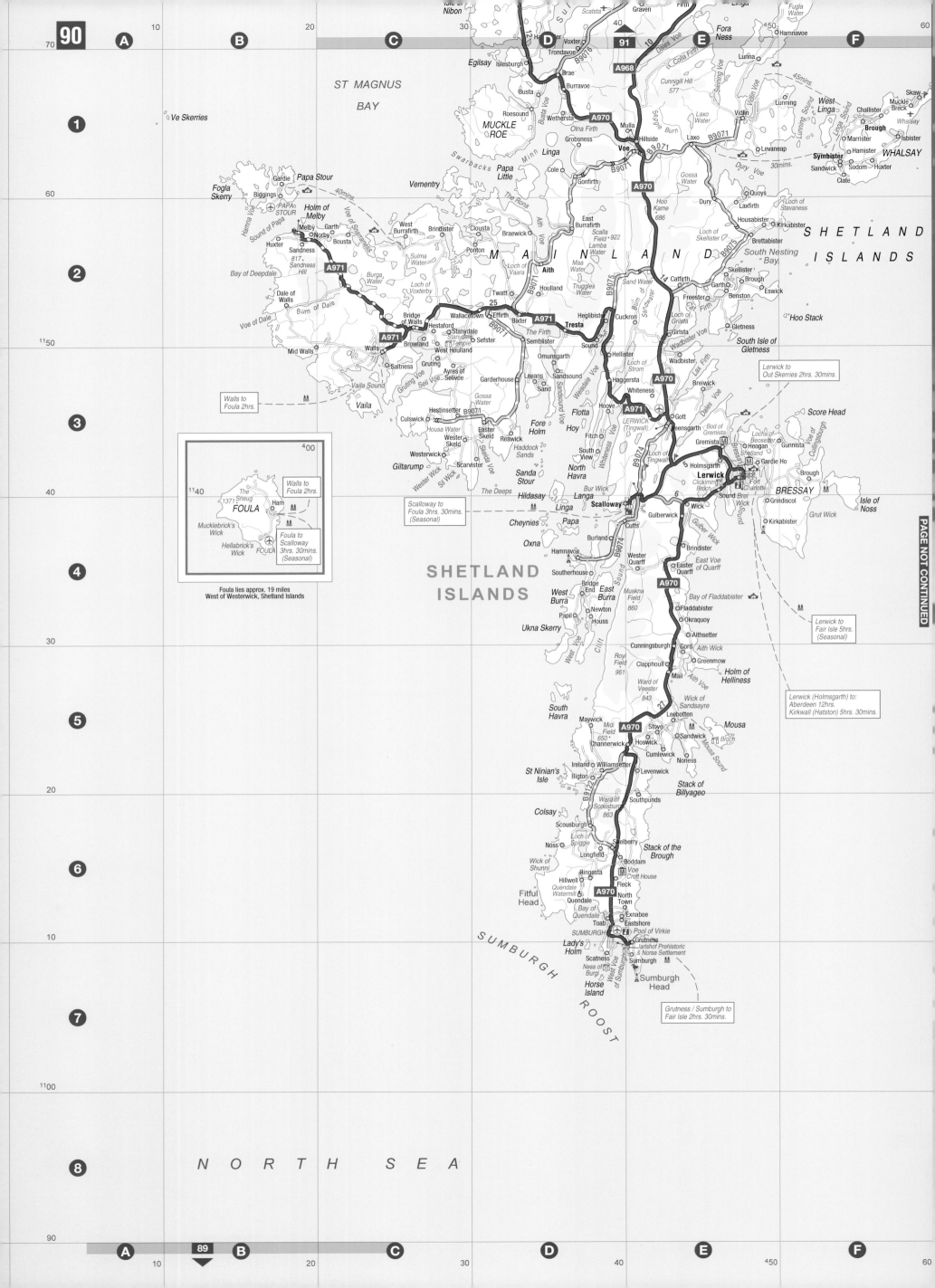

ST MAGNUS
BAY

MUCKLE
ROE

MAINLAND

SHETLAND
ISLANDS

SHETLAND
ISLANDS

LERWICK
(Tingwall)

Lerwick

BRESSAY

Scalloway

Walls to
Foula 2hrs.

Scalloway to
Foula 3hrs. 30mins.
(Seasonal)

FOULA

The
Sneug
1371

Muckle brick's
Wick

Hella brick's
Wick

Walls to
Foula 2hrs.

Foula to
Scalloway
3hrs. 30mins.
(Seasonal)

Foula lies approx. 19 miles
West of Westerwick, Shetland Islands

Lerwick to
Out Skerries 2hrs. 30mins.

Lerwick to
Fair Isle 5hrs.
(Seasonal)

Lerwick (Holmsgarth) to:
Aberdeen 12hrs.
Kirkwall (Hatston) 5hrs. 30mins.

Grutness / Sumburgh to
Fair Isle 2hrs. 30mins.

SUMBURGH ROOST

SUMBURGH

Sumburgh
Head

NORTH SEA

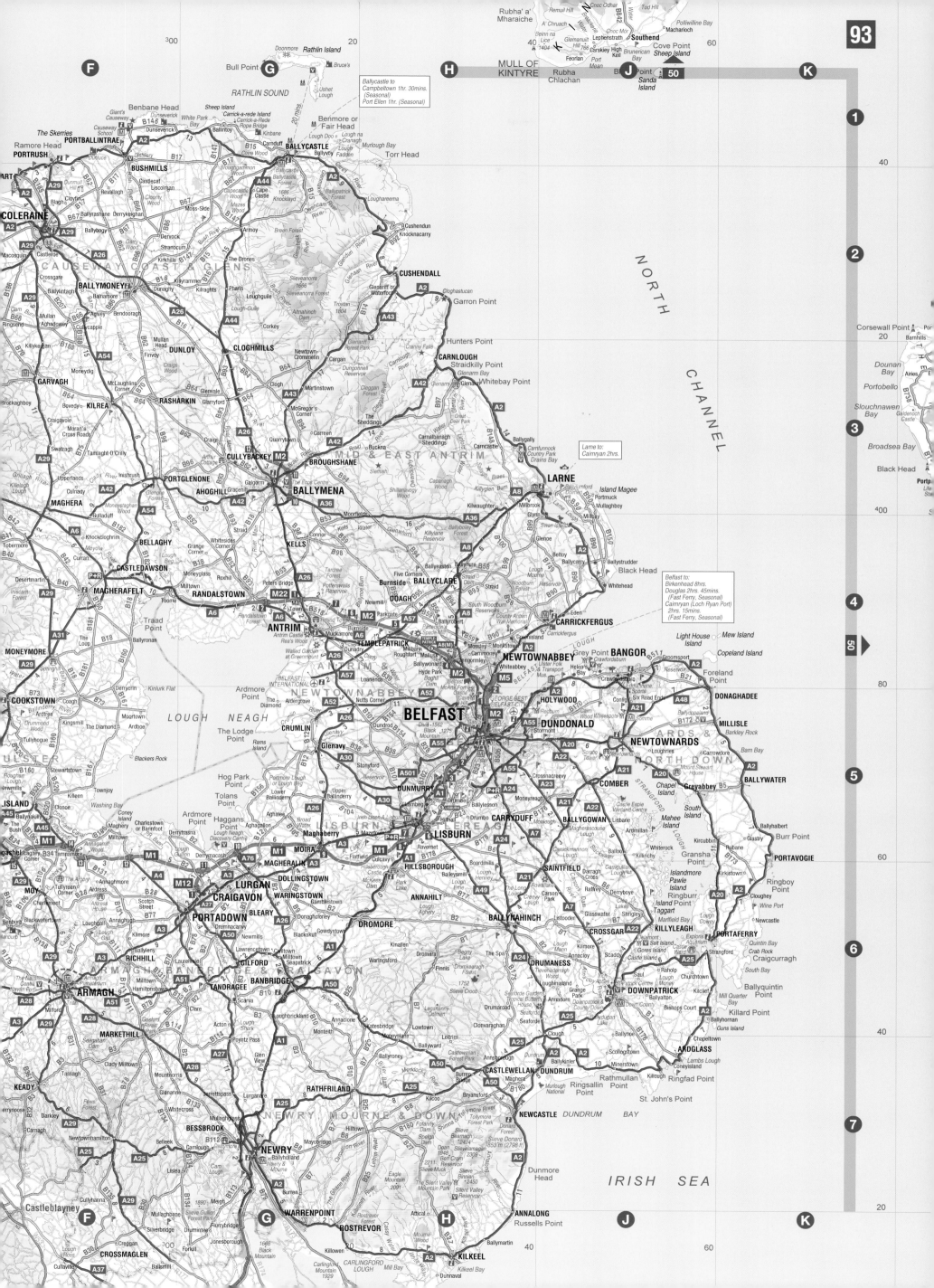

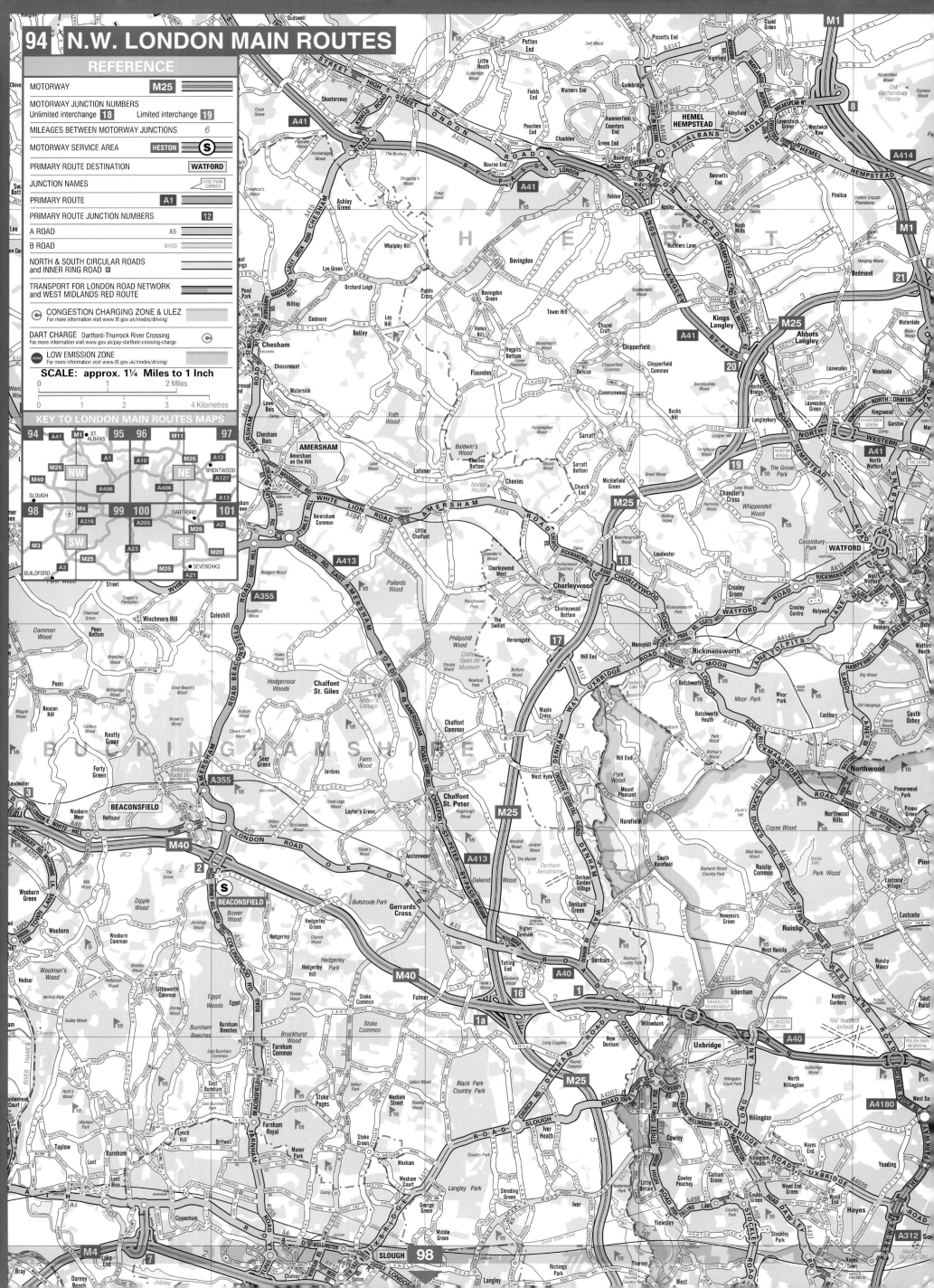

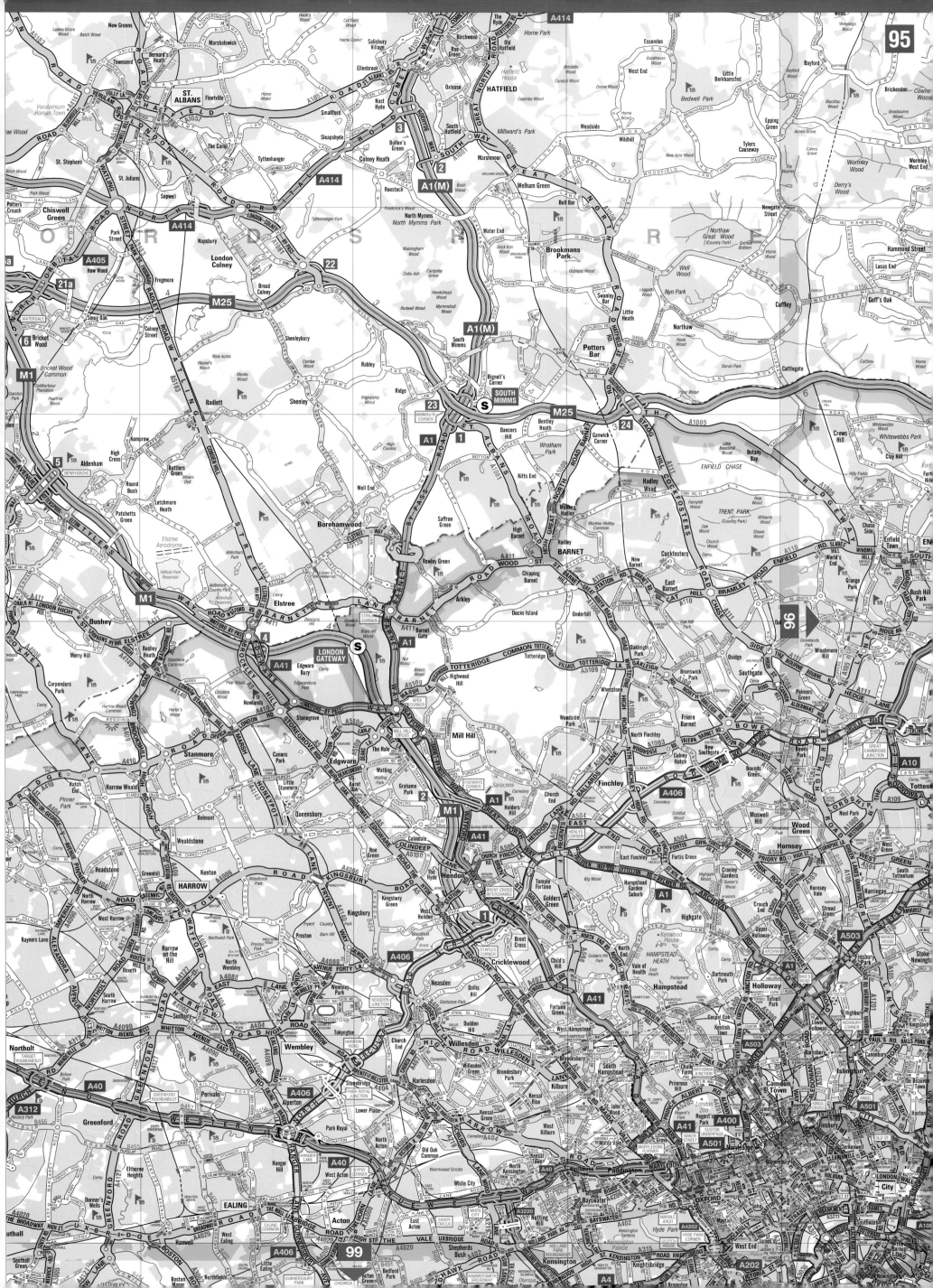

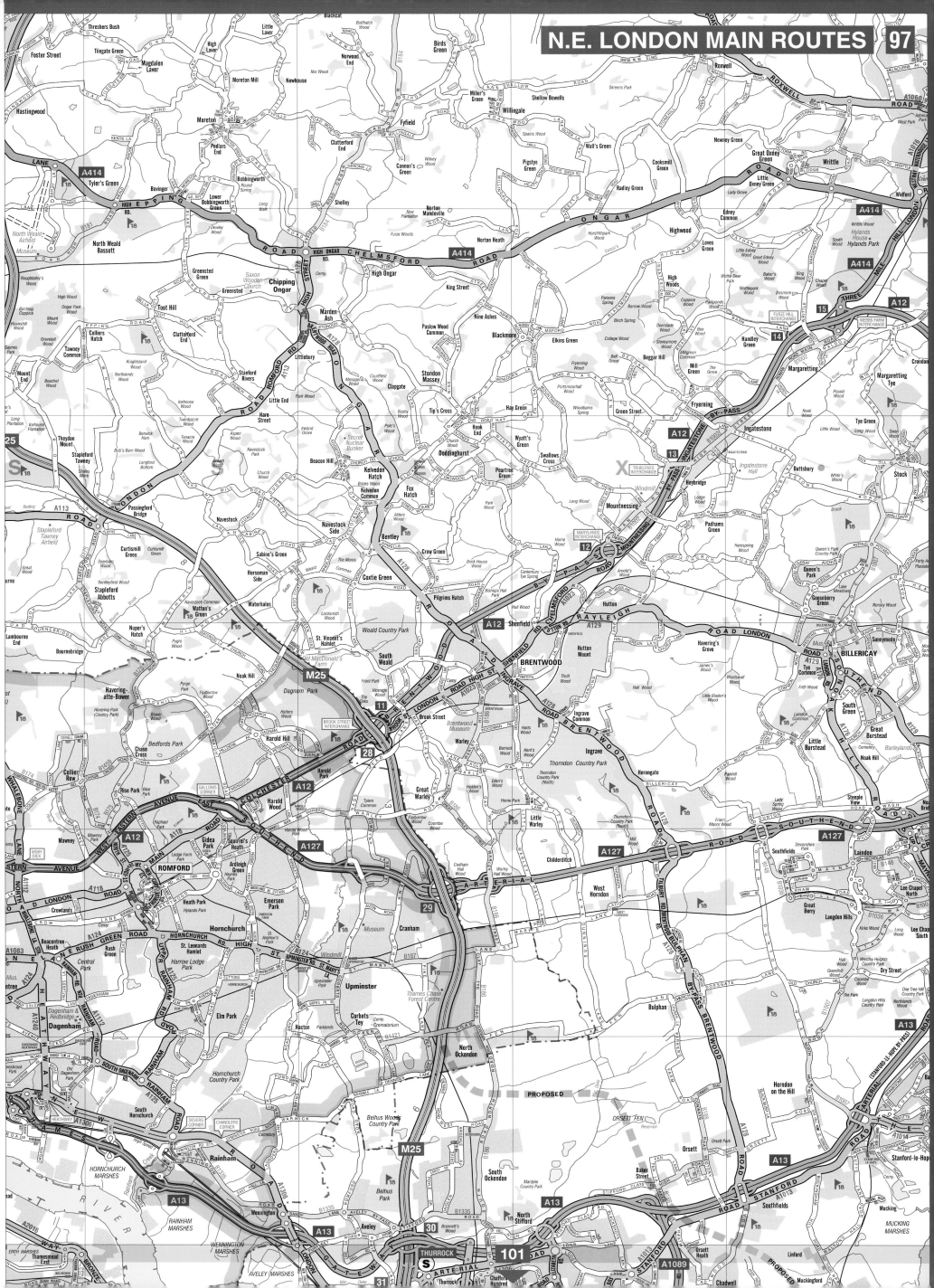

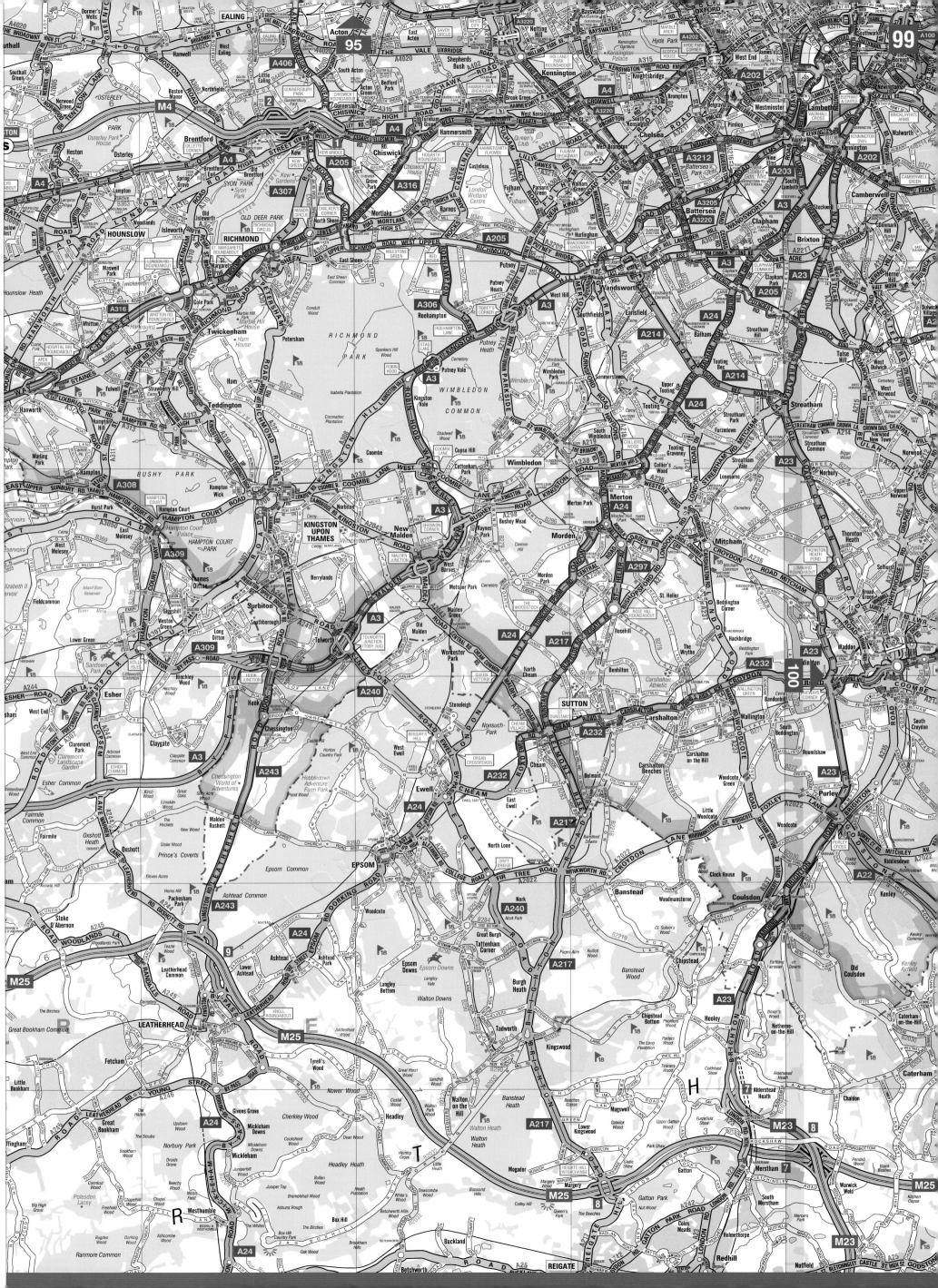

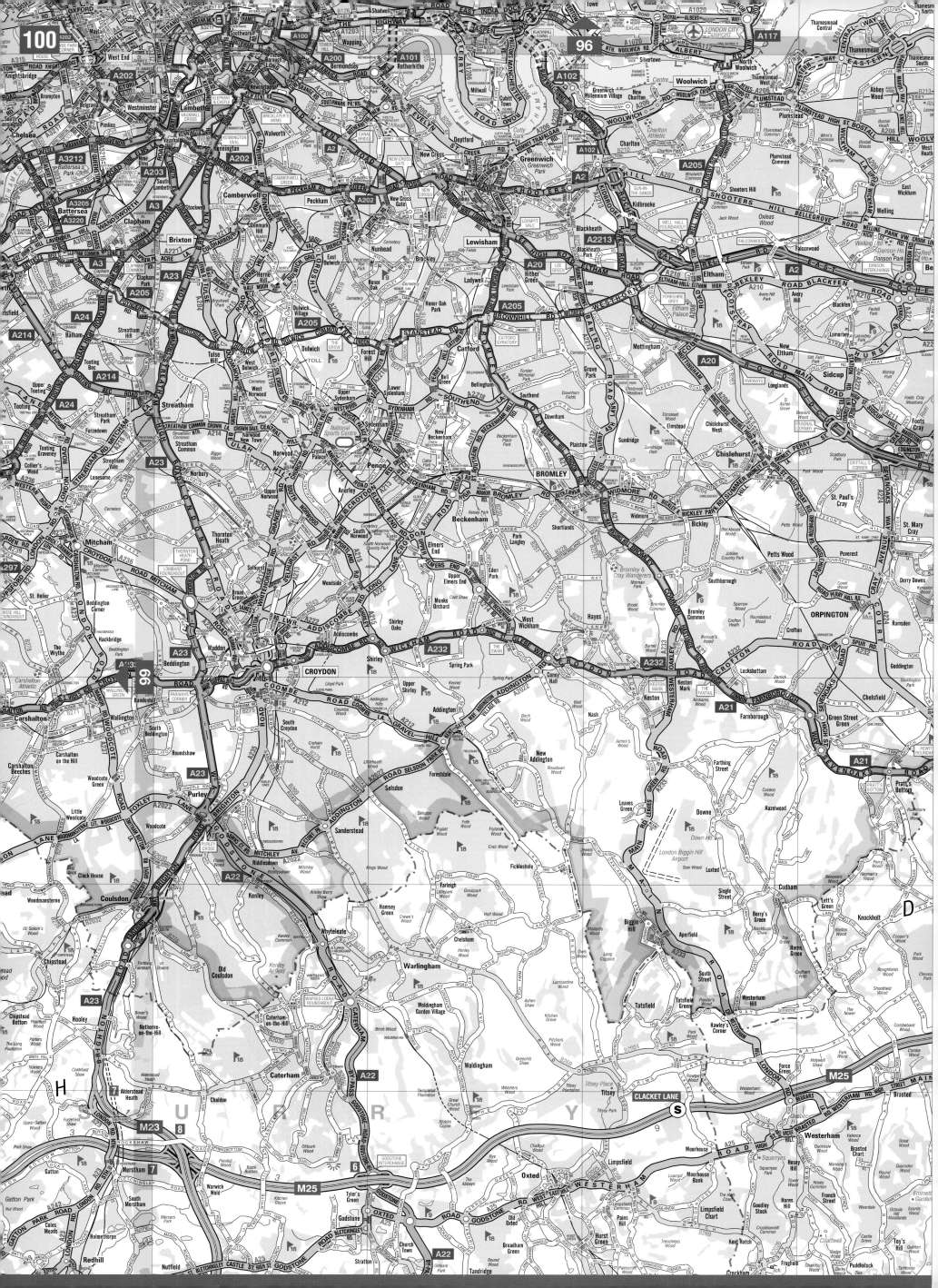

City & Town Centre Plans

Port Plans

Airport Plans

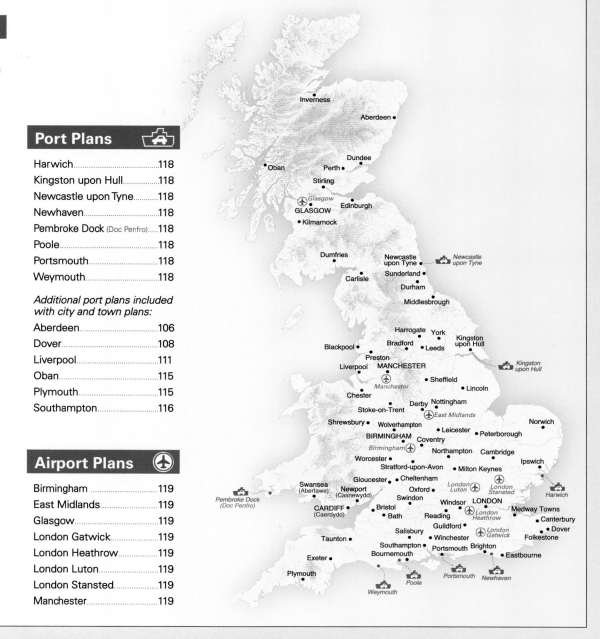

Reference to City & Town Plans — Légende — Zeichenerklärung

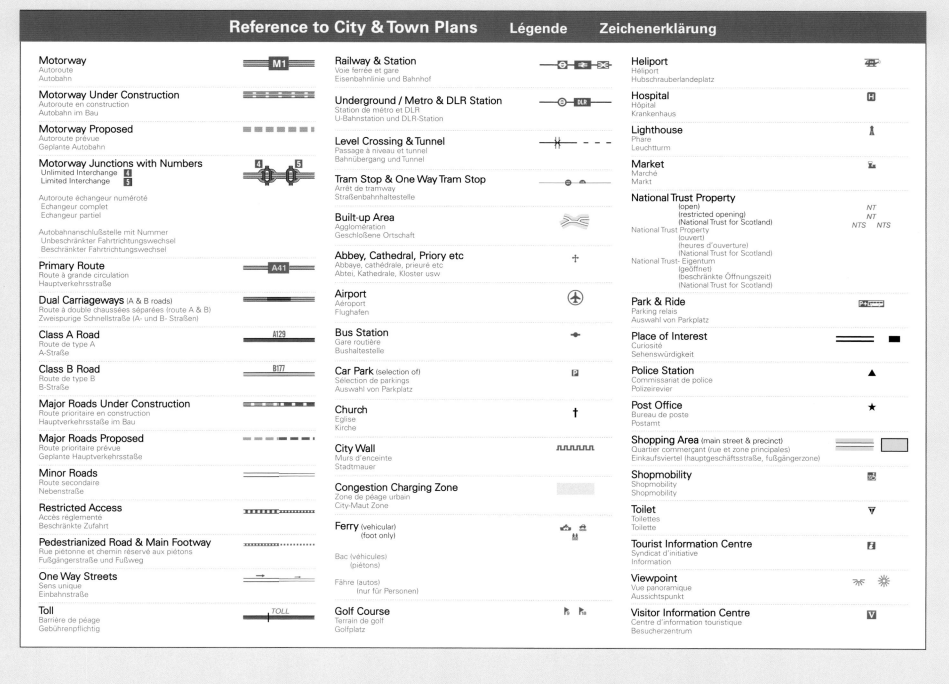

Motorway
Autoroute
Autobahn

Motorway Under Construction
Autoroute en construction
Autobahn im Bau

Motorway Proposed
Autoroute prévue
Geplante Autobahn

Motorway Junctions with Numbers
Unlimited Interchange
Limited Interchange
Autoroute échangeur numéroté
Echangeur complet
Echangeur partiel
Autobahnanschlußstelle mit Nummer
Unbeschränkter Fahrtrichtungswechsel
Beschränkter Fahrtrichtungswechsel

Primary Route
Route à grande circulation
Hauptverkehrsstraße

Dual Carriageways (A & B roads)
Route à double chaussées séparées (route A & B)
Zweispurige Schnellstraße (A- und B- Straßen)

Class A Road
Route de type A
A-Straße

Class B Road
Route de type B
B-Straße

Major Roads Under Construction
Route prioritaire en construction
Hauptverkehrsstraße im Bau

Major Roads Proposed
Route prioritaire prévue
Geplante Hauptverkehrsstraße

Minor Roads
Route secondaire
Nebenstraße

Restricted Access
Accès réglementé
Beschränkte Zufahrt

Pedestrianized Road & Main Footway
Rue piétonne et chemin réservé aux piétons
Fußgängerstraße und Fußweg

One Way Streets
Sens unique
Einbahnstraße

Toll
Barrière de péage
Gebührenpflichtig

Railway & Station
Voie ferrée et gare
Eisenbahnlinie und Bahnhof

Underground / Metro & DLR Station
Station de métro et DLR
U-Bahnstation und DLR-Station

Level Crossing & Tunnel
Passage à niveau et tunnel
Bahnübergang und Tunnel

Tram Stop & One Way Tram Stop
Arrêt de tramway
Straßenbahnhaltestelle

Built-up Area
Agglomération
Geschlossene Ortschaft

Abbey, Cathedral, Priory etc
Abbaye, cathédrale, prieuré etc
Abtei, Kathedrale, Kloster usw

Airport
Aéroport
Flughafen

Bus Station
Gare routière
Bushaltestelle

Car Park (selection of)
Sélection de parkings
Auswahl von Parkplatz

Church
Eglise
Kirche

City Wall
Murs d'enceinte
Stadtmauer

Congestion Charging Zone
Zone de péage urbain
City-Maut Zone

Ferry (vehicular)
(foot only)
Bac (véhicules)
(piétons)
Fähre (autos)
(nur für Personen)

Golf Course
Terrain de golf
Golfplatz

Heliport
Héliport
Hubschrauberlandeplatz

Hospital
Hôpital
Krankenhaus

Lighthouse
Phare
Leuchtturm

Market
Marché
Markt

National Trust Property
(open)
(restricted opening)
(National Trust for Scotland)   NT   NT   NTS   NTS
National Trust Property
(ouvert)
(heures d'ouverture)
(National Trust for Scotland)
National Trust- Eigentum
(geöffnet)
(beschränkte Öffnungszeit)
(National Trust for Scotland)

Park & Ride
Parking relais
Auswahl von Parkplatz

Place of Interest
Curiosité
Sehenswürdigkeit

Police Station
Commissariat de police
Polizeirevier

Post Office
Bureau de poste
Postamt

Shopping Area (main street & precinct)
Quartier commerçant (rue et zone principales)
Einkaufsviertel (hauptgeschäftsstraße, fußgängerzone)

Shopmobility
Shopmobility
Shopmobility

Toilet
Toilettes
Toilette

Tourist Information Centre
Syndicat d'initiative
Information

Viewpoint
Vue panoramique
Aussichtspunkt

Visitor Information Centre
Centre d'information touristique
Besucherzentrum

ABERDEEN

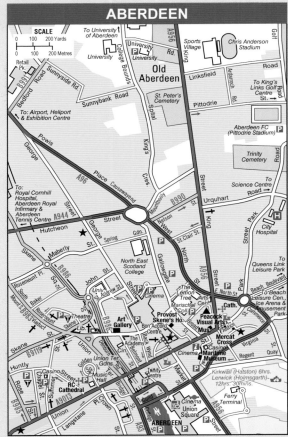

BATH

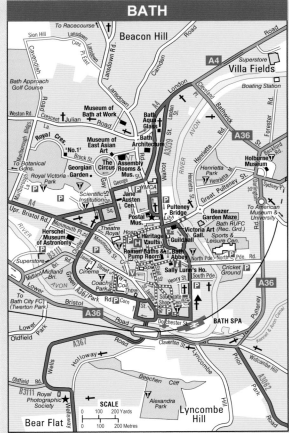

BLACKPOOL

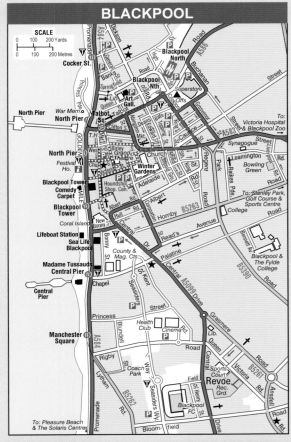

BIRMINGHAM (CITY CENTRE)

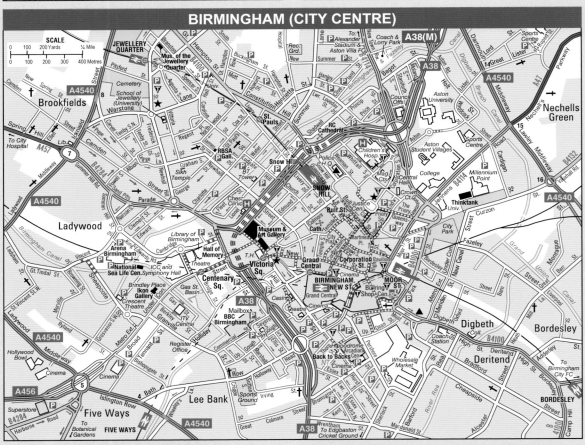

BOURNEMOUTH

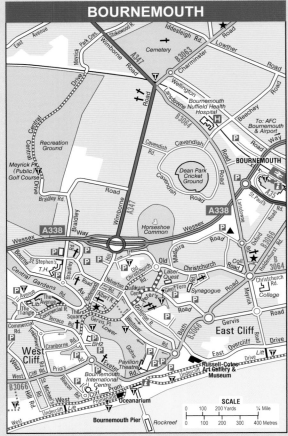

BRADFORD

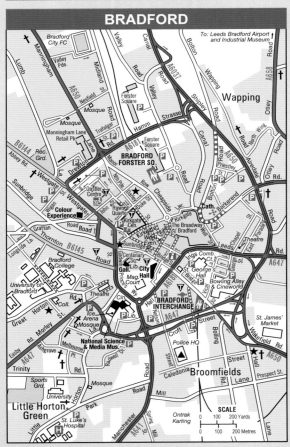

BRIGHTON and HOVE

BRISTOL

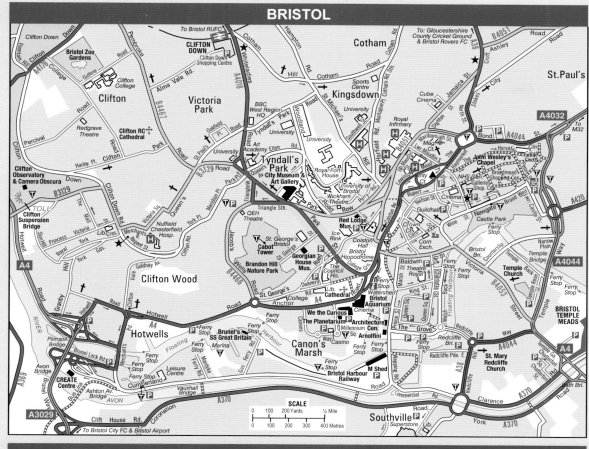

CANTERBURY

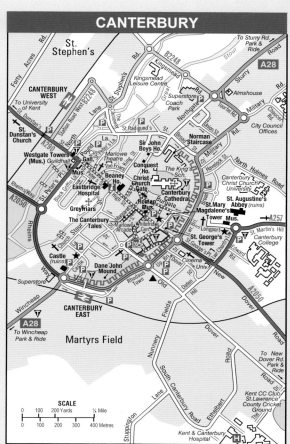

CAMBRIDGE

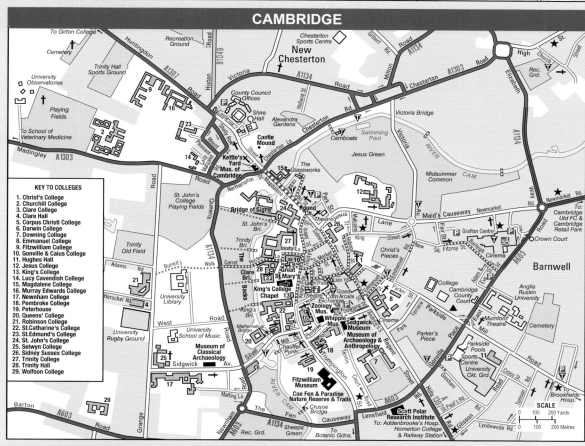

KEY TO COLLEGES
1. Christ's College
2. Churchill College
3. Clare College
4. Clare Hall
5. Corpus Christi College
6. Darwin College
7. Downing College
8. Emmanuel College
9. Fitzwilliam College
10. Gonville & Caius College
11. Hughes Hall
12. Jesus College
13. King's College
14. Lucy Cavendish College
15. Magdalene College
16. Murray Edwards College
17. Newnham College
18. Pembroke College
19. Peterhouse
20. Queens' College
21. Robinson College
22. St.Catharine's College
23. St.Edmund's College
24. St. John's College
25. Selwyn College
26. Sidney Sussex College
27. Trinity College
28. Trinity Hall
29. Wolfson College

CARLISLE

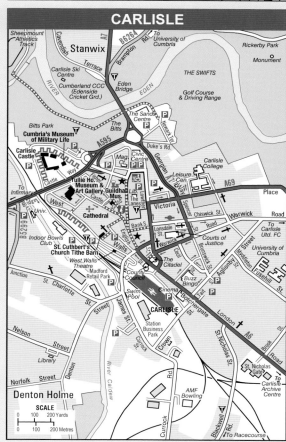

CARDIFF (CAERDYDD)

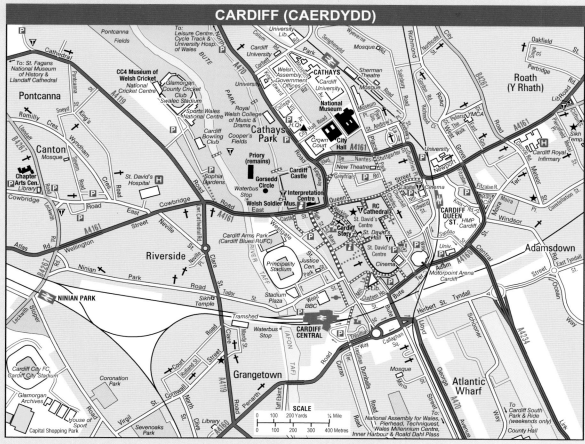

CHELTENHAM

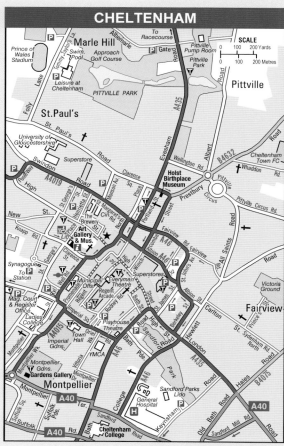

CHESTER

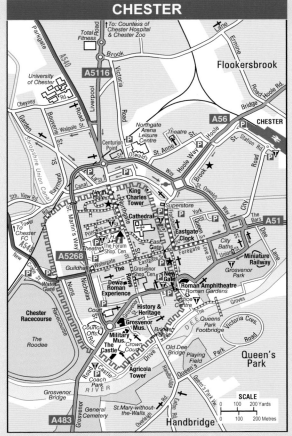

COVENTRY

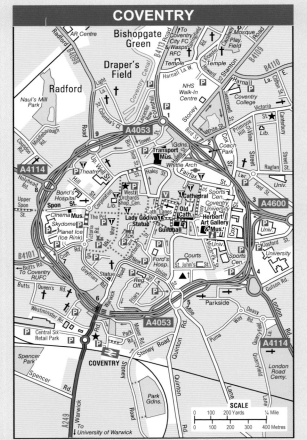

DERBY

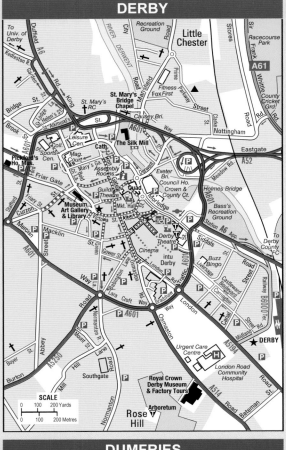

DOVER

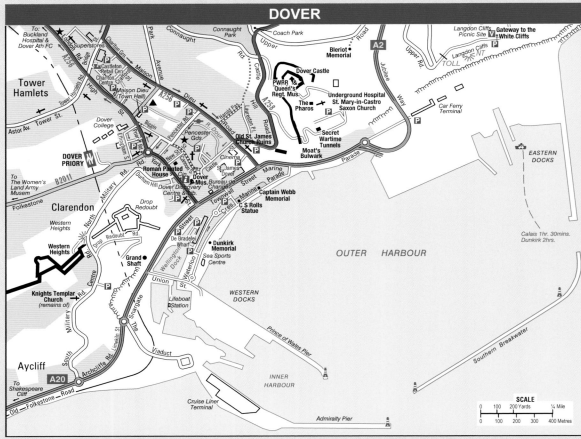

DUMFRIES

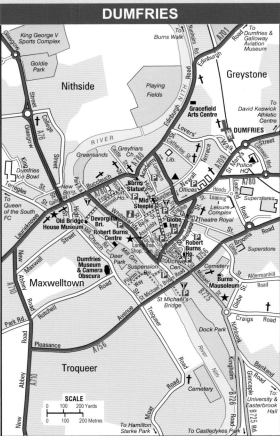

DUNDEE

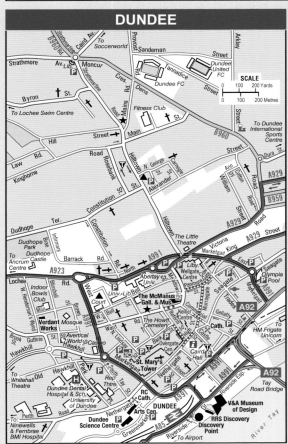

DURHAM

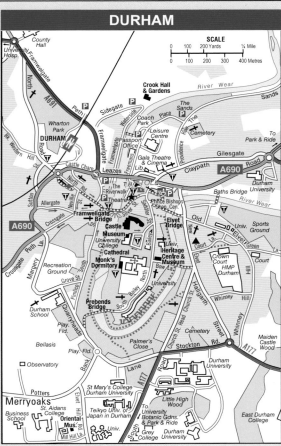

EASTBOURNE

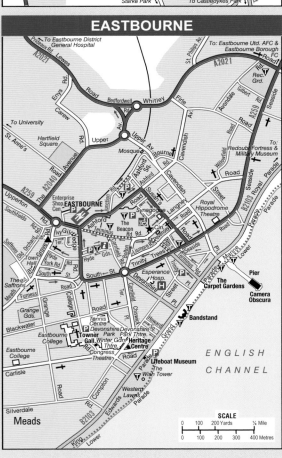

EDINBURGH

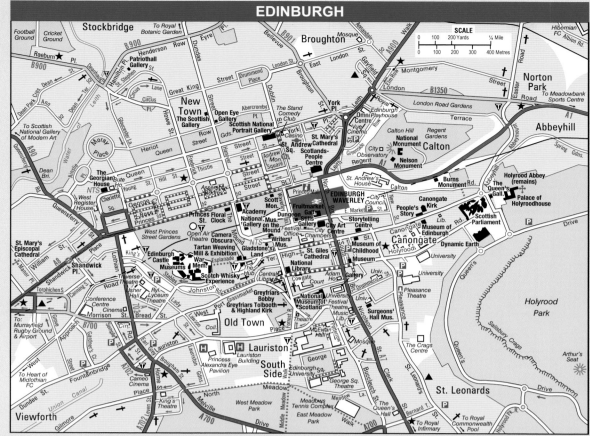

FOLKESTONE

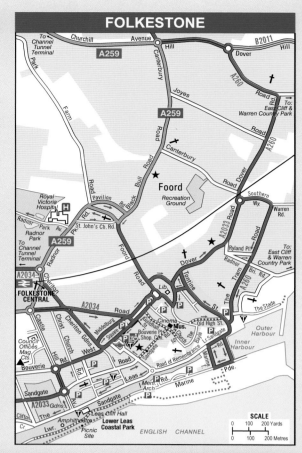

EXETER

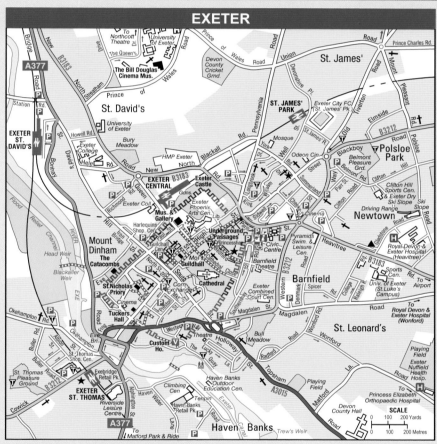

GUILDFORD

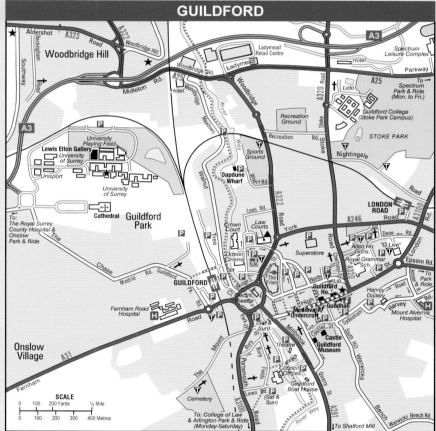

GLASGOW

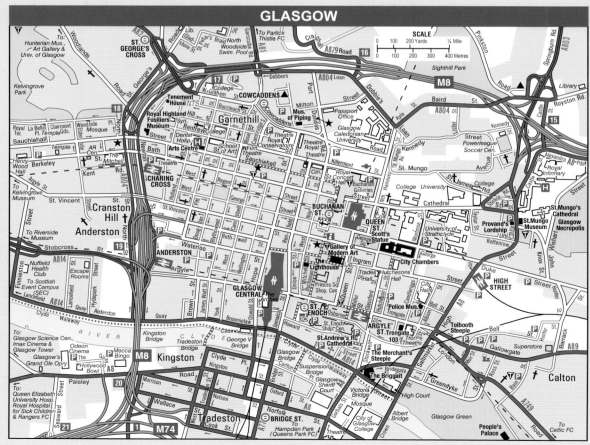

GLOUCESTER

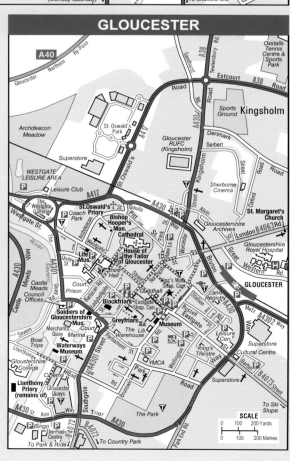

HARROGATE

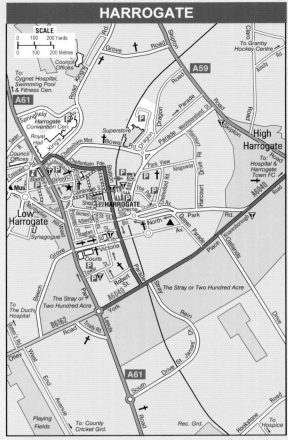

INVERNESS

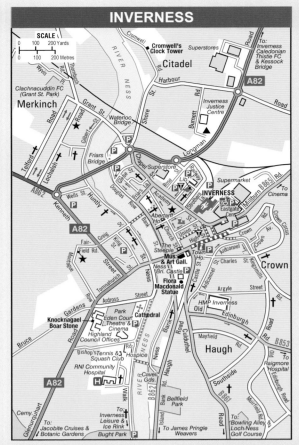

IPSWICH

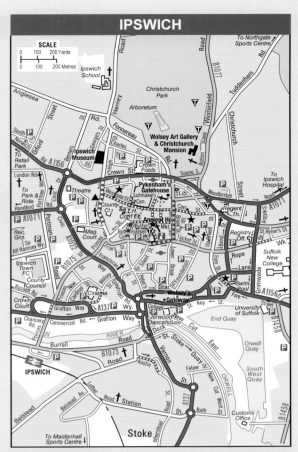

KILMARNOCK

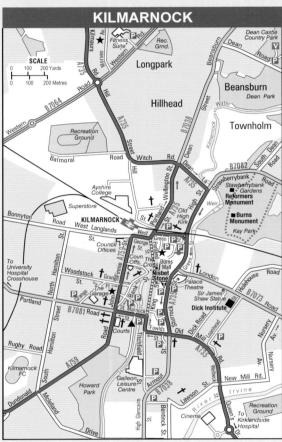

LEEDS

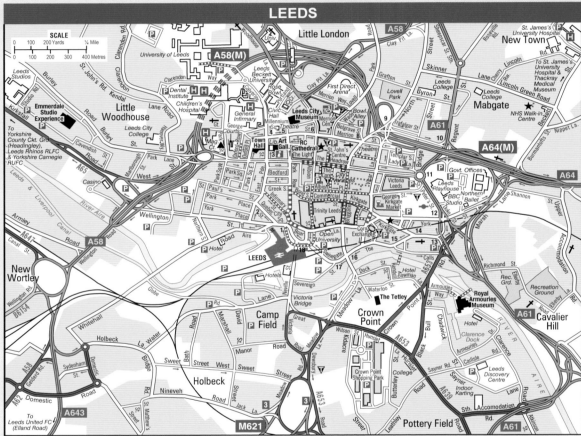

KINGSTON UPON HULL

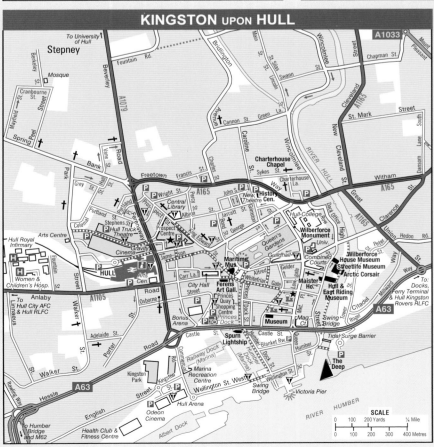

LEICESTER

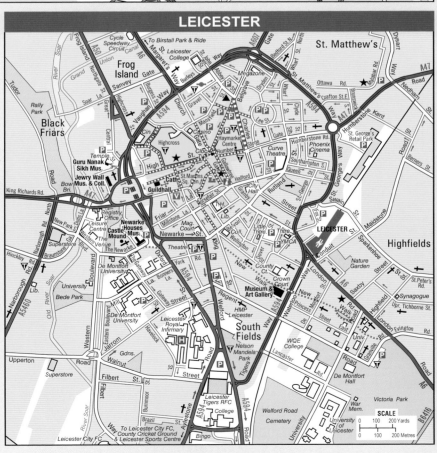

LINCOLN

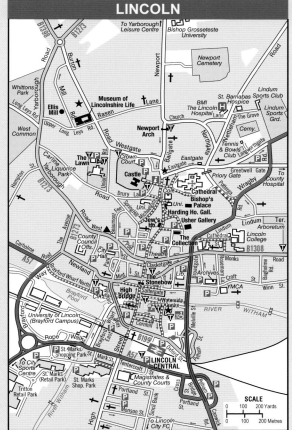

LIVERPOOL

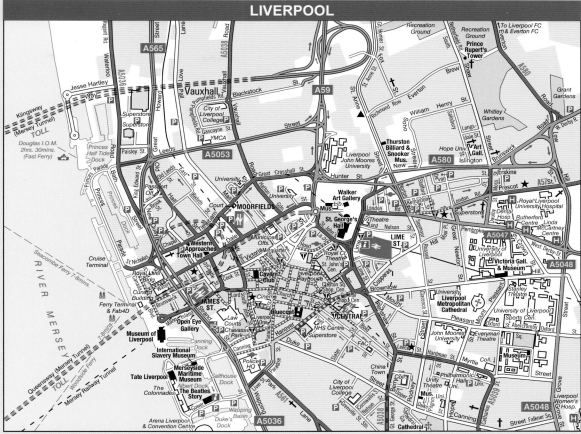

MANCHESTER (CITY CENTRE)

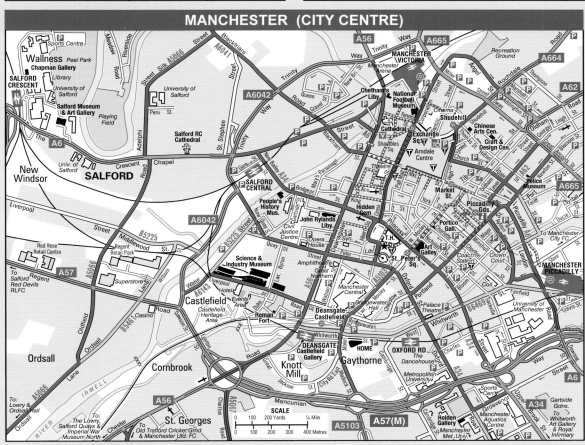

MIDDLESBROUGH

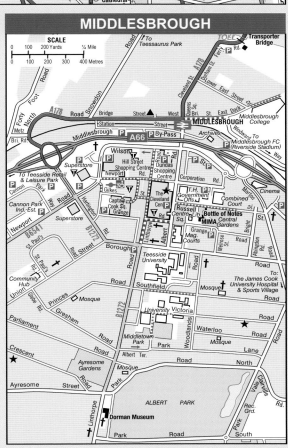

MEDWAY TOWNS

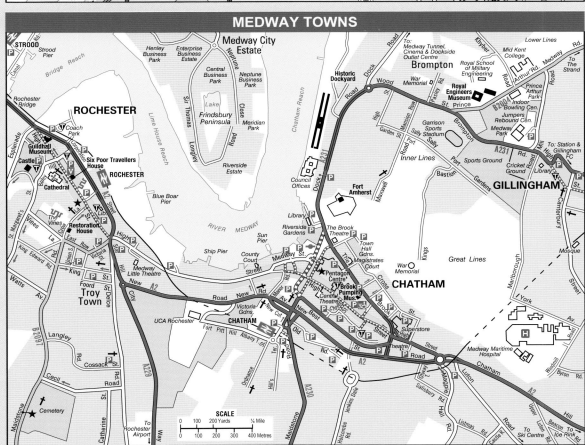

NEWCASTLE UPON TYNE

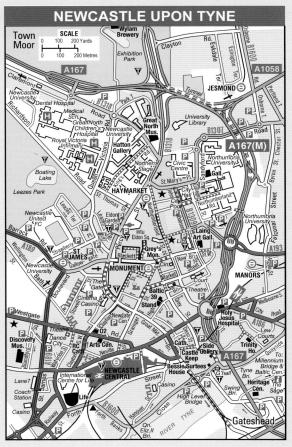

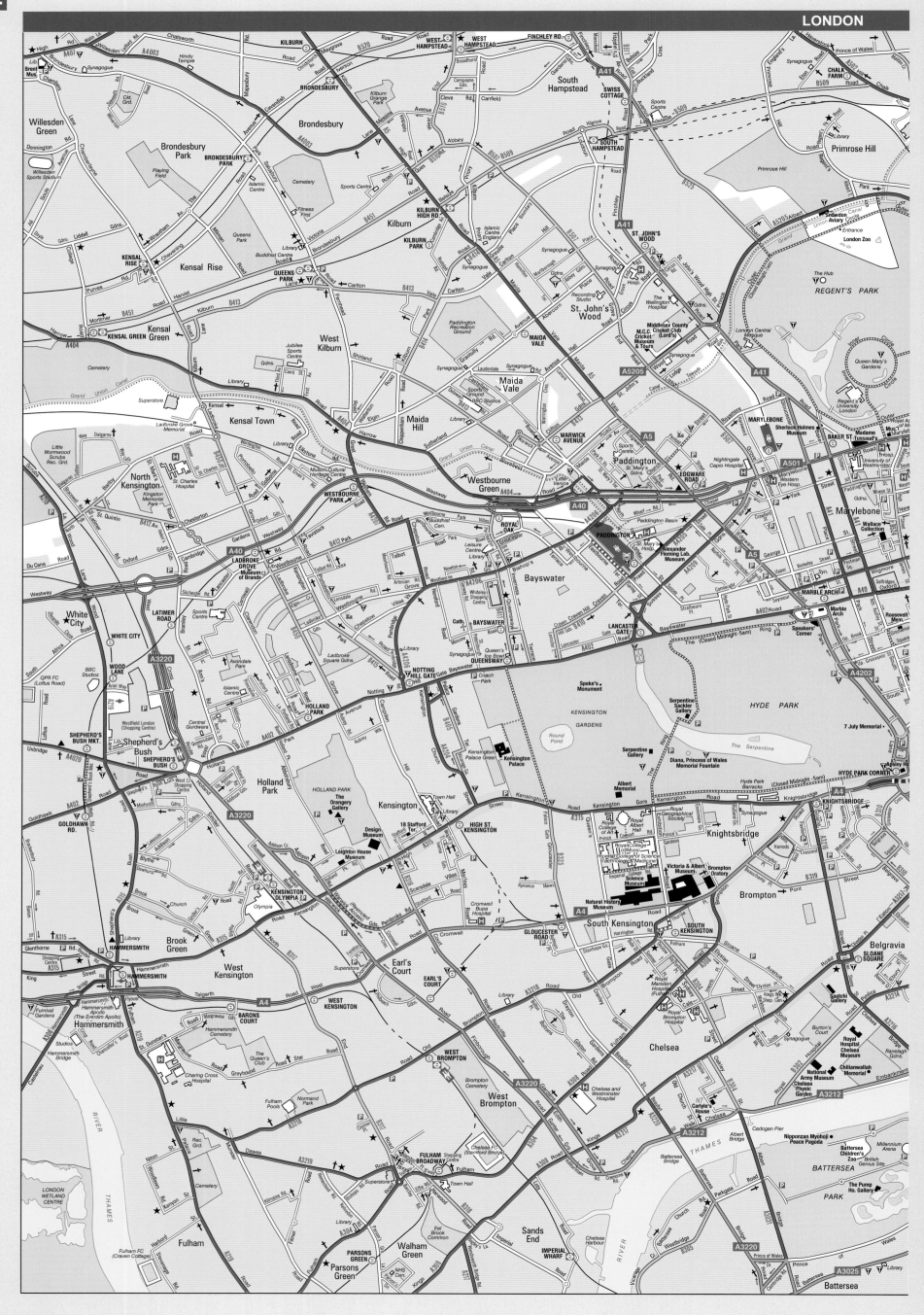

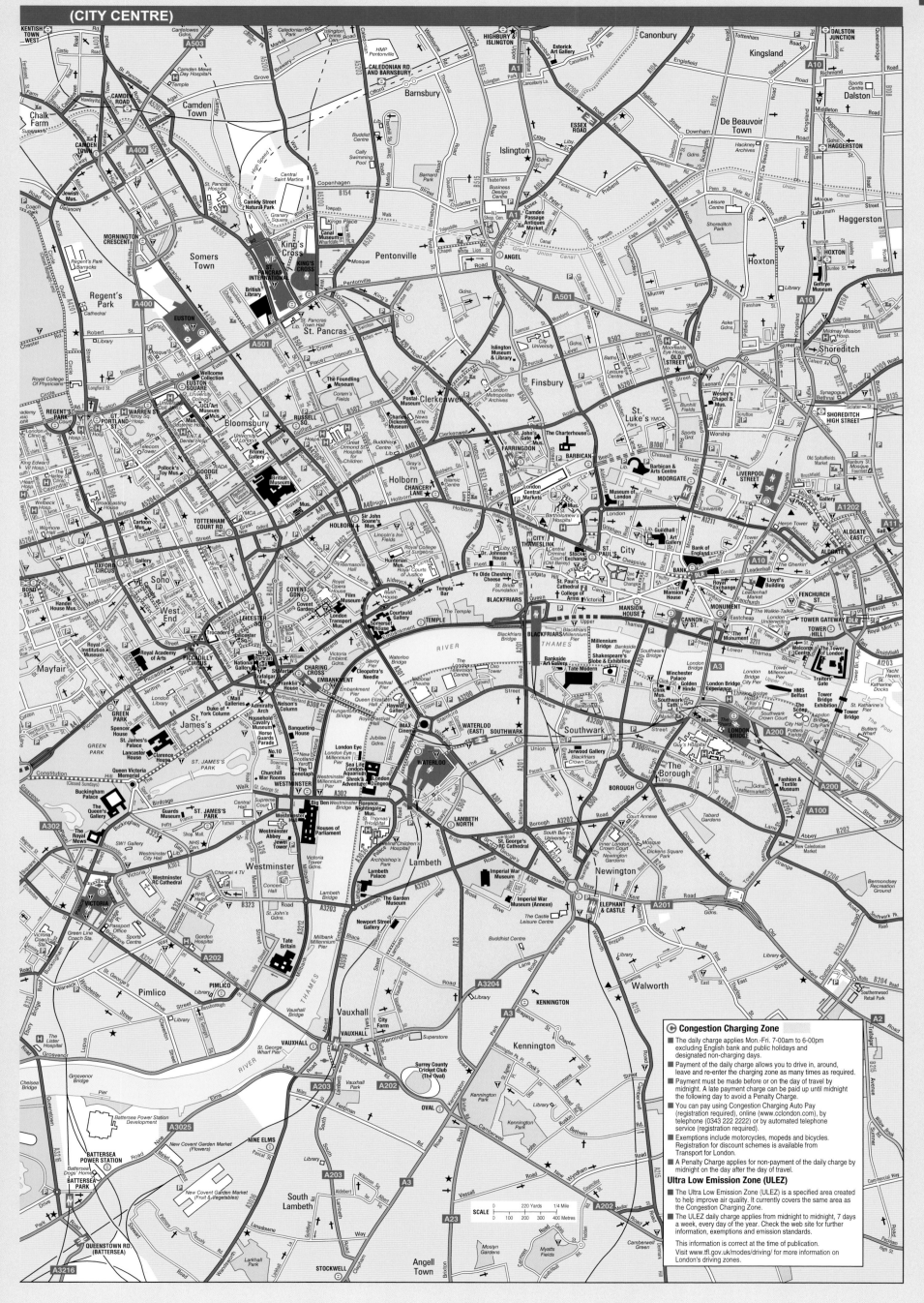

Congestion Charging Zone

- The daily charge applies Mon.-Fri. 7-00am to 6-00pm excluding English bank and public holidays and designated non-charging days.
- Payment of the daily charge allows you to drive in, around, leave and re-enter the charging zone as many times as required.
- Payment must be made before or on the day of travel by midnight. A late payment charge can be paid up until midnight the following day to avoid a Penalty Charge.
- You can pay using Congestion Charging Auto Pay (registration required), online (www.cclondon.com), by telephone (0343 222 2222) or by automated telephone service (registration required).
- Exemptions include motorcycles, mopeds and bicycles. Registration for discount schemes is available from Transport for London.
- A Penalty Charge applies for non-payment of the daily charge by midnight on the day after the day of travel.

Ultra Low Emission Zone (ULEZ)

- The Ultra Low Emission Zone (ULEZ) is a specified area created to help improve air quality. It currently covers the same area as the Congestion Charging Zone.
- The ULEZ daily charge applies from midnight to midnight, 7 days a week, every day of the year. Check the web site for further information, exemptions and emission standards.

This information is correct at the time of publication. Visit www.tfl.gov.uk/modes/driving/ for more information on London's driving zones.

SCALE
0   220 Yards   1/4 Mile
0 100 200 300 400 Metres

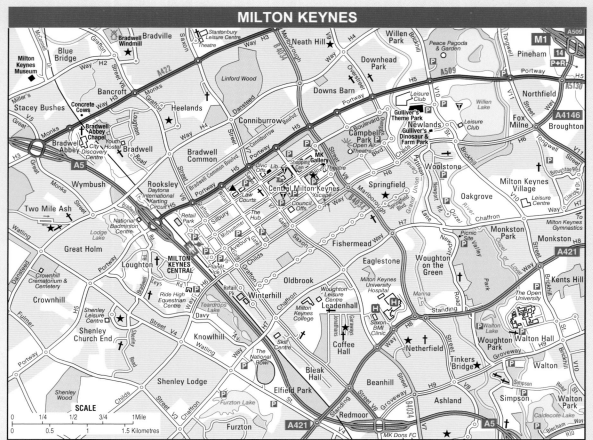

MILTON KEYNES

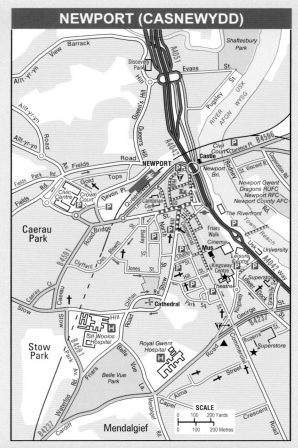

NEWPORT (CASNEWYDD)

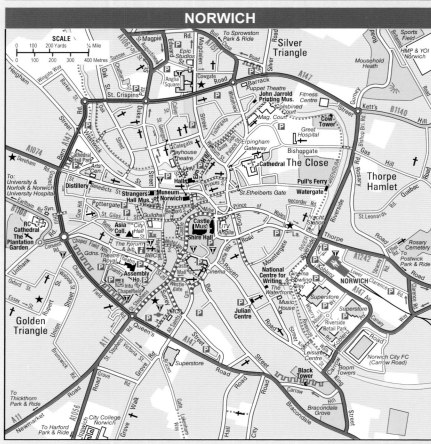

NORWICH

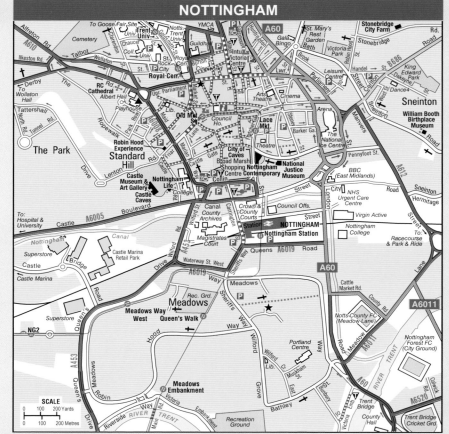

NOTTINGHAM

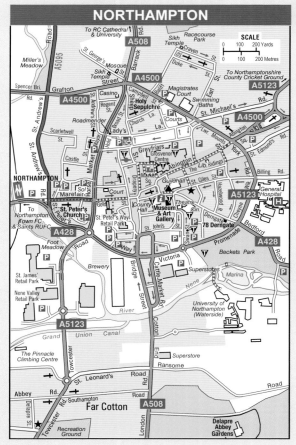

NORTHAMPTON

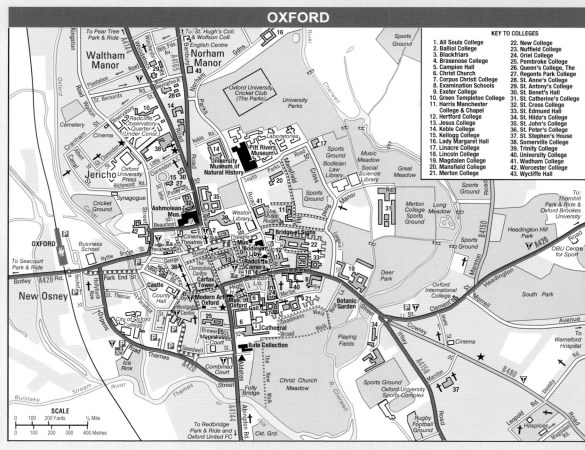

OXFORD

KEY TO COLLEGES

1. All Souls College
2. Balliol College
3. Blackfriars
4. Brasenose College
5. Campion Hall
6. Christ Church
7. Corpus Christi College
8. Examination Schools
9. Exeter College
10. Green Templeton College
11. Harris Manchester College & Chapel
12. Hertford College
13. Jesus College
14. Keble College
15. Kellogg College
16. Lady Margaret Hall
17. Linacre College
18. Lincoln College
19. Magdalen College
20. Mansfield College
21. Merton College
22. New College
23. Nuffield College
24. Oriel College
25. Pembroke College
26. Queen's College, The
27. Regents Park College
28. St. Anne's College
29. St. Antony's College
30. St. Benet's Hall
31. St. Catherine's College
32. St. Cross College
33. St. Edmund Hall
34. St. Hilda's College
35. St. John's College
36. St. Peter's College
37. St. Stephen's House
38. Somerville College
39. Trinity College
40. University College
41. Wadham College
42. Worcester College
43. Wycliffe Hall

115

OBAN
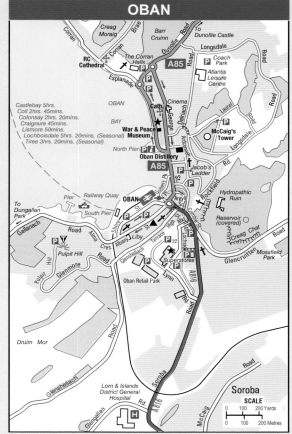

PERTH
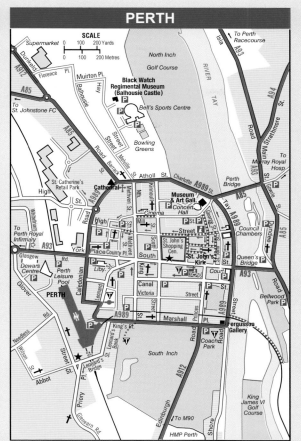

PETERBOROUGH
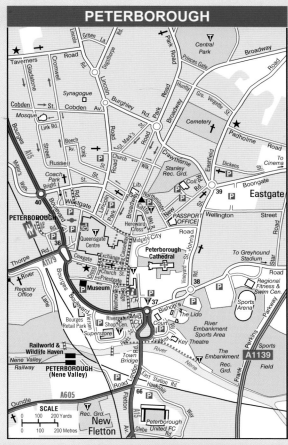

PLYMOUTH
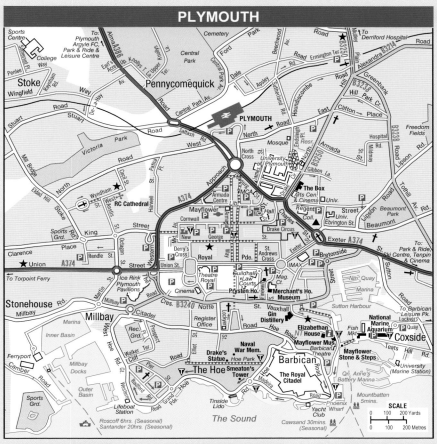

PORTSMOUTH
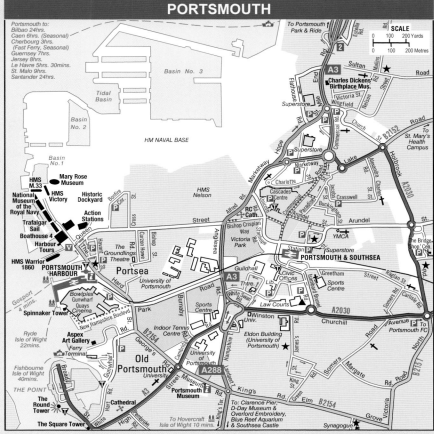

PRESTON
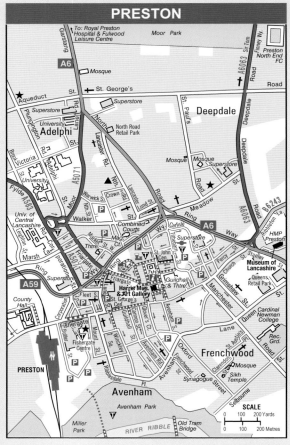

READING
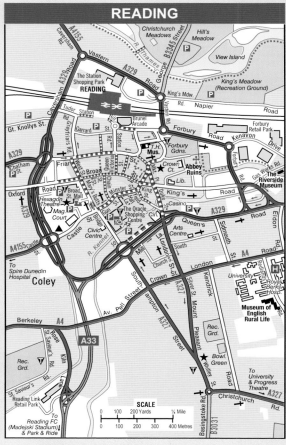

SALISBURY
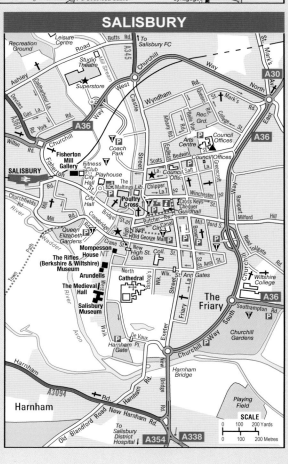

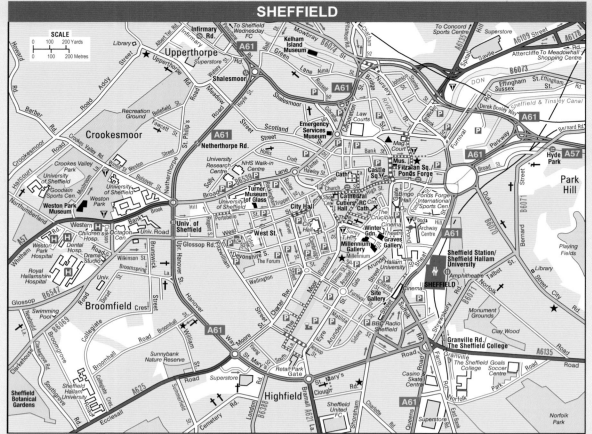

SHEFFIELD

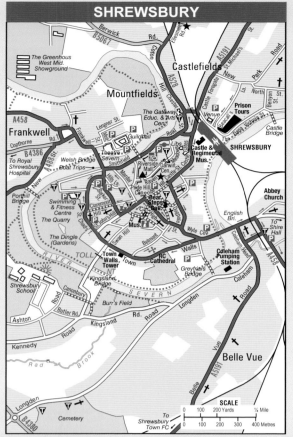

SHREWSBURY

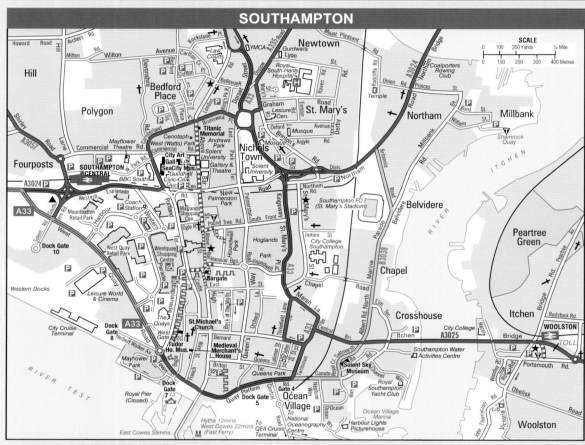

SOUTHAMPTON

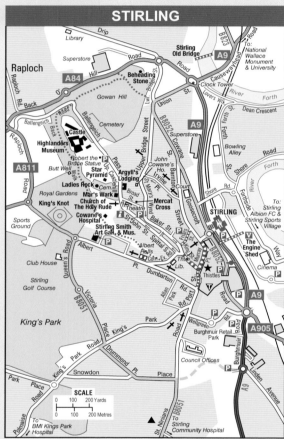

STIRLING

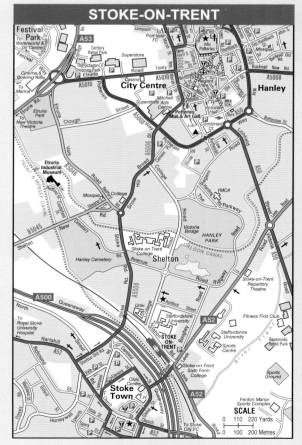

STOKE-ON-TRENT

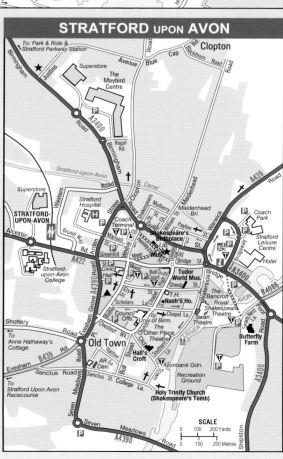

STRATFORD upon AVON

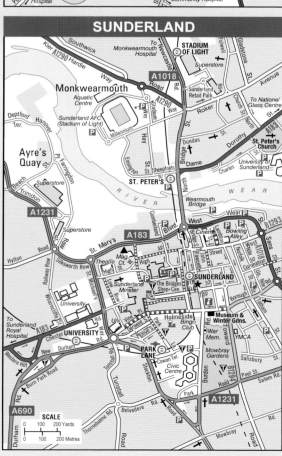

SUNDERLAND

SWANSEA (ABERTAWE)

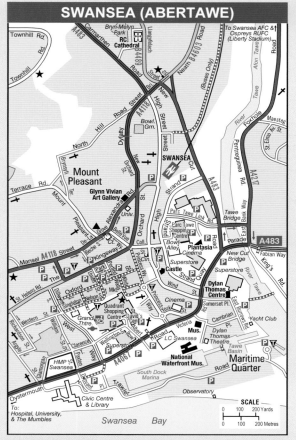

SWINDON

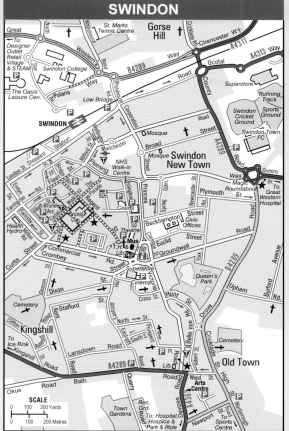

TAUNTON

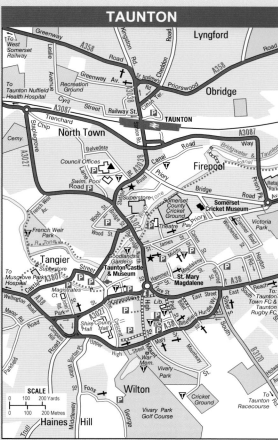

WINCHESTER

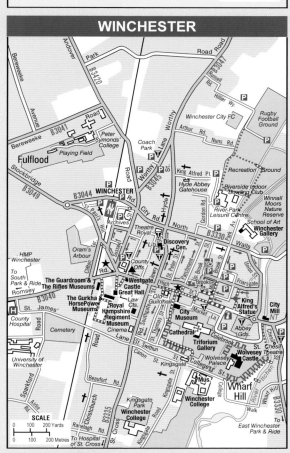

WINDSOR

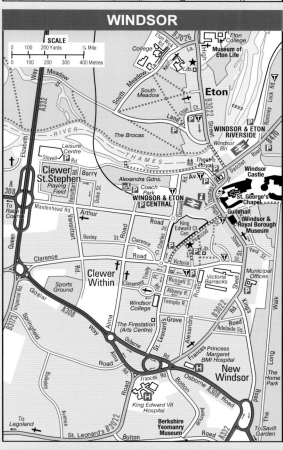

WOLVERHAMPTON

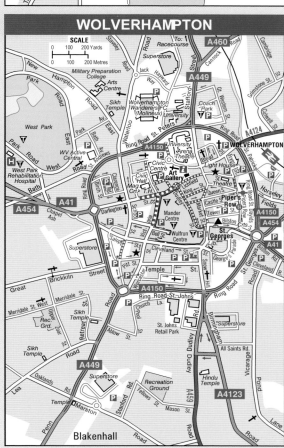

WORCESTER

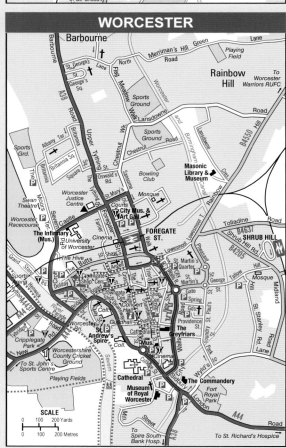

YORK

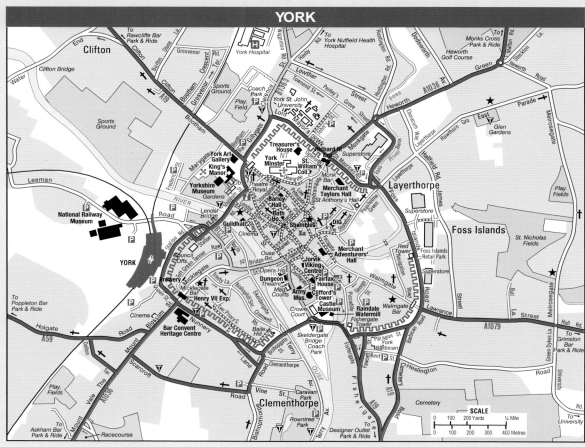

PORT PLANS

For detailed Plans of DOVER, PLYMOUTH and SOUTHAMPTON refer to Town Plans

HARWICH

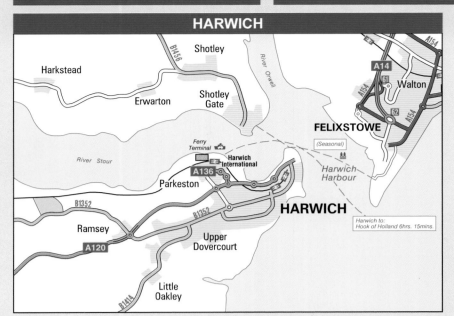

KINGSTON UPON HULL

NEWCASTLE UPON TYNE

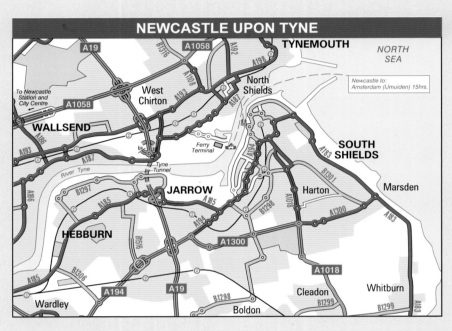

NEWHAVEN

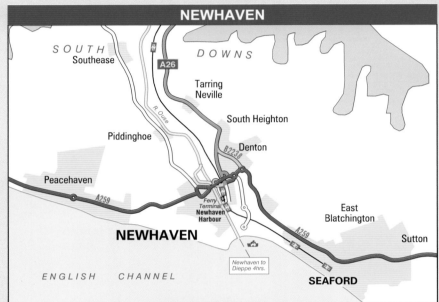

PEMBROKE DOCK (DOC PENFRO)

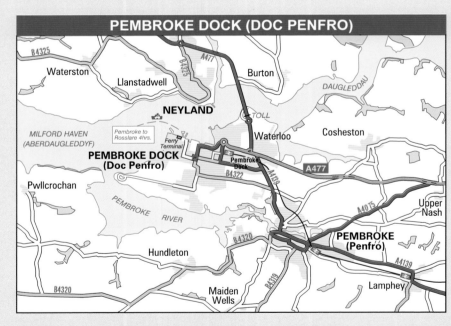

POOLE

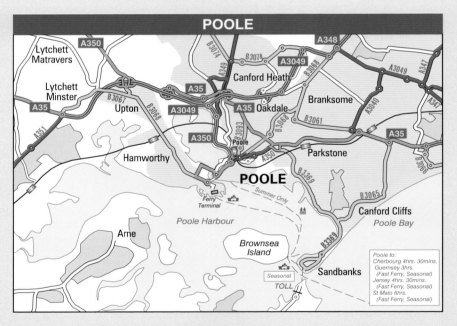

PORTSMOUTH

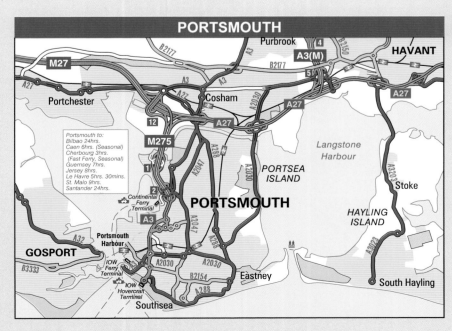

WEYMOUTH

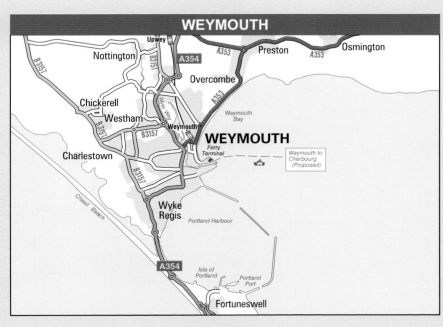

BIRMINGHAM

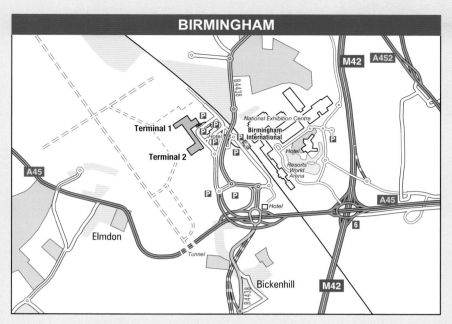

EAST MIDLANDS

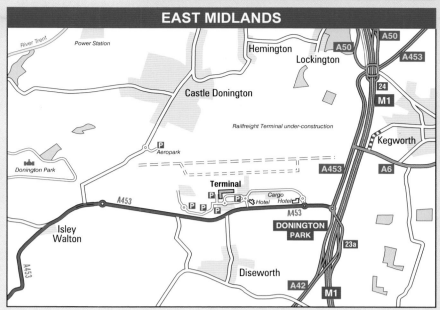

GLASGOW

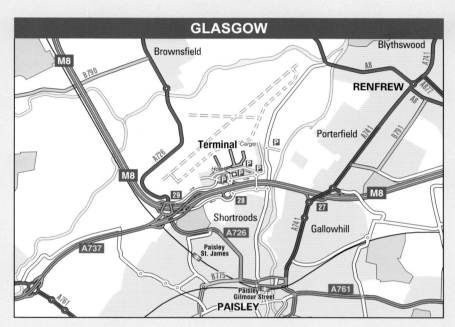

LONDON GATWICK

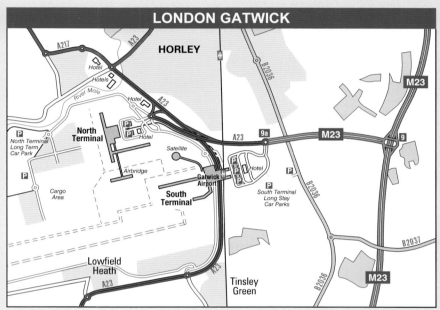

LONDON HEATHROW

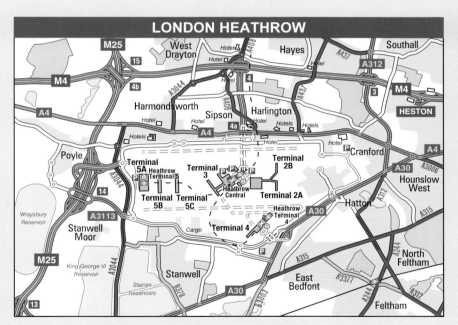

LONDON LUTON

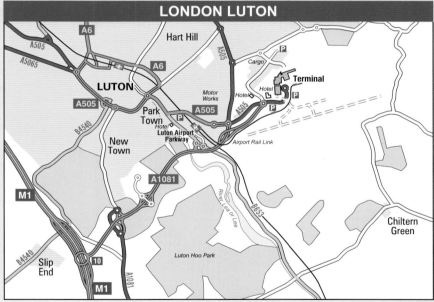

LONDON STANSTED

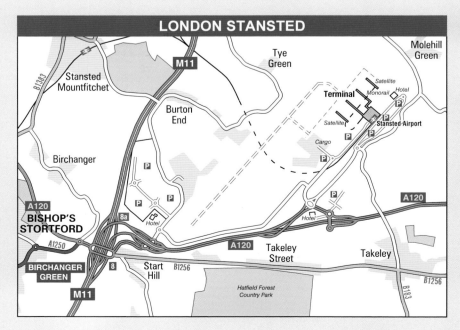

MANCHESTER

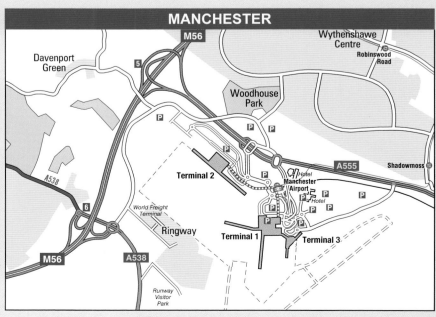

INDEX TO CITIES, TOWNS, VILLAGES, HAMLETS, LOCATIONS, AIRPORTS & PORTS

(1) A strict alphabetical order is used e.g. An Dùnan follows Andreas but precedes Andwell.

(2) The map reference given refers to the actual map square in which the town spot or built-up area is located and not to the place name.

(3) Major towns and destinations are shown in bold, i.e. **Aberdeen.** *Aber* **106** (5J **73**)
Page references for Town Plan entries are shown first.

(4) Where two or more places of the same name occur in the same County or Unitary Authority, the nearest large town is also given; e.g. Achiemore. *High* nr. Durness . . . .5F **84** indicates that Achiemore is located in square 5F on page **84** and is situated near Durness in the Unitary Authority of Highland.

(5) Only one reference is given although due to page overlaps the place may appear on more than one page.

COUNTIES and UNITARY AUTHORITIES with the abbreviations used in this index

Aberdeen : *Aber*
Aberdeenshire : *Abers*
Angus : *Ang*
Antrim & Newtownabbey : *Ant*
Ards & North Down : *Ards*
Argyll & Bute : *Arg*
Armagh, Banbridge & Craigavon : *Arm*
Bath & N E Somerset : *Bath*
Bedford : *Bed*
Belfast : *Bel*
Blackburn with Darwen : *Bkbn*
Blackpool : *Bkpl*
Blaenau Gwent : *Blae*
Bournemouth : *Bour*
Bracknell Forest : *Brac*
Bridgend : *B'end*
Brighton & Hove : *Brig*
Bristol : *Bris*
Buckinghamshire : *Buck*
Caerphilly : *Cphy*
Cambridgeshire : *Cambs*
Cardiff : *Card*
Carmarthenshire : *Carm*
Causeway Coast & Glens : *Caus*
Central Bedfordshire : *C Beds*
Ceredigion : *Cdgn*
Cheshire East : *Ches E*
Cheshire West & Chester : *Ches W*
Clackmannanshire : *Clac*
Conwy : *Cnwy*
Cornwall : *Corn*
Cumbria : *Cumb*
Darlington : *Darl*
Denbighshire : *Den*
Derby : *Derb*
Derbyshire : *Derbs*
Derry & Strabane : *Derr*
Devon : *Devn*
Dorset : *Dors*
Dumfries & Galloway : *Dum*
Dundee : *D'dee*
Durham : *Dur*
East Ayrshire : *E Ayr*
East Dunbartonshire : *E Dun*
East Lothian : *E Lot*
East Renfrewshire : *E Ren*
East Riding of Yorkshire : *E Yor*
East Sussex : *E Sus*
Edinburgh : *Edin*
Essex : *Essx*
Falkirk : *Falk*
Fermanagh & Omagh : *Ferm*
Fife : *Fife*
Flintshire : *Flin*
Glasgow : *Glas*
Gloucestershire : *Glos*
Greater London : *G Lon*
Greater Manchester : *G Man*
Gwynedd : *Gwyn*
Halton : *Hal*
Hampshire : *Hants*
Hartlepool : *Hart*
Herefordshire : *Here*
Hertfordshire : *Herts*
Highland : *High*
Inverclyde : *Inv*
Isle of Anglesey : *IOA*
Isle of Man : *IOM*
Isle of Wight : *IOW*
Isles of Scilly : *IOS*
Kent : *Kent*
Kingston upon Hull : *Hull*
Lancashire : *Lanc*
Leicester : *Leic*
Leicestershire : *Leics*
Lincolnshire : *Linc*
Lisburn & Castlereagh : *Lis*
Luton : *Lutn*
Medway : *Medw*
Merseyside : *Mers*
Merthyr Tydfil : *Mer T*
Mid & East Antrim : *ME Ant*
Middlesbrough : *Midd*
Midlothian : *Midl*
Mid Ulster : *M Ulst*
Milton Keynes : *Mil*
Monmouthshire : *Mon*
Moray : *Mor*
Neath Port Talbot : *Neat*
Newport : *Newp*
Newry, Mourne & Down : *New M*
Norfolk : *Norf*
Northamptonshire : *Nptn*
North Ayrshire : *N Ayr*
North East Lincolnshire : *NE Lin*
North Lanarkshire : *N Lan*
North Lincolnshire : *N Lin*
North Somerset : *N Som*
Northumberland : *Nmbd*
North Yorkshire : *N Yor*
Nottingham : *Nott*
Nottinghamshire : *Notts*
Orkney : *Orkn*
Oxfordshire : *Oxon*
Pembrokeshire : *Pemb*
Perth & Kinross : *Per*
Peterborough : *Pet*
Plymouth : *Plym*
Poole : *Pool*
Portsmouth : *Port*
Powys : *Powy*
Reading : *Read*
Redcar & Cleveland : *Red C*
Renfrewshire : *Ren*
Rhondda Cynon Taff : *Rhon*
Rutland : *Rut*
Scottish Borders : *Bord*
Shetland : *Shet*
Shropshire : *Shrp*
Slough : *Slo*
Somerset : *Som*
Southampton : *Sotn*
South Ayrshire : *S Ayr*
Southend-on-Sea : *S'end*
South Gloucestershire : *S Glo*
South Lanarkshire : *S Lan*
South Yorkshire : *S Yor*
Staffordshire : *Staf*
Stirling : *Stir*
Stockton-on-Tees : *Stoc T*
Stoke-on-Trent : *Stoke*
Suffolk : *Suff*
Surrey : *Surr*
Swansea : *Swan*
Swindon : *Swin*
Telford & Wrekin : *Telf*
Thurrock : *Thur*
Torbay : *Torb*
Torfaen : *Torf*
Tyne & Wear : *Tyne*
Vale of Glamorgan, The : *V Glam*
Warrington : *Warr*
Warwickshire : *Warw*
West Berkshire : *W Ber*
West Dunbartonshire : *W Dun*
Western Isles : *W Isl*
West Lothian : *W Lot*
West Midlands : *W Mid*
West Sussex : *W Sus*
West Yorkshire : *W Yor*
Wiltshire : *Wilts*
Windsor & Maidenhead : *Wind*
Wokingham : *Wok*
Worcestershire : *Worc*
Wrexham : *Wrex*
York : *York*

INDEX

A

Ashurst—Bewaldeth

Ashurst. Kent 2B 12
Ashurst. Lanc 7C 40
Ashurst. W Sus 4J 11
Ashurst Wood. W Sus 2M 11
Ash Vale. Surr 8F 20
Ashwater. Devn 6C 6
Ashwell. Herts 8K 29
Ashwell. Rut 8F 36
Ashwellthorpe. Norf 2H 31
Ashwick. Som 1E 8
Ashwicken. Norf 8D 38
Ashwood. Staf 3G 27
Askam in Furness. Cumb 7M 45
Askern. S Yor 6C 42
Askerswell. Dors 6D 8
Askett. Buck 3F 20
Askham. Cumb 3D 46
Askham. Notts 2E 36
Askham Bryan. York 3C 42
Askham Richard. York 3C 42
Askrigg. N Yor 6H 47
Askwith. N Yor 3K 41
Aslackby. Linc 6H 37
Aslacton. Norf 2H 31
Aslockton. Notts 5E 36
Aspatria. Cumb 7F 52
Aspenden. Herts 1L 21
Asperton. Linc 6K 37
Aspley Guise. C Beds 8G 29
Aspley Heath. C Beds 8G 29
Aspull. G Man 7E 40
Asselby. E Yor 5E 42
Assington. Suff 8F 30
Assington Green. Suff 6D 30
Astbury. Ches E 3G 35
Astcote. Nptn 6D 28
Asterby. Linc 2K 37
Asterley. Shrp 1B 26
Asterton. Shrp 2B 26
Asthall. Oxon 2L 19
Asthall Leigh. Oxon 2M 19
Astle. High 4H 79
Astley. G Man 7F 40
Astley. Shrp 8D 34
Astley. Warw 3M 27
Astley. Worc 5F 26
Astley Abbotts. Shrp 2F 26
Astley Bridge. G Man 6F 40
Astley Cross. Worc 5G 27
Aston. Ches E 5E 34
Aston. Ches W 2D 34
Aston. Derbs
nr. Hope 1K 35
nr. Sudbury 6K 35
Aston. Flin 3B 34
Aston. Here 5C 26
Aston. Herts 1K 21
Aston. Oxon 3M 19
Aston. Shrp
nr. Bridgnorth 2G 27
nr. Wem 7D 34
Aston. S Yor 1B 36
Aston. Staf 5F 34
Aston. Telf 1E 26
Aston. W Mid 2J 27
Aston. Wok 5E 20
Aston Abbotts. Buck 1F 20
Aston Botterell. Shrp 3E 26
Aston-by-Stone. Staf 6H 35
Aston Cantlow. Warw 6K 27
Aston Clinton. Buck 2F 20
Aston Crews. Here 1E 18
Aston Cross. Glos 8H 27
Aston End. Herts 1K 21
Aston Eyre. Shrp 2E 26
Aston Fields. Worc 5H 27
Aston Flamville. Leics 2B 28
Aston Ingham. Here 1E 18
Aston juxta Mondrum.
Ches E 4E 34
Astonlane. Shrp 2E 26
Aston le Walls. Nptn 6B 28
Aston Magna. Glos 8K 27
Aston Munslow. Shrp 3D 26
Aston on Carrant. Glos 8H 27
Aston on Clun. Shrp 3B 26
Aston-on-Trent. Derbs 7B 36
Aston Pigott. Shrp 1B 26
Aston Rogers. Shrp 1B 26
Aston Rowant. Oxon 4E 20
Aston Sandford. Buck 3E 20
Aston Somerville. Worc 8J 27
Aston Subedge. Glos 7K 27
Aston Tirrold. Oxon 5C 20
Aston Upthorpe. Oxon 5C 20
Astrop. Nptn 8C 28
Astwick. C Beds 8K 29
Astwood. Mil 7G 29
Astwood Bank. Worc 5J 27
Aswarby. Linc 6H 37
Aswardby. Linc 2L 37
Atcham. Shrp 1D 26
Atch Lench. Worc 6J 27
Athelhampton. Dors 6F 8
Athelington. Suff 4J 31
Athelney. Som 3B 8
Athelstaneford. E Lot 2C 60
Atherfield Green. IOW 8B 10
Atherington. Devn 3E 6
Atherington. W Sus 5H 11
Athersley. S Yor 7A 42
Atherstone. Warw 2M 27
Atherstone on Stour. Warw 6L 27
Atherton. G Man 7E 40
Ath-Tharracail. High 1A 64
Atlow. Derbs 5L 35
Attadale. High 2L 69
Attenborough. Notts 6C 36
Atterby. Linc 8G 43
Atterley. Shrp 2E 26
Atterton. Leics 2A 28
Attical. New M 7H 93
Attleborough. Norf 2G 31
Attleborough. Warw 2A 28
Attlebridge. Norf 8H 39
Atwick. E Yor 2J 43
Atworth. Wilts 7G 19
Auberrow. Here 7C 26
Aubourn. Linc 3G 37
Aucharnie. Abers 1F 72
Auchattie. Abers 6F 72
Auchavan. Ang 1E 66
Auchbreck. Mor 3B 72
Auchenback. E Ren 4D 58
Auchenblae. Abers 8G 73
Auchenbrack. Dum 2B 52
Auchenbreck. Arg 1K 57
Auchencairn. Dum
nr. Dalbeattie 6B 52
nr. Dumfries 3D 52
Auchencarroch. W Dun 1C 58
Auchencrow. Bord 3F 60
Auchendennan. Arg 1B 58
Auchendinny. Midl 3L 59
Auchengray. S Lan 4H 59
Auchenhalrig. Mor 7C 80
Auchenheath. S Lan 5G 59
Auchenlochan. Arg 2J 57
Auchenmade. N Ayr 5B 58
Auchenmalg. Dum 6H 51
Auchentiber. N Ayr 5B 58
Auchenvennel. Arg 1A 58
Auchindrain. Arg 7E 64
Auchininna. Abers 1F 72
Auchinleck. Dum 4K 51
Auchinleck. E Ayr 7D 58
Auchinloch. N Lan 2E 58
Auchinstarry. N Lan 2F 58
Auchleven. Abers 3F 72
Auchlochan. S Lan 6G 59
Auchlunachan. High 5B 78
Auchmillan. E Ayr 7D 58
Auchmithie. Ang 3K 67
Auchmuirbridge. Fife 7F 66
Auchmull. Ang 8E 72
Auchnacree. Ang 1H 67
Auchnafree. Per 4B 66
Auchnagallin. High 2L 71
Auchnagatt. Abers 1J 73
Aucholzie. Abers 6C 72
Auchreddie. Abers 1H 73
Auchterarder. Per 6C 66
Auchteraw. High 5D 70
Auchterderran. Fife 8F 66
Auchterhouse. Ang 4G 67
Auchtermuchty. Fife 6F 66
Auchterneed. High 8E 78
Auchtertool. Fife 8F 66
Auchtertyre. High 3K 69
Auchtubh. Stir 5K 65
Auckengill. High 5E 86
Auckley. S Yor 7D 42
Audenshaw. G Man 8H 41
Audlem. Ches E 5E 34
Audley. Staf 4F 34
Audley End. Essx 8B 30
Audmore. Staf 7G 35
Auds. Abers 7F 80
Augher. M Ulst 6D 92
Aughertree. Cumb 8G 53
Aughnacloy. M Ulst 6E 92
Aughton. E Yor 4E 42
Aughton. Lanc
nr. Lancaster 1D 40
nr. Ormskirk 7B 40
Aughton. S Yor 1B 36
Aughton. Wilts 8L 19
Aughton Park. Lanc 7C 40
Auldearn. High 8K 79
Aulden. Here 6C 26
Auldgirth. Dum 3D 52
Auldhouse. S Lan 4E 58
Ault a' chruinn. High 3L 69
Aultbea. High 5K 77
Aultdearg. High 7C 78
Aultgrishan. High 5J 77
Aultguish Inn. High 6D 78
Ault Hucknall. Derbs 3B 36
Aultibea. High 1L 79
Aultiphurst. High 5L 85
Aultivullin. High 5L 85
Aultmore. Mor 8D 80
Aultnamain Inn. High 5G 79
Aunby. Linc 8H 37
Aunsby. Linc 6H 37
Aust. S Glo 5D 18
Austerfield. S Yor 8D 42
Austin Fen. Linc 8L 43
Austrey. Warw 1L 27
Austwick. N Yor 1F 40
Authorpe. Linc 1M 37
Authorpe Row. Linc 2B 38
Avebury. Wilts 7K 19
Avebury Trusloe. Wilts 7J 19
Aveley. Thur 5B 22
Avening. Glos 4G 19
Averham. Notts 4E 36
Aveton Gifford. Devn 7J 5
Avielochan. High 4K 71
Aviemore. High 4J 71
Avington. Hants 2C 10
Avoch. High 8H 79
Avon. Hants 6K 9
Avonbridge. Falk 2H 59
Avon Dassett. Warw 6B 28
Avonmouth. Bris 6D 18
Avonwick. Devn 6K 5
Awbridge. Hants 3M 9
Awliscombe. Devn 5L 7
Awre. Glos 3F 18
Awsworth. Notts 5B 36
Axbridge. Som 8C 18
Axford. Hants 1D 10
Axford. Wilts 7L 19
Axminster. Devn 6B 8
Axmouth. Devn 6A 8
Aycliffe Village. Dur 3L 47
Aydon. Nmbd 5D 54
Aykley Heads. Dur 7F 54
Aylburton. Glos 3E 18
Aylburton Common. Glos 3E 18
Ayle. Nmbd 7M 53
Aylesbeare. Devn 6K 7
Aylesbury. Buck 2F 20
Aylesby. NE Lin 7K 43
Aylescott. Devn 4F 6
Aylesford. Kent 8D 22
Aylesham. Kent 8J 23
Aylestone. Leic 1C 28
Aylmerton. Norf 6H 39
Aylsham. Norf 7H 39
Aylton. Here 8E 26
Aylworth. Glos 1K 19
Aymestrey. Here 5C 26
Aynho. Nptn 8C 28
Ayot Green. Herts 2K 21
Ayot St Lawrence. Herts 2J 21
Ayot St Peter. Herts 2K 21
Ayr. S Ayr 7B 58
Ayres of Selivoe. Shet 3C 90
Ayreville. Torb 5L 5
Aysgarth. N Yor 7J 47
Ayshford. Devn 4K 7
Ayside. Cumb 7B 46
Ayston. Rut 1F 28
Ayton. Bord 3G 61
Aywick. Shet 5K 91
Azerley. N Yor 8L 47

B

Babbacombe. Torb 5M 5
Babbinswood. Shrp 6B 34
Babbs Green. Herts 2L 21
Babcary. Som 3D 8
Babel. Carm 1H 17
Babell. Flin 3L 33
Babingley. Norf 7C 38
Bablock Hythe. Oxon 3B 20
Babraham. Cambs 6B 30
Babworth. Notts 1D 36
Bac. W Isl 7H 83
Bachau. IOA 2D 32
Bacheldre. Powy 3M 25
Bachymbyd Fawr. Den 4K 33
Backaland. Orkn 6E 88
Backaskaill. Orkn 4D 88
Backbarrow. Cumb 7B 46
Backe. Carm 5J 15
Backfolds. Abers 8K 81
Backford. Ches W 2C 34
Backhill. Abers 2G 73
Backhill of Clackriach.
Abers 1J 73
Backies. High 3J 79
Backmuir of New Gilston.
Fife 7H 67
Back of Keppoch. High 7H 69
Back Street. Suff 6D 30
Backwell. N Som 7C 18
Backworth. Tyne 4G 55
Bacon End. Essx 2C 22
Baconsthorpe. Norf 6H 39
Bacton. Here 8B 26
Bacton. Norf 6K 39
Bacton. Suff 5G 31
Bacton Green. Norf 6K 39
Bacup. Lanc 5G 41
Badachonacher. High 6G 79
Badachro. High 6J 77
Badanloch Lodge. High 8K 85
Badavanich. High 8B 78
Badbury. Swin 5K 19
Badby. Nptn 6C 28
Badcall. High 6E 84
Badcaul. High 4M 77
Baddeley Green. Stoke 4H 35
Baddesley Clinton. W Mid 4L 27
Baddesley Ensor. Warw 2L 27
Baddidarach. High 1A 78
Baddoch. Abers 7M 71
Badenscallie. High 3M 77
Badenscoth. Abers 2G 73
Badentarbat. High 2M 77
Badgall. Corn 7B 6
Badgers Mount. Kent 7A 22
Badgeworth. Glos 2H 19
Badgworth. Som 8B 18
Badicaul. High 3J 69
Badingham. Suff 5K 31
Badlesmere. Kent 8G 23
Badlipster. High 7D 86
Badluarach. High 4L 77
Badminton. S Glo 5G 19
Badnaban. High 1A 78
Badnabay. High 7E 84
Badnagie. High 8C 86
Badnellan. High 3J 79
Badninish. High 4H 79
Badrallach. High 4A 78
Badsey. Worc 7J 27
Badshot Lea. Surr 1F 10
Badsworth. W Yor 6B 42
Badwell Ash. Suff 5F 30
Bae Cinmel. Cnwy 2J 33
Bae Colwyn. Cnwy 3H 33
Bae Penrhyn. Cnwy 2H 33
Bagby. N Yor 7B 48
Bag Enderby. Linc 2L 37
Bagendon. Glos 3J 19
Bagginswood. Shrp 3E 26
Bàgh a Chàise. W Isl 6A 76
Bàgh a' Chaisteil. W Isl 6C 74
Bagham. Kent 8G 23
Baghasdal. W Isl 4D 74
Bagh Mor. W Isl 8K 75
Bagh Shiarabhagh. W Isl 5D 74
Bagillt. Flin 3M 33
Baginton. Warw 4M 27
Baglan. Neat 5G 17
Bagley. Shrp 7C 34
Bagley. Som 1C 8
Bagnall. Staf 4H 35
Bagnor. W Ber 7B 20
Bagshot. Surr 7G 21
Bagshot. Wilts 7M 19
Bagstone. S Glo 5E 18
Bagthorpe. Norf 6D 38
Bagthorpe. Notts 4B 36
Bagworth. Leics 1B 28
Bagwy Llydiart. Here 1C 18
Baildon. W Yor 4K 41
Baildon Green. W Yor 4K 41
Baile. W Isl 5L 75
Baile Ailein. W Isl 1D 76
Baile an Truiseil. W Isl 6G 83
Baile Boidheach. Arg 2G 57
Baile Glas. W Isl 8K 75
Bailemeonach. Arg 3A 64
Baile Mhanaich. W Isl 8J 75
Baile Mhartainn. W Isl 6J 75
Baile MhicPhail. W Isl 6K 75
Baile Mor. W Isl 7J 75
Baile Mór. Arg 5H 63
Baile nan Cailleach. W Isl 8J 75
Baile Raghaill. W Isl 7J 75
Bailey Green. Hants 3D 10
Baileyhead. Cumb 3K 53
Baileysmill. Lis 6H 93
Bailiesward. Abers 2D 72
Bail' Iochdrach. W Isl 8K 75
Baillieston. Glas 3E 58
Bailrigg. Lanc 2C 40
Bail Uachdraich. W Isl 7K 75
Bail' Ur Tholastaidh. W Isl 7J 83
Bainbridge. N Yor 6H 47
Bainsford. Falk 1G 59
Bainshole. Abers 2F 72
Bainton. E Yor 2G 43
Bainton. Oxon 1C 20
Bainton. Pet 1H 29
Baintown. Fife 7G 67
Baker Street. Thur 5C 22
Bakewell. Derbs 3L 35
Bala. Gwyn 7J 33
Y Bala. Gwyn 7J 33
Balachuirn. High 1G 69
Balbeg. High
nr. Cannich 2E 70
nr. Loch Ness 3E 70
Balbeggie. Per 5E 66
Balblair. High
nr. Bonar Bridge 4F 78
nr. Invergordon 7H 79
nr. Inverness 1F 70
Balby. S Yor 7C 42
Balcathie. Ang 4K 67
Balchladich. High 8C 84
Balchraggan. High 1F 70
Balchrick. High 6D 84
Balcombe. W Sus 2L 11
Balcombe Lane. W Sus 2L 11
Balcurvie. Fife 7G 67
Baldersby. N Yor 8A 48
Baldersby St James. N Yor 8A 48
Balderstone. Lanc 4E 40
Balderton. Ches W 3B 34
Balderton. Notts 4F 36
Baldinnie. Fife 6H 67
Baldock. Herts 8K 29
Baldrine. IOM 6D 44
Baldslow. E Sus 4E 12
Baldwin. IOM 6C 44
Baldwinholme. Cumb 6H 53
Baldwin's Gate. Staf 6F 34
Bale. Norf 6G 39
Balearn. Abers 8K 81
Balemartine. Arg 3E 62
Balephetrish. Arg 3F 62
Balephuil. Arg 3E 62
Balerno. Edin 3K 59
Balevullin. Arg 3E 62
Balfield. Ang 1J 67
Balfour. Orkn 8D 88
Balfron. Stir 1D 58
Balgaveny. Abers 1F 72
Balgonar. Fife 8D 66
Balgowan. High 6G 71
Balgown. High 7E 76
Balgrochan. E Dun 2E 58
Balgy. High 8K 77
Balhalgardy. Abers 3G 73
Baliasta. Shet 3L 91
Baligill. High 5L 85
Balintore. Ang 2F 66
Balintore. High 6J 79
Balintraid. High 6H 79
Balk. N Yor 7B 48
Balkeerie. Ang 3G 67
Balkholme. E Yor 5E 42
Ball. Shrp 7B 34
Ballabeg. IOM 7B 44
Ballacannell. IOM 6D 44
Ballacarnane Beg. IOM 6C 44
Ballachulish. High 2E 64
Ballagyr. IOM 6B 44
Ballajora. IOM 5D 44
Ballaleigh. IOM 6C 44
Ballamodha. IOM 7B 44
Ballantrae. S Ayr 3F 50
Ballards Gore. Essx 4F 22
Ballasalla. IOM
nr. Castletown 7B 44
nr. Kirk Michael 5C 44
Ballater. Abers 6C 72
Ballaugh. IOM 5C 44
Ballencrieff. E Lot 2B 60
Ballencrieff Toll. W Lot 2H 59
Ballentoul. Per 1B 66
Ball Hill. Hants 7B 20
Ballidon. Derbs 4L 35
Balliemore. Arg
nr. Dunoon 1K 57
nr. Oban 5C 64
Ballieward. High 2L 71
Ballig. IOM 6B 44
Ballimore. Stir 6K 65
Ballinamallard. Ferm 6C 92
Ballindarragh. Ferm 7C 92
Ballingdon. Suff 7E 30
Ballinger Common. Buck 3G 21
Ballingham. Here 8D 26
Ballingry. Fife 8E 66
Ballinluig. Per 2C 66
Ballintoy. Caus 1G 93
Ballintuim. Per 2E 66
Balliveolan. Arg 3C 64
Balloan. High 3F 78
Balloch. High 1H 71
Balloch. N Lan 2F 58
Balloch. Per 6B 66
Balloch. W Dun 1B 58
Ballochan. Abers 6E 72
Ballochgoy. Arg 3K 57
Ballochmyle. E Ayr 7D 58
Ballochroy. Arg 4G 57
Balloo. Ards 5J 93
Balls Cross. W Sus 3G 11
Ball's Green. E Sus 2A 12
Ballsmill. New M 7F 93
Ballyalton. New M 6J 93
Ballybogy. Caus 2F 93
Ballycarry. ME Ant 4J 93
Ballycassidy. Ferm 6C 92
Ballycastle. Caus 1G 93
Ballyclare. Ant 4H 93
Ballyeaston. Ant 4H 93
Ballygally. ME Ant 3H 93
Ballygawley. M Ulst 6E 92
Ballygowan. Ards 5J 93
Ballygown. Arg 3K 63
Ballygrant. Arg 3C 56
Ballyhalbert. Ards 5K 93
Ballyholland. New M 7G 93
Ballyhornan. New M 6J 93
Ballykelly. Caus 2E 92
Ballykinler. New M 7J 93
Ballylesson. Lis 5H 93
Ballymagorry. Derr 3C 92
Ballymartin. New M 7H 93
Ballymena. ME Ant 3G 93
Ballymichael. N Ayr 6J 57
Ballymoney. Caus 2F 93
Ballynagard. Derr 2D 92
Ballynahinch. New M 6H 93
Ballynakilly. M Ulst 5F 93
Ballynoe. New M 6J 93
Ballynure. Ant 4H 93
Ballyrashane. Caus 2F 93
Ballyrobert. Ant 4H 93
Ballyronan. M Ulst 4F 93
Ballyroney. Arm 7H 93
Ballyscullion. Caus 2E 92
Ballystrudder. ME Ant 4J 93
Ballyvoy. Caus 1G 93
Ballyward. New M 7H 93
Ballywater. Ards 5K 93
Ballywonard. Ant 4H 93
Balmacara. High 3K 69
Balmaclellan. Dum 4A 52
Balmacqueen. High 6F 76
Balmaha. Stir 8J 65
Balmalcolm. Fife 7G 67
Balmalloch. N Lan 2F 58
Balmeanach. High 2G 69
Balmedie. Abers 4J 73
Balmerino. Fife 5G 67
Balmerlawn. Hants 5M 9
Balmore. E Dun 2E 58
Balmore. High 1D 68
Balmullo. Fife 5H 67
Balmurrie. Dum 5H 51
Balnaboth. Ang 1G 67
Balnabruaich. High 6H 79
Balnabruich. High 1A 80
Balnacoil. High 2J 79
Balnacra. High 1L 69
Balnacroft. Abers 6B 72
Balnageith. Mor 8L 79
Balnaglaic. High 2E 70
Balnagrantach. High 2E 70
Balnaguard. Per 2C 66
Balnahard. Arg 8K 63
Balnain. High 2E 70
Balnakeil. High 5F 84
Balnaknock. High 7F 76
Balnamoon. Abers 8J 81
Balnamoon. Ang 1J 67
Balnamore. Caus 2F 93
Balnapaling. High 7H 79
Balornock. Glas 3E 58
Balquhidder. Stir 5K 65
Balsall. W Mid 4L 27
Balsall Common. W Mid 4L 27
Balscote. Oxon 7A 28
Balsham. Cambs 6B 30
Balstonia. Thur 5C 22
Baltasound. Shet 3L 91
Balterley. Staf 4F 34
Baltersan. Dum 5K 51
Balthangie. Abers 8H 81
Baltonsborough. Som 2D 8
Balvaird. High 8F 78
Balvaird. Per 6E 66
Balvenie. Mor 1C 72
Balvicar. Arg 6B 64
Balvraid. High 4K 69
Balvraid Lodge. High 2J 71
Bamber Bridge. Lanc 5D 40
Bamber's Green. Essx 1B 22
Bamburgh. Nmbd 6J 61
Bamford. Derbs 1L 35
Bamfurlong. G Man 7D 40
Bampton. Cumb 4D 46
Bampton. Devn 3J 7
Bampton. Oxon 3M 19
Bampton Grange. Cumb 4D 46
Banavie. High 8B 70
Banbridge. Arm 6G 93
Banbury. Oxon 7B 28
Bancffosfelen. Carm 5L 15
Banchory. Abers 6F 72
Banchory-Devenick. Abers 5J 73
Bancycapel. Carm 5L 15
Bancyfelin. Carm 5K 15
Banc-y-ffordd. Carm 3L 15
Banff. Abers 7F 80
Bangor. Ards 4J 93
Bangor. Gwyn 3E 32
Bangor-is-y-coed. Wrex 5B 34
Bangors. Corn 6B 6
Bangor's Green. Lanc 7B 40
Banham. Norf 3G 31
Bank. Hants 5L 9
The Bank. Ches E 4G 35
The Bank. Shrp 2E 26
Bankend. Dum 5E 52
Bankfoot. Per 4D 66
Bankglen. E Ayr 8E 58
Bankhead. Aber 4H 73
Bankhead. Abers 5F 72
Bankhead. S Lan 5G 59
Bankland. Som 3B 8
Bank Newton. N Yor 2H 41
Banknock. Falk 2F 58
Banks. Cumb 5K 53
Banks. Lanc 5B 40
Bankshill. Dum 3F 52
Bank Street. Worc 5E 26
Bank Top. Lanc 7D 40
Banners Gate. W Mid 2J 27
Banningham. Norf 7J 39
Banniskirk. High 6C 86
Bannister Green. Essx 1C 22
Bannockburn. Stir 8B 66
Banstead. Surr 8K 21
Bantham. Devn 7J 5
Banton. N Lan 2F 58
Banwell. N Som 8B 18
Banyard's Green. Suff 4K 31
Bapchild. Kent 7F 22
Bapton. Wilts 2H 9
Barabhas. W Isl 6G 83
Barabhas Iarach. W Isl 7G 83
Baramore. High 8H 69
Barassie. S Ayr 6B 58
Baravullin. Arg 3D 64
Barbaraville. High 6H 79
Barber Booth. Derbs 1K 35
Barber Green. Cumb 7B 46
Barbhas Uarach. W Isl 6G 83
Barbieston. S Ayr 8C 58
Barbon. Cumb 7E 46
Barbourne. Worc 6G 27
Barbridge. Ches E 4E 34
Barbrook. Devn 1G 7
Barby. Nptn 4C 28
Barby Nortoft. Nptn 4C 28
Barcaldine. Arg 3D 64
Barcheston. Warw 8L 27
Barclose. Cumb 5J 53
Barcombe. E Sus 4M 11
Barcombe Cross. E Sus 4M 11
Barden. N Yor 6K 47
Barden Scale. N Yor 2J 41
Bardfield End Green. Essx 8C 30
Bardfield Saling. Essx 1C 22
Bardister. Shet 6H 91
Bardnabeinne. High 4H 79
Bardney. Linc 3J 37
Bardon. Leics 8B 36
Bardon Mill. Nmbd 5A 54
Bardowie. E Dun 2D 58
Bardrainney. Inv 2B 58
Bardsea. Cumb 8B 46
Bardsey. W Yor 3A 42
Bardsley. G Man 7H 41
Bardwell. Suff 4F 30
Bare. Lanc 1C 40
Barelees. Nmbd 6F 60
Barewood. Here 6B 26
Barford. Hants 2F 10
Barford. Norf 1H 31
Barford. Warw 5L 27
Barford St John. Oxon 8B 28
Barford St Martin. Wilts 2J 9
Barford St Michael. Oxon 8B 28
Barfrestone. Kent 8J 23
Bargeddie. N Lan 3E 58
Bargod. Cphy 5L 17
Bargoed. Cphy 5L 17
Bargrennan. Dum 4J 51
Barham. Cambs 4J 29
Barham. Kent 8J 23
Barham. Suff 6H 31
Barharrow. Dum 6M 51
Bar Hill. Cambs 5L 29
Barholm. Linc 8H 37
Barkby. Leics 1D 28
Barkestone-le-Vale. Leics 6E 36
Barkham. Wok 7E 20
Barking. G Lon 5M 21
Barking. Suff 6G 31
Barkingside. G Lon 5A 22
Barking Tye. Suff 6G 31
Barkisland. W Yor 6J 41
Barkston. Linc 5G 37
Barkston Ash. N Yor 4B 42
Barkway. Herts 8L 29
Barlanark. Glas 3E 58
Barlaston. Staf 6G 35
Barlavington. W Sus 4G 11
Barlborough. Derbs 2B 36
Barlby. N Yor 4D 42
Barlestone. Leics 1B 28
Barley. Herts 8L 29
Barley. Lanc 3G 41
Barley Mow. Tyne 6F 54
Barleythorpe. Rut 1F 28
Barling. Essx 5F 22
Barlings. Linc 2H 37
Barlow. Derbs 2M 35
Barlow. N Yor 5D 42
Barlow. Tyne 5E 54
Barmby Moor. E Yor 3E 42
Barmby on the Marsh.
E Yor 5D 42
Barmer. Norf 6E 38
Barming. Kent 8D 22
Barming Heath. Kent 8D 22
Barmoor. Nmbd 6H 61
Barmouth. Gwyn 1F 24
Barmpton. Darl 4M 47
Barmston. E Yor 2J 43
Barmulloch. Glas 3E 58
Barnack. Pet 1H 29
Barnacle. Warw 3A 28
Barnard Castle. Dur 4J 47
Barnard Gate. Oxon 2B 20
Barnardiston. Suff 7D 30
Barnbarroch. Dum 6C 52
Barnburgh. S Yor 7B 42
Barnby. Suff 3L 31
Barnby Dun. S Yor 7D 42
Barnby in the Willows.
Notts 4F 36
Barnby Moor. Notts 1D 36
Barnes. G Lon 6K 21
Barnes Street. Kent 1C 12
Barnet. G Lon 4K 21
Barnetby le Wold. N Lin 7H 43
Barney. Norf 6F 38
Barnham. Suff 4E 30
Barnham. W Sus 5G 11
Barnham Broom. Norf 1G 31
Barnhead. Ang 2K 67
Barnhill. D'dee 4H 67
Barnhill. Mor 8M 79
Barnhill. Per 5E 66
Barnhills. Dum 4E 50
Barningham. Dur 4J 47
Barningham. Suff 4F 30
Barnoldby le Beck. NE Lin 7K 43
Barnoldswick. Lanc 3G 41
Barns Green. W Sus 3J 11
Barnsley. Glos 3J 19
Barnsley. Shrp 2F 26
Barnsley. S Yor 7M 41
Barnstaple. Devn 2E 6
Barnston. Essx 2C 22
Barnston. Mers 1A 34
Barnstone. Notts 6E 36
Barnt Green. Worc 4J 27
Barnton. Ches W 2E 34
Barnwell. Cambs 6A 30
Barnwell. Nptn 3H 29
Barnwood. Glos 2G 19
Barons Cross. Here 6C 26
The Barony. Orkn 7B 88
Barr. Dum 1B 52
Barr. S Ayr 2H 51
Barra Airport. W Isl 5C 74
Barrachan. Dum 7J 51
Barraglom. W Isl 8E 82
Barrahormid. Arg 1G 57
Barrapol. Arg 3E 62
Barrasford. Nmbd 4C 54
Barravullin. Arg 7C 64
Barregarrow. IOM 6C 44
Barrhead. E Ren 4D 58
Barrhill. S Ayr 3H 51
Barri. V Glam 8L 17
Barrington. Cambs 7L 29
Barrington. Som 4B 8
Barripper. Corn 5K 3
Barrmill. N Ayr 4B 58
Barrock. High 4D 86
Barrow. Lanc 4F 40
Barrow. Rut 8F 36
Barrow. Shrp 1E 26
Barrow. Som 2F 8
Barrow. Suff 5D 30
Barroway Drove. Norf 1B 30
Barrow Bridge. G Man 6E 40
Barrowburn. Nmbd 8F 60
Barrowby. Linc 6F 36
Barrowcliff. N Yor 7H 49
Barrow Common. N Som 7D 18
Barrowden. Rut 1G 29
Barrowford. Lanc 4G 41
Barrow Gurney. N Som 7D 18
Barrow Haven. N Lin 5H 43
Barrow Hill. Derbs 2B 36
Barrow-in-Furness. Cumb 8M 45
Barrow Nook. Lanc 7C 40
Barrow's Green. Hal 1D 34
Barrows Green. Cumb 7D 46
Barrow Street. Wilts 2G 9
Barrow upon Humber.
N Lin 5H 43
Barrow upon Soar. Leics 8C 36
Barrow upon Trent. Derbs 7A 36
Barry. Ang 4J 67
Barry. V Glam 8L 17
Barry Island. V Glam 8L 17
Barsby. Leics 8D 36
Barsham. Suff 3K 31
Barston. W Mid 4L 27
Bartestree. Here 7D 26
Barthol Chapel. Abers 2H 73
Bartholomew Green. Essx 1D 22
Barthomley. Ches E 4F 34
Bartley. Hants 4M 9
Bartley Green. W Mid 3J 27
Bartlow. Cambs 7B 30
Barton. Cambs 6M 29
Barton. Ches W 4C 34
Barton. Cumb 3C 46
Barton. Glos 1K 19
Barton. IOW 7C 10
Barton. Lanc
nr. Ormskirk 7B 40
nr. Preston 4D 40
Barton. N Som 8B 18
Barton. N Yor 5L 47
Barton. Oxon 3C 20
Barton. Torb 5M 5
Barton. Warw 6K 27
Barton Bendish. Norf 1D 30
Barton Gate. Staf 8K 35
Barton Green. Staf 8K 35
Barton Hartshorn. Buck 8D 28
Barton Hill. N Yor 1E 42
Barton in Fabis. Notts 6C 36
Barton in the Beans. Leics 1A 28
Barton-le-Clay. C Beds 8H 29
Barton-le-Street. N Yor 8E 48
Barton-le-Willows. N Yor 1E 42
Barton Mills. Suff 4D 30
Barton on Sea. Hants 6L 9
Barton-on-the-Heath. Warw 8L 27
Barton St David. Som 2D 8
Barton Seagrave. Nptn 4F 28
Barton Stacey. Hants 1B 10
Barton Town. Devn 1F 6
Barton Turf. Norf 7K 39
Barton-Under-Needwood.
Staf 8K 35
Barton-upon-Humber.
N Lin 5H 43
Barton Waterside. N Lin 5H 43
Barugh Green. S Yor 7M 41
Barway. Cambs 4B 30
Barwell. Leics 2B 28
Barwick. Herts 2L 21
Barwick. Som 4D 8
Barwick in Elmet. W Yor 4A 42
Baschurch. Shrp 7C 34
Bascote. Warw 5B 28
Basford Green. Staf 4H 35
Bashall Eaves. Lanc 3E 40
Bashall Town. Lanc 3F 40
Bashley. Hants 6L 9
Basildon. Essx 5D 22
Basingstoke. Hants 8D 20
Baslow. Derbs 2L 35
Bason Bridge. Som 1B 8
Bassaleg. Newp 5A 18
Bassendean. Bord 5D 60
Bassenthwaite. Cumb 8G 53
Bassett. Sotn 4B 10
Bassingbourn. Cambs 7L 29
Bassingfield. Notts 6D 36
Bassingham. Linc 3G 37
Bassingthorpe. Linc 7G 37
Bassus Green. Herts 1L 21
Basta. Shet 4K 91
Baston. Linc 8J 37
Bastonford. Worc 6G 27
Bastwick. Norf 8L 39
Batchley. Worc 5J 27
Batchworth. Herts 4H 21
Batcombe. Dors 5E 8
Batcombe. Som 2E 8
Bate Heath. Ches E 2E 34
Bath. Bath 106 (7F 18)
Bathampton. Bath 7F 18
Bathealton. Som 3K 7
Batheaston. Bath 7F 18
Bathford. Bath 7F 18
Bathgate. W Lot 3H 59
Bathley. Notts 4E 36
Bathpool. Corn 8B 6
Bathpool. Som 3A 8
Bathville. W Lot 3H 59
Bathway. Som 8D 18
Batley. W Yor 5L 41
Batsford. Glos 8K 27
Batson. Devn 8K 5
Battersby. N Yor 5C 48
Battersea. G Lon 6K 21
Battisborough Cross. Devn 7J 5
Battisford. Suff 6G 31
Battisford Tye. Suff 6G 31
Battle. E Sus 4D 12
Battle. Powy 1K 17
Battleborough. Som 8B 18
Battledown. Glos 1H 19
Battlefield. Shrp 8D 34
Battlesbridge. Essx 4D 22
Battlesden. C Beds 1G 21
Battlesea Green. Suff 4J 31
Battleton. Som 3J 7
Battram. Leics 1B 28
Battramsley. Hants 6M 9
Batt's Corner. Surr 1F 10
Bauds of Cullen. Mor 7D 80
Baugh. Arg 3F 62
Baughton. Worc 7G 27
Baughurst. Hants 7C 20
Baulking. Oxon 4M 19
Baumber. Linc 2K 37
Baunton. Glos 3J 19
Baverstock. Wilts 2J 9
Bawburgh. Norf 1H 31
Bawdeswell. Norf 7G 39
Bawdrip. Som 2B 8
Bawdsey. Suff 7K 31
Bawsey. Norf 8C 38
Bawtry. S Yor 8D 42
Baxenden. Lanc 5F 40
Baxterley. Warw 2L 27
Baxter's Green. Suff 6D 30
Bay. High 8D 76
Baybridge. Hants 3C 10
Baybridge. Nmbd 6C 54
Baycliff. Cumb 8A 46
Baydon. Wilts 6L 19
Bayford. Herts 3L 21
Bayford. Som 3F 8
Bayles. Cumb 7M 53
Baylham. Suff 6H 31
Baynard's Green. Oxon 1C 20
Bayston Hill. Shrp 1C 26
Baythorne End. Essx 7D 30
Baythorpe. Linc 5K 37
Bayton. Worc 4E 26
Bayton Common. Worc 4F 26
Bayworth. Oxon 3C 20
Beach. S Glo 6F 18
Beachampton. Buck 8E 28
Beachamwell. Norf 1D 30
Beachley. Glos 4D 18
Beacon. Devn 5L 7
Beacon End. Essx 1F 22
Beacon Hill. Surr 2F 10
Beacon's Bottom. Buck 4E 20
Beaconsfield. Buck 4G 21
Beacrabhaic. W Isl 4C 76
Beadlam. N Yor 7D 48
Beadnell. Nmbd 7K 61
Beaford. Devn 4E 6
Beal. Nmbd 5H 61
Beal. N Yor 5C 42
Bealsmill. Corn 8C 6
Beam Hill. Staf 7L 35
Beamhurst. Staf 6J 35
Beaminster. Dors 5C 8
Beamish. Dur 6F 54
Beamond End. Buck 4G 21
Beamsley. N Yor 2J 41
Bean. Kent 6B 22
Beanacre. Wilts 7H 19
Beanley. Nmbd 8H 61
Beaquoy. Orkn 7C 88
Beardwood. Bkbn 5E 40
Beare Green. Surr 1J 11
Bearley. Warw 5K 27
Bearpark. Dur 7F 54
Bearsbridge. Nmbd 6A 54
Bearsden. E Dun 2D 58
Bearsted. Kent 8D 22
Bearstone. Shrp 6F 34
Bearwood. Pool 6J 9
Bearwood. W Mid 3J 27
Beattock. Dum 1E 52
Beauchamp Roding. Essx 2B 22
Beauchief. S Yor 1M 35
Beaufort. Blae 3L 17
Beaulieu. Hants 5A 10
Beauly. High 1F 70
Beaumaris. IOA 3F 32
Beaumont. Cumb 6H 53
Beaumont. Essx 1H 23
Beaumont Hill. Darl 4L 47
Beaumont Leys. Leic 1C 28
Beausale. Warw 4L 27
Beauvale. Notts 5B 36
Beauworth. Hants 3C 10
Beaworthy. Devn 6D 6
Beazley End. Essx 1D 22
Bebington. Mers 1B 34
Bebside. Nmbd 3F 54
Beccles. Suff 3L 31
Becconsall. Lanc 5C 40
Beckbury. Shrp 1F 26
Beckenham. G Lon 7L 21
Beckermet. Cumb 4K 45
Beckett End. Norf 2D 30
Beck Foot. Cumb 6E 46
Beckfoot. Cumb
nr. Broughton in Furness 6L 45
nr. Seascale 4L 45
nr. Silloth 7E 52
Beckford. Worc 8H 27
Beckhampton. Wilts 7J 19
Beck Hole. N Yor 5F 48
Beckingham. Linc 4F 36
Beckingham. Notts 8E 42
Beckington. Som 8G 19
Beckley. E Sus 3E 12
Beckley. Hants 6L 9
Beckley. Oxon 2C 20
Beck Row. Suff 4C 30
Beck Side. Cumb
nr. Cartmel 7B 46
nr. Ulverston 6M 45
Beckside. Cumb 7E 46
Beckton. G Lon 5M 21
Beckwithshaw. N Yor 2L 41
Becontree. G Lon 5A 22
Bedale. N Yor 7L 47
Bedburn. Dur 8E 54
Bedchester. Dors 4G 9
Beddau. Rhon 6K 17
Beddgelert. Gwyn 6E 32
Beddingham. E Sus 5M 11
Beddington. G Lon 7L 21
Bedfield. Suff 5J 31
Bedford. Bed 7H 29
Bedford. G Man 8E 40
Bedham. W Sus 3H 11
Bedhampton. Hants 5E 10
Bedingfield. Suff 5H 31
Bedingham Green. Norf 2J 31
Bedlam. N Yor 1L 41
Bedlar's Green. Essx 1B 22
Bedlington. Nmbd 3F 54
Bedlinog. Mer T 4K 17
Bedminster. Bris 6D 18
Bedmond. Herts 3H 21
Bednall. Staf 8H 35
Bedrule. Bord 8D 60
Bedstone. Shrp 4B 26
Bedwas. Cphy 6L 17
Bedwellty. Cphy 4L 17
Bedworth. Warw 3A 28
Beeby. Leics 1D 28
Beech. Hants 2D 10
Beech. Staf 6G 35
Beechcliffe. W Yor 3J 41
Beech Hill. W Ber 7D 20
Beechingstoke. Wilts 8J 19
Beedon. W Ber 6B 20
Beeford. E Yor 2J 43
Beeley. Derbs 3L 35
Beelsby. NE Lin 7K 43
Beenham. W Ber 7C 20
Beeny. Corn 2D 4
Beer. Devn 7M 7
Beer. Som 2C 8
Beercrocombe. Som 3B 8
Beer Hackett. Dors 4E 8
Beesands. Devn 7L 5
Beesby. Linc 1A 38
Beeson. Devn 7L 5
Beeston. C Beds 7J 29
Beeston. Ches W 4D 34
Beeston. Norf 8F 38
Beeston. Notts 6C 36
Beeston. W Yor 4L 41
Beeston Regis. Norf 5H 39
Beeswing. Dum 5C 52
Beetham. Cumb 8C 46
Beetham. Som 4A 8
Beetley. Norf 8F 38
Beffcote. Staf 8G 35
Began. Card 6M 17
Begbroke. Oxon 2B 20
Begdale. Cambs 1A 30
Begelly. Pemb 6H 15
Beggar Hill. Essx 3C 22
Beggar's Bush. Powy 5A 26
Beggearn Huish. Som 2K 7
Beguildy. Powy 5L 25
Beighton. Norf 1K 31
Beighton. S Yor 1B 36
Beighton Hill. Derbs 4L 35
Beinn Casgro. W Isl 1F 76
Beith. N Ayr 4B 58
Bekesbourne. Kent 8H 23
Belaugh. Norf 8J 39
Belbroughton. Worc 4H 27
Belchalwell. Dors 5F 8
Belchalwell Street. Dors 5F 8
Belchamp Otten. Essx 7E 30
Belchamp St Paul. Essx 7D 30
Belchamp Walter. Essx 7E 30
Belchford. Linc 2K 37
Belcoo. Ferm 7B 92
Belfast. Bel 5H 93
Belfast City George Best Airport.
Bel 5H 93
Belfast International Airport.
Ant 4G 93
Belfatton. Abers 8K 81
Belford. Nmbd 6J 61
Belgrano. Cnwy 3J 33
Belhaven. E Lot 2D 60
Belhelvie. Abers 4J 73
Belhinnie. Abers 3D 72
Bellabeg. Abers 4C 72
Belladrum. High 1F 70
Bellaghy. M Ulst 4F 93
Bellamore. S Ayr 3H 51
Bellanaleck. Ferm 7C 92
Bellanoch. Arg 8C 64
Bell Busk. N Yor 2H 41
Belleau. Linc 2M 37
Belleek. Ferm 6A 92
Belleek. New M 7F 93
Belleheiglash. Mor 2A 72
Bell End. Worc 4H 27
Bellerby. N Yor 6K 47
Bellerby Camp. N Yor 6J 47
Bellever. Devn 8F 6
Belle Vue. Cumb 8F 52
Belle Vue. Shrp 8C 34
Bellfield. S Lan 6G 59
Belliehill. Ang 1J 67
Bellingdon. Buck 3G 21
Bellingham. Nmbd 3B 54
Bellmount. Norf 7B 38
Bellochantuy. Arg 6F 56
Bellsbank. E Ayr 1K 51
Bell's Cross. Suff 6H 31
Bellshill. N Lan 4F 58
Bellshill. Nmbd 6J 61
Bellside. N Lan 4G 59
Bellspool. Bord 6K 59
Bellsquarry. W Lot 3J 59
Bells Yew Green. E Sus 2C 12
Belmaduthy. High 8G 79
Belmesthorpe. Rut 8H 37
Belmont. Bkbn 6E 40
Belmont. Shet 3K 91
Belmont. S Ayr 7B 58
Belnacraig. Abers 4C 72
Belnie. Linc 6K 37
Belowda. Corn 5B 4
Belper. Derbs 5A 36
Belper Lane End. Derbs 5M 35
Belph. Derbs 2C 36
Belsay. Nmbd 4E 54
Belsford. Devn 6K 5
Belsize. Herts 3H 21
Belstead. Suff 7H 31
Belston. S Ayr 7B 58
Belstone. Devn 6F 6
Belstone Corner. Devn 6F 6
Belthorn. Lanc 5F 40
Beltinge. Kent 7H 23
Beltoft. N Lin 7F 42
Belton. Leics 7B 36
Belton. Linc 6G 37
Belton. Norf 1L 31
Belton. N Lin 7E 42
Belton-in-Rutland. Rut 1F 28
Beltring. Kent 1C 12
Belts of Collonach. Abers 6F 72
Belvedere. G Lon 6A 22
Belvoir. Leics 6F 36
Bembridge. IOW 7D 10
Bemersyde. Bord 6C 60
Bemerton. Wilts 2K 9
Bempton. E Yor 8J 49
Benacre. Suff 3M 31
Ben Alder Lodge. High 8F 70
Ben Armine Lodge. High 2H 79
Benbecula Airport. W Isl 8J 75
Benbuie. Dum 2B 52
Benburb. M Ulst 6F 93
Benchill. G Man 1G 35
Benderloch. Arg 4D 64
Bendish. Herts 1J 21
Bendooragh. Caus 2F 93
Bendronaig Lodge. High 2M 69
Benenden. Kent 2E 12
Benfieldside. Dur 6D 54
Bengate. Norf 7K 39
Bengeworth. Worc 7J 27
Benhall Green. Suff 5K 31
Benholm. Abers 1M 67
Beningbrough. N Yor 2C 42
Benington. Herts 1K 21
Benington. Linc 5L 37
Benington Sea End. Linc 5M 37
Benllech. IOA 2E 32
Benmore Lodge. High 2D 78
Bennacott. Corn 6B 6
Bennah. Devn 7H 7
Bennecarrigan. N Ayr 7J 57
Bennethead. Cumb 3C 46
Benniworth. Linc 1K 37
Benover. Kent 1D 12
Benson. Oxon 4D 20
Benston. Shet 2E 90
Benstonhall. Orkn 6E 88
Bent. Abers 8F 72
Benthall. Shrp 1E 26
Bentham. Glos 2H 19
Bentlawnt. Shrp 1B 26
Bentley. E Yor 4H 43
Bentley. Hants 1E 10
Bentley. S Yor 7C 42
Bentley. Suff 8H 31
Bentley. Warw 2L 27
Bentley. W Mid 2H 27
Bentley Heath. Herts 4K 21
Bentley Heath. W Mid 4K 27
Bentpath. Dum 2H 53
Bents. W Lot 3H 59
Bentworth. Hants 1D 10
Benvie. D'dee 4G 67
Benville. Dors 5D 8
Benwell. Tyne 5F 54
Benwick. Cambs 2L 29
Beoley. Worc 5J 27
Beoraidbeg. High 6H 69
Bepton. W Sus 4F 10
Beragh. Ferm 5D 92
Berden. Essx 1A 22
Bere Alston. Devn 5G 5
Bere Ferrers. Devn 5G 5
Berepper. Corn 6K 3
Bere Regis. Dors 6G 9
Bergh Apton. Norf 1K 31
Berinsfield. Oxon 4C 20
Berkeley. Glos 4E 18
Berkhamsted. Herts 3G 21
Berkley. Som 1G 9
Berkswell. W Mid 4L 27
Bermondsey. G Lon 6L 21
Bernera. High 3K 69
Bernice. Arg 8F 64
Bernisdale. High 8F 76
Berrick Salome. Oxon 4D 20
Berriedale. High 1M 79
Berrier. Cumb 3B 46
Berriew. Powy 2L 25
Berrington. Nmbd 5H 61
Berrington. Shrp 1D 26
Berrington. Worc 5D 26
Berrington Green. Worc 5D 26
Berrington Law. Nmbd 5G 61
Berrow. Som 8B 18
Berrow Green. Worc 6F 26
Berry Cross. Devn 4D 6
Berry Down Cross. Devn 1E 6
Berry Hill. Glos 2D 18
Berry Hill. Pemb 2G 15
Berryhillock. Mor 7E 80
Berrynarbor. Devn 1E 6
Berry Pomeroy. Devn 5L 5
Berryscaur. Dum 2F 52
Berry's Green. G Lon 8M 21
Bersham. Wrex 5B 34
Berthengam. Flin 3L 33
Berwick. E Sus 5B 12
Berwick Bassett. Wilts 6K 19
Berwick Hill. Nmbd 4E 54
Berwick St James. Wilts 2J 9
Berwick St John. Wilts 3H 9
Berwick St Leonard. Wilts 2H 9
Berwick-upon-Tweed.
Nmbd 4G 61
Berwyn. Den 6L 33
Bescaby. Leics 7F 36
Bescar. Lanc 6B 40
Besford. Worc 7H 27
Bessacarr. S Yor 7D 42
Bessbrook. New M 7G 93
Bessels Leigh. Oxon 3B 20
Bessingby. E Yor 1J 43
Bessingham. Norf 6H 39
Best Beech Hill. E Sus 2C 12
Besthorpe. Norf 2G 31
Besthorpe. Notts 3F 36
Bestwood Village. Notts 5C 36
Beswick. E Yor 3H 43
Betchworth. Surr 8K 21
Bethania. Cdgn 6E 24
Bethania. Gwyn
nr. Blaenau Ffestiniog 6G 33
nr. Caernarfon 5F 32
Bethel. Gwyn
nr. Bala 7J 33
nr. Caernarfon 4E 32
Bethel. IOA 3C 32
Bethersden. Kent 1F 12
Bethesda. Gwyn 4F 32
Bethesda. Pemb 5G 15
Bethlehem. Carm 2F 16
Bethnal Green. G Lon 5L 21
Betley. Staf 5F 34
Betsham. Kent 6C 22
Betteshanger. Kent 8K 23
Bettiscombe. Dors 6C 8
Bettisfield. Wrex 6C 34
Betton. Shrp 6E 34
Betton Strange. Shrp 1D 26
Bettws. B'end 6J 17
Bettws. Newp 4A 18
Bettws Bledrws. Cdgn 7E 24
Bettws Cedewain. Powy 3L 25
Bettws Gwerfil Goch. Den 6K 33
Bettws Ifan. Cdgn 2K 15
Bettws Newydd. Mon 3B 18
Bettyhill. High 5K 85
Betws. Carm 3F 16
Betws Garmon. Gwyn 5E 32
Betws-y-Coed. Cnwy 5G 33
Betws-yn-Rhos. Cnwy 3J 33
Beulah. Cdgn 2J 15
Beulah. Powy 7J 25
Beul an Atha. Arg 3C 56
Bevendean. Brig 5L 11
Bevercotes. Notts 2E 36
Beverley. E Yor 4H 43
Beverston. Glos 4G 19
Bevington. Glos 4E 18
Bewaldeth. Cumb 8G 53

Bridport—Carlton-on-Trent

Bridport. Dors 6C 8
Bridstow. Here 1D 18
Brierfield. Lanc 4G 41
Brierley. Glos 2E 18
Brierley. Here 6C 26
Brierley. S Yor 6B 42
Brierley Hill. W Mid 3H 27
Brierton. Hart 8H 55
Briestfield. W Yor 6L 41
Brigg. N Lin 7H 43
Briggate. Norf 7K 39
Briggswath. N Yor 5F 48
Brigham. Cumb 8E 52
Brigham. E Yor 2H 43
Brighouse. W Yor 5K 41
Brighstone. IOW 7B 10
Brightgate. Derbs 4L 35
Brighthampton. Oxon 3A 20
Brightholmlee. S Yor 8L 41
Brightley. Devn 6F 6
Brightling. E Sus 3C 12
Brightlingsea. Essx 2G 23
Brighton. Brig 106 (5L 11)
Brighton. Corn 6B 4
Brighton Hill. Hants 1D 10
Brightons. Falk 2H 59
Brightwalton. W Ber 6B 20
Brightwalton Green. W Ber 6B 20
Brightwell. Suff 7J 31
Brightwell Baldwin. Oxon 4D 20
Brightwell-cum-Sotwell. Oxon 4C 20
Brigmerston. Wilts 1K 9
Brignall. Dur 4J 47
Brig o' Turk. Stir 7K 65
Brigsley. NE Lin 7K 43
Brigsteer. Cumb 7C 46
Brigstock. Nptn 3G 29
Brill. Buck 2D 20
Brill. Corn 6L 3
Brilley. Here 7A 26
Brimaston. Pemb 4F 14
Brimfield. Here 5D 26
Brimington. Derbs 2B 36
Brimley. Devn 8H 7
Brimpsfield. Glos 2H 19
Brimpton. W Ber 7C 20
Brims. Orkn 3D 86
Brimscombe. Glos 3G 19
Brimstage. Mers 1B 34
Brincliffe. S Yor 1M 35
Brind. E Yor 4E 42
Brindister. Shet
nr. West Burrafirth 2C 90
nr. West Lerwick 4E 90
Brindle. Lanc 5D 40
Brindley. Ches E 4D 34
Brindley Ford. Stoke 4G 35
Brineton. Staf 8G 35
Bringhurst. Leics 2F 28
Bringsty Common. Here 6E 26
Brington. Cambs 4H 29
Brinian. Orkn 7D 88
Briningham. Norf 6G 39
Brinkhill. Linc 2L 37
Brinkley. Cambs 6C 30
Brinklow. Warw 4B 28
Brinkworth. Wilts 5J 19
Brinscall. Lanc 5E 40
Brinscombe. Som 8C 18
Brinsley. Notts 5B 36
Brinsworth. S Yor 1B 36
Brinton. Norf 6G 39
Brisco. Cumb 6J 53
Brisley. Norf 7F 38
Brislington. Bris 6E 18
Brissenden Green. Kent 2F 12
Bristol. Bris 107 (6D 18)
Bristol Airport. N Som 7D 18
Briston. Norf 6G 39
Britannia. Lanc 5G 41
Britford. Wilts 3K 9
Brithdir. Cphy 4L 17
Brithdir. Cdgn 2K 15
Brithdir. Gwyn 1G 25
Briton Ferry. Neat 5G 17
Britwell Salome. Oxon 4D 20
Brixham. Torb 6M 5
Brixton. Devn 6H 5
Brixton. G Lon 6L 21
Brixton Deverill. Wilts 2G 9
Brixworth. Nptn 4E 28
Brize Norton. Oxon 3M 19
The Broad. Here 5C 26
Broad Alley. Worc 5G 27
Broad Blunsdon. Swin 4K 19
Broadbottom. G Man 8H 41
Broadbridge. W Sus 5F 10
Broadbridge Heath. W Sus 2J 11
Broad Campden. Glos 8K 27
Broad Chalke. Wilts 3J 9
Broadclyst. Devn 6J 7
Broadfield. Inv 2B 58
Broadfield. Pemb 6H 15
Broadfield. W Sus 2K 11
Broadford. High 3H 69
Broadford Bridge. W Sus 3H 11
Broadgate. Cumb 6L 45
Broad Green. Cambs 6C 30
Broad Green. C Beds 7G 29
Broad Green. Worc
nr. Bromsgrove 4H 27
nr. Worcester 6F 26
Broad Haven. Pemb 5E 14
Broadhaven. High 6E 86
Broad Heath. Staf 7G 35
Broadheath. G Man 1F 34
Broadheath. Worc 5E 26
Broadheath Common. Worc 6G 27
Broadhembury. Devn 5L 7
Broadhempston. Devn 5L 5
Broad Hill. Cambs 4B 30
Broad Hinton. Wilts 6K 19
Broadholme. Derbs 5A 36
Broadholme. Linc 2F 36
Broadlay. Carm 6K 15
Broad Laying. Hants 7B 20
Broadley. Lanc 6G 41
Broadley. Mor 7C 80
Broadley Common. Essx 3M 21
Broad Marston. Worc 7K 27
Broadmayne. Dors 7F 8
Broadmere. Hants 1D 10
Broadmoor. Pemb 6G 15
Broad Oak. Carm 2E 16
Broad Oak. Cumb 5L 45
Broad Oak. Devn 6K 7
Broad Oak. Dors 4F 8
Broad Oak. E Sus
nr. Hastings 4E 12
nr. Heathfield 3C 12
Broad Oak. Here 1C 18
Broad Oak. Kent 7H 23
Broadoak. Dors 6C 8
Broadoak. Glos 2E 18
Broadoak. Hants 4C 10
Broadrashes. Mor 8D 80
Broadsea. Abers 7J 81
Broad's Green. Essx 2C 22
Broadshard. Som 4C 8
Broadstairs. Kent 7K 23
Broadstone. Pool 6J 9
Broadstone. Shrp 3D 26
Broad Street. E Sus 4E 12
Broad Street. Kent
nr. Ashford 1H 13
nr. Maidstone 8E 22
Broad Street Green. Essx 3E 22
Broad Town. Wilts 6J 19
Broadwas. Worc 6F 26
Broadwath. Cumb 6J 53
Broadway. Carm
nr. Kidwelly 6K 15
nr. Laugharne 6J 15
Broadway. Pemb 5E 14
Broadway. Som 4B 8
Broadway. Suff 4K 31
Broadway. Worc 8J 27
Broadwell. Glos
nr. Cinderford 2D 18
nr. Stow-on-the-Wold 1L 19
Broadwell. Oxon 3L 19
Broadwell. Warw 5B 28
Broadwell House. Nmbd 6C 54
Broadwey. Dors 7E 8
Broadwindsor. Dors 5C 8
Broadwoodkelly. Devn 5F 6
Broadwoodwidger. Devn 7D 6
Broallan. High 1E 70
Brobury. Here 7B 26
Brochel. High 1G 69
Brockaghboy. Caus 3F 93
Brockamin. Worc 6F 26
Brockbridge. Hants 4D 10
Brockdish. Norf 4J 31
Brockencote. Worc 4G 27
Brockenhurst. Hants 5L 9
Brocketsbrae. S Lan 6G 59
Brockford Street. Suff 5H 31
Brockhall. Nptn 5D 28
Brockham. Surr 1J 11
Brockhampton. Glos
nr. Bishop's Cleeve 1H 19
nr. Sevenhampton 1J 19
Brockhampton. Here 8D 26
Brockhill. Bord 7A 60
Brockholes. W Yor 6K 41
Brockhurst. Hants 5C 10
Brocklesby. Linc 6J 43
Brockley. N Som 7C 18
Brockley Corner. Suff 4E 30
Brockley Green. Suff
nr. Bury St Edmunds 7D 30
nr. Haverhill 6E 30
Brockleymoor. Cumb 8J 53
Brockmoor. W Mid 3H 27
Brockton. Shrp
nr. Bishop's Castle 3B 26
nr. Madeley 1F 26
nr. Much Wenlock 2D 26
nr. Pontesbury 1B 26
Brockton. Staf 6G 35
Brockton. Telf 8F 34
Brockweir. Glos 3D 18
Brockworth. Glos 2G 19
Brocton. Staf 8H 35
Brodick. N Ayr 6K 57
Brodie. Mor 8K 79
Brodiesord. Abers 8E 80
Brodsworth. S Yor 7C 42
Brogaig. High 7F 76
Brogborough. C Beds 8G 29
Brokenborough. Wilts 5H 19
Broken Cross. Ches E 2G 35
Bromborough. Mers 1B 34
Bromdon. Shrp 3E 26
Brome. Suff 4H 31
Brome Street. Suff 4H 31
Bromeswell. Suff 6K 31
Bromfield. Cumb 7F 52
Bromfield. Shrp 4C 26
Bromford. W Mid 2K 27
Bromham. Bed 6H 29
Bromham. Wilts 7H 19
Bromley. G Lon 7M 21
Bromley. Herts 1M 21
Bromley. Shrp 2F 26
Bromley Cross. G Man 6F 40
Bromley Green. Kent 2F 12
Bromley Wood. Staf 7K 35
Brompton. Medw 7D 22
Brompton. N Yor
nr. Northallerton 6A 48
nr. Scarborough 7G 49
Brompton. Shrp 1D 26
Brompton-on-Swale. N Yor 6L 47
Brompton Ralph. Som 2K 7
Brompton Regis. Som 2J 7
Bromsash. Here 1E 18
Bromsberrow. Glos 8F 26
Bromsberrow Heath. Glos 8F 26
Bromsgrove. Worc 4H 27
Bromstead Heath. Staf 8F 34
Bromyard. Here 6E 26
Bromyard Downs. Here 6E 26
Bronaber. Gwyn 7G 33
Broncroft. Shrp 3D 26
Brongest. Cdgn 2K 15
Brongwyn. Cdgn 2J 15
Bronington. Wrex 6C 34
Bronllys. Powy 1L 17
Bronnant. Cdgn 6F 24
Bronwydd Arms. Carm 4L 15
Bronydd. Powy 8M 25
Bronygarth. Shrp 6A 34
Brook. Carm 6J 15
Brook. Hants
nr. Cadnam 4L 9
nr. Romsey 3M 9
Brook. IOW 7A 10
Brook. Kent 1G 13
Brook. Surr
nr. Guildford 1H 11
nr. Haslemere 2G 11
Brooke. Norf 2J 31
Brooke. Rut 1F 28
Brookeborough. Ferm 6C 92
Brookenby. Linc 8K 43
Brook End. Worc 7G 27
Brookend. Glos 3E 18
Brookfield. Lanc 4D 40
Brookfield. Ren 3C 58
Brookhouse. Lanc 1D 40
Brookhouse. S Yor 1C 36
Brookhouse Green. Ches E 3G 35
Brookhouses. Staf 5H 35
Brookhurst. Mers 1B 34
Brookland. Kent 3F 12
Brooklands. G Man 8F 40
Brooklands. Shrp 5D 34
Brookmans Park. Herts 3K 21
Brooks. Powy 3L 25
Brooksby. Leics 8D 36
Brooks Green. W Sus 3J 11
Brook Street. Essx 4B 22
Brook Street. Kent 2F 12
Brook Street. W Sus 3L 11
Brookthorpe. Glos 2G 19
Brookville. Norf 2D 30
Brookwood. Surr 8G 21
Broom. C Beds 7J 29
Broom. Fife 7G 67
Broom. Warw 6J 27
Broome. Norf 2K 31
Broome. Shrp
nr. Cardington 2D 26
nr. Craven Arms 3C 26
Broome. Worc 4H 27
Broomedge. Warr 1F 34
Broomend. Abers 4G 73
Broomer's Corner. W Sus 3J 11
Broomfield. Abers 2J 73
Broomfield. Essx 2D 22
Broomfield. Kent
nr. Herne Bay 7H 23
nr. Maidstone 8E 22
Broomfield. Som 2M 7
Broomfleet. E Yor 5F 42
Broom Green. Norf 7F 38
Broomhall. Ches E 5E 34
Broomhall. Wind 7G 21
Broomhaugh. Nmbd 5D 54
Broom Hill. Dors 5J 9
Broom Hill. Worc 4H 27
Broomhill. High
nr. Grantown-on-Spey 3K 71
nr. Invergordon 6H 79
Broomhill. Norf 1C 30
Broomhill. S Yor 7B 42
Broomhillbank. Dum 2F 52
Broomholm. Norf 6K 39
Broomlands. Dum 1E 52
Broomley. Nmbd 5D 54
Broom of Moy. Mor 8L 79
Broompark. Dur 7F 54
Broom's Green. Glos 8F 26
Brora. High 3K 79
Broseley. Shrp 1E 26
Brotherhouse Bar. Linc 8K 37
Brotheridge Green. Worc 7G 27
Brotherlee. Dur 8C 54
Brothertoft. Linc 5K 37
Brotherton. N Yor 5B 42
Brotton. Red C 4D 48
Broubster. High 5B 86
Brough. Cumb 4F 46
Brough. Derbs 1K 35
Brough. E Yor 5G 43
Brough. High 4D 86
Brough. Notts 4F 36
Brough. Orkn
nr. Finstown 8C 88
nr. St Margaret's Hope 3F 86
Brough. Shet
nr. Benston 2E 90
nr. Booth of Toft 6J 91
on Bressay 3F 90
on Whalsay 1F 90
Broughall. Shrp 5D 34
Brougham. Cumb 3D 46
Brough Lodge. Shet 4K 91
Broughshane. ME Ant 3G 93
Brough Sowerby. Cumb 4F 46
Broughton. Cambs 4K 29
Broughton. Flin 3B 34
Broughton. Hants 2M 9
Broughton. Lanc 4D 40
Broughton. Mil 8F 28
Broughton. Nptn 4F 28
Broughton. N Lin 7G 43
Broughton. N Yor
nr. Malton 8E 48
nr. Skipton 2H 41
Broughton. Orkn 5D 88
Broughton. Oxon 8B 28
Broughton. Bord 6K 59
Broughton. Staf 6F 34
Broughton. V Glam 7J 17
Broughton Astley. Leics 2C 28
Broughton Beck. Cumb 7A 46
Broughton Cross. Cumb 8E 52
Broughton Gifford. Wilts 7G 19
Broughton Green. Worc 5H 27
Broughton Hackett. Worc 6H 27
Broughton in Furness. Cumb 6M 45
Broughton Mills. Cumb 5M 45
Broughton Moor. Cumb 8E 52
Broughton Park. G Man 7G 41
Broughton Poggs. Oxon 3L 19
Broughtown. Orkn 5F 88
Broughty Ferry. D'dee 4H 67
Browland. Shet 2C 90
Brownbread Street. E Sus 4C 12
Brown Candover. Hants 2C 10
Brown Edge. Lanc 6B 40
Brown Edge. Staf 4H 35
Brownhill. Bkbn 4E 40
Brownhill. Shrp 7C 34
Brownhills. Shrp 6E 34
Brownhills. W Mid 1J 27
Brown Knowl. Ches W 4C 34
Brownlow. Ches E 3G 35
Brownlow Heath. Ches E 3G 35
Brown's Green. W Mid 2J 27
Brownshill. Glos 3G 19
Brownston. Devn 6J 5
Brownstone. Devn 5G 7
Browston Green. Norf 1L 31
Broxa. N Yor 6G 49
Broxbourne. Herts 3L 21
Broxburn. E Lot 2D 60
Broxburn. W Lot 2J 59
Broxholme. Linc 2G 37
Broxted. Essx 1B 22
Broxton. Ches W 4C 34
Broxwood. Here 6B 26
Broyle Side. E Sus 4A 12
Brù. W Isl 7G 83
Bruach Mairi. W Isl 8H 83
Bruairnis. W Isl 5D 74
Bruan. High 8E 86
Bruar Lodge. Per 8J 71
Brucehill. W Dun 2B 58
Brucklay. Abers 8J 81
Bruera. Ches W 3C 34
Bruern Abbey. Oxon 1L 19
Bruichladdich. Arg 3B 56
Bruisyard. Suff 5K 31
Bruisyard Street. Suff 5K 31
Brund. Staf 3K 35
Brundall. Norf 1K 31
Brundish. Norf 2K 31
Brundish. Suff 5J 31
Brundish Street. Suff 4J 31
Brunery. High 8J 69
Brunswick Village. Tyne 4F 54
Brunthwaite. W Yor 3J 41
Bruntingthorpe. Leics 2D 28
Brunton. Fife 5G 67
Brunton. Nmbd 7K 61
Brunton. Wilts 8L 19
Brushford. Devn 5F 6
Brushford. Som 3J 7
Brusta. W Isl 5L 75
Bruton. Som 2E 8
Bryansford. New M 7H 93
Bryanston. Dors 5G 9
Bryant's Bottom. Buck 4F 20
Brydekirk. Dum 4F 52
Brymbo. Cnwy 3H 33
Brymbo. Wrex 4A 34
Brympton D'Evercy. Som 4D 8
Bryn. Carm 6M 15
Bryn. G Man 7D 40
Bryn. Neat 5H 17
Bryn. Shrp 3A 26
Brynamman. Carm 3G 17
Brynberian. Pemb 3H 15
Brynbryddan. Neat 5G 17
Bryncae. Rhon 6J 17
Bryncethin. B'end 6J 17
Bryncir. Gwyn 6D 32
Bryncoch. Neat 5G 17
Bryncroes. Gwyn 7B 32
Bryncrug. Gwyn 2F 24
Bryn Du. IOA 3C 32
Bryn Eden. Gwyn 8G 33
Bryn Eglwys. Gwyn 4F 32
Bryneglwys. Den 6L 33
Brynford. Flin 3L 33
Bryn Gates. G Man 7D 40
Bryn Golau. Rhon 6K 17
Bryngwran. IOA 3C 32
Bryngwyn. Mon 3B 18
Bryngwyn. Powy 8L 25
Bryn-henllan. Pemb 3G 15
Brynhoffnant. Cdgn 1K 15
Bryn-llwyn. Den 2K 33
Brynllywarch. Powy 4L 25
Bryn-mawr. Gwyn 7B 32
Brynmawr. Blae 3L 17
Brynmenyn. B'end 6J 17
Brynmill. Swan 5F 16
Brynna. Rhon 6J 17
Brynrefail. Gwyn 4E 32
Brynrefail. IOA 2D 32
Brynsadler. Rhon 6K 17
Bryn-Saith Marchog. Den 5K 33
Brynsiencyn. IOA 4D 32
Brynteg. IOA 2D 32
Brynteg. Wrex 4B 34
Brynygwenyn. Mon 2B 18
Bryn-y-maen. Cnwy 3H 33
Buaile nam Bodach. W Isl 5D 74
Bualintur. High 3F 68
Bubbenhall. Warw 4A 28
Bubwith. E Yor 4E 42
Buccleuch. Bord 8M 59
Buchanan Smithy. Stir 1C 58
Buchanhaven. Abers 1L 73
Buchanty. Per 5C 66
Buchany. Stir 7M 65
Buchley. E Dun 2D 58
Buchlyvie. Stir 8K 65
Buckabank. Cumb 7H 53
Buckden. Cambs 5J 29
Buckden. N Yor 8H 47
Buckenham. Norf 1K 31
Buckerell. Devn 5L 7
Buckfast. Devn 5K 5
Buckfastleigh. Devn 5K 5
Buckhaven. Fife 8G 67
Buckholm. Bord 6B 60
Buckholt. Here 2D 18
Buckhorn Weston. Dors 3F 8
Buckhurst Hill. Essx 4M 21
Buckie. Mor 7D 80
Buckingham. Buck 8D 28
Buckland. Buck 2F 20
Buckland. Glos 8J 27
Buckland. Here 6D 26
Buckland. Herts 8L 29
Buckland. Kent 1K 13
Buckland. Oxon 4M 19
Buckland. Surr 8K 21
Buckland Brewer. Devn 3D 6
Buckland Common. Buck 3G 21
Buckland Dinham. Som 8F 18
Buckland Filleigh. Devn 5D 6
Buckland in the Moor. Devn 8G 7
Buckland Monachorum. Devn 5G 5
Buckland Newton. Dors 5E 8
Buckland Ripers. Dors 7E 8
Buckland St Mary. Som 4A 8
Buckland-tout-Saints. Devn 7K 5
Bucklebury. W Ber 6C 20
Bucklegate. Linc 6L 37
Buckleigh. Devn 3D 6
Buckler's Hard. Hants 6B 10
Bucklesham. Suff 7J 31
Buckley. Flin 3A 34
Buckley Green. Warw 5K 27
Buckley Hill. Mers 8B 40
Bucklow Hill. Ches E 1F 34
Buckminster. Leics 7F 36
Bucknall. Linc 3J 37
Bucknall. Stoke 5H 35
Bucknell. Oxon 1C 20
Bucknell. Shrp 4B 26
Buckpool. Mor 7D 80
Bucksburn. Aber 5H 73
Buck's Cross. Devn 3C 6
Bucks Green. W Sus 2H 11
Buckshaw Village. Lanc 5D 40
Bucks Hill. Herts 3H 21
Bucks Horn Oak. Hants 1F 10
Buck's Mills. Devn 3C 6
Buckton. E Yor 8J 49
Buckton. Here 4B 26
Buckton. Nmbd 6H 61
Buckton Vale. G Man 7H 41
Buckworth. Cambs 4J 29
Budby. Notts 3D 36
Bude. Corn 5B 6
Budge's Shop. Corn 6F 4
Budlake. Devn 5J 7
Budle. Nmbd 6J 61
Budleigh Salterton. Devn 7K 7
Budock Water. Corn 5L 3
Buerton. Ches E 5E 34
Buffler's Holt. Buck 8D 28
Bugbrooke. Nptn 6D 28
Buglawton. Ches E 3G 35
Bugle. Corn 6C 4
Bugthorpe. E Yor 2E 42
Buildwas. Shrp 1E 26
Builth Road. Powy 7K 25
Builth Wells. Powy 7K 25
Bulbourne. Herts 2G 21
Bulby. Linc 7H 37
Bulcote. Notts 5D 36
Buldoo. High 5A 86
Bulford. Wilts 1K 9
Bulford Camp. Wilts 1K 9
Bulkeley. Ches E 4D 34
Bulkington. Warw 3A 28
Bulkington. Wilts 8H 19
Bulkworthy. Devn 4C 6
Bullamoor. N Yor 6A 48
Bull Bay. IOA 1D 32
Bullbridge. Derbs 4A 36
Bullgill. Cumb 8E 52
Bull Hill. Hants 6M 9
Bullinghope. Here 8D 26
Bull's Green. Herts 2K 21
Bullwood. Arg 2L 57
Bulmer. Essx 7E 30
Bulmer. N Yor 1D 42
Bulmer Tye. Essx 8E 30
Bulphan. Thur 5C 22
Bulverhythe. E Sus 5D 12
Bulwark. Abers 1J 73
Bulwell. Nott 5C 36
Bulwick. Nptn 2G 29
Bumble's Green. Essx 3M 21
Bun Abhainn Eadarra. W Isl 3C 76
Bunacaimb. High 7H 69
Bun a' Mhuillinn. W Isl 4D 74
Bunarkaig. High 7B 70
Bunbury. Ches E 4D 34
Bunchrew. High 1G 71
Bundalloch. High 3K 69
Buness. Shet 3L 91
Bunessan. Arg 5J 63
Bungay. Suff 3K 31
Bunkegivie. High 4F 70
Bunker's Hill. Cambs 1M 29
Bunker's Hill. Suff 1M 31
Bunkers Hill. Linc 4K 37
Bunloit. High 3F 70
Bunnahabhain. Arg 2D 56
Bunny. Notts 7C 36
Bunoich. High 5D 70
Bunree. High 1E 64
Bunroy. High 7C 70
Buntait. High 2E 70
Buntingford. Herts 1L 21
Bunting's Green. Essx 8E 30
Bunwell. Norf 2H 31
Burbage. Derbs 2J 35
Burbage. Leics 2B 28
Burbage. Wilts 7L 19
Burcher. Here 5B 26
Burchett's Green. Wind 5F 20
Burcombe. Wilts 2J 9
Burcot. Oxon 4C 20
Burcot. Worc 4H 27
Burcote. Shrp 2F 26
Burcott. Buck 1F 20
Burcott. Som 1D 8
Burdale. N Yor 1F 42
Burdrop. Oxon 8A 28
Bures. Suff 8F 30
The Burf. Worc 5G 27
Burford. Oxon 2L 19
Burford. Shrp 5D 26
Burg. Arg 3J 63
Burgate Great Green. Suff 4G 31
Burgate Little Green. Suff 4G 31
Burgess Hill. W Sus 4L 11
Burgh. Suff 6J 31
Burgh by Sands. Cumb 6H 53
Burgh Castle. Norf 1L 31
Burghclere. Hants 7B 20
Burghead. Mor 7M 79
Burghfield. W Ber 7D 20
Burghfield Common. W Ber 7D 20
Burghfield Hill. W Ber 7D 20
Burgh Heath. Surr 8K 21
Burghill. Here 7C 26
Burgh le Marsh. Linc 3B 38
Burgh Muir. Abers 4G 73
Burgh next Aylsham. Norf 7J 39
Burgh on Bain. Linc 1K 37
Burgh St Margaret. Norf 8L 39
Burgh St Peter. Norf 2L 31
Burghwallis. S Yor 6C 42
Burham. Kent 7D 22
Buriton. Hants 3E 10
Burland. Ches E 4E 34
Burland. Shet 4D 90
Burlawn. Corn 5B 4
Burleigh. Glos 3G 19
Burleigh. Wind 6F 20
Burlescombe. Devn 4K 7
Burleston. Dors 6F 8
Burlestone. Devn 7L 5
Burley. Hants 5L 9
Burley. Rut 8F 36
Burley. W Yor 4L 41
Burleydam. Ches E 5E 34
Burley Gate. Here 7D 26
Burley in Wharfedale. W Yor 3K 41
Burley Street. Hants 5L 9
Burley Woodhead. W Yor 3K 41
Burlingjobb. Powy 6A 26
Burlington. Shrp 8F 34
Burlton. Shrp 7C 34
Burmantofts. W Yor 4M 41
Burmarsh. Kent 2H 13
Burmington. Warw 8L 27
Burn. N Yor 5C 42
Burnage. G Man 8G 41
Burnaston. Derbs 6L 35
Burnbanks. Cumb 4D 46
Burnby. E Yor 3F 42
Burncross. S Yor 8M 41
Burneside. Cumb 6D 46
Burness. Orkn 5F 88
Burneston. N Yor 7M 47
Burnett. Bath 7E 18
Burnfoot. E Ayr 1K 51
Burnfoot. Per 7C 66
Burnfoot. Bord
nr. Hawick 8C 60
nr. Roberton 8B 60
Burngreave. S Yor 1A 36
Burnham. Buck 5G 21
Burnham. N Lin 6H 43
Burnham Deepdale. Norf 5E 38
Burnham Green. Herts 2K 21
Burnham Market. Norf 5E 38
Burnham Norton. Norf 5E 38
Burnham-on-Crouch. Essx 4F 22
Burnham-on-Sea. Som 1B 8
Burnham Overy Staithe. Norf 5E 38
Burnham Overy Town. Norf 5E 38
Burnham Thorpe. Norf 5E 38
Burnhaven. Abers 1L 73
Burnhead. Dum 2C 52
Burnhervie. Abers 4G 73
Burnhill Green. Staf 1F 26
Burnhope. Dur 7E 54
Burnhouse. N Ayr 4B 58
Burniston. N Yor 6H 49
Burnlee. W Yor 7K 41
Burnley. Lanc 4G 41
Burnmouth. Bord 3G 61
Burn Naze. Lanc 3B 40
Burn of Cambus. Stir 7M 65
Burnopfield. Dur 6E 54
Burnsall. N Yor 1J 41
Burnside. Ang 2J 67
Burnside. Ant
nr. Antrim 4G 93
nr. Ballyclare 4H 93
Burnside. E Ayr 8D 58
Burnside. Per 7E 66
Burnside. Shet 6G 91
Burnside. S Lan 4E 58
Burnside. W Lot
nr. Broxburn 2J 59
nr. Winchburgh 2J 59
Burntcommon. Surr 8H 21
Burnt Heath. Essx 1G 23
Burntheath. Derbs 6L 35
Burnt Hill. W Ber 6C 20
Burnt Houses. Dur 3K 47
Burntisland. Fife 1L 59
Burnt Oak. G Lon 4K 21
Burnton. E Ayr 1K 51
Burntstalk. Norf 6D 38
Burntwood. Staf 1J 27
Burntwood Green. Staf 1J 27
Burnt Yates. N Yor 1L 41
Burnwynd. Edin 3K 59
Burpham. Surr 8H 21
Burpham. W Sus 5H 11
Burradon. Nmbd 1C 54
Burradon. Tyne 4F 54
Burrafirth. Shet 2L 91
Burragarth. Shet 3K 91
Burras. Corn 5K 3
Burraton. Corn 6G 5
Burravoe. Shet
nr. North Roe 5H 91
on Mainland 1D 90
on Yell 6K 91
Burray Village. Orkn 2F 86
Burrells. Cumb 4E 46
Burrelton. Per 4E 66
Burren. New M 7G 93
Burren Bridge. New M 7H 93
Burridge. Hants 4C 10
Burridge. Som 5B 8
Burrigill. High 8D 86
Burrill. N Yor 7L 47
Burringham. N Lin 7F 42
Burrington. Devn 4F 6
Burrington. Here 4C 26
Burrington. N Som 8C 18
Burrough End. Cambs 6C 30
Burrough Green. Cambs 6C 30
Burrough on the Hill. Leics 8E 36
Burroughston. Orkn 7E 88
Burrow. Devn 7K 7
Burrow. Som 1J 7
Burrowbridge. Som 3B 8
Burrowhill. Surr 7G 21
Burry. Swan 7L 15
Burry Green. Swan 7L 15
Burry Port. Carm 6L 15
Burscough. Lanc 6C 40
Burscough Bridge. Lanc 6C 40
Bursea. E Yor 4F 42
Burshill. E Yor 3H 43
Bursledon. Hants 5B 10
Burslem. Stoke 5G 35
Burstall. Suff 7G 31
Burstock. Dors 5C 8
Burston. Devn 5G 7
Burston. Norf 3H 31
Burston. Staf 6H 35
Burstow. Surr 1L 11
Burstwick. E Yor 5K 43
Burtersett. N Yor 7G 47
Burtholme. Cumb 5K 53
Burthorpe. Suff 5D 30
Burthwaite. Cumb 7J 53
Burtle. Som 1C 8
Burtoft. Linc 6K 37
Burton. Ches W
nr. Kelsall 3D 34
nr. Neston 2B 34
Burton. Dors
nr. Christchurch 6K 9
nr. Dorchester 6E 8
Burton. Nmbd 6J 61
Burton. Pemb 6F 14
Burton. Som 1L 7
Burton. Wilts
nr. Chippenham 6G 19
nr. Warminster 2G 9
Burton. Wrex 4B 34
Burton Agnes. E Yor 1J 43
Burton Bradstock. Dors 7C 8
Burton-by-Lincoln. Linc 2G 37
Burton Coggles. Linc 7G 37
Burton Constable. E Yor 4J 43
Burton Corner. Linc 5L 37
Burton End. Cambs 7C 30
Burton End. Essx 1B 22
Burton Fleming. E Yor 8H 49
Burton Green. Warw 4L 27
Burton Green. Wrex 4B 34
Burton Hastings. Warw 3B 28
Burton-in-Kendal. Cumb 8D 46
Burton in Lonsdale. N Yor 8E 46
Burton Joyce. Notts 5D 36
Burton Latimer. Nptn 4G 29
Burton Lazars. Leics 8E 36
Burton Leonard. N Yor 1M 41
Burton on the Wolds. Leics 7C 36
Burton Overy. Leics 2D 28
Burton Pedwardine. Linc 5J 37
Burton Pidsea. E Yor 4K 43
Burton Salmon. N Yor 5B 42
Burton's Green. Essx 1E 22
Burton Stather. N Lin 6F 42
Burton upon Stather. N Lin 6F 42
Burton upon Trent. Staf 7L 35
Burton Wolds. Leics 7D 36
Burtonwood. Warr 8D 40
Burwardsley. Ches W 4D 34
Burwarton. Shrp 3E 26
Burwash. E Sus 3C 12
Burwash Common. E Sus 3C 12
Burwash Weald. E Sus 3C 12
Burwell. Cambs 5B 30
Burwell. Linc 2L 37
Burwen. IOA 1D 32
Burwick. Orkn 3F 86
Bury. Cambs 3K 29
Bury. G Man 6G 41
Bury. Som 3J 7
Bury. W Sus 4H 11
Burybank. Staf 6G 35
Bury End. Worc 8J 27
Bury Green. Herts 1A 22
Bury St Edmunds. Suff 5E 30
Burythorpe. N Yor 1E 42
Busbridge. Surr 1G 11
Busby. E Ren 4D 58
Busby. Per 5D 66
Buscot. Oxon 4L 19
Bush. Corn 5B 6
The Bush. M Ulst 5F 93
Bush Bank. Here 6C 26
Bushbury. W Mid 1H 27
Bushby. Leics 1D 28
Bushey. Dors 7H 9
Bushey. Herts 4J 21
Bushey Heath. Herts 4J 21
Bush Green. Norf
nr. Attleborough 2G 31
nr. Harleston 3J 31
Bush Green. Suff 6F 30
Bushley. Worc 8G 27
Bushley Green. Worc 8G 27
Bushmead. Bed 5J 29
Bushmills. Caus 1F 93
Bushmoor. Shrp 3C 26
Bushton. Wilts 6J 19
Bushy Common. Norf 8F 38
Busk. Cumb 7L 53
Buslingthorpe. Linc 1H 37
Bussage. Glos 3G 19
Bussex. Som 2B 8
Busta. Shet 1D 90
Butcher's Cross. E Sus 3B 12
Butcombe. N Som 7D 18
Bute Town. Cphy 4L 17
Butleigh. Som 2D 8
Butleigh Wootton. Som 2D 8
Butlers Marston. Warw 7M 27
Butley. Suff 6K 31
Butley High Corner. Suff 7K 31
Butlocks Heath. Hants 5B 10
Butterburn. Cumb 4L 53
Buttercrambe. N Yor 2E 42
Butterknowle. Dur 3K 47
Butterleigh. Devn 5J 7
Buttermere. Cumb 3L 45
Buttermere. Wilts 7M 19
Buttershaw. W Yor 5K 41
Butterstone. Per 3D 66
Butterton. Staf
nr. Leek 4J 35
nr. Stoke-on-Trent 5G 35
Butterwick. Dur 3A 48
Butterwick. Linc 5L 37
Butterwick. N Yor
nr. Malton 8E 48
nr. Weaverthorpe 8G 49
Butteryhaugh. Nmbd 2L 53
Butt Green. Ches E 4E 34
Buttington. Powy 1A 26
Buttonbridge. Shrp 4F 26
Buttonoak. Shrp 4F 26
Buttsash. Hants 5B 10
Butt's Green. Essx 3D 22
Butt Yeats. Lanc 1D 40
Buxhall. Suff 6G 31
Buxted. E Sus 3A 12
Buxton. Derbs 2J 35
Buxton. Norf 7J 39
Buxworth. Derbs 1J 35
Bwcle. Flin 3A 34
Bwlch. Powy 2L 17
Bwlchderwin. Gwyn 6D 32
Bwlchgwyn. Wrex 4A 34
Bwlch-Llan. Cdgn 7E 24
Bwlchnewydd. Carm 4K 15
Bwlchtocyn. Gwyn 8C 32
Bwlch-y-cibau. Powy 1L 25
Bwlchyddar. Powy 8L 33
Bwlch-y-fadfa. Cdgn 2L 15
Bwlch-y-ffridd. Powy 3K 25
Bwlch y Garreg. Powy 3K 25
Bwlch-y-groes. Pemb 3J 15
Bwlch-y-sarnau. Powy 5K 25
Bybrook. Kent 1G 13
Byermoor. Tyne 6E 54
Byers Garth. Dur 7G 55
Byers Green. Dur 8F 54
Byfield. Nptn 6C 28
Byfleet. Surr 7H 21
Byford. Here 7B 26
Bygrave. Herts 8K 29
Byker. Tyne 5F 54
Byland Abbey. N Yor 8C 48
Bylchau. Cnwy 4J 33
Byley. Ches W 3F 34
Bynea. Carm 7M 15
Byram. N Yor 5B 42
Byrness. Nmbd 1A 54
Bystock. Devn 7K 7
Bythorn. Cambs 4H 29
Byton. Here 5B 26
Bywell. Nmbd 5D 54
Byworth. W Sus 3G 11

C

Cabharstadh. W Isl 2E 76
Cabourne. Linc 7J 43
Cabrach. Arg 3D 56
Cabrach. Mor 3C 72
Cabragh. M Ulst 5E 92
Cabus. Lanc 3C 40
Cadbury. Devn 5J 7
Cadder. E Dun 2E 58
Caddington. C Beds 2H 21
Caddonfoot. Bord 6B 60
Cadeby. Leics 1B 28
Cadeby. S Yor 7C 42
Cadeleigh. Devn 5J 7
Cade Street. E Sus 3C 12
Cadgwith. Corn 7L 3
Cadham. Fife 7F 66
Cadishead. G Man 8F 40
Cadle. Swan 5F 16
Cadley. Lanc 4D 40
Cadley. Wilts
nr. Ludgershall 8L 19
nr. Marlborough 7L 19
Cadmore End. Buck 4E 20
Cadnam. Hants 4L 9
Cadney. N Lin 7H 43
Cadole. Flin 4M 33
Cadoxton-juxta-Neath. Neat 5G 17
Cadwell. Herts 8J 29
Cadwst. Den 7K 33
Caeathro. Gwyn 4E 32
Caehopkin. Powy 3H 17
Caenby. Linc 1H 37
Caerau. B'end 5H 17
Caerau. Card 7L 17
Cae'r-bont. Powy 3H 17
Cae'r-bryn. Carm 3E 16
Caerdeon. Gwyn 1F 24
Caerdydd. Card 107 (7L 17)
Caerfarchell. Pemb 4D 14
Caerffili. Cphy 6L 17
Caerfyrddin. Carm 5L 15
Caergeiliog. IOA 3C 32
Caergwrle. Flin 4B 34
Caergybi. IOA 2B 32
Caerlaverock. Per 6B 66
Caerleon. Newp 4B 18
Caerlleon. Carm 4J 15
Caerllion. Newp 4B 18
Caernarfon. Gwyn 4D 32
Caerphilly. Cphy 6L 17
Caersws. Powy 3K 25
Caerwedros. Cdgn 1K 15
Caerwent. Mon 4C 18
Caerwys. Flin 3L 33
Caim. IOA 2F 32
Caio. Carm 1F 16
Cairinis. W Isl 7K 75
Cairisiadar. W Isl 8D 82
Cairminis. W Isl 5B 76
Cairnbaan. Arg 8C 64
Cairnbulg. Abers 7K 81
Cairncross. Ang 8D 72
Cairndow. Arg 6F 64
Cairness. Abers 7K 81
Cairneyhill. Fife 1J 59
Cairngarroch. Dum 7F 50
Cairnhill. Abers 2F 72
Cairnie. Abers 1D 72
Cairnorrie. Abers 1H 73
Cairnryan. Dum 5F 50
Cairston. Orkn 8B 88
Caister-on-Sea. Norf 8M 39
Caistor. Linc 7J 43
Caistor St Edmund. Norf 1J 31
Caistron. Nmbd 1C 54
Cakebole. Worc 4G 27
Calais Street. Suff 7F 30
Calanais. W Isl 8F 82
Calbost. W Isl 2F 76
Calbourne. IOW 7B 10
Calceby. Linc 2L 37
Calcot. Glos 2J 19
Calcot Row. W Ber 6D 20
Calcott. Kent 7H 23
Calcott. Shrp 8C 34
Caldback. Shet 3L 91
Caldbeck. Cumb 8H 53
Caldbergh. N Yor 7J 47
Caldecote. Cambs
nr. Cambridge 6L 29
nr. Peterborough 3J 29
Caldecote. Herts 8K 29
Caldecote. Nptn 6D 28
Caldecote. Warw 2A 28
Caldecott. Nptn 5G 29
Caldecott. Oxon 4B 20
Caldecott. Rut 2F 28
Calderbank. N Lan 3F 58
Calder Bridge. Cumb 4K 45
Calderbrook. G Man 6H 41
Caldercruix. N Lan 3G 59
Calder Grove. W Yor 6M 41
Calder Mains. High 6B 86
Caldermill. S Lan 5E 58
Calder Vale. Lanc 3D 40
Calderwood. S Lan 4E 58
Caldicot. Mon 5C 18
Caldwell. Derbs 8L 35
Caldwell. N Yor 4K 47
Caldy. Mers 2M 33
Calebrack. Cumb 8H 53
Caledon. M Ulst 6E 92
Calf Heath. Staf 1H 27
Calford Green. Suff 7C 30
Calfsound. Orkn 6E 88
Calgary. Arg 2J 63
Califer. Mor 8L 79
California. Cambs 3B 30
California. Falk 2H 59
California. Norf 8M 39
California. Suff 7H 31
Calke. Derbs 7A 36
Callakille. High 8H 77
Callaly. Nmbd 1D 54
Callander. Stir 7L 65
Callaughton. Shrp 2E 26
Callendoun. Arg 1B 58
Callestick. Corn 3L 3
Calligarry. High 5H 69
Callington. Corn 5F 4
Callingwood. Staf 7K 35
Callow. Here 8C 26
Callowell. Glos 3G 19
Callow End. Worc 7G 27
Callow Hill. Wilts 5J 19
Callow Hill. Worc
nr. Bewdley 4F 26
nr. Redditch 5J 27
Calmore. Hants 4M 9
Calmsden. Glos 3J 19
Calne. Wilts 6H 19
Calow. Derbs 2B 36
Calshot. Hants 5B 10
Calstock. Corn 5G 5
Calstone Wellington. Wilts 7J 19
Calthorpe. Norf 6H 39
Calthorpe Street. Norf 7L 39
Calthwaite. Cumb 7J 53
Calton. N Yor 2H 41
Calton. Staf 4K 35
Calveley. Ches E 4D 34
Calver. Derbs 2L 35
Calverhall. Shrp 6E 34
Calverleigh. Devn 4J 7
Calverley. W Yor 4L 41
Calvert. Buck 1D 20
Calverton. Mil 8E 28
Calverton. Notts 5D 36
Calvine. Per 1B 66
Calvo. Cumb 6F 52
Cam. Glos 4F 18
Camaghael. High 8B 70
Camas-luinie. High 3L 69
Camasnacroise. High 2C 64
Camastianavaig. High 2G 69
Camasunary. High 4G 69
Camault Muir. High 1F 70
Camb. Shet 4K 91
Camber. E Sus 4F 12
Camberley. Surr 7F 20
Camberwell. G Lon 6L 21
Camblesforth. N Yor 5D 42
Cambo. Nmbd 3D 54
Cambois. Nmbd 3G 55
Camborne. Corn 5K 3
Cambourne. Cambs 6L 29
Cambridge. Cambs 107 (6A 30)
Cambridge. Glos 3F 18
Cambrose. Corn 4K 3
Cambus. Clac 8B 66
Cambusbarron. Stir 8A 66
Cambuskenneth. Stir 8B 66
Cambuslang. S Lan 3E 58
Cambusnethan. N Lan 4G 59
Cambus o' May. Abers 6D 72
Camden Town. G Lon 5K 21
Cameley. Bath 8E 18
Camelford. Corn 3D 4
Camelon. Falk 1G 59
Camelsdale. W Sus 2F 10
Camer's Green. Worc 8F 26
Camerton. Bath 8E 18
Camerton. Cumb 8E 52
Camerton. E Yor 5K 43
Camghouran. Per 2K 65
Camlough. New M 7G 93
Cammachmore. Abers 6J 73
Cammeringham. Linc 1G 37
Camore. High 4H 79
The Camp. Glos 3H 19
Campbelton. N Ayr 4L 57
Campbeltown. Arg 7G 57
Campbeltown Airport. Arg 7F 56
Cample. Dum 2C 52
Campmuir. Per 4F 66
Campsall. S Yor 6C 42
Campsea Ashe. Suff 6K 31
Camps End. Cambs 7C 30
Campsey. Derr 2D 92
Campton. C Beds 8J 29
Camptoun. E Lot 2C 60
Camptown. Bord 8D 60
Camrose. Pemb 4F 14
Camserney. Per 3B 66
Camster. High 7D 86
Camus Croise. High 4H 69
Camuscross. High 4H 69
Camusdarach. High 6H 69
Camusnagaul. High
nr. Fort William 8A 70
nr. Little Loch Broom 5A 78
Camus Park. Derr 4C 92
Camusteel. High 1J 69
Camusterrach. High 1J 69
Camusvrachan. Per 3L 65
Canada. Hants 4L 9
Canadia. E Sus 4D 12
Canaston Bridge. Pemb 5G 15
Candlesby. Linc 3A 38
Candle Street. Suff 4G 31
Candy Mill. S Lan 5J 59
Cane End. Oxon 6D 20
Canewdon. Essx 4F 22
Canford Cliffs. Pool 7J 9
Canford Heath. Pool 6J 9
Canford Magna. Pool 6J 9
Cangate. Norf 8K 39
Canham's Green. Suff 5G 31
Canholes. Derbs 2J 35
Canisbay. High 4E 86
Canley. W Mid 4M 27
Cann. Dors 3G 9
Cann Common. Dors 3G 9
Cannich. High 2D 70
Cannington. Som 2A 8
Cannock. Staf 8H 35
Cannock Wood. Staf 8J 35
Canonbie. Dum 4H 53
Canon Bridge. Here 7C 26
Canon Frome. Here 7E 26
Canon Pyon. Here 7C 26
Canons Ashby. Nptn 6C 28
Canonstown. Corn 5J 3
Canterbury. Kent 107 (8H 23)
Cantley. Norf 1K 31
Cantley. S Yor 7D 42
Cantlop. Shrp 1D 26
Canton. Card 7L 17
Cantray. High 1H 71
Cantraybruich. High 1H 71
Cantraywood. High 1H 71
Cantsdam. Fife 8E 66
Cantsfield. Lanc 8E 46
Canvey Island. Essx 5D 22
Canwick. Linc 3G 37
Canworthy Water. Corn 6B 6
Caol. High 8B 70
Caolas. Arg 3F 62
Caolas. W Isl 6C 74
Caolas Liubharsaigh. W Isl 1E 74
Caolas Scalpaigh. W Isl 4D 76
Caolas Stocinis. W Isl 4C 76
Caol Ila. Arg 2D 56
Caol Loch Ailse. High 3J 69
Caol Reatha. High 3J 69
Capel. Kent 1C 12
Capel. Surr 1J 11
Capel Bangor. Cdgn 4F 24
Capel Betws Lleucu. Cdgn 7F 24
Capel Coch. IOA 2D 32
Capel Curig. Cnwy 5G 33
Capel Cynon. Cdgn 2K 15
Capel Dewi. Carm 4L 15
Capel Dewi. Cdgn
nr. Aberystwyth 4F 24
nr. Llandysul 2L 15
Capel Garmon. Cnwy 5H 33
Capel Green. Suff 7K 31
Capel Gwyn. IOA 3C 32
Capel Gwynfe. Carm 2G 17
Capel Hendre. Carm 3E 16
Capel Isaac. Carm 2E 16
Capel Iwan. Carm 3J 15
Capel-le-Ferne. Kent 2J 13
Capel Llanilltern. Card 7K 17
Capel Mawr. IOA 3D 32
Capel Newydd. Pemb 3J 15
Capel St Andrew. Suff 7K 31
Capel St Mary. Suff 8G 31
Capel Seion. Carm 5M 15
Capel Seion. Cdgn 5F 24
Capel Uchaf. Gwyn 6D 32
Capel-y-ffin. Powy 8A 26
Capenhurst. Ches W 2B 34
Capernwray. Lanc 8D 46
Capheaton. Nmbd 3D 54
Cappagh. M Ulst 5E 92
Cappercleuch. Bord 7L 59
Capplegill. Dum 1F 52
Capton. Devn 6L 5
Capton. Som 2K 7
Caputh. Per 4D 66
Caradon Town. Corn 8B 6
Carbis Bay. Corn 5J 3
Carbost. High
nr. Loch Harport 2E 68
nr. Portree 1F 68
Carbrook. S Yor 1A 36
Carbrooke. Norf 1F 30
Carburton. Notts 2D 36
Carcluie. S Ayr 8B 58
Car Colston. Notts 5E 36
Carcroft. S Yor 7C 42
Cardenden. Fife 8F 66
Cardeston. Shrp 8B 34
Cardewlees. Cumb 6H 53
Cardiff. Card 107 (7L 17)
Cardiff Airport. V Glam 8K 17
Cardigan. Cdgn 2H 15
Cardinal's Green. Cambs 7C 30
Cardington. Bed 7H 29
Cardington. Shrp 2D 26
Cardinham. Corn 5D 4
Cardno. Abers 7J 81
Cardow. Mor 1A 72
Cardross. Arg 2B 58
Cardurnock. Cumb 6F 52
Careby. Linc 8H 37
Careston. Ang 1J 67
Carew. Pemb 6G 15
Carew Cheriton. Pemb 6G 15
Carew Newton. Pemb 6G 15
Carey. Here 8D 26
Carfin. N Lan 4F 58
Carfrae. Bord 4C 60
Cargan. ME Ant 3G 93
Cargate Green. Norf 8K 39
Cargenbridge. Dum 4D 52
Cargill. Per 4E 66
Cargo. Cumb 6H 53
Cargreen. Corn 5G 5
Carham. Nmbd 6F 60
Carhampton. Som 1K 7
Carharrack. Corn 4L 3
Carie. Per
nr. Loch Rannah 2L 65
nr. Loch Tay 4L 65
Carisbrooke. IOW 7B 10
Cark. Cumb 8B 46
Carkeel. Corn 5G 5
Carlabhagh. W Isl 7F 82
Carland Cross. Corn 3M 3
Carlbury. Darl 4L 47
Carlby. Linc 8H 37
Carlecotes. S Yor 7K 41
Carleen. Corn 6K 3
Carlesmoor. N Yor 8K 47
Carleton. Cumb
nr. Carlisle 6J 53
nr. Egremont 4K 45
nr. Penrith 3D 46
Carleton. Lanc 3B 40
Carleton. N Yor 3H 41
Carleton. W Yor 5B 42
Carleton Forehoe. Norf 1G 31
Carleton Rode. Norf 2H 31
Carleton St Peter. Norf 1K 31
Carlidnack. Corn 6L 3
Carlingcott. Bath 8E 18
Carlin How. Red C 4E 48
Carlisle. Cumb 107 (6J 53)
Carloonan. Arg 6E 64
Carlops. Bord 4K 59
Carlton. Bed 6G 29
Carlton. Cambs 6C 30
Carlton. Leics 1A 28
Carlton. N Yor
nr. Helmsley 7D 48
nr. Middleham 7J 47
nr. Selby 5D 42
Carlton. Notts 5D 36
Carlton. S Yor 6A 42
Carlton. Stoc T 3A 48
Carlton. Suff 5K 31
Carlton. W Yor 5M 41
Carlton Colville. Suff 2M 31
Carlton Curlieu. Leics 2D 28
Carlton Husthwaite. N Yor 8B 48
Carlton in Cleveland. N Yor 5C 48
Carlton in Lindrick. Notts 1C 36
Carlton-le-Moorland. Linc 4G 37
Carlton Miniott. N Yor 7A 48
Carlton-on-Trent. Notts 3F 36

A-Z Great Britain Road Atlas 123

Carlton Scroop—Coddenham Green

Carlton Scroop. Linc 5G 37
Carluke. S Lan 4G 59
Carlyon Bay. Corn 6C 4
Carmarthen. Carm 5L 15
Carmel. Carm 3E 16
Carmel. Flin 3L 33
Carmel. Gwyn 5D 32
Carmel. IOA 2C 32
Carmichael. S Lan 6H 59
Carmunnock. Glas 4E 58
Carmyle. Glas 3E 58
Carmyllie. Ang 3J 67
Carnaby. E Yor 1J 43
Carnach. High
nr. Lochcarron 3M 69
nr. Ullapool 4M 77
Carnach. Mor 1L 71
Carnach. W Isl 4D 76
Carnachy. High 6K 85
Carnain. Arg 3C 56
Carnais. W Isl 8D 82
Carnan. Arg 3F 62
Carnan. W Isl 1D 74
Carnbee. Fife 7J 67
Carnbo. Per 7D 66
Carn Brea Village. Corn 4K 3
Carndu. High 3K 69
Carnduff. Caus 1G 93
Carne. Corn 8B 4
Carnell. S Ayr 6C 58
Carnforth. Lanc 8D 46
Carn-gorm. High 3L 69
Carnhedryn. Pemb 4E 14
Carnhell Green. Corn 5K 3
Carnie. Abers 5H 73
Carnkie. Corn
nr. Falmouth 5L 3
nr. Redruth 5K 3
Carnkief. Corn 3L 3
Carnlough. ME Ant 3H 93
Carnmoney. Ant 4H 93
Carno. Powy 3J 25
Carnock. Fife 1J 59
Carnon Downs. Corn 4L 3
Carnoustie. Ang 4J 67
Carnteel. M Ulst 6E 92
Carntyne. Glas 3E 58
Carnwath. S Lan 5H 59
Carnyorth. Corn 5G 3
Carol Green. W Mid 4L 27
Carpalla. Corn 6B 4
Carperby. N Yor 7J 47
Carradale. Arg 6H 57
Carragraich. W Isl 4C 76
Carrbridge. High 3K 71
Carr Cross. Lanc 6B 40
Carreglefn. IOA 2C 32
Carrhouse. N Lin 7E 42
Carrick Castle. Arg 8F 64
Carrickfergus. ME Ant 4J 93
Carrick Ho. Orkn 6E 88
Carrickmore. Ferm 5E 92
Carriden. Falk 1J 59
Carrington. G Man 8F 40
Carrington. Linc 4L 37
Carrington. Midl 3M 59
Carrog. Cnwy 6G 33
Carrog. Den 6L 33
Carron. Falk 1G 59
Carron. Mor 1B 72
Carronbridge. Dum 2C 52
Carronshore. Falk 1G 59
Carrowclare. Caus 2E 92
Carrowdore. Ards 5J 93
Carrow Hill. Mon 4C 18
Carr Shield. Nmbd 7B 54
Carrutherstown. Dum 4F 52
Carr Vale. Derbs 3B 36
Carrville. Dur 7G 55
Carryduff. Lis 5H 93
Carsaig. Arg 5L 63
Carscreugh. Dum 5H 51
Carsegowan. Dum 6K 51
Carse House. Arg 3G 57
Carseriggan. Dum 5J 51
Carsethorn. Dum 6D 52
Carshalton. G Lon 7K 21
Carsington. Derbs 4L 35
Carskiey. Arg 1M 49
Carsluith. Dum 6K 51
Carson Park. New M 7H 93
Carsphairn. Dum 2L 51
Carstairs. S Lan 5H 59
Carstairs Junction. S Lan 5H 59
Cartbridge. Surr 8H 21
Carterhaugh. Ang 3H 67
Carter's Clay. Hants 3M 9
Carterton. Oxon 3L 19
Carterway Heads. Nmbd 6D 54
Carthew. Corn 6C 4
Carthorpe. N Yor 7M 47
Cartington. Nmbd 1D 54
Cartland. S Lan 5G 59
Cartmel. Cumb 8B 46
Cartmel Fell. Cumb 7C 46
Cartworth. W Yor 7K 41
Carwath. Cumb 7H 53
Carway. Carm 6L 15
Carwinley. Cumb 4J 53
Cascob. Powy 6M 25
Cas-gwent. Mon 4D 18
Cash Feus. Fife 7F 66
Cashlie. Per 3J 65
Cashmoor. Dors 4H 9
Cas-Mael. Pemb 4G 15
Casnewydd. Newp 114 (5B 18)
Cassington. Oxon 2B 20
Cassop. Dur 8G 55
Castell. Cnwy 4G 33
Castell. Den 4L 33
Castell Hendre. Pemb 4G 15
Castell-Nedd. Neat 5G 17
Castell Newydd Emlyn. Carm 2K 15
Castell-y-bwch. Torf 4A 18
Casterton. Cumb 8E 46
Castle. Som 1D 8
Castle Acre. Norf 8E 38
Castle Ashby. Nptn 6F 28
Castlebay. W Isl 6C 74
Castle Bolton. N Yor 6J 47
Castle Bromwich. W Mid 3K 27
Castle Bytham. Linc 8G 37
Castlebythe. Pemb 4G 15
Castle Caereinion. Powy 2L 25
Castle Camps. Cambs 7C 30
Castle Carrock. Cumb 6K 53
Castle Cary. Som 2E 8
Castlecary. N Lan 2F 58
Castlecaulfield. M Ulst 5E 92
Castle Combe. Wilts 6G 19
Castlecraig. High 7J 79
Castledawson. M Ulst 4F 93
Castlederg. Derr 4C 92
Castle Donington. Leics 7B 36
Castle Douglas. Dum 5B 52
Castle Eaton. Swin 4K 19
Castle Eden. Dur 8H 55
Castleford. W Yor 5B 42
Castle Frome. Here 7E 26
Castle Green. Surr 7G 21
Castle Green. Warw 4L 27
Castle Gresley. Derbs 8L 35
Castle Heaton. Nmbd 5G 61
Castle Hedingham. Essx 8D 30
Castle Hill. Kent 1C 12
Castle Hill. Suff 7H 31
Castlehill. Per 4F 66
Castlehill. S Lan 4G 59
Castlehill. W Dun 2B 58
Castle Kennedy. Dum 6G 51
Castle Lachlan. Arg 8E 64
Castlemartin. Pemb 7F 14
Castlemilk. Glas 4E 58
Castlemorris. Pemb 3F 14
Castlemorton. Worc 8F 26
Castle O'er. Dum 2G 53
Castle Park. N Yor 4F 48
Castlerigg. Cumb 3A 46
Castle Rising. Norf 7C 38
Castlerock. Caus 2E 92
Castleroe. Caus 2F 93
Castleside. Dur 7D 54
Castlethorpe. Mil 7E 28
Castleton. Abers 6A 72
Castleton. Arg 1H 57
Castleton. Derbs 1K 35
Castleton. G Man 6G 41
Castleton. Mor 3A 72
Castleton. Newp 5A 18
Castleton. N Yor 5D 48
Castleton. Per 6C 66
Castletown. Cumb 8K 53
Castletown. Dors 8E 8
Castletown. High 5C 86
Castletown. IOM 8B 44
Castletown. Tyne 6G 55
Castlewellan. New M 7H 93
Castley. N Yor 3L 41
Caston. Norf 2F 30
Castor. Pet 2J 29
Caswell. Swan 6E 16
Catacol. N Ayr 5J 57
Catbrook. Mon 3D 18
Catchems End. Worc 4F 26
Catchgate. Dur 6E 54
Catcleugh. Nmbd 1M 53
Catcliffe. S Yor 1B 36
Catcott. Som 2B 8
Caterham. Surr 8L 21
Catfield. Norf 7K 39
Catfield Common. Norf 7K 39
Catfirth. Shet 2E 90
Catford. G Lon 6L 21
Catforth. Lanc 4C 40
Cathcart. Glas 3D 58
Cathedine. Powy 2L 17
Catherine-de-Barnes. W Mid 3K 27
Catherington. Hants 4D 10
Catherston Leweston. Dors 6B 8
Catherton. Shrp 4E 26
Catisfield. Hants 5C 10
Catlodge. High 6G 71
Catlowdy. Cumb 4J 53
Catmore. W Ber 5B 20
Caton. Devn 8G 7
Caton. Lanc 1D 40
Catrine. E Ayr 7D 58
Cat's Ash. Newp 4B 18
Catsfield. E Sus 4D 12
Catsgore. Som 3D 8
Catshill. Worc 4H 27
Cattal. N Yor 2B 42
Cattawade. Suff 8H 31
Catterall. Lanc 3D 40
Catterick. N Yor 6L 47
Catterick Bridge. N Yor 6L 47
Catterick Garrison. N Yor 6K 47
Catterlen. Cumb 8J 53
Catterline. Abers 8H 73
Catterton. N Yor 3C 42
Catteshall. Surr 1G 11
Catthorpe. Leics 4C 28
Cattistock. Dors 6D 8
Catton. Nmbd 6B 54
Catton. N Yor 8A 48
Catwick. E Yor 3J 43
Catworth. Cambs 4H 29
Caudle Green. Glos 2H 19
Caulcott. Oxon 1C 20
Cauldhame. Stir 8L 65
Cauldmill. Bord 8C 60
Cauldon. Staf 5J 35
Cauldon Lowe. Staf 5J 35
Cauldwells. Abers 8G 81
Caulkerbush. Dum 6D 52
Caulside. Dum 3J 53
Caunsall. Worc 3G 27
Caunton. Notts 3E 36
Causewayend. S Lan 6J 59
Causewayhead. Stir 8B 66
Causey Park. Nmbd 2E 54
Caute. Devn 4D 6
Cautley. Cumb 6E 46
Cavendish. Suff 7E 30
Cavendish Bridge. Leics 7B 36
Cavenham. Suff 5D 30
Caversfield. Oxon 1C 20
Caversham. Read 6E 20
Caversham Heights. Read 6E 20
Caverswall. Staf 5H 35
Cawdor. High 1J 71
Cawkwell. Linc 1K 37
Cawood. N Yor 4C 42
Cawsand. Corn 6G 5
Cawston. Norf 7H 39
Cawston. Warw 4B 28
Cawthorne. N Yor 7E 48
Cawthorne. S Yor 7L 41
Cawthorpe. Linc 7H 37
Cawton. N Yor 8D 48
Caxton. Cambs 6L 29
Caynham. Shrp 4D 26
Caythorpe. Linc 5G 37
Caythorpe. Notts 5D 36
Cayton. N Yor 7H 49
Ceallan. W Isl 8K 75
Ceann a Bhaigh. W Isl
on North Uist 7J 75
on Scalpay 4D 76
on South Harris 4C 76
Ceann a Bhàigh. W Isl 5B 76
Ceannacroc Lodge. High 4C 70
Ceann a Deas Loch Baghasdail. W Isl 4D 74
Ceann an Leothaid. High 7H 69
Ceann a Tuath Loch Baghasdail. W Isl 3D 74
Ceann Loch Ailleart. High 7J 69
Ceann Loch Muideirt. High 8J 69
Ceann-na-Cleithe. W Isl 4C 76
Ceann Shiphoirt. W Isl 2D 76
Ceann Tarabhaigh. W Isl 2D 76
Cearsiadar. W Isl 1E 76
Ceathramh Meadhanach. W Isl 6K 75
Cefn Berain. Cnwy 4J 33
Cefn-brith. Cnwy 5J 33
Cefn-bryn-brain. Carm 3G 17
Cefn Bychan. Cphy 5M 17
Cefn-bychan. Flin 4L 33
Cefncaeau. Carm 7M 15
Cefn Canol. Powy 7M 33
Cefn Coch. Powy 2K 25
Cefn-coch. Powy 8L 33
Cefn-coed-y-cymmer. Mer T 4K 17
Cefn Cribwr. B'end 6H 17
Cefn-ddwysarn. Gwyn 7J 33
Cefn Einion. Shrp 3A 26
Cefneithin. Carm 5M 15
Cefn Glas. B'end 6H 17
Cefngorwydd. Powy 8J 25
Cefn Llwyd. Cdgn 4F 24
Cefn-mawr. Wrex 5A 34
Cefn-y-bedd. Flin 4B 34
Cefn-y-coed. Powy 3L 25
Cefn-y-pant. Carm 4H 15
Cegidfa. Powy 1M 25
Ceinewydd. Cdgn 1K 15
Cellan. Cdgn 8F 24
Cellardyke. Fife 7J 67
Cellarhead. Staf 5H 35
Cemaes. IOA 1C 32
Cemmaes. Powy 2H 25
Cemmaes Road. Powy 2H 25
Cenarth. Cdgn 2J 15
Cenin. Gwyn 6D 32
Ceos. W Isl 1E 76
Ceres. Fife 6H 67
Ceri. Powy 4L 25
Cerist. Powy 4J 25
Cerne Abbas. Dors 5E 8
Cerney Wick. Glos 4J 19
Cerrigceinwen. IOA 3D 32
Cerrigydrudion. Cnwy 6J 33
Cess. Norf 8L 39
Cessford. Bord 7E 60
Ceunant. Gwyn 4E 32
Chaceley. Glos 8G 27
Chacewater. Corn 4L 3
Chackmore. Buck 8D 28
Chacombe. Nptn 7B 28
Chadderton. G Man 7H 41
Chaddesden. Derb 6A 36
Chaddesden Common. Derb 6A 36
Chaddesley Corbett. Worc 4G 27
Chaddlehanger. Devn 8D 6
Chaddleworth. W Ber 6B 20
Chadlington. Oxon 1M 19
Chadshunt. Warw 6M 27
Chadstone. Nptn 6F 28
Chad Valley. W Mid 3J 27
Chadwell. Leics 8E 36
Chadwell. Shrp 8F 34
Chadwell Heath. G Lon 5A 22
Chadwell St Mary. Thur 6C 22
Chadwick End. W Mid 4L 27
Chadwick Green. Mers 8D 40
Chaffcombe. Som 4B 8
Chafford Hundred. Thur 6C 22
Chagford. Devn 7G 7
Chailey. E Sus 4L 11
Chain Bridge. Linc 5L 37
Chainbridge. Cambs 1M 29
Chainhurst. Kent 1D 12
Chalbury. Dors 5J 9
Chalbury Common. Dors 5J 9
Chaldon. Surr 8L 21
Chaldon Herring. Dors 7F 8
Chale. IOW 8B 10
Chale Green. IOW 8B 10
Chalfont Common. Buck 4H 21
Chalfont St Giles. Buck 4G 21
Chalfont St Peter. Buck 5H 21
Chalford. Glos 3G 19
Chalgrove. Oxon 4D 20
Chalk. Kent 6C 22
Chalk End. Essx 2C 22
Chalk Hill. Glos 1K 19
Challaborough. Devn 7J 5
Challacombe. Devn 1F 6
Challister. Shet 1F 90
Challoch. Dum 5J 51
Challock. Kent 8G 23
Chalton. C Beds
nr. Bedford 6J 29
nr. Luton 1H 21
Chalton. Hants 4E 10
Chalvington. E Sus 5B 12
Champany. Falk 2J 59
Chance Inn. Fife 6G 67
Chancery. Cdgn 5E 24
Chandler's Cross. Herts 4H 21
Chandler's Cross. Worc 8F 26
Chandler's Ford. Hants 3B 10
Chanlockfoot. Dum 1B 52
Channel's End. Bed 6J 29
Channel Tunnel. Kent 2H 13
Channerwick. Shet 5E 90
Chantry. Som 1F 8
Chantry. Suff 7H 31
Chapel. Cumb 8G 53
Chapel. Fife 8F 66
Chapel Allerton. Som 8C 18
Chapel Allerton. W Yor 4M 41
Chapel Amble. Corn 4B 4
Chapel Brampton. Nptn 5E 28
Chapelbridge. Cambs 2K 29
Chapel Chorlton. Staf 6G 35
Chapel Cleeve. Som 1K 7
Chapel End. C Beds 7H 29
Chapel-en-le-Frith. Derbs 1J 35
Chapelfield. Abers 1L 67
Chapelgate. Linc 7M 37
Chapel Green. Warw
nr. Coventry 3L 27
nr. Southam 5B 28
Chapel Haddlesey. N Yor 5C 42
Chapelhall. N Lan 3F 58
Chapel Hill. Abers 2K 73
Chapel Hill. Linc 4K 37
Chapel Hill. Mon 3D 18
Chapelhill. Per
nr. Glencarse 5F 66
nr. Harrietfield 4D 66
Chapelknowe. Dum 4H 53
Chapel Lawn. Shrp 4B 26
Chapel le Dale. N Yor 8F 46
Chapel Milton. Derbs 1J 35
Chapel of Garioch. Abers 3G 73
Chapel Row. W Ber 7C 20
Chapels. Cumb 6M 45
Chapel St Leonards. Linc 2B 38
Chapel Stile. Cumb 5B 46
Chapelthorpe. W Yor 6M 41
Chapelton. Ang 3K 67
Chapelton. Devn 3E 6
Chapelton. High
nr. Grantown-on-Spey 4K 71
nr. Inverness 5F 78
Chapelton. S Lan 5E 58
Chapeltown. Bkbn 6F 40
Chapel Town. Corn 6A 4
Chapeltown. Mor 3B 72
Chapeltown. New M 7J 93
Chapeltown. S Yor 8A 42
Chapmanslade. Wilts 1G 9
Chapmans Well. Devn 6C 6
Chapmore End. Herts 2L 21
Chappel. Essx 1E 22
Chard. Som 5B 8
Chard Junction. Dors 5B 8
Chardstock. Devn 5B 8
Charfield. S Glo 4F 18
Charing. Kent 1F 12
Charing Heath. Kent 1F 12
Charing Hill. Kent 8F 22
Charingworth. Glos 8L 27
Charlbury. Oxon 2A 20
Charlcombe. Bath 7F 18
Charlcutt. Wilts 6H 19
Charlecote. Warw 6L 27
Charlemont. Arm 6F 93
Charles. Devn 2F 6
Charlesfield. Dum 5F 52
Charleshill. Surr 1F 10
Charleston. Ang 3G 67
Charleston. Ren 3C 58
Charlestown. Aber 5J 73
Charlestown. Abers 7K 81
Charlestown. Corn 6C 4
Charlestown. Dors 8E 8
Charlestown. Fife 1J 59
Charlestown. G Man 7G 41
Charlestown. High
nr. Gairloch 6K 77
nr. Inverness 1G 71
Charlestown. W Yor 5H 41
Charlestown of Aberlour. Mor 1B 72
Charles Tye. Suff 6G 31
Charlesworth. Derbs 8J 41
Charlton. G Lon 6M 21
Charlton. Hants 1A 10
Charlton. Herts 1J 21
Charlton. Nptn 8C 28
Charlton. Nmbd 3B 54
Charlton. Oxon 5B 20
Charlton. Som
nr. Radstock 8E 18
nr. Shepton Mallet 1E 8
nr. Taunton 3A 8
Charlton. Telf 8D 34
Charlton. W Sus 4F 10
Charlton. Wilts
nr. Malmesbury 5H 19
nr. Pewsey 8K 19
nr. Shaftesbury 3H 9
Charlton. Worc
nr. Evesham 7J 27
nr. Stourport-on-Severn 4G 27
Charlton Abbots. Glos 1J 19
Charlton Adam. Som 3D 8
Charlton All Saints. Wilts 3K 9
Charlton Down. Dors 6E 8
Charlton Horethorne. Som 3E 8
Charlton Kings. Glos 1H 19
Charlton Mackrell. Som 3D 8
Charlton Marshall. Dors 5G 9
Charlton Musgrove. Som 3F 8
Charlton-on-Otmoor. Oxon 2C 20
Charlton on the Hill. Dors 5G 9
Charlwood. Hants 2D 10
Charlwood. Surr 1K 11
Charlynch. Som 2M 7
Charminster. Dors 6E 8
Charmouth. Dors 6B 8
Charndon. Buck 1D 20
Charney Bassett. Oxon 4A 20
Charnock Green. Lanc 6D 40
Charnock Richard. Lanc 6D 40
Charsfield. Suff 6J 31
The Chart. Kent 8A 22
Chart Corner. Kent 8D 22
Charter Alley. Hants 8C 20
Charterhouse. Som 8C 18
Charterville Allotments. Oxon 2M 19
Chartham. Kent 8H 23
Chartham Hatch. Kent 8H 23
Chartridge. Buck 3G 21
Chart Sutton. Kent 8D 22
Charvil. Wok 6E 20
Charwelton. Nptn 6C 28
Chase Terrace. Staf 1J 27
Chasetown. Staf 1J 27
Chastleton. Oxon 1L 19
Chasty. Devn 5C 6
Chatburn. Lanc 3F 40
Chatcull. Staf 6F 34
Chatham. Medw
Medway Towns 111 (7D 22)
Chatham Green. Essx 2D 22
Chathill. Nmbd 7J 61
Chatley. Worc 5G 27
Chattenden. Medw 6D 22
Chatteris. Cambs 3L 29
Chattisham. Suff 7G 31
Chatton. Nmbd 7H 61
Chatwall. Shrp 2C 26
Chaulden. Herts 3H 21
Chaul End. C Beds 1H 21
Chawleigh. Devn 4G 7
Chawley. Oxon 3B 20
Chawston. Bed 6J 29
Chawton. Hants 2E 10
Chaxhill. Glos 2F 18
Cheadle. G Man 1G 35
Cheadle. Staf 5J 35
Cheadle Hulme. G Man 1G 35
Cheam. G Lon 7K 21
Cheapside. Wind 7G 21
Chearsley. Buck 2E 20
Chebsey. Staf 7G 35
Checkendon. Oxon 5D 20
Checkley. Ches E 5F 34
Checkley. Here 8D 26
Checkley. Staf 6J 35
Chedburgh. Suff 6D 30
Cheddar. Som 8C 18
Cheddington. Buck 2G 21
Cheddleton. Staf 4H 35
Cheddon Fitzpaine. Som 3M 7
Chedglow. Wilts 4H 19
Chedgrave. Norf 2K 31
Chedington. Dors 5C 8
Chediston. Suff 4K 31
Chediston Green. Suff 4K 31
Chedworth. Glos 2J 19
Chedzoy. Som 2B 8
Cheeseman's Green. Kent 2G 13
Cheetham Hill. G Man 7G 41
Cheglinch. Devn 1E 6
Cheldon. Devn 4G 7
Chelford. Ches E 2G 35
Chellaston. Derb 6A 36
Chellington. Bed 6G 29
Chelmarsh. Shrp 3F 26
Chelmick. Shrp 2C 26
Chelmondiston. Suff 8J 31
Chelmorton. Derbs 3K 35
Chelmsford. Essx 3D 22
Chelsea. G Lon 6K 21
Chelsfield. G Lon 7A 22
Chelsham. Surr 8L 21
Chelston. Som 3L 7
Chelsworth. Suff 7F 30
Cheltenham. Glos 107 (1H 19)
Chelveston. Nptn 5G 29
Chelvey. N Som 7C 18
Chelwood. Bath 7E 18
Chelwood Common. E Sus 3M 11
Chelwood Gate. E Sus 3M 11
Chelworth. Wilts 4H 19
Chelworth Lower Green. Wilts 4J 19
Chelworth Upper Green. Wilts 4J 19
Chelynch. Som 1E 8
Cheney Longville. Shrp 3C 26
Chenies. Buck 4H 21
Chepstow. Mon 4D 18
Chequerfield. W Yor 5B 42
Chequers Corner. Norf 1M 29
Cherhill. Wilts 6J 19
Cherington. Glos 4H 19
Cherington. Warw 8L 27
Cheriton. Devn 1G 7
Cheriton. Hants 3C 10
Cheriton. Kent 2J 13
Cheriton. Pemb 8F 14
Cheriton. Swan 7L 15
Cheriton Bishop. Devn 6G 7
Cheriton Cross. Devn 6G 7
Cheriton Fitzpaine. Devn 5H 7
Cherrington. Telf 7E 34
Cherrybank. Per 5E 66
Cherry Burton. E Yor 3G 43
Cherry Green. Herts 1L 21
Cherry Hinton. Cambs 6A 30
Cherry Willingham. Linc 2H 37
Chertsey. Surr 7H 21
Cheselbourne. Dors 6F 8
Chesham. Buck 3G 21
Chesham. G Man 6G 41
Chesham Bois. Buck 4G 21
Cheshunt. Herts 3L 21
Cheslyn Hay. Staf 1H 27
Chessetts Wood. Warw 4K 27
Chessington. G Lon 7J 21
Chester. Ches W 108 (3C 34)
Chesterblade. Som 1E 8
Chesterfield. Derbs 2A 36
Chesterfield. Staf 1K 27
Chesterhope. Nmbd 3B 54
Chester-le-Street. Dur 6F 54
Chester Moor. Dur 7F 54
Chesters. Bord 8D 60
Chesterton. Cambs
nr. Cambridge 5A 30
nr. Peterborough 2J 29
Chesterton. Glos 3J 19
Chesterton. Oxon 1C 20
Chesterton. Shrp 2F 26
Chesterton. Staf 5G 35
Chesterton Green. Warw 6M 27
Chesterwood. Nmbd 5B 54
Chestfield. Kent 7H 23
Cheston. Devn 6J 5
Cheswardine. Shrp 6F 34
Cheswell. Telf 8F 34
Cheswick. Nmbd 5H 61
Cheswick Green. W Mid 4K 27
Chetnole. Dors 5E 8
Chettiscombe. Devn 4J 7
Chettisham. Cambs 3B 30
Chettle. Dors 4H 9
Chetton. Shrp 2E 26
Chetwode. Buck 1D 20
Chetwynd Aston. Telf 8F 34
Cheveley. Cambs 5C 30
Chevening. Kent 8A 22
Chevington. Suff 6D 30
Chevithorne. Devn 4J 7
Chew Magna. Bath 7D 18
Chew Moor. G Man 7E 40
Chew Stoke. Bath 7D 18
Chewton Keynsham. Bath 7E 18
Chewton Mendip. Som 8D 18
Chichacott. Devn 6F 6
Chicheley. Mil 7G 29
Chichester. W Sus 5F 10
Chickerell. Dors 7E 8
Chickering. Suff 4J 31
Chicklade. Wilts 2H 9
Chicksands. C Beds 8J 29
Chickward. Here 6A 26
Chidden. Hants 4D 10
Chiddingfold. Surr 2G 11
Chiddingly. E Sus 4B 12
Chiddingstone. Kent 1B 12
Chiddingstone Causeway. Kent 1B 12
Chiddingstone Hoath. Kent 1A 12
Chideock. Dors 6C 8
Chidgley. Som 2K 7
Chidham. W Sus 5E 10
Chieveley. W Ber 6B 20
Chignal St James. Essx 3C 22
Chignal Smealy. Essx 2C 22
Chigwell. Essx 4M 21
Chigwell Row. Essx 4A 22
Chilbolton. Hants 1A 10
Chilcomb. Hants 3C 10
Chilcombe. Dors 6D 8
Chilcompton. Som 8E 18
Chilcote. Leics 8L 35
Childer Thornton. Ches W 2B 34
Child Okeford. Dors 4G 9
Childrey. Oxon 5A 20
Child's Ercall. Shrp 7E 34
Childswickham. Worc 8J 27
Childwall. Mers 1C 34
Childwick Green. Herts 2J 21
Chilfrome. Dors 6D 8
Chilgrove. W Sus 4F 10
Chilham. Kent 8G 23
Chilhampton. Wilts 2J 9
Chilla. Devn 5D 6
Chilland. Hants 2C 10
Chillaton. Devn 7D 6
Chillenden. Kent 8J 23
Chillerton. IOW 7B 10
Chillesford. Suff 6K 31
Chillingham. Nmbd 7H 61
Chillington. Devn 7K 5
Chillington. Som 4B 8
Chilmark. Wilts 2H 9
Chilmington Green. Kent 1F 12
Chilson. Oxon 2M 19
Chilsworthy. Corn 8D 6
Chilsworthy. Devn 5C 6
Chiltern Green. C Beds 2J 21
Chilthorne Domer. Som 4D 8
Chilton. Buck 2D 20
Chilton. Devn 5H 7
Chilton. Dur 3L 47
Chilton. Oxon 5B 20
Chilton Candover. Hants 1C 10
Chilton Cantelo. Som 3D 8
Chilton Foliat. Wilts 6M 19
Chilton Lane. Dur 8G 55
Chilton Polden. Som 2B 8
Chilton Street. Suff 7D 30
Chilton Trinity. Som 2A 8
Chilwell. Notts 6C 36
Chilworth. Hants 4B 10
Chilworth. Surr 1H 11
Chimney. Oxon 3A 20
Chimney Street. Suff 7D 30
Chineham. Hants 8D 20
Chingford. G Lon 4L 21
Chinley. Derbs 1J 35
Chinnor. Oxon 3E 20
Chipley. Som 3L 7
Chipnall. Shrp 6F 34
Chippenham. Cambs 5C 30
Chippenham. Wilts 6H 19
Chipperfield. Herts 3H 21
Chipping. Herts 8L 29
Chipping. Lanc 3E 40
Chipping Campden. Glos 8K 27
Chipping Hill. Essx 2E 22
Chipping Norton. Oxon 1M 19
Chipping Ongar. Essx 3B 22
Chipping Sodbury. S Glo 5F 18
Chipping Warden. Nptn 7B 28
Chipstable. Som 3K 7
Chipstead. Kent 8B 22
Chipstead. Surr 8K 21
Chirbury. Shrp 2A 26
Chirk. Wrex 6A 34
Chirmorie. S Ayr 4H 51
Chirnside. Bord 4F 60
Chirnsidebridge. Bord 4F 60
Chirton. Wilts 8J 19
Chisbridge Cross. Buck 5F 20
Chisbury. Wilts 7L 19
Chiselborough. Som 4C 8
Chiseldon. Swin 6K 19
Chiselhampton. Oxon 4C 20
Chiserley. W Yor 5J 41
Chislehurst. G Lon 6M 21
Chislet. Kent 7J 23
Chiswell. Dors 8E 8
Chiswell Green. Herts 3J 21
Chiswick. G Lon 6K 21
Chisworth. Derbs 8H 41
Chitcombe. E Sus 3E 12
Chithurst. W Sus 3F 10
Chittering. Cambs 5A 30
Chitterley. Devn 5J 7
Chitterne. Wilts 1H 9
Chittlehamholt. Devn 3F 6
Chittlehampton. Devn 3F 6
Chittoe. Wilts 7H 19
Chivelstone. Devn 8K 5
Chivenor. Devn 2E 6
Chobham. Surr 7G 21
Cholderton. Wilts 1L 9
Cholesbury. Buck 3G 21
Chollerford. Nmbd 4C 54
Chollerton. Nmbd 4C 54
Cholsey. Oxon 5C 20
Cholstrey. Here 6C 26
Chop Gate. N Yor 6C 48
Choppington. Nmbd 3F 54
Chopwell. Tyne 6E 54
Chorley. Ches E 4D 34
Chorley. Lanc 6D 40
Chorley. Shrp 3E 26
Chorley. Staf 8J 35
Chorleywood. Herts 4H 21
Chorlton. Ches E 4F 34
Chorlton-cum-Hardy. G Man 8G 41
Chorlton Lane. Ches W 5C 34
Choulton. Shrp 3B 26
Chrishall. Essx 8M 29
Christchurch. Cambs 2A 30
Christchurch. Dors 6K 9
Christchurch. Glos 2D 18
Christian Malford. Wilts 6H 19
Christleton. Ches W 3C 34
Christmas Common. Oxon 4E 20
Christon. N Som 8B 18
Christon Bank. Nmbd 7K 61
Christow. Devn 7H 7
Chryston. N Lan 2E 58
Chuck Hatch. E Sus 2A 12
Chudleigh. Devn 8H 7
Chudleigh Knighton. Devn 8H 7
Chulmleigh. Devn 4F 6
Chunal. Derbs 8J 41
Church. Lanc 5F 40
Churcham. Glos 2F 18
Church Aston. Telf 8F 34
Church Brampton. Nptn 5E 28
Church Brough. Cumb 4F 46
Church Broughton. Derbs 6L 35
Church Corner. Suff 3L 31
Church Crookham. Hants 8F 20
Churchdown. Glos 1G 19
Church Eaton. Staf 8G 35
Church End. Cambs
nr. Cambridge 6A 30
nr. Over 4L 29
nr. Sawtry 3K 29
nr. Wisbech 1L 29
Church End. C Beds
nr. Stotfold 8J 29
nr. Totternhoe 1G 21
Church End. E Yor 2J 43
Church End. Essx
nr. Braintree 1D 22
nr. Great Dunmow 1C 22
nr. Saffron Walden 7B 30
Church End. Glos 8G 27
Church End. Hants 8D 20
Church End. Linc
nr. Donington 6K 37
nr. North Somercotes 8M 43
Church End. Norf 8B 38
Church End. Warw
nr. Coleshill 2L 27
nr. Nuneaton 2L 27
Church End. Wilts 6J 19
Churchend. Essx 4G 23
Church Enstone. Oxon 1A 20
Church Fenton. N Yor 4C 42
Church Green. Devn 6L 7
Church Gresley. Derbs 8L 35
Church Hanborough. Oxon 2B 20
Church Hill. Ches W 3E 34
Church Hill. Worc 5J 27
Church Hougham. Kent 1J 13
Church Houses. N Yor 6D 48
Churchill. Devn
nr. Axminster 5B 8
nr. Barnstaple 1E 6
Churchill. N Som 8C 18
Churchill. Oxon 1L 19
Churchill. Worc
nr. Kidderminster 4G 27
nr. Worcester 6H 27
Churchinford. Som 4M 7
Church Knowle. Dors 7H 9
Church Laneham. Notts 2F 36
Church Langley. Essx 3A 22
Church Langton. Leics 2E 28
Church Lawford. Warw 4B 28
Church Lawton. Ches E 4G 35
Church Leigh. Staf 6J 35
Church Lench. Worc 6J 27
Church Mayfield. Staf 5K 35
Church Minshull. Ches E 3E 34
Church Norton. W Sus 6F 10
Churchover. Warw 3C 28
Church Preen. Shrp 2D 26
Church Pulverbatch. Shrp 1C 26
Churchstanton. Som 4L 7
Church Stoke. Powy 2A 26
Churchstow. Devn 7K 5
Church Stowe. Nptn 6D 28
Church Street. Kent 6D 22
Church Stretton. Shrp 2C 26
Churchtown. Cumb 7H 53
Churchtown. Derbs 3L 35
Churchtown. Devn 1F 6
Churchtown. IOM 5D 44
Churchtown. Lanc 3C 40
Churchtown. Mers 6B 40
Churchtown. New M 6J 93
Churchtown. Shrp 3A 26
Church Village. Rhon 6K 17
Church Warsop. Notts 3C 36
Church Westcote. Glos 1L 19
Church Wilne. Derbs 6B 36
Churnsike Lodge. Nmbd 4L 53
Churston Ferrers. Torb 6M 5
Churt. Surr 2F 10
Churton. Ches W 4C 34
Churwell. W Yor 5L 41
Chute Standen. Wilts 8M 19
Chwilog. Gwyn 7D 32
Chwitffordd. Flin 3L 33
Chyandour. Corn 5H 3
Cilan Uchaf. Gwyn 8B 32
Cilcain. Flin 4L 33
Cilcennin. Cdgn 6E 24
Cilfrew. Neat 4G 17
Cilfynydd. Rhon 5K 17
Cilgerran. Pemb 2H 15
Cilgeti. Pemb 6H 15
Cilgwyn. Carm 2G 17
Cilgwyn. Pemb 3G 15
Ciliau Aeron. Cdgn 1L 15
Cill Amhlaidh. W Isl 4K 75
Cill Donnain. W Isl 3D 74
Cille a' Bhacstair. High 7E 76
Cille Bhrighde. W Isl 4D 74
Cille Pheadair. W Isl 4D 74
Cilmaengwyn. Neat 4G 17
Cilmeri. Powy 7K 25
Cilmery. Powy 7K 25
Cilrhedyn. Pemb 3J 15
Cilsan. Carm 5E 16
Ciltalgarth. Gwyn 6H 33
Ciltwrch. Powy 8L 25
Cilybebyll. Neat 4G 17
Cilycwm. Carm 8G 25
Cimla. Neat 5G 17
Cinderford. Glos 2E 18
Cinderhill. Derbs 5A 36
Cippenham. Slo 5G 21
Cippyn. Pemb 2H 15
Cirbhig. W Isl 7E 82
Circebost. W Isl 8E 82
Cirencester. Glos 3J 19
City. Powy 3M 25
City. V Glam 7J 17
The City. Buck 4E 20
City Airport. G Lon 5M 21
City Centre. Stoke
Stoke 116 (5G 35)
City Dulas. IOA 2D 32
City of Derry Airport. Derr 2D 92
City of London. G Lon
London 113 (5L 21)
Civiltown. Arm 6G 93
Clabby. Ferm 6D 92
Clabhach. Arg 2G 63
Clachaig. Arg 1L 57
Clachaig. High
nr. Kinlochleven 2F 64
nr. Nethy Bridge 4L 71
Clachamish. High 8E 76
Clachan. Arg
on Kintyre 4G 57
on Lismore 3C 64
Clachan. High
nr. Bettyhill 5K 85
nr. Staffin 7F 76
nr. Uig 6F 76
on Raasay 2G 69
Clachan Farm. Arg 6F 64
Clachan na Luib. W Isl 7K 75
Clachan of Campsie. E Dun 2E 58
Clachan of Glendaruel. Arg 1J 57
Clachan-Seil. Arg 6B 64
Clachan Shannda. W Isl 6K 75
Clachan Strachur. Arg 7E 64
Clachbreck. Arg 2G 57
Clachnaharry. High 1G 71
Clachtoll. High 1M 77
Clackmannan. Clac 8C 66
Clackmannanshire Bridge. Clac 1H 59
Clackmarras. Mor 8B 80
Clacton-on-Sea. Essx 2H 23
Cladach a Chaolais. W Isl 7J 75
Cladach Chairinis. W Isl 8K 75
Cladach Chirceboist. W Isl 7J 75
Cladach Iolaraigh. W Isl 7J 75
Cladich. Arg 5E 64
Cladswell. Worc 6J 27
Clady. Derr 4C 92
Clady. M Ulst 3F 93
Claggan. High
nr. Fort William 8B 70
nr. Lochaline 3A 64
Claigan. High 8D 76
Clandown. Bath 8E 18
Clanfield. Hants 4D 10
Clanfield. Oxon 3L 19
Clanville. Hants 1M 9
Clanville. Som 2E 8
Claonaig. Arg 4H 57
Clapgate. Dors 5J 9
Clapgate. Herts 1M 21
Clapham. Bed 6H 29
Clapham. Devn 7H 7
Clapham. G Lon 6K 21
Clapham. N Yor 1F 40
Clapham. W Sus 5H 11
Clap Hill. Kent 2G 13
Clappers. Bord 4G 61
Clappersgate. Cumb 5B 46
Clapphoull. Shet 5E 90
Clapton. Som
nr. Crewkerne 5C 8
nr. Radstock 8E 18
Clapton in Gordano. N Som 6C 18
Clapton-on-the-Hill. Glos 2K 19
Clapworthy. Devn 3F 6
Clara Vale. Tyne 5E 54
Clarbeston. Pemb 4G 15
Clarbeston Road. Pemb 4G 15
Clarborough. Notts 1E 36
Clare. Arm 6G 93
Clare. Suff 7D 30
Clarebrand. Dum 5B 52
Clarencefield. Dum 5E 52
Clarilaw. Bord 8C 60
Clark's Green. Surr 2J 11
Clark's Hill. Linc 7L 37
Clarkston. E Ren 4D 58
Clasheddy. High 5J 85
Clashindarroch. Abers 2D 72
Clashmore. High
nr. Dornoch 5H 79
nr. Stoer 8C 84
Clashnessie. High 8C 84
Clashnoir. Mor 3B 72
Clate. Shet 1F 90
Clathick. Per 5B 66
Clathy. Per 6C 66
Clatt. Abers 3E 72
Clatter. Powy 3J 25
Clatterford. IOW 7B 10
Clatworthy. Som 2K 7
Claudy. Derr 3D 92
Claughton. Lanc
nr. Caton 1D 40
nr. Garstang 3D 40
Claughton. Mers 1A 34
Claverdon. Warw 5K 27
Claverham. N Som 7C 18
Clavering. Essx 8A 30
Claverley. Shrp 2F 26
Claverton. Bath 7F 18
Clawdd-côch. V Glam 7K 17
Clawdd-newydd. Den 5K 33
Clawson Hill. Leics 7E 36
Clawton. Devn 6C 6
Claxby. Linc
nr. Alford 2A 38
nr. Market Rasen 8J 43
Claxton. Norf 1K 31
Claxton. N Yor 1D 42
Claybrooke Magna. Leics 3B 28
Claybrooke Parva. Leics 3B 28
Clay Common. Suff 3L 31
Clay Coton. Nptn 4C 28
Clay Cross. Derbs 3A 36
Claydon. Oxon 6B 28
Claydon. Suff 6H 31
Clay End. Herts 1L 21
Claygate. Dum 4H 53
Claygate. Kent 1D 12
Claygate. Surr 7J 21
Claygate Cross. Kent 8C 22
Clayhall. Hants 6D 10
Clayhanger. Devn 3K 7
Clayhanger. W Mid 1J 27
Clayhidon. Devn 4L 7
Clay Hill. Bris 6E 18
Clayhill. E Sus 3E 12
Clayhill. Hants 5M 9
Clayhithe. Cambs 5B 30
Clayholes. Ang 4J 67
Clay Lake. Linc 7K 37
Claylock. High 6C 86
Claypits. Glos 3F 18
Claypole. Linc 5F 36
Claythorpe. Linc 2M 37
Clayton. G Man 8G 41
Clayton. S Yor 7B 42
Clayton. Staf 5G 35
Clayton. W Sus 4K 11
Clayton. W Yor 4K 41
Clayton Green. Lanc 5D 40
Clayton-le-Moors. Lanc 4F 40
Clayton-le-Woods. Lanc 5D 40
Clayton West. W Yor 6L 41
Clayworth. Notts 1E 36
Cleadale. High 7F 68
Cleadon. Tyne 5G 55
Clearbrook. Devn 5H 5
Clearwell. Glos 3D 18
Cleasby. N Yor 4L 47
Cleat. Orkn
nr. Braehead 5D 88
nr. St Margaret's Hope 3F 86
Cleatlam. Dur 4K 47
Cleator. Cumb 3K 45
Cleator Moor. Cumb 3K 45
Cleckheaton. W Yor 5K 41
Cleedownton. Shrp 3D 26
Cleehill. Shrp 4D 26
Cleekhimin. N Lan 4F 58
Clee St Margaret. Shrp 3D 26
Cleestanton. Shrp 4D 26
Cleethorpes. NE Lin 7L 43
Cleeton St Mary. Shrp 4E 26
Cleeve. N Som 7C 18
Cleeve. Oxon 5D 20
Cleeve Hill. Glos 1H 19
Cleeve Prior. Worc 7J 27
Clehonger. Here 8C 26
Cleigh. Arg 5C 64
Cleish. Per 8D 66
Cleland. N Lan 4G 59
Clench Common. Wilts 7K 19
Clenchwarton. Norf 7B 38
Clennell. Nmbd 1C 54
Clent. Worc 4H 27
Cleobury Mortimer. Shrp 4E 26
Cleobury North. Shrp 3E 26
Clephanton. High 8J 79
Clerkhill. High 5K 85
Clestrain. Orkn 1E 86
Clevancy. Wilts 6J 19
Clevedon. N Som 6C 18
Cleveley. Oxon 1A 20
Cleveleys. Lanc 3B 40
Clevelode. Worc 7G 27
Cleverton. Wilts 5H 19
Clewer. Som 8C 18
Cley next the Sea. Norf 5G 39
Cliaid. W Isl 5C 74
Cliasmol. W Isl 3B 76
Clibberswick. Shet 2L 91
Cliburn. Cumb 3D 46
Cliddesden. Hants 1D 10
Clieves Hills. Lanc 7B 40
Cliff. Warw 2L 27
Cliffburn. Ang 3K 67
Cliffe. Medw 6D 22
Cliffe. N Yor
nr. Darlington 4L 47
nr. Selby 4D 42
Cliff End. E Sus 4E 12
Cliffe Woods. Medw 6D 22
Clifford. Here 8M 25
Clifford. W Yor 3B 42
Clifford Chambers. Warw 6K 27
Clifford's Mesne. Glos 1F 18
Cliffsend. Kent 7K 23
Clifton. Bris 6D 18
Clifton. C Beds 8J 29
Clifton. Cumb 3D 46
Clifton. Derbs 5K 35
Clifton. Devn 1F 6
Clifton. G Man 7F 40
Clifton. Lanc 4C 40
Clifton. Nmbd 3F 54
Clifton. N Yor 3K 41
Clifton. Nott 6C 36
Clifton. Oxon 8B 28
Clifton. S Yor 8C 42
Clifton. Stir 4H 65
Clifton. W Yor 5K 41
Clifton. Worc 7G 27
Clifton. York 2C 42
Clifton Campville. Staf 8L 35
Clifton Hampden. Oxon 4C 20
Clifton Hill. Worc 5F 26
Clifton Reynes. Mil 6G 29
Clifton upon Dunsmore. Warw 4C 28
Clifton upon Teme. Worc 5F 26
Cliftonville. Kent 6K 23
Cliftonville. Norf 6K 39
Climping. W Sus 5G 11
Climpy. S Lan 4H 59
Clink. Som 1F 8
Clint. N Yor 2L 41
Clint Green. Norf 8G 39
Clintmains. Bord 6D 60
Cliobh. W Isl 8D 82
Clipiau. Gwyn 1H 25
Clippesby. Norf 8L 39
Clippings Green. Norf 8G 39
Clipsham. Rut 8G 37
Clipston. Nptn 3E 28
Clipston. Notts 6D 36
Clipstone. Notts 3C 36
Clitheroe. Lanc 3F 40
Cliuthar. W Isl 4C 76
Clive. Shrp 7D 34
Clivocast. Shet 3K 91
Clixby. Linc 7H 43
Clocaenog. Den 5K 33
Clochan. Mor 7D 80
Clochforbie. Abers 8H 81
Clock Face. Mers 8D 40
Cloddiau. Powy 2M 25
Cloddymoss. Mor 7K 79
Clodock. Here 1B 18
Cloford. Som 1F 8
Clogh. ME Ant 3G 93
Clogher. M Ulst 6D 92
Cloghmills. Caus 3G 93
Clola. Abers 1K 73
Clonoe. M Ulst 5F 93
Clonvaraghan. New M 6H 93
Clophill. C Beds 8H 29
Clopton. Nptn 3H 29
Clopton Corner. Suff 6J 31
Clopton Green. Suff 6D 30
Closeburn. Dum 2C 52
Close Clark. IOM 7B 44
Closworth. Som 4D 8
Clothall. Herts 8K 29
Clotton. Ches W 3D 34
Clough. G Man 6H 41
Clough. New M 7J 93
Clough. W Yor 6J 41
Cloughey. Ards 6K 93
Clough Foot. W Yor 5H 41
Cloughton. N Yor 6H 49
Cloughton Newlands. N Yor 6H 49
Clousta. Shet 2D 90
Clouston. Orkn 8B 88
Clova. Abers 3D 72
Clova. Ang 8C 72
Clovelly. Devn 3C 6
Clovenfords. Bord 6B 60
Clovenstone. Abers 4G 73
Clovullin. High 1E 64
Clowne. Derbs 2B 36
Clows Top. Worc 4F 26
Cloy. Wrex 5B 34
Cloyfin. Caus 2F 93
Cluanie Inn. High 4A 70
Cluanie Lodge. High 4A 70
Cluddley. Telf 8E 34
Clun. Shrp 3B 26
Y Clun. Neat 4H 17
Clunas. High 1J 71
Clunbury. Shrp 3B 26
Clunderwen. Pemb 5H 15
Clune. High 3H 71
Clunes. High 7C 70
Clungunford. Shrp 4B 26
Clunie. Per 3E 66
Clunton. Shrp 3B 26
Cluny. Fife 8F 66
Clutton. Bath 8E 18
Clutton. Ches W 4C 34
Clwt-y-bont. Gwyn 4E 32
Clwydfagwyr. Mer T 4K 17
Clydach. Mon 3M 17
Clydach. Swan 4F 16
Clydach Vale. Rhon 5J 17
Clydebank. W Dun 3D 58
Clydey. Pemb 3J 15
Clyffe Pypard. Wilts 6J 19
Clynder. Arg 1M 57
Clyne. Neat 4H 17
Clynelish. High 3J 79
Clynnog-fawr. Gwyn 6D 32
Clyro. Powy 8M 25
Clyst Honiton. Devn 6J 7
Clyst Hydon. Devn 5K 7
Clyst St George. Devn 7J 7
Clyst St Lawrence. Devn 5K 7
Clyst St Mary. Devn 6J 7
Clyth. High 8D 86
Cnip. W Isl 8D 82
Cnoc Amhlaigh. W Isl 8J 83
Cnwcau. Pemb 2J 15
Cnwch Coch. Cdgn 5F 24
Coad's Green. Corn 8B 6
Coagh. M Ulst 5F 93
Coal Aston. Derbs 2A 36
Coalbrookdale. Telf 1E 26
Coalbrookvale. Blae 4L 17
Coalburn. S Lan 6G 59
Coalburns. Tyne 5E 54
Coalcleugh. Nmbd 7B 54
Coaley. Glos 3F 18
Coalford. Abers 6H 73
Coalhall. E Ayr 8C 58
Coalhill. Essx 4D 22
Coalisland. M Ulst 5F 93
Coalpit Heath. S Glo 5E 18
Coal Pool. W Mid 1J 27
Coalport. Telf 1F 26
Coalsnaughton. Clac 8C 66
Coaltown of Balgonie. Fife 8G 67
Coaltown of Wemyss. Fife 8G 67
Coalville. Leics 8B 36
Coalway. Glos 2D 18
Coanwood. Nmbd 6L 53
Coat. Som 3C 8
Coatbridge. N Lan 3F 58
Coatdyke. N Lan 3F 58
Coate. Swin 5K 19
Coate. Wilts 7J 19
Coates. Cambs 2L 29
Coates. Glos 3H 19
Coates. Linc 1G 37
Coates. W Sus 4G 11
Coatham. Red C 3C 48
Coatham Mundeville. Darl 3L 47
Cobbaton. Devn 3F 6
Coberley. Glos 2H 19
Cobhall Common. Here 8C 26
Cobham. Kent 7C 22
Cobham. Surr 8J 21
Cobnash. Here 5C 26
Coburg. Devn 8H 7
Cockayne. N Yor 6D 48
Cockayne Hatley. C Beds 7K 29
Cock Bank. Wrex 5B 34
Cock Bridge. Abers 5B 72
Cockburnspath. Bord 2E 60
Cock Clarks. Essx 3E 22
Cockenzie and Port Seton. E Lot 2B 60
Cockerham. Lanc 2C 40
Cockermouth. Cumb 8F 52
Cockernhoe. Herts 1J 21
Cockfield. Dur 3K 47
Cockfield. Suff 6F 30
Cockfosters. G Lon 4K 21
Cock Gate. Here 5C 26
Cock Green. Essx 2C 22
Cocking. W Sus 4F 10
Cocking Causeway. W Sus 4F 10
Cockington. Torb 5L 5
Cocklake. Som 1C 8
Cocklaw. Abers 1K 73
Cocklaw. Nmbd 4C 54
Cockley Beck. Cumb 4M 45
Cockley Cley. Norf 1D 30
Cockmuir. Abers 8J 81
Cockpole Green. Wok 5E 20
Cockshutford. Shrp 3D 26
Cockshutt. Shrp 7C 34
Cockthorpe. Norf 5F 38
Cockwood. Devn 7J 7
Cockyard. Derbs 2J 35
Cockyard. Here 8C 26
Codda. Corn 8A 6
Coddenham. Suff 6H 31
Coddenham Green. Suff 6H 31

124 A-Z Great Britain Road Atlas

Coddington—Cwmtillery

Coddington. *Ches W* 4C 34
Coddington. *Here* 7F 26
Coddington. *Notts* 4F 36
Codford. *Wilts* 2H 9
Codicote. *Herts* 2K 21
Codmore Hill. *W Sus* 3H 11
Codnor. *Derbs* 5B 36
Codrington. *S Glo* 6F 18
Codsall. *Staf* 1G 27
Codsall Wood. *Staf* 1G 27
Coed Duon. *Cphy* 5L 17
Coedely. *Rhon* 6K 17
Coedglasson. *Powy* 6K 25
Coedkernew. *Newp* 5A 18
Coed Morgan. *Mon* 2B 18
Coedpoeth. *Wrex* 4A 34
Coedway. *Powy* 8B 34
Coed-y-bryn. *Cdgn* 2K 15
Coed-y-paen. *Mon* 4B 18
Coed Ystumgwern. *Gwyn* 8E 32
Coelbren. *Powy* 3H 17
Coffinswell. *Devn* 5L 5
Cofton Hackett. *Worc* 4J 27
Cogan. *V Glam* 7L 17
Cogenhoe. *Nptn* 5F 28
Cogges. *Oxon* 3A 20
Coggeshall. *Essx* 1E 22
Coggeshall Hamlet. *Essx* 1E 22
Coggins Mill. *E Sus* 3B 12
Coignafearn Lodge. *High* 4G 71
Coig Peighinnean. *W Isl* 5J 83
Coig Peighinnean Bhuirgh.
  W Isl 6H 83
Coilleag. *W Isl* 4D 74
Coillemore. *High* 6G 79
Coillore. *High* 2E 68
Coire an Fhuarain. *W Isl* 8F 82
Coity. *B'end* 6J 17
Cokhay Green. *Derbs* 7L 35
Col. *W Isl* 7H 83
Colaboll. *High* 2F 78
Colan. *Corn* 5A 4
Colaton Raleigh. *Devn* 7K 7
Colbost. *High* 1D 68
Colburn. *N Yor* 6K 47
Colby. *Cumb* 3E 46
Colby. *IOM* 7B 44
Colby. *Norf* 6J 39
Colchester. *Essx* 1G 23
Cold Ash. *W Ber* 7C 20
Cold Ashby. *Nptn* 4D 28
Cold Ashton. *S Glo* 6F 18
Cold Aston. *Glos* 2K 19
Coldbackie. *High* 6J 85
Cold Blow. *Pemb* 5H 15
Cold Brayfield. *Mil* 6G 29
Cold Cotes. *N Yor* 8F 46
Coldean. *Brig* 5L 11
Coldeast. *Devn* 8H 7
Colden. *W Yor* 5H 41
Colden Common. *Hants* 3B 10
Coldfair Green. *Suff* 5L 31
Coldham. *Cambs* 1M 29
Coldham. *Staf* 1G 27
Cold Hanworth. *Linc* 1H 37
Cold Harbour. *Dors* 6H 9
Coldharbour. *Corn* 4L 3
Coldharbour. *Glos* 3D 18
Coldharbour. *Kent* 8B 22
Coldharbour. *Surr* 1J 11
Cold Hatton. *Telf* 7E 34
Cold Hatton Heath. *Telf* 7E 34
Cold Hesledon. *Dur* 7H 55
Cold Hiendley. *W Yor* 6A 42
Cold Higham. *Nptn* 6D 28
Coldingham. *Bord* 3G 61
Cold Kirby. *N Yor* 7C 48
Coldmeece. *Staf* 6G 35
Cold Northcott. *Corn* 7B 6
Cold Norton. *Essx* 3E 22
Cold Overton. *Leics* 8F 36
Coldrain. *Per* 7D 66
Coldred. *Kent* 1J 13
Coldridge. *Devn* 5F 6
Cold Row. *Lanc* 3B 40
Coldstream. *Bord* 5F 60
Coldwaltham. *W Sus* 4H 11
Coldwell. *Here* 8C 26
Coldwells. *Abers* 2L 73
Coldwells Croft. *Abers* 3E 72
Cole. *Shet* 1D 90
Cole. *Som* 2E 8
Colebatch. *Shrp* 3B 26
Colebrook. *Devn* 5K 7
Colebrooke. *Devn* 6G 7
Coleburn. *Mor* 8B 80
Coleby. *Linc* 3G 37
Coleby. *N Lin* 6F 42
Cole End. *Warw* 3L 27
Coleford. *Devn* 5G 7
Coleford. *Glos* 2D 18
Coleford. *Som* 1E 8
Colegate End. *Norf* 3H 31
Cole Green. *Herts* 2K 21
Cole Henley. *Hants* 8B 20
Colehill. *Dors* 5J 9
Coleman Green. *Herts* 2J 21
Coleman's Hatch. *E Sus* 2A 12
Colemere. *Shrp* 6C 34
Colemore. *Hants* 2E 10
Colemore Green. *Shrp* 2F 26
Coleorton. *Leics* 8B 36
Coleraine. *Caus* 2F 93
Colerne. *Wilts* 6G 19
Colesbourne. *Glos* 2J 19
Colesden. *Bed* 6J 29
Coles Green. *Worc* 6F 26
Coleshill. *Buck* 4G 21
Coleshill. *Oxon* 4L 19
Coleshill. *Warw* 3L 27
Colestocks. *Devn* 5K 7
Colethrop. *Glos* 2G 19
Coley. *Bath* 8D 18
Colgate. *W Sus* 2K 11
Colinsburgh. *Fife* 7H 67
Colinton. *Edin* 3L 59
Colintraive. *Arg* 2K 57
Colkirk. *Norf* 7F 38
Collace. *Per* 4F 66
Collam. *W Isl* 4C 76
Collaton. *Devn* 8K 5
Collaton St Mary. *Torb* 5L 5
College of Roseisle. *Mor* 7M 79
Collessie. *Fife* 6F 66
Collier Row. *G Lon* 4A 22
Colliers End. *Herts* 1L 21
Collier Street. *Kent* 1D 12
Colliery Row. *Tyne* 7G 55
Collieston. *Abers* 3K 73
Collin. *Dum* 4E 52
Collingbourne Ducis. *Wilts* 8L 19
Collingbourne Kingston.
  Wilts 8L 19
Collingham. *Notts* 3F 36
Collingham. *W Yor* 3A 42
Collingtree. *Nptn* 6E 28
Collins Green. *Warr* 8D 40
Collins Green. *Worc* 6F 26
Colliston. *Ang* 3K 67
Colliton. *Devn* 5K 7
Collydean. *Fife* 7F 66
Collyweston. *Nptn* 1G 29
Colmonell. *S Ayr* 3G 51
Colmworth. *Bed* 6J 29
Colnbrook. *Slo* 6H 21
Colne. *Cambs* 4L 29
Colne. *Lanc* 3G 41
Colne Engaine. *Essx* 8E 30
Colney. *Norf* 1H 31
Colney Heath. *Herts* 3K 21
Colney Street. *Herts* 3J 21
Coln Rogers. *Glos* 3J 19
Coln St Aldwyns. *Glos* 3K 19
Coln St Dennis. *Glos* 2J 19
Colpitts Grange. *Nmbd* 6C 54
Colpy. *Abers* 2F 72
Colscott. *Devn* 4C 6
Colsterdale. *N Yor* 7K 47
Colsterworth. *Linc* 7G 37
Colston Bassett. *Notts* 6E 36
Colstoun House. *E Lot* 2C 60
Coltfield. *Mor* 7M 79
Colthouse. *Cumb* 6B 46
Coltishall. *Norf* 8J 39
Coltness. *N Lan* 4G 59
Colton. *Cumb* 7B 46
Colton. *Norf* 1H 31
Colton. *N Yor* 3C 42
Colton. *Staf* 7J 35
Colton. *W Yor* 4A 42
Colt's Hill. *Kent* 1C 12
Col Uarach. *W Isl* 8H 83
Colvend. *Dum* 6C 52
Colvister. *Shet* 4K 91
Colwall. *Here* 7F 26
Colwall Green. *Here* 7F 26
Colwell. *Nmbd* 4C 54
Colwich. *Staf* 7J 35
Colwick. *Notts* 5D 36
Colwinston. *V Glam* 7J 17
Colworth. *W Sus* 5G 11
Colwyn Bay. *Cnwy* 3H 33
Colyford. *Devn* 6A 8
Colyton. *Devn* 6M 7
Combe. *Devn* 5K 5
Combe. *Here* 5B 26
Combe. *Oxon* 2B 20
Combe. *W Ber* 7A 20
Combe Almer. *Dors* 6H 9
Combebow. *Devn* 7D 6
Combe Down. *Bath* 7F 18
Combe Fishacre. *Devn* 5L 5
Combe Florey. *Som* 2L 7
Combe Hay. *Bath* 7F 18
Combeinteignhead. *Devn* 8J 7
Combe Martin. *Devn* 1E 6
Combe Moor. *Here* 5B 26
Comber. *Ards* 5J 93
Combe Raleigh. *Devn* 5L 7
Comberbach. *Ches W* 2E 34
Comberford. *Staf* 1K 27
Comberton. *Cambs* 6L 29
Comberton. *Here* 5C 26
Combe St Nicholas. *Som* 4B 8
Combpyne. *Devn* 6A 8
Combridge. *Staf* 6J 35
Combrook. *Warw* 6M 27
Combs. *Derbs* 2J 35
Combs. *Suff* 6G 31
Combs Ford. *Suff* 6G 31
Combwich. *Som* 1A 8
Comers. *Abers* 5F 72
Comhampton. *Worc* 5G 27
Comins Coch. *Cdgn* 4F 24
Comley. *Shrp* 2C 26
Commercial End. *Cambs* 5B 30
Commins. *Powy* 8L 33
Commins Coch. *Powy* 2H 25
The Common. *Wilts*
  nr. Salisbury 2L 9
  nr. Swindon 5J 19
Commondale. *N Yor* 4D 48
Common End. *Cumb* 2K 45
Common Hill. *Here* 8D 26
Common Moor. *Corn* 5E 4
Common Side. *Derbs* 2M 35
Commonside. *Ches W* 2D 34
Commonside. *Derbs* 5L 35
Compstall. *G Man* 8H 41
Compton. *Devn* 5L 5
Compton. *Hants* 3B 10
Compton. *Staf* 3G 27
Compton. *Surr* 1G 11
Compton. *W Ber* 6C 20
Compton. *W Sus* 4E 10
Compton. *Wilts* 8K 19
Compton Abbas. *Dors* 4G 9
Compton Abdale. *Glos* 2J 19
Compton Bassett. *Wilts* 6J 19
Compton Beauchamp. *Oxon* 5L 19
Compton Bishop. *Som* 8B 18
Compton Chamberlayne.
  Wilts 3J 9
Compton Dando. *Bath* 7E 18
Compton Dundon. *Som* 2C 8
Compton Greenfield. *S Glo* 5D 18
Compton Martin. *Bath* 8D 18
Compton Pauncefoot. *Som* 3E 8
Compton Valence. *Dors* 6D 8
Comrie. *Fife* 1J 59
Comrie. *Per* 5A 66
Conaglen. *High* 1E 64
Conchra. *Arg* 1K 57
Conchra. *High* 3K 69
Conder Green. *Lanc* 2C 40
Conderton. *Worc* 8H 27
Condicote. *Glos* 1K 19
Condorrat. *N Lan* 2F 58
Condover. *Shrp* 1C 26
Coneyhurst. *W Sus* 3J 11
Coneyisland. *New M* 7J 93
Coneysthorpe. *N Yor* 8E 48
Coneythorpe. *N Yor* 2A 42
Coney Weston. *Suff* 4F 30
Conford. *Hants* 2F 10
Congdon's Shop. *Corn* 8B 6
Congerstone. *Leics* 1A 28
Congham. *Norf* 7D 38
Congleton. *Ches E* 3G 35
Congl-y-wal. *Gwyn* 6G 33
Congresbury. *N Som* 7C 18
Congreve. *Staf* 8H 35
Conham. *S Glo* 6E 18
Conicaval. *Mor* 8K 79
Coningsby. *Linc* 4K 37
Conington. *Cambs*
  nr. Fenstanton 5L 29
  nr. Sawtry 3J 29
Conisbrough. *S Yor* 8C 42
Conisby. *Arg* 3B 56
Conisholme. *Linc* 8M 43
Coniston. *Cumb* 6B 46
Coniston. *E Yor* 4J 43
Coniston Cold. *N Yor* 2H 41
Conistone. *N Yor* 1H 41
Conlig. *Ards* 5J 93
Connah's Quay. *Flin* 2A 34
Connel. *Arg* 4D 64
Connel Park. *E Ayr* 8E 58
Connista. *High* 6F 76
Connor. *ME Ant* 4G 93
Connor Downs. *Corn* 5J 3
Conock. *Wilts* 8J 19
Conon Bridge. *High* 8F 78
Cononley. *N Yor* 3H 41
Cononsyth. *Ang* 3J 67
Conordan. *High* 2G 69
Consall. *Staf* 5H 35
Consett. *Dur* 6E 54
Constable Burton. *N Yor* 6K 47
Constantine. *Corn* 6L 3
Constantine Bay. *Corn* 4A 4
Contin. *High* 8E 78
Contullich. *High* 6G 79
Conwy. *Cnwy* 3G 33
Conyer. *Kent* 7F 22
Conyer's Green. *Suff* 5E 30
Cooden. *E Sus* 5D 12
Cooil. *IOM* 7C 44
Cookbury. *Devn* 5D 6
Cookbury Wick. *Devn* 5C 6
Cookham. *Wind* 5F 20
Cookham Dean. *Wind* 5F 20
Cookham Rise. *Wind* 5F 20
Cookhill. *Worc* 6J 27
Cookley. *Suff* 4K 31
Cookley. *Worc* 3G 27
Cookley Green. *Oxon* 4D 20
Cookney. *Abers* 6H 73
Cooksbridge. *E Sus* 4M 11
Cooksey Green. *Worc* 5H 27
Cookshill. *Staf* 5H 35
Cooksmill Green. *Essx* 3C 22
Cookstown. *M Ulst* 5F 93
Coolham. *W Sus* 3J 11
Cooling. *Medw* 6D 22
Cooling Street. *Medw* 6D 22
Coombe. *Corn*
  nr. Bude 4B 6
  nr. St Austell 6B 4
  nr. Truro 4M 3
Coombe. *Devn*
  nr. Sidmouth 6L 7
  nr. Teignmouth 8J 7
Coombe. *Glos* 4F 18
Coombe. *Hants* 3D 10
Coombe. *Wilts* 8K 19
Coombe Bissett. *Wilts* 3K 9
Coombe Hill. *Glos* 1G 19
Coombe Keynes. *Dors* 7G 9
Coombes. *W Sus* 5J 11
Coopersale. *Essx* 3A 22
Coopersale Street. *Essx* 3A 22
Cooper's Corner. *Kent* 1A 12
Cooper Street. *Kent* 8K 23
Cootham. *W Sus* 4H 11
Copalder Corner. *Cambs* 2L 29
Copdock. *Suff* 7H 31
Copford. *Essx* 1F 22
Copford Green. *Essx* 1F 22
Copgrove. *N Yor* 1M 41
Copister. *Shet* 6J 91
Cople. *Bed* 7J 29
Copley. *Dur* 3J 47
Coplow Dale. *Derbs* 2K 35
Copmanthorpe. *York* 3C 42
Copp. *Lanc* 4C 40
Coppathorne. *Corn* 5B 6
Coppenhall. *Ches E* 4F 34
Coppenhall. *Staf* 8H 35
Coppenhall Moss. *Ches E* 4F 34
Copperhouse. *Corn* 5J 3
Coppicegate. *Shrp* 3F 26
Coppingford. *Cambs* 3J 29
Copplestone. *Devn* 5G 7
Coppull. *Lanc* 6D 40
Coppull Moor. *Lanc* 6D 40
Copsale. *W Sus* 3J 11
Copshaw Holm. *Bord* 3J 53
Copster Green. *Lanc* 4E 40
Copston Magna. *Warw* 3B 28
Copt Green. *Warw* 5K 27
Copthall Green. *Essx* 3M 21
Copt Heath. *W Mid* 4K 27
Copt Hewick. *N Yor* 8M 47
Copthill. *Dur* 7B 54
Copthorne. *W Sus* 2L 11
Coptiviney. *Shrp* 6C 34
Copy's Green. *Norf* 6F 38
Copythorne. *Hants* 4M 9
Corbridge. *Nmbd* 5C 54
Corby. *Nptn* 3F 28
Corby Glen. *Linc* 7G 37
Cordon. *N Ayr* 6K 57
Coreley. *Shrp* 4E 26
Corfe. *Som* 4M 7
Corfe Castle. *Dors* 7H 9
Corfe Mullen. *Dors* 6H 9
Corfton. *Shrp* 3C 26
Corgarff. *Abers* 5B 72
Corhampton. *Hants* 3D 10
Corkey. *Caus* 2G 93
Corlae. *Dum* 2A 52
Corlannau. *Neat* 5G 17
Corley. *Warw* 3M 27
Corley Ash. *Warw* 3L 27
Corley Moor. *Warw* 3L 27
Cormiston. *S Lan* 6J 59
Cornaa. *IOM* 6D 44
Cornaigbeg. *Arg* 3E 62
Cornaigmore. *Arg*
  on Coll 1H 63
  on Tiree 3E 62
Corner Row. *Lanc* 4C 40
Corney. *Cumb* 5L 45
Cornforth. *Dur* 8G 55
Cornhill. *Abers* 8E 80
Cornhill. *High* 4F 78
Cornhill-on-Tweed. *Nmbd* 6F 60
Cornholme. *W Yor* 5H 41
Cornish Hall End. *Essx* 8C 30
Cornquoy. *Orkn* 1G 87
Cornriggs. *Dur* 7B 54
Cornsay. *Dur* 7E 54
Cornsay Colliery. *Dur* 7E 54
Corntown. *High* 8F 78
Corntown. *V Glam* 7J 17
Cornwall Airport Newquay.
  Corn 5A 4
Cornwell. *Oxon* 1L 19
Cornwood. *Devn* 6J 5
Cornworthy. *Devn* 6L 5
Corpach. *High* 8A 70
Corpusty. *Norf* 7H 39
Corra. *Dum* 5C 52
Corran. *High*
  nr. Arnisdale 1E 64
  nr. Fort William 5K 69
Corrany. *IOM* 6D 44
Corribeg. *High* 8L 69
Corrie. *N Ayr* 5K 57
Corrie Common. *Dum* 3G 53
Corriecravie. *N Ayr* 7J 57
Corriekinloch. *High* 1D 78
Corriemoillie. *High* 7D 78
Corrievarkie Lodge. *Per* 8F 70
Corrievorrie. *High* 3H 71
Corrigall. *Orkn* 8C 88
Corrimony. *High* 2D 70
Corringham. *Linc* 8F 42
Corringham. *Thur* 5D 22
Corris. *Gwyn* 2G 25
Corris Uchaf. *Gwyn* 2G 25
Corrour Shooting Lodge.
  High 1J 65
Corry. *High* 3H 69
Corrybrough. *High* 3J 71
Corrygills. *N Ayr* 6K 57
Corry of Ardnagrask. *High* 1F 70
Corsback. *High*
  nr. Dunnet 4D 86
  nr. Halkirk 6D 86
Corscombe. *Dors* 5D 8
Corse. *Abers* 1F 72
Corse. *Glos* 1F 18
Corsehill. *Abers* 8J 81
Corse Lawn. *Worc* 8G 27
Corse of Kinnoir. *Abers* 1E 72
Corsham. *Wilts* 6G 19
Corsley. *Wilts* 1G 9
Corsley Heath. *Wilts* 1G 9
Corsock. *Dum* 4B 52
Corston. *Bath* 7E 18
Corston. *Wilts* 5H 19
Corstorphine. *Edin* 2L 59
Cortachy. *Ang* 2G 67
Corton. *Suff* 2M 31
Corton. *Wilts* 1H 9
Corton Denham. *Som* 3E 8
Corwar House. *S Ayr* 3H 51
Corwen. *Den* 6K 33
Coryates. *Dors* 7E 8
Coryton. *Devn* 7D 6
Coryton. *Thur* 5D 22
Cosby. *Leics* 2C 28
Coscote. *Oxon* 5C 20
Coseley. *W Mid* 2H 27
Cosgrove. *Nptn* 7E 28
Cosham. *Port* 5D 10
Cosheston. *Pemb* 6G 15
Coskills. *N Lin* 6H 43
Cosmeston. *V Glam* 8L 17
Cossall. *Notts* 5B 36
Cossington. *Leics* 8D 36
Cossington. *Som* 1B 8
Costa. *Orkn* 7C 88
Costessey. *Norf* 8H 39
Costock. *Notts* 7C 36
Coston. *Leics* 7F 36
Coston. *Norf* 1G 31
Cote. *Oxon* 3A 20
Cotebrook. *Ches W* 3D 34
Cotehill. *Cumb* 6J 53
Cotes. *Cumb* 7C 46
Cotes. *Leics* 7C 36
Cotes. *Staf* 6G 35
Cotesbach. *Leics* 3C 28
Cotes Heath. *Staf* 6G 35
Cotford St Luke. *Som* 3L 7
Cotgrave. *Notts* 6D 36
Cothal. *Abers* 4H 73
Cotham. *Notts* 5E 36
Cothelstone. *Som* 2L 7
Cotheridge. *Worc* 6F 26
Cotherstone. *Dur* 4J 47
Cothill. *Oxon* 4B 20
Cotland. *Mon* 3D 18
Cotleigh. *Devn* 5M 7
Cotmanhay. *Derbs* 5B 36
Coton. *Cambs* 6M 29
Coton. *Nptn* 4D 28
Coton. *Staf*
  nr. Gnosall 7G 35
  nr. Stone 6H 35
  nr. Tamworth 1K 27
Coton Clanford. *Staf* 7G 35
Coton Hayes. *Staf* 6H 35
Coton Hill. *Shrp* 8C 34
Coton in the Clay. *Staf* 7K 35
Coton in the Elms. *Derbs* 8L 35
Cotonwood. *Shrp* 6D 34
Cotonwood. *Staf* 7G 35
Cott. *Devn* 5K 5
Cott. *Orkn* 7F 88
Cottam. *E Yor* 1G 43
Cottam. *Lanc* 4D 40
Cottam. *Notts* 2F 36
Cottartown. *High* 2L 71
Cottarville. *Nptn* 5E 28
Cottenham. *Cambs* 5A 30
Cotterdale. *N Yor* 6G 47
Cottered. *Herts* 1L 21
Cotterstock. *Nptn* 2H 29
Cottesbrooke. *Nptn* 4E 28
Cottesmore. *Rut* 8G 37
Cotteylands. *Devn* 4J 7
Cottingham. *E Yor* 4H 43
Cottingham. *Nptn* 2F 28
Cottingley. *W Yor* 4K 41
Cottisford. *Oxon* 8C 28
Cotton. *Staf* 5J 35
Cotton. *Suff* 5G 31
Cotton End. *Bed* 7H 29
Cottown. *Abers* 1H 73
Cotts. *Devn* 5G 5
Cotwalton. *Staf* 6H 35
Couch's Mill. *Corn* 6D 4
Coughton. *Here* 1D 18
Coughton. *Warw* 5J 27
Coulags. *High* 1L 69
Coulby Newham. *Midd* 4C 48
Coulderton. *Cumb* 4J 45
Coulin Lodge. *High* 8M 77
Coull. *Abers* 5E 72
Coulport. *Arg* 1M 57
Coulsdon. *G Lon* 8K 21
Coulston. *Wilts* 8H 19
Coulter. *S Lan* 6J 59
Coultings. *Som* 1M 7
Coulton. *N Yor* 8D 48
Cound. *Shrp* 1D 26
Coundon. *Dur* 3L 47
Coundon Grange. *Dur* 3L 47
Countersett. *N Yor* 7H 47
Countess. *Wilts* 1K 9
Countess Cross. *Essx* 8E 30
Countesthorpe. *Leics* 2C 28
Countisbury. *Devn* 1G 7
Coupar Angus. *Per* 3F 66
Coupe Green. *Lanc* 5D 40
Coupland. *Cumb* 4F 46
Coupland. *Nmbd* 6G 61
Cour. *Arg* 5H 57
Courance. *Dum* 2E 52
Court-at-Street. *Kent* 2G 13
Courteachan. *High* 6H 69
Courteenhall. *Nptn* 6E 28
Court Henry. *Carm* 2E 16
Courtsend. *Essx* 4G 23
Courtway. *Som* 2M 7
Cousland. *Midl* 3A 60
Cousley Wood. *E Sus* 2C 12
Coustonn. *Arg* 2K 57
Cove. *Arg* 1M 57
Cove. *Devn* 4J 7
Cove. *Hants* 8F 20
Cove. *High* 4K 77
Cove. *Bord* 2E 60
Cove Bay. *Aber* 5J 73
Covehithe. *Suff* 3M 31
Coven. *Staf* 1H 27
Coveney. *Cambs* 3A 30
Covenham St Bartholomew.
  Linc 8L 43
Covenham St Mary. *Linc* 8L 43
Coven Heath. *Staf* 1H 27
Coventry. *W Mid* 108 (4M 27)
Coverack. *Corn* 7L 3
Coverham. *N Yor* 7K 47
Covesea. *Mor* 6A 80
Covingham. *Swin* 5K 19
Covington. *Cambs* 4H 29
Covington. *S Lan* 6H 59
Cowan Bridge. *Lanc* 8E 46
Cowan Head. *Cumb* 6C 46
Cowbar. *Red C* 4E 48
Cowbeech. *E Sus* 4C 12
Cowbit. *Linc* 8K 37
Cowbridge. *V Glam* 7J 17
Cowden. *Kent* 1A 12
Cowdenbeath. *Fife* 8E 66
Cowdenburn. *Bord* 4L 59
Cowdenend. *Fife* 8E 66
Cowers Lane. *Derbs* 5M 35
Cowes. *IOW* 6B 10
Cowesby. *N Yor* 7B 48
Cowfold. *W Sus* 3K 11
Cowfords. *Mor* 7C 80
Cowgill. *Cumb* 7F 46
Cowie. *Abers* 7H 73
Cowie. *Stir* 1G 59
Cowlam. *E Yor* 1G 43
Cowley. *Devn* 6J 7
Cowley. *Glos* 2H 19
Cowley. *G Lon* 5H 21
Cowley. *Oxon* 3C 20
Cowley. *Staf* 8G 35
Cowleymoor. *Devn* 4J 7
Cowling. *Lanc* 6D 40
Cowling. *N Yor*
  nr. Bedale 7L 47
  nr. Glusburn 3H 41
Cowlinge. *Suff* 6D 30
Cowmes. *W Yor* 6K 41
Cowpe. *Lanc* 5G 41
Cowpen. *Nmbd* 3F 54
Cowpen Bewley. *Stoc T* 3B 48
Cowplain. *Hants* 4D 10
Cowshill. *Dur* 7B 54
Cowslip Green. *N Som* 7C 18
Cowstrandburn. *Fife* 8D 66
Cowthorpe. *N Yor* 2B 42
Coxall. *Here* 4B 26
Coxbank. *Ches E* 5E 34
Coxbench. *Derbs* 5A 36
Cox Common. *Suff* 3L 31
Coxford. *Norf* 7E 38
Cox Green. *Surr* 2H 11
Cox Green. *Tyne* 6G 55
Coxgreen. *Staf* 3G 27
Coxheath. *Kent* 8D 22
Coxhoe. *Dur* 8G 55
Coxley. *Som* 1D 8
Coxwold. *N Yor* 8C 48
Coychurch. *B'end* 6J 17
Coylton. *S Ayr* 8C 58
Coylumbridge. *High* 4K 71
Coynach. *Abers* 5D 72
Coynachie. *Abers* 2D 72
Coytrahen. *B'end* 6H 17
Crabbs Cross. *Worc* 5J 27
Crabgate. *Norf* 7G 39
Crab Orchard. *Dors* 5J 9
Crabtree. *W Sus* 3K 11
Crabtree Green. *Wrex* 5B 34
Crackaig. *High* 2K 79
Crackenthorpe. *Cumb* 3E 46
Crackington Haven. *Corn* 2D 4
Crackley. *Staf* 4G 35
Crackley. *Warw* 4L 27
Crackleybank. *Shrp* 8F 34
Crackpot. *N Yor* 6H 47
Cracoe. *N Yor* 1H 41
Craddock. *Devn* 4K 7
Cradhlastadh. *W Isl* 8D 82
Cradley. *Here* 7F 26
Cradley. *W Mid* 3H 27
Cradoc. *Powy* 1K 17
Crafthole. *Corn* 6F 4
Crafton. *Buck* 2F 20
Cragabus. *Arg* 5C 56
Crag Foot. *Lanc* 8C 46
Craggan. *High* 3L 71
Cragganmore. *Mor* 2A 72
Cragganvallie. *High* 2F 70
Craggie. *High* 2J 79
Craggiemore. *High* 2H 71
Cragg Vale. *W Yor* 5J 41
Craghead. *Dur* 6F 54
Crai. *Powy* 2H 17
Craichie. *Ang* 3J 67
Craig. *Arg* 4E 64
Craig. *Dum* 4A 52
Craig. *High*
  nr. Achnashellach 1M 69
  nr. Lower Diabaig 7J 77
  nr. Stromeferry 2K 69
Craiganour Lodge. *Per* 2L 65
Craigavon. *Arm* 6G 93
Craigbrack. *Arg* 8F 64
Craig-Cefn-Parc. *Swan* 4F 16
Craigdallie. *Per* 5F 66
Craigdam. *Abers* 2H 73
Craigdarragh. *Derr* 3D 92
Craigdarroch. *E Ayr* 1M 51
Craigdarroch. *High* 8E 78
Craigdhu. *High* 1E 70
Craigearn. *Abers* 4G 73
Craigellachie. *Mor* 1B 72
Craigend. *Per* 5E 66
Craigendoran. *Arg* 1B 58
Craigends. *Ren* 3C 58
Craigenputtock. *Dum* 3B 52
Craigens. *E Ayr* 8D 58
Craighall. *Edin* 2K 59
Craighead. *Fife* 6K 67
Craighouse. *Arg* 3E 56
Craigie. *Abers* 4J 73
Craigie. *D'dee* 4H 67
Craigie. *Per*
  nr. Blairgowrie 3E 66
  nr. Perth 5E 66
Craigie. *S Ayr* 6C 58
Craigielaw. *E Lot* 2B 60
Craiglemine. *Dum* 8K 51
Craig-llwyn. *Shrp* 8M 33
Craiglockhart. *Edin* 2L 59
Craig Lodge. *Arg* 2K 57
Craigmalloch. *E Ayr* 2K 51
Craigmaud. *Abers* 8H 81
Craigmill. *Stir* 8B 66
Craigmillar. *Edin* 2L 59
Craigmore. *Arg* 3L 57
Craigmuie. *Dum* 3B 52
Craignair. *Dum* 5C 52
Craignant. *Shrp* 6A 34
Craigneuk. *N Lan*
  nr. Airdrie 3F 58
  nr. Motherwell 4F 58
Craignure. *Arg* 4B 64
Craigo. *Ang* 1K 67
Craigrory. *High* 1G 71
Craigrothie. *Fife* 6G 67
Craigs. *Dum* 4G 53
The Craigs. *High* 4E 78
Craigshill. *W Lot* 3J 59
Craigton. *Aber* 5H 73
Craigton. *Abers* 5G 73
Craigton. *Ang*
  nr. Carnoustie 4J 67
  nr. Kirriemuir 2G 67
Craigton. *High* 1G 71
Craigtown. *High* 6L 85
Craig-y-Duke. *Neat* 4G 17
Craig-y-nos. *Powy* 3H 17
Craik. *Bord* 1H 53
Crail. *Fife* 7K 67
Crailing. *Bord* 7D 60
Crailinghall. *Bord* 7D 60
Crakehill. *N Yor* 8B 48
Crakemarsh. *Staf* 6J 35
Crambe. *N Yor* 1E 42
Crambeck. *N Yor* 1E 42
Cramlington. *Nmbd* 4F 54
Cramond. *Edin* 2K 59
Cramond Bridge. *Edin* 2K 59
Cranage. *Ches E* 3F 34
Cranagh. *Derr* 4D 92
Cranberry. *Staf* 6G 35
Cranborne. *Dors* 4J 9
Cranbourne. *Brac* 6G 21
Cranbrook. *Devn* 6K 7
Cranbrook. *Kent* 2D 12
Cranbrook Common. *Kent* 2D 12
Crane Moor. *S Yor* 7M 41
Crane's Corner. *Norf* 8F 38
Cranfield. *C Beds* 7G 29
Cranford. *G Lon* 6J 21
Cranford St Andrew. *Nptn* 4G 29
Cranford St John. *Nptn* 4G 29
Cranham. *Glos* 2G 19
Cranham. *G Lon* 5B 22
Crank. *Mers* 8D 40
Cranleigh. *Surr* 2H 11
Cranley. *Suff* 4H 31
Cranloch. *Mor* 8B 80
Cranmer Green. *Suff* 4G 31
Cranmore. *IOW* 6B 10
Cranmore. *Linc* 1J 29
Crannich. *Arg* 3L 63
Crannoch. *Mor* 8D 80
Cranoe. *Leics* 2E 28
Cransford. *Suff* 5K 31
Cranshaws. *Bord* 3D 60
Cranstal. *IOM* 4D 44
Crantock. *Corn* 2L 3
Cranwell. *Linc* 5H 37
Cranwich. *Norf* 2D 30
Cranworth. *Norf* 1F 30
Craobh Haven. *Arg* 7B 64
Craobhnaclag. *High* 1E 70
Crapstone. *Devn* 5H 5
Crarae. *Arg* 8D 64
Crask. *High*
  nr. Bettyhill 5K 85
  nr. Lairg 1F 78
Crask of Aigas. *High* 1E 70
Craster. *Nmbd* 7K 61
Craswall. *Here* 8A 26
Cratfield. *Suff* 4K 31
Crathes. *Abers* 6G 73
Crathie. *Abers* 6B 72
Crathie. *High* 6F 70
Crathorne. *N Yor* 5B 48
Craven Arms. *Shrp* 3C 26
Crawcrook. *Tyne* 5E 54
Crawford. *Lanc* 7C 40
Crawford. *S Lan* 7H 59
Crawforddyke. *S Lan* 4G 59
Crawfordjohn. *S Lan* 7G 59
Crawfordsburn. *Ards* 4J 93
Crawick. *Dum* 8F 58
Crawley. *Devn* 5A 8
Crawley. *Hants* 2B 10
Crawley. *Oxon* 2M 19
Crawley. *W Sus* 2K 11
Crawley Down. *W Sus* 2L 11
Crawley End. *Essx* 7M 29
Crawley Side. *Dur* 7C 54
Crawshawbooth. *Lanc* 5G 41
Crawton. *Abers* 7H 73
Cray. *N Yor* 8H 47
Cray. *Per* 1E 66
Crayford. *G Lon* 6B 22
Crayke. *N Yor* 8C 48
Craymere Beck. *Norf* 6G 39
Crays Hill. *Essx* 4D 22
Cray's Pond. *Oxon* 5D 20
Crazies Hill. *Wok* 5E 20
Creacombe. *Devn* 4H 7
Creagan. *Arg* 3D 64
Creag Aoil. *High* 8B 70
Creag Ghoraidh. *W Isl* 1D 74
Creaguaineach Lodge. *High* 1H 65
Creamore Bank. *Shrp* 6D 34
Creaton. *Nptn* 4E 28
Creca. *Dum* 4G 53
Credenhill. *Here* 7C 26
Crediton. *Devn* 5H 7
Creebridge. *Dum* 5K 51
Creech. *Dors* 7H 9
Creech Heathfield. *Som* 3A 8
Creech St Michael. *Som* 3A 8
Creed. *Corn* 7B 4
Creekmoor. *Pool* 6H 9
Creekmouth. *G Lon* 5A 22
Creeting St Mary. *Suff* 6G 31
Creeting St Peter. *Suff* 6G 31
Creeton. *Linc* 7H 37
Creetown. *Dum* 6K 51
Creggan. *Ferm* 5E 92
Creggan. *New M* 7F 93
Creggans. *Arg* 7E 64
Cregneash. *IOM* 8A 44
Cregrina. *Powy* 7L 25
Creich. *Arg* 5J 63
Creich. *Fife* 5G 67
Creighton. *Staf* 6J 35
Creigiau. *Card* 6K 17
Cremyll. *Corn* 6G 5
Crendell. *Dors* 4J 9
Crepkill. *High* 1F 68
Cressage. *Shrp* 1D 26
Cressbrook. *Derbs* 2K 35
Cresselly. *Pemb* 6G 15
Cressing. *Essx* 1D 22
Cresswell. *Nmbd* 2F 54
Cresswell. *Staf* 6H 35
Cresswell Quay. *Pemb* 6G 15
Creswell. *Derbs* 2C 36
Creswell Green. *Staf* 8J 35
Cretingham. *Suff* 5J 31
Crewe. *Ches E* 4F 34
Crewe-by-Farndon. *Ches W* 4C 34
Crewgreen. *Powy* 8B 34
Crewkerne. *Som* 5C 8
Crews Hill. *G Lon* 3L 21
Crewton. *Derb* 6A 36
Crianlarich. *Stir* 5H 65
Cribbs Causeway. *S Glo* 5D 18
Cribyn. *Cdgn* 1M 15
Criccieth. *Gwyn* 7D 32
Crich. *Derbs* 4A 36
Crichton. *Midl* 3A 60
Crick. *Mon* 4C 18
Crick. *Nptn* 4C 28
Crickadarn. *Powy* 8K 25
Cricket Hill. *Hants* 7F 20
Cricket Malherbie. *Som* 4B 8
Cricket St Thomas. *Som* 5B 8
Crickham. *Som* 1C 8
Crickheath. *Shrp* 7A 34
Crickhowell. *Powy* 3M 17
Cricklade. *Wilts* 4K 19
Cricklewood. *G Lon* 5K 21
Cridling Stubbs. *N Yor* 5C 42
Crieff. *Per* 5B 66
Criftins. *Shrp* 6B 34
Criggion. *Powy* 8A 34
Crigglestone. *W Yor* 6M 41
Crimchard. *Som* 5B 8
Crimdon Park. *Dur* 8H 55
Crimond. *Abers* 8K 81
Crimonmogate. *Abers* 8K 81
Crimplesham. *Norf* 1C 30
Crimscote. *Warw* 7L 27
Crinan. *Arg* 8B 64
Cringleford. *Norf* 1H 31
Crinow. *Pemb* 5H 15
Cripplesease. *Corn* 5J 3
Cripplestyle. *Dors* 4J 9
Cripp's Corner. *E Sus* 3D 12
Croanford. *Corn* 4C 4
Crockenhill. *Kent* 7B 22
Crocker End. *Oxon* 5E 20
Crockerhill. *Hants* 5C 10
Crockernwell. *Devn* 6G 7
Crocker's Ash. *Here* 2D 18
Crockerton. *Wilts* 1G 9
Crocketford. *Dum* 4C 52
Crockey Hill. *York* 3D 42
Crockham Hill. *Kent* 8M 21
Crockhurst Street. *Kent* 1C 12
Crockleford Heath. *Essx* 1G 23
Croeserw. *Neat* 5H 17
Croes-Goch. *Pemb* 3E 14
Croes Hywel. *Mon* 2B 18
Croes-lan. *Cdgn* 2K 15
Croesor. *Gwyn* 6F 32
Croesoswallt. *Shrp* 7A 34
Croesyceiliog. *Carm* 5L 15
Croesyceiliog. *Torf* 4B 18
Croes-y-mwyalch. *Torf* 4B 18
Croesywaun. *Gwyn* 5E 32
Croford. *Som* 3L 7
Croft. *Leics* 2C 28
Croft. *Linc* 3B 38
Croft. *Warr* 8E 40
Croftamie. *Stir* 1C 58
Croftfoot. *Glas* 3D 58
Croftmill. *Per* 4B 66
Crofton. *Cumb* 6H 53
Crofton. *W Yor* 6A 42
Crofton. *Wilts* 7L 19
Croft-on-Tees. *N Yor* 5L 47
Crofts. *Dum* 4B 52
Crofts of Benachielt. *High* 8C 86
Crofts of Dipple. *Mor* 8C 80
Crofty. *Swan* 7M 15
Croggan. *Arg* 5B 64
Croglin. *Cumb* 7K 53
Croich. *High* 4E 78
Croick. *High* 6L 85
Croig. *Arg* 2J 63
Cromarty. *High* 7H 79
Crombie. *Fife* 1J 59
Cromdale. *High* 3L 71
Cromer. *Herts* 1K 21
Cromer. *Norf* 5J 39
Cromford. *Derbs* 4L 35
Cromhall. *S Glo* 4E 18
Cromor. *W Isl* 1F 76
Cromra. *High* 7F 70
Cromwell. *Notts* 3E 36
Cronberry. *E Ayr* 7E 58
Crondall. *Hants* 1E 10
The Cronk. *IOM* 5C 44
Cronk-y-Voddy. *IOM* 6C 44
Cronton. *Mers* 1C 34
Crook. *Cumb* 6C 46
Crook. *Dur* 8E 54
Crookdake. *Cumb* 7F 52
Crooke. *G Man* 7D 40
Crookedholm. *E Ayr* 6C 58
Crooked Soley. *Wilts* 6M 19
Crookes. *S Yor* 1M 35
Crookgate Bank. *Dur* 6E 54
Crookhall. *Dur* 6E 54
Crookham. *Nmbd* 6G 61
Crookham. *W Ber* 7C 20
Crookham Village. *Hants* 8E 20
Crooklands. *Cumb* 7D 46
Crook of Devon. *Per* 7D 66
Crookston. *Glas* 3D 58
Cropredy. *Oxon* 7B 28
Cropston. *Leics* 8C 36
Cropthorne. *Worc* 7H 27
Cropton. *N Yor* 7E 48
Cropwell Bishop. *Notts* 6D 36
Cropwell Butler. *Notts* 6D 36
Cros. *W Isl* 5J 83
Crosbie. *N Ayr* 4M 57
Crosbost. *W Isl* 1E 76
Crosby. *Cumb* 8E 52
Crosby. *IOM* 7C 44
Crosby. *Mers* 8B 40
Crosby. *N Lin* 6F 42
Crosby Court. *N Yor* 6A 48
Crosby Garrett. *Cumb* 5F 46
Crosby Ravensworth. *Cumb* 4E 46
Crosby Villa. *Cumb* 8E 52
Croscombe. *Som* 1D 8
Crosland Moor. *W Yor* 6K 41
Cross. *Som* 8C 18
Crossaig. *Arg* 4H 57
Crossapol. *Arg* 3E 62
Cross Ash. *Mon* 2C 18
Cross-at-Hand. *Kent* 1D 12
Crossbush. *W Sus* 5H 11
Crosscanonby. *Cumb* 8E 52
Crossdale Street. *Norf* 6J 39
Cross End. *Essx* 8E 30
Crossens. *Mers* 5B 40
Crossford. *Fife* 1J 59
Crossford. *S Lan* 5G 59
Cross Foxes. *Gwyn* 1G 25
Crossgar. *New M* 6J 93
Crossgate. *Orkn* 8D 88
Crossgate. *Staf* 6H 35
Crossgatehall. *E Lot* 3A 60
Cross Gates. *W Yor* 4A 42
Crossgates. *Fife* 1K 59
Crossgates. *N Yor* 7H 49
Crossgates. *Powy* 6K 25
Crossgill. *Lanc* 1D 40
Cross Green. *Devn* 7C 6
Cross Green. *Staf* 1H 27
Cross Green. *Suff*
  nr. Cockfield 6E 30
  nr. Hitcham 6F 30
Cross Hands. *Carm* 3E 16
Crosshands. *Carm* 4H 15
Crosshands. *E Ayr* 6C 58
Cross Hill. *Derbs* 5B 36
Cross Hill. *Glos* 4D 18
Crosshill. *E Ayr* 7C 58
Crosshill. *Fife* 8E 66
Crosshill. *S Ayr* 1J 51
Cross Hills. *N Yor* 3J 41
Crosshills. *High* 6G 79
Cross Holme. *N Yor* 6C 48
Crosshouse. *E Ayr* 6B 58
Cross Houses. *Shrp* 1D 26
Crossings. *Cumb* 4K 53
Cross in Hand. *E Sus* 3B 12
Cross Inn. *Cdgn*
  nr. Aberaeron 6E 24
  nr. New Quay 1K 15
Cross Inn. *Rhon* 6K 17
Crosskeys. *Cphy* 5M 17
Crosskirk. *High* 5B 86
Crosslands. *Cumb* 7B 46
Cross Lane Head. *Shrp* 2F 26
Cross Lanes. *Corn* 6K 3
Cross Lanes. *Dur* 4J 47
Cross Lanes. *N Yor* 1C 42
Cross Lanes. *Wrex* 5B 34
Crosslanes. *Shrp* 8B 34
Crosslee. *Ren* 3C 58
Crossmaglen. *New M* 7F 93
Crossmichael. *Dum* 5B 52
Crossmoor. *Lanc* 4C 40
Crossnacreevy. *Lis* 5H 93
Cross Oak. *Powy* 2L 17
Cross of Jackston. *Abers* 2G 73
Cross o' th' Hands. *Derbs* 5L 35
Crossroads. *Abers*
  nr. Aberdeen 5J 73
  nr. Banchory 6G 73
Crossroads. *E Ayr* 6C 58
Cross Side. *Devn* 3H 7
Cross Street. *Suff* 4H 31
Crosston. *Ang* 2J 67
Cross Town. *Ches E* 2F 34
Crossway. *Mon* 2C 18
Crossway. *Powy* 7K 25
Crossway Green. *Mon* 4D 18
Crossway Green. *Worc* 5G 27
Crossways. *Dors* 7F 8
Crosswell. *Pemb* 3H 15
Crosswood. *Cdgn* 5F 24
Crosthwaite. *Cumb* 6C 46
Croston. *Lanc* 6C 40
Crostwick. *Norf* 8J 39
Crostwight. *Norf* 7K 39
Crothair. *W Isl* 8E 82
Crouch. *Kent* 8C 22
Croucheston. *Wilts* 3J 9
Crouch Hill. *Dors* 4F 8
Croughton. *Nptn* 8C 28
Crovie. *Abers* 7H 81
Crow. *Hants* 5K 9
Crowan. *Corn* 5K 3
Crowborough. *E Sus* 2B 12
Crowcombe. *Som* 2L 7
Crowcroft. *Worc* 6F 26
Crowdecote. *Derbs* 3K 35
Crowden. *Derbs* 8J 41
Crowden. *Devn* 6D 6
Crowdhill. *Hants* 4B 10
Crowdon. *N Yor* 6G 49
Crow Edge. *S Yor* 7K 41
Crow End. *Cambs* 6L 29
Crowfield. *Nptn* 7D 28
Crowfield. *Suff* 6H 31
Crow Green. *Essx* 4B 22
Crow Hill. *Here* 1E 18
Crowhurst. *E Sus* 4D 12
Crowhurst. *Surr* 1L 11
Crowhurst Lane End. *Surr* 1L 11
Crowland. *Linc* 8K 37
Crowland. *Suff* 4G 31
Crowlas. *Corn* 5J 3
Crowle. *N Lin* 6E 42
Crowle. *Worc* 6H 27
Crowle Green. *Worc* 6H 27
Crowmarsh Gifford. *Oxon* 5D 20
Crown Corner. *Suff* 4J 31
Crownthorpe. *Norf* 1G 31
Crowntown. *Corn* 5K 3
Crows-an-wra. *Corn* 6G 3
Crowshill. *Norf* 1F 30
Crowthorne. *Brac* 7F 20
Crowton. *Ches W* 2D 34
Croxall. *Staf* 8K 35
Croxby. *Linc* 8J 43
Croxdale. *Dur* 8F 54
Croxden. *Staf* 6J 35
Croxley Green. *Herts* 4H 21
Croxton. *Cambs* 5K 29
Croxton. *Norf*
  nr. Fakenham 6F 38
  nr. Thetford 3E 30
Croxton. *N Lin* 6H 43
Croxton. *Staf* 6F 34
Croxtonbank. *Staf* 6F 34
Croxton Green. *Ches E* 4D 34
Croxton Kerrial. *Leics* 7F 36
Croy. *High* 1H 71
Croy. *N Lan* 2F 58
Croyde. *Devn* 2D 6
Croydon. *Cambs* 7L 29
Croydon. *G Lon* 7L 21
Crubenbeg. *High* 6G 71
Crubenmore Lodge. *High* 6G 71
Cruckmeole. *Shrp* 1C 26
Cruckton. *Shrp* 8C 34
Cruden Bay. *Abers* 2K 73
Crudgington. *Telf* 8E 34
Crudie. *Abers* 8G 81
Crudwell. *Wilts* 4H 19
Cruft. *Devn* 6E 6
Crug. *Powy* 5L 25
Crughywel. *Powy* 3M 17
Crugmeer. *Corn* 4B 4
Crugybar. *Carm* 1F 16
Crug-y-byddar. *Powy* 4L 25
Crulabhig. *W Isl* 8E 82
Crumlin. *Ant* 5G 93
Crumlin. *Cphy* 5M 17
Crumpsall. *G Man* 7G 41
Crumpsbrook. *Shrp* 4E 26
Crundale. *Kent* 1G 13
Crundale. *Pemb* 5F 14
Cruwys Morchard. *Devn* 4H 7
Crux Easton. *Hants* 8B 20
Cruxton. *Dors* 6E 8
Crwbin. *Carm* 5L 15
Cryers Hill. *Buck* 4F 20
Crymych. *Pemb* 3H 15
Crynant. *Neat* 4G 17
Crystal Palace. *G Lon* 6L 21
Cuaich. *High* 7G 71
Cuaig. *High* 8J 77
Cuan. *Arg* 6B 64
Cubbington. *Warw* 5M 27
Cubert. *Corn* 3L 3
Cubley. *S Yor* 7L 41
Cubley Common. *Derbs* 6K 35
Cublington. *Buck* 1F 20
Cublington. *Here* 8B 26
Cuckfield. *W Sus* 3L 11
Cucklington. *Som* 3F 8
Cuckney. *Notts* 2C 36
Cuckron. *Shet* 2E 90
Cuddesdon. *Oxon* 3D 20
Cuddington. *Buck* 2E 20
Cuddington. *Ches W* 2E 34
Cuddington Heath. *Ches W* 5C 34
Cuddy Hill. *Lanc* 4C 40
Cudham. *G Lon* 8M 21
Cudlipptown. *Devn* 8E 6
Cudworth. *Som* 4B 8
Cudworth. *S Yor* 7A 42
Cudworth. *Surr* 1K 11
Cuerdley Cross. *Warr* 1D 34
Cuffley. *Herts* 3L 21
Cuidhir. *W Isl* 5C 74
Cuidhsiadar. *W Isl* 6J 83
Cuidhtinis. *W Isl* 5B 76
Culbo. *High* 7G 79
Culbokie. *High* 8G 79
Culburnie. *High* 1E 70
Culcabock. *High* 1G 71
Culcavy. *Lis* 5H 93
Culcharry. *High* 8J 79
Culcheth. *Warr* 8E 40
Culduie. *High* 1J 69
Culeave. *High* 4F 78
Culford. *Suff* 4E 30
Culgaith. *Cumb* 3E 46
Culham. *Oxon* 4C 20
Culkein. *High* 8C 84
Culkein Drumbeg. *High* 8D 84
Culkerton. *Glos* 4H 19
Cullaville. *New M* 7F 93
Cullen. *Mor* 7E 80
Cullercoats. *Tyne* 4G 55
Cullicudden. *High* 7G 79
Cullingworth. *W Yor* 4J 41
Cullipool. *Arg* 6B 64
Cullivoe. *Shet* 3K 91
Culloch. *Per* 6A 66
Culloden. *High* 1H 71
Cullompton. *Devn* 5K 7
Cullybackey. *ME Ant* 3G 93
Cullycapple. *Caus* 2F 93
Cullyhanna. *New M* 7F 93
Culm Davy. *Devn* 4L 7
Culmington. *Shrp* 3C 26
Culmore. *Derr* 2D 92
Culmstock. *Devn* 4L 7
Cul na Caepaich. *High* 7H 69
Culnacnoc. *High* 7G 77
Culnacraig. *High* 3A 78
Culnady. *M Ulst* 3F 93
Culrain. *High* 4F 78
Culross. *Fife* 1H 59
Culroy. *S Ayr* 8B 58
Culswick. *Shet* 3C 90
Cults. *Aber* 5H 73
Cults. *Abers* 2E 72
Cults. *Fife* 7G 67
Cultybraggan Camp. *Per* 5A 66
Culver. *Devn* 6H 7
Culverlane. *Devn* 5K 5
Culverstone Green. *Kent* 7C 22
Culverthorpe. *Linc* 5H 37
Culworth. *Nptn* 7C 28
Culzie Lodge. *High* 6F 78
Cumberlow Green. *Herts* 8L 29
Cumbernauld. *N Lan* 2F 58
Cumbernauld Village. *N Lan* 2F 58
Cumberworth. *Linc* 2B 38
Cumdivock. *Cumb* 7H 53
Cuminestown. *Abers* 8H 81
Cumledge Mill. *Bord* 4E 60
Cumlewick. *Shet* 5E 90
Cummersdale. *Cumb* 6H 53
Cummertrees. *Dum* 5F 52
Cummingstown. *Mor* 7M 79
Cumnock. *E Ayr* 7D 58
Cumnor. *Oxon* 3B 20
Cumrew. *Cumb* 6K 53
Cumwhinton. *Cumb* 6J 53
Cumwhitton. *Cumb* 6K 53
Cundall. *N Yor* 8B 48
Cunninghamhead. *N Ayr* 5B 58
Cunning Park. *S Ayr* 8B 58
Cunningsburgh. *Shet* 5E 90
Cunnister. *Shet* 4K 91
Cupar. *Fife* 6G 67
Cupar Muir. *Fife* 6G 67
Cupernham. *Hants* 3A 10
Curbar. *Derbs* 2L 35
Curborough. *Staf* 8K 35
Curbridge. *Hants* 4C 10
Curbridge. *Oxon* 3M 19
Curdridge. *Hants* 4C 10
Curdworth. *Warw* 2K 27
Curland. *Som* 4A 8
Curland Common. *Som* 4A 8
Curran. *M Ulst* 4F 93
Curridge. *W Ber* 6B 20
Currie. *Edin* 3K 59
Curry Mallet. *Som* 3B 8
Curry Rivel. *Som* 3B 8
Curtisden Green. *Kent* 1D 12
Curtisknowle. *Devn* 6K 5
Cury. *Corn* 6K 3
Cusgarne. *Corn* 4L 3
Cushendall. *Caus* 2H 93
Cushendun. *Caus* 2H 93
Cusop. *Here* 8M 25
Cusworth. *S Yor* 7C 42
Cutcombe. *Som* 2J 7
Cuthill. *E Lot* 2A 60
Cutiau. *Gwyn* 1F 24
Cutlers Green. *Essx* 8B 30
Cutmadoc. *Corn* 5C 4
Cutnall Green. *Worc* 5G 27
Cutsdean. *Glos* 8J 27
Cutthorpe. *Derbs* 2M 35
Cuttiford's Door. *Som* 4B 8
Cuttivett. *Corn* 5F 4
Cutts. *Shet* 4D 90
Cuttybridge. *Pemb* 5F 14
Cuttyhill. *Abers* 8K 81
Cuxham. *Oxon* 4D 20
Cuxton. *Medw* 7D 22
Cuxwold. *Linc* 7J 43
Cwm. *Blae* 4L 17
Cwm. *Den* 3K 33
Cwm. *Powy* 2A 26
Cwmafan. *Neat* 5G 17
Cwmaman. *Rhon* 5J 17
Cwmann. *Carm* 8E 24
Cwmbach. *Carm* 4J 15
Cwmbach. *Powy* 1L 17
Cwmbach. *Rhon* 4K 17
Cwmbach Llechrhyd. *Powy* 7K 25
Cwmbelan. *Powy* 4J 25
Cwmbran. *Torf* 4A 18
Cwmbrwyno. *Cdgn* 4G 25
Cwm Capel. *Carm* 6L 15
Cwmcarn. *Cphy* 5M 17
Cwmcarvan. *Mon* 3C 18
Cwm-celyn. *Blae* 4M 17
Cwmcerdinen. *Swan* 4F 16
Cwm-Cewydd. *Gwyn* 1H 25
Cwm-cou. *Cdgn* 2J 15
Cwmcych. *Pemb* 3J 15
Cwmdare. *Rhon* 4J 17
Cwmdu. *Carm* 1F 16
Cwmdu. *Powy* 2L 17
Cwmduad. *Carm* 3K 15
Cwm Dulais. *Swan* 4F 16
Cwmerfyn. *Cdgn* 4F 24
Cwmfelin. *B'end* 6H 17
Cwmfelin Boeth. *Carm* 5H 15
Cwmfelinfach. *Cphy* 5L 17
Cwmfelin Mynach. *Carm* 4J 15
Cwmffrwd. *Carm* 5L 15
Cwmgiedd. *Powy* 3G 17
Cwmgors. *Neat* 3G 17
Cwmgwili. *Carm* 3E 16
Cwmgwrach. *Neat* 4H 17
Cwmhiraeth. *Carm* 3K 15
Cwmifor. *Carm* 2F 16
Cwmisfael. *Carm* 5L 15
Cwm-Llinau. *Powy* 2H 25
Cwmllynfell. *Neat* 3G 17
Cwm-mawr. *Carm* 5M 15
Cwm-miles. *Carm* 4H 15
Cwmorgan. *Carm* 3J 15
Cwmparc. *Rhon* 5J 17
Cwm Penmachno. *Cnwy* 6G 33
Cwmpennar. *Rhon* 4K 17
Cwm Plysgog. *Pemb* 2H 15
Cwmrhos. *Powy* 2L 17
Cwmsychpant. *Cdgn* 2L 15
Cwmsyfiog. *Cphy* 4L 17
Cwmsymlog. *Cdgn* 4F 24
Cwmtillery. *Blae* 4M 17

Cwm-twrch Isaf—East Hagbourne

Cwm-twrch Isaf. Powy .4G 17
Cwm-twrch Uchaf. Powy .3G 17
Cwmwysg. Powy .2H 17
Cwm-y-glo. Gwyn .4E 32
Cwmyoy. Mon .1B 18
Cwmystwyth. Cdgn .5G 25
Cwrt. Gwyn .2F 24
Cwrtnewydd. Cdgn .2L 15
Cwrt-y-Cadno. Carm .8F 24
Cydweli. Carm .6L 15
Cyffylliog. Den .5K 33
Cymau. Flin .4A 34
Cymer. Neat .5H 17
Cymmer. Neat .5H 17
Cymmer. Rhon .5K 17
Cyncoed. Card .6L 17
Cynghordy. Carm .1H 17
Cynheidre. Carm .6L 15
Cynonville. Neat .5H 17
Cynwyd. Den .6K 33
Cynwyl Elfed. Carm .4K 15
Cywarch. Gwyn .1H 25

D

Dacre. Cumb .3C 46
Dacre. N Yor .1K 41
Dacre Banks. N Yor .1K 41
Daddry Shield. Dur .8B 54
Dadford. Buck .8D 28
Dadlington. Leics .2B 28
Dafen. Carm .6M 15
Daffy Green. Norf .1F 30
Dagdale. Staf .6J 35
Dagenham. G Lon .5A 22
Daggons. Dors .4K 9
Daglingworth. Glos .3H 19
Dagnall. Buck .2G 21
Dagtail End. Worc .5J 27
Dail. Arg .4E 64
Dail Beag. W Isl .7F 82
Dail bho Dheas. W Isl .5H 83
Dailly. S Ayr .1H 51
Dail Mor. W Isl .7F 82
Dairsie. Fife .6H 67
Daisy Bank. W Mid .2J 27
Daisy Hill. G Man .7E 40
Daisy Hill. W Yor .4K 41
Dalabrog. W Isl .3D 74
Dalavich. Arg .6D 64
Dalbeattie. Dum .5C 52
Dalblair. E Ayr .8E 58
Dalbury. Derbs .6L 35
Dalby. IOM .7B 44
Dalby Wolds. Leics .7D 36
Dalchalm. High .3K 79
Dalcharn. High .6J 85
Dalchork. High .2F 78
Dalchreichart. High .4C 70
Dalchruin. Per .6M 65
Dalcross. High .1H 71
Dalderby. Linc .3K 37
Dale. Cumb .7K 53
Dale. Pemb .6E 14
Dale Abbey. Derbs .6B 36
Dalebank. Derbs .3A 36
Dale Bottom. Cumb .3A 46
Dale Head. Cumb .4C 46
Dalehouse. N Yor .4E 48
Dalelia. High .1B 64
Dale of Walls. Shet .2B 90
Dalgarven. N Ayr .5A 58
Dalgety Bay. Fife .1K 59
Dalginross. Per .5A 66
Dalguise. Per .3C 66
Dalhalvaig. High .6L 85
Dalham. Suff .5D 30
Dalintart. Arg .5C 64
Dalkeith. Midl .3M 59
Dallas. Mor .8M 79
Dalleagles. E Ayr .8D 58
Dall House. Per .2K 65
Dallinghoo. Suff .6J 31
Dallington. E Sus .4C 12
Dallow. N Yor .8K 47
Dalmally. Arg .5F 64
Dalmarnock. Glas .3E 58
Dalmellington. E Ayr .1K 51
Dalmeny. Edin .2K 59
Dalmigavie. High .4H 71
Dalmilling. S Ayr .7B 58
Dalmore. High
nr. Alness .7G 79
nr. Rogart .3H 79
Dalmuir. W Dun .2C 58
Dalmunach. Mor .1B 72
Dalnabreck. High .1B 64
Dalnacardoch Lodge. Per .8H 71
Dalnamein Lodge. Per .1A 66
Dalnaspidal Lodge. Per .8G 71
Dalnatrat. High .2D 64
Dalnavie. High .6G 79
Dalnawillan Lodge. High .7B 86
Dalness. High .2F 64
Dalnessie. High .2G 79
Dalqueich. Per .7D 66
Dalquhairn. S Ayr .2J 51
Dalreavoch. High .3H 79
Dalreoch. Per .6D 66
Dalry. Edin .2L 59
Dalry. N Ayr .5A 58
Dalrymple. E Ayr .8B 58
Dalscote. Nptn .6D 28
Dalserf. S Lan .4G 59
Dalsmirren. Arg .8F 56
Dalston. Cumb .6H 53
Dalswinton. Dum .3D 52
Dalton. Dum .4F 52
Dalton. Lanc .7C 40
Dalton. Nmbd
nr. Hexham .6C 54
nr. Ponteland .4E 54
Dalton. N Yor
nr. Richmond .5K 47
nr. Thirsk .8B 48
Dalton. S Lan .4E 58
Dalton. S Yor .8B 42
Dalton-in-Furness. Cumb .7M 45
Dalton-le-Dale. Dur .7H 55
Dalton Magna. S Yor .8B 42
Dalton-on-Tees. N Yor .5L 47
Dalton Piercy. Hart .8H 55
Daltot. Arg .1G 57
Dalvey. High .2M 71
Dalwhinnie. High .7G 71
Dalwood. Devn .5A 8
Damerham. Hants .4K 9
Damgate. Norf
nr. Acle .1L 31
nr. Martham .8L 39
Dam Green. Norf .3G 31
Damhead. Mor .8L 79
Danaway. Kent .7E 22
Danbury. Essx .3D 22
Danby. N Yor .5E 48
Danby Botton. N Yor .5D 48
Danby Wiske. N Yor .6M 47
Danderhall. Midl .3M 59
Danebank. Ches E .1H 35
Danebridge. Ches E .3H 35
Dane End. Herts .1L 21
Danehill. E Sus .3M 11
Danesford. Shrp .2F 26
Daneshill. Hants .8D 20
Danesmoor. Derbs .3B 36
Danestone. Aber .4J 73
Dangerous Corner. Lanc .6D 40
Daniel's Water. Kent .1F 12
Dan's Castle. Dur .8E 54
Danzey Green. Warw .5K 27
Dapple Heath. Staf .7J 35
Daren. Powy .3M 17
Darenth. Kent .6B 22
Daresbury. Hal .1D 34
Darfield. S Yor .7B 42
Dargate. Kent .7G 23
Dargill. Per .6B 66
Darite. Corn .5E 4
Darkley. Arm .7F 93
Darlaston. W Mid .2H 27
Darley. N Yor .2L 41
Darley Abbey. Derb .6M 35
Darley Bridge. Derbs .3L 35
Darley Dale. Derbs .3L 35
Darley Head. N Yor .2K 41
Darlingscott. Warw .7L 27
Darlington. Darl .4L 47
Darliston. Shrp .6D 34
Darlton. Notts .2E 36
Darmsden. Suff .6G 31
Darnall. S Yor .1A 36
Darnford. Abers .6G 73
Darnford. Staf .1K 27
Darnhall. Ches W .3E 34
Darnick. Bord .6C 60
Darowen. Powy .2H 25
Darra. Abers .1G 73
Darracott. Devn .2D 6
Darragh Cross. New M .6J 93
Darras Hall. Nmbd .4E 54
Darrington. W Yor .5B 42
Darrow Green. Norf .3J 31
Darsham. Suff .5L 31
Dartfield. Abers .8K 81
Dartford. Kent .6B 22
Dartford-Thurrock River Crossing. Kent .6B 22
Dartington. Devn .5K 5
Dartmeet. Devn .8F 6
Dartmouth. Devn .6L 5
Darton. S Yor .6M 41
Darvel. E Ayr .6D 58
Darwen. Bkbn .5E 40
Dassels. Herts .1L 21
Datchet. Wind .6G 21
Datchworth. Herts .2K 21
Datchworth Green. Herts .2K 21
Daubhill. G Man .7F 40
Dauntsey. Wilts .5H 19
Dauntsey Green. Wilts .5H 19
Dauntsey Lock. Wilts .5H 19
Dava. Mor .2L 71
Davenham. Ches W .2E 34
Daventry. Nptn .5C 28
Davidson's Mains. Edin .2L 59
Davidston. High .7H 79
Davidstow. Corn .7A 6
David's Well. Powy .5K 25
Davington. Dum .1G 53
Daviot. Abers .3G 73
Daviot. High .2H 71
Davyhulme. G Man .8F 40
Daw Cross. N Yor .2L 41
Dawdon. Dur .7H 55
Dawesgreen. Surr .1K 11
Dawley. Telf .1E 26
Dawlish. Devn .8J 7
Dawlish Warren. Devn .8J 7
Dawn. Cnwy .3H 33
Daws Heath. Essx .5E 22
Dawshill. Worc .6G 27
Daw's House. Corn .7C 6
Dawsmere. Linc .6M 37
Dayhills. Staf .6H 35
Dayhouse Bank. Worc .4H 27
Daylesford. Glos .1L 19
Daywall. Shrp .6A 34
Ddol. Flin .3L 33
Ddol Cownwy. Powy .1K 25
Deadman's Cross. C Beds .7J 29
Deadwater. Nmbd .2L 53
Deaf Hill. Dur .8G 55
Deal. Kent .8K 23
Dean. Cumb .2K 45
Dean. Devn
nr. Combe Martin .1F 6
nr. Lynton .1G 7
Dean. Dors .4H 9
Dean. Hants
nr. Bishop's Waltham .4C 10
nr. Winchester .2B 10
Dean. Oxon .1M 19
Dean. Som .1E 8
Dean Bank. Dur .8F 54
Deanburnhaugh. Bord .8A 60
Dean Cross. Devn .1E 6
Deane. Hants .8C 20
Deanich Lodge. High .5D 78
Deanland. Dors .4H 9
Deanlane End. W Sus .4E 10
Dean Park. Shrp .5E 26
Dean Prior. Devn .5K 5
Dean Row. Ches E .1G 35
Deans. W Lot .3J 59
Deanscales. Cumb .2K 45
Deanshanger. Nptn .7E 28
Deanston. Stir .7M 65
Dearham. Cumb .8E 52
Dearne Valley. S Yor .7A 42
Debach. Suff .6J 31
Debden. Essx .8B 30
Debden Green. Essx
nr. Loughton .4M 21
nr. Saffron Walden .8B 30
Debenham. Suff .5H 31
Dechmont. W Lot .2J 59
Deddington. Oxon .8B 28
Dedham. Essx .8G 31
Dedham Heath. Essx .8G 31
Deebank. Abers .6F 72
Deene. Nptn .2G 29
Deenethorpe. Nptn .2G 29
Deepcar. S Yor .8L 41
Deepcut. Surr .8G 21
Deepdale. Cumb .7F 46
Deepdale. N Lin .6H 43
Deepdale. N Yor .8G 47
Deeping Gate. Pet .1J 29
Deeping St James. Linc .8J 37
Deeping St Nicholas. Linc .8K 37
Deerhill. Mor .8D 80
Deerhurst. Glos .1G 19
Deerhurst Walton. Glos .1G 19
Deerness. Orkn .1G 87
Defford. Worc .7H 27
Defynnog. Powy .2J 17
Deganwy. Cnwy .3G 33
Deighton. N Yor .5A 48
Deighton. W Yor .6K 41
Deighton. York .3D 42
Deiniolen. Gwyn .4E 32
Delabole. Corn .3C 4
Delamere. Ches W .3D 34
Delfour. High .5J 71
The Dell. Suff .2L 31
Delliefure. High .2L 71
Delly End. Oxon .2A 20
Delny. High .6H 79
Delph. G Man .7H 41
Delves. Dur .7E 54
The Delves. W Mid .2J 27
Delvin End. Essx .8D 30
Dembleby. Linc .6H 37
Demelza. Corn .5B 4
The Den. N Ayr .4B 58
Denaby Main. S Yor .8B 42
Denbeath. Fife .8G 67
Denbigh. Den .4K 33
Denbury. Devn .5L 5
Denby. Derbs .5A 36
Denby Common. Derbs .5B 36
Denby Dale. W Yor .7L 41
Denchworth. Oxon .4A 20
Dendron. Cumb .7M 45
Deneside. Dur .7H 55
Denford. Nptn .4G 29
Dengie. Essx .3F 22
Denham. Buck .5H 21
Denham. Suff
nr. Bury St Edmunds .5D 30
nr. Eye .4H 31
Denham Green. Buck .5H 21
Denham Street. Suff .4H 31
Denhead. Abers
nr. Ellon .2J 73
nr. Strichen .8J 81
Denhead. Fife .6H 67
Denholm. Bord .8C 60
Denholme. W Yor .4J 41
Denholme Clough. W Yor .4J 41
Denholme Gate. W Yor .4J 41
Denio. Gwyn .7C 32
Denmead. Hants .4D 10
Dennington. Suff .5J 31
Denny. Falk .1G 59
Denny End. Cambs .5A 30
Dennyloanhead. Falk .1G 59
Den of Lindores. Fife .6F 66
Denshaw. G Man .6H 41
Denside. Abers .6H 73
Densole. Kent .1J 13
Denston. Suff .6D 30
Denstone. Staf .5K 35
Denstroude. Kent .7H 23
Dent. Cumb .7F 46
Denton. Cambs .3J 29
Denton. Darl .4L 47
Denton. E Sus .5A 12
Denton. G Man .8H 41
Denton. Kent .1J 13
Denton. Linc .6F 36
Denton. Norf .3J 31
Denton. Nptn .6F 28
Denton. N Yor .3K 41
Denton. Oxon .3C 20
Denver. Norf .1C 30
Denwick. Nmbd .8K 61
Deopham. Norf .1G 31
Deopham Green. Norf .2G 31
Depden. Suff .6D 30
Depden Green. Suff .6D 30
Deptford. G Lon .6L 21
Deptford. Wilts .2J 9
Derby. Derb .108 (6A 36)
Derbyhaven. IOM .8B 44
Derculich. Per .2B 66
Dereham. Norf .8F 38
Deri. Cphy .4L 17
Derril. Devn .5C 6
Derringstone. Kent .1J 13
Derrington. Shrp .2E 26
Derrington. Staf .7G 35
Derriton. Devn .5C 6
Derry. Derr .3D 92
Derryboye. New M .6J 93
Derrycrin. M Ulst .5F 93
Derrygonnelly. Ferm .6B 92
Derryguaig. Arg .4K 63
Derry Hill. Wilts .6H 19
Derrykeighan. Caus .2F 93
Derrylin. Ferm .7C 92
Derrymacash. Arm .6G 93
Derrythorpe. N Lin .7F 42
Derrytrasna. Arm .5F 93
Dersingham. Norf .6C 38
Dervaig. Arg .2K 63
Dervock. Caus .2F 93
Derwen. Den .5K 33
Derwen Gam. Cdgn .1L 15
Derwenlas. Powy .3G 25
Desborough. Nptn .3F 28
Desertmartin. M Ulst .4F 93
Desford. Leics .1B 28
Detchant. Nmbd .6H 61
Dethick. Derbs .4M 35
Detling. Kent .8D 22
Deuchar. Ang .1H 67
Deuddwr. Powy .1M 25
Devauden. Mon .4C 18
Devil's Bridge. Cdgn .5G 25
Devitts Green. Warw .2L 27
Devizes. Wilts .7J 19
Devonport. Plym .6G 5
Devonside. Clac .8C 66
Devoran. Corn .5L 3
Dewartown. Midl .3A 60
Dewlish. Dors .6F 8
Dewsall Court. Here .8C 26
Dewsbury. W Yor .5L 41
Dexbeer. Devn .5B 6
Dhoon. IOM .6D 44
Dhoor. IOM .5D 44
Dhowin. IOM .4D 44
Dial Green. W Sus .3G 11
Dial Post. W Sus .4J 11
The Diamond. M Ulst .5F 93
Dibberford. Dors .5C 8
Dibden. Hants .5B 10
Dibden Purlieu. Hants .5B 10
Dickleburgh. Norf .3H 31
Didbrook. Glos .8J 27
Didcot. Oxon .4C 20
Diddington. Cambs .5J 29
Diddlebury. Shrp .3D 26
Didley. Here .8C 26
Didling. W Sus .4F 10
Didmarton. Glos .5G 19
Didsbury. G Man .8G 41
Didworthy. Devn .5J 5
Digby. Linc .4H 37
Digg. High .7F 76
Diggle. G Man .7J 41
Digmoor. Lanc .7C 40
Digswell. Herts .2K 21
Dihewyd. Cdgn .1L 15
Dilham. Norf .7K 39
Dilhorne. Staf .5H 35
Dillarburn. S Lan .5G 59
Dillington. Cambs .5J 29
Dilston. Nmbd .5C 54
Dilton Marsh. Wilts .1G 9
Dilwyn. Here .6C 26
Dimmer. Som .2E 8
Dimple. G Man .6F 40
Dinas. Carm .3J 15
Dinas. Gwyn
nr. Caernarfon .5D 32
nr. Tudweiliog .7B 32
Dinas Cross. Pemb .3G 15
Dinas Dinlle. Gwyn .5D 32
Dinas Mawddwy. Gwyn .1H 25
Dinas Powys. V Glam .7L 17
Dinbych. Den .4K 33
Dinbych-y-Pysgod. Pemb .6H 15
Dinckley. Lanc .4E 40
Dinder. Som .1D 8
Dinedor. Here .8D 26
Dinedor Cross. Here .8D 26
Dingestow. Mon .2C 18
Dingle. Mers .1B 34
Dingleden. Kent .2E 12
Dingleton. Bord .6C 60
Dingley. Nptn .3E 28
Dingwall. High .8F 78
Dinmael. Cnwy .6K 33
Dinnet. Abers .6D 72
Dinnington. Som .4C 8
Dinnington. S Yor .1C 36
Dinnington. Tyne .4F 54
Dinorwig. Gwyn .4E 32
Dinton. Buck .2E 20
Dinton. Wilts .2J 9
Dinworthy. Devn .4C 6
Dipley. Hants .8E 20
Dippen. Arg .6G 57
Dippenhall. Surr .1F 10
Dippertown. Devn .7D 6
Dippin. N Ayr .7K 57
Dipple. S Ayr .1H 51
Diptford. Devn .6K 5
Dipton. Dur .6E 54
Dirleton. E Lot .1C 60
Dirt Pot. Nmbd .7B 54
Discoed. Powy .5A 26
Diseworth. Leics .7B 36
Dishes. Orkn .7F 88
Dishforth. N Yor .8A 48
Disley. Ches E .1H 35
Diss. Norf .4H 31
Disserth. Powy .7K 25
Distington. Cumb .2K 45
Ditchampton. Wilts .2J 9
Ditcheat. Som .2E 8
Ditchingham. Norf .2K 31
Ditchling. E Sus .4L 11
Ditteridge. Wilts .7G 19
Dittisham. Devn .6L 5
Ditton. Hal .1C 34
Ditton. Kent .8D 22
Ditton Green. Cambs .6C 30
Ditton Priors. Shrp .3E 26
Divach. High .3E 70
Dixonfield. High .5C 86
Dixton. Glos .8H 27
Dixton. Mon .2D 18
Dizzard. Corn .6A 6
Doagh. Ant .4H 93
Dobcross. G Man .7H 41
Dobs Hill. Flin .3B 34
Dobson's Bridge. Shrp .6C 34
Dobwalls. Corn .5E 4
Doccombe. Devn .7G 7
Dochgarroch. High .1G 71
Docking. Norf .6D 38
Docklow. Here .6D 26
Dockray. Cumb .3B 46
Doc Penfro. Pemb .6F 14
Dodbrooke. Devn .7K 5
Doddenham. Worc .6F 26
Doddinghurst. Essx .4B 22
Doddington. Cambs .2L 29
Doddington. Kent .8F 22
Doddington. Linc .2G 37
Doddington. Nmbd .6G 61
Doddington. Shrp .4E 26
Doddiscombsleigh. Devn .7H 7
Doddshill. Norf .6D 38
Dodford. Nptn .5D 28
Dodford. Worc .4H 27
Dodington. Som .1L 7
Dodington. S Glo .5F 18
Dodleston. Ches W .3B 34
Dods Leigh. Staf .6J 35
Dodworth. S Yor .7M 41
Doe Lea. Derbs .3B 36
Dogdyke. Linc .4K 37
Dogmersfield. Hants .8E 20
Dogsthorpe. Pet .1K 29
Dog Village. Devn .6J 7
Dolanog. Powy .1K 25
Dolau. Powy .6L 25
Dolau. Rhon .6K 17
Dolbenmaen. Gwyn .6E 32
Doley. Staf .7F 34
Dol-fâch. Powy .2J 25
Dolfach. Powy .5J 25
Dolfor. Powy .4L 25
Dolgarrog. Cnwy .4G 33
Dolgellau. Gwyn .1G 25
Dolgoch. Gwyn .2F 24
Dol-gran. Carm .3L 15
Dolhelfa. Powy .5J 25
Doll. High .3J 79
Dollar. Clac .8C 66
Dolley Green. Powy .5A 26
Dollingstown. Arm .6G 93
Dollwen. Cdgn .4F 24
Dolphin. Flin .3L 33
Dolphinholme. Lanc .2D 40
Dolphinton. S Lan .5K 59
Dolton. Devn .4E 6
Dolwen. Cnwy .3H 33
Dolwyddelan. Cnwy .5G 33
Dol-y-Bont. Cdgn .4F 24
Dolyhir. Powy .7M 25
Domgay. Powy .8A 34
Donagh. Ferm .7C 92
Donaghadee. Ards .5J 93
Donaghcloney. Arm .6G 93
Donaghmore. M Ulst .5E 92
Doncaster. S Yor .7C 42
Doncaster Sheffield Airport. S Yor .8D 42
Donhead St Andrew. Wilts .3H 9
Donhead St Mary. Wilts .3H 9
Doniford. Som .1K 7
Donington. Linc .6K 37
Donington. Shrp .1G 27
Donington Eaudike. Linc .6K 37
Donington le Heath. Leics .8B 36
Donington on Bain. Linc .1K 37
Donington South Ing. Linc .6K 37
Donisthorpe. Leics .8M 35
Donkey Street. Kent .2H 13
Donkey Town. Surr .7G 21
Donna Nook. Linc .8M 43
Donnington. Glos .1K 19
Donnington. Here .8F 26
Donnington. Shrp .1D 26
Donnington. Telf .8F 34
Donnington. W Ber .7B 20
Donnington. W Sus .5F 10
Donyatt. Som .4B 8
Doomsday Green. W Sus .3J 11
Doonfoot. S Ayr .8B 58
Doonholm. S Ayr .8B 58
Dorback Lodge. High .4L 71
Dorchester. Dors .6E 8
Dorchester on Thames. Oxon .4C 20
Dordon. Warw .1L 27
Dore. S Yor .1M 35
Dores. High .2F 70
Dorking. Surr .1J 11
Dorking Tye. Suff .8F 30
Dormansland. Surr .1M 11
Dormans Park. Surr .1L 11
Dormanstown. Red C .3C 48
Dormington. Here .7D 26
Dormston. Worc .6H 27
Dorn. Glos .8L 27
Dorney. Buck .6G 21
Dornie. High .3K 69
Dornoch. High .5H 79
Dornock. Dum .5G 53
Dorrery. High .6B 86
Dorridge. W Mid .4K 27
Dorrington. Linc .4H 37
Dorrington. Shrp .1C 26
Dorsington. Warw .7K 27
Dorstone. Here .7B 26
Dorton. Buck .2D 20
Dosthill. Staf .1L 27
Dotham. IOA .3C 32
Dottery. Dors .6C 8
Doublebois. Corn .5D 4
Dougarie. N Ayr .6H 57
Doughton. Glos .4G 19
Douglas. IOM .7C 44
Douglas. S Lan .6G 59
Douglas Bridge. Derr .4C 92
Douglastown. Ang .3H 67
Douglas Water. S Lan .6G 59
Doulting. Som .1E 8
Dounby. Orkn .7B 88
Doune. High
nr. Kingussie .4J 71
nr. Lairg .3E 78
Doune. Stir .7M 65
Dounie. High
nr. Bonar Bridge .4F 78
nr. Tain .5G 79
Dounreay, Upper & Lower. High .5A 86
Doura. N Ayr .5B 58
Dousland. Devn .5H 5
Dovaston. Shrp .7B 34
Dove Holes. Derbs .2J 35
Dovenby. Cumb .8E 52
Dover. Kent .108 (1K 13)
Dovercourt. Essx .8J 31
Doverdale. Worc .5G 27
Doveridge. Derbs .6K 35
Doversgreen. Surr .1K 11
Dowally. Per .3D 66
Dowbridge. Lanc .4C 40
Dowdeswell. Glos .2J 19
Dowlais. Mer T .4K 17
Dowland. Devn .4E 6
Dowlands. Devn .6A 8
Dowles. Worc .4F 26
Dowlesgreen. Wok .7F 20
Dowlish Wake. Som .4B 8
The Down. Shrp .2E 26
Downall Green. Mers .7D 40
Down Ampney. Glos .4K 19
Downderry. Corn
nr. Looe .6F 4
nr. St Austell .6B 4
Downe. G Lon .7M 21
Downend. IOW .7C 10
Downend. S Glo .6E 18
Downend. W Ber .6B 20
Down Field. Cambs .4C 30
Downfield. D'dee .4G 67
Downgate. Corn
nr. Kelly Bray .8C 6
nr. Upton Cross .8B 6
Downham. Essx .4D 22
Downham. Lanc .3F 40
Downham. Nmbd .6F 60
Downham Market. Norf .1C 30
Down Hatherley. Glos .1G 19
Downhead. Som
nr. Frome .1E 8
nr. Yeovil .3D 8
Downhill. Caus .2E 92
Downholland Cross. Lanc .7B 40
Downholme. N Yor .6K 47
Downies. Abers .6J 73
Downley. Buck .4F 20
Downpatrick. New M .6J 93
Down St Mary. Devn .5G 7
Downside. Som
nr. Chilcompton .8E 18
nr. Shepton Mallet .1E 8
Downside. Surr .8J 21
Down Thomas. Devn .6H 5
Downton. Hants .6L 9
Downton. Wilts .3K 9
Downton on the Rock. Here .4C 26
Dowsby. Linc .7J 37
Dowsdale. Linc .8K 37
Dowthwaitehead. Cumb .3B 46
Doxey. Staf .7H 35
Doxford. Nmbd .7J 61
Doynton. S Glo .6F 18
Drabblegate. Norf .7J 39
Draethen. Cphy .6M 17
Draffan. S Lan .5F 58
Dragonby. N Lin .6G 43
Dragon's Green. W Sus .3J 11
Drakelow. Worc .3G 27
Drakemyre. N Ayr .4A 58
Drakes Broughton. Worc .7H 27
Drakes Cross. Worc .4J 27
Drakewalls. Corn .8D 6
Draperstown. M Ulst .4E 92
Draughton. Nptn .4E 28
Draughton. N Yor .2J 41
Drax. N Yor .5D 42
Draycot. Oxon .3D 20
Draycote. Warw .4B 28
Draycot Foliat. Swin .6K 19
Draycott. Derbs .6B 36
Draycott. Glos .8K 27
Draycott. Shrp .2G 27
Draycott. Som
nr. Cheddar .8C 18
nr. Yeovil .3D 8
Draycott. Worc .7G 27
Draycott in the Clay. Staf .7K 35
Draycott in the Moors. Staf .5H 35
Drayford. Devn .4G 7
Drayton. Leics .2F 28
Drayton. Linc .6K 37
Drayton. Norf .8H 39
Drayton. Nptn .5C 28
Drayton. Oxon
nr. Abingdon .4B 20
nr. Banbury .7B 28
Drayton. Port .5D 10
Drayton. Som .3C 8
Drayton. Warw .6K 27
Drayton. Worc .4H 27
Drayton Bassett. Staf .1K 27
Drayton Beauchamp. Buck .2G 21
Drayton Parslow. Buck .1F 20
Drayton St Leonard. Oxon .4C 20
Drebley. N Yor .2J 41
Dreenhill. Pemb .5F 14
Y Dref. Gwyn .7D 32
Drefach. Carm
nr. Meidrim .5M 15
nr. Newcastle Emlyn .3K 15
nr. Tumble .4J 15
Drefach. Cdgn .2L 15
Dreghorn. N Ayr .6B 58
Drellingore. Kent .1J 13
Drem. E Lot .2C 60
Y Drenewydd. Powy .3L 25
Dreumasdal. W Isl .2D 74
Drewsteignton. Devn .6G 7
Driby. Linc .2L 37
Driffield. E Yor .2H 43
Driffield. Glos .4J 19
Drift. Corn .6H 3
Drigg. Cumb .5K 45
Drighlington. W Yor .5L 41
Drimnin. High .2L 63
Drimpton. Dors .5C 8
Dringhoe. E Yor .2J 43
Drinisiadar. W Isl .4C 76
Drinkstone. Suff .5F 30
Drinkstone Green. Suff .5F 30
Drointon. Staf .7J 35
Droitwich Spa. Worc .5G 27
Droman. High .6D 84
Dromara. Lis .6H 93
Dromore. Arm .5C 92
Dromore. Ferm .5C 92
Dron. Per .6E 66
Dronfield. Derbs .2A 36
Dronfield Woodhouse. Derbs .2M 35
Drongan. E Ayr .8C 58
Dronley. Ang .4G 67
Droop. Dors .5F 8
Drope. V Glam .7L 17
Droxford. Hants .4D 10
Droylsden. G Man .8G 41
Druggers End. Worc .8F 26
Druid. Den .6K 33
Druid's Heath. W Mid .1J 27
Druidston. Pemb .5E 14
Druim. High .8K 79
Druimarbin. High .8A 70
Druim Fhearna. High .4H 69
Druimindarroch. High .7H 69
Druim Saighdinis. W Isl .7K 75
Drum. Per .7D 66
Drumaness. New M .6H 93
Drumaroad. New M .6H 93
Drumbeg. High .8D 84
Drumblade. Abers .1E 72
Drumbo. Lis .5H 93
Drumbuie. Dum .3L 51
Drumbuie. High .2J 69
Drumburgh. Cumb .6G 53
Drumburn. Dum .5D 52
Drumchapel. Glas .2D 58
Drumchardine. High .1F 70
Drumchork. High .5K 77
Drumclog. S Lan .6E 58
Drumeldrie. Fife .7H 67
Drumelzier. Bord .6K 59
Drumfearn. High .4H 69
Drumgask. High .6G 71
Drumgelloch. N Lan .3F 58
Drumgley. Ang .2H 67
Drumguish. High .6H 71
Drumin. Mor .2A 72
Drumindorsair. High .1E 70
Drumintee. New M .7G 93
Drumlamford House. S Ayr .4H 51
Drumlasie. Abers .5F 72
Drumlemble. Arg .8F 56
Drumlithie. Abers .7G 73
Drummoddie. Dum .7J 51
Drummond. High .7G 79
Drummore. Dum .8G 51
Drummuir. Mor .1C 72
Drumnacanvy. Arm .6G 93
Drumnadrochit. High .2F 70
Drumnagorrach. Mor .8E 80
Drumnakilly. Ferm .5D 92
Drumoak. Abers .6G 73
Drumquin. Ferm .5C 92
Drumraighland. Caus .2E 92
Drumrunie. High .3B 78
Drumry. W Dun .2D 58
Drums. Abers .3J 73
Drumsleet. Dum .4D 52
Drumsmittal. High .1G 71
Drums of Park. Abers .8E 80
Drumsturdy. Ang .4H 67
Drumsurn. Caus .3E 92
Drumtochty Castle. Abers .7F 72
Drumuie. High .1F 68
Drumuillie. High .3K 71
Drumvaich. Stir .7L 65
Drumwhindle. Abers .2J 73
Drunkendub. Ang .3K 67
Drury. Flin .3A 34
Drury Square. Norf .8F 38
Drybeck. Cumb .4E 46
Drybridge. Mor .7D 80
Drybridge. N Ayr .6B 58
Drybrook. Glos .2E 18
Drybrook. Here .2D 18
Dryburgh. Bord .6C 60
Dry Doddington. Linc .5F 36
Dry Drayton. Cambs .5L 29
Drym. Corn .5K 3
Drymen. Stir .1C 58
Drymuir. Abers .1J 73
Drynachan Lodge. High .2J 71
Drynie Park. High .8F 78
Drynoch. High .2F 68
Dry Sandford. Oxon .3B 20
Dryslwyn. Carm .2E 16
Dry Street. Essx .5C 22
Dryton. Shrp .1D 26
Dubford. Abers .7G 81
Dubiton. Abers .8F 80
Dubton. Ang .2J 67
Duchally. High .2D 78
Duck End. Essx .1C 22
Duckington. Ches W .4C 34
Ducklington. Oxon .3A 20
Duckmanton. Derbs .2B 36
Duck Street. Hants .1M 9
Dudbridge. Glos .3G 19
Duddenhoe End. Essx .8A 30
Duddingston. Edin .2L 59
Duddington. Nptn .1G 29
Duddleswell. E Sus .3A 12
Duddo. Nmbd .5G 61
Duddon. Ches W .3D 34
Duddon Bridge. Cumb .6L 45
Dudleston. Shrp .6B 34
Dudleston Heath. Shrp .6B 34
Dudley. Tyne .4F 54
Dudley. W Mid .3H 27
Dudston. Shrp .3M 25
Dudwells. Pemb .4F 14
Duffield. Derbs .5M 35
Duffryn. Neat .5H 17
Dufftown. Mor .1C 72
Duffus. Mor .7A 80
Dufton. Cumb .3E 46
Duggleby. N Yor .1F 42
Duirinish. High .2J 69
Duisdalemore. High .4H 69
Duisdeil Mòr. High .4H 69
Duisky. High .8M 69
Dukesfield. Nmbd .6C 54
Dukestown. Blae .4L 17
Dukinfield. G Man .8H 41
Dulas. IOA .2D 32
Dulcote. Som .1D 8
Dulford. Devn .5K 7
Dull. Per .3B 66
Dullatur. N Lan .2F 58
Dullingham. Cambs .6C 30
Dullingham Ley. Cambs .6C 30
Dulnain Bridge. High .3K 71
Duloe. Bed .5J 29
Duloe. Corn .6E 4
Dulverton. Som .3J 7
Dulwich. G Lon .6L 21
Dumbarton. W Dun .2C 58
Dumbleton. Glos .8J 27
Dumfin. Arg .1B 58
Dumfries. Dum .108 (4D 52)
Dumgoyne. Stir .1D 58
Dummer. Hants .1C 10
Dumpford. W Sus .3F 10
Dun. Ang .1K 67
Dunadry. Ant .4G 93
Dunaghy. Caus .2F 93
Dunagoil. Arg .4K 57
Dunalastair. Per .2M 65
Dunan. High .3G 69
Dunball. Som .1B 8
Dunbar. E Lot .2D 60
Dunbeath. High .1A 80
Dunbeg. Arg .4C 64
Dunblane. Stir .7A 66
Dunbog. Fife .6F 66
Dunbridge. Hants .3M 9
Duncanston. Abers .3E 72
Duncanston. High .8F 78
Dun Charlabhaigh. W Isl .7E 82
Dunchideock. Devn .7H 7
Dunchurch. Warw .4B 28
Duncote. Nptn .6D 28
Duncow. Dum .3D 52
Duncrievie. Per .7E 66
Duncton. W Sus .4G 11
Dundee. D'dee .108 (4H 67)
Dundee Airport. D'dee .5G 67
Dundon. Som .2C 8
Dundonald. Lis .5J 93
Dundonald. S Ayr .6B 58
Dundonnell. High .5A 78
Dundraw. Cumb .7G 53
Dundreggan. High .4D 70
Dundrennan. Dum .7B 52
Dundridge. Hants .4C 10
Dundrod. Lis .5H 93
Dundrum. New M .7J 93
Dundry. N Som .7D 18
Dunecht. Abers .5G 73
Dunfermline. Fife .1J 59
Dunford Bridge. S Yor .7K 41
Dungannon. M Ulst .5E 92
Dungate. Kent .8F 22
Dunge. Wilts .8G 19
Dungeness. Kent .4G 13
Dungiven. Caus .3E 92
Dungworth. S Yor .1L 35
Dunham-on-the-Hill. Ches W .2C 34
Dunham-on-Trent. Notts .2F 36
Dunhampton. Worc .5G 27
Dunham Town. G Man .1F 34
Dunham Woodhouses. G Man .1F 34
Dunholme. Linc .2H 37
Dunino. Fife .6J 67
Dunipace. Falk .1G 59
Dunira. Per .5M 65
Dunkeld. Per .3D 66
Dunkerton. Bath .8F 18
Dunkeswell. Devn .5L 7
Dunkeswick. N Yor .3M 41
Dunkirk. Kent .8G 23
Dunkirk. S Glo .5F 18
Dunkirk. Staf .4G 35
Dunkirk. Wilts .7H 19
Dunk's Green. Kent .8C 22
Dunlappie. Ang .1J 67
Dunley. Hants .8B 20
Dunley. Worc .5F 26
Dunlichity Lodge. High .2G 71
Dunlop. E Ayr .5C 58
Dunloy. Caus .3G 93
Dunmaglass Lodge. High .3F 70
Dunmore. Arg .3G 57
Dunmore. Falk .1G 59
Dunmore. High .1F 70
Dunmurry. Bel .5H 93
Dunnamanagh. Derr .3D 92
Dunnaval. New M .7H 93
Dunnet. High .4D 86
Dunnichen. Ang .3J 67
Dunning. Per .6D 66
Dunnington. E Yor .2J 43
Dunnington. Warw .6J 27
Dunnington. York .2D 42
Dunningwell. Cumb .6L 45
Dunnockshaw. Lanc .5G 41
Dunoon. Arg .2L 57
Dunphail. Mor .1L 71
Dunragit. Dum .6G 51
Dunrostan. Arg .1G 57
Duns. Bord .4F 60
Dunsby. Linc .7J 37
Dunscar. G Man .6F 40
Dunscore. Dum .3C 52
Dunscroft. S Yor .7D 42
Dunsdale. Red C .4D 48
Dunsden Green. Oxon .6E 20
Dunsfold. Surr .2H 11
Dunsford. Devn .7H 7
Dunshalt. Fife .6F 66
Dunshillock. Abers .1J 73
Dunsley. N Yor .4F 48
Dunsley. Staf .3G 27
Dunsmore. Buck .3F 20
Dunsop Bridge. Lanc .2E 40
Dunstable. C Beds .1H 21
Dunstal. Staf .7J 35
Dunstall. Staf .7K 35
Dunstall Green. Suff .5D 30
Dunstall Hill. W Mid .1H 27
Dunstan. Nmbd .8K 61
Dunster. Som .1J 7
Duns Tew. Oxon .1B 20
Dunston. Linc .3H 37
Dunston. Norf .1J 31
Dunston. Staf .8H 35
Dunston. Tyne .5F 54
Dunstone. Devn .6H 5
Dunston Heath. Staf .8H 35
Dunsville. S Yor .7D 42
Dunswell. E Yor .4H 43
Dunsyre. S Lan .5J 59
Dunterton. Devn .8C 6
Duntisbourne Abbots. Glos .3H 19
Duntisbourne Leer. Glos .3H 19
Duntisbourne Rouse. Glos .3H 19
Duntish. Dors .5E 8
Duntocher. W Dun .2C 58
Dunton. Buck .1F 20
Dunton. C Beds .7K 29
Dunton. Norf .6E 38
Dunton Bassett. Leics .2C 28
Dunton Green. Kent .8B 22
Dunton Patch. Norf .6E 38
Duntulm. High .6F 76
Dunure. S Ayr .8A 58
Dunvant. Swan .5E 16
Dunvegan. High .1D 68
Dunwich. Suff .4L 31
Dunwood. Staf .4H 35
Durdar. Cumb .6J 53
Durgates. E Sus .2C 12
Durham. Dur .108 (7F 54)
Durham Tees Valley Airport. Darl .4A 48
Durisdeer. Dum .1C 52
Durisdeermill. Dum .1C 52
Durkar. W Yor .6M 41
Durleigh. Som .2A 8
Durley. Hants .4C 10
Durley. Wilts .7L 19
Durley Street. Hants .4C 10
Durlow Common. Here .8E 26
Durnamuck. High .4M 77
Durness. High .5G 85
Durno. Abers .3G 73
Durns Town. Hants .6L 9
Duror. High .2D 64
Durran. Arg .7D 64
Durran. High .5C 86
Durrant Green. Kent .2E 12
Durrants. Hants .4E 10
Durrington. W Sus .5J 11
Durrington. Wilts .1K 9
Dursley. Glos .4F 18
Dursley Cross. Glos .2E 18
Durston. Som .3A 8
Durweston. Dors .5G 9
Dury. Shet .2E 90
Duston. Nptn .5E 28
Duthil. High .3K 71
Dutlas. Powy .5M 25
Duton Hill. Essx .1C 22
Dutson. Corn .7C 6
Dutton. Ches W .2D 34
Duxford. Cambs .7A 30
Duxford. Oxon .4A 20
Dwygyfylchi. Cnwy .3G 33
Dwyran. IOA .4D 32
Dyce. Aber .4H 73
Dyffryn. B'end .5H 17
Dyffryn. Carm .4K 15
Dyffryn. Pemb .3F 14
Dyffryn. V Glam .7K 17
Dyffryn Ardudwy. Gwyn .8E 32
Dyffryn Castell. Cdgn .4G 25
Dyffryn Ceidrych. Carm .2G 17
Dyffryn Cellwen. Neat .4H 17
Dyke. Linc .7J 37
Dyke. Mor .8K 79
Dykehead. Ang .1G 67
Dykehead. N Lan .3G 59
Dykehead. Stir .8K 65
Dykend. Ang .2F 66
Dykesfield. Cumb .6H 53
Dylife. Powy .3H 25
Dymchurch. Kent .3H 13
Dymock. Glos .8F 26
Dyrham. S Glo .6F 18
Dysart. Fife .8G 67
Dyserth. Den .3K 33

E

Eachwick. Nmbd .4E 54
Eadar Dha Fhadhail. W Isl .8D 82
Eagland Hill. Lanc .3C 40
Eagle. Linc .3F 36
Eagle Barnsdale. Linc .3F 36
Eagle Moor. Linc .3F 36
Eaglescliffe. Stoc T .4B 48
Eaglesfield. Cumb .2K 45
Eaglesfield. Dum .4G 53
Eaglesham. E Ren .4D 58
Eaglethorpe. Nptn .2H 29
Eagley. G Man .6F 40
Eairy. IOM .7B 44
Eakley Lanes. Mil .6F 28
Eakring. Notts .3D 36
Ealand. N Lin .6E 42
Ealing. G Lon .5J 21
Eallabus. Arg .3C 56
Eals. Nmbd .6L 53
Eamont Bridge. Cumb .3D 46
Earby. Lanc .3H 41
Earcroft. Bkbn .5E 40
Eardington. Shrp .2F 26
Eardisland. Here .6C 26
Eardisley. Here .7B 26
Eardiston. Shrp .7B 34
Eardiston. Worc .5E 26
Earith. Cambs .4L 29
Earlais. High .7E 76
Earle. Nmbd .7G 61
Earlesfield. Linc .6G 37
Earlestown. Mers .8D 40
Earley. Wok .6E 20
Earlham. Norf .1H 31
Earlish. High .7E 76
Earls Barton. Nptn .5F 28
Earls Colne. Essx .1E 22
Earls Common. Worc .6H 27
Earl's Croome. Worc .7G 27
Earlsdon. W Mid .4M 27
Earlsferry. Fife .7H 67
Earlsford. Abers .2H 73
Earl's Green. Suff .5G 31
Earlsheaton. W Yor .5L 41
Earl Shilton. Leics .2B 28
Earl Soham. Suff .5J 31
Earl Sterndale. Derbs .3J 35
Earlston. E Ayr .6C 58
Earlston. Bord .6C 60
Earl Stonham. Suff .6H 31
Earlstoun. Dum .3M 51
Earlswood. Mon .4C 18
Earlswood. Warw .4K 27
Earlyvale. Bord .4L 59
Earnley. W Sus .6F 10
Earsairidh. W Isl .6D 74
Earsdon. Tyne .4G 55
Earsham. Norf .3K 31
Earsham Street. Suff .4J 31
Earswick. York .2D 42
Eartham. W Sus .5G 11
Earthcott Green. S Glo .5E 18
Easby. N Yor
nr. Great Ayton .5C 48
nr. Richmond .5K 47
Easdale. Arg .6B 64
Easebourne. W Sus .3F 10
Easenhall. Warw .4B 28
Eashing. Surr .1G 11
Easington. Buck .2D 20
Easington. Dur .7H 55
Easington. E Yor .6L 43
Easington. Nmbd .6J 61
Easington. Oxon
nr. Banbury .8B 28
nr. Watlington .4D 20
Easington. Red C .4E 48
Easington Colliery. Dur .7H 55
Easington Lane. Tyne .7G 55
Easingwold. N Yor .8C 48
Eassie. Ang .3G 67
Eassie and Nevay. Ang .3G 67
East Aberthaw. V Glam .8K 17
Eastacombe. Devn .3E 6
Eastacott. Devn .3F 6
East Allington. Devn .7K 5
East Anstey. Devn .3H 7
East Anton. Hants .1A 10
East Appleton. N Yor .6L 47
East Ardsley. W Yor .5M 41
East Ashley. Devn .4F 6
East Ashling. W Sus .5F 10
East Aston. Hants .1B 10
East Ayton. N Yor .7G 49
East Barkwith. Linc .1J 37
East Barnby. N Yor .4F 48
East Barnet. G Lon .4K 21
East Barns. E Lot .2E 60
East Barsham. Norf .6F 38
East Beach. W Sus .6F 10
East Beckham. Norf .6H 39
East Bedfont. G Lon .6H 21
East Bennan. N Ayr .7J 57
East Bergholt. Suff .8G 31
East Bierley. W Yor .5L 41
East Bilney. Norf .8F 38
East Blatchington. E Sus .5A 12
East Bloxworth. Dors .6G 9
East Boldre. Hants .5A 10
East Bolton. Nmbd .8J 61
Eastbourne. Darl .4L 47
Eastbourne. E Sus .108 (6C 12)
East Brent. Som .8B 18
East Bridge. Suff .5L 31
East Bridgford. Notts .5D 36
East Briscoe. Dur .4H 47
East Buckland. Devn
nr. Barnstaple .2F 6
nr. Thurlestone .7J 5
East Budleigh. Devn .7K 7
Eastburn. W Yor .3J 41
East Burnham. Buck .5G 21
East Burrafirth. Shet .2D 90
East Burton. Dors .7G 9
Eastbury. Herts .4H 21
Eastbury. W Ber .6M 19
East Butsfield. Dur .7E 54
East Butterleigh. Devn .5J 7
East Butterwick. N Lin .7F 42
Eastby. N Yor .2J 41
East Calder. W Lot .3J 59
East Carleton. Norf .1H 31
East Carlton. Nptn .3F 28
East Carlton. W Yor .3L 41
East Chaldon. Dors .7F 8
East Challow. Oxon .5A 20
East Charleton. Devn .7K 5
East Chelborough. Dors .5D 8
East Chiltington. E Sus .4L 11
East Chinnock. Som .4C 8
East Chisenbury. Wilts .8K 19
Eastchurch. Kent .6F 22
East Clandon. Surr .8H 21
East Claydon. Buck .1E 20
East Clevedon. N Som .6C 18
East Clyne. High .3J 79
East Clyth. High .8D 86
East Coker. Som .4D 8
East Combe. Som .2L 7
Eastcombe. Glos .3G 19
East Common. N Yor .4D 42
East Compton. Som .1E 8
East Cornworthy. Devn .6L 5
Eastcote. G Lon .5J 21
Eastcote. Nptn .6D 28
Eastcote. W Mid .4K 27
Eastcott. Corn .4B 6
Eastcott. Wilts .8J 19
East Cottingwith. E Yor .3E 42
Eastcourt. Wilts
nr. Pewsey .7L 19
nr. Tetbury .4H 19
East Cowes. IOW .6C 10
East Cowick. E Yor .5D 42
East Cowton. N Yor .5M 47
East Cramlington. Nmbd .4F 54
East Cranmore. Som .1E 8
East Creech. Dors .7H 9
East Croachy. High .3G 71
East Dean. E Sus .6B 12
East Dean. Glos .1E 18
East Dean. Hants .3L 9
East Dean. W Sus .4G 11
East Down. Devn .1F 6
East Drayton. Notts .2E 36
East Dundry. N Som .7D 18
East Ella. Hull .5H 43
East End. Cambs .4L 29
East End. Dors .6H 9
East End. E Yor
nr. Ulrome .2J 43
nr. Withernsea .5K 43
East End. Hants
nr. Lymington .6A 10
nr. Newbury .7B 20
East End. Herts .1A 22
East End. Kent
nr. Minster .6F 22
nr. Tenterden .2E 12
East End. N Som .6C 18
East End. Oxon .2A 20
East End. Som .8D 18
East End. Suff .8H 31
Easter Ardross. High .6G 79
Easter Balgedie. Per .7E 66
Easter Balmoral. Abers .6B 72
Easter Brae. High .7G 79
Easter Buckieburn. Stir .1F 58
Easter Compton. S Glo .5D 18
Easter Fearn. High .5G 79
Easter Galcantray. High .1J 71
Eastergate. W Sus .5G 11
Easterhouse. Glas .3E 58
Easter Howgate. Midl .3L 59
Easter Kinkell. High .8F 78
Easter Lednathie. Ang .1G 67
Easter Ogil. Ang .1H 67
Easter Ord. Abers .5H 73
Easter Quarff. Shet .4E 90
Easter Rhynd. Per .6E 66
Easter Skeld. Shet .3D 90
Easter Suddie. High .8G 79
Easterton. Wilts .8J 19
Eastertown. Som .8B 18
Easter Tulloch. Abers .8G 73
East Everleigh. Wilts .8L 19
East Farleigh. Kent .8D 22
East Farndon. Nptn .3E 28
East Ferry. Linc .8F 42
Eastfield. N Lan
nr. Caldercruix .3G 59
nr. Harthill .3G 59
Eastfield. N Yor .7H 49
Eastfield. S Lan .3E 58
Eastfield Hall. Nmbd .1F 54
East Fortune. E Lot .2C 60
East Garforth. W Yor .4B 42
East Garston. W Ber .6A 20
Eastgate. Dur .8C 54
Eastgate. Norf .7H 39
East Ginge. Oxon .5B 20
East Gores. Essx .1E 22
East Goscote. Leics .8D 36
East Grafton. Wilts .7L 19
East Green. Suff .6C 30
East Grimstead. Wilts .3L 9
East Grinstead. W Sus .2L 11
East Guldeford. E Sus .3F 12
East Haddon. Nptn .5D 28
East Hagbourne. Oxon .5C 20

F

Ford—Great Hockham

Ford. *Nmbd* 6G 61
Ford. *Plym* 6G 5
Ford. *Shrp* 8C 34
Ford. *Som*
nr. Wells 8D 18
nr. Wiveliscombe 3K 7
Ford. *Staf* 4J 35
Ford. *W Sus* 5H 11
Ford. *Wilts*
nr. Chippenham 6G 19
nr. Salisbury 2K 9
Forda. *Devn* 2D 6
Ford Barton. *Devn* 4J 7
Fordcombe. *Kent* 1B 12
Fordell. *Fife* 1K 59
Forden. *Powy* 2M 25
Ford End. *Essx* 2C 22
Forder Green. *Devn* 5K 5
Ford Green. *Lanc* 3C 40
Fordham. *Cambs* 4C 30
Fordham. *Essx* 1F 22
Fordham. *Norf* 2C 30
Fordham Heath. *Essx* 1F 22
Ford Heath. *Shrp* 8C 34
Fordhouses. *W Mid* 1H 27
Fordie. *Per* 5A 66
Fordingbridge. *Hants* 4K 9
Fordington. *Linc* 2M 37
Fordon. *E Yor* 8H 49
Fordoun. *Abers* 8G 73
Ford Street. *Essx* 1F 22
Ford Street. *Som* 4L 7
Fordton. *Devn* 6H 7
Fordwells. *Oxon* 2M 19
Fordwich. *Kent* 8H 23
Fordyce. *Abers* 7E 80
Forebridge. *Staf* 7H 35
Foreglen. *Caus* 3E 92
Foremark. *Derbs* 7M 35
Forest. *N Yor* 5L 47
Forestburn Gate. *Nmbd* 2D 54
Foresterseat. *Mor* 8A 80
Forest Green. *Glos* 4G 19
Forest Green. *Surr* 1J 11
Forest Hall. *Cumb* 5D 46
Forest Head. *Cumb* 6K 53
Forest Hill. *Oxon* 3C 20
Forest-in-Teesdale. *Dur* 3G 47
Forest Lodge. *Per* 8K 71
Forest Mill. *Clac* 8C 66
Forest Row. *E Sus* 2M 11
Forestside. *W Sus* 4E 10
Forest Town. *Notts* 3C 36
Forfar. *Ang* 2H 67
Forgandenny. *Per* 6D 66
Forge. *Powy* 3G 25
The Forge. *Here* 6B 26
Forge Side. *Torf* 4M 17
Forgewood. *N Lan* 4F 58
Forgie. *Mor* 8C 80
Forgue. *Abers* 1F 72
Forkill. *New M* 7G 93
Formby. *Mers* 7B 40
Forncett End. *Norf* 2H 31
Forncett St Mary. *Norf* 2H 31
Forncett St Peter. *Norf* 2H 31
Forneth. *Per* 3D 66
Fornham All Saints. *Suff* 5E 30
Fornham St Martin. *Suff* 5E 30
Forres. *Mor* 8L 79
Forrestfield. *N Lan* 3G 59
Forrest Lodge. *Dum* 3L 51
Forsbrook. *Staf* 5H 35
Forse. *High* 8D 86
Forsinard. *High* 7L 85
Forss. *High* 5B 86
The Forstal. *Kent* 2G 13
Forston. *Dors* 6E 8
Fort Augustus. *High* 5D 70
Forteviot. *Per* 6D 66
Fort George. *High* 8H 79
Forth. *S Lan* 4H 59
Forthampton. *Glos* 8G 27
Forthay. *Glos* 4F 18
Fortingall. *Per* 3M 65
Fort Matilda. *Inv* 2A 58
Forton. *Hants* 1B 10
Forton. *Lanc* 2C 40
Forton. *Shrp* 8C 34
Forton. *Som* 5B 8
Forton. *Staf* 7F 34
Forton Heath. *Shrp* 8C 34
Fortrie. *Abers* 1F 72
Fortrose. *High* 8H 79
Fortuneswell. *Dors* 8E 8
Fort William. *High* 8B 70
Forty Green. *Buck* 4G 21
Forty Hill. *G Lon* 4L 21
Forward Green. *Suff* 6G 31
Fosbury. *Wilts* 8M 19
Foscot. *Oxon* 1L 19
Fosdyke. *Linc* 6L 37
Foss. *Per* 2A 66
Fossebridge. *Glos* 2J 19
Foster Street. *Essx* 3A 22
Foston. *Derbs* 6K 35
Foston. *Leics* 2D 28
Foston. *Linc* 5F 36
Foston. *N Yor* 1D 42
Foston on the Wolds. *E Yor* 2J 43
Fotherby. *Linc* 8L 43
Fothergill. *Cumb* 8E 52
Fotheringhay. *Nptn* 2H 29
Foubister. *Orkn* 1G 87
Foula Airport. *Shet* 4B 90
Foul Anchor. *Cambs* 8A 38
Foulbridge. *Cumb* 7J 53
Foulden. *Norf* 2D 30
Foulden. *Bord* 4G 61
Foul Mile. *E Sus* 4C 12
Foulridge. *Lanc* 3G 41
Foulsham. *Norf* 7G 39
Fountainhall. *Bord* 5B 60
The Four Alls. *Shrp* 6E 34
Four Ashes. *Staf*
nr. Cannock 1H 27
nr. Kinver 3G 27
Four Ashes. *Suff* 4G 31
Four Crosses. *Powy*
nr. Llanerfyl 2K 25
nr. Llanymynech 8A 34
Four Crosses. *Staf* 1H 27
Four Elms. *Kent* 1A 12
Four Forks. *Som* 2M 7
Four Gotes. *Cambs* 8A 38
Four Lane End. *S Yor* 7L 41
Four Lane Ends. *Lanc* 2D 40
Four Lanes. *Corn* 5K 3
Fourlanes End. *Ches E* 4G 35
Four Marks. *Hants* 2D 10
Four Mile Bridge. *IOA* 3B 32
Four Oaks. *E Sus* 3E 12
Four Oaks. *Glos* 1E 18
Four Oaks. *W Mid* 3L 27
Four Roads. *Carm* 6L 15
Four Roads. *IOM* 8B 44
Fourstones. *Nmbd* 5B 54
Four Throws. *Kent* 3D 12
Fovant. *Wilts* 3J 9
Foveran. *Abers* 3J 73
Fowey. *Corn* 6D 4
Fowlershill. *Aber* 4J 73
Fowley Common. *Warr* 8E 40
Fowlis. *Ang* 4G 67
Fowlis Wester. *Per* 5C 66
Fowlmere. *Cambs* 7M 29
Fownhope. *Here* 8D 26
Fox Corner. *Surr* 8G 21
Foxcote. *Glos* 2J 19
Foxcote. *Som* 8F 18
Foxdale. *IOM* 7B 44
Foxearth. *Essx* 7E 30
Foxfield. *Cumb* 6M 45
Foxham. *Wilts* 6H 19
Fox Hatch. *Essx* 4B 22
Foxhole. *Corn* 6B 4
Foxholes. *N Yor* 8H 49
Foxhunt Green. *E Sus* 4B 12
Fox Lane. *Hants* 8F 20
Foxley. *Norf* 7G 39
Foxley. *Nptn* 6D 28
Foxley. *Wilts* 5G 19
Foxlydiate. *Worc* 5J 27
Fox Street. *Essx* 1G 23
Foxt. *Staf* 5J 35
Foxton. *Cambs* 7M 29
Foxton. *Dur* 3A 48
Foxton. *Leics* 3D 28
Foxton. *N Yor* 6B 48
Foxup. *N Yor* 8G 47
Foxwist Green. *Ches W* 3E 34
Foxwood. *Shrp* 4E 26
Foy. *Here* 1D 18
Foyers. *High* 3E 70
Foynesfield. *High* 8J 79
Fraddam. *Corn* 5J 3
Fraddon. *Corn* 6B 4
Fradley. *Staf* 8K 35
Fradley South. *Staf* 8K 35
Fradswell. *Staf* 6H 35
Fraisthorpe. *E Yor* 1J 43
Framfield. *E Sus* 3A 12
Framingham Earl. *Norf* 1J 31
Framingham Pigot. *Norf* 1J 31
Framlingham. *Suff* 5J 31
Frampton. *Dors* 6E 8
Frampton. *Linc* 6L 37
Frampton Cotterell. *S Glo* 5E 18
Frampton Mansell. *Glos* 3H 19
Frampton on Severn. *Glos* 3F 18
Frampton West End. *Linc* 5K 37
Framsden. *Suff* 6H 31
Framwellgate Moor. *Dur* 7F 54
Franche. *Worc* 4G 27
Frandley. *Ches W* 2E 34
Frankby. *Mers* 2M 33
Frankfort. *Norf* 7K 39
Frankley. *Worc* 3H 27
Frank's Bridge. *Powy* 7L 25
Frankton. *Warw* 4B 28
Frankwell. *Shrp* 8C 34
Frant. *E Sus* 2B 12
Fraserburgh. *Abers* 7J 81
Frating Green. *Essx* 1G 23
Fratton. *Port* 5D 10
Freathy. *Corn* 6G 5
Freckenham. *Suff* 4C 30
Freckleton. *Lanc* 5C 40
Freeby. *Leics* 7F 36
Freefolk Priors. *Hants* 1B 10
Freehay. *Staf* 5J 35
Freeland. *Oxon* 2B 20
Freester. *Shet* 2E 90
Freethorpe. *Norf* 1L 31
Freiston. *Linc* 5L 37
Freiston Shore. *Linc* 5L 37
Fremington. *Devn* 2E 6
Fremington. *N Yor* 6J 47
Frenchay. *S Glo* 6E 18
Frenchbeer. *Devn* 7F 6
Frenich. *Stir* 7J 65
Frensham. *Surr* 1F 10
Frenze. *Norf* 3H 31
Fresgoe. *High* 5A 86
Freshfield. *Mers* 7A 40
Freshford. *Bath* 7F 18
Freshwater. *IOW* 7M 9
Freshwater Bay. *IOW* 7M 9
Freshwater East. *Pemb* 7G 15
Fressingfield. *Suff* 4J 31
Freston. *Suff* 8H 31
Freswick. *High* 5E 86
Fretherne. *Glos* 3F 18
Frettenham. *Norf* 8J 39
Freuchie. *Fife* 7F 66
Freystrop. *Pemb* 5F 14
Friar's Gate. *E Sus* 2A 12
Friar Waddon. *Dors* 7E 8
Friday Bridge. *Cambs* 1A 30
Friday Street. *E Sus* 5C 12
Friday Street. *Surr* 1J 11
Fridaythorpe. *E Yor* 2F 42
Friden. *Derbs* 3K 35
Friern Barnet. *G Lon* 4K 21
Friesthorpe. *Linc* 1H 37
Frieston. *Linc* 5G 37
Frieth. *Buck* 4E 20
Friezeland. *Notts* 4B 36
Frilford. *Oxon* 4B 20
Frilsham. *W Ber* 6C 20
Frimley. *Surr* 8F 20
Frimley Green. *Surr* 8F 20
Frindsbury. *Medw* 7D 22
Fring. *Norf* 6D 38
Fringford. *Oxon* 1D 20
Frinsted. *Kent* 8E 22
Frinton-on-Sea. *Essx* 2J 23
Friockheim. *Ang* 3J 67
Friog. *Gwyn* 1F 24
Frisby. *Leics* 1E 28
Frisby on the Wreake. *Leics* 8D 36
Friskney. *Linc* 4A 38
Friskney Eaudyke. *Linc* 4A 38
Friston. *E Sus* 6B 12
Friston. *Suff* 5L 31
Fritchley. *Derbs* 4A 36
Fritham. *Hants* 4L 9
Frith Bank. *Linc* 5L 37
Frith Common. *Worc* 5E 26
Frithelstock. *Devn* 4D 6
Frithelstock Stone. *Devn* 4D 6
Frithsden. *Herts* 3H 21
Frithville. *Linc* 4L 37
Frittenden. *Kent* 1E 12
Frittiscombe. *Devn* 7L 5
Fritton. *Norf*
nr. Great Yarmouth 1L 31
nr. Long Stratton 2J 31
Fritwell. *Oxon* 1C 20
Frizinghall. *W Yor* 4K 41
Frizington. *Cumb* 3K 45
Frobost. *W Isl* 3D 74
Frocester. *Glos* 3F 18
Frochas. *Powy* 2L 25
Frodesley. *Shrp* 1D 26
Frodingham. *N Lin* 6G 43
Frodsham. *Ches W* 2D 34
Froggatt. *Derbs* 2L 35
Froghall. *Staf* 5J 35
Frogham. *Hants* 4K 9
Frogham. *Kent* 8J 23
Frogmore. *Devn* 7K 5
Frogmore. *Hants* 7F 20
Frogmore. *Herts* 3J 21
Frognall. *Linc* 8J 37
Frogshall. *Norf* 6J 39
Frogwell. *Corn* 5F 4
Frolesworth. *Leics* 2C 28
Frome. *Som* 1F 8
Fromefield. *Som* 1F 8
Frome St Quintin. *Dors* 5D 8
Fromes Hill. *Here* 7E 26
Fron. *Gwyn* 7C 32
Fron. *Powy*
nr. Llandrindod Wells 6K 25
nr. Newtown 3L 25
nr. Welshpool 2M 25
Y Fron. *Gwyn* 5E 32
Froncysyllte. *Wrex* 5A 34
Frongoch. *Gwyn* 7J 33
Fron Isaf. *Wrex* 5A 34
Fronoleu. *Gwyn* 7G 33
Frosterley. *Dur* 8D 54
Frotoft. *Orkn* 7D 88
Froxfield. *C Beds* 8G 29
Froxfield. *Wilts* 7L 19
Froxfield Green. *Hants* 3E 10
Fryern Hill. *Hants* 3B 10
Fryerning. *Essx* 3C 22
Fryton. *N Yor* 8D 48
Fugglestone St Peter. *Wilts* 2K 9
Fulbeck. *Linc* 4G 37
Fulbourn. *Cambs* 6B 30
Fulbrook. *Oxon* 2L 19
Fulflood. *Hants* 2B 10
Fulford. *Som* 3M 7
Fulford. *Staf* 6H 35
Fulford. *York* 3D 42
Fulham. *G Lon* 6K 21
Fulking. *W Sus* 4K 11
Fuller's Moor. *Ches W* 4C 34
Fuller Street. *Essx* 2D 22
Fullerton. *Hants* 2A 10
Fulletby. *Linc* 2K 37
Full Sutton. *E Yor* 2E 42
Fullwood. *E Ayr* 4C 58
Fulmer. *Buck* 5G 21
Fulmodestone. *Norf* 6F 38
Fulnetby. *Linc* 2H 37
Fulney. *Linc* 7K 37
Fulstow. *Linc* 8L 43
Fulthorpe. *Stoc T* 3B 48
Fulwell. *Tyne* 6G 55
Fulwood. *Lanc* 4D 40
Fulwood. *Notts* 4B 36
Fulwood. *Som* 4M 7
Fulwood. *S Yor* 1L 35
Fundenhall. *Norf* 2H 31
Funtington. *W Sus* 5F 10
Funtley. *Hants* 5C 10
Funzie. *Shet* 4L 91
Furley. *Devn* 5A 8
Furnace. *Arg* 7E 64
Furnace. *Carm* 6M 15
Furnace. *Cdgn* 3F 24
Furner's Green. *E Sus* 3M 11
Furness Vale. *Derbs* 1J 35
Furneux Pelham. *Herts* 1M 21
Furzebrook. *Dors* 7H 9
Furzehill. *Devn* 1G 7
Furzehill. *Dors* 5J 9
Furzeley Corner. *Hants* 4D 10
Furzey Lodge. *Hants* 5A 10
Furzley. *Hants* 4L 9
Fyfield. *Essx* 3B 22
Fyfield. *Glos* 3L 19
Fyfield. *Hants* 1L 9
Fyfield. *Oxon* 4B 20
Fyfield. *Wilts* 7K 19
The Fylde. *Lanc* 4B 40
Fylingthorpe. *N Yor* 5G 49
Fyning. *W Sus* 3F 10
Fyvie. *Abers* 2G 73

G

Gabhsann bho Dheas. *W Isl* 6H 83
Gabhsann bho Thuath. *W Isl* 6H 83
Gabroc Hill. *E Ayr* 4C 58
Gadbrook. *Surr* 1K 11
Gaddesby. *Leics* 8D 36
Gadfa. *IOA* 2D 32
Gadgirth. *S Ayr* 7C 58
Gaer. *Powy* 2L 17
Gaerwen. *IOA* 3D 32
Gagingwell. *Oxon* 1B 20
Gaick Lodge. *High* 7H 71
Gailey. *Staf* 8H 35
Gainford. *Dur* 4K 47
Gainsborough. *Linc* 8F 42
Gainsborough. *Suff* 7H 31
Gainsford End. *Essx* 8D 30
Gairletter. *Arg* 1L 57
Gairloch. *Abers* 5G 73
Gairloch. *High* 6K 77
Gairlochy. *High* 7B 70
Gairney Bank. *Per* 8E 66
Gairnshiel Lodge. *Abers* 5B 72
Gaisgill. *Cumb* 5E 46
Gaitsgill. *Cumb* 7H 53
Galashiels. *Bord* 6B 60
Galgate. *Lanc* 2C 40
Galgorm. *ME Ant* 3G 93
Galhampton. *Som* 3E 8
Gallatown. *Fife* 8F 66
Galley Common. *Warw* 2M 27
Galleyend. *Essx* 3D 22
Galleywood. *Essx* 3D 22
Gallin. *Per* 3K 65
Gallowfauld. *Ang* 3H 67
Gallowhill. *Per* 4E 66
Gallowhill. *Ren* 3C 58
Gallowhills. *Abers* 8K 81
Gallows Green. *Staf* 5J 35
Gallows Green. *Worc* 5H 27
Gallowstree Common. *Oxon* 5D 20
Galltair. *High* 3K 69
Gallt Melyd. *Den* 2K 33
Galmington. *Som* 3M 7
Galmisdale. *High* 7F 68
Galmpton. *Devn* 7J 5
Galmpton. *Torb* 6L 5
Galmpton Warborough. *Torb* 6L 5
Galphay. *N Yor* 8L 47
Galston. *E Ayr* 6C 58
Galton. *Dors* 7F 8
Galtrigill. *High* 8C 76
Gamblesby. *Cumb* 8L 53
Gamblestown. *Arm* 6G 93
Gamelsby. *Cumb* 6G 53
Gamesley. *Derbs* 8J 41
Gamlingay. *Cambs* 6K 29
Gamlingay Cinques. *Cambs* 6K 29
Gamlingay Great Heath. *Cambs* 6K 29
Gammaton. *Devn* 3D 6
Gammersgill. *N Yor* 7J 47
Gamston. *Notts*
nr. Nottingham 6D 36
nr. Retford 2E 36
Ganarew. *Here* 2D 18
Ganavan. *Arg* 4C 64
Ganborough. *Glos* 1K 19
Gang. *Corn* 5F 4
Ganllwyd. *Gwyn* 8G 33
Gannochy. *Ang* 8E 72
Gannochy. *Per* 5E 66
Gansclet. *High* 7E 86
Ganstead. *E Yor* 4J 43
Ganthorpe. *N Yor* 8D 48
Ganton. *N Yor* 8G 49
Gants Hill. *G Lon* 5M 21
Gappah. *Devn* 8H 7
Garafad. *High* 7F 76
Garboldisham. *Norf* 3G 31
Garden City. *Flin* 3B 34
Gardeners Green. *Wok* 7F 20
Gardenstown. *Abers* 7H 81
Garden Village. *S Yor* 8L 41
Garden Village. *Swan* 5E 16
Garderhouse. *Shet* 3D 90
Gardham. *E Yor* 3G 43
Gardie. *Shet*
on Papa Stour 1B 90
on Unst 2L 91
Gardie Ho. *Shet* 3E 90
Gare Hill. *Wilts* 1F 8
Garelochhead. *Arg* 8G 65
Garford. *Oxon* 4B 20
Garforth. *W Yor* 4B 42
Gargrave. *N Yor* 2H 41
Gargunnock. *Stir* 8M 65
Garleffin. *S Ayr* 3F 50
Garlieston. *Dum* 7K 51
Garlinge Green. *Kent* 8H 23
Garlogie. *Abers* 5G 73
Garmelow. *Staf* 7F 34
Garmond. *Abers* 8H 81
Garmondsway. *Dur* 8G 55
Garmony. *Arg* 3A 64
Garmouth. *Mor* 7C 80
Garmston. *Shrp* 1E 26
Garnant. *Carm* 3F 16
Garndiffaith. *Torf* 3A 18
Garndolbenmaen. *Gwyn* 6D 32
Garnett Bridge. *Cumb* 6D 46
Garnfadryn. *Gwyn* 7B 32
Garnkirk. *N Lan* 3E 58
Garnlydan. *Blae* 3L 17
Garnsgate. *Linc* 7M 37
Garnswllt. *Swan* 4F 16
Garn yr Erw. *Torf* 3M 17
Garrabost. *W Isl* 8J 83
Garrallan. *E Ayr* 8D 58
Garras. *Corn* 6L 3
Garreg. *Gwyn* 6F 32
Garrigill. *Cumb* 7M 53
Garrison. *Ferm* 6A 92
Garriston. *N Yor* 6K 47
Garrogie Lodge. *High* 4F 70
Garros. *High* 7F 76
Garrow. *Per* 3B 66
Garsdale. *Cumb* 7F 46
Garsdale Head. *Cumb* 6F 46
Garsdon. *Wilts* 5H 19
Garshall Green. *Staf* 6H 35
Garsington. *Oxon* 3C 20
Garstang. *Lanc* 3C 40
Garston. *Mers* 1C 34
Garswood. *Mers* 8D 40
Gartcosh. *N Lan* 3E 58
Garth. *B'end* 5H 17
Garth. *Cdgn* 4F 24
Garth. *Gwyn* 7E 32
Garth. *IOM* 7C 44
Garth. *Powy*
nr. Builth Wells 8J 25
nr. Knighton 4A 26
Garth. *Shet*
nr. Sandness 2C 90
nr. Skellister 2E 90
Garth. *Wrex* 5A 34
Garthamlock. *Glas* 3E 58
Garthbrengy. *Powy* 1K 17
Gartheli. *Cdgn* 7E 24
Garthmyl. *Powy* 3L 25
Garthorpe. *Leics* 7F 36
Garthorpe. *N Lin* 6F 42
Garth Owen. *Powy* 3L 25
Garth Place. *Cphy* 6L 17
Garth Row. *Cumb* 6D 46
Gartly. *Abers* 2E 72
Gartmore. *Stir* 8K 65
Gartness. *N Lan* 3F 58
Gartness. *Stir* 1D 58
Gartocharn. *W Dun* 1C 58
Garton. *E Yor* 4K 43
Garton-on-the-Wolds. *E Yor* 2G 43
Gartsherrie. *N Lan* 3F 58
Gartymore. *High* 2L 79
Garvagh. *Caus* 3F 93
Garvaghy. *Ferm* 5D 92
Garvald. *E Lot* 2C 60
Garvamore. *High* 6F 70
Garvard. *Arg* 8J 63
Garvault. *High* 8K 85
Garve. *High* 7D 78
Garvestone. *Norf* 1G 31
Garvetagh. *Derr* 4C 92
Garvie. *Arg* 8E 64
Garvock. *Abers* 8G 73
Garvock. *Inv* 2A 58
Garway. *Here* 1C 18
Garway Common. *Here* 1C 18
Garway Hill. *Here* 1C 18
Garwick. *Linc* 5J 37
Gaskan. *High* 8K 69
Gasper. *Wilts* 2F 8
Gastard. *Wilts* 7G 19
Gasthorpe. *Norf* 3F 30
Gatcombe. *IOW* 7B 10
Gateacre. *Mers* 1C 34
Gatebeck. *Cumb* 7D 46
Gate Burton. *Linc* 1F 36
Gateforth. *N Yor* 5C 42
Gatehead. *E Ayr* 6B 58
Gate Helmsley. *N Yor* 2D 42
Gatehouse. *Nmbd* 3A 54
Gatehouse of Fleet. *Dum* 6M 51
Gatelawbridge. *Dum* 2D 52
Gateley. *Norf* 7F 38
Gatenby. *N Yor* 7M 47
Gatesgarth. *Cumb* 3L 45
Gateshead. *Tyne* 5F 54
Gatesheath. *Ches W* 3C 34
Gateside. *Ang*
nr. Forfar 3H 67
nr. Kirriemuir 3G 67
Gateside. *Fife* 7E 66
Gateside. *N Ayr* 4B 58
Gathurst. *G Man* 7D 40
Gatley. *G Man* 1G 35
Gatton. *Surr* 8K 21
Gattonside. *Bord* 6C 60
Gatwick Airport. *W Sus* **119** (1K 11)
Gaufron. *Powy* 6J 25
Gaulby. *Leics* 1D 28
Gauldry. *Fife* 5G 67
Gaultree. *Norf* 1A 30
Gaunt's Common. *Dors* 5J 9
Gaunt's Earthcott. *S Glo* 5E 18
Gautby. *Linc* 2J 37
Gavinton. *Bord* 4E 60
Gawber. *S Yor* 7M 41
Gawcott. *Buck* 8D 28
Gawsworth. *Ches E* 3G 35
Gawthorpe. *W Yor* 5L 41
Gawthrop. *Cumb* 7E 46
Gawthwaite. *Cumb* 7A 46
Gay Bowers. *Essx* 3D 22
Gaydon. *Warw* 6A 28
Gayfield. *Orkn* 4D 88
Gayhurst. *Mil* 7F 28
Gayle. *N Yor* 7G 47
Gayles. *N Yor* 5K 47
Gay Street. *W Sus* 3H 11
Gayton. *Mers* 1A 34
Gayton. *Norf* 8D 38
Gayton. *Nptn* 6E 28
Gayton. *Staf* 7H 35
Gayton le Marsh. *Linc* 1M 37
Gayton le Wold. *Linc* 1K 37
Gayton Thorpe. *Norf* 8D 38
Gaywood. *Norf* 7C 38
Gazeley. *Suff* 5D 30
Geanies. *High* 6J 79
Gearraidh Bhailteas. *W Isl* 3D 74
Gearraidh Bhaird. *W Isl* 2E 76
Gearraidh ma Monadh. *W Isl* 4D 74
Gearraidh na h-Aibhne. *W Isl* 8F 82
Geary. *High* 7D 76
Geddes. *High* 8J 79
Gedding. *Suff* 6F 30
Geddington. *Nptn* 3F 28
Gedintailor. *High* 2G 69
Gedling. *Notts* 5D 36
Gedney. *Linc* 7M 37
Gedney Broadgate. *Linc* 7M 37
Gedney Drove End. *Linc* 7A 38
Gedney Dyke. *Linc* 7M 37
Gedney Hill. *Linc* 8L 37
Gee Cross. *G Man* 8H 41
Geeston. *Rut* 1G 29
Geilston. *Arg* 2B 58
Geirinis. *W Isl* 1D 74
Geise. *High* 5C 86
Geisiadar. *W Isl* 8E 82
Gelder Shiel. *Abers* 7B 72
Geldeston. *Norf* 2K 31
Gell. *Cnwy* 4H 33
Gelli. *Pemb* 5G 15
Gelli. *Rhon* 5J 17
Gellifor. *Den* 4L 33
Gelligaer. *Cphy* 5L 17
Y Gelli Gandryll. *Powy* 8M 25
Gellilydan. *Gwyn* 7F 32
Gellinudd. *Neat* 4G 17
Gellyburn. *Per* 4D 66
Gellywen. *Carm* 4J 15
Gelston. *Dum* 6B 52
Gelston. *Linc* 5G 37
Gembling. *E Yor* 2J 43
Geneva. *Cdgn* 1L 15
Gentleshaw. *Staf* 8J 35
Geocrab. *W Isl* 4C 76
George Best Belfast City Airport. *Bel* 5H 93
George Green. *Buck* 5G 21
Georgeham. *Devn* 2D 6
George Nympton. *Devn* 3G 7
Georgetown. *Blae* 4L 17
Georgetown. *Ren* 3C 58
Georth. *Orkn* 7C 88
Gerlan. *Gwyn* 4F 32
Germansweek. *Devn* 6D 6
Germoe. *Corn* 6J 3
Gerrans. *Corn* 8A 4
Gerrard's Bromley. *Staf* 6F 34
Gerrards Cross. *Buck* 5G 21
Gerston. *High* 6C 86
Gestingthorpe. *Essx* 8E 30
Gethsemane. *Pemb* 2G 15
Geuffordd. *Powy* 1M 25
Gibraltar. *Buck* 2E 20
Gibraltar. *Linc* 4B 38
Gibraltar. *Suff* 6H 31
Gibsmere. *Notts* 5E 36
Giddeahall. *Wilts* 6G 19
Gidea Park. *G Lon* 5B 22
Gidleigh. *Devn* 7F 6
Giffnock. *E Ren* 4D 58
Gifford. *E Lot* 3C 60
Giffordtown. *Fife* 6F 66
Giggetty. *Staf* 2G 27
Giggleswick. *N Yor* 1G 41
Gignog. *Pemb* 4E 14
Gilberdyke. *E Yor* 5F 42
Gilbert's End. *Worc* 7G 27
Gilbert's Green. *Warw* 4K 27
Gilchriston. *E Lot* 3B 60
Gilcrux. *Cumb* 8F 52
Gildersome. *W Yor* 5L 41
Gildingwells. *S Yor* 1C 36
Gilesgate Moor. *Dur* 7F 54
Gileston. *V Glam* 8K 17
Gilfach. *Cphy* 5L 17
Gilfach Goch. *Rhon* 6J 17
Gilfachreda. *Cdgn* 1L 15
Gilford. *Arm* 6G 93
Gilgarran. *Cumb* 2K 45
Gillamoor. *N Yor* 6D 48
Gillan. *Corn* 6L 3
Gillar's Green. *Mers* 8C 40
Gillen. *High* 8D 76
Gilling East. *N Yor* 8D 48
Gillingham. *Dors* 3G 9
Gillingham. *Medw* Medway Towns **111** (7D 22)
Gillingham. *Norf* 2L 31
Gilling West. *N Yor* 5K 47
Gillock. *High* 6D 86
Gillow Heath. *Staf* 4G 35
Gills. *High* 4E 86
Gill's Green. *Kent* 2D 12
Gilmanscleuch. *Bord* 7M 59
Gilmerton. *Edin* 3L 59
Gilmerton. *Per* 5B 66
Gilmonby. *Dur* 4H 47
Gilmorton. *Leics* 3C 28
Gilsland. *Nmbd* 5L 53
Gilsland Spa. *Cumb* 5L 53
Gilston. *Bord* 4B 60
Giltbrook. *Notts* 5B 36
Gilwern. *Mon* 3M 17
Gimingham. *Norf* 6J 39
Giosla. *W Isl* 1C 76
Gipping. *Suff* 5G 31
Gipsey Bridge. *Linc* 5K 37
Gipton. *W Yor* 4M 41
Girdle Toll. *N Ayr* 5B 58
Girlsta. *Shet* 2E 90
Girsby. *N Yor* 5A 48
Girthon. *Dum* 6M 51
Girton. *Cambs* 5M 29
Girton. *Notts* 3F 36
Girvan. *S Ayr* 2G 51
Gisburn. *Lanc* 3G 41
Gisleham. *Suff* 3M 31
Gislingham. *Suff* 4G 31
Gissing. *Norf* 3H 31
Gittisham. *Devn* 6L 7
Gladestry. *Powy* 7M 25
Gladsmuir. *E Lot* 2B 60
Glaichbea. *High* 2F 70
Glais. *Swan* 4G 17
Glaisdale. *N Yor* 5E 48
Glame. *High* 1G 69
Glamis. *Ang* 3G 67
Glanaman. *Carm* 3F 16
Glan-Conwy. *Cnwy* 5H 33
Glandford. *Norf* 5G 39
Glan Duar. *Carm* 2M 15
Glandwr. *Blae* 4M 17
Glandwr. *Pemb* 4H 15
Glan-Dwyfach. *Gwyn* 6D 32
Glandy Cross. *Carm* 4H 15
Glandyfi. *Cdgn* 3F 24
Glangrwyney. *Powy* 3M 17
Glanmule. *Powy* 3L 25
Glan-rhyd. *Pemb* 3H 15
Glan-rhyd. *Powy* 4G 17
Glanrhyd. *Gwyn* 7B 32
Glanrhyd. *Pemb* 2H 15
Glanton. *Nmbd* 8H 61
Glanton Pyke. *Nmbd* 8H 61
Glanvilles Wootton. *Dors* 5E 8
Glan-y-don. *Flin* 3L 33
Glan-y-nant. *Powy* 4J 25
Glan-yr-afon. *Gwyn* 6K 33
Glan-yr-afon. *IOA* 2F 32
Glan-yr-afon. *Powy* 2K 25
Glan-y-wern. *Gwyn* 7F 32
Glapthorn. *Nptn* 2H 29
Glapwell. *Derbs* 3B 36
Glarryford. *ME Ant* 3G 93
Glas Aird. *Arg* 8J 63
Glas-allt Shiel. *Abers* 7B 72
Glasbury. *Powy* 1L 17
Glaschoil. *High* 2L 71
Glascoed. *Den* 3J 33
Glascoed. *Mon* 3B 18
Glascote. *Staf* 1L 27
Glascwm. *Powy* 7L 25
Glasfryn. *Cnwy* 5J 33
Glasgow. *Glas* **109** (3D 58)
Glasgow Airport. *Ren* **118** (3C 58)
Glasgow Prestwick Airport. *S Ayr* 7B 58
Glashvin. *High* 7F 76
Glasinfryn. *Gwyn* 4E 32
Glas na Cardaich. *High* 6H 69
Glasnacardoch. *High* 6H 69
Glasnakille. *High* 4G 69
Glaspwll. *Cdgn* 3G 25
Glassburn. *High* 2D 70
Glassenbury. *Kent* 2D 12
Glasserton. *Dum* 8K 51
Glassford. *S Lan* 5F 58
Glassgreen. *Mor* 7B 80
Glasshouse. *Glos* 1F 18
Glasshouses. *N Yor* 1K 41
Glasson. *Cumb* 5G 53
Glasson. *Lanc* 2C 40
Glassonby. *Cumb* 8K 53
Glasswater. *New M* 6J 93
Glasterlaw. *Ang* 2J 67
Glaston. *Rut* 1F 28
Glastonbury. *Som* 2C 8
Glatton. *Cambs* 3J 29
Glazebrook. *Warr* 8E 40
Glazebury. *Warr* 8E 40
Glazeley. *Shrp* 3F 26
Gleadless. *S Yor* 1A 36
Gleadsmoss. *Ches E* 3G 35
Gleann Dail bho Dheas. *W Isl* 4D 74
Gleann Tholastaidh. *W Isl* 7J 83
Gleann Uige. *High* 8H 69
Gleaston. *Cumb* 8A 46
Glebe. *Derr* 4C 92
Glecknabae. *Arg* 3K 57
Gledrid. *Shrp* 6A 34
Gleiniant. *Powy* 3J 25
Glemsford. *Suff* 7E 30
Glen. *Dum* 6L 51
Glenancross. *High* 6H 69
Glenanne. *Arm* 7F 93
Glenariff. *Caus* 2H 93
Glenarm. *ME Ant* 3H 93
Glen Auldyn. *IOM* 5D 44
Glenavy. *Lis* 5G 93
Glenbarr. *Arg* 6F 56
Glenbeg. *High* 1L 63
Glen Bernisdale. *High* 1F 68
Glenbervie. *Abers* 7G 73
Glenboig. *N Lan* 3F 58
Glenborrodale. *High* 1M 63
Glenbranter. *Arg* 8F 64
Glenbreck. *Bord* 7J 59
Glenbrein Lodge. *High* 4E 70
Glenbrittle. *High* 3F 68
Glenbuchat Lodge. *Abers* 4C 72
Glenbuck. *E Ayr* 7F 58
Glenburn. *Ren* 3C 58
Glencalvie Lodge. *High* 5E 78
Glencaple. *Dum* 5D 52
Glencarron Lodge. *High* 8A 78
Glencarse. *Per* 5E 66
Glencassley Castle. *High* 3E 78
Glencat. *Abers* 6E 72
Glencoe. *High* 2F 64
Glen Cottage. *High* 7H 69
Glencraig. *Fife* 8E 66
Glendale. *High* 1C 68
Glendevon. *Per* 7C 66
Glendoebeg. *High* 5E 70
Glendoick. *Per* 5F 66
Glendoune. *S Ayr* 2G 51
Glenduckie. *Fife* 6F 66
Gleneagles. *Per* 7C 66
Glenegedale. *Arg* 4C 56
Glenegedale Lots. *Arg* 4C 56
Glenelg. *High* 4K 69
Glenernie. *Mor* 1L 71
Glenesslin. *Dum* 3C 52
Glenfarg. *Per* 6E 66
Glenfarquhar Lodge. *Abers* 7G 73
Glenferness Mains. *High* 1K 71
Glenfeshie Lodge. *High* 6J 71
Glenfiddich Lodge. *Mor* 2C 72
Glenfield. *Leics* 1C 28
Glenfinnan. *High* 7L 69
Glenfintaig Lodge. *High* 7C 70
Glenfoot. *Per* 6E 66
Glenfyne Lodge. *Arg* 6G 65
Glengap. *Dum* 6A 52
Glengarnock. *N Ayr* 4B 58
Glengolly. *High* 5C 86
Glengorm Castle. *Arg* 2K 63
Glengormley. *Ant* 4H 93
Glengrasco. *High* 1F 68
Glenhead Farm. *Ang* 1F 66
Glenholm. *Bord* 6K 59
Glen House. *Bord* 6L 59
Glenhurich. *High* 1C 64
Glenkerry. *Bord* 8L 59
Glenkiln. *Dum* 4C 52
Glenkindie. *Abers* 4D 72
Glenkinglass Lodge. *Arg* 4F 64
Glenkirk. *Bord* 7J 59
Glenlean. *Arg* 1K 57
Glenlee. *Dum* 3M 51
Glenleraig. *High* 8D 84
Glenlichorn. *Per* 6A 66
Glenlivet. *Mor* 3A 72
Glenlochar. *Dum* 5B 52
Glenlochsie Lodge. *Per* 8L 71
Glenluce. *Dum* 6G 51
Glenmarksie. *High* 8D 78
Glenmassan. *Arg* 1L 57
Glenmavis. *N Lan* 3F 58
Glen Maye. *IOM* 7B 44
Glenmazeran Lodge. *High* 3H 71
Glenmidge. *Dum* 3C 52
Glen Mona. *IOM* 6D 44
Glenmore. *High*
nr. Glenborrodale 1L 63
nr. Kingussie 5K 71
on Isle of Skye 1F 68
Glenmoy. *Ang* 1H 67
Glennoe. *Arg* 4E 64
Glen of Coachford. *Abers* 1D 72
Glenogil. *Ang* 1H 67
Glen Parva. *Leics* 2C 28
Glenprosen Village. *Ang* 1G 67
Glenree. *N Ayr* 7J 57
Glenridding. *Cumb* 4B 46
Glenrosa. *N Ayr* 6K 57
Glenrothes. *Fife* 7F 66
Glensanda. *High* 3C 64
Glensaugh. *Abers* 8F 72
Glenshero Lodge. *High* 6F 70
Glensluain. *Arg* 8E 64
Glenstockadale. *Dum* 5F 50
Glenstriven. *Arg* 2K 57
Glen Tanar House. *Abers* 6D 72
Glentham. *Linc* 8H 43
Glenton. *Abers* 3F 72
Glentress. *Bord* 6L 59
Glentromie Lodge. *High* 6H 71
Glentrool Lodge. *Dum* 3K 51
Glentrool Village. *Dum* 4J 51
Glentruim House. *High* 6G 71
Glentworth. *Linc* 1G 37
Glenuig. *High* 8H 69
Glen View. *New M* 7G 93
Glen Village. *Falk* 2G 59
Glen Vine. *IOM* 7C 44
Glenwhilly. *Dum* 4G 51
Glenzierfoot. *Dum* 4H 53
Glespin. *S Lan* 7G 59
Gletness. *Shet* 2E 90
Glewstone. *Here* 1D 18
Glib Cheois. *W Isl* 1E 76
Glinton. *Pet* 1J 29
Glooston. *Leics* 2E 28
Glossop. *Derbs* 8J 41
Gloster Hill. *Nmbd* 1F 54
Gloucester. *Glos* **109** (2G 19)
Gloucestershire Airport. *Glos* 1G 19
Gloup. *Shet* 3K 91
Glusburn. *N Yor* 3J 41
Glutt Lodge. *High* 8A 86
Glutton Bridge. *Derbs* 3J 35
Gluvian. *Corn* 5B 4
Glympton. *Oxon* 1B 20
Glyn. *Cnwy* 3H 33
Glynarthen. *Cdgn* 2K 15
Glynbrochan. *Powy* 4J 25
Glyn Ceiriog. *Wrex* 7M 33
Glyncoch. *Rhon* 5K 17
Glyncorrwg. *Neat* 5H 17
Glynde. *E Sus* 5A 12
Glyndebourne. *E Sus* 4A 12
Glyndyfrdwy. *Den* 6L 33
Glyn Ebwy. *Blae* 4L 17
Glynllan. *B'end* 6J 17
Glynn. *ME Ant* 4J 93
Glyn-neath. *Neat* 4H 17
Glynogwr. *B'end* 6J 17
Glyntaff. *Rhon* 6K 17
Glyntawe. *Powy* 3H 17
Glynteg. *Carm* 3K 15
Gnosall. *Staf* 7G 35
Gnosall Heath. *Staf* 7G 35
Goadby. *Leics* 2E 28
Goadby Marwood. *Leics* 7E 36
Goatacre. *Wilts* 6J 19
Goathill. *Dors* 4E 8
Goathland. *N Yor* 5F 48
Goathurst. *Som* 2A 8
Goathurst Common. *Kent* 8A 22
Goat Lees. *Kent* 1G 13
Gobernuisgach Lodge. *High* 7G 85
Gobernuisgeach. *High* 8A 86
Gobhaig. *W Isl* 3B 76
Gobowen. *Shrp* 6B 34
Godalming. *Surr* 1G 11
Goddard's Corner. *Suff* 5J 31
Goddard's Green. *Kent*
nr. Benenden 2E 12
nr. Cranbrook 2D 12
Goddards' Green. *W Sus* 3K 11
Godford Cross. *Devn* 5L 7
Godleybrook. *Staf* 5H 35
Godmanchester. *Cambs* 4K 29
Godmanstone. *Dors* 6E 8
Godmersham. *Kent* 8G 23
Godolphin Cross. *Corn* 5K 3
Godre'r-graig. *Neat* 4G 17
Godshill. *Hants* 4K 9
Godshill. *IOW* 7C 10
Godstone. *Staf* 6J 35
Godstone. *Surr* 8L 21
Goetre. *Mon* 3B 18
Goff's Oak. *Herts* 3L 21
Gogar. *Edin* 2K 59
Goginan. *Cdgn* 4F 24
Golan. *Gwyn* 6E 32
Golant. *Corn* 6D 4
Golberdon. *Corn* 8C 6
Golborne. *G Man* 8E 40
Golcar. *W Yor* 6J 41
Goldcliff. *Newp* 5B 18
Golden Cross. *E Sus* 4B 12
Golden Green. *Kent* 1C 12
Golden Grove. *Carm* 3E 16
Golden Grove. *N Yor* 5F 48
Golden Hill. *Pemb* 4F 14
Goldenhill. *Stoke* 4G 35
Golden Pot. *Hants* 1E 10
Golden Valley. *Glos* 1H 19
Golders Green. *G Lon* 5K 21
Goldhanger. *Essx* 3F 22
Gold Hill. *Norf* 2B 30
Golding. *Shrp* 1D 26
Goldington. *Bed* 6H 29
Goldsborough. *N Yor*
nr. Harrogate 2A 42
nr. Whitby 4F 48
Goldsithney. *Corn* 5J 3
Goldstone. *Kent* 7J 23
Goldstone. *Shrp* 7F 34
Goldthorpe. *S Yor* 7B 42
Goldworthy. *Devn* 3C 6
Golfa. *Powy* 8L 33
Gollanfield. *High* 8J 79
Gollinglith Foot. *N Yor* 7K 47
Golsoncott. *Som* 2K 7
Golspie. *High* 4J 79
Gomeldon. *Wilts* 2K 9
Gomersal. *W Yor* 5L 41
Gometra House. *Arg* 3J 63
Gomshall. *Surr* 1H 11
Gonalston. *Notts* 5D 36
Gonerby Hill Foot. *Linc* 6G 37
Gonfirth. *Shet* 1D 90
Good Easter. *Essx* 2C 22
Gooderstone. *Norf* 1D 30
Goodleigh. *Devn* 2F 6
Goodmanham. *E Yor* 3F 42
Goodmayes. *G Lon* 5A 22
Goodnestone. *Kent*
nr. Aylesham 8J 23
nr. Faversham 7G 23
Goodrich. *Here* 2D 18
Goodrington. *Torb* 6L 5
Goodshaw. *Lanc* 5G 41
Goodshaw Fold. *Lanc* 5G 41
Goodstone. *Devn* 8G 7
Goodwick. *Pemb* 3F 14
Goodworth Clatford. *Hants* 1A 10
Goole. *E Yor* 5E 42
Goom's Hill. *Worc* 6J 27
Goonabarn. *Corn* 6B 4
Goonbell. *Corn* 4L 3
Goonhavern. *Corn* 3L 3
Goonlaze. *Corn* 5L 3
Goonvrea. *Corn* 4L 3
Goose Green. *Cumb* 7D 46
Goose Green. *S Glo* 5F 18
Gooseham. *Corn* 4B 6
Goosewell. *Plym* 6H 5
Goosey. *Oxon* 4A 20
Goosnargh. *Lanc* 4D 40
Goostrey. *Ches E* 2F 34
Gorcott Hill. *Warw* 5J 27
Gord. *Shet* 5E 90
Gordon. *Bord* 5D 60
Gordonbush. *High* 3J 79
Gordonstown. *Abers*
nr. Cornhill 8E 80
nr. Fyvie 2G 73
Gorebridge. *Midl* 3M 59
Gorefield. *Cambs* 8M 37
Gores. *Wilts* 8K 19
Gorgie. *Edin* 2L 59
Goring. *Oxon* 5D 20
Goring-by-Sea. *W Sus* 5J 11
Goring Heath. *Oxon* 6D 20
Gorleston-on-Sea. *Norf* 1M 31
Gornalwood. *W Mid* 2H 27
Gorran Churchtown. *Corn* 7B 4
Gorran Haven. *Corn* 7C 4
Gorran High Lanes. *Corn* 7B 4
Gors. *Cdgn* 5F 24
Gorsedd. *Flin* 3L 33
Gorseinon. *Swan* 5E 16
Gorseness. *Orkn* 8D 88
Gorseybank. *Derbs* 4L 35
Gorsgoch. *Cdgn* 1L 15
Gorslas. *Carm* 3E 16
Gorsley. *Glos* 1E 18
Gorsley Common. *Here* 1E 18
Gorstan. *High* 7D 78
Gorstella. *Ches W* 3B 34
Gorsty Common. *Here* 8C 26
Gorsty Hill. *Staf* 7K 35
Gortantaoid. *Arg* 2C 56
Gorteneorn. *High* 1M 63
Gortenfern. *High* 1M 63
Gortin. *Ferm* 4D 92
Gortnahey. *Caus* 3E 92
Gorton. *G Man* 8G 41
Gosbeck. *Suff* 6H 31
Gosberton. *Linc* 6K 37
Gosberton Cheal. *Linc* 7K 37
Gosberton Clough. *Linc* 7J 37
Goseley Dale. *Derbs* 7M 35
Gosfield. *Essx* 1D 22
Gosford. *Oxon* 2C 20
Gosforth. *Cumb* 4K 45
Gosforth. *Tyne* 5F 54
Gosmore. *Herts* 1J 21
Gospel End. *Staf* 2G 27
Gosport. *Hants* 6D 10
Gossabrough. *Shet* 5K 91
Gossington. *Glos* 3F 18
Gossops Green. *W Sus* 2K 11
Goswick. *Nmbd* 5H 61
Gotham. *Notts* 6C 36
Gotherington. *Glos* 1H 19
Gott. *Arg* 3F 62
Gott. *Shet* 3E 90
Goudhurst. *Kent* 2D 12
Goulceby. *Linc* 2K 37
Gourdon. *Abers* 8H 73
Gourock. *Inv* 2M 57
Govan. *Glas* 3D 58
Govanhill. *Glas* 3D 58
Goverton. *Notts* 5E 36
Goveton. *Devn* 7K 5
Govilon. *Mon* 2A 18
Gowanhill. *Abers* 7K 81
Gowdall. *E Yor* 5D 42
Gowdystown. *Arm* 6G 93
Gowerton. *Swan* 5E 16
Gowkhall. *Fife* 1J 59
Gowthorpe. *E Yor* 2E 42
Goxhill. *E Yor* 3J 43
Goxhill. *N Lin* 5J 43
Goxhill Haven. *N Lin* 5J 43
Goytre. *Neat* 6G 17
Grabhair. *W Isl* 2E 76
Graby. *Linc* 7H 37
Gracehill. *ME Ant* 3G 93
Graffham. *W Sus* 4G 11
Grafham. *Cambs* 5J 29
Grafham. *Surr* 1H 11
Grafton. *Here* 8C 26
Grafton. *N Yor* 1B 42
Grafton. *Oxon* 3L 19
Grafton. *Shrp* 8C 34
Grafton. *Worc*
nr. Evesham 8H 27
nr. Leominster 5D 26
Grafton Flyford. *Worc* 6H 27
Grafton Regis. *Nptn* 7E 28
Grafton Underwood. *Nptn* 3G 29
Grafty Green. *Kent* 1E 12
Graianrhyd. *Den* 5M 33
Graig. *Carm* 6L 15
Graig. *Cnwy* 3H 33
Graig. *Den* 3K 33
Graig-fechan. *Den* 5L 33
Graig Penllyn. *V Glam* 7J 17
Grain. *Medw* 6E 22
Grainsby. *Linc* 8K 43
Grainthorpe. *Linc* 8L 43
Grainthorpe Fen. *Linc* 8L 43
Graiselound. *N Lin* 8E 42
Gramasdail. *W Isl* 8K 75
Grampound. *Corn* 7B 4
Grampound Road. *Corn* 6B 4
Granborough. *Buck* 1E 20
Granby. *Notts* 6E 36
Grandborough. *Warw* 5B 28
Grandpont. *Oxon* 3C 20
Grandtully. *Per* 2C 66
Grange. *Cumb* 4A 46
Grange. *E Ayr* 6C 58
Grange. *Here* 4C 26
Grange. *Mers* 2M 33
Grange. *Per* 5F 66
The Grange. *N Yor* 6C 48
Grange Corner. *ME Ant* 4G 93
Grange Crossroads. *Mor* 8D 80
Grange Hill. *Essx* 4M 21
Grangemill. *Derbs* 4L 35
Grange Moor. *W Yor* 6L 41
Grangemouth. *Falk* 1H 59
Grange of Lindores. *Fife* 6F 66
Grange-over-Sands. *Cumb* 8C 46
Grangepans. *Falk* 1J 59
Grange Park. *New M* 6J 93
Grangetown. *Card* 7L 17
Grangetown. *Red C* 3C 48
Grange Villa. *Dur* 6F 54
Granish. *High* 4J 71
Gransmoor. *E Yor* 2J 43
Granston. *Pemb* 3E 14
Grantchester. *Cambs* 6M 29
Grantham. *Linc* 6G 37
Grantley. *N Yor* 1L 41
Grantlodge. *Abers* 4G 73
Granton. *Edin* 2L 59
Granton-on-Spey. *High* 3L 71
Grantshouse. *Bord* 3F 60
Grappenhall. *Warr* 1E 34
Grasby. *Linc* 7H 43
Grasmere. *Cumb* 5B 46
Grasscroft. *G Man* 7H 41
Grassendale. *Mers* 1B 34
Grassgarth. *Cumb* 7H 53
Grassholme. *Dur* 3H 47
Grassington. *N Yor* 1J 41
Grassmoor. *Derbs* 3B 36
Grassthorpe. *Notts* 3E 36
Grateley. *Hants* 1L 9
Gratton. *Devn* 4C 6
Gratton. *Staf* 4H 35
Gratwich. *Staf* 6J 35
Graveley. *Cambs* 5K 29
Graveley. *Herts* 1K 21
Gravelhill. *Shrp* 8C 34
Gravel Hole. *G Man* 7H 41
Gravelly Hill. *W Mid* 2K 27
Graven. *Shet* 6J 91
Graveney. *Kent* 7G 23
Gravesend. *Kent* 6C 22
Grayingham. *Linc* 8G 43
Grayrigg. *Cumb* 6D 46
Grays. *Thur* 6C 22
Grayshott. *Hants* 2F 10
Grayson Green. *Cumb* 2J 45
Grayswood. *Surr* 2G 11
Graythorp. *Hart* 3C 48
Grazeley. *Wok* 7D 20
Grealin. *High* 7G 77
Greasbrough. *S Yor* 8B 42
Greasby. *Mers* 1A 34
Great Abington. *Cambs* 7B 30
Great Addington. *Nptn* 4G 29
Great Alne. *Warw* 6K 27
Great Altcar. *Lanc* 7B 40
Great Amwell. *Herts* 2L 21
Great Asby. *Cumb* 4E 46
Great Ashfield. *Suff* 5F 30
Great Ayton. *N Yor* 4C 48
Great Baddow. *Essx* 3D 22
Great Bardfield. *Essx* 8C 30
Great Barford. *Bed* 6J 29
Great Barr. *W Mid* 2J 27
Great Barrington. *Glos* 2L 19
Great Barrow. *Ches W* 3C 34
Great Barton. *Suff* 5E 30
Great Barugh. *N Yor* 8E 48
Great Bavington. *Nmbd* 3C 54
Great Bealings. *Suff* 7J 31
Great Bedwyn. *Wilts* 7L 19
Great Bentley. *Essx* 1H 23
Great Billing. *Nptn* 5F 28
Great Bircham. *Norf* 6D 38
Great Blakenham. *Suff* 6H 31
Great Blencow. *Cumb* 8J 53
Great Bolas. *Telf* 7E 34
Great Bookham. *Surr* 8J 21
Great Bosullow. *Corn* 5H 3
Great Bourton. *Oxon* 7B 28
Great Bowden. *Leics* 3E 28
Great Bradley. *Suff* 6C 30
Great Braxted. *Essx* 2E 22
Great Bricett. *Suff* 6G 31
Great Brickhill. *Buck* 8G 29
Great Bridgeford. *Staf* 7G 35
Great Brington. *Nptn* 5D 28
Great Bromley. *Essx* 1G 23
Great Broughton. *Cumb* 8E 52
Great Broughton. *N Yor* 5C 48
Great Budworth. *Ches W* 2E 34
Great Burdon. *Darl* 4M 47
Great Burstead. *Essx* 4C 22
Great Busby. *N Yor* 5C 48
Great Canfield. *Essx* 2B 22
Great Carlton. *Linc* 1M 37
Great Casterton. *Rut* 1G 29
Great Chalfield. *Wilts* 7G 19
Great Chart. *Kent* 1F 12
Great Chatwell. *Staf* 8F 34
Great Chesterford. *Essx* 7B 30
Great Cheverell. *Wilts* 8H 19
Great Chilton. *Dur* 8F 54
Great Chishill. *Cambs* 8M 29
Great Clacton. *Essx* 2H 23
Great Cliff. *W Yor* 6M 41
Great Clifton. *Cumb* 2K 45
Great Coates. *NE Lin* 6K 43
Great Comberton. *Worc* 7H 27
Great Corby. *Cumb* 6J 53
Great Cornard. *Suff* 7E 30
Great Cowden. *E Yor* 3K 43
Great Coxwell. *Oxon* 4L 19
Great Crakehall. *N Yor* 6L 47
Great Cransley. *Nptn* 4F 28
Great Cressingham. *Norf* 1E 30
Great Crosby. *Mers* 7B 40
Great Cubley. *Derbs* 6K 35
Great Dalby. *Leics* 8E 36
Great Doddington. *Nptn* 5F 28
Great Doward. *Here* 2D 18
Great Dunham. *Norf* 8E 38
Great Dunmow. *Essx* 1C 22
Great Durnford. *Wilts* 2K 9
Great Easton. *Essx* 1C 22
Great Easton. *Leics* 2F 28
Great Eccleston. *Lanc* 3C 40
Great Edstone. *N Yor* 7E 48
Great Ellingham. *Norf* 2G 31
Great Elm. *Som* 1F 8
Great Eppleton. *Tyne* 7G 55
Great Eversden. *Cambs* 6L 29
Great Fencote. *N Yor* 6L 47
Great Finborough. *Suff* 6G 31
Greatford. *Linc* 8H 37
Great Fransham. *Norf* 8E 38
Great Gaddesden. *Herts* 2H 21
Great Gate. *Staf* 5J 35
Great Gidding. *Cambs* 3J 29
Great Givendale. *E Yor* 2F 42
Great Glemham. *Suff* 5K 31
Great Glen. *Leics* 2D 28
Great Gonerby. *Linc* 6F 36
Great Gransden. *Cambs* 6K 29
Great Green. *Norf* 3J 31
Great Green. *Suff*
nr. Lavenham 6F 30
nr. Palgrave 4H 31
Great Habton. *N Yor* 8E 48
Great Hale. *Linc* 5J 37
Great Hallingbury. *Essx* 2B 22
Greatham. *Hants* 2E 10
Greatham. *Hart* 3B 48
Greatham. *W Sus* 4H 11
Great Hampden. *Buck* 3F 20
Great Harrowden. *Nptn* 4F 28
Great Harwood. *Lanc* 4F 40
Great Haseley. *Oxon* 3D 20
Great Hatfield. *E Yor* 3J 43
Great Haywood. *Staf* 7H 35
Great Heath. *W Mid* 3M 27
Great Heck. *N Yor* 5C 42
Great Henny. *Essx* 8E 30
Great Hinton. *Wilts* 8H 19
Great Hockham. *Norf* 2F 30

Hendon—Inchbrook

Hendon. G Lon 5K 21
Hendon. Tyne 6H 55
Hendra. Corn 6B 4
Hendre. B'end 6J 17
Hendreforgan. Rhon 6J 17
Hendy. Carm 4E 16
Heneglwys. IOA 3D 32
Henfeddau Fawr. Pemb 3J 15
Henfield. S Glo 6E 18
Henfield. W Sus 4K 11
Henford. Devn 6C 6
Hengoed. Cphy 5L 17
Hengoed. Shrp 6A 34
Hengrave. Suff 5E 30
Henham. Essx 1B 22
Heniarth. Powy 2L 25
Henlade. Som 3A 8
Henley. Dors 5E 8
Henley. Shrp
nr. Church Stretton 3C 26
nr. Ludlow 4D 26
Henley. Som 2C 8
Henley. Suff 6H 31
Henley. W Sus 3F 10
Henley Down. E Sus 4D 12
Henley-in-Arden. Warw 5K 27
Henley-on-Thames. Oxon 5E 20
Henley Street. Kent 7C 22
Henllan. Cdgn 2K 15
Henllan. Den 4K 33
Henllan. Mon 1A 18
Henllan Amgoed. Carm 5H 15
Henllys. Torf 4A 18
Henlow. C Beds 8J 29
Hennock. Devn 7H 7
Henny Street. Essx 8E 30
Henryd. Cnwy 3G 33
Henry's Moat. Pemb 4G 15
Hensall. N Yor 5C 42
Henshaw. Nmbd 5A 54
Hensingham. Cumb 3J 45
Henstead. Suff 3L 31
Hensting. Hants 3B 10
Henstridge. Som 4F 8
Henstridge Ash. Som 3F 8
Henstridge Bowden. Som 3E 8
Henstridge Marsh. Som 3F 8
Henton. Oxon 3E 20
Henton. Som 1C 8
Henwood. Corn 8B 6
Heogan. Shet 3E 90
Heolgerrig. Mer T 4K 17
Heol Senni. Powy 2J 17
Heol-y-Cyw. B'end 6J 17
Hepburn. Nmbd 7H 61
Hepple. Nmbd 1C 54
Hepscott. Nmbd 3F 54
Heptonstall. W Yor 5H 41
Hepworth. Suff 4F 30
Hepworth. W Yor 7K 41
Herbrandston. Pemb 6E 14
Hereford. Here 8D 26
Heribusta. High 6F 76
Heriot. Bord 4B 60
Hermiston. Edin 2K 59
Hermitage. Dors 5E 8
Hermitage. Bord 2K 53
Hermitage. W Ber 6C 20
Hermitage. W Sus 5E 10
Hermon. Carm
nr. Llandeilo 2F 16
nr. Newcastle Emlyn 3K 15
Hermon. IOA 4C 32
Hermon. Pemb 3J 15
Herne. Kent 7H 23
Herne Bay. Kent 7H 23
Herne Common. Kent 7H 23
Herne Pound. Kent 8C 22
Herner. Devn 3E 6
Hernhill. Kent 7G 23
Herodsfoot. Corn 5E 4
Heronden. Kent 8J 23
Herongate. Essx 4C 22
Heronsford. S Ayr 3G 51
Heronsgate. Herts 4H 21
Heron's Ghyll. E Sus 3A 12
Herra. Shet 4L 91
Herriard. Hants 1D 10
Herringfleet. Suff 2L 31
Herringswell. Suff 5D 30
Herrington. Tyne 6G 55
Hersden. Kent 7J 23
Hersham. Corn 5B 6
Hersham. Surr 7J 21
Herstmonceux. E Sus 4C 12
Herston. Dors 8J 9
Herston. Orkn 2F 86
Hertford. Herts 2L 21
Hertford Heath. Herts 2L 21
Hertingfordbury. Herts 2L 21
Hesketh. Lanc 5C 40
Hesketh Bank. Lanc 5C 40
Hesketh Lane. Lanc 3E 40
Hesket Newmarket. Cumb 8H 53
Heskin Green. Lanc 6D 40
Hesleden. Dur 8H 55
Hesleyside. Nmbd 3B 54
Heslington. York 2D 42
Hessay. York 2C 42
Hessenford. Corn 6F 4
Hessett. Suff 5F 30
Hessilhead. N Ayr 4B 58
Hessle. E Yor 5H 43
Hestaford. Shet 2C 90
Hest Bank. Lanc 1C 40
Hester's Way. Glos 1H 19
Hestinsetter. Shet 3C 90
Heston. G Lon 6J 21
Hestwall. Orkn 8B 88
Heswall. Mers 1A 34
Hethe. Oxon 1C 20
Hethelpit Cross. Glos 1F 18
Hethersett. Norf 1H 31
Hethersgill. Cumb 5J 53
Hetherside. Cumb 5J 53
Hethpool. Nmbd 7F 60
Hett. Dur 8F 54
Hetton. N Yor 2H 41
Hetton-le-Hole. Tyne 7G 55
Hetton Steads. Nmbd 6H 61
Heugh. Nmbd 4D 54
Heugh-head. Abers 4C 72
Heveningham. Suff 4K 31
Hever. Kent 1A 12
Heversham. Cumb 7C 46
Hevingham. Norf 7H 39
Hewas Water. Corn 7B 4
Hewelsfield. Glos 3D 18
Hewish. N Som 7C 18
Hewish. Som 5C 8
Hewood. Dors 5B 8
Heworth. York 2D 42
Hexham. Nmbd 5C 54
Hextable. Kent 6B 22
Hexton. Herts 8J 29
Hexworthy. Devn 8F 6
Heybridge. Essx
nr. Brentwood 4C 22
nr. Maldon 3E 22
Heybridge Basin. Essx 3E 22
Heybrook Bay. Devn 7G 5
Heydon. Cambs 7M 29
Heydon. Norf 7H 39
Heydour. Linc 6H 37
Heylipol. Arg 3E 62
Heyop. Powy 5M 25
Heysham. Lanc 1C 40
Heyshott. W Sus 4F 10
Heytesbury. Wilts 1H 9
Heythrop. Oxon 1A 20
Heywood. G Man 6G 41
Heywood. Wilts 8G 19
Hibaldstow. N Lin 7G 43
Hickleton. S Yor 7B 42
Hickling. Norf 7L 39
Hickling. Notts 7D 36
Hickling Green. Norf 7L 39
Hickling Heath. Norf 7L 39
Hickstead. W Sus 3K 11
Hidcote Bartrim. Glos 7K 27
Hidcote Boyce. Glos 7K 27
Higford. Shrp 1F 26
High Ackworth. W Yor 6B 42
Higham. Derbs 4A 36
Higham. Kent 6D 22
Higham. Lanc 4G 41
Higham. S Yor 7M 41
Higham. Suff
nr. Ipswich 8G 31
nr. Newmarket 5D 30
Higham Dykes. Nmbd 4E 54
Higham Ferrers. Nptn 5G 29
Higham Gobion. C Beds 8J 29
Higham on the Hill. Leics 2A 28
Highampton. Devn 5D 6
Higham Wood. Kent 1C 12
High Angerton. Nmbd 3D 54
High Auldgirth. Dum 3D 52
High Bankhill. Cumb 7K 53
High Banton. N Lan 1F 58
High Barnet. G Lon 4K 21
High Beech. Essx 4M 21
High Bentham. N Yor 1E 40
High Bickington. Devn 3F 6
High Biggins. Cumb 8D 46
High Birkwith. N Yor 8F 46
High Blantyre. S Lan 4E 58
High Bonnybridge. Falk 2G 59
High Borrans. Cumb 5C 46
High Bradfield. S Yor 8L 41
High Bray. Devn 2F 6
Highbridge. Cumb 7H 53
Highbridge. High 7C 70
Highbridge. Som 1B 8
Highbrook. W Sus 2L 11
High Brooms. Kent 1B 12
High Bullen. Devn 3E 6
Highburton. W Yor 6K 41
Highbury. Som 1E 8
High Buston. Nmbd 1F 54
High Callerton. Nmbd 4E 54
High Carlingill. Cumb 5E 46
High Catton. E Yor 2E 42
High Church. Nmbd 3E 54
Highclere. Hants 7B 20
Highcliffe. Dors 6L 9
High Cogges. Oxon 3A 20
High Common. Norf 1F 30
High Coniscliffe. Darl 4L 47
High Crosby. Cumb 6J 53
High Cross. Hants 3E 10
High Cross. Herts 2L 21
High Easter. Essx 2C 22
High Eggborough. N Yor 5C 42
High Ellington. N Yor 7K 47
Higher Alham. Som 1E 8
Higher Ansty. Dors 5F 8
Higher Ashton. Devn 7H 7
Higher Ballam. Lanc 4B 40
Higher Bartle. Lanc 4D 40
Higher Bockhampton. Dors 6F 8
Higher Bojewyan. Corn 5G 3
High Ercall. Telf 8D 34
Higher Cheriton. Devn 5L 7
Higher Clovelly. Devn 3C 6
Higher Compton. Plym 6G 5
Higher Dean. Devn 5K 5
Higher Dinting. Derbs 8J 41
Higher Dunstone. Devn 8G 7
Higher End. G Man 7D 40
Higherford. Lanc 3G 41
Higher Gabwell. Devn 5M 5
Higher Halstock Leigh. Dors 5D 8
Higher Heysham. Lanc 1C 40
Higher Hurdsfield. Ches E 2H 35
Higher Kingcombe. Dors 6D 8
Higher Kinnerton. Flin 3B 34
Higher Melcombe. Dors 5F 8
Higher Penwortham. Lanc 5D 40
Higher Porthpean. Corn 6C 4
Higher Poynton. Ches E 1H 35
Higher Shotton. Flin 3B 34
Higher Shurlach. Ches W 2E 34
Higher Slade. Devn 1E 6
Higher Tale. Devn 5K 7
Higher Town. IOS 1H 3
Higher Town. Som 1J 7
Highertown. Corn 4M 3
Higher Vexford. Som 2L 7
Higher Walton. Lanc 5D 40
Higher Walton. Warr 1D 34
Higher Whatcombe. Dors 5G 9
Higher Wheelton. Lanc 5E 40
Higher Whiteleigh. Corn 6B 6
Higher Whitley. Ches W 1E 34
Higher Wincham. Ches W 2E 34
Higher Wraxall. Dors 5D 8
Higher Wych. Ches W 5C 34
Higher Yalberton. Torb 6L 5
High Etherley. Dur 3K 47
High Ferry. Linc 5L 37
Highfield. E Yor 4E 42
Highfield. N Ayr 4B 58
Highfield. Tyne 6E 54
Highfields Caldecote.
Cambs 6L 29
High Gallowhill. E Dun 2E 58
High Garrett. Essx 1D 22
Highgate. G Lon 5K 21
Highgate. N Ayr 4B 58
Highgate. Powy 3L 25
High Grange. Dur 8E 54
High Green. Cumb 5C 46
High Green. Norf 1H 31
High Green. Shrp 3F 26
High Green. S Yor 8M 41
High Green. W Yor 6K 41
High Green. Worc 7G 27
Highgreen Manor. Nmbd 2B 54
High Halden. Kent 2E 12
High Halstow. Medw 6D 22
High Ham. Som 2C 8
High Harrington. Cumb 2K 45
High Haswell. Dur 7G 55
High Hatton. Shrp 7E 34
High Hawsker. N Yor 5G 49
High Hesket. Cumb 7J 53
High Hesleden. Dur 8H 55
High Hoyland. S Yor 6L 41
High Hunsley. E Yor 4G 43
High Hurstwood. E Sus 3A 12
High Hutton. N Yor 1E 42
High Ireby. Cumb 8G 53
High Keil. Arg 1B 50
High Kelling. Norf 6H 39
High Kilburn. N Yor 8C 48
High Knipe. Cumb 4D 46
High Lands. Dur 3K 47
The Highlands. Shrp 3E 26
High Lane. G Man 1H 35
High Lane. Worc 5E 26
Highlane. Ches E 3G 35
Highlane. Derbs 1B 36
High Laver. Essx 3B 22
Highlaws. Cumb 7F 52
Highleadon. Glos 1F 18
High Legh. Ches E 1F 34
Highleigh. W Sus 6F 10
High Leven. Stoc T 4B 48
Highley. Shrp 3F 26
High Littleton. Bath 8E 18
High Longthwaite. Cumb 7G 53
High Lorton. Cumb 2L 45
High Marishes. N Yor 8F 48
High Marnham. Notts 2F 36
High Melton. S Yor 7C 42
High Mickley. Nmbd 5D 54
High Moor. Lanc 6D 40
Highmoor. Cumb 7G 53
Highmoor. Oxon 5E 20
Highmoor Cross. Oxon 5E 20
Highmoor Hill. Mon 5C 18
Highnam. Glos 2F 18
High Newport. Tyne 6G 55
High Newton. Cumb 7C 46
High Newton-by-the-Sea.
Nmbd 7K 61
High Nibthwaite. Cumb 7A 46
High Offley. Staf 7F 34
High Ongar. Essx 3B 22
High Onn. Staf 8G 35
High Orchard. Glos 2G 19
High Park. Mers 6B 40
High Roding. Essx 2C 22
High Row. Cumb 8H 53
High Salvington. W Sus 5J 11
High Scales. Cumb 7F 52
High Shaw. N Yor 6G 47
High Shincliffe. Dur 7F 54
High Side. Cumb 8G 53
High Spen. Tyne 5E 54
Highsted. Kent 7F 22
High Stoop. Dur 7E 54
High Street. Corn 6B 4
High Street. Suff
nr. Aldeburgh 6L 31
nr. Bungay 3K 31
nr. Yoxford 4L 31
High Street Green. Suff 6G 31
Highstreet Green. Essx 8D 30
Highstreet Green. Surr 2G 11
Hightae. Dum 4E 52
High Throston. Hart 8H 55
High Town. Staf 8H 35
Hightown. Ches E 3G 35
Hightown. Mers 7A 40
Hightown Green. Suff 6F 30
High Toynton. Linc 3K 37
High Trewhitt. Nmbd 1D 54
High Valleyfield. Fife 1J 59
Highway. Here 7C 26
Highweek. Devn 8H 7
High Westwood. Dur 6E 54
Highwood. Staf 6J 35
Highwood. Worc 5E 26
High Worsall. N Yor 5A 48
Highworth. Swin 4L 19
High Wray. Cumb 6B 46
High Wych. Herts 2A 22
High Wycombe. Buck 4F 20
Hilborough. Norf 1E 30
Hilcott. Wilts 8K 19
Hildenborough. Kent 1B 12
Hildersham. Cambs 7B 30
Hilderstone. Staf 6H 35
Hilderthorpe. E Yor 1J 43
Hilfield. Dors 5E 8
Hilgay. Norf 2C 30
Hill. S Glo 4E 18
Hill. Warw 5B 28
Hill. Worc 7H 27
The Hill. Cumb 6L 45
Hillam. N Yor 5C 42
Hillbeck. Cumb 4F 46
Hillberry. IOM 7C 44
Hillborough. Kent 7J 23
Hillbourne. Pool 6J 9
Hillbrae. Abers
nr. Aberchirder 1F 72
nr. Inverurie 3G 73
nr. Methlick 2H 73
Hill Brow. Hants 3E 10
Hillbutts. Dors 5H 9
Hillclifflane. Derbs 5L 35
Hillcommon. Som 3L 7
Hill Deverill. Wilts 1G 9
Hilldyke. Linc 5L 37
Hill End. Dur 8D 54
Hill End. Fife 8D 66
Hill End. N Yor 2J 41
Hillend. Fife 1K 59
Hillend. N Lan 3G 59
Hillend. Shrp 2G 27
Hillend. Swan 7L 15
Hillersland. Glos 2D 18
Hillerton. Devn 6G 7
Hillesden. Buck 1D 20
Hillesley. Glos 5F 18
Hillfarrance. Som 3L 7
Hill Gate. Here 1C 18
Hill Green. Essx 8A 30
Hill Green. W Ber 6B 20
Hillhall. Lis 5H 93
Hill Head. Hants 5C 10
Hillhead. Abers 2E 72
Hillhead. Devn 6M 5
Hillhead. S Ayr 8C 58
Hillhead of Auchentumb.
Abers 8J 81
Hilliard's Cross. Staf 8K 35
Hilliclay. High 5C 86
Hillingdon. G Lon 5H 21
Hillington. Glas 3D 58
Hillington. Norf 7D 38
Hillmorton. Warw 4C 28
Hill of Beath. Fife 8E 66
Hill of Fearn. High 6J 79
Hill of Fiddes. Abers 3J 73
Hill of Keillor. Ang 3F 66
Hill of Overbrae. Abers 7H 81
Hill Ridware. Staf 8J 35
Hillsborough. Lis 6H 93
Hillsborough. S Yor 8M 41
Hill Side. W Yor 6K 41
Hillside. Abers 6J 73
Hillside. Ang 1L 67
Hillside. Devn 5K 5
Hillside. Mers 6B 40
Hillside. Orkn 7C 88
Hillside. Shet 1E 90
Hillside. Shrp 3E 26
Hillside. Worc 5F 26
Hillside of Prieston. Ang 4G 67
Hill Somersal. Derbs 6K 35
Hillstown. Derbs 3B 36
Hillstreet. Hants 4M 9
Hillswick. Shet 6G 91
Hill Top. Dur
nr. Barnard Castle 3H 47
nr. Durham 7F 54
nr. Stanley 6E 54
Hilltown. New M 7H 93
Hill View. Dors 6H 9
Hillwell. Shet 6D 90
Hill Wootton. Warw 5M 27
Hillyland. Per 5D 66
Hilmarton. Wilts 6J 19
Hilperton. Wilts 8G 19
Hilperton Marsh. Wilts 8G 19
Hilsea. Port 5D 10
Hilston. E Yor 4K 43
Hiltingbury. Hants 3B 10
Hilton. Cambs 5K 29
Hilton. Cumb 3F 46
Hilton. Derbs 6L 35
Hilton. Dors 5F 8
Hilton. Dur 3K 47
Hilton. High 5H 79
Hilton. Shrp 2F 26
Hilton. Staf 1J 27
Hilton. Stoc T 4B 48
Hilton of Cadboll. High 6J 79
Himbleton. Worc 6H 27
Himley. Staf 2G 27
Hincaster. Cumb 7D 46
Hinchwick. Glos 1K 19
Hinckley. Leics 2B 28
Hinderclay. Suff 4G 31
Hinderwell. N Yor 4E 48
Hindford. Shrp 6B 34
Hindhead. Surr 2F 10
Hindley. G Man 7E 40
Hindley. Nmbd 6D 54
Hindley Green. G Man 7E 40
Hindlip. Worc 6G 27
Hindolveston. Norf 7G 39
Hindon. Wilts 2H 9
Hindringham. Norf 6F 38
Hingham. Norf 1G 31
Hinksford. Staf 3G 27
Hinstock. Shrp 7E 34
Hintlesham. Suff 7G 31
Hinton. Hants 6L 9
Hinton. Here 8B 26
Hinton. Nptn 6C 28
Hinton. Shrp 1C 26
Hinton. S Glo 6F 18
Hinton Ampner. Hants 3C 10
Hinton Blewett. Bath 8D 18
Hinton Charterhouse. Bath 8F 18
Hinton-in-the-Hedges. Nptn 8C 28
Hinton Martell. Dors 5J 9
Hinton on the Green. Worc 7J 27
Hinton Parva. Swin 5L 19
Hinton St George. Som 4C 8
Hinton St Mary. Dors 4F 8
Hinton Waldrist. Oxon 4A 20
Hints. Shrp 4E 26
Hints. Staf 1K 27
Hinwick. Bed 5G 29
Hinxhill. Kent 1G 13
Hinxton. Cambs 7A 30
Hinxworth. Herts 7K 29
Hipley. Hants 4D 10
Hipperholme. W Yor 5K 41
Hipsburn. Nmbd 8K 61
Hipswell. N Yor 6K 47
Hiraeth. Carm 4H 15
Hirn. Abers 5G 73
Hirnant. Powy 8K 33
Hirst. N Lan 3G 59
Hirst. Nmbd 3F 54
Hirst Courtney. N Yor 5D 42
Hirwaen. Den 4L 33
Hirwaun. Rhon 4J 17
Hiscott. Devn 3E 6
Histon. Cambs 5M 29
Hitcham. Suff 6F 30
Hitchin. Herts 1J 21
Hittisleigh. Devn 6G 7
Hittisleigh Barton. Devn 6G 7
Hive. E Yor 4F 42
Hixon. Staf 7J 35
Hoaden. Kent 8J 23
Hoar Cross. Staf 7K 35
Hoarwithy. Here 1D 18
Hoath. Kent 7J 23
Yr Hôb. Flin 4B 34
Hobarris. Shrp 4B 26
Hobbister. Orkn 1E 86
Hobbles Green. Suff 6D 30
Hobbs Cross. Essx 4A 22
Hobkirk. Bord 8C 60
Hobson. Dur 6E 54
Hoby. Leics 8D 36
Hockering. Norf 8G 39
Hockering Heath. Norf 8G 39
Hockerton. Notts 4E 36
Hockley. Essx 4E 22
Hockley. Staf 1L 27
Hockley. W Mid 4L 27
Hockley Heath. W Mid 4K 27
Hockliffe. C Beds 1G 21
Hockwold cum Wilton.
Norf 3D 30
Hockworthy. Devn 4K 7
Hoddesdon. Herts 3L 21
Hoddlesden. Bkbn 5F 40
Hoddomcross. Dum 4F 52
Hodgeston. Pemb 7G 15
Hodley. Powy 3L 25
Hodnet. Shrp 7E 34
Hodsoll Street. Kent 7C 22
Hodson. Swin 5K 19
Hodthorpe. Derbs 2C 36
Hoe. Norf 8F 38
The Hoe. Plym 6G 5
Hoe Gate. Hants 4D 10
Hoff. Cumb 4E 46
Hoffleet Stow. Linc 6K 37
Hogaland. Shet 6H 91
Hogben's Hill. Kent 8G 23
Hoggard's Green. Suff 6E 30
Hoggeston. Buck 1F 20
Hoggrill's End. Warw 2L 27
Hogha Gearraidh. W Isl 6J 75
Hoghton. Lanc 5E 40
Hoghton Bottoms. Lanc 5E 40
Hognaston. Derbs 4L 35
Hogsthorpe. Linc 2B 38
Hogstock. Dors 5H 9
Holbeach. Linc 7L 37
Holbeach Bank. Linc 7L 37
Holbeach Clough. Linc 7L 37
Holbeach Drove. Linc 8L 37
Holbeach Hurn. Linc 7L 37
Holbeach St Johns. Linc 8L 37
Holbeach St Marks. Linc 6L 37
Holbeach St Matthew. Linc 6M 37
Holbeck. Notts 2C 36
Holbeck. W Yor 4L 41
Holbeck Woodhouse. Notts 2C 36
Holberrow Green. Worc 6J 27
Holbeton. Devn 6J 5
Holborn. G Lon 5L 21
Holbrook. Derbs 5A 36
Holbrook. S Yor 1B 36
Holbrook. Suff 8H 31
Holburn. Nmbd 6H 61
Holbury. Hants 5B 10
Holcombe. Devn 8J 7
Holcombe. G Man 6F 40
Holcombe. Som 1E 8
Holcombe Brook. G Man 6F 40
Holcombe Rogus. Devn 4K 7
Holcot. Nptn 5E 28
Holden. Lanc 3F 40
Holdenby. Nptn 5D 28
Holder's Green. Essx 1C 22
Holdgate. Shrp 3D 26
Holdingham. Linc 5H 37
Holditch. Dors 5B 8
Holemoor. Devn 5D 6
Hole Street. W Sus 4J 11
Holford. Som 1L 7
Holker. Cumb 8B 46
Holkham. Norf 5E 38
Hollacombe. Devn 5C 6
Holland. Orkn
on Papa Westray 4D 88
on Stronsay 7F 88
Holland Fen. Linc 5K 37
Holland Lees. Lanc 7D 40
Holland-on-Sea. Essx 2J 23
Holland Park. W Mid 1J 27
Hollandstoun. Orkn 4G 89
Hollesley. Suff 7K 31
Hollinfare. Warr 8E 40
Hollingbourne. Kent 8E 22
Hollingbury. Brig 5L 11
Hollingdon. Buck 1F 20
Hollingrove. E Sus 3C 12
Hollington. Derbs 6L 35
Hollington. E Sus 4D 12
Hollington. Staf 6J 35
Hollington Grove. Derbs 6L 35
Hollingworth. G Man 8J 41
Hollins. Derbs 2M 35
Hollins. G Man
nr. Bury 7G 41
nr. Middleton 7G 41
Hollinsclough. Staf 3J 35
Hollinswood. Telf 1F 26
Hollinthorpe. W Yor 4A 42
Hollinwood. G Man 7H 41
Hollinwood. Shrp 6D 34
Hollocombe. Devn 4F 6
Holloway. Derbs 4M 35
Hollowell. Nptn 4D 28
Hollow Meadows. S Yor 1L 35
Hollows. Dum 4H 53
Hollybush. Cphy 4L 17
Hollybush. E Ayr 8B 58
Hollybush. Worc 8F 26
Holly End. Norf 1A 30
Holly Hill. N Yor 5K 47
Hollyhurst. Shrp 5D 34
Hollym. E Yor 5L 43
Hollywood. Worc 4J 27
Holmacott. Devn 3E 6
Holmbridge. W Yor 7K 41
Holmbury St Mary. Surr 1J 11
Holmbush. Corn 6C 4
Holmcroft. Staf 7H 35
Holme. Cambs 3J 29
Holme. Cumb 8D 46
Holme. N Lin 7G 43
Holme. N Yor 7A 48
Holme. Notts 4F 36
Holme. W Yor 7K 41
Holmebridge. Dors 7G 9
Holme Chapel. Lanc 5G 41
Holme Hale. Norf 1E 30
Holme Lacy. Here 8D 26
Holme Marsh. Here 6B 26
Holmend. Dum 1E 52
Holme next the Sea. Norf 5D 38
Holme-on-Spalding-Moor.
E Yor 4F 42
Holme on the Wolds. E Yor 3G 43
Holme Pierrepont. Notts 6D 36
Holmer. Here 7D 26
Holmer Green. Buck 4G 21
Holmes. Lanc 6C 40
Holme St Cuthbert. Cumb 7F 52
Holmes Chapel. Ches E 3F 34
Holmesfield. Derbs 2M 35
Holmeswood. Lanc 6C 40
Holmewood. Derbs 3B 36
Holmfirth. W Yor 7K 41
Holmhead. E Ayr 7D 58
Holmisdale. High 1C 68
Holm of Drumlanrig. Dum 2C 52
Holmpton. E Yor 5L 43
Holmrook. Cumb 5K 45
Holmsgarth. Shet 3E 90
Holmside. Dur 7F 54
Holmwrangle. Cumb 7K 53
Holne. Devn 5K 5
Holsworthy. Devn 5C 6
Holsworthy Beacon. Devn 5C 6
Holt. Dors 5J 9
Holt. Norf 6G 39
Holt. Wilts 7G 19
Holt. Worc 5G 27
Holt. Wrex 4C 34
Holtby. York 2D 42
Holt End. Hants 2D 10
Holt End. Worc 5J 27
Holt Fleet. Worc 5G 27
Holt Green. Lanc 7B 40
Holt Heath. Dors 5J 9
Holt Heath. Worc 5G 27
Holton. Oxon 3C 20
Holton. Som 3E 8
Holton. Suff 4K 31
Holton cum Beckering. Linc 1J 37
Holton Heath. Dors 6H 9
Holton le Clay. Linc 7K 43
Holton le Moor. Linc 8H 43
Holton St Mary. Suff 8G 31
Holt Pound. Hants 1F 10
Holtsmere End. Herts 2H 21
Holtye. E Sus 2A 12
Holwell. Dors 4F 8
Holwell. Herts 8J 29
Holwell. Leics 7E 36
Holwell. Oxon 3L 19
Holwell. Som 1F 8
Holwick. Dur 3H 47
Holworth. Dors 7F 8
Holybourne. Hants 1E 10
Holy City. Devn 5B 8
Holy Cross. Worc 4H 27
Holyfield. Essx 3L 21
Holyhead. IOA 2B 32
Holy Island. Nmbd 5J 61
Holymoorside. Derbs 3M 35
Holyport. Wind 6F 20
Holystone. Nmbd 1C 54
Holytown. N Lan 3F 58
Holywell. Cambs 4L 29
Holywell. Corn 3L 3
Holywell. Dors 5D 8
Holywell. Flin 3L 33
Holywell. Glos 4F 18
Holywell. Nmbd 4G 55
Holywell. Warw 5K 27
Holywell Green. W Yor 6J 41
Holywell Lake. Som 3L 7
Holywell Row. Suff 4D 30
Holywood. Ards 5J 93
Holywood. Dum 3D 52
Homer. Shrp 1E 26
Homer Green. Mers 7B 40
Homersfield. Suff 3J 31
Hom Green. Here 1D 18
Homington. Wilts 3K 9
Honeyborough. Pemb 6F 14
Honeybourne. Worc 7K 27
Honeychurch. Devn 5F 6
Honeydon. Bed 6J 29
Honey Hill. Kent 7H 23
Honey Street. Wilts 7K 19
Honey Tye. Suff 8F 30
Honeywick. C Beds 1G 21
Honiley. Warw 4L 27
Honing. Norf 7K 39
Honingham. Norf 8H 39
Honington. Linc 5G 37
Honington. Suff 4F 30
Honington. Warw 7L 27
Honiton. Devn 5L 7
Honley. W Yor 6K 41
Honnington. Telf 8F 34
Hoo. Suff 6J 31
Hoobrook. Worc 4G 27
Hood Green. S Yor 7M 41
Hooe. E Sus 5C 12
Hooe. Plym 6H 5
Hooe Common. E Sus 4C 12
Hoo Green. Ches E 1F 34
Hoohill. Bkpl 4B 40
Hook. Cambs 2M 29
Hook. E Yor 5E 42
Hook. G Lon 7J 21
Hook. Hants
nr. Basingstoke 8E 20
nr. Fareham 5C 10
Hook. Pemb 5F 14
Hook. Wilts 5J 19
Hook-a-Gate. Shrp 1C 26
Hook Bank. Worc 7G 27
Hooke. Dors 5D 8
Hooker Gate. Tyne 6E 54
Hookgate. Staf 6F 34
Hook Green. Kent
nr. Lamberhurst 2C 12
nr. Meopham 7C 22
nr. Southfleet 6C 22
Hook Norton. Oxon 8A 28
Hook's Cross. Herts 1K 21
Hook Street. Glos 4E 18
Hookway. Devn 6H 7
Hookwood. Surr 1K 11
Hoole. Ches W 3C 34
Hooley. Surr 8K 21
Hooley Bridge. G Man 6G 41
Hooley Brow. G Man 6G 41
Hoo St Werburgh. Medw 6D 22
Hooton. Ches W 2B 34
Hooton Levitt. S Yor 8C 42
Hooton Pagnell. S Yor 7B 42
Hooton Roberts. S Yor 8B 42
Hoove. Shet 3D 90
Hope. Derbs 1K 35
Hope. Flin 4B 34
Hope. High 5G 85
Hope. Powy 1A 26
Hope. Shrp 1B 26
Hope. Staf 4K 35
Hope Bagot. Shrp 4D 26
Hope Bowdler. Shrp 2C 26
Hopedale. Staf 4K 35
Hope Green. Ches E 1H 35
Hopeman. Mor 7M 79
Hope Mansell. Here 2E 18
Hopesay. Shrp 3B 26
Hope's Green. Essx 5D 22
Hopetown. W Yor 5A 42
Hope under Dinmore. Here 6D 26
Hopley's Green. Here 6B 26
Hopperton. N Yor 2B 42
Hop Pole. Linc 8J 37
Hopstone. Shrp 2F 26
Hopton. Derbs 4L 35
Hopton. Powy 3M 25
Hopton. Shrp
nr. Oswestry 7B 34
nr. Wem 7D 34
Hopton. Staf 7H 35
Hopton. Suff 4F 30
Hopton Cangeford. Shrp 3D 26
Hopton Castle. Shrp 4B 26
Hopton Heath. Staf 7H 35
Hoptonheath. Shrp 4B 26
Hopton on Sea. Norf 1M 31
Hopton Wafers. Shrp 4E 26
Hopwas. Staf 1K 27
Hopwood. Worc 4J 27
Horam. E Sus 4B 12
Horbling. Linc 6J 37
Horbury. W Yor 6L 41
Horcott. Glos 3K 19
Horden. Dur 7H 55
Horderley. Shrp 3C 26
Hordle. Hants 6L 9
Hordley. Shrp 6B 34
Horeb. Carm
nr. Brechfa 4M 15
nr. Llanelli 6L 15
Horeb. Cdgn 2K 15
Horfield. Bris 6D 18
Horgabost. W Isl 4B 76
Horham. Suff 4J 31
Horkstow. N Lin 6G 43
Horley. Oxon 7B 28
Horley. Surr 1K 11
Horn Ash. Dors 5B 8
Hornblotton Green. Som 2D 8
Hornby. Lanc 1D 40
Hornby. N Yor
nr. Appleton Wiske 5A 48
nr. Catterick Garrison 6L 47
Horncastle. Linc 3K 37
Hornchurch. G Lon 5B 22
Horncliffe. Nmbd 5G 61
Horndean. Hants 4E 10
Horndean. Bord 5F 60
Horndon. Devn 7E 6
Horndon on the Hill. Thur 5C 22
Horne. Surr 1L 11
Horner. Som 1J 7
Horning. Norf 8K 39
Horninghold. Leics 2F 28
Horninglow. Staf 7L 35
Horningsea. Cambs 5A 30
Horningsham. Wilts 1G 9
Horningtoft. Norf 7F 38
Hornsbury. Som 4B 8
Hornsby. Cumb 6K 53
Hornsbygate. Cumb 6K 53
Horns Corner. Kent 3D 12
Horns Cross. Devn 3C 6
Hornsea. E Yor 3K 43
Hornsea Burton. E Yor 3K 43
Hornsey. G Lon 5L 21
Hornton. Oxon 7A 28
Horpit. Swin 5L 19
Horrabridge. Devn 5H 5
Horringer. Suff 5E 30
Horringford. IOW 7C 10
Horrocks Fold. G Man 6F 40
Horrocksford. Lanc 3F 40
Horsbrugh Ford. Bord 6L 59
Horsebridge. Devn 8D 6
Horsebridge. Hants 2M 9
Horsebrook. Staf 8G 35
Horsecastle. N Som 7C 18
Horsehay. Telf 1E 26
Horseheath. Cambs 7C 30
Horsehouse. N Yor 7J 47
Horsell. Surr 8G 21
Horseman's Green. Wrex 5C 34
Horsenden. Buck 3E 20
Horseway. Cambs 3M 29
Horsey. Norf 7L 39
Horsey. Som 2B 8
Horsford. Norf 8H 39
Horsforth. W Yor 4L 41
Horsham. W Sus 2J 11
Horsham. Worc 6F 26
Horsham St Faith. Norf 8J 39
Horsington. Linc 3J 37
Horsington. Som 3F 8
Horsley. Derbs 5A 36
Horsley. Glos 4G 19
Horsley. Nmbd
nr. Prudhoe 5D 54
nr. Rochester 2B 54
Horsley Cross. Essx 1H 23
Horsleycross Street. Essx 1H 23
Horsleyhill. Bord 8C 60
Horsleyhope. Dur 7D 54
Horsley Woodhouse. Derbs 5A 36
Horsmonden. Kent 1C 12
Horspath. Oxon 3C 20
Horstead. Norf 8J 39
Horsted Keynes. W Sus 3L 11
Horton. Buck 2G 21
Horton. Dors 5J 9
Horton. Lanc 2G 41
Horton. Nptn 6F 28
Horton. Shrp 6C 34
Horton. Som 4B 8
Horton. S Glo 5F 18
Horton. Staf 4H 35
Horton. Swan 8L 15
Horton. Wilts 7J 19
Horton. Wind 6H 21
Horton Cross. Som 4B 8
Horton-cum-Studley. Oxon 2C 20
Horton Grange. Nmbd 4F 54
Horton Green. Ches W 5C 34
Horton Heath. Hants 4B 10
Horton in Ribblesdale.
N Yor 8G 47
Horton Kirby. Kent 7B 22
Hortonwood. Telf 8E 34
Horwich. G Man 6E 40
Horwich End. Derbs 1J 35
Horwood. Devn 3E 6
Hoscar. Lanc 6C 40
Hose. Leics 7E 36
Hosh. Per 5B 66
Hosta. W Isl 6J 75
Hoswick. Shet 5E 90
Hotham. E Yor 4F 42
Hothfield. Kent 1F 12
Hoton. Leics 7C 36
Houbie. Shet 4L 91
Hough. Arg 3E 62
Hough. Ches E
nr. Crewe 4F 34
nr. Wilmslow 2G 35
Hougham. Linc 5F 36
Hough Green. Hal 1C 34
Hough-on-the-Hill. Linc 5G 37
Houghton. Cambs 4K 29
Houghton. Cumb 6J 53
Houghton. Hants 2M 9
Houghton. Nmbd 5E 54
Houghton. Pemb 6F 14
Houghton. W Sus 4H 11
Houghton Bank. Darl 3L 47
Houghton Conquest.
C Beds 7H 29
Houghton Green. E Sus 3F 12
Houghton-le-Side. Darl 3L 47
Houghton-le-Spring. Tyne 6G 55
Houghton on the Hill. Leics 1D 28
Houghton Regis. C Beds 1H 21
Houghton St Giles. Norf 6F 38
Houlland. Shet
on Mainland 2D 90
on Yell 6K 91
Houlsyke. N Yor 5E 48
Houlton. Warw 4C 28
Hound. Hants 5B 10
Hound Green. Hants 8E 20
Houndslow. Bord 5D 60
Houndsmoor. Som 3L 7
Houndwood. Bord 3F 60
Hounsdown. Hants 4M 9
Hounslow. G Lon 6J 21
Housabister. Shet 2E 90
Housay. Shet 6L 91
Househill. High 8J 79
Housetter. Shet 5H 91
Houss. Shet 4D 90
Houston. Ren 3C 58
Housty. High 8C 86
Houton. Orkn 1E 86
Hove. Brig 106 (5K 11)
Hoveringham. Notts 5D 36
Hoveton. Norf 8K 39
Hovingham. N Yor 8D 48
How. Cumb 6K 53
How Caple. Here 8E 26
Howden. E Yor 5E 42
Howden-le-Wear. Dur 8E 54
Howe. High 5E 86
Howe. Norf 1J 31
Howe. N Yor 7A 48
The Howe. Cumb 7C 46
The Howe. IOM 8A 44
Howe Green. Essx 3D 22
Howe Green. Warw 3M 27
Howegreen. Essx 3E 22
Howell. Linc 5J 37
How End. C Beds 7H 29
Howe of Teuchar. Abers 1G 73
Howes. Dum 5F 52
Howe Street. Essx
nr. Chelmsford 2C 22
nr. Finchingfield 8C 30
Howey. Powy 7K 25
Howgate. Midl 4L 59
Howgill. Lanc 3G 41
Howgill. N Yor 2J 41
How Green. Kent 1A 12
How Hill. Norf 8K 39
Howick. Nmbd 8K 61
Howle. Telf 7E 34
Howle Hill. Here 1E 18
Howleigh. Som 4M 7
Howlett End. Essx 8B 30
Howley. Som 5A 8
Howley. Warr 1E 34
Hownam. Bord 8E 60
Howsham. N Lin 7H 43
Howsham. N Yor 1E 42
Howtel. Nmbd 6F 60
Howt Green. Kent 7E 22
Howton. Here 1C 18
Howwood. Ren 3B 58
Hoxne. Suff 4H 31
Hoylake. Mers 2M 33
Hoyland. S Yor 7A 42
Hoylandswaine. S Yor 7L 41
Hoyle. W Sus 4G 11
Hubberholme. N Yor 8H 47
Hubberston. Pemb 6E 14
Hubbert's Bridge. Linc 5K 37
Huby. N Yor
nr. Harrogate 3L 41
nr. York 1C 42
Hucclecote. Glos 2G 19
Hucking. Kent 8E 22
Hucknall. Notts 5C 36
Huddersfield. W Yor 6K 41
Huddington. Worc 6H 27
Huddlesford. Staf 1K 27
Hudswell. N Yor 5K 47
Huggate. E Yor 2F 42
Hugglescote. Leics 8B 36
Hughenden Valley. Buck 4F 20
Hughley. Shrp 2D 26
Hughton. High 1E 70
Hugh Town. IOS 1H 3
Hugus. Corn 4L 3
Huish. Devn 4E 6
Huish. Wilts 7K 19
Huish Champflower. Som 3K 7
Huish Episcopi. Som 3C 8
Huisinis. W Isl 2A 76
Hulcote. Nptn 7E 28
Hulcott. Buck 2F 20
Hulham. Devn 7K 7
Hull. Hull
Kingston upon Hull 110 (5J 43)
Hulland. Derbs 5L 35
Hulland Moss. Derbs 5L 35
Hulland Ward. Derbs 5L 35
Hullavington. Wilts 5G 19
Hullbridge. Essx 4E 22
Hulme. G Man 8G 41
Hulme. Staf 5H 35
Hulme End. Staf 4K 35
Hulme Walfield. Ches E 3G 35
Hulverstone. IOW 7A 10
Hulver Street. Suff 3L 31
Humber. Devn 8J 7
Humber. Here 6D 26
Humber Bridge. N Lin 5H 43
Humberside Airport. N Lin 6H 43
Humberston. NE Lin 7L 43
Humberstone. Leic 1D 28
Humbie. E Lot 3B 60
Humbleton. E Yor 4K 43
Humbleton. Nmbd 7G 61
Humby. Linc 6H 37
Hume. Bord 5E 60
Humshaugh. Nmbd 4C 54
Huna. High 4E 86
Huncoat. Lanc 4F 40
Huncote. Leics 2C 28
Hundall. Derbs 2A 36
Hunderthwaite. Dur 3H 47
Hundleby. Linc 3L 37
Hundle Houses. Linc 4K 37
Hundleton. Pemb 6F 14
Hundon. Suff 7D 30
The Hundred. Here 5D 26
Hundred Acres. Hants 4C 10
Hundred House. Powy 7L 25
Hungarton. Leics 1D 28
Hungerford. Hants 4K 9
Hungerford. Shrp 3D 26
Hungerford. Som 1K 7
Hungerford. W Ber 7M 19
Hungerford Newtown.
W Ber 6A 20
Hunger Hill. G Man 7E 40
Hungerton. Linc 6F 36
Hungladder. High 6E 76
Hungryhatton. Shrp 7E 34
Hunmanby. N Yor 8H 49
Hunmanby Sands. N Yor 8J 49
Hunningham. Warw 5A 28
Hunnington. Worc 3H 27
Hunny Hill. IOW 7B 10
Hunsdon. Herts 2M 21
Hunsdonbury. Herts 2M 21
Hunsingore. N Yor 2B 42
Hunslet. W Yor 4M 41
Hunslet Carr. W Yor 4M 41
Hunsonby. Cumb 8K 53
Hunspow. High 4D 86
Hunstanton. Norf 5C 38
Hunstanworth. Dur 7C 54
Hunston. Suff 5F 30
Hunston. W Sus 5F 10
Hunstrete. Bath 7E 18
Hunt End. Worc 5J 27
Hunterfield. Midl 3M 59
Hunters Forstal. Kent 7H 23
Hunter's Quay. Arg 2L 57
Huntham. Som 3B 8
Hunthill Lodge. Ang 8D 72
Huntingdon. Cambs 4K 29
Huntingfield. Suff 4K 31
Huntingford. Wilts 3G 9
Huntington. Ches W 3C 34
Huntington. E Lot 2B 60
Huntington. Here 6A 26
Huntington. Staf 8H 35
Huntington. Telf 1E 26
Huntington. York 2D 42
Huntingtower. Per 5D 66
Huntley. Glos 2F 18
Huntley. Staf 5J 35
Huntly. Abers 2E 72
Huntlywood. Bord 5D 60
Hunton. Hants 2B 10
Hunton. Kent 1D 12
Hunton. N Yor 6K 47
Hunton Bridge. Herts 4H 21
Hunt's Corner. Norf 3G 31
Huntscott. Som 1J 7
Hunt's Cross. Mers 1C 34
Hunts Green. Warw 2K 27
Huntsham. Devn 3K 7
Huntshaw. Devn 3E 6
Huntspill. Som 1B 8
Huntstile. Som 2A 8
Huntworth. Som 2B 8
Hunwick. Dur 8E 54
Hunworth. Norf 6G 39
Hurcott. Som
nr. Ilminster 4B 8
nr. Somerton 3D 8
Hurdcott. Wilts 2K 9
Hurdley. Powy 2A 26
Hurdsfield. Ches E 2H 35
Hurlet. Glas 3D 58
Hurley. Warw 2L 27
Hurley. Wind 5F 20
Hurlford. E Ayr 6C 58
Hurliness. Orkn 3D 86
Hurlston Green. Lanc 6C 40
Hurn. Dors 6K 9
Hursey. Dors 5C 8
Hursley. Hants 3B 10
Hurst. G Man 7H 41
Hurst. N Yor 5J 47
Hurst. Som 4C 8
Hurst. Wok 6E 20
Hurstbourne Priors. Hants 1B 10
Hurstbourne Tarrant. Hants 8A 20
Hurst Green. Ches E 5D 34
Hurst Green. E Sus 3D 12
Hurst Green. Essx 2G 23
Hurst Green. Lanc 4E 40
Hurst Green. Surr 8L 21
Hurstley. Here 7B 26
Hurstpierpoint. W Sus 4K 11
Hurstway Common. Here 7B 26
Hurst Wickham. W Sus 4K 11
Hurstwood. Lanc 4G 41
Hurtmore. Surr 1G 11
Hurworth-on-Tees. Darl 4M 47
Hurworth Place. Darl 5L 47
Hury. Dur 4H 47
Husbands Bosworth. Leics 3D 28
Husborne Crawley. C Beds 8G 29
Husthwaite. N Yor 8C 48
Hutcherleigh. Devn 6K 5
Hut Green. N Yor 5C 42
Huthwaite. Notts 4B 36
Huttoft. Linc 2B 38
Hutton. Cumb 3C 46
Hutton. E Yor 2H 43
Hutton. Essx 4C 22
Hutton. Lanc 5C 40
Hutton. N Som 8B 18
Hutton. Bord 4G 61
Hutton Bonville. N Yor 5M 47
Hutton Buscel. N Yor 7G 49
Hutton Conyers. N Yor 8M 47
Hutton Cranswick. E Yor 2H 43
Hutton End. Cumb 8J 53
Hutton Gate. Red C 4C 48
Hutton Henry. Dur 8H 55
Hutton-le-Hole. N Yor 7E 48
Hutton Magna. Dur 4K 47
Hutton Mulgrave. N Yor 5F 48
Hutton Roof. Cumb
nr. Kirkby Lonsdale 8D 46
nr. Penrith 8H 53
Hutton Rudby. N Yor 5B 48
Huttons Ambo. N Yor 1E 42
Hutton Sessay. N Yor 8B 48
Hutton Village. Red C 4D 48
Hutton Wandesley. N Yor 2C 42
Huxham. Devn 6J 7
Huxham Green. Som 2D 8
Huxley. Ches W 3D 34
Huxter. Shet
on Mainland 2B 90
on Whalsay 1F 90
Huyton. Mers 8C 40
Hwlffordd. Pemb 5F 14
Hycemoor. Cumb 6K 45
Hyde. Glos
nr. Stroud 3G 19
nr. Winchcombe 1J 19
Hyde. G Man 8H 41
Hyde Heath. Buck 3G 21
Hyde Lea. Staf 8H 35
Hyde Park. S Yor 7C 42
Hydestile. Surr 1G 11
Hyndford Bridge. S Lan 5H 59
Hynish. Arg 4E 62
Hyssington. Powy 2B 26
Hythe. Hants 5B 10
Hythe. Kent 2H 13
Hythe End. Wind 6H 21
Hythie. Abers 8K 81
Hyton. Cumb 6K 45

I

Ianstown. Mor 7D 80
Iarsiadar. W Isl 8E 82
Ibberton. Dors 5F 8
Ible. Derbs 4L 35
Ibrox. Glas 3D 58
Ibsley. Hants 5K 9
Ibstock. Leics 8B 36
Ibstone. Buck 4E 20
Ibthorpe. Hants 8A 20
Iburndale. N Yor 5F 48
Ibworth. Hants 8C 20
Icelton. N Som 7B 18
Ichrachan. Arg 4E 64
Ickburgh. Norf 2E 30
Ickenham. G Lon 5H 21
Ickenthwaite. Cumb 7B 46
Ickford. Buck 3D 20
Ickham. Kent 8J 23
Ickleford. Herts 8J 29
Icklesham. E Sus 4E 12
Ickleton. Cambs 7A 30
Icklingham. Suff 4D 30
Ickwell. C Beds 7J 29
Icomb. Glos 1L 19
Idbury. Oxon 2L 19
Iddesleigh. Devn 5E 6
Ide. Devn 6H 7
Ideford. Devn 8H 7
Ide Hill. Kent 8A 22
Iden. E Sus 3F 12
Iden Green. Kent
nr. Benenden 2E 12
nr. Goudhurst 2D 12
Idle. W Yor 4K 41
Idless. Corn 4M 3
Idlicote. Warw 7L 27
Idmiston. Wilts 2K 9
Idole. Carm 5L 15
Idridgehay. Derbs 5L 35
Idrigill. High 7E 76
Idstone. Oxon 5L 19
Iffley. Oxon 3C 20
Ifield. W Sus 2K 11
Ifieldwood. W Sus 2K 11
Ifold. W Sus 2H 11
Iford. E Sus 5M 11
Ifton Heath. Shrp 6B 34
Ightfield. Shrp 6D 34
Ightham. Kent 8B 22
Iken. Suff 6L 31
Ilam. Staf 4K 35
Ilchester. Som 3D 8
Ilderton. Nmbd 7H 61
Ilford. G Lon 5M 21
Ilford. Som 4B 8
Ilfracombe. Devn 1E 6
Ilkeston. Derbs 5B 36
Ilketshall St Andrew. Suff 3K 31
Ilketshall St Lawrence. Suff 3K 31
Ilketshall St Margaret. Suff 3K 31
Ilkley. W Yor 3K 41
Illand. Corn 8B 6
Illey. W Mid 3H 27
Illidge Green. Ches E 3F 34
Illington. Norf 3F 30
Illingworth. W Yor 5J 41
Illogan. Corn 4K 3
Illogan Highway. Corn 4K 3
Illston on the Hill. Leics 2E 28
Ilmer. Buck 3E 20
Ilmington. Warw 7L 27
Ilminster. Som 4B 8
Ilsington. Devn 8G 7
Ilsington. Dors 6F 8
Ilston. Swan 5E 16
Ilton. N Yor 8K 47
Ilton. Som 4B 8
Imachar. N Ayr 5H 57
Imber. Wilts 1H 9
Immingham. NE Lin 6J 43
Immingham Dock. NE Lin 6K 43
Impington. Cambs 5M 29
Ince. Ches W 2C 34
Ince Blundell. Mers 7B 40
Ince-in-Makerfield. G Man 7D 40
Inchbae Lodge. High 7E 78
Inchbare. Ang 1K 67
Inchberry. Mor 8C 80
Inchbraoch. Ang 2L 67
Inchbrook. Glos 3G 19

Incheril—Lanark

Incheril. High 7M 77
Inchinnan. Ren 3C 58
Inchlaggan. High 5B 70
Inchmichael. Per 5F 66
Inchnadamph. High 1C 78
Inchree. High 1E 64
Inchture. Per 5F 66
Inchyra. Per 5E 66
Indian Queens. Corn 6B 4
Ingatestone. Essx 4C 22
Ingbirchworth. S Yor 7L 41
Ingestre. Staf 7H 35
Ingham. Linc 1G 37
Ingham. Norf 7K 39
Ingham. Suff 4E 30
Ingham Corner. Norf 7K 39
Ingleborough. Norf 8A 38
Ingleby. Derbs 7M 35
Ingleby Arncliffe. N Yor 5B 48
Ingleby Barwick. Stoc T 4B 48
Ingleby Greenhow. N Yor 5C 48
Ingleigh Green. Devn 5F 6
Inglemire. Hull 4H 43
Inglesbatch. Bath 7F 18
Ingleton. Dur 3K 47
Ingleton. N Yor 8E 46
Inglewhite. Lanc 3D 40
Ingoe. Nmbd 4D 54
Ingol. Lanc 4D 40
Ingoldisthorpe. Norf 6C 38
Ingoldmells. Linc 3B 38
Ingoldsby. Linc 6H 37
Ingon. Warw 6L 27
Ingram. Nmbd 8H 61
Ingrave. Essx 4C 22
Ingrow. W Yor 4J 41
Ings. Cumb 6C 46
Ingst. S Glo 5D 18
Ingthorpe. Rut 1G 29
Ingworth. Norf 7H 39
Inishrush. M Ulst 3F 93
Inkberrow. Worc 6J 27
Inkford. Worc 4J 27
Inkpen. W Ber 7A 20
Inkstack. High 4D 86
Innellan. Arg 3L 57
Inner Hope. Devn 8J 5
Innerleith. Fife 6F 66
Innerleithen. Bord 6M 59
Innerleven. Fife 7G 67
Innermessan. Dum 5F 50
Innerwick. E Lot 2E 60
Innerwick. Per 3K 65
Innsworth. Glos 1G 19
Insch. Abers 3F 72
Insh. High 5J 71
Inshegra. High 6E 84
Inshore. High 4F 84
Inskip. Lanc 4C 40
Instow. Devn 2D 6
Intwood. Norf 1H 31
Inver. Abers 6B 72
Inver. High 5J 79
Inver. Per 3D 66
Inverailort. High 7J 69
Inveralligin. High 8K 77
Inverallochy. Abers 7K 81
Inveramsay. Abers 3G 73
Inveran. High 4F 78
Inveraray. Arg 7E 64
Inverarish. High 2G 69
Inverarity. Ang 3H 67
Inverarnan. Stir 6H 65
Inverarnie. High 2G 71
Inverbeg. Arg 8H 65
Inverbervie. Abers 8H 73
Inverboyndie. Abers 7F 80
Invercassley. High 3E 78
Invercharnan. High 3F 64
Inverchoran. High 8C 78
Invercreran. Arg 3E 64
Inverdruie. High 4K 71
Inverebrie. Abers 2J 73
Invereck. Arg 1L 57
Inveresk. E Lot 2M 59
Inveresragan. Arg 4D 64
Inverey. Abers 7L 71
Inverfarigaig. High 3F 70
Invergarry. High 5D 70
Invergeldie. Per 5M 65
Invergordon. High 7H 79
Invergowrie. Per 4G 67
Inverguseran. High 5J 69
Inverharroch. Mor 2C 72
Inverie. High 5J 69
Inverinan. Arg 6D 64
Inverinate. High 3L 69
Inverkeilor. Ang 3K 67
Inverkeithing. Fife 1K 59
Inverkeithny. Abers 1F 72
Inverkip. Inv 2M 57
Inverkirkaig. High 2A 78
Inverlael. High 5B 78
Inverliever Lodge. Arg 7C 64
Inverliver. Arg 4E 64
Inverlochlarig. Stir 6J 65
Inverlochy. High 8B 70
Inverlussa. Arg 1F 56
Inver Mallie. High 7B 70
Invermarkie. Abers 2D 72
Invermoriston. High 4E 70
Invernaver. High 5K 85
Inverneil House. Arg 1H 57
Inverness. High 110 (1G 71)
Inverness Airport. High 8H 79
Invernettie. Abers 1L 73
Inverpolly Lodge. High 2A 78
Inverquhomery. Abers 1K 73
Inverroy. High 7C 70
Inversanda. High 2D 64
Invershiel. High 4L 69
Invershin. High 4F 78
Invershore. High 8D 86
Inversnaid. Stir 7H 65
Inverugie. Abers 1L 73
Inveruglas. Arg 7H 65
Inverurie. Abers 3G 73
Invervar. Per 3L 65
Inverythan. Abers 1G 73
Inwardleigh. Devn 6E 6
Inworth. Essx 2E 22
Iochdar. W Isl 1D 74
Iping. W Sus 3F 10
Ipplepen. Devn 5L 5
Ipsden. Oxon 5D 20
Ipstones. Staf 5J 35
Ipswich. Suff 110 (7H 31)
Irby. Mers 1A 34
Irby in the Marsh. Linc 3A 38
Irby upon Humber. NE Lin 7J 43
Irchester. Nptn 5G 29
Ireby. Cumb 8G 53
Ireby. Lanc 8E 46
Ireland. Shet 5D 90
Ireleth. Cumb 7M 45
Ireshopeburn. Dur 8B 54
Ireton Wood. Derbs 5L 35
Irlam. G Man 8F 40
Irnham. Linc 7H 37
Iron Acton. S Glo 5E 18
Iron Bridge. Cambs 2A 30
Ironbridge. Telf 1E 26
Iron Cross. Warw 6J 27
Ironville. Derbs 4B 36
Irstead. Norf 7K 39
Irthington. Cumb 5J 53
Irthlingborough. Nptn 4G 29
Irton. N Yor 7H 49
Irvine. N Ayr 6B 58
Irvine Mains. N Ayr 6B 58
Irvinestown. Ferm 6C 92
Isabella Pit. Nmbd 3G 55
Isauld. High 5A 86
Isbister. Orkn 8C 88
Isbister. Shet
on Mainland 4H 91
on Whalsay 1F 90
Isfield. E Sus 4A 12
Isham. Nptn 4F 28
Island Carr. N Lin 7G 43
Islay Airport. Arg 4C 56
Isle Abbotts. Som 3B 8
Isle Brewers. Som 3B 8
Isleham. Cambs 4C 30
Isle of Man Airport. IOM 8B 44
Isle of Thanet. Kent 7K 23
Isle of Whithorn. Dum 8K 51
Isle of Wight. IOW 7B 10
Isleornsay. High 4J 69
Islesburgh. Shet 1D 90
Isles of Scilly Airport. IOS 1H 3
Islesteps. Dum 4D 52
Isleworth. G Lon 6J 21
Isley Walton. Leics 7B 36
Islibhig. W Isl 1A 76
Islington. G Lon 5L 21
Islington. Telf 7F 34
Islip. Nptn 4G 29
Islip. Oxon 2C 20
Isombridge. Telf 8E 34
Istead Rise. Kent 7C 22
Itchen. Sotn 4B 10
Itchen Abbas. Hants 2C 10
Itchenor. W Sus 5E 10
Itchen Stoke. Hants 2C 10
Itchingfield. W Sus 3J 11
Itchington. S Glo 5E 18
Itlaw. Abers 8F 80
Itteringham. Norf 6H 39
Itteringham Common. Norf 7H 39
Itton. Devn 6F 6
Itton Common. Mon 4C 18
Ivegill. Cumb 7J 53
Ivelet. N Yor 6H 47
Iverchaolain. Arg 2K 57
Iver Heath. Buck 5H 21
Iveston. Dur 6E 54
Ivetsey Bank. Staf 8G 35
Ivinghoe. Buck 2G 21
Ivinghoe Aston. Buck 2G 21
Ivington. Here 6C 26
Ivington Green. Here 6C 26
Ivybridge. Devn 6J 5
Ivychurch. Kent 3G 13
Ivy Hatch. Kent 8B 22
Ivy Todd. Norf 1E 30
Iwade. Kent 7F 22
Iwerne Courtney. Dors 4G 9
Iwerne Minster. Dors 4G 9
Ixworth. Suff 4F 30
Ixworth Thorpe. Suff 4F 30

J

Jackfield. Shrp 1E 26
Jack Hill. N Yor 2K 41
Jacksdale. Notts 4B 36
Jackton. S Lan 4D 58
Jacobstow. Corn 6A 6
Jacobstowe. Devn 5E 6
Jacobs Well. Surr 8G 21
Jameston. Pemb 7G 15
Jamestown. Dum 2H 53
Jamestown. Fife 1K 59
Jamestown. High 8E 78
Jamestown. W Dun 1B 58
Janetstown. High
nr. Thurso 5B 86
nr. Wick 6E 86
Jarrow. Tyne 5G 55
Jarvis Brook. E Sus 3B 12
Jasper's Green. Essx 1D 22
Jaywick. Essx 2H 23
Jedburgh. Bord 7D 60
Jeffreyston. Pemb 6G 15
Jemimaville. High 7H 79
Jenkins Park. High 5D 70
Jersey Marine. Neat 5G 17
Jesmond. Tyne 5F 54
Jevington. E Sus 5B 12
Jingle Street. Mon 2C 18
Jockey End. Herts 2H 21
Jodrell Bank. Ches E 2F 34
Johnby. Cumb 8J 53
John O'Gaunts. W Yor 5M 41
John o' Groats. High 4E 86
John's Cross. E Sus 3D 12
Johnshaven. Abers 1L 67
Johnson Street. Norf 8K 39
Johnston. Pemb 5F 14
Johnstone. Ren 3C 58
Johnstonebridge. Dum 2E 52
Johnstown. Carm 5L 15
Johnstown. Wrex 5B 34
Jonesborough. New M 7G 93
Joppa. Edin 2M 59
Joppa. S Ayr 8C 58
Jordan Green. Norf 7G 39
Jordans. Buck 4G 21
Jordanston. Pemb 3F 14
Jump. S Yor 7A 42
Jumpers Common. Dors 6K 9
Juniper. Nmbd 6C 54
Juniper Green. Edin 3K 59
Jurby East. IOM 5C 44
Jurby West. IOM 5C 44
Jury's Gap. E Sus 4F 12

K

Kaber. Cumb 4F 46
Kaimend. S Lan 5H 59
Kaimes. Edin 3L 59
Kaimrig End. Bord 5J 59
Kames. Arg 2J 57
Kames. E Ayr 7E 58
Katesbridge. Arm 6H 93
Kea. Corn 4M 3
Keadby. N Lin 6F 42
Keady. Arm 7F 93
Keal Cotes. Linc 3L 37
Kearsley. G Man 7F 40
Kearsney. Kent 1J 13
Kearstwick. Cumb 7E 46
Kearton. N Yor 6H 47
Kearvaig. High 4E 84
Keasden. N Yor 1F 40
Keason. Corn 5F 4
Keckwick. Hal 1D 34
Keddington. Linc 1L 37
Keddington Corner. Linc 1L 37
Kedington. Suff 7D 30
Kedleston. Derbs 5M 35
Kedlock Feus. Fife 6G 67
Keekle. Cumb 3K 45
Keelby. Linc 6J 43
Keele. Staf 5G 35
Keeley Green. Bed 7H 29
Keeston. Pemb 5F 14
Keevil. Wilts 8H 19
Kegworth. Leics 7B 36
Kehelland. Corn 4K 3
Keig. Abers 4F 72
Keighley. W Yor 3J 41
Keilarsbrae. Clac 8B 66
Keillmore. Arg 1F 56
Keillor. Per 3F 66
Keillour. Per 5C 66
Keills. Arg 3D 56
Keiloch. Abers 6A 72
Keils. Arg 3E 56
Keinton Mandeville. Som 2D 8
Keir Mill. Dum 2C 52
Keirsleywell Row. Nmbd 6A 54
Keisby. Linc 7H 37
Keisley. Cumb 3F 46
Keiss. High 5E 86
Keith. Mor 8D 80
Keith Inch. Abers 1L 73
Kelbrook. Lanc 3H 41
Kelby. Linc 5H 37
Keld. Cumb 4D 46
Keld. N Yor 5G 47
Keldholme. N Yor 7E 48
Kelfield. N Lin 7F 42
Kelfield. N Yor 4C 42
Kelham. Notts 4E 36
Kellacott. Devn 7D 6
Kellan. Arg 3L 63
Kellas. Ang 4H 67
Kellas. Mor 8A 80
Kellaton. Devn 8L 5
Kelleth. Cumb 5E 46
Kelling. Norf 5G 39
Kellingley. N Yor 5C 42
Kellington. N Yor 5C 42
Kelloe. Dur 8G 55
Kelloholm. Dum 8F 58
Kells. Cumb 3J 45
Kells. ME Ant 4G 93
Kelly. Devn 7C 6
Kelly Bray. Corn 8C 6
Kelmarsh. Nptn 4E 28
Kelmscott. Oxon 4L 19
Kelsale. Suff 5K 31
Kelsall. Ches W 3D 34
Kelshall. Herts 8L 29
Kelsick. Cumb 6F 52
Kelso. Bord 6E 60
Kelstedge. Derbs 3M 35
Kelstern. Linc 8K 43
Kelsterton. Flin 2A 34
Kelston. Bath 7F 18
Keltneyburn. Per 3A 66
Kelton. Dum 4D 52
Kelton Hill. Dum 6B 52
Kelty. Fife 8E 66
Kelvedon. Essx 2E 22
Kelvedon Hatch. Essx 4B 22
Kelvinside. Glas 3D 58
Kelynack. Corn 5G 3
Kemback. Fife 6H 67
Kemberton. Shrp 1F 26
Kemble. Glos 4H 19
Kemerton. Worc 8H 27
Kemeys Commander. Mon 3B 18
Kemnay. Abers 4G 73
Kempe's Corner. Kent 1G 13
Kempley. Glos 1E 18
Kempley Green. Glos 1E 18
Kempsey. Worc 7G 27
Kempsford. Glos 4K 19
Kemps Green. Warw 4K 27
Kempshott. Hants 1D 10
Kempston. Bed 7H 29
Kempston Hardwick. Bed 7H 29
Kempton. Shrp 3B 26
Kemp Town. Brig 5L 11
Kemsing. Kent 8B 22
Kemsley. Kent 7F 22
Kenardington. Kent 2F 12
Kenchester. Here 7C 26
Kencot. Oxon 3L 19
Kendal. Cumb 6D 46
Kendleshire. S Glo 6E 18
Kendray. S Yor 7A 42
Kenfig. B'end 6H 17
Kenfig Hill. B'end 6H 17
Kengharair. Arg 3K 63
Kenilworth. Warw 4L 27
Kenknock. Stir 4J 65
Kenley. G Lon 8L 21
Kenley. Shrp 1D 26
Kenmore. High 8J 77
Kenmore. Per 3A 66
Kenn. Devn 7J 7
Kenn. N Som 7C 18
Kennacraig. Arg 3H 57
Kenneggy Downs. Corn 6J 3
Kennerleigh. Devn 5H 7
Kennet. Clac 8C 66
Kennethmont. Abers 3E 72
Kennett. Cambs 5D 30
Kennford. Devn 7J 7
Kenninghall. Norf 3G 31
Kennington. Kent 1G 13
Kennington. Oxon 3C 20
Kennoway. Fife 7G 67
Kennyhill. Suff 4C 30
Kennythorpe. N Yor 1E 42
Kenovay. Arg 3E 62
Kensaleyre. High 8F 76
Kensington. G Lon 6K 21
Kenstone. Shrp 7D 34
Kensworth. C Beds 2H 21
Kensworth Common.
C Beds 2H 21
Kentallen. High 2E 64
Kentchurch. Here 1C 18
Kentford. Suff 5D 30
Kentisbeare. Devn 5K 7
Kentisbury. Devn 1F 6
Kentisbury Ford. Devn 1F 6
Kentmere. Cumb 5C 46
Kenton. Devn 7J 7
Kenton. G Lon 5J 21
Kenton. Suff 5H 31
Kenton Bankfoot. Tyne 5F 54
Kentra. High 1M 63
Kentrigg. Cumb 6D 46
Kents Bank. Cumb 8B 46
Kent's Green. Glos 1F 18
Kent's Oak. Hants 3M 9
Kent Street. E Sus 4D 12
Kent Street. Kent 8C 22
Kent Street. W Sus 3K 11
Kenwick. Shrp 6C 34
Kenwyn. Corn 4M 3
Kenyon. Warr 8E 40
Keoldale. High 5F 84
Keppoch. High 3L 69
Kepwick. N Yor 6B 48
Keresley. W Mid 3M 27
Keresley Newland. Warw 3M 27
Keristal. IOM 7C 44
Kerne Bridge. Here 2D 18
Kerridge. Ches E 2H 35
Kerris. Corn 6H 3
Kerrow. High 2D 70
Kerry. Powy 4L 25
Kerrycroy. Arg 3L 57
Kerry's Gate. Here 8B 26
Kersall. Notts 3E 36
Kersbrook. Devn 7K 7
Kerse. Ren 4B 58
Kersey. Suff 7G 31
Kershopefoot. Cumb 3J 53
Kersoe. Worc 7H 27
Kerswell. Devn 5K 7
Kerswell Green. Worc 7G 27
Kesgrave. Suff 7J 31
Kesh. Ferm 5B 92
Kessingland. Suff 3M 31
Kessingland Beach. Suff 3M 31
Kestle. Corn 7B 4
Kestle Mill. Corn 6A 4
Keston. G Lon 7M 21
Keswick. Cumb 3A 46
Keswick. Norf
nr. North Walsham 6K 39
nr. Norwich 1J 31
Ketsby. Linc 2L 37
Kettering. Nptn 4F 28
Ketteringham. Norf 1H 31
Kettins. Per 4F 66
Kettlebaston. Suff 6F 30
Kettlebridge. Fife 7G 67
Kettlebrook. Staf 1L 27
Kettleburgh. Suff 5J 31
Kettleholm. Dum 4F 52
Kettleness. N Yor 4F 48
Kettleshulme. Ches E 2H 35
Kettlesing. N Yor 2L 41
Kettlesing Bottom. N Yor 2L 41
Kettlestone. Norf 6F 38
Kettlethorpe. Linc 2F 36
Kettletoft. Orkn 6F 88
Kettlewell. N Yor 8H 47
Ketton. Rut 1G 29
Kew. G Lon 6J 21
Kewaigue. IOM 7C 44
Kewstoke. N Som 7B 18
Kexbrough. S Yor 7L 41
Kexby. Linc 1F 36
Kexby. York 2E 42
Keyford. Som 1F 8
Key Green. Ches E 3G 35
Key Green. N Yor 5F 48
Keyham. Leics 1D 28
Keyhaven. Hants 6M 9
Keyhead. Abers 8K 81
Keyingham. E Yor 5K 43
Keymer. W Sus 4L 11
Keynsham. Bath 7E 18
Keysoe. Bed 5H 29
Keysoe Row. Bed 5H 29
Key's Toft. Linc 4A 38
Keyston. Cambs 4H 29
Key Street. Kent 7E 22
Keyworth. Notts 6D 36
Kibblesworth. Tyne 6F 54
Kibworth Beauchamp.
Leics 2D 28
Kibworth Harcourt. Leics 2D 28
Kidbrooke. G Lon 6M 21
Kidburngill. Cumb 2K 45
Kiddemore Green. Staf 1G 27
Kidderminster. Worc 4G 27
Kiddington. Oxon 1B 20
Kidd's Moor. Norf 1H 31
Kidlington. Oxon 2B 20
Kidmore End. Oxon 6D 20
Kidnal. Ches W 5C 34
Kidsgrove. Staf 4G 35
Kidstones. N Yor 7H 47
Kidwelly. Carm 6L 15
Kiel Crofts. Arg 4D 64
Kielder. Nmbd 2L 53
Kilbagie. Fife 8C 66
Kilbarchan. Ren 3C 58
Kilbeg. High 5H 69
Kilberry. Arg 3G 57
Kilbirnie. N Ayr 4B 58
Kilbride. Arg 5C 64
Kilbride. High 3G 69
Kilbucho Place. Bord 6J 59
Kilburn. Derbs 5A 36
Kilburn. G Lon 5K 21
Kilburn. N Yor 8C 48
Kilby. Leics 2D 28
Kilchattan. Arg 8J 63
Kilchattan Bay. Arg 4L 57
Kilchenzie. Arg 7F 56
Kilcheran. Arg 4C 64
Kilchiaran. Arg 3B 56
Kilchoan. High
nr. Inverie 6J 69
nr. Tobermory 1K 63
Kilchoman. Arg 3B 56
Kilchrenan. Arg 5E 64
Kilclief. New M 6J 93
Kilconquhar. Fife 7H 67
Kilcoo. New M 7H 93
Kilcot. Glos 1E 18
Kilcoy. High 8F 78
Kilcreggan. Arg 1M 57
Kildale. N Yor 5D 48
Kildary. High 6H 79
Kildermorie Lodge. High 6F 78
Kildonan. Dum 6F 50
Kildonan. High
nr. Helmsdale 1K 79
on Isle of Skye 8E 76
Kildonan. N Ayr 7K 57
Kildonnan. High 7F 68
Kildrummy. Abers 4D 72
Kildwick. N Yor 3J 41
Kilfillan. Dum 6H 51
Kilfinan. Arg 2J 57
Kilfinnan. High 6C 70
Kilgetty. Pemb 6H 15
Kilgour. Fife 7F 66
Kilgrammie. S Ayr 1H 51
Kilham. E Yor 1H 43
Kilham. Nmbd 6F 60
Kilkeel. New M 7H 93
Kilkenneth. Arg 3E 62
Kilkhampton. Corn 4B 6
Killadeas. Ferm 6C 92
Killamarsh. Derbs 1B 36
Killandrist. Arg 3C 64
Killay. Swan 5F 16
Killean. Arg 5F 56
Killearn. Stir 1D 58
Killeen. M Ulst 5F 93
Killellan. Arg 8F 56
Killen. Derr 4C 92
Killen. High 8G 79
Killerby. Darl 4K 47
Killeter. Derr 4C 92
Killichonan. Per 2K 65
Killiechronan. Arg 3L 63
Killiecrankie. Per 1C 66
Killilan. High 2L 69
Killimster. High 6E 86
Killin. Stir 4K 65
Killinchy. Ards 5J 93
Killinghall. N Yor 2L 41
Killington. Cumb 7E 46
Killingworth. Tyne 4F 54
Killin Lodge. High 5F 70
Killinochonoch. Arg 8C 64
Killochyett. Bord 5B 60
Killough. New M 7J 93
Killowen. New M 7G 93
Killundine. High 3L 63
Killylea. Arm 6E 92
Killyleagh. New M 6J 93
Killyrammer. Caus 2F 93
Kilmacolm. Inv 3B 58
Kilmahog. Stir 7L 65
Kilmahumaig. Arg 8B 64
Kilmalieu. High 2C 64
Kilmaluag. High 6F 76
Kilmany. Fife 5G 67
Kilmarie. High 4G 69
Kilmarnock. E Ayr 110 (6C 58)
Kilmaron. Fife 6G 67
Kilmartin. Arg 8C 64
Kilmaurs. E Ayr 5C 58
Kilmelford. Arg 6C 64
Kilmeny. Arg 3C 56
Kilmersdon. Som 8E 18
Kilmeston. Hants 3C 10
Kilmichael Glassary. Arg 8C 64
Kilmichael of Inverlussa.
Arg 1G 57
Kilmington. Devn 6A 8
Kilmington. Wilts 2F 8
Kilmoluaig. Arg 3E 62
Kilmorack. High 1E 70
Kilmore. Arg 5C 64
Kilmore. Arm 6F 93
Kilmore. High 5H 69
Kilmore. New M 6J 93
Kilmory. Arg 2G 57
Kilmory. High
nr. Kilchoan 8G 69
on Rùm 5E 68
Kilmory. N Ayr 7J 57
Kilmory Lodge. Arg 7B 64
Kilmote. High 2K 79
Kilmuir. High
nr. Dunvegan 1D 68
nr. Invergordon 6H 79
nr. Inverness 1G 71
nr. Uig 6E 76
Kilmun. Arg 1L 57
Kilnave. Arg 2B 56
Kilncadzow. S Lan 5G 59
Kilndown. Kent 2D 12
Kiln Green. Here 2E 18
Kiln Green. Wok 6F 20
Kilnhill. Cumb 8G 53
Kilnhurst. S Yor 8B 42
Kilninian. Arg 3J 63
Kilninver. Arg 5C 64
Kiln Pit Hill. Nmbd 6D 54
Kilnsea. E Yor 6M 43
Kilnsey. N Yor 1H 41
Kilnwick. E Yor 3G 43
Kiloran. Arg 8J 63
Kilpatrick. N Ayr 7J 57
Kilpeck. Here 8C 26
Kilpin. E Yor 5E 42
Kilpin Pike. E Yor 5E 42
Kilrea. Caus 3F 93
Kilrenny. Fife 7J 67
Kilsby. Nptn 4C 28
Kilspindie. Per 5F 66
Kilsyth. N Lan 2F 58
Kiltarlity. High 1F 70
Kilton. Som 1L 7
Kilton Thorpe. Red C 4D 48
Kilvaxter. High 7E 76
Kilve. Som 1L 7
Kilvington. Notts 5F 36
Kilwinning. N Ayr 5A 58
Kimberley. Norf 1G 31
Kimberley. Notts 5B 36
Kimblesworth. Dur 7F 54
Kimble Wick. Buck 3F 20
Kimbolton. Cambs 5H 29
Kimbolton. Here 5D 26
Kimcote. Leics 3C 28
Kimmeridge. Dors 8H 9
Kimmerston. Nmbd 6G 61
Kimpton. Hants 1L 9
Kimpton. Herts 2J 21
Kinallen. Arm 6H 93
Kinawley. Ferm 7C 92
Kinbeachie. High 7G 79
Kinbrace. High 8L 85
Kinbuck. Stir 7A 66
Kincaple. Fife 6H 67
Kincardine. Fife 1H 59
Kincardine. High 5G 79
Kincardine Bridge. Falk 1H 59
Kincardine O'Neil. Abers 6E 72
Kinchrackine. Arg 5F 64
Kincorth. Aber 5J 73
Kincraig. High 5J 71
Kincraigie. Per 3C 66
Kindallachan. Per 2C 66
Kineton. Glos 1J 19
Kineton. Warw 6M 27
Kinfauns. Per 5E 66
Kingairloch. High 2C 64
Kingarth. Arg 4K 57
Kingcoed. Mon 3C 18
King Edward. Abers 8G 81
Kingerby. Linc 8H 43
Kingham. Oxon 1L 19
Kingholm Quay. Dum 4D 52
Kinghorn. Fife 1L 59
Kingie. High 5B 70
Kinglassie. Fife 8F 66
Kingledores. Bord 7K 59
King o' Muirs. Clac 8B 66
Kingoodie. Per 5G 67
King's Acre. Here 7C 26
Kingsand. Corn 6G 5
Kingsash. Buck 3F 20
Kingsbarns. Fife 6J 67
Kingsbridge. Devn 7K 5
Kingsbridge. Som 2J 7
King's Bromley. Staf 8K 35
Kingsburgh. High 8E 76
Kingsbury. G Lon 5J 21
Kingsbury. Warw 2L 27
Kingsbury Episcopi. Som 3C 8
Kings Caple. Here 1D 18
Kingscavil. W Lot 2J 59
Kingsclere. Hants 8C 20
King's Cliffe. Nptn 2H 29
Kings Clipstone. Notts 3D 36
Kingscote. Glos 4G 19
Kingscott. Devn 4E 6
Kings Coughton. Warw 6J 27
Kingscross. N Ayr 7K 57
Kingsdon. Som 3D 8
Kingsdown. Kent 1K 13
Kingsdown. Swin 5K 19
Kingsdown. Wilts 7G 19
Kingseat. Fife 8E 66
Kingsey. Buck 3E 20
Kingsfold. Lanc 5D 40
Kingsfold. W Sus 2J 11
Kingsford. E Ayr 5C 58
Kingsford. Worc 3G 27
Kingsforth. N Lin 6H 43
Kingsgate. Kent 6K 23
King's Green. Glos 8F 26
Kingshall Street. Suff 5F 30
Kingsheanton. Devn 2E 6
King's Heath. W Mid 3J 27
Kings Hill. Kent 8C 22
Kingsholm. Glos 2G 19
Kingshouse. High 2G 65
Kingshouse. Stir 5K 65
Kingshurst. W Mid 3K 27
Kingskerswell. Devn 5L 5
Kingskettle. Fife 7G 67
Kingsland. Here 5C 26
Kingsland. IOA 2B 32
Kings Langley. Herts 3H 21
Kingsley. Ches W 2D 34
Kingsley. Hants 2E 10
Kingsley. Staf 5J 35
Kingsley Green. W Sus 2F 10
Kingsley Holt. Staf 5J 35
King's Lynn. Norf 7C 38
King's Meaburn. Cumb 3E 46
Kings Moss. Mers 7D 40
Kings Muir. Bord 6L 59
Kingsmuir. Ang 3H 67
Kingsmuir. Fife 7J 67
King's Newnham. Warw 4B 28
King's Newton. Derbs 7A 36
Kingsnorth. Kent 2G 13
Kingsnorth. Medw 6E 22
King's Norton. Leics 1D 28
Kings Norton. W Mid 4J 27
King's Nympton. Devn 4F 6
King's Pyon. Here 6C 26
Kings Ripton. Cambs 4K 29
King's Somborne. Hants 2A 10
King's Stag. Dors 4F 8
King's Stanley. Glos 3G 19
King's Sutton. Nptn 8B 28
Kingstanding. W Mid 2J 27
Kingsteignton. Devn 8H 7
Kingsteps. High 8K 79
King Sterndale. Derbs 2J 35
King's Thorn. Here 8D 26
Kingsthorpe. Nptn 5E 28
Kingston. Cambs 6L 29
Kingston. Devn 7J 5
Kingston. Dors
nr. Sturminster Newton 5F 8
nr. Swanage 8H 9
Kingston. E Lot 1C 60
Kingston. Hants 5K 9
Kingston. IOW 7B 10
Kingston. Kent 8H 23
Kingston. Mor 7C 80
Kingston. W Sus 5H 11
Kingston Bagpuize. Oxon 4B 20
Kingston Blount. Oxon 4E 20
Kingston by Sea. W Sus 5K 11
Kingston Deverill. Wilts 2G 9
Kingstone. Here 8C 26
Kingstone. Som 4B 8
Kingstone. Staf 7J 35
Kingston Lisle. Oxon 5M 19
Kingston Maurward. Dors 6F 8
Kingston near Lewes.
E Sus 5L 11
Kingston on Soar. Notts 7C 36
Kingston Russell. Dors 6D 8
Kingston St Mary. Som 3M 7
Kingston Seymour. N Som 7C 18
Kingston Stert. Oxon 3E 20
Kingston upon Hull.
Hull 110 (5J 43)
Kingston upon Thames.
G Lon 7J 21
King's Walden. Herts 1J 21
Kingswear. Devn 6L 5
Kingswells. Aber 5H 73
Kingswinford. W Mid 3G 27
Kingswood. Buck 2D 20
Kingswood. Glos 4F 18
Kingswood. Here 6A 26
Kingswood. Kent 8E 22
Kingswood. Per 4D 66
Kingswood. Powy 2M 25
Kingswood. Som 2L 7
Kingswood. S Glo 6E 18
Kingswood. Surr 8K 21
Kingswood. Warw 4K 27
Kingswood Common. Staf 1G 27
Kings Worthy. Hants 2B 10
Kingthorpe. Linc 2J 37
Kington. Here 6A 26
Kington. S Glo 4E 18
Kington. Worc 6H 27
Kington Langley. Wilts 6H 19
Kington Magna. Dors 3F 8
Kington St Michael. Wilts 6H 19
Kingussie. High 5H 71
Kingweston. Som 2D 8
Kinharrachie. Abers 2J 73
Kinhrive. High 6G 79
Kinkell Bridge. Per 6C 66
Kinknockie. Abers 1K 73
Kinkry Hill. Cumb 4K 53
Kinlet. Shrp 3F 26
Kinloch. High
nr. Lochaline 2A 64
nr. Loch More 8F 84
on Rùm 6E 68
Kinloch. Per 3E 66
Kinlochard. Stir 7J 65
Kinlochbervie. High 6E 84
Kinlocheil. High 8L 69
Kinlochewe. High 7M 77
Kinloch Hourn. High 5L 69
Kinloch Laggan. High 7F 70
Kinlochleven. High 1F 64
Kinloch Lodge. High 6H 85
Kinlochmoidart. High 8J 69
Kinlochmore. High 1F 64
Kinloch Rannoch. Per 2L 65
Kinlochspelve. Arg 5A 64
Kinloid. High 7H 69
Kinloss. Mor 7L 79
Kinmel Bay. Cnwy 2J 33
Kinmuck. Abers 4H 73
Kinnadie. Abers 1J 73
Kinnaird. Per 5F 66
Kinneff. Abers 8H 73
Kinnelhead. Dum 1E 52
Kinnell. Ang 2K 67
Kinnerley. Shrp 7B 34
Kinnernie. Abers 5G 73
Kinnersley. Here 7B 26
Kinnersley. Worc 7G 27
Kinnerton. Powy 6M 25
Kinnerton. Shrp 2B 26
Kinnesswood. Per 7E 66
Kinninvie. Dur 3J 47
Kinnordy. Ang 2G 67
Kinoulton. Notts 6D 36
Kinross. Per 7E 66
Kinrossie. Per 4E 66
Kinsbourne Green. Herts 2J 21
Kinsey Heath. Ches E 5E 34
Kinsham. Here 5B 26
Kinsham. Worc 8H 27
Kinsley. W Yor 6B 42
Kinson. Bour 6J 9
Kintbury. W Ber 7A 20
Kintessack. Mor 7L 79
Kintillo. Per 6E 66
Kinton. Here 4C 26
Kinton. Shrp 8B 34
Kintore. Abers 4G 73
Kintour. Arg 4D 56
Kintra. Arg 5J 63
Kintraw. Arg 7C 64
Kinveachy. High 4K 71
Kinver. Staf 3G 27
Kinwarton. Warw 6K 27
Kiplingcotes. E Yor 3G 43
Kippax. W Yor 4B 42
Kippen. Stir 8L 65
Kippford. Dum 6C 52
Kipping's Cross. Kent 1C 12
Kirbister. Orkn
nr. Hobbister 1E 86
nr. Quholm 8B 88
Kirbuster. Orkn 7F 88
Kirby Bedon. Norf 1J 31
Kirby Bellars. Leics 8E 36
Kirby Cane. Norf 2K 31
Kirby Cross. Essx 1J 23
Kirby Fields. Leics 1C 28
Kirby Green. Norf 2K 31
Kirby Grindalythe. N Yor 1G 43
Kirby Hill. N Yor
nr. Richmond 5K 47
nr. Ripon 1A 42
Kirby Knowle. N Yor 7B 48
Kirby-le-Soken. Essx 1J 23
Kirby Misperton. N Yor 8E 48
Kirby Muxloe. Leics 1C 28
Kirby Sigston. N Yor 6B 48
Kirby Underdale. E Yor 2F 42
Kirby Wiske. N Yor 7A 48
Kircubbin. Ards 5K 93
Kirdford. W Sus 3H 11
Kirk. High 6D 86
Kirkabister. Shet
on Bressay 4E 90
on Mainland 2E 90
Kirkandrews. Dum 7M 51
Kirkandrews-on-Eden.
Cumb 6H 53
Kirkapol. Arg 3F 62
Kirkbampton. Cumb 6H 53
Kirkbean. Dum 6D 52
Kirk Bramwith. S Yor 6D 42
Kirkbride. Cumb 6G 53
Kirkbridge. N Yor 6L 47
Kirkbuddo. Ang 3J 67
Kirkburn. E Yor 2G 43
Kirkburton. W Yor 6K 41
Kirkby. Linc 8H 43
Kirkby. Mers 8C 40
Kirkby. N Yor 5C 48
Kirkby Fenside. Linc 3L 37
Kirkby Fleetham. N Yor 6L 47
Kirkby Green. Linc 4H 37
Kirkby-in-Ashfield. Notts 4C 36
Kirkby-in-Furness. Cumb 6M 45
Kirkby la Thorpe. Linc 5J 37
Kirkby Lonsdale. Cumb 8E 46
Kirkby Malham. N Yor 1G 41
Kirkby Mallory. Leics 1B 28
Kirkby Malzeard. N Yor 8L 47
Kirkby Mills. N Yor 7E 48
Kirkbymoorside. N Yor 7D 48
Kirkby on Bain. Linc 3K 37
Kirkby Overblow. N Yor 3M 41
Kirkby Stephen. Cumb 5F 46
Kirkby Thore. Cumb 3E 46
Kirkby Underwood. Linc 7H 37
Kirkby Wharfe. N Yor 3C 42
Kirkcaldy. Fife 8F 66
Kirkcambeck. Cumb 5K 53
Kirkcolm. Dum 5F 50
Kirkconnel. Dum 8F 58
Kirkconnell. Dum 5D 52
Kirkcowan. Dum 5J 51
Kirkcudbright. Dum 6A 52
Kirkdale. Mers 8B 40
Kirk Deighton. N Yor 2A 42
Kirk Ella. E Yor 5H 43
Kirkfieldbank. S Lan 5G 59
Kirkforthar Feus. Fife 7F 66
Kirkgunzeon. Dum 5C 52
Kirk Hallam. Derbs 5B 36
Kirkham. Lanc 4C 40
Kirkham. N Yor 1E 42
Kirkhamgate. W Yor 5L 41
Kirk Hammerton. N Yor 2B 42
Kirkharle. Nmbd 3D 54
Kirkheaton. Nmbd 4D 54
Kirkheaton. W Yor 6K 41
Kirkhill. Ang 1K 67
Kirkhill. High 1F 70
Kirkhope. S Lan 1D 52
Kirkhouse. Bord 6M 59
Kirkibost. High 4G 69
Kirkinch. Ang 3G 67
Kirkinner. Dum 6K 51
Kirkintilloch. E Dun 2E 58
Kirk Ireton. Derbs 4L 35
Kirkland. Cumb
nr. Cleator Moor 3K 45
nr. Penrith 8L 53
nr. Wigton 7G 53
Kirkland. Dum
nr. Kirkconnel 8F 58
nr. Moniaive 2C 52
Kirkland Guards. Cumb 7F 52
Kirk Langley. Derbs 6L 35
Kirklauchline. Dum 6F 50
Kirkleatham. Red C 3C 48
Kirklevington. Stoc T 5B 48
Kirkley. Suff 2M 31
Kirklington. N Yor 7M 47
Kirklington. Notts 4D 36
Kirklinton. Cumb 5J 53
Kirkliston. Edin 2K 59
Kirkmabreck. Dum 6K 51
Kirkmaiden. Dum 8G 51
Kirk Merrington. Dur 8F 54
Kirk Michael. IOM 5C 44
Kirkmichael. Per 1D 66
Kirkmichael. S Ayr 1J 51
Kirkmuirhill. S Lan 5F 58
Kirknewton. Nmbd 6G 61
Kirknewton. W Lot 3K 59
Kirkney. Abers 2E 72
Kirk of Shotts. N Lan 3G 59
Kirkoswald. Cumb 7K 53
Kirkoswald. S Ayr 1H 51
Kirkpatrick. Dum 2D 52
Kirkpatrick Durham. Dum 4B 52
Kirkpatrick-Fleming. Dum 4G 53
Kirk Sandall. S Yor 7D 42
Kirksanton. Cumb 6L 45
Kirk Smeaton. N Yor 6C 42
Kirkstall. W Yor 4L 41
Kirkstile. Dum 2H 53
Kirkstyle. High 4E 86
Kirkthorpe. W Yor 5A 42
Kirkton. Abers
nr. Alford 4F 72
nr. Insch 3F 72
nr. Turriff 1H 73
Kirkton. Ang
nr. Dundee 4H 67
nr. Forfar 3H 67
nr. Tarfside 7D 72
Kirkton. Dum 3D 52
Kirkton. Fife 5G 67
Kirkton. High
nr. Golspie 4H 79
nr. Kyle of Lochalsh 3K 69
nr. Lochcarron 1L 69
Kirkton. Bord 8C 60
Kirkton. S Lan 7H 59
Kirktonhill. W Dun 2B 58
Kirkton Manor. Bord 6L 59
Kirkton of Airlie. Ang 2G 67
Kirkton of Auchterhouse.
Ang 4G 67
Kirkton of Bourtie. Abers 3H 73
Kirkton of Collace. Per 4E 66
Kirkton of Craig. Ang 2L 67
Kirkton of Culsalmond.
Abers 2F 72
Kirkton of Durris. Abers 6G 73
Kirkton of Glenbuchat.
Abers 4C 72
Kirkton of Glenisla. Ang 1F 66
Kirkton of Kingoldrum. Ang 2G 67
Kirkton of Largo. Fife 7H 67
Kirkton of Lethendy. Per 3E 66
Kirkton of Logie Buchan.
Abers 3J 73
Kirkton of Maryculter.
Abers 6H 73
Kirkton of Menmuir. Ang 1J 67
Kirkton of Monikie. Ang 4J 67
Kirkton of Oyne. Abers 3F 72
Kirkton of Rayne. Abers 2F 72
Kirkton of Skene. Abers 5H 73
Kirktown. Abers
nr. Fraserburgh 7J 81
nr. Peterhead 8K 81
Kirktown of Alvah. Abers 7F 80
Kirktown of Auchterless.
Abers 1G 73
Kirktown of Deskford. Mor 7E 80
Kirktown of Fetteresso.
Abers 7H 73
Kirktown of Mortlach. Mor 2C 72
Kirktown of Slains. Abers 3K 73
Kirkurd. Bord 5K 59
Kirkwall. Orkn 8D 88
Kirkwall Airport. Orkn 1F 86
Kirkwhelpington. Nmbd 3C 54
Kirk Yetholm. Bord 7F 60
Kirmington. N Lin 6J 43
Kirmond le Mire. Linc 8J 43
Kirn. Arg 2L 57
Kirriemuir. Ang 2G 67
Kirstead Green. Norf 2J 31
Kirtlebridge. Dum 4G 53
Kirtleton. Dum 4G 53
Kirtling. Cambs 6C 30
Kirtling Green. Cambs 6C 30
Kirtlington. Oxon 2C 20
Kirtomy. High 5K 85
Kirton. Linc 6L 37
Kirton. Notts 3D 36
Kirton. Suff 8J 31
Kirton End. Linc 5K 37
Kirton Holme. Linc 5K 37
Kirton in Lindsey. N Lin 8G 43
Kishorn. High 1K 69
Kislingbury. Nptn 6D 28
Kites Hardwick. Warw 5B 28
Kittisford. Som 3K 7
Kittle. Swan 6E 16
Kittybrewster. Aber 5J 73
Kitwood. Hants 2D 10
Kivernoll. Here 8C 26
Kiveton Park. S Yor 1B 36
Knaith. Linc 1F 36
Knaith Park. Linc 1F 36
Knaphill. Surr 8G 21
Knapp. Hants 3B 10
Knapp. Per 4F 66
Knapp. Som 3B 8
Knapperfield. High 6D 86
Knapton. Norf 6K 39
Knapton. York 2C 42
Knapton Green. Here 6C 26
Knapwell. Cambs 5L 29
Knaresborough. N Yor 2A 42
Knarsdale. Nmbd 6L 53
Knatts Valley. Kent 7B 22
Knaven. Abers 1H 73
Knayton. N Yor 7B 48
Knebworth. Herts 1K 21
Knedlington. E Yor 5E 42
Kneesall. Notts 3E 36
Kneesworth. Cambs 7L 29
Kneeton. Notts 5E 36
Knelston. Swan 8L 15
Knenhall. Staf 6H 35
Knightacott. Devn 2F 6
Knightcote. Warw 6B 28
Knightcott. N Som 8B 18
Knightley. Staf 7G 35
Knightley Dale. Staf 7G 35
Knightlow Hill. Warw 4B 28
Knighton. Devn 7H 5
Knighton. Dors 4E 8
Knighton. Leic 1C 28
Knighton. Powy 4A 26
Knighton. Som 1L 7
Knighton. Staf
nr. Eccleshall 7F 34
nr. Woore 5F 34
Knighton. Wilts 6L 19
Knighton. Worc 6J 27
Knighton Common. Worc 4E 26
Knight's End. Cambs 2M 29
Knightswood. Glas 3D 58
Knightwick. Worc 6F 26
Knill. Here 5A 26
Knipton. Leics 6F 36
Knitsley. Dur 7E 54
Kniveton. Derbs 4L 35
Knock. Arg 4L 63
Knock. Cumb 3E 46
Knock. Mor 8E 80
Knockally. High 1M 79
Knockan. Arg 5K 63
Knockan. High 2C 78
Knockandhu. Mor 3B 72
Knockando. Mor 1A 72
Knockarthur. High 3H 79
Knockbain. High 8G 79
Knockbreck. High 7D 76
Knockcloghrim. M Ulst 4F 93
Knockdee. High 5C 86
Knockdolian. S Ayr 3G 51
Knockdon. S Ayr 8B 58
Knockdown. Glos 5G 19
Knockenbaird. Abers 3F 72
Knockenkelly. N Ayr 7K 57
Knockentiber. E Ayr 6B 58
Knockfarrel. High 8F 78
Knockglass. High 5B 86
Knockholt. Kent 8A 22
Knockholt Pound. Kent 8A 22
Knockie Lodge. High 4E 70
Knockin. Shrp 7B 34
Knockinlaw. E Ayr 6C 58
Knockinnon. High 8C 86
Knocknacarry. Caus 2H 93
Knockrome. Arg 2E 56
Knocksharry. IOM 6B 44
Knockshinnoch. E Ayr 8C 58
Knockvennie. Dum 4B 52
Knockvologan. Arg 6J 63
Knodishall. Suff 5L 31
Knole. Som 3C 8
Knollbury. Mon 5C 18
Knolls Green. Ches E 2G 35
Knolton. Wrex 6B 34
Knook. Wilts 1H 9
Knossington. Leics 1F 28
Knott. High 8E 76
Knott End-on-Sea. Lanc 3B 40
Knotting. Bed 5H 29
Knotting Green. Bed 5H 29
Knottingley. W Yor 5B 42
Knotts. Cumb 3C 46
Knotty Ash. Mers 8C 40
Knotty Green. Buck 4G 21
Knowbury. Shrp 4D 26
Knowe. Dum 4J 51
Knowefield. Cumb 6J 53
Knowehead. Dum 2M 51
Knowes. E Lot 2D 60
Knowesgate. Nmbd 3C 54
Knoweside. S Ayr 8A 58
Knowes of Elrick. Abers 8F 80
Knowle. Bris 6E 18
Knowle. Devn
nr. Braunton 2D 6
nr. Budleigh Salterton 7K 7
nr. Crediton 5G 7
Knowle. Shrp 4D 26
Knowle. W Mid 4K 27
Knowle Green. Lanc 4E 40
Knowle St Giles. Som 4B 8
Knowlesands. Shrp 2F 26
Knowle Village. Hants 5C 10
Knowl Hill. Wind 6F 20
Knowlton. Kent 8J 23
Knowsley. Mers 8C 40
Knowstone. Devn 3H 7
Knucklas. Powy 4A 26
Knuston. Nptn 5G 29
Knutsford. Ches E 2F 34
Knypersley. Staf 4G 35
Krumlin. W Yor 6J 41
Kuggar. Corn 7L 3
Kyleakin. High 3J 69
Kyle of Lochalsh. High 3J 69
Kylerhea. High 3J 69
Kylesku. High 8E 84
Kyles Lodge. W Isl 5A 76
Kylesmorar. High 6K 69
Kylestrome. High 8E 84
Kymin. Mon 2D 18
Kynaston. Here 8E 26
Kynaston. Shrp 7B 34
Kynnersley. Telf 8E 34
Kyre Green. Worc 5E 26
Kyre Park. Worc 5E 26
Kyrewood. Worc 5E 26

L

Labost. W Isl 7F 82
Lacasaidh. W Isl 1E 76
Lacasdail. W Isl 8H 83
Laceby. NE Lin 7K 43
Lacey Green. Buck 3F 20
Lach Dennis. Ches W 2F 34
Lache. Ches W 3B 34
Lack. Ferm 5C 92
Lackagh. Caus 3E 92
Lackford. Suff 4D 30
Lacock. Wilts 7H 19
Ladbroke. Warw 6B 28
Laddingford. Kent 1C 12
Lade Bank. Linc 4L 37
Ladock. Corn 6A 4
Lady. Orkn 5F 88
Ladybank. Fife 6G 67
Ladycross. Corn 7C 6
Lady Green. Mers 7B 40
Lady Hall. Cumb 6L 45
Ladykirk. Bord 5F 60
Ladysford. Abers 7J 81
Ladywood. W Mid 3J 27
Ladywood. Worc 5G 27
Laga. High 1M 63
Lagavulin. Arg 5D 56
Lagg. Arg 2E 56
Lagg. N Ayr 7J 57
Laggan. Arg 4B 56
Laggan. High
nr. Fort Augustus 6C 70
nr. Newtonmore 6G 71
Laggan. Mor 2C 72
Lagganlia. High 5J 71
Lagganulva. Arg 3K 63
Laghey Corner. M Ulst 5F 93
Laglingarten. Arg 7F 64
Lagness. W Sus 5F 10
Laid. High 6G 85
Laide. High 4K 77
Laigh Fenwick. E Ayr 5C 58
Laindon. Essx 5C 22
Lairg. High 3F 78
Lairg Muir. High 3F 78
Laithes. Cumb 8J 53
Laithkirk. Dur 3H 47
Lake. Devn 2E 6
Lake. IOW 7C 10
Lake. Wilts 2K 9
Lakenham. Norf 1J 31
Lakenheath. Suff 3D 30
Lakesend. Norf 2B 30
Lakeside. Cumb 7B 46
Laleham. Surr 7H 21
Laleston. B'end 6H 17
Lamancha. Bord 4L 59
Lamarsh. Essx 8E 30
Lamas. Norf 7J 39
Lamb Corner. Essx 8G 31
Lambden. Bord 5E 60
Lamberhead Green. G Man 7D 40
Lamberhurst. Kent 2C 12
Lamberhurst Quarter. Kent 2C 12
Lamberton. Bord 4G 61
Lambeth. G Lon 6L 21
Lambfell Moar. IOM 6B 44
Lambhill. Glas 3D 58
Lambley. Nmbd 6L 53
Lambley. Notts 5D 36
Lambourn. W Ber 6M 19
Lambourne End. Essx 4A 22
Lambourn Woodlands.
W Ber 6M 19
Lambs Green. Dors 6H 9
Lambs Green. W Sus 2K 11
Lambston. Pemb 5F 14
Lamellion. Corn 5E 4
Lamerton. Devn 8D 6
Lamesley. Tyne 6F 54
Laminess. Orkn 6F 88
Lamington. High 6H 79
Lamington. S Lan 6H 59
Lamlash. N Ayr 6K 57
Lamonby. Cumb 8J 53
Lamorick. Corn 5C 4
Lamorna. Corn 6H 3
Lamorran. Corn 7A 4
Lampeter. Cdgn 8E 24
Lampeter Velfrey. Pemb 5H 15
Lamphey. Pemb 6G 15
Lamplugh. Cumb 2K 45
Lamport. Nptn 4E 28
Lamyatt. Som 2E 8
Lana. Devn
nr. Ashwater 6C 6
nr. Holsworthy 5C 6
Lanark. S Lan 5G 59

Lanarth—Llansanffraid Glan Conwy

Lanarth. Corn 6L 3
Lancaster. Lanc 1C 40
Lanchester. Dur 7E 54
Lancing. W Sus 5J 11
Landbeach. Cambs 5A 30
Landcross. Devn 3D 6
Landerberry. Abers 5G 73
Landford. Wilts 4L 9
Land Gate. G Man 7D 40
Landhallow. High 8C 86
Landimore. Swan 7L 15
Landkey. Devn 2E 6
Landkey Newland. Devn 2E 6
Landore. Swan 5F 16
Landport. Port 5D 10
Landrake. Corn 5F 4
Landscove. Devn 5K 5
Land's End Airport. Corn 6G 3
Landshipping. Pemb 5G 15
Landulph. Corn 5G 5
Landywood. Staf 1H 27
Lane. Corn 2M 3
Laneast. Corn 7B 6
Lane Bottom. Lanc 4G 41
Lane End. Buck 4F 20
Lane End. Hants 3C 10
Lane End. IOW 7D 10
Lane End. Wilts 1G 9
Lane Ends. Derbs 6L 35
Lane Ends. Dur 8E 54
Lane Ends. Lanc 2F 40
Laneham. Notts 2F 36
Lane Head. Dur
nr. Hutton Magna 4K 47
nr. Woodland 3J 47
Lane Head. G Man 8E 40
Lane Head. W Yor 7K 41
Lanehead. Dur 7B 54
Lanehead. Nmbd 3A 54
Lane Heads. Lanc 4C 40
Lanercost. Cumb 5K 53
Laneshaw Bridge. Lanc 3H 41
Laney Green. Staf 1H 27
Langais. W Isl 7K 75
Langal. High 1B 64
Langar. Notts 6E 36
Langbank. Ren 2B 58
Langbar. N Yor 2J 41
Langburnshiels. Bord 1K 53
Langcliffe. N Yor 1G 41
Langdale End. N Yor 6G 49
Langdon. Corn 6B 6
Langdon Beck. Dur 8B 54
Langdon Cross. Corn 7C 6
Langdon Hills. Essx 5C 22
Langdown. Hants 5B 10
Langdyke. Fife 7G 67
Langenhoe. Essx 2G 23
Langford. C Beds 7J 29
Langford. Devn 5K 7
Langford. Essx 3E 22
Langford. Notts 4F 36
Langford. Oxon 3L 19
Langford. Som 3M 7
Langford Budville. Som 3L 7
Langham. Dors 3F 8
Langham. Essx 8G 31
Langham. Norf 5G 39
Langham. Rut 8F 36
Langham. Suff 5F 30
Langho. Lanc 4F 40
Langholm. Dum 3H 53
Langland. Swan 6F 16
Langleeford. Nmbd 7G 61
Langley. Ches E 2H 35
Langley. Derbs 5B 36
Langley. Essx 8M 29
Langley. Glos 1J 19
Langley. Hants 5B 10
Langley. Herts 1K 21
Langley. Kent 8E 22
Langley. Nmbd 5B 54
Langley. Slo 6H 21
Langley. Som 3K 7
Langley. Warw 5K 27
Langley. W Sus 3F 10
Langley Burrell. Wilts 6H 19
Langleybury. Herts 3H 21
Langley Common. Derbs 6L 35
Langley Green. Derbs 6L 35
Langley Green. Norf 1K 31
Langley Green. Warw 5K 27
Langley Green. W Sus 2K 11
Langley Heath. Kent 8E 22
Langley Marsh. Som 3K 7
Langley Moor. Dur 7F 54
Langley Park. Dur 7F 54
Langley Street. Norf 1K 31
Langney. E Sus 5C 12
Langold. Notts 1C 36
Langore. Corn 7B 6
Langport. Som 3C 8
Langrick. Linc 5K 37
Langridge. Bath 7F 18
Langridgeford. Devn 3E 6
Langrigg. Cumb 7F 52
Langrish. Hants 3E 10
Langsett. S Yor 7L 41
Langshaw. Bord 6C 60
Langstone. Hants 5E 10
Langthorne. N Yor 6L 47
Langthorpe. N Yor 1A 42
Langthwaite. N Yor 5J 47
Langtoft. E Yor 1H 43
Langtoft. Linc 8J 37
Langton. Dur 4K 47
Langton. Linc
nr. Horncastle 3K 37
nr. Spilsby 2L 37
Langton. N Yor 1E 42
Langton by Wragby. Linc 2J 37
Langton Green. Kent 2B 12
Langton Herring. Dors 7E 8
Langton Long Blandford.
Dors 5G 9
Langton Matravers. Dors 8H 9
Langtree. Devn 4D 6
Langwathby. Cumb 8K 53
Langwith. Derbs 2C 36
Langworth. Linc 2H 37
Lanivet. Corn 5C 4
Lanjeth. Corn 6B 4
Lank. Corn 4C 4
Lanlivery. Corn 6C 4
Lanner. Corn 5L 3
Lanreath. Corn 6D 4
Lansallos. Corn 6D 4
Lansdown. Bath 7F 18
Lansdown. Glos 1H 19
Lanteglos Highway. Corn 6D 4
Lanton. Nmbd 6G 61
Lanton. Bord 7D 60
Lapford. Devn 5G 7
Lapford Cross. Devn 5G 7
Laphroaig. Arg 5C 56
Lapley. Staf 8G 35
Lapworth. Warw 4K 27
Larachbeg. High 3A 64
Larbert. Falk 1G 59
Larden Green. Ches E 4D 34
Larel. High 6C 86
Largie. Abers 2F 72
Largiemore. Arg 1J 57
Largoward. Fife 7H 67
Largs. N Ayr 4M 57
Largue. Abers 1F 72
Largybeg. N Ayr 7K 57
Largymeanoch. N Ayr 7K 57
Largymore. N Ayr 7K 57
Larkfield. Inv 2M 57
Larkfield. Kent 8D 22
Larkhall. Bath 7F 18
Larkhall. S Lan 4F 58
Larkhill. Wilts 1K 9
Larling. Norf 3F 30
Larne. ME Ant 3J 93
Larport. Here 8D 26
Lartington. Dur 4J 47
Lary. Abers 5C 72
Lasham. Hants 1D 10
Lashenden. Kent 1E 12
Lasswade. Midl 3M 59
Lastingham. N Yor 6E 48
Latchford. Herts 1L 21
Latchford. Oxon 3D 20
Latchingdon. Essx 3E 22
Latchley. Corn 8D 6
Latchmere Green. Hants 8D 20
Lathbury. Mil 7F 28
Latheron. High 8C 86
Latheronwheel. High 8C 86
Lathom. Lanc 7C 40
Lathones. Fife 7H 67
Latimer. Buck 4H 21
Latteridge. S Glo 5E 18
Lattiford. Som 3E 8
Latton. Wilts 4J 19
Laudale House. High 2B 64
Lauder. Bord 5C 60
Laugharne. Carm 5K 15
Laughterton. Linc 2F 36
Laughton. E Sus 4B 12
Laughton. Leics 3D 28
Laughton. Linc
nr. Gainsborough 8F 42
nr. Grantham 6H 37
Laughton Common. S Yor 1C 36
Laughton en le Morthen.
S Yor 1C 36
Launcells. Corn 5B 6
Launceston. Corn 7C 6
Launcherley. Som 1D 8
Launton. Oxon 1D 20
Laurelvale. Arm 6G 93
Laurencekirk. Abers 8G 73
Laurieston. Dum 5A 52
Laurieston. Falk 2H 59
Lavendon. Mil 6G 29
Lavenham. Suff 7F 30
Laverhay. Dum 2F 52
Laversdale. Cumb 5J 53
Laverstock. Wilts 2K 9
Laverstoke. Hants 1B 10
Laverton. Glos 8J 27
Laverton. N Yor 8L 47
Laverton. Som 8F 18
Lavister. Wrex 4B 34
Law. S Lan 4G 59
Lawers. Per 4L 65
Lawford. Essx 8G 31
Lawhitton. Corn 7C 6
Lawkland. N Yor 1F 40
Lawley. Telf 1E 26
Lawnhead. Staf 7G 35
Lawrencetown. Arm 6G 93
Lawrenny. Pemb 6G 15
Lawshall. Suff 6E 30
Lawton. Here 6C 26
Laxey. IOM 6D 44
Laxfield. Suff 4J 31
Laxfirth. Shet 2E 90
Laxo. Shet 1E 90
Laxton. E Yor 5E 42
Laxton. Nptn 2G 29
Laxton. Notts 3E 36
Laycock. W Yor 3J 41
Layer Breton. Essx 2F 22
Layer-de-la-Haye. Essx 1F 22
Layer Marney. Essx 2F 22
Laymore. Dors 5B 8
Laysters Pole. Here 5D 26
Layter's Green. Buck 4G 21
Laytham. E Yor 4E 42
Lazenby. Red C 4C 48
Lazonby. Cumb 8K 53
Lea. Derbs 4M 35
Lea. Here 1E 18
Lea. Linc 1F 36
Lea. Shrp
nr. Bishop's Castle 3B 26
nr. Shrewsbury 1C 26
Lea. Wilts 5H 19
Leabrooks. Derbs 4B 36
Leac a Li. W Isl 4C 76
Leachd. Arg 8E 64
Leachkin. High 1G 71
Leachpool. Pemb 5F 14
Leadburn. Midl 4L 59
Leadenham. Linc 4G 37
Leaden Roding. Essx 2B 22
Leaderfoot. Bord 6C 60
Leadgate. Cumb 7M 53
Leadgate. Dur 6E 54
Leadgate. Nmbd 6E 54
Leadhills. S Lan 8G 59
Leadingcross Green. Kent 8E 22
Lea End. Worc 4J 27
Leafield. Oxon 2M 19
Leagrave. Lutn 1H 21
Lea Hall. W Mid 3K 27
Lea Heath. Staf 7J 35
Leake. N Yor 6B 48
Leake Common Side. Linc 4L 37
Leake Fold Hill. Linc 4M 37
Leake Hurn's End. Linc 5M 37
Lealholm. N Yor 5E 48
Lealt. Arg 8A 64
Lealt. High 7G 77
Leam. Derbs 2L 35
Lea Marston. Warw 2L 27
Leamington Hastings.
Warw 5B 28
Leamington Spa, Royal.
Warw 5M 27
Leamonsley. Staf 1K 27
Leamside. Dur 7G 55
Leargybreck. Arg 2E 56
Lease Rigg. N Yor 5F 48
Leasgill. Cumb 7C 46
Leasingham. Linc 5H 37
Leasingthorne. Dur 8F 54
Leasowe. Mers 8A 40
Leatherhead. Surr 8J 21
Leathley. N Yor 3L 41
Leaths. Dum 5B 52
Leaton. Shrp 8C 34
Leaton. Telf 8E 34
Lea Town. Lanc 4C 40
Leaveland. Kent 8G 23
Leavenheath. Suff 8F 30
Leavening. N Yor 1E 42
Leaves Green. G Lon 7M 21
Lea Yeat. Cumb 7F 46
Leazes. Dur 6E 54
Lebberston. N Yor 7H 49
Lechlade on Thames. Glos 4L 19
Leck. Lanc 8E 46
Leckford. Hants 2A 10
Leckfurin. High 6K 85
Leckgruinart. Arg 3B 56
Leckhampstead. Buck 8E 28
Leckhampstead. W Ber 6B 20
Leckhampton. Glos 2H 19
Leckmelm. High 4B 78
Leckwith. V Glam 7L 17
Leconfield. E Yor 3H 43
Ledaig. Arg 4D 64
Ledburn. Buck 1G 21
Ledbury. Here 8F 26
Ledgemoor. Here 6C 26
Ledgowan. High 8B 78
Ledicot. Here 5C 26
Ledmore. High 2C 78
Lednabirichen. High 4H 79
Lednagullin. High 5L 85
Ledsham. Ches W 2B 34
Ledsham. W Yor 5B 42
Ledston. W Yor 5B 42
Ledstone. Devn 7K 5
Ledwell. Oxon 1B 20
Lee. Devn
nr. Ilfracombe 1D 6
nr. South Molton 3H 7
Lee. G Lon 6L 21
Lee. Hants 4A 10
Lee. Lanc 2D 40
Lee. Shrp 6C 34
The Lee. Buck 3G 21
Leeans. Shet 3D 90
Leebotten. Shet 5E 90
Leebotwood. Shrp 2C 26
Lee Brockhurst. Shrp 7D 34
Leece. Cumb 8M 45
Leechpool. Mon 5D 18
Lee Clump. Buck 3G 21
Leeds. Kent 8E 22
Leeds. W Yor 110 (4L 41)
Leeds Bradford Airport.
W Yor 3L 41
Leedstown. Corn 5K 3
Leegomery. Telf 8E 34
Lee Head. Derbs 8J 41
Leek. Staf 4H 35
Leekbrook. Staf 4H 35
Leek Wootton. Warw 5L 27
Lee Mill. Devn 6H 5
Leeming. N Yor 7L 47
Leeming Bar. N Yor 6L 47
Lee Moor. Devn 5H 5
Lee Moor. W Yor 5M 41
Lee-on-the-Solent. Hants 5C 10
Lees. Derbs 6L 35
Lees. G Man 7H 41
Lees. W Yor 4J 41
The Lees. Kent 8G 23
Leeswood. Flin 3A 34
Leetown. Per 5F 66
Leftwich. Ches W 2E 34
Legbourne. Linc 1L 37
Legburthwaite. Cumb 4B 46
Legerwood. Bord 5C 60
Legsby. Linc 1J 37
Leicester. Leic 110 (1C 28)
Leicester Forest East. Leics 1C 28
Leigh. Dors 5E 8
Leigh. G Man 7E 40
Leigh. Kent 1B 12
Leigh. Shrp 1B 26
Leigh. Surr 1K 11
Leigh. Wilts 4J 19
Leigh. Worc 6F 26
The Leigh. Glos 1G 19
Leigham. Plym 6H 5
Leigh Beck. Essx 5E 22
Leigh Common. Som 3F 8
Leigh Delamere. Wilts 6G 19
Leigh Green. Kent 2F 12
Leighland Chapel. Som 2K 7
Leigh-on-Sea. S'end 5E 22
Leigh Park. Hants 5E 10
Leigh Sinton. Worc 6F 26
Leighterton. Glos 4G 19
Leighton. N Yor 8K 47
Leighton. Powy 2M 25
Leighton. Shrp 1E 26
Leighton. Som 1F 8
Leighton Bromswold.
Cambs 4J 29
Leighton Buzzard. C Beds 1G 21
Leigh-upon-Mendip. Som 1E 8
Leinthall Earls. Here 5C 26
Leinthall Starkes. Here 5C 26
Leintwardine. Here 4C 26
Leire. Leics 2C 28
Leirinmore. High 5G 85
Leishmore. High 1E 70
Leiston. Suff 5L 31
Leitfie. Per 3F 66
Leith. Edin 2L 59
Leitholm. Bord 5E 60
Leitrim. New M 7H 93
Lelant. Corn 5J 3
Lelant Downs. Corn 5J 3
Lelley. E Yor 4K 43
Lem Hill. Shrp 4F 26
Lemington. Tyne 5E 54
Lempitlaw. Bord 6E 60
Lemsford. Herts 2K 21
Lenacre. Cumb 7E 46
Lenchie. Abers 2E 72
Lenchwick. Worc 7J 27
Lendalfoot. S Ayr 3G 51
Lendrick. Stir 7K 65
Lenham. Kent 8E 22
Lenham Heath. Kent 1F 12
Lenimore. N Ayr 5H 57
Lennel. Bord 5F 60
Lennoxtown. E Dun 2E 58
Lenton. Linc 6H 37
Lentran. High 1F 70
Lenwade. Norf 8G 39
Lenzie. E Dun 2E 58
Leochel Cushnie. Abers 4E 72
Leogh. Shet 2M 89
Leominster. Here 6C 26
Leonard Stanley. Glos 3G 19
Lepe. Hants 6B 10
Lephenstrath. Arg 1B 50
Lephin. High 1C 68
Lephinchapel. Arg 8D 64
Lephinmore. Arg 8D 64
Leppington. N Yor 1E 42
Lepton. W Yor 6L 41
Lerryn. Corn 6D 4
Lerwick. Shet 3E 90
Lerwick (Tingwall) Airport.
Shet 3E 90
Lesbury. Nmbd 8K 61
Leslie. Abers 3E 72
Leslie. Fife 7F 66
Lesmahagow. S Lan 6G 59
Lesnewth. Corn 2D 4
Lessingham. Norf 7K 39
Lessonhall. Cumb 6G 53
Leswalt. Dum 5F 50
Letchmore Heath. Herts 4J 21
Letchworth Garden City.
Herts 8K 29
Letcombe Bassett. Oxon 5A 20
Letcombe Regis. Oxon 5A 20
Letham. Ang 3J 67
Letham. Falk 1G 59
Letham. Fife 6G 67
Lethanhill. E Ayr 8C 58
Lethenty. Abers 1H 73
Letheringham. Suff 6J 31
Letheringsett. Norf 6G 39
Lettaford. Devn 7G 7
Lettan. Orkn 5G 89
Letter. Abers 4G 73
Letterewe. High 6L 77
Letterfearn. High 3K 69
Lettermore. Arg 3K 63
Letters. High 5B 78
Lettershendoney. Derr 3D 92
Letterston. Pemb 4F 14
Letton. Here
nr. Kington 7B 26
nr. Leintwardine 4B 26
Letty Green. Herts 2K 21
Letwell. S Yor 1C 36
Leuchars. Fife 5H 67
Leumrabhagh. W Isl 2E 76
Leusdon. Devn 8G 7
Levaneap. Shet 1E 90
Levedale. Staf 8G 35
Leven. E Yor 3J 43
Leven. Fife 7G 67
Levencorroch. N Ayr 7K 57
Levenhall. E Lot 2A 60
Levens. Cumb 7C 46
Levens Green. Herts 1L 21
Levenshulme. G Man 8G 41
Levenwick. Shet 5E 90
Leverburgh. W Isl 5B 76
Leverington. Cambs 8M 37
Leverton. Linc 5L 37
Leverton. W Ber 6M 19
Leverton Lucasgate. Linc 5M 37
Leverton Outgate. Linc 5M 37
Levington. Suff 8J 31
Levisham. N Yor 6F 48
Levishie. High 4E 70
Lew. Oxon 3M 19
Lewaigue. IOM 5D 44
Lewannick. Corn 7B 6
Lewdown. Devn 7D 6
Lewes. E Sus 4M 11
Leweston. Pemb 4F 14
Lewisham. G Lon 6L 21
Lewiston. High 3F 70
Lewistown. B'end 6J 17
Lewknor. Oxon 4E 20
Leworthy. Devn
nr. Barnstaple 2F 6
nr. Holsworthy 5C 6
Lewson Street. Kent 7F 22
Lewthorn Cross. Devn 8G 7
Lewtrenchard. Devn 7D 6
Ley. Corn 5D 4
Leybourne. Kent 8C 22
Leyburn. N Yor 6K 47
Leycett. Staf 5F 34
Leyfields. Staf 1L 27
Ley Green. Herts 1J 21
Ley Hill. Buck 3G 21
Leyland. Lanc 5D 40
Leylodge. Abers 4G 73
Leymoor. W Yor 6K 41
Leys. Per 4F 66
Leysdown-on-Sea. Kent 6G 23
Leysmill. Ang 3K 67
Leyton. G Lon 5L 21
Leytonstone. G Lon 5M 21
Lezant. Corn 8C 6
Leziate. Norf 8C 38
Lhanbryde. Mor 7B 80
The Lhen. IOM 4C 44
Liatrie. High 2C 70
Libanus. Powy 2J 17
Libberton. S Lan 5H 59
Libbery. Worc 6H 27
Liberton. Edin 3L 59
Liceasto. W Isl 4C 76
Lichfield. Staf 1K 27
Lickey. Worc 4H 27
Lickey End. Worc 4H 27
Lickfold. W Sus 3G 11
Liddaton. Devn 7D 6
Liddington. Swin 5L 19
Liddle. Orkn 3F 86
Lidgate. Suff 6D 30
Lidgett. Notts 3D 36
Lidham Hill. E Sus 4E 12
Lidlington. C Beds 8G 29
Lidsey. W Sus 5G 11
Lidstone. Oxon 1A 20
Lienassie. High 3L 69
Liff. Ang 4G 67
Lifford. W Mid 3J 27
Lifton. Devn 7C 6
Liftondown. Devn 7C 6
Lighthorne. Warw 6M 27
Light Oaks. Stoke 4H 35
Lightwater. Surr 7G 21
Lightwood. Staf 5J 35
Lightwood. Stoke 5H 35
Lightwood Green. Ches E 5E 34
Lightwood Green. Wrex 5B 34
Lilbourne. Nptn 4C 28
Lilburn Tower. Nmbd 7H 61
Lillesdon. Som 3B 8
Lilleshall. Telf 8F 34
Lilley. Herts 1J 21
Lilliesleaf. Bord 7C 60
Lillingstone Dayrell. Buck 8E 28
Lillingstone Lovell. Buck 7E 28
Lillington. Dors 4E 8
Lilstock. Som 1L 7
Lilybank. Inv 2B 58
Lilyhurst. Shrp 8F 34
Limavady. Caus 2E 92
Limbrick. Lanc 6E 40
Limbury. Lutn 1H 21
Limekilnburn. S Lan 4F 58
Limekilns. Fife 1J 59
Limerigg. Falk 2G 59
Limestone Brae. Nmbd 7A 54
Lime Street. Worc 8G 27
Limington. Som 3D 8
Limpenhoe. Norf 1K 31
Limpley Stoke. Wilts 7F 18
Limpsfield. Surr 8M 21
Limpsfield Chart. Surr 8M 21
Linburn. W Lot 3K 59
Linby. Notts 4C 36
Linchmere. W Sus 2F 10
Lincluden. Dum 4D 52
Lincoln. Linc 111 (2G 37)
Lincomb. Worc 5G 27
Lindale. Cumb 7C 46
Lindal in Furness. Cumb 8A 46
Lindean. Bord 6B 60
Linden. Glos 2G 19
Lindfield. W Sus 3L 11
Lindford. Hants 2F 10
Lindores. Fife 6F 66
Lindridge. Worc 5E 26
Lindsell. Essx 1C 22
Lindsey. Suff 7F 30
Lindsey Tye. Suff 7F 30
Linford. Hants 5K 9
Linford. Thur 6C 22
Lingague. IOM 7B 44
Lingdale. Red C 4D 48
Lingen. Here 5B 26
Lingfield. Surr 1L 11
Lingreabhagh. W Isl 5B 76
Lingwood. Norf 1K 31
Lingy Close. Cumb 6H 53
Linicro. High 7E 76
Linkend. Worc 8G 27
Linkenholt. Hants 8A 20
Linkinhorne. Corn 8C 6
Linklater. Orkn 3F 86
Linksness. Orkn 8E 88
Linktown. Fife 8F 66
Linkwood. Mor 7B 80
Linley. Shrp
nr. Bishop's Castle 2B 26
nr. Bridgnorth 2E 26
Linley Green. Here 6E 26
Linlithgow. W Lot 2H 59
Linlithgow Bridge. Falk 2H 59
Linneraineach. High 3B 78
Linshiels. Nmbd 1B 54
Linsiadar. W Isl 8F 82
Linsidemore. High 4F 78
Linslade. C Beds 1G 21
Linstead Parva. Suff 4K 31
Linstock. Cumb 6J 53
Linthwaite. W Yor 6K 41
Lintlaw. Bord 4F 60
Lintmill. Mor 7E 80
Linton. Cambs 7B 30
Linton. Derbs 8L 35
Linton. Here 1E 18
Linton. Kent 1D 12
Linton. N Yor 1H 41
Linton. Bord 7E 60
Linton. W Yor 3A 42
Linton Colliery. Nmbd 2F 54
Linton Hill. Here 1E 18
Linton-on-Ouse. N Yor 1B 42
Lintzford. Dur 6E 54
Lintzgarth. Dur 7C 54
Linwood. Hants 5K 9
Linwood. Linc 1J 37
Linwood. Ren 3C 58
Lionacleit. W Isl 1D 74
Lionacro. High 7E 76
Lionacuidhe. W Isl 1D 74
Lional. W Isl 5J 83
Liphook. Hants 2F 10
Lipley. Shrp 6F 34
Lipyeate. Som 8E 18
Liquo. N Lan 4G 59
Lisbane. Ards 5J 93
Lisbellaw. Ferm 6C 92
Lisburn. Lis 5H 93
Liscard. Mers 8B 40
Liscolman. Caus 2F 93
Liscombe. Som 2H 7
Lishahawley. Derr 2D 92
Liskeard. Corn 5E 4
Lislea. New M 7G 93
Lisle Court. Hants 6M 9
Lisnarick. Ferm 6B 92
Lisnaskea. Ferm 7C 92
Liss. Hants 3E 10
Lissett. E Yor 2J 43
Liss Forest. Hants 3E 10
Lissington. Linc 1J 37
Liston. Essx 7E 30
Listooder. New M 6J 93
Lisvane. Card 6L 17
Liswerry. Newp 5B 18
Litcham. Norf 8E 38
Litchard. B'end 6J 17
Litchborough. Nptn 6D 28
Litchfield. Hants 8B 20
Litherland. Mers 8B 40
Litlington. Cambs 7L 29
Litlington. E Sus 5B 12
Littemill. Nmbd 8K 61
Litterty. Abers 8G 81
Little Abington. Cambs 7B 30
Little Addington. Nptn 4G 29
Little Airmyn. N Yor 5E 42
Little Alne. Warw 5K 27
Little Ardo. Abers 2H 73
Little Asby. Cumb 5E 46
Little Aston. Staf 1J 27
Little Atherfield. IOW 7B 10
Little Ayton. N Yor 4C 48
Little Baddow. Essx 3D 22
Little Badminton. S Glo 5G 19
Little Ballinluig. Per 2C 66
Little Bampton. Cumb 6G 53
Little Bardfield. Essx 8C 30
Little Barford. Bed 6J 29
Little Barningham. Norf 6H 39
Little Barrington. Glos 2L 19
Little Barrow. Ches W 3C 34
Little Barugh. N Yor 8E 48
Little Bavington. Nmbd 4C 54
Little Bealings. Suff 7J 31
Littlebeck. Cumb 4E 46
Little Bedwyn. Wilts 7L 19
Little Bentley. Essx 1H 23
Little Berkhamsted. Herts 3K 21
Little Billing. Nptn 5F 28
Little Billington. C Beds 1G 21
Little Birch. Here 8D 26
Little Bispham. Bkpl 3B 40
Little Blakenham. Suff 7H 31
Little Blencow. Cumb 8J 53
Little Bognor. W Sus 3H 11
Little Bolas. Shrp 7E 34
Little Bollington. Ches E 1F 34
Little Bookham. Surr 8J 21
Littleborough. Devn 4H 7
Littleborough. G Man 6H 41
Littleborough. Notts 1F 36
Littlebourne. Kent 8J 23
Little Bourton. Oxon 7B 28
Little Bowden. Leics 3E 28
Little Bradley. Suff 6C 30
Little Brampton. Shrp 3B 26
Little Brechin. Ang 1J 67
Littlebredy. Dors 7D 8
Little Brickhill. Mil 8G 29
Little Bridgeford. Staf 7G 35
Little Brington. Nptn 5D 28
Little Bromley. Essx 1G 23
Little Broughton. Cumb 8E 52
Little Budworth. Ches W 3D 34
Little Burstead. Essx 4C 22
Little Burton. E Yor 3J 43
Littlebury. Essx 8B 30
Littlebury Green. Essx 8A 30
Little Bytham. Linc 8H 37
Little Canfield. Essx 1B 22
Little Canford. Dors 6J 9
Little Carlton. Linc 1L 37
Little Carlton. Notts 4E 36
Little Casterton. Rut 1H 29
Little Catwick. E Yor 3J 43
Little Catworth. Cambs 4J 29
Little Cawthorpe. Linc 1L 37
Little Chalfont. Buck 4G 21
Little Chart. Kent 1F 12
Little Chesterford. Essx 7B 30
Little Cheverell. Wilts 8H 19
Little Chishill. Cambs 8M 29
Little Clacton. Essx 2H 23
Little Clanfield. Oxon 3L 19
Little Clifton. Cumb 2K 45
Little Coates. NE Lin 7K 43
Little Comberton. Worc 7H 27
Little Common. E Sus 5D 12
Little Compton. Warw 8L 27
Little Cornard. Suff 8E 30
Littlecote. Buck 1F 20
Littlecott. Wilts 8K 19
Little Cowarne. Here 6E 26
Little Coxwell. Oxon 4L 19
Little Crakehall. N Yor 6L 47
Little Crawley. Mil 7G 29
Little Creich. High 5G 79
Little Cressingham. Norf 1E 30
Little Crosby. Mers 7B 40
Little Crosthwaite. Cumb 2M 45
Little Cubley. Derbs 6K 35
Little Dalby. Leics 8E 36
Little Dawley. Telf 1E 26
Littledean. Glos 2E 18
Little Dens. Abers 1K 73
Little Dewchurch. Here 8D 26
Little Ditton. Cambs 6C 30
Little Down. Hants 8A 20
Little Downham. Cambs 3B 30
Little Drayton. Shrp 6E 34
Little Driffield. E Yor 2H 43
Little Dunham. Norf 8E 38
Little Dunkeld. Per 3D 66
Little Dunmow. Essx 1C 22
Little Easton. Essx 1C 22
Little Eaton. Derbs 5A 36
Little Eccleston. Lanc 3C 40
Little Ellingham. Norf 2G 31
Little Elm. Som 1F 8
Little End. Essx 3B 22
Little Everdon. Nptn 6C 28
Little Eversden. Cambs 6L 29
Little Faringdon. Oxon 3L 19
Little Fencote. N Yor 6L 47
Little Fenton. N Yor 4C 42
Littleferry. High 4J 79
Little Fransham. Norf 8F 38
Little Gaddesden. Herts 2G 21
Little Garway. Here 1C 18
Little Gidding. Cambs 3J 29
Little Glemham. Suff 6K 31
Little Glenshee. Per 4C 66
Little Gransden. Cambs 6K 29
Little Green. Suff 4G 31
Little Green. Wrex 5C 34
Little Grimsby. Linc 8L 43
Little Habton. N Yor 8E 48
Little Hadham. Herts 1M 21
Little Hale. Linc 5J 37
Little Hallingbury. Essx 2A 22
Littleham. Devn
nr. Bideford 3D 6
nr. Exmouth 7K 7
Little Hampden. Buck 3F 20
Littlehampton. W Sus 5H 11
Little Haresfield. Glos 3G 19
Little Harrowden. Nptn 4F 28
Little Haseley. Oxon 3D 20
Little Hatfield. E Yor 3J 43
Little Hautbois. Norf 7J 39
Little Haven. Pemb 5E 14
Little Hay. Staf 1K 27
Little Hayfield. Derbs 1J 35
Little Haywood. Staf 7J 35
Little Heath. W Mid 3M 27
Little Heck. N Yor 5C 42
Littlehempston. Devn 5L 5
Little Herbert's. Glos 2H 19
Little Hereford. Here 5D 26
Little Horkesley. Essx 8F 30
Little Hormead. Herts 1L 21
Little Horsted. E Sus 4A 12
Little Horton. W Yor 4K 41
Little Horwood. Buck 8E 28
Little Houghton. Nptn 6F 28
Little Houghton. S Yor 7B 42
Littlehoughton. Nmbd 8K 61
Little Hucklow. Derbs 2K 35
Little Hulton. G Man 7F 40
Little Irchester. Nptn 5G 29
Little Kelk. E Yor 1H 43
Little Kimble. Buck 3F 20
Little Kineton. Warw 6M 27
Little Kingshill. Buck 4F 20
Little Langdale. Cumb 5B 46
Little Langford. Wilts 2J 9
Little Laver. Essx 3B 22
Little Lawford. Warw 4B 28
Little Leigh. Ches W 2E 34
Little Leighs. Essx 2D 22
Little Leven. E Yor 3H 43
Little Lever. G Man 7F 40
Little Linford. Mil 7F 28
Little London. Buck 2D 20
Little London. E Sus 4B 12
Little London. Hants
nr. Andover 1A 10
nr. Basingstoke 8D 20
Little London. Linc
nr. Long Sutton 7M 37
nr. Spalding 7K 37
Little London. Norf
nr. North Walsham 6J 39
nr. Northwold 2D 30
nr. Saxthorpe 6H 39
nr. Southery 2C 30
Little London. Powy 4K 25
Little Longstone. Derbs 2K 35
Little Malvern. Worc 7F 26
Little Maplestead. Essx 8E 30
Little Marcle. Here 8E 26
Little Marlow. Buck 5F 20
Little Massingham. Norf 7D 38
Little Melton. Norf 1H 31
Little Mill. Mon 3B 18
Littlemill. Abers 6C 72
Littlemill. E Ayr 8C 58
Littlemill. High 1K 71
Little Milton. Oxon 3D 20
Little Missenden. Buck 4G 21
Littlemoor. Derbs 3A 36
Littlemoor. Dors 7E 8
Littlemore. Oxon 3C 20
Little Mountain. Flin 3A 34
Little Musgrave. Cumb 4F 46
Little Ness. Shrp 8C 34
Little Neston. Ches W 2A 34
Little Newcastle. Pemb 4F 14
Little Newsham. Dur 4K 47
Little Oakley. Essx 1J 23
Little Oakley. Nptn 3F 28
Little Onn. Staf 8G 35
Little Ormside. Cumb 4F 46
Little Orton. Cumb 6H 53
Little Orton. Leics 1M 27
Little Ouse. Cambs 3C 30
Little Ouseburn. N Yor 1B 42
Littleover. Derb 6M 35
Little Packington. Warw 3L 27
Little Paxton. Cambs 5J 29
Little Petherick. Corn 4B 4
Little Plumpton. Lanc 4B 40
Little Plumstead. Norf 8K 39
Little Ponton. Linc 6G 37
Littleport. Cambs 3B 30
Little Posbrook. Hants 5C 10
Little Potheridge. Devn 4E 6
Little Preston. Nptn 6C 28
Little Raveley. Cambs 4K 29
Little Reynoldston. Swan 8L 15
Little Ribston. N Yor 2A 42
Little Rissington. Glos 2K 19
Little Rogart. High 3H 79
Little Rollright. Oxon 8L 27
Little Ryburgh. Norf 7F 38
Little Ryle. Nmbd 8H 61
Little Ryton. Shrp 1C 26
Little Salkeld. Cumb 8K 53
Little Sampford. Essx 8C 30
Little Sandhurst. Brac 7F 20
Little Saredon. Staf 1H 27
Little Saxham. Suff 5D 30
Little Scatwell. High 8D 78
Little Shelford. Cambs 6A 30
Little Shoddesden. Hants 1L 9
Little Singleton. Lanc 4B 40
Little Smeaton. N Yor 6C 42
Little Snoring. Norf 6F 38
Little Sodbury. S Glo 5F 18
Little Somborne. Hants 2A 10
Little Somerford. Wilts 5H 19
Little Soudley. Shrp 7F 34
Little Stainforth. N Yor 1G 41
Little Stainton. Darl 4M 47
Little Stanney. Ches W 2C 34
Little Staughton. Bed 5J 29
Little Steeping. Linc 3M 37
Littlester. Shet 5K 91
Little Stoke. Staf 6H 35
Littlestone-on-Sea. Kent 3G 13
Little Stonham. Suff 5H 31
Little Stretton. Leics 1D 28
Little Stretton. Shrp 2C 26
Little Strickland. Cumb 4D 46
Little Stukeley. Cambs 4K 29
Little Sugnall. Staf 6G 35
Little Sutton. Ches W 2B 34
Little Sutton. Linc 7A 38
Little Swinburne. Nmbd 4C 54
Little Tew. Oxon 1A 20
Little Tey. Essx 1E 22
Little Thetford. Cambs 4B 30
Little Thirkleby. N Yor 8B 48
Little Thornage. Norf 6G 39
Little Thornton. Lanc 3B 40
Little Thorpe. W Yor 5K 41
Littlethorpe. Leics 2C 28
Littlethorpe. N Yor 1M 41
Little Thurlow. Suff 6C 30
Little Thurrock. Thur 6C 22
Littleton. Ches W 3C 34
Littleton. Hants 2B 10
Littleton. Som 2C 8
Littleton. Surr
nr. Guildford 1G 11
nr. Staines 7H 21
Littleton Drew. Wilts 5G 19
Littleton Pannell. Wilts 8J 19
Littleton-upon-Severn.
S Glo 5D 18
Little Torboll. High 4H 79
Little Torrington. Devn 4D 6
Little Totham. Essx 2E 22
Little Town. Cumb 3M 45
Little Town. Lanc 4E 40
Littletown. Dur 7G 55
Littletown. High 5H 79
Little Twycross. Leics 1M 27
Little Urswick. Cumb 8A 46
Little Wakering. Essx 5F 22
Little Walden. Essx 7B 30
Little Waldingfield. Suff 7F 30
Little Walsingham. Norf 6F 38
Little Waltham. Essx 2D 22
Little Warley. Essx 4C 22
Little Weighton. E Yor 4G 43
Little Wenham. Suff 8G 31
Little Wenlock. Telf 1E 26
Little Whelnetham. Suff 5E 30
Little Whittingham Green.
Suff 4J 31
Littlewick Green. Wind 6F 20
Little Wilbraham. Cambs 6B 30
Littlewindsor. Dors 5C 8
Little Wisbeach. Linc 6J 37
Little Witcombe. Glos 2H 19
Little Witley. Worc 5F 26
Little Wittenham. Oxon 4C 20
Little Wolford. Warw 8L 27
Littleworth. Bed 7H 29
Littleworth. Glos 8K 27
Littleworth. Oxon 4M 19
Littleworth. Staf
nr. Cannock 8J 35
nr. Eccleshall 7F 34
nr. Stafford 7H 35
Littleworth. W Sus 3J 11
Littleworth. Worc
nr. Redditch 5H 27
nr. Worcester 6G 27
Little Wratting. Suff 7C 30
Little Wymondley. Herts 1K 21
Little Wyrley. Staf 1J 27
Little Yeldham. Essx 8D 30
Littley Green. Essx 2C 22
Litton. Derbs 2K 35
Litton. N Yor 8H 47
Litton. Som 8D 18
Litton Cheney. Dors 6D 8
Liurbost. W Isl 1E 76
Liverpool. Mers 111 (8B 40)
Liverpool John Lennon Airport.
Mers 1C 34
Liversedge. W Yor 5K 41
Liverton. Devn 8H 7
Liverton. Red C 4E 48
Liverton Mines. Red C 4E 48
Livingston. W Lot 3J 59
Livingston Village. W Lot 3J 59
Lixwm. Flin 3L 33
Lizard. Corn 7L 3
Llaingoch. IOA 2B 32
Llaithddu. Powy 4K 25
Llampha. V Glam 7J 17
Llan. Powy 2H 25
Llanaber. Gwyn 1F 24
Llanaelhaearn. Gwyn 6C 32
Llanaeron. Cdgn 6D 24
Llanafan. Cdgn 5F 24
Llanafan-fawr. Powy 7J 25
Llanafan-fechan. Powy 7J 25
Llanallgo. IOA 2D 32
Llanandras. Powy 5B 26
Llananno. Powy 5K 25
Llanarmon. Gwyn 7D 32
Llanarmon Dyffryn Ceiriog.
Wrex 7L 33
Llanarmon-yn-Ial. Den 5L 33
Llanarth. Cdgn 1L 15
Llanarth. Mon 2B 18
Llanarthne. Carm 4M 15
Llanasa. Flin 2L 33
Llanbabo. IOA 2C 32
Llanbadarn Fawr. Cdgn 4F 24
Llanbadarn Fynydd. Powy 5L 25
Llanbadarn-y-garreg. Powy 8L 25
Llanbadoc. Mon 3B 18
Llanbadrig. IOA 1C 32
Llanbeder. Newp 4B 18
Llanbedr. Gwyn 8E 32
Llanbedr. Powy
nr. Crickhowell 2M 17
nr. Hay-on-Wye 8L 25
Llanbedr-Dyffryn-Clwyd.
Den 5L 33
Llanbedrgoch. IOA 2E 32
Llanbedrog. Gwyn 7C 32
Llanbedr Pont Steffan.
Cdgn 8E 24
Llanbedr-y-cennin. Cnwy 4G 33
Llanberis. Gwyn 4E 32
Llanbethery. V Glam 8K 17
Llanbister. Powy 5L 25
Llanblethian. V Glam 7J 17
Llanboidy. Carm 4J 15
Llanbradach. Cphy 5L 17
Llanbrynmair. Powy 2H 25
Llanbydderi. V Glam 8K 17
Llancadle. V Glam 8K 17
Llancarfan. V Glam 7K 17
Llancatal. V Glam 8K 17
Llancayo. Mon 3B 18
Llancloudy. Here 1C 18
Llancoch. Powy 5M 25
Llancynfelyn. Cdgn 3F 24
Llandaff. Card 7L 17
Llandanwg. Gwyn 8E 32
Llandarcy. Neat 5G 17
Llandawke. Carm 5J 15
Llanddaniel Fab. IOA 3D 32
Llanddarog. Carm 5M 15
Llanddeiniol. Cdgn 5E 24
Llanddeiniolen. Gwyn 4E 32
Llandderfel. Gwyn 7J 33
Llanddeusant. Carm 2G 17
Llanddeusant. IOA 2C 32
Llanddew. Powy 1K 17
Llanddewi. Swan 8L 15
Llanddewi Brefi. Cdgn 7F 24
Llanddewi'r Cwm. Powy 8K 25
Llanddewi Rhydderch. Mon 2B 18
Llanddewi Velfrey. Pemb 5H 15
Llanddewi Ystradenni.
Powy 6L 25
Llanddoged. Cnwy 4H 33
Llanddona. IOA 3E 32
Llanddowror. Carm 5J 15
Llanddulas. Cnwy 3J 33
Llanddwywe. Gwyn 8E 32
Llanddyfnan. IOA 3E 32
Llandecwyn. Gwyn 7F 32
Llandefaelog Fach. Powy 1K 17
Llandefaelog-tre'r-graig.
Powy 1L 17
Llandefalle. Powy 1L 17
Llandegfan. IOA 3E 32
Llandegla. Den 5L 33
Llandegley. Powy 6L 25
Llandegveth. Mon 4B 18
Llandeilo. Carm 2F 16
Llandeilo Graban. Powy 8K 25
Llandeilo'r Fan. Powy 1H 17
Llandeloy. Pemb 4E 14
Llandenny. Mon 3C 18
Llandevaud. Newp 4C 18
Llandevenny. Mon 5C 18
Llandilo. Pemb 4H 15
Llandinabo. Here 1D 18
Llandinam. Powy 4K 25
Llandissilio. Pemb 4H 15
Llandogo. Mon 3D 18
Llandough. V Glam
nr. Cowbridge 7J 17
nr. Penarth 7L 17
Llandovery. Carm 1G 17
Llandow. V Glam 7J 17
Llandre. Cdgn 4F 24
Llandrillo. Den 7K 33
Llandrillo-yn-Rhos. Cnwy 2H 33
Llandrindod. Powy 6K 25
Llandrindod Wells. Powy 6K 25
Llandrinio. Powy 8A 34
Llandudno. Cnwy 2G 33
Llandudno Junction. Cnwy 3G 33
Llandudoch. Pemb 2H 15
Llandw. V Glam 7J 17
Llandwrog. Gwyn 5D 32
Llandybie. Carm 3F 16
Llandyfaelog. Carm 5L 15
Llandyfan. Carm 3F 16
Llandyfriog. Cdgn 2K 15
Llandyfrydog. IOA 2D 32
Llandygai. Gwyn 3F 32
Llandygwydd. Cdgn 2J 15
Llandynan. Den 6L 33
Llandyrnog. Den 4L 33
Llandysilio. Powy 8A 34
Llandyssil. Powy 3L 25
Llandysul. Cdgn 2L 15
Llanedeyrn. Card 6M 17
Llaneglwys. Powy 1K 17
Llanegryn. Gwyn 2F 24
Llanegwad. Carm 4M 15
Llaneilian. IOA 1D 32
Llanelian-yn-Rhos. Cnwy 3H 33
Llanelidan. Den 5L 33
Llanelieu. Powy 1L 17
Llanellen. Mon 2B 18
Llanelli. Carm 7M 15
Llanelltyd. Gwyn 1G 25
Llanelly. Mon 3M 17
Llanelly Hill. Mon 3M 17
Llanelwedd. Powy 7K 25
Llan-Elwy. Den 3K 33
Llanenddwyn. Gwyn 8E 32
Llanengan. Gwyn 8B 32
Llanerch. Powy 2B 26
Llanerchymedd. IOA 2D 32
Llanerfyl. Powy 2K 25
Llaneuddog. IOA 2D 32
Llanfachraeth. IOA 2C 32
Llanfachreth. Gwyn 8G 33
Llanfaelog. IOA 3C 32
Llanfaelrhys. Gwyn 8B 32
Llanfaenor. Mon 2C 18
Llanfaes. IOA 3F 32
Llanfaes. Powy 2K 17
Llanfaethlu. IOA 2C 32
Llanfaglan. Gwyn 4D 32
Llanfair. Gwyn 8E 32
Llanfair. Here 7A 26
Llanfair Caereinion. Powy 2L 25
Llanfair Clydogau. Cdgn 7F 24
Llanfair Dyffryn Clwyd. Den 5L 33
Llanfairfechan. Cnwy 3F 32
Llanfair-Nant-Gwyn. Pemb 3H 15
Llanfair Pwllgwyngyll. IOA 3E 32
Llanfair Talhaiarn. Cnwy 3J 33
Llanfair Waterdine. Shrp 5M 25
Llanfair-ym-Muallt. Powy 7K 25
Llanfairyneubwll. IOA 3C 32
Llanfairynghornwy. IOA 1C 32
Llanfallteg. Carm 5H 15
Llanfallteg West. Carm 5H 15
Llanfaredd. Powy 7K 25
Llanfarian. Cdgn 5E 24
Llanfechain. Powy 8L 33
Llanfechell. IOA 1C 32
Llanfendigaid. Gwyn 2E 24
Llanferres. Den 4L 33
Llan Ffestiniog. Gwyn 6G 33
Llanfflewyn. IOA 2C 32
Llanfihangel-ar-Arth. Carm 3L 15
Llanfihangel Glyn Myfyr.
Cnwy 6J 33
Llanfihangel Nant Bran.
Powy 1J 17
Llanfihangel-Nant-Melan.
Powy 7L 25
Llanfihangel near Rogiet.
Mon 5C 18
Llanfihangel Rhydithon.
Powy 6L 25
Llanfihangel Tal-y-llyn.
Powy 2L 17
Llanfihangel-uwch-Gwili.
Carm 4L 15
Llanfihangel-y-Creuddyn.
Cdgn 5F 24
Llanfihangel-yng-Ngwynfa.
Powy 1K 25
Llanfihangel yn Nhowyn.
IOA 3C 32
Llanfihangel-y-pennant.
Gwynnr. Golan 6E 32
nr. Tywyn 2F 24
Llanfihangel-y-traethau.
Gwyn 7E 32
Llanfilo. Powy 1L 17
Llanfleiddan. V Glam 7J 17
Llanfoist. Mon 2A 18
Llanfor. Gwyn 7J 33
Llanfrechfa. Torf 4B 18
Llanfrothen. Gwyn 6F 32
Llanfrynach. Powy 2K 17
Llanfwrog. Den 5L 33
Llanfwrog. IOA 2C 32
Llanfyllin. Powy 1L 25
Llanfynydd. Carm 2E 16
Llanfynydd. Flin 4A 34
Llanfyrnach. Pemb 3J 15
Llangadfan. Powy 1K 25
Llangadog. Carm
nr. Llandovery 2G 17
nr. Llanelli 6L 15
Llangadwaladr. IOA 4C 32
Llangadwaladr. Powy 7L 33
Llangaffo. IOA 4D 32
Llangain. Carm 5K 15
Llangammarch Wells. Powy 8J 25
Llangan. V Glam 7J 17
Llangarron. Here 1D 18
Llangasty-Talyllyn. Powy 2L 17
Llangathen. Carm 2E 16
Llangattock. Powy 3M 17
Llangattock Lingoed. Mon 1B 18
Llangattock-Vibon-Avel.
Mon 2C 18
Llangedwyn. Powy 8L 33
Llangefni. IOA 3D 32
Llangeinor. B'end 6J 17
Llangeitho. Cdgn 7F 24
Llangeler. Carm 3K 15
Llangelynin. Gwyn 2E 24
Llangendeirne. Carm 5L 15
Llangennech. Carm 4E 16
Llangennith. Swan 7L 15
Llangenny. Powy 3M 17
Llangernyw. Cnwy 4H 33
Llangian. Gwyn 8B 32
Llangiwg. Neat 4G 17
Llangloffan. Pemb 3F 14
Llanglydwen. Carm 4H 15
Llangoed. IOA 3F 32
Llangoedmor. Cdgn 2H 15
Llangollen. Den 6M 33
Llangolman. Pemb 4H 15
Llangorse. Powy 2L 17
Llangorwen. Cdgn 4F 24
Llangovan. Mon 3C 18
Llangower. Gwyn 7J 33
Llangranog. Cdgn 1K 15
Llangristiolus. IOA 3D 32
Llangrove. Here 2D 18
Llangua. Mon 1B 18
Llangunllo. Powy 5M 25
Llangunnor. Carm 4L 15
Llangurig. Powy 5J 25
Llangwm. Cnwy 6J 33
Llangwm. Mon 3C 18
Llangwm. Pemb 6F 14
Llangwm-isaf. Mon 3C 18
Llangwnnadl. Gwyn 7B 32
Llangwyfan. Den 4L 33
Llangwyfan-isaf. IOA 4C 32
Llangwyllog. IOA 3D 32
Llangwyryfon. Cdgn 5F 24
Llangybi. Cdgn 7F 24
Llangybi. Gwyn 6D 32
Llangybi. Mon 4B 18
Llangyfelach. Swan 5F 16
Llangynhafal. Den 4L 33
Llangynidr. Powy 3L 17
Llangynin. Carm 5J 15
Llangynog. Carm 5K 15
Llangynog. Powy 8K 33
Llangynwyd. B'end 6H 17
Llanhamlach. Powy 2K 17
Llanharan. Rhon 6K 17
Llanharry. Rhon 6K 17
Llanhennock. Mon 4B 18
Llanhilleth. Blae 4M 17
Llanidloes. Powy 4J 25
Llaniestyn. Gwyn 7B 32
Llanigon. Powy 8M 25
Llanilar. Cdgn 5F 24
Llanilid. Rhon 6J 17
Llanilltud Fawr. V Glam 8J 17
Llanishen. Card 6L 17
Llanishen. Mon 3C 18
Llanllawddog. Carm 4L 15
Llanllechid. Gwyn 4F 32
Llanllowell. Mon 4B 18
Llanllugan. Powy 2K 25
Llanllwch. Carm 5K 15
Llanllwchaiarn. Powy 3L 25
Llanllwni. Carm 3L 15
Llanllyfni. Gwyn 5D 32
Llanmadoc. Swan 7L 15
Llanmaes. V Glam 8J 17
Llanmartin. Newp 5B 18
Llanmerwig. Powy 3L 25
Llanmihangel. V Glam 7J 17
Llan-mill. Pemb 5H 15
Llanmiloe. Carm 6J 15
Llanmorlais. Swan 7M 15
Llannefydd. Cnwy 3J 33
Llan-non. Cdgn 6E 24
Llannon. Carm 6M 15
Llannor. Gwyn 7C 32
Llanover. Mon 3B 18
Llanpumsaint. Carm 4L 15
Llanrhaeadr. Den 4K 33
Llanrhaeadr-ym-Mochnant.
Powy 8L 33
Llanrhian. Pemb 3E 14
Llanrhidian. Swan 7L 15
Llanrhos. Cnwy 2G 33
Llanrhyddlad. IOA 2C 32
Llanrhystud. Cdgn 6E 24
Llanrothal. Here 2C 18
Llanrug. Gwyn 4E 32
Llanrumney. Card 6M 17
Llanrwst. Cnwy 4G 33
Llansadurnen. Carm 5J 15
Llansadwrn. Carm 1F 16
Llansadwrn. IOA 3E 32
Llansaint. Carm 6K 15
Llansamlet. Swan 5F 16
Llansanffraid Glan Conwy.
Cnwy 3H 33

Llansannan—Meadgate

Llansannan. Cnwy 4J 33
Llansannor. V Glam 7J 17
Llansantffraed. Cdgn 6E 24
Llansantffraed. Powy 2L 17
Llansantffraed Cwmdeuddwr. Powy 6J 25
Llansantffraed-in-Elwel. Powy 7K 25
Llansantffraid-ym-Mechain. Powy 8M 33
Llansawel. Carm 1F 16
Llansawel. Neat 5G 17
Llansilin. Powy 8M 33
Llansoy. Mon 3C 18
Llanspyddid. Powy 2K 17
Llanstadwell. Pemb 6F 14
Llansteffan. Carm 5K 15
Llanstephan. Powy 8L 25
Llantarnam. Torf 4B 18
Llanteg. Pemb 5H 15
Llanthony. Mon 1A 18
Llantilio Crossenny. Mon 2B 18
Llantilio Pertholey. Mon 2B 18
Llantood. Pemb 2H 15
Llantrisant. Mon 4B 18
Llantrisant. Rhon 6K 17
Llantrithyd. V Glam 7K 17
Llantwit Fardre. Rhon 6K 17
Llantwit Major. V Glam 8J 17
Llanuwchllyn. Gwyn 7H 33
Llanvaches. Newp 4C 18
Llanvair Discoed. Mon 4C 18
Llanvapley. Mon 2B 18
Llanvetherine. Mon 2B 18
Llanveynoe. Here 8B 26
Llanvihangel Crucorney. Mon 1B 18
Llanvihangel Gobion. Mon 3B 18
Llanvihangel Ystern-Llewern. Mon 2C 18
Llanwarne. Here 1D 18
Llanwddyn. Powy 1K 25
Llanwenarth. Mon 2A 18
Llanwenog. Cdgn 2L 15
Llanwern. Newp 5B 18
Llanwinio. Carm 4J 15
Llanwnda. Gwyn 5D 32
Llanwnda. Pemb 3F 14
Llanwnnen. Cdgn 2M 15
Llanwnog. Powy 3K 25
Llanwrda. Carm 1G 17
Llanwrin. Powy 2G 25
Llanwrthwl. Powy 6J 25
Llanwrtud. Powy 8H 25
Llanwrtyd. Powy 8H 25
Llanwrtyd Wells. Powy 8H 25
Llanwyddelan. Powy 2K 25
Llanyblodwel. Shrp 8M 33
Llanybri. Carm 5K 15
Llanybydder. Carm 2M 15
Llanycefn. Pemb 4G 15
Llanychaer. Pemb 3F 14
Llanycil. Gwyn 7J 33
Llanymawddwy. Gwyn 1J 25
Llanymddyfri. Carm 1G 17
Llanymynech. Powy 7A 34
Llanynghenedl. IOA 2C 32
Llanynys. Den 4L 33
Llan-y-pwll. Wrex 4B 34
Llanyrafon. Torf 4B 18
Llanyre. Powy 6K 25
Llanystumdwy. Gwyn 7D 32
Llanywern. Powy 2L 17
Llawhaden. Pemb 5G 15
Llawndy. Flin 2L 33
Llawnt. Shrp 6A 34
Llawr Dref. Gwyn 8B 32
Llawryglyn. Powy 3J 25
Llay. Wrex 4B 34
Llechfaen. Powy 2K 17
Llechryd. Cphy 4L 17
Llechryd. Cdgn 2J 15
Llechrydau. Wrex 7M 33
Lledrod. Cdgn 5F 24
Llethrid. Swan 7M 15
Llidiad-Nenog. Carm 3M 15
Llidiardau. Gwyn 7H 33
Llidiart y Parc. Den 6L 33
Llithfaen. Gwyn 6C 32
Lloc. Flin 3L 33
Llong. Flin 3A 34
Llowes. Powy 8L 25
Lloyney. Powy 5M 25
Llundain-fach. Cdgn 7E 24
Llwydcoed. Rhon 4J 17
Llwyncelyn. Cdgn 1L 15
Llwyncelyn. Swan 4F 16
Llwyndafydd. Cdgn 1K 15
Llwynderw. Powy 2M 25
Llwyn-du. Mon 2A 18
Llwyngwril. Gwyn 2E 24
Llwynhendy. Carm 7M 15
Llwynmawr. Wrex 7M 33
Llwyn-on Village. Mer T 3K 17
Llwyn-têg. Carm 4E 16
Llwyn-y-brain. Carm 5H 15
Llwynygog. Powy 3H 25
Llwyn-y-groes. Cdgn 7E 24
Llwynypia. Rhon 5J 17
Llynclys. Shrp 7A 34
Llynfaes. IOA 3D 32
Llysfaen. Cnwy 3H 33
Llyswen. Powy 1L 17
Llysworney. V Glam 7J 17
Llys-y-fran. Pemb 4G 15
Llywel. Powy 1H 17
Llywernog. Cdgn 4G 25
Loan. Falk 2H 59
Loanend. Nmbd 4G 61
Loanhead. Midl 3L 59
Loaningfoot. Dum 6D 52
Loanreoch. High 6G 79
Loans. S Ayr 6B 58
Loansdean. Nmbd 3E 54
Lobb. Devn 2D 6
Lobhillcross. Devn 7D 6
Lochaber. Mor 8L 79
Loch a Charnain. W Isl 1E 74
Loch a Ghainmhich. W Isl 1D 76
Lochailort. High 7J 69
Lochaline. High 3A 64
Lochans. Dum 6F 50
Locharbriggs. Dum 3D 52
Lochardil. High 1G 71
Lochassynt Lodge. High 1B 78
Lochavich. Arg 6D 64
Lochawe. Arg 5F 64
Loch Baghasdail. W Isl 4D 74
Lochboisdale. W Isl 4D 74
Lochbuie. Arg 5M 63
Lochcarron. High 2K 69
Loch Choire Lodge. High 8J 85
Lochdochart House. Stir 5J 65
Lochdon. Arg 4B 64
Lochearnhead. Stir 5K 65
Lochee. D'dee 4G 67
Lochend. High
nr. Inverness 2F 70
nr. Thurso 5D 86
Locherben. Dum 2D 52
Loch Euphort. W Isl 7K 75
Lochfoot. Dum 4C 52
Lochgair. Arg 8D 64
Lochgarthside. High 4F 70
Lochgelly. Fife 8E 66
Lochgilphead. Arg 1H 57
Lochgoilhead. Arg 7F 64
Loch Head. Dum 7J 51
Lochhill. Mor 7B 80
Lochindorb Lodge. High 2K 71
Lochinver. High 1A 78
Lochlane. Per 5B 66
Loch Lomond. Arg 7H 65
Loch Loyal Lodge. High 7J 85
Lochluichart. High 7D 78
Lochmaben. Dum 3E 52
Lochmaddy. W Isl 7L 75
Loch nam Madadh. W Isl 7L 75
Lochore. Fife 8E 66
Lochportain. W Isl 6L 75
Lochranza. N Ayr 4J 57
Loch Sgioport. W Isl 2E 74
Lochside. Abers 1L 67
Lochside. High
nr. Achentoul 8L 85
nr. Nairn 8J 79
Lochslin. High 5J 79
Lochstack Lodge. High 7E 84
Lochton. Abers 6G 73
Lochty. Fife 7J 67
Lochuisge. High 2B 64
Lochussie. High 8E 78
Lochwinnoch. Ren 4B 58
Lochyside. High 8B 70
Lockengate. Corn 5C 4
Lockerbie. Dum 3F 52
Lockeridge. Wilts 7K 19
Lockerley. Hants 3L 9
Lockhills. Cumb 7K 53
Locking. N Som 8B 18
Lockington. E Yor 3G 43
Lockington. Leics 7B 36
Lockleywood. Shrp 7E 34
Locksgreen. IOW 6B 10
Locks Heath. Hants 5C 10
Lockton. N Yor 6F 48
Loddington. Leics 1E 28
Loddington. Nptn 4F 28
Loddiswell. Devn 7K 5
Loddon. Norf 2K 31
Lode. Cambs 5B 30
Loders. Dors 6C 8
Lodsworth. W Sus 3G 11
Lofthouse. N Yor 8K 47
Lofthouse. W Yor 5M 41
Lofthouse Gate. W Yor 5M 41
Loftus. Red C 4E 48
Logan. E Ayr 7D 58
Loganlea. W Lot 3H 59
Logaston. Here 6B 26
Loggerheads. Den 4L 33
Loggerheads. Staf 6F 34
Loggie. High 4B 78
Logie. Ang 1K 67
Logie. Fife 5H 67
Logie. Mor 8L 79
Logie Coldstone. Abers 5D 72
Logie Pert. Ang 1K 67
Logierait. Per 2C 66
Login. Carm 4H 15
Lolworth. Cambs 5L 29
Lonbain. High 8H 77
Londesborough. E Yor 3F 42
London. G Lon 112-113 (5L 21)
London Apprentice. Corn 6C 4
London Ashford Airport. Kent 3G 13
London City Airport. G Lon 5M 21
London Colney. Herts 3J 21
Londonderry. Derr 3D 92
Londonderry. N Yor 7M 47
London Gatwick Airport. W Sus 119 (1K 11)
London Heathrow Airport. G Lon 119 (6H 21)
London Luton Airport. Lutn 119 (1J 21)
London Southend Airport. Essx 5E 22
London Stansted Airport. Essx 119 (1B 22)
Londonthorpe. Linc 6G 37
Londubh. High 5K 77
Lone. High 7F 84
Lonemore. High
nr. Dornoch 5H 79
nr. Gairloch 6J 77
Long Ashton. N Som 6D 18
Long Bank. Worc 4F 26
Longbar. N Ayr 4B 58
Long Bennington. Linc 5F 36
Longbenton. Tyne 5F 54
Longborough. Glos 1K 19
Long Bredy. Dors 6D 8
Longbridge. Warw 5L 27
Longbridge. W Mid 4J 27
Longbridge Deverill. Wilts 1G 9
Long Buckby. Nptn 5D 28
Long Buckby Wharf. Nptn 5D 28
Longburgh. Cumb 6H 53
Longburton. Dors 4E 8
Long Clawson. Leics 7E 36
Longcliffe. Derbs 4L 35
Long Common. Hants 4C 10
Long Compton. Staf 7G 35
Long Compton. Warw 8L 27
Longcot. Oxon 4L 19
Long Crendon. Buck 3D 20
Long Crichel. Dors 4H 9
Longcroft. Cumb 6G 53
Longcroft. Falk 2F 58
Longcross. Surr 7G 21
Longdale. Cumb 5E 46
Longdales. Cumb 7K 53
Longden. Shrp 1C 26
Longden Common. Shrp 1C 26
Long Ditton. Surr 7J 21
Longdon. Staf 8J 35
Longdon. Worc 8G 27
Longdon Green. Staf 8J 35
Longdon on Tern. Telf 8E 34
Longdown. Devn 6H 7
Longdowns. Corn 5L 3
Long Drax. N Yor 5D 42
Long Duckmanton. Derbs 2B 36
Long Eaton. Derbs 6B 36
Longfield. Kent 7C 22
Longfield. Shet 6D 90
Longfield Hill. Kent 7C 22
Longford. Derbs 6L 35
Longford. Glos 1G 19
Longford. G Lon 6H 21
Longford. Shrp 6E 34
Longford. Telf 8F 34
Longford. W Mid 3A 28
Longforgan. Per 4G 67
Longformacus. Bord 4D 60
Longframlington. Nmbd 1E 54
Long Gardens. Essx 8E 30
Long Green. Ches W 2C 34
Long Green. Worc 8G 27
Longham. Dors 6J 9
Longham. Norf 8F 38
Long Hanborough. Oxon 2B 20
Longhedge. Wilts 1G 9
Longhill. Abers 8K 81
Longhirst. Nmbd 3F 54
Longhope. Glos 2E 18
Longhope. Orkn 2E 86
Longhorsley. Nmbd 2E 54
Longhoughton. Nmbd 8K 61
Long Itchington. Warw 5B 28
Longlands. Cumb 8G 53
Long Lane. Telf 8E 34
Longlane. Derbs 6L 35
Longlane. W Ber 6B 20
Long Lawford. Warw 4B 28
Long Lease. N Yor 5G 49
Longley Green. Worc 6F 26
Long Load. Som 3C 8
Longmanhill. Abers 7G 81
Long Marston. Herts 2F 20
Long Marston. N Yor 2C 42
Long Marston. Warw 7K 27
Long Marton. Cumb 3E 46
Long Meadow. Cambs 5B 30
Long Meadowend. Shrp 3C 26
Long Melford. Suff 7E 30
Longmoor Camp. Hants 2E 10
Longmorn. Mor 8B 80
Longmoss. Ches E 2G 35
Long Newnton. Glos 4H 19
Long Newton. Stoc T 4A 48
Longnewton. Bord 7C 60
Longney. Glos 2F 18
Longniddry. E Lot 2B 60
Longnor. Shrp 1C 26
Longnor. Staf
nr. Leek 3J 35
nr. Stafford 8G 35
Longparish. Hants 1B 10
Longpark. Cumb 5J 53
Long Preston. N Yor 2G 41
Longridge. Lanc 4E 40
Longridge. Staf 8H 35
Longridge. W Lot 3H 59
Longriggend. N Lan 2G 59
Long Riston. E Yor 3J 43
Longrock. Corn 5J 3
Longsdon. Staf 4H 35
Longshaw. G Man 7D 40
Longshaw. Staf 5J 35
Longside. Abers 1K 73
Longslow. Shrp 6E 34
Longstanton. Cambs 5L 29
Longstock. Hants 2A 10
Longstowe. Cambs 6L 29
Long Stratton. Norf 2H 31
Long Street. Mil 7E 28
Longstreet. Wilts 8K 19
Long Sutton. Hants 1E 10
Long Sutton. Linc 7M 37
Long Sutton. Som 3C 8
Longthorpe. Pet 2J 29
Long Thurlow. Suff 5G 31
Longthwaite. Cumb 3C 46
Longton. Lanc 5C 40
Longton. Stoke 5H 35
Longtown. Cumb 5H 53
Longtown. Here 1B 18
Longville in the Dale. Shrp 2D 26
Long Whatton. Leics 7B 36
Longwick. Buck 3E 20
Long Wittenham. Oxon 4C 20
Longwitton. Nmbd 3D 54
Longworth. Oxon 4A 20
Longyester. E Lot 3C 60
Lonmore. High 1D 68
Looe. Corn 6E 4
Loose. Kent 8D 22
Loosegate. Linc 7L 37
Loosley Row. Buck 3F 20
Lopcombe Corner. Wilts 2L 9
Lopen. Som 4C 8
Loppington. Shrp 7C 34
Lorbottle. Nmbd 1D 54
Lordington. W Sus 5E 10
Loscoe. Derbs 5B 36
Loscombe. Dors 6D 8
Losgaintir. W Isl 4B 76
Lossiemouth. Mor 7B 80
Lossit. Arg 4A 56
Lostock Gralam. Ches W 2E 34
Lostock Green. Ches W 2E 34
Lostock Hall. Lanc 5D 40
Lostock Junction. G Man 7E 40
Lostwithiel. Corn 6D 4
Lothbeg. High 2K 79
Lothersdale. N Yor 3H 41
Lothianbridge. Midl 3M 59
Lothianburn. Midl 3L 59
Lothmore. High 2K 79
Lottisham. Som 2D 8
Loudwater. Buck 4G 21
Loughborough. Leics 8C 36
Loughbrickland. Arm 6G 93
Loughgall. Arm 6F 93
Loughguile. Caus 2G 93
Loughinisland. New M 6J 93
Loughmacrory. Ferm 5D 92
Loughor. Swan 5E 16
Loughries. Ards 5J 93
Loughton. Essx 4M 21
Loughton. Mil 8F 28
Loughton. Shrp 3E 26
Lound. Linc 8H 37
Lound. Notts 1D 36
Lound. Suff 2M 31
Lount. Leics 8A 36
The Loup. M Ulst 4F 93
Louth. Linc 1L 37
Love Clough. Lanc 5G 41
Lovedean. Hants 4D 10
Lover. Wilts 3L 9
Loversall. S Yor 8C 42
Loves Green. Essx 3C 22
Loveston. Pemb 6G 15
Lovington. Som 2D 8
Low Ackworth. W Yor 6B 42
Low Angerton. Nmbd 3D 54
Low Ardwell. Dum 7F 50
Low Ballochdowan. S Ayr 4F 50
Lowbands. Glos 8F 26
Low Barlings. Linc 2H 37
Low Bell End. N Yor 6E 48
Low Bentham. N Yor 1E 40
Low Borrowbridge. Cumb 5E 46
Low Bradfield. S Yor 8L 41
Low Bradley. N Yor 3J 41
Low Braithwaite. Cumb 7J 53
Low Brunton. Nmbd 4C 54
Low Burnham. N Lin 7E 42
Lowca. Cumb 2J 45
Low Catton. E Yor 2E 42
Low Coniscliffe. Darl 4L 47
Low Coylton. S Ayr 8C 58
Low Crosby. Cumb 6J 53
Low Dalby. N Yor 7F 48
Lowdham. Notts 5D 36
Low Dinsdale. Darl 4M 47
Lowe. Shrp 6D 34
Low Ellington. N Yor 7L 47
Lower Amble. Corn 4B 4
Lower Ansty. Dors 5F 8
Lower Arboll. High 5J 79
Lower Arncott. Oxon 2D 20
Lower Ashton. Devn 7H 7
Lower Assendon. Oxon 5E 20
Lower Auchenreath. Mor 7C 80
Lower Badcall. High 7D 84
Lower Ballam. Lanc 4B 40
Lower Ballinderry. Lis 5G 93
Lower Basildon. W Ber 6D 20
Lower Beeding. W Sus 3K 11
Lower Benefield. Nptn 3G 29
Lower Bentley. Worc 5H 27
Lower Beobridge. Shrp 2F 26
Lower Bockhampton. Dors 6F 8
Lower Boddington. Nptn 6B 28
Lower Bordean. Hants 3D 10
Lower Brailes. Warw 8M 27
Lower Breakish. High 3H 69
Lower Broadheath. Worc 6G 27
Lower Brynamman. Neat 3G 17
Lower Bullingham. Here 8D 26
Lower Bullington. Hants 1B 10
Lower Burgate. Hants 4K 9
Lower Cam. Glos 3F 18
Lower Catesby. Nptn 6C 28
Lower Chapel. Powy 1K 17
Lower Cheriton. Devn 5L 7
Lower Chicksgrove. Wilts 2H 9
Lower Chute. Wilts 8M 19
Lower Clopton. Warw 6K 27
Lower Common. Hants 1D 10
Lower Crossings. Derbs 1J 35
Lower Cumberworth. W Yor 7L 41
Lower Darwen. Bkbn 5E 40
Lower Dean. Bed 5H 29
Lower Dean. Devn 5K 5
Lower Diabaig. High 7J 77
Lower Dicker. E Sus 4B 12
Lower Dounreay. High 5A 86
Lower Down. Shrp 3B 26
Lower Dunsforth. N Yor 1B 42
Lower East Carleton. Norf 1H 31
Lower Egleton. Here 7E 26
Lower Ellastone. Staf 5K 35
Lower End. Nptn 5F 28
Lower Everleigh. Wilts 8K 19
Lower Eype. Dors 6C 8
Lower Failand. N Som 6D 18
Lower Faintree. Shrp 3E 26
Lower Farringdon. Hants 2E 10
Lower Foxdale. IOM 7B 44
Lower Frankton. Shrp 6B 34
Lower Froyle. Hants 1E 10
Lower Gabwell. Devn 5M 5
Lower Gledfield. High 4F 78
Lower Godney. Som 1C 8
Lower Gravenhurst. C Beds 8J 29
Lower Green. Essx 8M 29
Lower Green. Norf 6F 38
Lower Green. W Ber 7A 20
Lower Halstow. Kent 7E 22
Lower Hardres. Kent 8H 23
Lower Hardwick. Here 6C 26
Lower Hartshay. Derbs 4A 36
Lower Hawthwaite. Cumb 6M 45
Lower Haysden. Kent 1B 12
Lower Hayton. Shrp 3D 26
Lower Hergest. Here 6A 26
Lower Heyford. Oxon 1B 20
Lower Heysham. Lanc 1C 40
Lower Higham. Kent 6D 22
Lower Holbrook. Suff 8H 31
Lower Holditch. Dors 5B 8
Lower Hordley. Shrp 7B 34
Lower Horncroft. W Sus 4H 11
Lower Horsebridge. E Sus 4B 12
Lower Kilcott. Glos 5F 18
Lower Killeyan. Arg 5B 56
Lower Kingcombe. Dors 6D 8
Lower Kingswood. Surr 8K 21
Lower Kinnerton. Ches W 3B 34
Lower Langford. N Som 7C 18
Lower Largo. Fife 7H 67
Lower Layham. Suff 7G 31
Lower Ledwyche. Shrp 4D 26
Lower Leigh. Staf 6J 35
Lower Lemington. Glos 8L 27
Lower Lenie. High 3F 70
Lower Ley. Glos 2F 18
Lower Llanfadog. Powy 6J 25
Lower Lode. Glos 8G 27
Lower Lovacott. Devn 3E 6
Lower Loxhore. Devn 2F 6
Lower Loxley. Staf 6J 35
Lower Lydbrook. Glos 2D 18
Lower Lye. Here 5C 26
Lower Machen. Newp 6M 17
Lower Maes-coed. Here 8B 26
Lower Meend. Glos 3D 18
Lower Midway. Derbs 7M 35
Lower Milovaig. High 8C 76
Lower Moor. Worc 7H 27
Lower Morton. S Glo 4E 18
Lower Mountain. Flin 4B 34
Lower Nazeing. Essx 3L 21
Lower Netchwood. Shrp 2E 26
Lower Nyland. Dors 3F 8
Lower Oakfield. Fife 8E 66
Lower Oddington. Glos 1L 19
Lower Ollach. High 2G 69
Lower Penarth. V Glam 8L 17
Lower Penn. Staf 2G 27
Lower Pennington. Hants 6M 9
Lower Peover. Ches W 2F 34
Lower Pilsley. Derbs 3B 36
Lower Pitkerrie. High 6J 79
Lower Place. G Man 6H 41
Lower Quinton. Warw 7K 27
Lower Rainham. Medw 7E 22
Lower Raydon. Suff 8G 31
Lower Seagry. Wilts 5H 19
Lower Shelton. C Beds 7G 29
Lower Shiplake. Oxon 6E 20
Lower Shuckburgh. Warw 5B 28
Lower Sketty. Swan 5F 16
Lower Slade. Devn 1E 6
Lower Slaughter. Glos 1K 19
Lower Soudley. Glos 2E 18
Lower Stanton St Quintin. Wilts 5H 19
Lower Stoke. Medw 6E 22
Lower Stondon. C Beds 8J 29
Lower Stonnall. Staf 1J 27
Lower Stow Bedon. Norf 2F 30
Lower Street. Norf 6J 39
Lower Strensham. Worc 7H 27
Lower Sundon. C Beds 1H 21
Lower Swanwick. Hants 5B 10
Lower Swell. Glos 1K 19
Lower Tale. Devn 5K 7
Lower Tean. Staf 6J 35
Lower Thurlton. Norf 2L 31
Lower Thurnham. Lanc 2C 40
Lower Thurvaston. Derbs 6L 35
Lower Town. Here 7E 26
Lower Town. IOS 1H 3
Lower Town. Pemb 3F 14
Lowertown. Corn 6K 3
Lowertown. Orkn 2F 86
Lower Tysoe. Warw 7M 27
Lower Upham. Hants 4C 10
Lower Upnor. Medw 6D 22
Lower Vexford. Som 2L 7
Lower Walton. Warr 1E 34
Lower Wear. Devn 7J 7
Lower Weare. Som 8C 18
Lower Welson. Here 6A 26
Lower Whatcombe. Dors 5G 9
Lower Whitley. Ches W 2E 34
Lower Wield. Hants 1D 10
Lower Withington. Ches E 3G 35
Lower Woodend. Buck 5F 20
Lower Woodford. Wilts 2K 9
Lower Wraxall. Dors 5D 8
Lower Wych. Ches W 5C 34
Lower Wyche. Worc 7F 26
Lowesby. Leics 1E 28
Lowestoft. Suff 2M 31
Loweswater. Cumb 2L 45
Low Etherley. Dur 3K 47
Lowfield Heath. W Sus 1K 11
Lowford. Hants 4B 10
Low Fulney. Linc 7K 37
Low Gate. Nmbd 5C 54
Lowgill. Cumb 6E 46
Lowgill. Lanc 1E 40
Low Grantley. N Yor 8L 47
Low Green. N Yor 2L 41
Low Habberley. Worc 4G 27
Low Ham. Som 3C 8
Low Hameringham. Linc 3L 37
Low Hawsker. N Yor 5G 49
Low Hesket. Cumb 7J 53
Low Hesleyhurst. Nmbd 2D 54
Lowick. Cumb 7A 46
Lowick. Nptn 3G 29
Lowick. Nmbd 6H 61
Lowick Bridge. Cumb 7A 46
Lowick Green. Cumb 7A 46
Low Knipe. Cumb 3D 46
Low Leighton. Derbs 1J 35
Low Lorton. Cumb 2L 45
Low Marishes. N Yor 8F 48
Low Marnham. Notts 3F 36
Low Mill. N Yor 6D 48
Low Moor. Lanc 3F 40
Low Moor. W Yor 5K 41
Low Moorsley. Tyne 7G 55
Low Newton-by-the-Sea. Nmbd 7K 61
Lownie Moor. Ang 3H 67
Lowood. Bord 6C 60
Low Row. Cumb
nr. Brampton 5K 53
nr. Wigton 7F 52
Low Row. N Yor 6H 47
Lowsonford. Warw 5K 27
Low Street. Norf 1G 31
Lowther. Cumb 3D 46
Lowthorpe. E Yor 1H 43
Lowton. Devn 5F 6
Lowton. G Man 8E 40
Lowton. Som 4L 7
Lowton Common. G Man 8E 40
Low Torry. Fife 1J 59
Low Toynton. Linc 2K 37
Low Valleyfield. Fife 1H 59
Low Westwood. Dur 6E 54
Low Whinnow. Cumb 6H 53
Low Wood. Cumb 7B 46
Low Worsall. N Yor 5A 48
Low Wray. Cumb 5B 46
Loxbeare. Devn 4J 7
Loxhill. Surr 2H 11
Loxhore. Devn 2F 6
Loxley. S Yor 1M 35
Loxley. Warw 6L 27
Loxley Green. Staf 6J 35
Loxton. N Som 8B 18
Loxwood. W Sus 2H 11
Lubcroy. High 3D 78
Lubenham. Leics 3E 28
Lubinvullin. High 5H 85
Luccombe. Som 1J 7
Luccombe Village. IOW 7C 10
Lucker. Nmbd 6J 61
Luckett. Corn 8C 6
Luckington. Wilts 5G 19
Lucklawhill. Fife 5H 67
Luckwell Bridge. Som 2J 7
Lucton. Here 5C 26
Ludag. W Isl 4D 74
Ludborough. Linc 8K 43
Ludchurch. Pemb 5H 15
Luddenden. W Yor 5J 41
Luddenden Foot. W Yor 5J 41
Luddenham. Kent 7F 22
Ludderburn. Cumb 6C 46
Luddesdown. Kent 7C 22
Luddington. N Lin 6F 42
Luddington. Warw 6K 27
Luddington in the Brook. Nptn 3J 29
Ludford. Linc 1J 37
Ludford. Shrp 4D 26
Ludgershall. Buck 2D 20
Ludgershall. Wilts 8L 19
Ludgvan. Corn 5J 3
Ludham. Norf 8K 39
Ludlow. Shrp 4D 26
Ludstone. Shrp 2G 27
Ludwell. Wilts 3H 9
Ludworth. Dur 7G 55
Luffenhall. Herts 1K 21
Luffincott. Devn 6C 6
Lugar. E Ayr 7D 58
Luggate Burn. E Lot 2D 60
Lugg Green. Here 5C 26
Luggiebank. N Lan 2F 58
Lugton. E Ayr 4C 58
Lugwardine. Here 7D 26
Luib. High 3G 69
Luib. Stir 5J 65
Lulham. Here 7C 26
Lullington. Derbs 8L 35
Lullington. E Sus 5B 12
Lullington. Som 8F 18
Lulsgate Bottom. N Som 7D 18
Lulsley. Worc 6F 26
Lulworth Camp. Dors 7G 9
Lumb. Lanc 5G 41
Lumby. N Yor 4B 42
Lumphanan. Abers 5E 72
Lumphinnans. Fife 8E 66
Lumsdaine. Bord 3F 60
Lumsden. Abers 3D 72
Lunan. Ang 2K 67
Lunanhead. Ang 2H 67
Luncarty. Per 5D 66
Lund. E Yor 3G 43
Lund. N Yor 4D 42
Lundie. Ang 4F 66
Lundin Links. Fife 7H 67
Lundy Green. Norf 2J 31
Lunna. Shet 1E 90
Lunning. Shet 1F 90
Lunnon. Swan 8M 15
Lunsford. Kent 8C 22
Lunsford's Cross. E Sus 4D 12
Lunt. Mers 7B 40
Luppitt. Devn 5L 7
Lupridge. Devn 6K 5
Lupset. W Yor 6M 41
Lupton. Cumb 7D 46
Lurgan. Arm 6G 93
Lurganare. New M 7G 93
Lurgashall. W Sus 3G 11
Lurley. Devn 4J 7
Lusby. Linc 3L 37
Luscombe. Devn 6K 5
Luson. Devn 7J 5
Luss. Arg 8H 65
Lussagiven. Arg 1F 56
Lusta. High 8D 76
Lustleigh. Devn 7G 7
Luston. Here 5C 26
Luthermuir. Abers 1K 67
Luthrie. Fife 6G 67
Lutley. Staf 3G 27
Luton. Devn
nr. Honiton 5K 7
nr. Teignmouth 8J 7
Luton. Lutn 1H 21
Luton Airport. Lutn 119 (1J 21)
Lutterworth. Leics 3C 28
Lutton. Devn
nr. Ivybridge 6H 5
nr. South Brent 5J 5
Lutton. Linc 7M 37
Lutton. Nptn 3J 29
Lutton Gowts. Linc 7M 37
Lutworthy. Devn 4G 7
Luxborough. Som 2J 7
Luxley. Glos 1E 18
Luxulyan. Corn 6C 4
Lybster. High 8D 86
Lydbury North. Shrp 3B 26
Lydcott. Devn 2F 6
Lydd. Kent 3G 13
Lydd Airport. Kent 3G 13
Lydden. Kent
nr. Dover 1J 13
nr. Margate 7K 23
Lyddington. Rut 2F 28
Lydd-on-Sea. Kent 3G 13
Lydeard St Lawrence. Som 2L 7
Lyde Green. Hants 8E 20
Lydford. Devn 7E 6
Lydford Fair Place. Som 2D 8
Lydgate. G Man 7H 41
Lydgate. W Yor 5H 41
Lydham. Shrp 2B 26
Lydiard Millicent. Wilts 5J 19
Lydiate. Mers 7B 40
Lydiate Ash. Worc 4H 27
Lydlinch. Dors 4F 8
Lydmarsh. Som 5B 8
Lydney. Glos 3E 18
Lydstep. Pemb 7G 15
Lye. W Mid 3H 27
The Lye. Shrp 2E 26
Lye Green. Buck 3G 21
Lye Green. E Sus 2B 12
Lye Head. Worc 4F 26
Lyford. Oxon 4A 20
Lyham. Nmbd 6H 61
Lylestone. N Ayr 5B 58
Lymbridge Green. Kent 1H 13
Lyme Regis. Dors 6B 8
Lyminge. Kent 1H 13
Lymington. Hants 6M 9
Lyminster. W Sus 5H 11
Lymm. Warr 1E 34
Lymore. Hants 6L 9
Lympne. Kent 2H 13
Lympsham. Som 8B 18
Lympstone. Devn 7J 7
Lynaberack Lodge. High 6H 71
Lynbridge. Devn 1G 7
Lynch. Som 1J 7
Lynchat. High 5H 71
Lynch Green. Norf 1H 31
Lyndhurst. Hants 5M 9
Lyndon. Rut 1G 29
Lyne. Bord 5L 59
Lyne. Surr 7H 21
Lyneal. Shrp 6C 34
Lyne Down. Here 8E 26
Lyneham. Oxon 1L 19
Lyneham. Wilts 6J 19
Lyneholmeford. Cumb 4K 53
Lynemouth. Nmbd 2F 54
Lyne of Gorthleck. High 3F 70
Lyne of Skene. Abers 4G 73
Lynesack. Dur 3J 47
Lyness. Orkn 2E 86
Lyng. Norf 8G 39
Lyngate. Norf
nr. North Walsham 6J 39
nr. Worstead 7K 39
Lynmouth. Devn 1G 7
Lynn. Staf 1J 27
Lynn. Telf 8F 34
Lynsted. Kent 7F 22
Lynstone. Corn 5B 6
Lynton. Devn 1G 7
Lynwilg. High 4J 71
Lyon's Gate. Dors 5E 8
Lyonshall. Here 6B 26
Lytchett Matravers. Dors 6H 9
Lytchett Minster. Dors 6H 9
Lyth. High 5D 86
Lytham. Lanc 5B 40
Lytham St Anne's. Lanc 5B 40
Lythe. N Yor 4F 48
Lythes. Orkn 3F 86
Lythmore. High 5B 86

M

Mabe Burnthouse. Corn 5L 3
Mabie. Dum 4D 52
Mablethorpe. Linc 1B 38
Macbiehill. Bord 4K 59
Macclesfield. Ches E 2H 35
Macclesfield Forest. Ches E 2H 35
Macduff. Abers 7G 81
Machan. S Lan 4F 58
Macharioch. Arg 1C 50
Machen. Cphy 6M 17
Machrie. N Ayr 6H 57
Machrihanish. Arg 7F 56
Machroes. Gwyn 8C 32
Machynlleth. Powy 2G 25
Mackerye End. Herts 2J 21
Mackworth. Derb 6M 35
Macmerry. E Lot 2B 60
Macosquin. Caus 2F 93
Madderty. Per 5C 66
Maddington. Wilts 1J 9
Maddiston. Falk 2H 59
Madehurst. W Sus 4G 11
Madeley. Staf 5F 34
Madeley. Telf 1E 26
Madeley Heath. Staf 5F 34
Madeley Heath. Worc 4H 27
Madford. Devn 4L 7
Madingley. Cambs 5L 29
Madley. Here 8C 26
Madresfield. Worc 7G 27
Madron. Corn 5H 3
Maenaddwyn. IOA 2D 32
Maenclochog. Pemb 4G 15
Maendy. V Glam 7K 17
Maenporth. Corn 6L 3
Maentwrog. Gwyn 6F 32
Maen-y-groes. Cdgn 1K 15
Maer. Staf 6F 34
Maerdy. Carm 2F 16
Maerdy. Cnwy 6K 33
Maerdy. Rhon 5J 17
Maesbrook. Shrp 7B 34
Maesbury. Shrp 7B 34
Maesbury Marsh. Shrp 7B 34
Maes-glas. Flin 3L 33
Maesgwyn-Isaf. Powy 1L 25
Maeshafn. Den 4M 33
Maes Llyn. Cdgn 2K 15
Maesmynis. Powy 8K 25
Maesteg. B'end 5H 17
Maestir. Cdgn 8E 24
Maesybont. Carm 3E 16
Maesycrugiau. Carm 2L 15
Maesycwmmer. Cphy 5L 17
Maesyrhandir. Powy 3K 25
Magdalen Laver. Essx 3B 22
Maggieknockater. Mor 1C 72
Maghaberry. Lis 5G 93
Magham Down. E Sus 4C 12
Maghera. M Ulst 3F 93
Maghera. New M 7H 93
Magherafelt. M Ulst 4F 93
Magheralin. Arm 6G 93
Magheramason. Derr 3C 92
Magheraveely. Ferm 7D 92
Maghery. Arm 5F 93
Maghull. Mers 7B 40
Magna Park. Leics 3C 28
Magor. Mon 5C 18
Magpie Green. Suff 4G 31
Maguiresbridge. Ferm 7C 92
Magwyr. Mon 5C 18
Maidenbower. W Sus 2K 11
Maiden Bradley. Wilts 2G 9
Maidencombe. Torb 5M 5
Maidenhayne. Devn 6A 8
Maidenhead. Wind 5F 20
Maiden Law. Dur 7E 54
Maiden Newton. Dors 6D 8
Maidens. S Ayr 1H 51
Maiden's Green. Brac 6F 20
Maidensgrove. Oxon 5E 20
Maidenwell. Corn 4D 4
Maidenwell. Linc 2L 37
Maiden Wells. Pemb 7F 14
Maidford. Nptn 6D 28
Maids Moreton. Buck 8E 28
Maidstone. Kent 8D 22
Maidwell. Nptn 4E 28
Mail. Shet 5E 90
Maindee. Newp 5B 18
Mainsforth. Dur 8G 55
Mains of Auchindachy. Mor 1D 72
Mains of Auchnagatt. Abers 1J 73
Mains of Drum. Abers 6H 73
Mains of Edingight. Mor 8E 80
Mainsriddle. Dum 6D 52
Mainstone. Shrp 3A 26
Maisemore. Glos 1G 19
Major's Green. Worc 4K 27
Makeney. Derbs 5A 36
Makerstoun. Bord 6D 60
Malacleit. W Isl 6J 75
Malaig. High 6H 69
Malaig Bheag. High 6H 69
Malborough. Devn 8K 5
Malcoff. Derbs 1J 35
Malcolmburn. Mor 8C 80
Malden Rushett. G Lon 7J 21
Maldon. Essx 3E 22
Malham. N Yor 1H 41
Maligar. High 7F 76
Malinslee. Telf 1E 26
Mallaig. High 6H 69
Malleny Mills. Edin 3K 59
Mallows Green. Essx 1A 22
Malltraeth. IOA 4D 32
Mallusk. Ant 4H 93
Mallwyd. Gwyn 1H 25
Malmesbury. Wilts 5H 19
Malmsmead. Devn 1G 7
Malpas. Ches W 5C 34
Malpas. Corn 4M 3
Malpas. Newp 4B 18
Malswick. Glos 1F 18
Maltby. S Yor 8C 42
Maltby. Stoc T 4B 48
Maltby le Marsh. Linc 1A 38
Malt Lane. Arg 7E 64
Maltman's Hill. Kent 1F 12
Malton. N Yor 8E 48
Malvern Link. Worc 7F 26
Malvern Wells. Worc 7F 26
Mamble. Worc 4E 26
Mamhilad. Mon 3B 18
Manaccan. Corn 6L 3
Manafon. Powy 2L 25
Manais. W Isl 5C 76
Manaton. Devn 7G 7
Manby. Linc 1L 37
Mancetter. Warw 2M 27
Manchester. G Man 111 (8G 41)
Manchester Airport. G Man 119 (1G 35)
Mancot. Flin 3B 34
Manea. Cambs 3A 30
Maney. W Mid 2K 27
Manfield. N Yor 4L 47
Mangotsfield. S Glo 6E 18
Mangurstadh. W Isl 8D 82
Mankinholes. W Yor 5H 41
Manley. Ches W 2D 34
Manmoel. Cphy 4L 17
Mannal. Arg 3E 62
Mannerston. Falk 2J 59
Manningford Bohune. Wilts 8K 19
Manningford Bruce. Wilts 8K 19
Manningham. W Yor 4K 41
Mannings Heath. W Sus 3K 11
Mannington. Dors 5J 9
Manningtree. Essx 8H 31
Mannofield. Aber 5J 73
Manorbier. Pemb 7G 15
Manorbier Newton. Pemb 7G 15
Manordeilo. Carm 2F 16
Manorowen. Pemb 3F 14
Manor Park. G Lon 5M 21
Mansell Gamage. Here 7B 26
Mansell Lacy. Here 7C 26
Mansergh. Cumb 7E 46
Mansewood. Glas 3D 58
Mansfield. E Ayr 8E 58
Mansfield. Notts 3C 36
Mansfield Woodhouse. Notts 3C 36
Mansriggs. Cumb 7A 46
Manston. Dors 4G 9
Manston. Kent 7K 23
Manston. W Yor 4A 42
Manswood. Dors 5H 9
Manthorpe. Linc
nr. Bourne 8H 37
nr. Grantham 6G 37
Manton. N Lin 7G 43
Manton. Notts 2C 36
Manton. Rut 1F 28
Manton. Wilts 7K 19
Manuden. Essx 1A 22
Maperton. Som 3E 8
Maplebeck. Notts 3E 36
Maple Cross. Herts 4H 21
Mapledurham. Oxon 6D 20
Mapledurwell. Hants 8D 20
Maplehurst. W Sus 3J 11
Maplescombe. Kent 7B 22
Mapleton. Derbs 5K 35
Mapperley. Derbs 5B 36
Mapperley. Nott 5C 36
Mapperley Park. Nott 5C 36
Mapperton. Dors
nr. Beaminster 6D 8
nr. Poole 6H 9
Mappleborough Green. Warw 5J 27
Mappleton. E Yor 3K 43
Mapplewell. S Yor 7M 41
Mappowder. Dors 5F 8
Maraig. W Isl 3D 76
Marazion. Corn 5J 3
Marbhig. W Isl 2F 76
Marbury. Ches E 5D 34
March. Cambs 2M 29
Marcham. Oxon 4B 20
Marchamley. Shrp 7D 34
Marchington. Staf 6K 35
Marchington Woodlands. Staf 7K 35
Marchwiel. Wrex 5B 34
Marchwood. Hants 4A 10
Marcross. V Glam 8J 17
Marden. Here 7D 26
Marden. Kent 1D 12
Marden. Wilts 8J 19
Marden Beech. Kent 1D 12
Marden Thorn. Kent 1D 12
Mardu. Shrp 3A 26
Mardy. Mon 2B 18
Marefield. Leics 1E 28
Mareham le Fen. Linc 3K 37
Mareham on the Hill. Linc 3K 37
Marehay. Derbs 5B 36
Marehill. W Sus 4H 11
Maresfield. E Sus 3A 12
Marfleet. Hull 5J 43
Marford. Wrex 4B 34
Margam. Neat 6G 17
Margaret Marsh. Dors 4G 9
Margaret Roding. Essx 2B 22
Margaretting. Essx 3C 22
Margaretting Tye. Essx 3C 22
Margate. Kent 6K 23
Margery. Surr 8K 21
Margnaheglish. N Ayr 6K 57
Marham. Norf 1D 30
Marhamchurch. Corn 5B 6
Marholm. Pet 1J 29
Marian Cwm. Den 3K 33
Mariandyrys. IOA 2F 32
Marian-glas. IOA 2E 32
Mariansleigh. Devn 3G 7
Marian-y-de. Gwyn 7C 32
Marian-y-mor. Gwyn 7C 32
Marine Town. Kent 6F 22
Marishader. High 7F 76
Marjoriebanks. Dum 3E 52
Mark. Dum 6G 51
Mark. Som 1B 8
Markbeech. Kent 1A 12
Markby. Linc 2A 38
Mark Causeway. Som 1B 8
Mark Cross. E Sus 2B 12
Markeaton. Derb 6M 35
Market Bosworth. Leics 1B 28
Market Deeping. Linc 8J 37
Market Drayton. Shrp 6E 34
Market End. Warw 3M 27
Market Harborough. Leics 3E 28
Markethill. Arm 7F 93
Markethill. Per 4F 66
Market Lavington. Wilts 8J 19
Market Overton. Rut 8F 36
Market Rasen. Linc 1J 37
Market Stainton. Linc 1K 37
Market Weighton. E Yor 3F 42
Market Weston. Suff 4F 30
Markfield. Leics 8B 36
Markham. Cphy 4L 17
Markinch. Fife 7F 66
Markington. N Yor 1L 41
Marksbury. Bath 7E 18
Mark's Corner. IOW 6B 10
Marks Tey. Essx 1F 22
Markwell. Corn 6F 4
Markyate. Herts 2H 21
Marlborough. Wilts 7K 19
Marlcliff. Warw 6J 27
Marldon. Devn 5L 5
Marle Green. E Sus 4B 12
Marlesford. Suff 6K 31
Marley Green. Ches E 5D 34
Marley Hill. Tyne 6F 54
Marlingford. Norf 1H 31
Mar Lodge. Abers 7L 71
Marloes. Pemb 6D 14
Marlow. Buck 5F 20
Marlow. Here 4B 26
Marlow Bottom. Buck 5F 20
Marlow Common. Buck 5F 20
Marlpit Hill. Kent 1M 11
Marlpits. E Sus 3M 11
Marlpool. Derbs 5B 36
Marnhull. Dors 4F 8
Marnoch. Abers 8E 80
Marnock. N Lan 3F 58
Marple. G Man 1H 35
Marr. S Yor 7C 42
Marrel. High 2L 79
Marrick. N Yor 6J 47
Marrister. Shet 1F 90
Marros. Carm 6J 15
Marsden. Tyne 5G 55
Marsden. W Yor 6J 41
Marsett. N Yor 7H 47
Marsh. Buck 3F 20
Marsh. Devn 4A 8
The Marsh. Powy 2B 26
The Marsh. Shrp 7E 34
Marshall Meadows. Nmbd 4G 61
Marshalsea. Dors 5B 8
Marshalswick. Herts 3J 21
Marsham. Norf 7H 39
Marshaw. Lanc 2D 40
Marsh Baldon. Oxon 4C 20
Marsh Benham. W Ber 7B 20
Marshborough. Kent 8K 23
Marshbrook. Shrp 3C 26
Marshchapel. Linc 8L 43
Marshfield. Newp 5A 18
Marshfield. S Glo 6F 18
Marshgate. Corn 6A 6
Marsh Gibbon. Buck 1D 20
Marsh Green. Devn 6K 7
Marsh Green. Kent 1M 11
Marsh Green. Staf 4G 35
Marsh Green. Telf 8E 34
Marsh Lane. Derbs 2B 36
Marsh Side. Norf 5D 38
Marshside. Kent 7J 23
Marshside. Mers 6B 40
Marsh Street. Som 1J 7
Marshwood. Dors 6B 8
Marske. N Yor 5K 47
Marske-by-the-Sea. Red C 3D 48
Marston. Ches W 2E 34
Marston. Here 6B 26
Marston. Linc 5F 36
Marston. Oxon 3C 20
Marston. Staf
nr. Stafford 7H 35
nr. Wheaton Aston 8G 35
Marston. Warw 2L 27
Marston. Wilts 8H 19
Marston Doles. Warw 6B 28
Marston Green. W Mid 3K 27
Marston Hill. Glos 4K 19
Marston Jabbett. Warw 3A 28
Marston Magna. Som 3D 8
Marston Meysey. Wilts 4K 19
Marston Montgomery. Derbs 6K 35
Marston Moretaine. C Beds 7G 29
Marston on Dove. Derbs 7L 35
Marston St Lawrence. Nptn 7C 28
Marston Stannett. Here 6D 26
Marston Trussell. Nptn 3D 28
Marstow. Here 2D 18
Marsworth. Buck 2G 21
Marten. Wilts 8L 19
Marthall. Ches E 2G 35
Martham. Norf 8L 39
Marthwaite. Cumb 6E 46
Martin. Hants 4J 9
Martin. Kent 1K 13
Martin. Linc
nr. Horncastle 3K 37
nr. Metheringham 4J 37
Martindale. Cumb 4C 46
Martin Dales. Linc 3J 37
Martin Drove End. Hants 3J 9
Martinhoe. Devn 1F 6
Martinhoe Cross. Devn 1F 6
Martin Hussingtree. Worc 5G 27
Martin Mill. Kent 1K 13
Martinscroft. Warr 1E 34
Martin's Moss. Ches E 3G 35
Martinstown. Dors 7E 8
Martinstown. ME Ant 3G 93
Martlesham. Suff 7J 31
Martlesham Heath. Suff 7J 31
Martletwy. Pemb 5G 15
Martley. Worc 5F 26
Martock. Som 4C 8
Marton. Ches E 3G 35
Marton. Cumb 7M 45
Marton. E Yor
nr. Bridlington 1K 43
nr. Hull 4J 43
Marton. Linc 1F 36
Marton. Midd 4C 48
Marton. N Yor
nr. Boroughbridge 1B 42
nr. Pickering 7E 48
Marton. Shrp
nr. Myddle 7C 34
nr. Worthen 1A 26
Marton. Warw 5B 28
Marton Abbey. N Yor 1C 42
Marton-le-Moor. N Yor 8A 48
Martyr's Green. Surr 8H 21
Martyr Worthy. Hants 2C 10
Marwick. Orkn 7B 88
Marwood. Devn 2E 6
Marybank. High
nr. Dingwall 8E 78
nr. Invergordon 6H 79
Maryburgh. High 8F 78
Maryfield. Corn 6G 5
Maryhill. Glas 3D 58
Marykirk. Abers 1K 67
Marylebone. G Lon 5K 21
Marylebone. G Man 7D 40
Marypark. Mor 2A 72
Maryport. Cumb 8E 52
Maryport. Dum 8G 51
Marystow. Devn 7D 6
Mary Tavy. Devn 8E 6
Maryton. Ang
nr. Kirriemuir 2G 67
nr. Montrose 2K 67
Marywell. Abers 6E 72
Marywell. Ang 3K 67
Masham. N Yor 7L 47
Mashbury. Essx 2C 22
Masongill. N Yor 8E 46
Masons Lodge. Abers 5H 73
Mastin Moor. Derbs 2B 36
Mastrick. Aber 5J 73
Matching. Essx 2B 22
Matching Green. Essx 2B 22
Matching Tye. Essx 2B 22
Matfen. Nmbd 4D 54
Matfield. Kent 1C 12
Mathern. Mon 4D 18
Mathon. Here 7F 26
Mathry. Pemb 3E 14
Matlaske. Norf 6H 39
Matlock. Derbs 4L 35
Matlock Bath. Derbs 4L 35
Matterdale End. Cumb 3B 46
Mattersey. Notts 1D 36
Mattersey Thorpe. Notts 1D 36
Mattingley. Hants 8E 20
Mattishall. Norf 8G 39
Mattishall Burgh. Norf 8G 39
Mauchline. E Ayr 7C 58
Maud. Abers 1J 73
Maudlin. Corn 5C 4
Maugersbury. Glos 1K 19
Maughold. IOM 5D 44
Maulden. C Beds 8H 29
Maulds Meaburn. Cumb 4E 46
Maunby. N Yor 7A 48
Maund Bryan. Here 6D 26
Mautby. Norf 8L 39
Mavesyn Ridware. Staf 8J 35
Mavis Enderby. Linc 3L 37
Mawbray. Cumb 7E 52
Mawdesley. Lanc 6C 40
Mawdlam. B'end 6H 17
Mawgan. Corn 6L 3
Mawgan Porth. Corn 2M 3
Maw Green. Ches E 4F 34
Mawla. Corn 4L 3
Mawnan. Corn 6L 3
Mawnan Smith. Corn 6L 3
Mawsley Village. Nptn 4E 28
Mawthorpe. Linc 2A 38
Maxey. Pet 1J 29
Maxstoke. Warw 3L 27
Maxted Street. Kent 1H 13
Maxton. Kent 1J 13
Maxton. Bord 6D 60
Maxwellheugh. Bord 6E 60
Maxwelltown. Dum 4D 52
Maxworthy. Corn 6B 6
Mayals. Swan 6F 16
Maybole. S Ayr 8B 58
Maybush. Sotn 4A 10
Maydown. Derr 3D 92
Mayes Green. Surr 2J 11
Mayfield. E Sus 3B 12
Mayfield. Midl 3A 60
Mayfield. Per 5D 66
Mayfield. Staf 5K 35
Mayford. Surr 8G 21
Mayhill. Swan 5F 16
Mayland. Essx 3F 22
Maylandsea. Essx 3F 22
Maynard's Green. E Sus 4B 12
Mayobridge. New M 7G 93
Maypole. IOS 1H 3
Maypole. Kent 7J 23
Maypole. Mon 2C 18
Maypole Green. Norf 2L 31
Maypole Green. Suff 6F 30
Maywick. Shet 5D 90
Mazetown. Lis 5H 93
Mead. Devn 4B 6
Meadgate. Bath 8E 18

Meadle—Nether Westcote

Meadle. Buck 3F 20
Meadowbank. Ches W 3E 34
Meadowfield. Dur 8F 54
Meadow Green. Here 6F 26
Meadowmill. E Lot 2B 60
Meadows. Nott 6C 36
Meadowtown. Shrp 1B 26
Meadwell. Devn 7D 6
Meaford. Staf 6G 35
Mealabost. W Isl
nr. Borgh 6H 83
nr. Stornoway 8H 83
Mealasta. W Isl 1A 76
Meal Bank. Cumb 6D 46
Mealrigg. Cumb 7F 52
Mealsgate. Cumb 7G 53
Meanwood. W Yor 4L 41
Mearbeck. N Yor 1G 41
Meare. Som 1C 8
Meare Green. Som
nr. Curry Mallet 3A 8
nr. Stoke St Gregory 3B 8
Mears Ashby. Nptn 5F 28
Measham. Leics 8M 35
Meath Green. Surr 1K 11
Meathop. Cumb 7C 46
Meaux. E Yor 4H 43
Meavy. Devn 5H 5
Medbourne. Leics 2E 28
Medburn. Nmbd 4E 54
Meddon. Devn 4B 6
Meden Vale. Notts 3C 36
Medlam. Linc 4L 37
Medlicott. Shrp 2C 26
Medmenham. Buck 5F 20
Medomsley. Dur 6E 54
Medstead. Hants 2D 10
Medway Towns.
Medw 111 (7D 22)
Meerbrook. Staf 3H 35
Meer End. W Mid 4L 27
Meers Bridge. Linc 1A 38
Meesden. Herts 8M 29
Meeson. Telf 7E 34
Meeth. Devn 5E 6
Meeting Green. Suff 6D 30
Meeting House Hill. Norf 7K 39
Meidrim. Carm 4J 15
Meifod. Powy 1L 25
Meigh. New M 7G 93
Meigle. Per 3F 66
Meikle Earnock. S Lan 4F 58
Meikle Kilchattan Butts.
Arg 4K 57
Meikleour. Per 4E 66
Meikle Tarty. Abers 3J 73
Meikle Wartle. Abers 2G 73
Meinciau. Carm 5L 15
Meir. Stoke 5H 35
Meir Heath. Staf 5H 35
Melbourn. Cambs 7L 29
Melbourne. Derbs 7A 36
Melbourne. E Yor 3E 42
Melbury Abbas. Dors 3G 9
Melbury Bubb. Dors 5D 8
Melbury Osmond. Dors 5D 8
Melbury Sampford. Dors 5D 8
Melby. Shet 2B 90
Melchbourne. Bed 5H 29
Melcombe Bingham. Dors 5F 8
Melcombe Regis. Dors 7E 8
Meldon. Devn 6E 6
Meldon. Nmbd 3E 54
Meldreth. Cambs 7L 29
Melfort. Arg 6C 64
Melgarve. High 6E 70
Meliden. Den 2K 33
Melinbyrhedyn. Powy 3H 25
Melincourt. Neat 4H 17
Melin-y-coed. Cnwy 4H 33
Melin-y-ddol. Powy 2K 25
Melin-y-wig. Den 6K 33
Melkington. Nmbd 5F 60
Melkinthorpe. Cumb 3D 46
Melkridge. Nmbd 5M 53
Melksham. Wilts 7H 19
Mellangaun. High 5K 77
Melldalloch. Arg 2J 57
Mellguards. Cumb 7J 53
Melling. Lanc 8D 46
Melling. Mers 7B 40
Melling Mount. Mers 7C 40
Mellis. Suff 4G 31
Mellon Charles. High 4K 77
Mellon Udrigle. High 4K 77
Mellor. G Man 1H 35
Mellor. Lanc 4E 40
Mellor Brook. Lanc 4E 40
Mells. Som 1F 8
Melmerby. Cumb 8L 53
Melmerby. N Yor
nr. Middleham 7J 47
nr. Ripon 8M 47
Melplash. Dors 6C 8
Melrose. Bord 6C 60
Melsetter. Orkn 3D 86
Melsonby. N Yor 5K 47
Meltham. W Yor 6K 41
Meltham Mills. W Yor 6K 41
Melton. E Yor 5G 43
Melton. Suff 6J 31
Meltonby. E Yor 2E 42
Melton Constable. Norf 6G 39
Melton Mowbray. Leics 8E 36
Melton Ross. N Lin 6H 43
Melvaig. High 5J 77
Melverley. Shrp 8B 34
Melverley Green. Shrp 8B 34
Melvich. High 5L 85
Membury. Devn 5A 8
Memsie. Abers 7J 81
Memus. Ang 2H 67
Menabilly. Corn 6C 4
Menai Bridge. IOA 3E 32
Mendham. Suff 3J 31
Mendlesham. Suff 5H 31
Mendlesham Green. Suff 5G 31
Menethorpe. N Yor 1E 42
Menheniot. Corn 5E 4
Menithwood. Worc 5F 26
Menna. Corn 6B 4
Mennock. Dum 1C 52
Menston. W Yor 3K 41
Menstrie. Clac 8B 66
Menthorpe. N Yor 4E 42
Mentmore. Buck 2G 21
Meole Brace. Shrp 8C 34
Meols. Mers 1M 33
Meon. Hants 5C 10
Meonstoke. Hants 3D 10
Meopham. Kent 7C 22
Meopham Green. Kent 7C 22
Meopham Station. Kent 7C 22
Mepal. Cambs 3M 29
Meppershall. C Beds 8J 29
Merbach. Here 7B 26
Mercaston. Derbs 5L 35
Merchiston. Edin 2L 59
Mere. Ches E 1F 34
Mere. Wilts 2G 9
Mere Brow. Lanc 6C 40
Mereclough. Lanc 4G 41
Mere Green. W Mid 2K 27
Mere Green. Worc 5H 27
Mere Heath. Ches W 2E 34
Mereside. Bkpl 4B 40
Meretown. Staf 7F 34
Mereworth. Kent 8C 22
Meriden. W Mid 3L 27
Merkadale. High 2E 68
Merkland. S Ayr 2H 51
Merkland Lodge. High 1D 78
Merley. Pool 6J 9
Merlin's Bridge. Pemb 5F 14
Merridge. Som 2M 7
Merrington. Shrp 7C 34
Merrion. Pemb 7F 14
Merriott. Som 4C 8
Merrivale. Devn 8E 6
Merrow. Surr 8H 21
Merrybent. Darl 4L 47
Merry Lees. Leics 1B 28
Merrymeet. Corn 5E 4
Mersham. Kent 2G 13
Merstham. Surr 8K 21
Merston. W Sus 5F 10
Merstone. IOW 7C 10
Merther. Corn 7A 4
Merthyr. Carm 4K 15
Merthyr Cynog. Powy 1J 17
Merthyr Dyfan. V Glam 7L 17
Merthyr Mawr. B'end 7H 17
Merthyr Tudful. Mer T 4K 17
Merthyr Tydfil. Mer T 4K 17
Merthyr Vale. Mer T 5K 17
Merton. Devn 4E 6
Merton. G Lon 7K 21
Merton. Norf 2F 30
Merton. Oxon 2C 20
Meshaw. Devn 4G 7
Messing. Essx 2E 22
Messingham. N Lin 7F 42
Metcombe. Devn 6K 7
Metfield. Suff 3J 31
Metherell. Corn 5G 5
Metheringham. Linc 3H 37
Methil. Fife 8G 67
Methilhill. Fife 8G 67
Methley. W Yor 5A 42
Methley Junction. W Yor 5A 42
Methlick. Abers 2H 73
Methven. Per 5D 66
Methwold. Norf 2D 30
Methwold Hythe. Norf 2D 30
Mettingham. Suff 3K 31
Metton. Norf 6H 39
Mevagissey. Corn 7C 4
Mexborough. S Yor 7B 42
Mey. High 4D 86
Meysey Hampton. Glos 4K 19
Miabhag. W Isl 4C 76
Miabhaig. W Isl
nr. Cliasmol 3B 76
nr. Timsgearraidh 8D 82
Mial. High 6J 77
Michaelchurch. Here 1D 18
Michaelchurch Escley. Here 8B 26
Michaelchurch-on-Arrow.
Powy 7M 25
Michaelston-le-Pit. V Glam 7L 17
Michaelston-y-Fedw. Newp 6M 17
Michaelstow. Corn 4C 4
Michelcombe. Devn 5J 5
Micheldever. Hants 2C 10
Micheldever Station. Hants 1C 10
Michelmersh. Hants 3M 9
Mickfield. Suff 5H 31
Micklebring. S Yor 8C 42
Mickleby. N Yor 4F 48
Micklefield. W Yor 4B 42
Micklefield Green. Herts 4H 21
Mickleham. Surr 8J 21
Mickleover. Derb 6M 35
Micklethwaite. Cumb 6G 53
Micklethwaite. W Yor 3K 41
Mickleton. Dur 3H 47
Mickleton. Glos 7K 27
Mickletown. W Yor 5A 42
Mickle Trafford. Ches W 3C 34
Mickley. N Yor 8L 47
Mickley Green. Suff 6E 30
Mickley Square. Nmbd 5D 54
Mid Ardlaw. Abers 7J 81
Midbea. Orkn 5D 88
Mid Beltie. Abers 5F 72
Mid Calder. W Lot 3J 59
Mid Clyth. High 8D 86
Middle Assendon. Oxon 5E 20
Middle Aston. Oxon 1B 20
Middle Barton. Oxon 1B 20
Middlebie. Dum 4G 53
Middle Chinnock. Som 4C 8
Middle Claydon. Buck 1E 20
Middlecliffe. S Yor 7B 42
Middlecott. Devn 7G 7
Middle Drums. Ang 2J 67
Middle Duntisbourne. Glos 3H 19
Middle Essie. Abers 8K 81
Middleforth Green. Lanc 5D 40
Middleham. N Yor 7K 47
Middle Handley. Derbs 2B 36
Middle Harling. Norf 3F 30
Middlehope. Shrp 3C 26
Middle Littleton. Worc 7J 27
Middle Maes-coed. Here 8B 26
Middlemarsh. Dors 5E 8
Middle Marwood. Devn 2E 6
Middle Mayfield. Staf 5K 35
Middlemoor. Devn 8D 6
Middlemuir. Abers
nr. New Deer 1H 73
nr. Strichen 8J 81
Middle Rainton. Tyne 7G 55
Middle Rasen. Linc 1H 37
The Middles. Dur 6F 54
Middlesbrough.
Midd 111 (4B 48)
Middlesceugh. Cumb 7H 53
Middleshaw. Cumb 7D 46
Middlesmoor. N Yor 8J 47
Middlestone. Dur 8F 54
Middlestone Moor. Dur 8F 54
Middle Stoughton. Som 1C 8
Middlestown. W Yor 6L 41
Middle Street. Glos 3F 18
Middle Taphouse. Corn 5D 4
Middleton. Ang 3J 67
Middleton. Arg 3E 62
Middleton. Cumb 7E 46
Middleton. Derbs
nr. Bakewell 3K 35
nr. Wirksworth 4L 35
Middleton. Essx 8E 30
Middleton. G Man 7G 41
Middleton. Hants 1B 10
Middleton. Hart 8J 55
Middleton. Here 5D 26
Middleton. IOW 7M 9
Middleton. Lanc 2C 40
Middleton. Midl 4A 60
Middleton. Norf 8C 38
Middleton. Nptn 3F 28
Middleton. Nmbd
nr. Belford 6J 61
nr. Morpeth 3D 54
Middleton. N Yor
nr. Ilkley 3K 41
nr. Pickering 7E 48
Middleton. Per 7E 66
Middleton. Shrp
nr. Ludlow 4D 26
nr. Oswestry 7B 34
Middleton. Suff 5L 31
Middleton. Swan 8L 15
Middleton. Warw 2K 27
Middleton. W Yor 5L 41
Middleton Cheney. Nptn 7C 28
Middleton Green. Staf 6H 35
Middleton-in-Teesdale. Dur 3H 47
Middleton One Row. Darl 4A 48
Middleton-on-Leven. N Yor 5B 48
Middleton-on-Sea. W Sus 5G 11
Middleton on the Hill.
Here 5D 26
Middleton-on-the-Wolds.
E Yor 3G 43
Middleton Priors. Shrp 2E 26
Middleton Quernhow.
N Yor 8M 47
Middleton St George. Darl 4M 47
Middleton Scriven. Shrp 3E 26
Middleton Stoney. Oxon 1C 20
Middleton Tyas. N Yor 5L 47
Middle Town. IOS 1H 3
Middletown. Arm 7E 92
Middletown. Cumb 4J 45
Middletown. Powy 8B 34
Middle Tysoe. Warw 7M 27
Middle Wallop. Hants 2L 9
Middlewich. Ches E 3F 34
Middle Winterslow. Wilts 2L 9
Middlewood. Corn 8B 6
Middlewood. S Yor 8M 41
Middle Woodford. Wilts 2K 9
Middlewood Green. Suff 5G 31
Middleyard. Glos 3G 19
Middlezoy. Som 2B 8
Middridge. Dur 3L 47
Midelney. Som 3C 8
Midfield. High 5H 85
Midford. Bath 7F 18
Mid Garrary. Dum 4L 51
Midge Hall. Lanc 5D 40
Midgeholme. Cumb 6L 53
Midgham. W Ber 7C 20
Midgley. W Yor
nr. Halifax 5J 41
nr. Horbury 6L 41
Mid Ho. Shet 4K 91
Midhopestones. S Yor 8L 41
Midhurst. W Sus 3F 10
Mid Kirkton. N Ayr 4L 57
Mid Lambrook. Som 4C 8
Midland. Orkn 1E 86
Mid Lavant. W Sus 5F 10
Midlem. Bord 7C 60
Midney. Som 3D 8
Midsomer Norton. Bath 8E 18
Midton. Inv 2M 57
Midtown. High
nr. Poolewe 5K 77
nr. Tongue 5H 85
Midville. Linc 4L 37
Mid Walls. Shet 3B 90
Mid Yell. Shet 4K 91
Migdale. High 4G 79
Migvie. Abers 5D 72
Milborne Port. Som 4E 8
Milborne St Andrew. Dors 6G 9
Milborne Wick. Som 3E 8
Milbourne. Nmbd 4E 54
Milbourne. Wilts 5H 19
Milburn. Cumb 3E 46
Milbury Heath. S Glo 4E 18
Milby. N Yor 1B 42
Milcombe. Oxon 8B 28
Milden. Suff 7F 30
Mildenhall. Suff 4D 30
Mildenhall. Wilts 7L 19
Milebrook. Powy 4B 26
Milebush. Kent 1D 12
Mile End. Cambs 3C 30
Mile End. Essx 1F 22
Mileham. Norf 8F 38
Mile Oak. Brig 5K 11
Miles Green. Staf 4G 35
Miles Hope. Here 5D 26
Milesmark. Fife 1J 59
Mile Town. Kent 6F 22
Milfield. Nmbd 6G 61
Milford. Arm 6F 93
Milford. Derbs 5A 36
Milford. Devn 3B 6
Milford. Powy 3K 25
Milford. Staf 7H 35
Milford. Surr 1G 11
Milford Haven. Pemb 6F 14
Milford on Sea. Hants 6L 9
Milkwall. Glos 3D 18
Milkwell. Wilts 3H 9
Milland. W Sus 3F 10
Mill Bank. W Yor 5J 41
Millbank. Ant 4H 93
Millbank. High 5C 86
Millbay. ME Ant 4J 93
Millbeck. Cumb 3A 46
Millbounds. Orkn 6E 88
Millbreck. Abers 1K 73
Millbridge. Surr 1F 10
Millbrook. C Beds 8H 29
Millbrook. Corn 6G 5
Millbrook. G Man 8H 41
Millbrook. ME Ant 3H 93
Millbrook. Sotn 4A 10
Mill Common. Suff 3L 31
Mill Corner. E Sus 3E 12
Milldale. Staf 4K 35
Millden Lodge. Ang 8E 72
Milldens. Ang 2J 67
Millearn. Per 6C 66
Mill End. Buck 5E 20
Mill End. Cambs 6C 30
Mill End. Glos 2K 19
Mill End. Herts 8L 29
Millend. Glos 4F 18
Millerhill. Midl 3M 59
Miller's Dale. Derbs 2K 35
Millers Green. Derbs 4L 35
Millerston. Glas 3E 58
Millfield. Abers 6D 72
Millfield. Pet 1J 29
Millgate. Lanc 6G 41
Mill Green. Essx 3C 22
Mill Green. Norf 3H 31
Mill Green. Shrp 7E 34
Mill Green. Staf 7J 35
Mill Green. Suff 7F 30
Millhalf. Here 7A 26
Millhall. E Ren 4D 58
Millhayes. Devn
nr. Honiton 5M 7
nr. Wellington 4L 7
Millhead. Lanc 8C 46
Millheugh. S Lan 4F 58
Mill Hill. Bkbn 5E 40
Mill Hill. G Lon 4K 21
Millholme. Cumb 6D 46
Millhouse. Arg 2J 57
Millhouse. Cumb 8H 53
Millhousebridge. Dum 3F 52
Millhouses. S Yor 1M 35
Millikenpark. Ren 3C 58
Millington. E Yor 2F 42
Millington Green. Derbs 5L 35
Millisle. Ards 5J 93
Mill Knowe. Arg 7G 57
Mill Lane. Hants 8E 20
Millmeece. Staf 6G 35
Mill of Craigievar. Abers 4E 72
Mill of Fintray. Abers 4H 73
Mill of Haldane. W Dun 1C 58
Millom. Cumb 6L 45
Millow. C Beds 7K 29
Millpool. Corn 4D 4
Millport. N Ayr 4L 57
Mill Side. Cumb 7C 46
Mill Street. Norf
nr. Lyng 8G 39
nr. Swanton Morley 8G 39
Millthorpe. Derbs 2M 35
Millthorpe. Linc 6J 37
Millthrop. Cumb 6E 46
Milltimber. Aber 5H 73
Mill Town. Ant 4G 93
Milltown. Abers
nr. Corgarff 5B 72
nr. Lumsden 4D 72
Milltown. Ant 4G 93
Milltown. Arm
nr. Banbridge 6G 93
nr. Coalisland 5F 93
nr. Richhill 6F 93
Milltown. Corn 6D 4
Milltown. Derbs 3A 36
Milltown. Devn 2E 6
Milltown. Dum 4H 53
Milltown of Aberdalgie.
Per 5D 66
Milltown of Auchindoun.
Mor 1C 72
Milltown of Campfield.
Abers 5F 72
Milltown of Edinvillie. Mor 1B 72
Milltown of Rothiemay.
Mor 1E 72
Milltown of Towie. Abers 4D 72
Milnacraig. Ang 2F 66
Milnathort. Per 7E 66
Milngavie. E Dun 2D 58
Milnholm. Stir 1F 58
Milnrow. G Man 6H 41
Milnthorpe. Cumb 7C 46
Milnthorpe. W Yor 6M 41
Milson. Shrp 4E 26
Milstead. Kent 8F 22
Milston. Wilts 1K 9
Milthorpe. Nptn 7C 28
Milton. Ang 3G 67
Milton. Cambs 5A 30
Milton. Cumb
nr. Brampton 5K 53
nr. Crooklands 7D 46
Milton. Derbs 7M 35
Milton. Dum
nr. Crocketford 4C 52
nr. Glenluce 6H 51
Milton. Glas 3D 58
Milton. High
nr. Achnasheen 8D 78
nr. Applecross 1J 69
nr. Drumnadrochit 2E 70
nr. Invergordon 6H 79
nr. Inverness 1F 70
nr. Wick 6E 86
Milton. Mor
nr. Cullen 7E 80
nr. Tomintoul 4A 72
Milton. N Som 7B 18
Milton. Notts 2E 36
Milton. Oxon
nr. Bloxham 8B 28
nr. Didcot 4B 20
Milton. Pemb 6G 15
Milton. Port 6D 10
Milton. Som 3C 8
Milton. S Ayr 7C 58
Milton. Stir
nr. Aberfoyle 7K 65
nr. Drymen 8J 65
Milton. Stoke 4H 35
Milton. W Dun 2C 58
Milton Abbas. Dors 5G 9
Milton Abbot. Devn 8D 6
Milton Auchlossan. Abers 5E 72
Milton Bridge. Midl 3L 59
Milton Bryan. C Beds 8G 29
Milton Clevedon. Som 2E 8
Milton Coldwells. Abers 2J 73
Milton Combe. Devn 5G 5
Milton Common. Oxon 3D 20
Milton Damerel. Devn 4C 6
Miltonduff. Mor 7A 80
Milton End. Glos 3K 19
Milton Ernest. Bed 6H 29
Milton Green. Ches W 4C 34
Milton Hill. Devn 8J 7
Milton Hill. Oxon 4B 20
Milton Keynes. Mil 114 (8F 28)
Milton Keynes Village. Mil 8F 28
Milton Lilbourne. Wilts 7K 19
Milton Malsor. Nptn 6E 28
Milton Morenish. Per 4L 65
Milton of Auchinhove.
Abers 5E 72
Milton of Balgonie. Fife 7G 67
Milton of Barras. Abers 8H 73
Milton of Campsie. E Dun 2E 58
Milton of Cultoquhey. Per 5B 66
Milton of Cushnie. Abers 4E 72
Milton of Finavon. Ang 2H 67
Milton of Gollanfield. High 8H 79
Milton of Lesmore. Abers 3D 72
Milton of Leys. High 1G 71
Milton of Tullich. Abers 6C 72
Milton on Stour. Dors 3F 8
Milton Regis. Kent 7E 22
Milton Street. E Sus 5B 12
Milton-under-Wychwood.
Oxon 2L 19
Milverton. Som 3L 7
Milverton. Warw 5M 27
Milwich. Staf 6H 35
Mimbridge. Surr 7G 21
Minard. Arg 8D 64
Minchington. Dors 4H 9
Minchinhampton. Glos 3G 19
Mindrum. Nmbd 6F 60
Minehead. Som 1J 7
Minera. Wrex 4A 34
Minerstown. New M 7J 93
Minety. Wilts 4J 19
Minffordd. Gwyn 7E 32
Mingarrypark. High 1A 64
Mingary. High 1L 63
Mingearraidh. W Isl 3D 74
Miningsby. Linc 3L 37
Minions. Corn 8B 6
Minishant. S Ayr 8B 58
Minllyn. Gwyn 1H 25
Minnigaff. Dum 5K 51
Minorca. IOM 6D 44
Minskip. N Yor 1A 42
Minstead. Hants 4L 9
Minsted. W Sus 3F 10
Minster. Kent
nr. Ramsgate 7K 23
Minster. Kent
nr. Sheerness 6F 22
Minsteracres. Nmbd 6D 54
Minsterley. Shrp 1B 26
Minster Lovell. Oxon 2M 19
Minsterworth. Glos 2F 18
Minterne Magna. Dors 5E 8
Minterne Parva. Dors 5E 8
Minting. Linc 2J 37
Mintlaw. Abers 1K 73
Minto. Bord 7C 60
Minton. Shrp 2C 26
Minwear. Pemb 5G 15
Minworth. W Mid 2K 27
Miodar. Arg 3F 62
Mirbister. Orkn 7C 88
Mirehouse. Cumb 3J 45
Mireland. High 5E 86
Mirfield. W Yor 6L 41
Miserden. Glos 3H 19
Miskin. Rhon 6K 17
Misson. Notts 8D 42
Misterton. Leics 3C 28
Misterton. Notts 8E 42
Misterton. Som 5C 8
Mistley. Essx 8H 31
Mistley Heath. Essx 8H 31
Mitcham. G Lon 7K 21
Mitcheldean. Glos 2E 18
Mitchell. Corn 6A 4
Mitchel Troy. Mon 2C 18
Mitcheltroy Common. Mon 3C 18
Mitford. Nmbd 3E 54
Mithian. Corn 3L 3
Mitton. Staf 8G 35
Mixbury. Oxon 8D 28
Mixenden. W Yor 5J 41
Mixon. Staf 4J 35
Moaness. Orkn 1D 86
Moarfield. Shet 3K 91
Moat. Cumb 4J 53
Moats Tye. Suff 6G 31
Mobberley. Ches E 2F 34
Mobberley. Staf 5J 35
Moccas. Here 7B 26
Mochdre. Cnwy 3H 33
Mochdre. Powy 4K 25
Mochrum. Dum 7J 51
Mockbeggar. Hants 5K 9
Mockerkin. Cumb 2K 45
Modbury. Devn 6J 5
Moddershall. Staf 6H 35
Modsarie. High 5J 85
Moelfre. Cnwy 3J 33
Moelfre. IOA 2E 32
Moelfre. Powy 8L 33
Moffat. Dum 1E 52
Moggerhanger. C Beds 7J 29
Mogworthy. Devn 4H 7
Moira. Leics 8M 35
Moira. Lis 5G 93
Molash. Kent 8G 23
Mol-chlach. High 4F 68
Mold. Flin 4M 33
Molehill Green. Essx 1B 22
Molescroft. E Yor 3H 43
Molesden. Nmbd 3E 54
Molesworth. Cambs 4H 29
Moll. High 3G 69
Molland. Devn 3H 7
Mollington. Ches W 2B 34
Mollington. Oxon 7B 28
Mollinsburn. N Lan 2F 58
Monachty. Cdgn 6E 24
Monachyle. Stir 6J 65
Monar Lodge. High 1C 70
Monaughty. Powy 6M 25
Monea. Ferm 6B 92
Monewden. Suff 6J 31
Moneydie. Per 5D 66
Moneyglass. Ant 4G 93
Moneymore. M Ulst 4F 93
Moneyneany. M Ulst 4E 92
Moneyreagh. Lis 5J 93
Moneyrow Green. Wind 6F 20
Moneyslane. Arm 7H 93
Moniaive. Dum 2B 52
Monifieth. Ang 4J 67
Monikie. Ang 4J 67
Monimail. Fife 6F 66
Monington. Pemb 2H 15
Monk Bretton. S Yor 7A 42
Monken Hadley. G Lon 4K 21
Monk Fryston. N Yor 5C 42
Monk Hesleden. Dur 8H 55
Monkhide. Here 7E 26
Monkhill. Cumb 6H 53
Monkhopton. Shrp 2E 26
Monkland. Here 6C 26
Monkleigh. Devn 3D 6
Monknash. V Glam 7J 17
Monkokehampton. Devn 5E 6
Monkseaton. Tyne 4G 55
Monks Eleigh. Suff 7F 30
Monk's Gate. W Sus 3K 11
Monk's Heath. Ches E 2G 35
Monk Sherborne. Hants 8D 20
Monkshill. Abers 1G 73
Monksilver. Som 2K 7
Monks Kirby. Warw 3B 28
Monk Soham. Suff 5J 31
Monk Soham Green. Suff 5J 31
Monkspath. W Mid 4K 27
Monks Risborough. Buck 3F 20
Monksthorpe. Linc 3M 37
Monkstown. Ant 4H 93
Monk Street. Essx 1C 22
Monkswood. Mon 3B 18
Monkton. Devn 5L 7
Monkton. Kent 7J 23
Monkton. Pemb 6F 14
Monkton. S Ayr 7B 58
Monkton Combe. Bath 7F 18
Monkton Deverill. Wilts 2G 9
Monkton Farleigh. Wilts 7G 19
Monkton Heathfield. Som 3A 8
Monktonhill. S Ayr 7B 58
Monkton Up Wimborne.
Dors 4J 9
Monkton Wyld. Dors 6B 8
Monkwearmouth. Tyne 6G 55
Monkwood. Dors 6C 8
Monkwood. Hants 2D 10
Monmarsh. Here 7D 26
Monmouth. Mon 2D 18
Monnington on Wye. Here 7B 26
Monreith. Dum 7J 51
Montacute. Som 4C 8
Monteith. Arm 6G 93
Montford. Arg 3L 57
Montford. Shrp 8C 34
Montford Bridge. Shrp 8C 34
Montgarrie. Abers 4E 72
Montgarswood. E Ayr 7D 58
Montgomery. Powy 3M 25
Montgreenan. N Ayr 5B 58
Montrave. Fife 7G 67
Montrose. Ang 2L 67
Monxton. Hants 1M 9
Monyash. Derbs 3K 35
Monymusk. Abers 4F 72
Monzie. Per 5B 66
Moodiesburn. N Lan 2E 58
Moon's Green. Kent 3E 12
Moonzie. Fife 6G 67
Moor. Som 4C 8
The Moor. Kent 3D 12
Moor Allerton. W Yor 4L 41
Moorbath. Dors 6C 8
Moorbrae. Shet 5J 91
Moorby. Linc 3K 37
Moorcot. Here 6B 26
Moor Crichel. Dors 5H 9
Moor Cross. Devn 6J 5
Moordown. Bour 6J 9
Moore. Hal 1D 34
Moor End. E Yor 4F 42
Moorend. Dum 4G 53
Moorend. Glos
nr. Dursley 3F 18
nr. Gloucester 2G 19
Moorends. S Yor 6D 42
Moorfields. ME Ant 4G 93
Moorgate. S Yor 8B 42
Moor Green. Wilts 7G 19
Moorgreen. Hants 4B 10
Moorgreen. Notts 5B 36
Moorhaigh. Notts 3C 36
Moorhall. Derbs 2M 35
Moorhampton. Here 7B 26
Moorhouse. Cumb
nr. Carlisle 6H 53
nr. Wigton 6G 53
Moorhouse. Notts 3E 36
Moorhouse. Surr 8M 21
Moorhouses. Linc 4K 37
Moorland. Som 2B 8
Moorlinch. Som 2C 8
Moor Monkton. N Yor 2C 42
Moor of Granary. Mor 8L 79
Moor Row. Cumb
nr. Whitehaven 3K 45
nr. Wigton 7G 53
Moorsholm. Red C 4D 48
Moorside. Dors 4F 8
Moorside. G Man 7H 41
Moortown. Devn 6C 6
Moortown. Hants 5K 9
Moortown. IOW 7B 10
Moortown. Linc 8H 43
Moortown. M Ulst 5F 93
Moortown. Telf 8E 34
Moortown. W Yor 4M 41
Morangie. High 5H 79
Morar. High 6H 69
Morborne. Cambs 2J 29
Morchard Bishop. Devn 5G 7
Morcombelake. Dors 6C 8
Morcott. Rut 1G 29
Morda. Shrp 7A 34
Morden. G Lon 7K 21
Mordiford. Here 8D 26
Mordon. Dur 3M 47
More. Shrp 2B 26
Morebath. Devn 3J 7
Morebattle. Bord 7E 60
Morecambe. Lanc 1C 40
Morefield. High 4B 78
Moreleigh. Devn 6K 5
Morenish. Per 4K 65
Moresby Parks. Cumb 3J 45
Morestead. Hants 3C 10
Moreton. Dors 7G 9
Moreton. Essx 3B 22
Moreton. Here 5D 26
Moreton. Mers 8A 40
Moreton. Oxon 3D 20
Moreton. Staf 8F 34
Moreton Corbet. Shrp 7D 34
Moretonhampstead. Devn 7G 7
Moreton-in-Marsh. Glos 8L 27
Moreton Jeffries. Here 7E 26
Moreton Morrell. Warw 6M 27
Moreton on Lugg. Here 7D 26
Moreton Pinkney. Nptn 7C 28
Moreton Say. Shrp 6E 34
Moreton Valence. Glos 3F 18
Morfa. Cdgn 1K 15
Morfa Bach. Carm 5K 15
Morfa Bychan. Gwyn 7E 32
Morfa Glas. Neat 4H 17
Morfa Nefyn. Gwyn 6B 32
Morganstown. Card 6L 17
Morgan's Vale. Wilts 3K 9
Morham. E Lot 2C 60
Moriah. Cdgn 5F 24
Morland. Cumb 3D 46
Morley. Ches E 1G 35
Morley. Derbs 5A 36
Morley. Dur 3K 47
Morley. W Yor 5L 41
Morley St Botolph. Norf 2G 31
Morningside. Edin 2L 59
Morningside. N Lan 4G 59
Morningthorpe. Norf 2J 31
Morpeth. Nmbd 3F 54
Morrey. Staf 8K 35
Morridge Side. Staf 4J 35
Morridge Top. Staf 3J 35
Morrington. Dum 3C 52
Morris Green. Essx 8D 30
Morriston. Swan 5F 16
Morston. Norf 5G 39
Mortehoe. Devn 1D 6
Morthen. S Yor 1B 36
Mortimer. W Ber 7D 20
Mortimer's Cross. Here 5C 26
Mortimer West End. Hants 7D 20
Mortomley. S Yor 8M 41
Morton. Cumb
nr. Calthwaite 8J 53
nr. Carlisle 6H 53
Morton. Derbs 3B 36
Morton. Linc
nr. Bourne 7H 37
nr. Gainsborough 8F 42
nr. Lincoln 3F 36
Morton. Norf 8H 39
Morton. Notts 4E 36
Morton. Shrp 7A 34
Morton. S Glo 4E 18
Morton Bagot. Warw 5K 27
Morton Mill. Shrp 7D 34
Morton-on-Swale. N Yor 6M 47
Morton Tinmouth. Dur 3K 47
Morvah. Corn 5H 3
Morval. Corn 6E 4
Morvich. High
nr. Golspie 3H 79
nr. Shiel Bridge 3L 69
Morvil. Pemb 3G 15
Morville. Shrp 2E 26
Morwenstow. Corn 4B 6
Morwick. Nmbd 1F 54
Mosborough. S Yor 1B 36
Moscow. E Ayr 5C 58
Mose. Shrp 2F 26
Mosedale. Cumb 8H 53
Moseley. W Mid
nr. Birmingham 3J 27
nr. Wolverhampton 1H 27
Moseley. Worc 6G 27
Moss. Arg 3E 62
Moss. High 1A 64
Moss. S Yor 6C 42
Moss. Wrex 4B 34
Mossatt. Abers 4D 72
Moss Bank. Mers 8D 40
Mossbank. Shet 6J 91
Mossblown. S Ayr 7C 58
Mossbrow. G Man 1F 34
Mossburnford. Bord 8D 60
Mossdale. Dum 4A 52
Mossedge. Cumb 5J 53
Mossend. N Lan 3F 58
Mossgate. Staf 6H 35
Moss Lane. Ches E 2H 35
Mossley. Ant 4H 93
Mossley. Ches E 3G 35
Mossley. G Man 7H 41
Mossley Hill. Mers 1B 34
Moss of Barmuckity. Mor 7B 80
Mosspark. Glas 3D 58
Mosspaul. Bord 2J 53
Moss Side. Cumb 6F 52
Moss Side. G Man 8G 41
Moss Side. Lanc
nr. Blackpool 4B 40
nr. Preston 5D 40
Moss Side. Mers 7B 40
Moss-Side. Caus 2G 93
Moss-side. High 8J 79
Moss-side of Cairness.
Abers 7K 81
Mosstodloch. Mor 7C 80
Mosswood. Nmbd 6D 54
Mossy Lea. Lanc 6D 40
Mosterton. Dors 5C 8
Moston. Shrp 7D 34
Moston Green. Ches E 3F 34
Mostyn. Flin 2L 33
Mostyn Quay. Flin 2L 33
Motcombe. Dors 3G 9
Mothecombe. Devn 7J 5
Motherby. Cumb 3C 46
Motherwell. N Lan 4F 58
Mottingham. G Lon 6M 21
Mottisfont. Hants 3M 9
Mottistone. IOW 7B 10
Mottram in Longdendale.
G Man 8H 41
Mottram St Andrew.
Ches E 2G 35
Mott's Mill. E Sus 2B 12
Mouldsworth. Ches W 2D 34
Moulin. Per 2C 66
Moulsecoomb. Brig 5L 11
Moulsford. Oxon 5C 20
Moulsoe. Mil 7G 29
Moulton. Ches W 3E 34
Moulton. Linc 7L 37
Moulton. Nptn 5E 28
Moulton. N Yor 5L 47
Moulton. Suff 5C 30
Moulton. V Glam 7K 17
Moulton Chapel. Linc 8K 37
Moulton Eaugate. Linc 8L 37
Moulton St Mary. Norf 1K 31
Moulton Seas End. Linc 7L 37
Mount. Corn
nr. Bodmin 5D 4
nr. Newquay 3L 3
Mountain Ash. Rhon 5K 17
Mountain Cross. Bord 5K 59
Mountain Street. Kent 8G 23
Mountain Water. Pemb 4F 14
Mount Ambrose. Corn 4L 3
Mountbenger. Bord 7M 59
Mountblow. W Dun 2C 58
Mount Bures. Essx 8F 30
Mountfield. E Sus 3D 12
Mountfield. Ferm 5D 92
Mountgerald. High 7F 78
Mount Hawke. Corn 4L 3
Mount High. High 7G 79
Mountjoy. Corn 5A 4
Mountjoy. Ferm 5D 92
Mount Lothian. Midl 4L 59
Mountnessing. Essx 4C 22
Mountnorris. Arm 7F 93
Mounton. Mon 4D 18
Mount Pleasant. Buck 8D 28
Mount Pleasant. Ches E 4G 35
Mount Pleasant. Derbs
nr. Derby 5M 35
nr. Swadlincote 8L 35
Mount Pleasant. E Sus 4M 11
Mount Pleasant. Hants 6L 9
Mount Pleasant. Norf 2F 30
Mount Skippett. Oxon 2A 20
Mountsorrel. Leics 8C 36
Mount Stuart. Arg 4L 57
Mousehole. Corn 6H 3
Mouswald. Dum 4E 52
Mow Cop. Ches E 4G 35
Mowden. Darl 4L 47
Mowhaugh. Bord 7F 60
Mowmacre Hill. Leic 1C 28
Mowsley. Leics 3D 28
Moy. High 2H 71
Moy. M Ulst 6F 93
Moygashel. M Ulst 5F 93
Moylgrove. Pemb 2H 15
Moy Lodge. High 7E 70
Muasdale. Arg 5F 56
Muchalls. Abers 6J 73
Much Birch. Here 8D 26
Much Cowarne. Here 7E 26
Much Dewchurch. Here 8C 26
Muchelney. Som 3C 8
Muchelney Ham. Som 3C 8
Much Hadham. Herts 2M 21
Much Hoole. Lanc 5C 40
Muchlarnick. Corn 6E 4
Much Marcle. Here 8E 26
Muchrachd. High 2C 70
Much Wenlock. Shrp 1E 26
Mucking. Thur 5C 22
Muckle Breck. Shet 1F 90
Muckleford. Dors 6E 8
Mucklestone. Staf 6F 34
Muckleton. Norf 6E 38
Muckleton. Shrp 7D 34
Muckley. Shrp 2E 26
Muckley Corner. Staf 1J 27
Muckton. Linc 1L 37
Mudale. High 8H 85
Muddiford. Devn 2E 6
Mudeford. Dors 6K 9
Mudford. Som 4D 8
Mudgley. Som 1C 8
Mugdock. Stir 2D 58
Mugeary. High 2F 68
Muggington. Derbs 5L 35
Muggintonlane End. Derbs 5L 35
Muggleswick. Dur 6D 54
Mugswell. Surr 8K 21
Muie. High 3G 79
Muirden. Abers 8G 81
Muirdrum. Ang 4J 67
Muiredge. Per 5F 66
Muirend. Glas 3D 58
Muirhead. Ang 4G 67
Muirhead. Fife 7F 66
Muirhead. N Lan 3E 58
Muirhouses. Falk 1J 59
Muirkirk. E Ayr 7E 58
Muir of Alford. Abers 4E 72
Muir of Fairburn. High 8E 78
Muir of Fowlis. Abers 4E 72
Muir of Miltonduff. Mor 8A 80
Muir of Ord. High 8F 78
Muir of Tarradale. High 8F 78
Muirshearlich. High 7B 70
Muirtack. Abers 2J 73
Muirton. High 7H 79
Muirton. Per 5E 66
Muirton of Ardblair. Per 3E 66
Muirtown. Per 6C 66
Muiryfold. Abers 8G 81
Muker. N Yor 6H 47
Mulbarton. Norf 1H 31
Mulben. Mor 8C 80
Mulindry. Arg 4C 56
Mulla. Shet 1E 90
Mullach Charlabhaigh.
W Isl 7F 82
Mullacott. Devn 1E 6
Mullaghbane. New M 7F 93
Mullaghboy. ME Ant 3J 93
Mullaghglass. New M 7G 93
Mullion. Corn 7K 3
Mullion Cove. Corn 7K 3
Mumbles. Swan 6F 16
Mumby. Linc 2B 38
Munderfield Row. Here 6E 26
Munderfield Stocks. Here 6E 26
Mundesley. Norf 6K 39
Mundford. Norf 2E 30
Mundham. Norf 2K 31
Mundon. Essx 3E 22
Munerigie. High 5C 70
Muness. Shet 3L 91
Mungasdale. High 4L 77
Mungrisdale. Cumb 8H 53
Munlochy. High 8G 79
Munsley. Here 7E 26
Munslow. Shrp 3D 26
Murchington. Devn 7F 6
Murcot. Worc 7J 27
Murcott. Oxon 2C 20
Murdishaw. Hal 1D 34
Murieston. W Lot 3J 59
Murkle. High 5C 86
Murlaggan. High 6M 69
Murra. Orkn 1D 86
The Murray. S Lan 4E 58
Murrayfield. Edin 2L 59
Murrell Green. Hants 8E 20
Murroes. Ang 4H 67
Murrow. Cambs 1L 29
Mursley. Buck 1F 20
Murthly. Per 4D 66
Murton. Cumb 3F 46
Murton. Dur 7G 55
Murton. Nmbd 5G 61
Murton. Swan 6E 16
Murton. York 2D 42
Musbury. Devn 6A 8
Muscoates. N Yor 7D 48
Muscott. Nptn 5D 28
Musselburgh. E Lot 2M 59
Muston. Leics 6F 36
Muston. N Yor 8H 49
Mustow Green. Worc 4G 27
Muswell Hill. G Lon 5K 21
Mutehill. Dum 7A 52
Mutford. Suff 3L 31
Muthill. Per 6B 66
Mutterton. Devn 5K 7
Muxton. Telf 8F 34
Mwmbwls. Swan 6F 16
Mybster. High 6C 86
Myddfai. Carm 1G 17
Myddle. Shrp 7C 34
Mydroilyn. Cdgn 1L 15
Myerscough. Lanc 4C 40
Mylor Bridge. Corn 5M 3
Mylor Churchtown. Corn 5M 3
Mynachlog-ddu. Pemb 3H 15
Mynydd-bach. Mon 4C 18
Mynydd Isa. Flin 3A 34
Mynyddislwyn. Cphy 5L 17
Mynydd Llandegai. Gwyn 4F 32
Mynydd Mechell. IOA 1C 32
Mynydd-y-briw. Powy 8L 33
Mynyddygarreg. Carm 6L 15
Mynytho. Gwyn 7C 32
Myrebird. Abers 6G 73
Myrelandhorn. High 6D 86
Mytchett. Surr 8F 20
The Mythe. Glos 8G 27
Mytholmroyd. W Yor 5J 41
Myton-on-Swale. N Yor 1B 42
Mytton. Shrp 8C 34

N

Naast. High 5K 77
Na Buirgh. W Isl 4B 76
Naburn. York 3C 42
Nab Wood. W Yor 4K 41
Nackington. Kent 8H 23
Nacton. Suff 7J 31
Nafferton. E Yor 2H 43
Na Gearrannan. W Isl 7E 82
Nailbridge. Glos 2E 18
Nailsbourne. Som 3M 7
Nailsea. N Som 6C 18
Nailstone. Leics 1B 28
Nailsworth. Glos 4G 19
Nairn. High 8J 79
Nalderswood. Surr 1K 11
Nancegollan. Corn 5K 3
Nancledra. Corn 5H 3
Nangreaves. G Man 6G 41
Nanhyfer. Pemb 3G 15
Nannerch. Flin 4L 33
Nanpantan. Leics 8C 36
Nanpean. Corn 6B 4
Nanstallon. Corn 5C 4
Nant-ddu. Powy 3K 17
Nanternis. Cdgn 1K 15
Nantgaredig. Carm 4L 15
Nantgarw. Rhon 6L 17
Nant Glas. Powy 6J 25
Nantglyn. Den 4K 33
Nantgwyn. Powy 5J 25
Nantlle. Gwyn 5E 32
Nantmawr. Shrp 7A 34
Nantmel. Powy 6K 25
Nantmor. Gwyn 6F 32
Nant Peris. Gwyn 5F 32
Nantwich. Ches E 4E 34
Nant-y-bai. Carm 8G 25
Nant-y-bwch. Blae 3L 17
Nant-y-Derry. Mon 3B 18
Nant-y-dugoed. Powy 1J 25
Nant-y-felin. Cnwy 3F 32
Nantyffyllon. B'end 5H 17
Nantyglo. Blae 3L 17
Nant-y-meichiaid. Powy 1L 25
Nant-y-moel. B'end 5J 17
Nant-y-pandy. Cnwy 3F 32
Naphill. Buck 4F 20
Nappa. N Yor 2G 41
Napton on the Hill. Warw 5B 28
Narberth. Pemb 5H 15
Narberth Bridge. Pemb 5H 15
Narborough. Leics 2C 28
Narborough. Norf 8D 38
Narkurs. Corn 6F 4
The Narth. Mon 3D 18
Narthwaite. Cumb 6F 46
Nasareth. Gwyn 5D 32
Naseby. Nptn 4D 28
Nash. Buck 8E 28
Nash. Here 5B 26
Nash. Kent 8J 23
Nash. Newp 5B 18
Nash. Shrp 4E 26
Nash Lee. Buck 3F 20
Nassington. Nptn 2H 29
Nasty. Herts 1L 21
Natcott. Devn 3B 6
Nateby. Cumb 5F 46
Nateby. Lanc 3C 40
Nately Scures. Hants 8E 20
Natland. Cumb 7D 46
Naughton. Suff 7G 31
Naunton. Glos 1K 19
Naunton. Worc 8G 27
Naunton Beauchamp. Worc 6H 27
Navenby. Linc 4G 37
Navestock. Essx 4B 22
Navestock Side. Essx 4B 22
Navidale. High 2L 79
Nawton. N Yor 7D 48
Nayland. Suff 8F 30
Nazeing. Essx 3M 21
Neacroft. Hants 6K 9
Nealhouse. Cumb 6H 53
Neal's Green. Warw 3M 27
Near Sawrey. Cumb 6B 46
Neasden. G Lon 5K 21
Neasham. Darl 4M 47
Neath. Neat 5G 17
Neath Abbey. Neat 5G 17
Neatishead. Norf 7K 39
Neaton. Norf 1F 30
Nebo. Cdgn 6E 24
Nebo. Cnwy 5H 33
Nebo. Gwyn 5D 32
Nebo. IOA 1D 32
Necton. Norf 1E 30
Nedd. High 8D 84
Nedderton. Nmbd 3F 54
Nedging. Suff 7G 31
Nedging Tye. Suff 7G 31
Needham. Norf 3J 31
Needham Market. Suff 6G 31
Needham Street. Suff 5D 30
Needingworth. Cambs 4L 29
Needwood. Staf 7K 35
Neen Savage. Shrp 4E 26
Neen Sollars. Shrp 4E 26
Neenton. Shrp 3E 26
Nefyn. Gwyn 6C 32
Neilston. E Ren 4C 58
Neithrop. Oxon 7B 28
Nelly Andrews Green.
Powy 1A 26
Nelson. Cphy 5L 17
Nelson. Lanc 4G 41
Nelson Village. Nmbd 4F 54
Nemphlar. S Lan 5G 59
Nempnett Thrubwell. Bath 7D 18
Nene Terrace. Linc 1K 29
Nenthall. Cumb 7A 54
Nenthead. Cumb 7A 54
Nenthorn. Bord 6D 60
Nercwys. Flin 4M 33
Neribus. Arg 4B 56
Nerston. S Lan 4E 58
Nesbit. Nmbd 6G 61
Nesfield. N Yor 3J 41
Ness. Ches W 2B 34
Nesscliffe. Shrp 8B 34
Ness of Tenston. Orkn 8B 88
Neston. Ches W 2A 34
Neston. Wilts 7G 19
Nethanfoot. S Lan 5G 59
Nether Alderley. Ches E 2G 35
Netheravon. Wilts 1K 9
Nether Blainslie. Bord 5C 60
Netherbrae. Abers 8G 81
Netherbrough. Orkn 8C 88
Nether Broughton. Leics 7D 36
Netherburn. S Lan 5G 59
Nether Burrow. Lanc 8E 46
Netherbury. Dors 6C 8
Netherby. Cumb 4H 53
Nether Careston. Ang 2J 67
Nether Cerne. Dors 6E 8
Nether Compton. Dors 4D 8
Nethercote. Glos 1K 19
Nethercote. Warw 5C 28
Nethercott. Devn 2D 6
Nethercott. Oxon 1B 20
Nether Dallachy. Mor 7C 80
Nether Durdie. Per 5F 66
Nether End. Derbs 2L 35
Netherend. Glos 3D 18
Nether Exe. Devn 5J 7
Netherfield. E Sus 4D 12
Netherfield. Notts 5D 36
Nethergate. Norf 7G 39
Netherhampton. Wilts 3K 9
Nether Handley. Derbs 2B 36
Nether Haugh. S Yor 8B 42
Nether Heage. Derbs 4A 36
Nether Heyford. Nptn 6D 28
Netherhouses. Cumb 7A 46
Nether Howcleugh. S Lan 8J 59
Nether Kellet. Lanc 1D 40
Nether Kinmundy. Abers 1K 73
Netherland Green. Staf 6K 35
Nether Langwith. Notts 2C 36
Netherlaw. Dum 7B 52
Netherley. Abers 6H 73
Nethermill. Dum 3E 52
Nethermills. Mor 8E 80
Nether Moor. Derbs 3A 36
Nether Padley. Derbs 2L 35
Netherplace. E Ren 4D 58
Nether Poppleton. York 2C 42
Netherseal. Derbs 8L 35
Nether Silton. N Yor 6B 48
Nether Stowey. Som 2L 7
Nether Street. Essx 2B 22
Netherstreet. Wilts 7H 19
Netherthird. E Ayr 8D 58
Netherthong. W Yor 7K 41
Netherton. Ang 2J 67
Netherton. Cumb 8E 52
Netherton. Devn 8H 7
Netherton. Hants 8A 20
Netherton. Here 1D 18
Netherton. Mers 8B 40
Netherton. N Lan 4F 58
Netherton. Nmbd 1C 54
Netherton. Per 2E 66
Netherton. Shrp 3F 26
Netherton. Stir 2D 58
Netherton. W Mid 3H 27
Netherton. W Yor
nr. Armitage Bridge 6K 41
nr. Horbury 6L 41
Netherton. Worc 7H 27
Nethertown. Cumb 4J 45
Nethertown. High 4E 86
Nethertown. Staf 8K 35
Nether Urquhart. Fife 7E 66
Nether Wallop. Hants 2M 9
Nether Wasdale. Cumb 4L 45
Nether Welton. Cumb 7H 53
Nether Westcote. Glos 1L 19

Otley—Poundland

Otley. Suff 6J 31
Otley. W Yor 3L 41
Otterbourne. Hants 3B 10
Otterburn. Nmbd 2B 54
Otterburn. N Yor 2G 41
Otterburn Camp. Nmbd 2B 54
Otterburn Hall. Nmbd 2B 54
Otter Ferry. Arg 1J 57
Otterford. Som 4M 7
Otterham. Corn 6A 6
Otterhampton. Som 1M 7
Otterham Quay. Medw 7E 22
Ottershaw. Surr 7H 21
Otterspool. Mers 1B 34
Otterswick. Shet 5K 91
Otterton. Devn 7K 7
Otterwood. Hants 5B 10
Ottery St Mary. Devn 6K 7
Ottinge. Kent 1H 13
Ottringham. E Yor 5K 43
Oughterby. Cumb 6G 53
Oughtershaw. N Yor 7G 47
Oughterside. Cumb 7F 52
Oughtibridge. S Yor 8M 41
Oughtrington. Warr 1E 34
Oulston. N Yor 8C 48
Oulton. Cumb 6G 53
Oulton. Norf 7H 39
Oulton. Staf
nr. Gnosall Heath 7F 34
nr. Stone 6H 35
Oulton. Suff 2M 31
Oulton. W Yor 5A 42
Oulton Broad. Suff 2M 31
Oulton Street. Norf 7H 39
Oundle. Nptn 3H 29
Ousby. Cumb 8L 53
Ousdale. High 2L 79
Ousden. Suff 6D 30
Ousefleet. E Yor 5F 42
Ouston. Dur 6F 54
Ouston. Nmbd
nr. Bearsbridge 6A 54
nr. Stamfordham 4D 54
Outer Hope. Devn 7J 5
Outertown. Orkn 8B 88
Outgate. Cumb 6B 46
Outhgill. Cumb 5F 46
Outlands. Staf 6F 34
Outlane. W Yor 6J 41
Out Newton. E Yor 5L 43
Out Rawcliffe. Lanc 3C 40
Outwell. Norf 1B 30
Outwick. Hants 4K 9
Outwood. Surr 1L 11
Outwood. W Yor 5M 41
Outwood. Worc 4H 27
Outwoods. Leics 8B 36
Outwoods. Staf 8F 34
Ouzlewell Green. W Yor 5M 41
Ovenden. W Yor 5J 41
Over. Cambs 4L 29
Over. Ches W 3E 34
Over. Glos 2G 19
Over. S Glo 5D 18
Overbister. Orkn 5F 88
Over Burrows. Derbs 6L 35
Overbury. Worc 8H 27
Overcombe. Dors 7E 8
Over Compton. Dors 4D 8
Over End. Cambs 2H 29
Over Finlarg. Ang 3H 67
Over Green. Warw 2K 27
Overgreen. Derbs 2M 35
Over Haddon. Derbs 3L 35
Over Hulton. G Man 7E 40
Over Kellet. Lanc 8D 46
Over Kiddington. Oxon 1B 20
Overleigh. Som 2C 8
Overley. Staf 8K 35
Over Monnow. Mon 2D 18
Over Norton. Oxon 1M 19
Over Peover. Ches E 2F 34
Overpool. Ches W 2B 34
Overscaig. High 1E 78
Overseal. Derbs 8L 35
Over Silton. N Yor 6B 48
Oversland. Kent 8G 23
Overstone. Nptn 5F 28
Over Stowey. Som 2L 7
Overstrand. Norf 5J 39
Over Stratton. Som 4C 8
Over Street. Wilts 2J 9
Overthorpe. Nptn 7B 28
Overton. Aber 4H 73
Overton. Ches W 2D 34
Overton. Hants 1C 10
Overton. High 8D 86
Overton. Lanc 2C 40
Overton. N Yor 2C 42
Overton. Shrp
nr. Bridgnorth 3E 26
nr. Ludlow 4D 26
Overton. Swan 8L 15
Overton. W Yor 6L 41
Overton. Wrex 5B 34
Overtown. Lanc 8E 46
Overtown. N Lan 4G 59
Overtown. Swin 6K 19
Over Wallop. Hants 2L 9
Over Whitacre. Warw 2L 27
Over Worton. Oxon 1B 20
Oving. Buck 1E 20
Oving. W Sus 5G 11
Ovingdean. Brig 5L 11
Ovingham. Nmbd 5D 54
Ovington. Dur 4K 47
Ovington. Essx 7D 30
Ovington. Hants 2C 10
Ovington. Norf 1F 30
Ovington. Nmbd 5D 54
Owen's Bank. Staf 7L 35
Ower. Hants
nr. Holbury 5B 10
nr. Totton 4M 9
Owermoigne. Dors 7F 8
Owlbury. Shrp 2B 26
Owler Bar. Derbs 2L 35
Owlerton. S Yor 8M 41
Owlsmoor. Brac 7F 20
Owlswick. Buck 3E 20
Owmby. Linc 7H 43
Owmby-by-Spital. Linc 1H 37
Ownham. W Ber 6B 20
Owrytn. Wrex 5B 34
Owslebury. Hants 3C 10
Owston. Leics 1E 28
Owston. S Yor 6C 42
Owston Ferry. N Lin 7F 42
Owstwick. E Yor 4K 43
Owthorne. E Yor 5L 43
Owthorpe. Notts 6D 36
Owton Manor. Hart 3B 48
Oxborough. Norf 1D 30
Oxbridge. Dors 6C 8
Oxcombe. Linc 2L 37
Oxen End. Essx 1C 22
Oxenhall. Glos 1F 18
Oxenholme. Cumb 6D 46
Oxenhope. W Yor 4J 41
Oxen Park. Cumb 7B 46
Oxenpill. Som 1C 8
Oxenton. Glos 8H 27
Oxenwood. Wilts 8M 19
Oxford. Oxon 114 (3C 20)
Oxgangs. Edin 3L 59
Oxhey. Herts 4J 21
Oxhill. Warw 7M 27
Oxley. W Mid 1H 27
Oxley Green. Essx 2F 22
Oxley's Green. E Sus 3C 12
Oxlode. Cambs 3A 30
Oxnam. Bord 8E 60
Oxshott. Surr 7J 21
Oxspring. S Yor 7L 41
Oxted. Surr 8L 21
Oxton. Mers 1B 34
Oxton. N Yor 3C 42
Oxton. Notts 4D 36
Oxton. Bord 4B 60
Oxwich. Swan 8L 15
Oxwich Green. Swan 8L 15
Oxwick. Norf 7F 38
Oykel Bridge. High 3D 78
Oyne. Abers 3F 72
Oystermouth. Swan 6F 16
Ozleworth. Glos 4F 18

P

Pabail Iarach. W Isl 8J 83
Pabail Uarach. W Isl 8J 83
Pachesham Park. Surr 8J 21
Packers Hill. Dors 4F 8
Packington. Leics 8A 36
Packmoor. Stoke 4G 35
Packmores. Warw 5L 27
Packwood. W Mid 4K 27
Packwood Gullet. W Mid 4K 27
Padanaram. Ang 2H 67
Padbury. Buck 8E 28
Paddington. G Lon 5K 21
Paddington. Warr 1E 34
Paddlesworth. Kent 2H 13
Paddock. Kent 8F 22
Paddockhole. Dum 3G 53
Paddock Wood. Kent 1C 12
Paddolgreen. Shrp 6D 34
Padeswood. Flin 3A 34
Padiham. Lanc 4F 40
Padside. N Yor 2K 41
Padson. Devn 6E 6
Padstow. Corn 4B 4
Padworth. W Ber 7D 20
Page Bank. Dur 8F 54
Pagham. W Sus 6F 10
Paglesham Churchend.
Essx 4F 22
Paglesham Eastend. Essx 4F 22
Paibeil. W Isl
on North Uist 7J 75
on Taransay 4B 76
Paiblesgearraidh. W Isl 7J 75
Paignton. Torb 5L 5
Pailton. Warw 3B 28
Paine's Corner. E Sus 3C 12
Painleyhill. Staf 6J 35
Painscastle. Powy 8L 25
Painshawfield. Nmbd 5D 54
Painsthorpe. E Yor 2F 42
Painswick. Glos 3G 19
Painter's Forstal. Kent 8F 22
Painthorpe. W Yor 6M 41
Pairc Shiaboist. W Isl 7F 82
Paisley. Ren 3C 58
Pakefield. Suff 2M 31
Pakenham. Suff 5F 30
Pale. Gwyn 7J 33
Palehouse Common. E Sus 4A 12
Palestine. Hants 1L 9
Paley Street. Wind 6F 20
Palgowan. Dum 3J 51
Palgrave. Suff 4H 31
Pallington. Dors 6F 8
Palmarsh. Kent 2H 13
Palmer Moor. Derbs 6K 35
Palmers Cross. W Mid 1G 27
Palmerstown. V Glam 8L 17
Palnackie. Dum 6C 52
Palnure. Dum 5K 51
Palterton. Derbs 3B 36
Pamber End. Hants 8D 20
Pamber Green. Hants 8D 20
Pamber Heath. Hants 7D 20
Pamington. Glos 8H 27
Pamphill. Dors 5H 9
Pampisford. Cambs 7A 30
Panborough. Som 1C 8
Panbride. Ang 4J 67
Pancrasweek. Devn 5B 6
Pandy. Gwyn
nr. Bala 7H 33
nr. Tywyn 2F 24
Pandy. Mon 1B 18
Pandy. Powy 2J 25
Pandy. Wrex 7L 33
Pandy Tudur. Cnwy 4H 33
Panfield. Essx 1D 22
Pangbourne. W Ber 6D 20
Pannal. N Yor 2M 41
Pannal Ash. N Yor 2L 41
Pannanich. Abers 6C 72
Pant. Shrp 7A 34
Pant. Wrex 5A 34
Pantasaph. Flin 3L 33
Pant Glas. Gwyn 6D 32
Pant-glas. Shrp 6A 34
Pantgwyn. Carm 2E 16
Pantgwyn. Cdgn 2J 15
Pant-lasau. Swan 4F 16
Panton. Linc 2J 37
Pant-pastynog. Den 4K 33
Pantperthog. Gwyn 2G 25
Pant-teg. Carm 4L 15
Pant-y-Caws. Carm 4H 15
Pant-y-dwr. Powy 5J 25
Pant-y-ffridd. Powy 2L 25
Pantyffynnon. Carm 3F 16
Pantygasseg. Torf 3A 18
Pant-y-llyn. Carm 3F 16
Pant-yr-awel. B'end 6J 17
Pant y Wacco. Flin 3L 33
Panxworth. Norf 8K 39
Papa Stour Airport. Shet 2B 90
Papa Westray Airport. Orkn 4D 88
Papcastle. Cumb 8F 52
Papigoe. High 6E 86
Papil. Shet 4D 90
Papple. E Lot 2C 60
Papplewick. Notts 4C 36
Papworth Everard. Cambs 5K 29
Papworth St Agnes. Cambs 5K 29
Par. Corn 6C 4
Paramour Street. Kent 7J 23
Parbold. Lanc 6C 40
Parbrook. Som 2D 8
Parbrook. W Sus 3H 11
Parc. Gwyn 7H 33
Parcllyn. Cdgn 1J 15
Parc-Seymour. Newp 4C 18
Pardown. Hants 1C 10
Pardshaw. Cumb 2K 45
Parham. Suff 5K 31
Park. Abers 6G 73
Park. Arg 3D 64
Park. Derr 3D 92
Park. Dum 2D 52
Park Bottom. Corn 4K 3
Parkburn. Abers 2G 73
Park Corner. E Sus 2B 12
Park Corner. Oxon 5D 20
Park End. Nmbd 4B 54
Parkend. Glos 3E 18
Parkeston. Essx 8J 31
Parkfield. Corn 5F 4
Park Gate. Hants 5C 10
Park Gate. Worc 4H 27
Parkgate. Ant 4H 93
Parkgate. Ches W 2A 34
Parkgate. Cumb 7G 53
Parkgate. Dum 3E 52
Parkgate. Surr 1K 11
Parkhall. W Dun 2C 58
Parkham. Devn 3C 6
Parkham Ash. Devn 3C 6
Parkhead. Cumb 7H 53
Parkhead. Glas 3E 58
Park Hill. Mers 7C 40
Parkhouse. Mon 3D 18
Parkhurst. IOW 6B 10
Park Lane. G Man 7F 40
Park Lane. Staf 1G 27
Park Mill. W Yor 6L 41
Parkmill. Swan 8M 15
Parkneuk. Abers 8G 73
Parkside. N Lan 4G 59
Parkstone. Pool 6J 9
Park Street. Herts 3J 21
Park Street. W Sus 2J 11
Park Town. Oxon 3C 20
Park Village. Nmbd 5L 53
Parkway. Here 8F 26
Parley Cross. Dors 6J 9
Parmoor. Buck 5E 20
Parr. Mers 8D 40
Parracombe. Devn 1F 6
Parrog. Pemb 3G 15
Parsonage Green. Essx 2D 22
Parsonby. Cumb 8F 52
Parson Cross. S Yor 8M 41
Parson Drove. Cambs 1L 29
Partick. Glas 3D 58
Partington. G Man 8F 40
Partney. Linc 3M 37
Parton. Cumb
nr. Whitehaven 2J 45
nr. Wigton 6G 53
Parton. Dum 4A 52
Partridge Green. W Sus 4J 11
Parwich. Derbs 4K 35
Passenham. Nptn 8E 28
Passfield. Hants 2F 10
Passingford Bridge. Essx 4B 22
Paston. Norf 6K 39
Pasturefields. Staf 7H 35
Patchacott. Devn 6D 6
Patcham. Brig 5L 11
Patchetts Green. Herts 4J 21
Patching. W Sus 5H 11
Patchole. Devn 1F 6
Patchway. S Glo 5E 18
Pateley Bridge. N Yor 1K 41
Pathe. Som 2B 8
Pathfinder Village. Devn 6H 7
Pathhead. Abers 1L 67
Pathhead. E Ayr 8E 58
Pathhead. Fife 8F 66
Pathhead. Midl 3A 60
Pathlow. Warw 6K 27
Path of Condie. Per 6D 66
Pathstruie. Per 6D 66
Patmore Heath. Herts 1M 21
Patna. E Ayr 8C 58
Patney. Wilts 8J 19
Patrick. IOM 6B 44
Patrick Brompton. N Yor 6L 47
Patrington. E Yor 5L 43
Patrington Haven. E Yor 5L 43
Patrixbourne. Kent 8H 23
Patterdale. Cumb 4B 46
Pattiesmuir. Fife 1J 59
Pattingham. Staf 2G 27
Pattishall. Nptn 6D 28
Pattiswick. Essx 1E 22
Patton Bridge. Cumb 6D 46
Paul. Corn 6H 3
Paulerspury. Nptn 7E 28
Paull. E Yor 5J 43
Paulton. Bath 8E 18
Pauperhaugh. Nmbd 2E 54
Pave Lane. Telf 8F 34
Pavenham. Bed 6G 29
Pawlett. Som 1A 8
Pawston. Nmbd 6F 60
Paxford. Glos 8K 27
Paxton. Bord 4G 61
Payhembury. Devn 5K 7
Paythorne. Lanc 2G 41
Payton. Som 3L 7
Peacehaven. E Sus 5M 11
Peak Dale. Derbs 2J 35
Peak Forest. Derbs 2K 35
Peak Hill. Linc 8K 37
Peakirk. Pet 1J 29
Pearsie. Ang 2G 67
Peasedown St John. Bath 8F 18
Peaseland Green. Norf 8G 39
Peasemore. W Ber 6B 20
Peasenhall. Suff 5K 31
Pease Pottage. W Sus 2K 11
Peaslake. Surr 1H 11
Peasley Cross. Mers 8D 40
Peasmarsh. E Sus 3E 12
Peasmarsh. Som 4B 8
Peasmarsh. Surr 1G 11
Peaston. E Lot 3B 60
Peastonbank. E Lot 3B 60
Peathill. Abers 7J 81
Peat Inn. Fife 7H 67
Peatling Magna. Leics 2C 28
Peatling Parva. Leics 3C 28
Peaton. Arg 1M 57
Peaton. Shrp 3D 26
Peats Corner. Suff 5H 31
Pebmarsh. Essx 8E 30
Pebworth. Worc 7K 27
Pecket Well. W Yor 5H 41
Peckforton. Ches E 4D 34
Peckham Bush. Kent 8C 22
Peckleton. Leics 1B 28
Pedair-ffordd. Powy 8L 33
Pedham. Norf 8K 39
Pedlinge. Kent 2H 13
Pedmore. W Mid 3H 27
Pedwell. Som 2C 8
Peebles. Bord 5L 59
Peel. IOM 6B 44
Peel. Bord 6B 60
Peel Common. Hants 5C 10
Peening Quarter. Kent 3E 12
Peggs Green. Leics 8B 36
Pegsdon. C Beds 8J 29
Pegswood. Nmbd 3F 54
Peinchorran. High 2G 69
Peinlich. High 8F 76
Pelaw. Tyne 5F 54
Pelcomb Bridge. Pemb 5F 14
Pelcomb Cross. Pemb 5F 14
Peldon. Essx 2F 22
Pelsall. W Mid 1J 27
Pelton. Dur 6F 54
Pelutho. Cumb 7F 52
Pelynt. Corn 6E 4
Pemberton. Carm 6M 15
Pembrey. Carm 6L 15
Pembridge. Here 6B 26
Pembroke. Pemb 6F 14
Pembroke Dock.
Pemb 118 (6F 14)
Pembroke Ferry. Pemb 6F 14
Pembury. Kent 1C 12
Penallt. Mon 2D 18
Penally. Pemb 7H 15
Penalt. Here 1D 18
Penalum. Pemb 7H 15
Penare. Corn 7B 4
Penarth. V Glam 7L 17
Penbeagle. Corn 5J 3
Penberth. Corn 6H 3
Pen-bont Rhydybeddau.
Cdgn 4F 24
Penbryn. Cdgn 1J 15
Pencader. Carm 3L 15
Pen-cae. Cdgn 1L 15
Pencaenewydd. Gwyn 6D 32
Pencaerau. Neat 5G 17
Pencaitland. E Lot 3B 60
Pencarnisiog. IOA 3C 32
Pencarreg. Carm 2M 15
Pencarrow. Corn 3D 4
Pencelli. Powy 2K 17
Pen-clawdd. Swan 7M 15
Pencoed. B'end 6J 17
Pencombe. Here 6D 26
Pencraig. Here 1D 18
Pencraig. Powy 8K 33
Pendeen. Corn 5G 3
Pendeford. W Mid 1G 27
Penderyn. Rhon 4J 17
Pendine. Carm 6J 15
Pendlebury. G Man 7F 40
Pendleton. G Man 8G 41
Pendleton. Lanc 4F 40
Pendock. Worc 8F 26
Pendoggett. Corn 4C 4
Pendomer. Som 4D 8
Pendoylan. V Glam 7K 17
Pendre. B'end 6J 17
Penegoes. Powy 2G 25
Penelewey. Corn 4M 3
Penffordd. Pemb 4G 15
Penffordd-Lâs. Powy 3H 25
Penfro. Pemb 6F 14
Pengam. Cphy 5L 17
Pengam. Card 7M 17
Penge. G Lon 7L 21
Pengelly. Corn 3C 4
Pengenffordd. Powy 1L 17
Pengersick. Corn 6J 3
Pengorffwysfa. IOA 1D 32
Pengover Green. Corn 5E 4
Pengwern. Den 3K 33
Penhale. Corn
nr. Mullion 7K 3
nr. St Austell 6B 4
Penhale Camp. Corn 3L 3
Penhallow. Corn 3L 3
Penhalvean. Corn 5L 3
Penhelig. Gwyn 3F 24
Penhill. Swin 5K 19
Penhow. Newp 4C 18
Penhurst. E Sus 4C 12
Peniarth. Gwyn 2F 24
Penicuik. Midl 3L 59
Peniel. Carm 4L 15
Penifiler. High 1F 68
Peninver. Arg 7G 57
Penisa'r Waun. Gwyn 4E 32
Penistone. S Yor 7L 41
Penketh. Warr 1D 34
Penkill. S Ayr 2H 51
Penkridge. Staf 8H 35
Penley. Wrex 6C 34
Penllech. Gwyn 7B 32
Penllergaer. Swan 5F 16
Pen-llyn. IOA 2C 32
Penmachno. Cnwy 5G 33
Penmaen. Swan 8M 15
Penmaenmawr. Cnwy 3G 33
Penmaenpool. Gwyn 1F 24
Penmaen Rhos. Cnwy 3H 33
Pen-marc. V Glam 8K 17
Penmark. V Glam 8K 17
Penmarth. Corn 5L 3
Penmon. IOA 2F 32
Penmorfa. Gwyn 6E 32
Penmynydd. IOA 3E 32
Penn. Buck 4G 21
Penn. Dors 6B 8
Penn. W Mid 2G 27
Pennal. Gwyn 2G 25
Pennan. Abers 7H 81
Pennant. Cdgn 6E 24
Pennant. Den 7K 33
Pennant. Gwyn 8J 33
Pennant. Powy 3H 25
Pennant Melangell. Powy 8K 33
Pennar. Pemb 6F 14
Pennard. Swan 6E 16
Pennerley. Shrp 2B 26
Pennington. Cumb 8A 46
Pennington. G Man 8E 40
Pennington. Hants 6M 9
Pennorth. Powy 2L 17
Penn Street. Buck 4G 21
Pennsylvania. Devn 6J 7
Pennsylvania. S Glo 6F 18
Penny Bridge. Cumb 7B 46
Pennycross. Plym 6G 5
Pennygate. Norf 7K 39
Pennyghael. Arg 5L 63
Penny Hill. Linc 7L 37
Pennylands. Lanc 7C 40
Pennymoor. Devn 4H 7
Pennyvenie. E Ayr 1K 51
Pennywell. Tyne 6G 55
Penparc. Cdgn 2J 15
Penparcau. Cdgn 4E 24
Pen-pedair-heol. Cphy 5L 17
Penperlleni. Mon 3B 18
Penpillick. Corn 6C 4
Penpol. Corn 5M 3
Penpoll. Corn 6D 4
Penponds. Corn 5K 3
Penpont. Corn 4C 4
Penpont. Dum 2C 52
Penpont. Powy 2J 17
Penprysg. B'end 6J 17
Penquit. Devn 6J 5
Penrherber. Carm 3J 15
Penrhiw. Pemb 2J 15
Penrhiwceiber. Rhon 5K 17
Pen-Rhiw-fawr. Neat 3G 17
Penrhiw-llan. Cdgn 2K 15
Penrhiw-pal. Cdgn 2K 15
Penrhos. Gwyn 7C 32
Penrhos. Here 6B 26
Penrhos. IOA 2B 32
Penrhos. Mon 2C 18
Penrhos. Powy 3H 17
Penrhos Garnedd. Gwyn 3E 32
Penrhyn. IOA 1C 32
Penrhyn Bay. Cnwy 2H 33
Penrhyn-coch. Cdgn 4F 24
Penrhyndeudraeth. Gwyn 7F 32
Penrhyn-side. Cnwy 2H 33
Penrice. Swan 8L 15
Penrith. Cumb 3D 46
Penrose. Corn 4A 4
Penruddock. Cumb 3C 46
Penryn. Corn 5L 3
Pen-sarn. Carm 5L 15
Pen-sarn. Gwyn 8E 32
Pensax. Worc 5F 26
Pensby. Mers 1A 34
Penselwood. Som 2F 8
Pensford. Bath 7E 18
Pensham. Worc 7H 27
Penshaw. Tyne 6G 55
Penshurst. Kent 1B 12
Pensilva. Corn 5E 4
Pensnett. W Mid 3H 27
Penston. E Lot 2B 60
Penstone. Devn 5G 7
Pentewan. Corn 7C 4
Pentir. Gwyn 4E 32
Pentire. Corn 2L 3
Pentlepoir. Pemb 6H 15
Pentlow. Essx 7E 30
Pentney. Norf 8D 38
Penton Mewsey. Hants 1M 9
Pentraeth. IOA 3E 32
Pentre. Powy
nr. Church Stoke 2A 26
nr. Kerry 4L 25
nr. Mochdre 4K 25
Pentre. Rhon 5J 17
Pentre. Shrp 8B 34
Pentre. Wrex
nr. Chirk 5A 34
nr. Llanarmon Dyffryn Ceiriog 7L 33
Pentre-bach. Cdgn 2M 15
Pentre-bach. Powy 1J 17
Pentrebach. Carm 1H 17
Pentrebach. Mer T 4K 17
Pentrebach. Swan 4F 16
Pentre Berw. IOA 3D 32
Pentre-bont. Cnwy 5G 33
Pentrecagal. Carm 2K 15
Pentre-celyn. Den 5L 33
Pentre-clawdd. Shrp 6A 34
Pentreclwydau. Neat 4H 17
Pentre-cwrt. Carm 3K 15
Pentre Dolau Honddu.
Powy 8J 25
Pentre-dwr. Swan 5F 16
Pentrefelin. Carm 2E 16
Pentrefelin. Cdgn 8F 24
Pentrefelin. Cnwy 3H 33
Pentrefelin. Gwyn 7E 32
Pentrefoelas. Cnwy 5H 33
Pentre Galar. Pemb 3H 15
Pentregat. Cdgn 1K 15
Pentre Gwenlais. Carm 3F 16
Pentre Gwynfryn. Gwyn 8E 32
Pentre Halkyn. Flin 3M 33
Pentre Hodre. Shrp 4B 26
Pentre-Llanrhaeadr. Den 4K 33
Pentre Llifior. Powy 3L 25
Pentrellwyn. IOA 2E 32
Pentre-llwyn-llwyd. Powy 7J 25
Pentre-llyn-cymmer. Cnwy 5J 33
Pentre Meyrick. V Glam 7J 17
Pentre-piod. Gwyn 7H 33
Pentre-poeth. Newp 5A 18
Pentre'r beirdd. Powy 1L 25
Pentre'r-felin. Powy 1J 17
Pentre-tafarn-y-fedw. Cnwy 4H 33
Pentre-ty-gwyn. Carm 1H 17
Pentre-uchaf. Gwyn 7C 32
Pentrich. Derbs 4A 36
Pentridge. Dors 4J 9
Pen-twyn. Cphy 4M 17
Pentwyn. Cphy 4L 17
Pentwyn. Card 6M 17
Pentyrch. Card 6L 17
Pentywyn. Carm 6J 15
Penuwch. Cdgn 6E 24
Penwithick. Corn 6C 4
Penwyllt. Powy 3H 17
Pen-y-banc. Carm 2F 16
Penybanc. Carm 3F 16
Pen-y-bont. Carm 4K 15
Pen-y-bont. Powy 8M 33
Penybont. Powy 6L 25
Pen-y-Bont Ar Ogwr. B'end 6J 17
Penybontfawr. Powy 8K 33
Pen-y-bryn. Pemb 2H 15
Pen-y-bryn. Wrex 5A 34
Penybryn. Cphy 5L 17
Pen-y-cae. Powy 3H 17
Penycae. Wrex 5A 34
Pen-y-cae mawr. Mon 4C 18
Penycaerau. Gwyn 8A 32
Pen-y-cefn. Flin 3L 33
Pen-y-clawdd. Mon 3C 18
Pen-y-coedcae. Rhon 6K 17
Penycwm. Pemb 4E 14
Pen-y-Darren. Mer T 4K 17
Pen-y-fai. B'end 6H 17
Pen-y-ffordd. Flin 2L 33
Penyffordd. Flin 3B 34
Penyffridd. Gwyn 5E 32
Pen-y-garn. Cdgn 4F 24
Pen-y-garnedd. IOA 3E 32
Penygarnedd. Powy 8L 33
Pen-y-graig. Gwyn 7B 32
Penygraig. Rhon 5J 17
Penygraigwen. IOA 2D 32
Pen-y-groes. Carm 3E 16
Penygroes. Gwyn 5D 32
Penygroes. Pemb 3H 15
Pen-y-Mynydd. Carm 6L 15
Penymynydd. Flin 3B 34
Pen-yr-heol. Mon 2C 18
Penyrheol. Cphy 6L 17
Penyrheol. Swan 5E 16
Penysarn. IOA 1D 32
Pen-y-stryt. Den 5L 33
Penywaun. Rhon 4J 17
Penzance. Corn 5H 3
Peopleton. Worc 6H 27
Peover Heath. Ches E 2F 34
Peper Harow. Surr 1G 11
Peplow. Shrp 7E 34
Pepper Arden. N Yor 5L 47
Perceton. N Ayr 5B 58
Percyhorner. Abers 7J 81
Perham Down. Wilts 1L 9
Periton. Som 1J 7
Perkinsville. Dur 6F 54
Perlethorpe. Notts 2D 36
Perranarworthal. Corn 5L 3
Perranporth. Corn 3L 3
Perranuthnoe. Corn 6J 3
Perranwell. Corn 5L 3
Perranzabuloe. Corn 3L 3
Perrott's Brook. Glos 3J 19
Perry. W Mid 2J 27
Perry Barr. W Mid 2J 27
Perry Crofts. Staf 1L 27
Perry Green. Essx 1E 22
Perry Green. Herts 2M 21
Perry Green. Wilts 5H 19
Perry Street. Kent 6C 22
Perry Street. Som 5B 8
Perrywood. Kent 8G 23
Pershall. Staf 7G 35
Pershore. Worc 7H 27
Pertenhall. Bed 5H 29
Perth. Per 115 (5E 66)
Perthy. Shrp 6B 34
Perton. Staf 2G 27
Pertwood. Wilts 2G 9
Peterborough. Pet 115 (2J 29)
Peterburn. High 5J 77
Peterchurch. Here 8B 26
Peterculter. Aber 5H 73
Peterhead. Abers 1L 73
Peterlee. Dur 7H 55
Petersfield. Hants 3E 10
Petersfinger. Wilts 3K 9
Peters Green. Herts 2J 21
Peters Marland. Devn 4D 6
Peterstone Wentlooge.
Newp 5A 18
Peterston-super-Ely.
V Glam 7K 17
Peterstow. Here 1D 18
Peters Village. Kent 7D 22
Peter Tavy. Devn 8E 6
Petertown. Orkn 1E 86
Petham. Kent 8H 23
Petherwin Gate. Corn 7B 6
Petrockstowe. Devn 5E 6
Petsoe End. Mil 7F 28
Pett. E Sus 4E 12
Pettaugh. Suff 6H 31
Pett Bottom. Kent 8H 23
Petteridge. Kent 1C 12
Pettinain. S Lan 5H 59
Pettistree. Suff 6J 31
Petton. Devn 3K 7
Petton. Shrp 7C 34
Petts Wood. G Lon 7M 21
Pettycur. Fife 1L 59
Pettywell. Norf 7G 39
Petworth. W Sus 3G 11
Pevensey. E Sus 5C 12
Pevensey Bay. E Sus 5C 12
Pewsey. Wilts 7K 19
Pheasants Hill. Buck 5E 20
Philadelphia. Tyne 6G 55
Philham. Devn 3B 6
Philiphaugh. Bord 7B 60
Phillack. Corn 5J 3
Philleigh. Corn 8A 4
Philpstoun. W Lot 2J 59
Phocle Green. Here 1E 18
Phoenix Green. Hants 8E 20
Pibsbury. Som 3C 8
Pibwrlwyd. Carm 5L 15
Pica. Cumb 2K 45
Piccadilly. Warw 2L 27
Piccadilly Corner. Norf 3J 31
Piccotts End. Herts 3H 21
Pickering. N Yor 7E 48
Picket Piece. Hants 1A 10
Picket Post. Hants 5K 9
Pickford. W Mid 3L 27
Pickhill. N Yor 7M 47
Picklenash. Glos 1F 18
Picklescott. Shrp 2C 26
Pickletillem. Fife 5H 67
Pickmere. Ches E 2E 34
Pickstock. Telf 7F 34
Pickwell. Devn 1D 6
Pickwell. Leics 8E 36
Pickworth. Linc 6H 37
Pickworth. Rut 8G 37
Picton. Ches W 2C 34
Picton. Flin 2L 33
Picton. N Yor 5B 48
Pict's Hill. Som 3C 8
Piddinghoe. E Sus 5M 11
Piddington. Buck 4F 20
Piddington. Nptn 6F 28
Piddington. Oxon 2D 20
Piddlehinton. Dors 6F 8
Piddletrenthide. Dors 5F 8
Pidley. Cambs 4L 29
Pidney. Dors 5F 8
Pie Corner. Here 5E 26
Piercebridge. Darl 4L 47
Pierowall. Orkn 5D 88
Pigdon. Nmbd 3E 54
Pightley. Som 2M 7
Pikehall. Derbs 4K 35
Pikeshill. Hants 5L 9
Pilford. Dors 5J 9
Pilgrims Hatch. Essx 4B 22
Pilham. Linc 8F 42
Pill. N Som 6D 18
The Pill. Mon 5C 18
Pillaton. Corn 5F 4
Pillaton. Staf 8H 35
Pillerton Hersey. Warw 7M 27
Pillerton Priors. Warw 7L 27
Pilleth. Powy 5A 26
Pilley. Hants 6M 9
Pilley. S Yor 7M 41
Pillgwenlly. Newp 5B 18
Pilling. Lanc 3C 40
Pilling Lane. Lanc 3B 40
Pillowell. Glos 3E 18
Pillwell. Dors 4F 8
Pilning. S Glo 5D 18
Pilsbury. Derbs 3K 35
Pilsdon. Dors 6C 8
Pilsgate. Pet 1H 29
Pilsley. Derbs
nr. Bakewell 2L 35
nr. Clay Cross 3B 36
Pilson Green. Norf 8K 39
Piltdown. E Sus 3M 11
Pilton. Edin 2L 59
Pilton. Nptn 3H 29
Pilton. Rut 1G 29
Pilton. Som 1D 8
Pilton Green. Swan 8L 15
Pimperne. Dors 5H 9
Pinchbeck. Linc 7K 37
Pinchbeck Bars. Linc 7J 37
Pinchbeck West. Linc 7K 37
Pinfold. Lanc 6B 40
Pinford End. Suff 6E 30
Pinged. Carm 6L 15
Pinhoe. Devn 6J 7
Pinkerton. E Lot 2E 60
Pinkneys Green. Wind 5F 20
Pinley. W Mid 4A 28
Pinley Green. Warw 5L 27
Pinmill. Suff 8J 31
Pinmore. S Ayr 2H 51
Pinner. G Lon 5J 21
Pins Green. Worc 7F 26
Pinsley Green. Ches E 5D 34
Pinvin. Worc 7H 27
Pinwherry. S Ayr 3G 51
Pinxton. Derbs 4B 36
Pipe and Lyde. Here 7D 26
Pipe Aston. Here 4C 26
Pipe Gate. Shrp 5F 34
Pipehill. Staf 1J 27
Piperhill. High 8J 79
Pipe Ridware. Staf 8J 35
Pipers Pool. Corn 7B 6
Pipewell. Nptn 3F 28
Pippacott. Devn 2E 6
Pipton. Powy 1L 17
Pirbright. Surr 8G 21
Pirnmill. N Ayr 5H 57
Pirton. Herts 8J 29
Pirton. Worc 7G 27
Pisgah. Stir 7A 66
Pishill. Oxon 5E 20
Pistyll. Gwyn 6C 32
Pitagowan. Per 1B 66
Pitcairn. Per 2B 66
Pitcairngreen. Per 5D 66
Pitcalnie. High 6J 79
Pitcaple. Abers 3G 73
Pitchcombe. Glos 3G 19
Pitchcott. Buck 1E 20
Pitchford. Shrp 1D 26
Pitch Green. Buck 3E 20
Pitch Place. Surr 8G 21
Pitcombe. Som 2E 8
Pitcox. E Lot 2D 60
Pitcur. Per 4F 66
Pitfichie. Abers 4F 72
Pitgrudy. High 4H 79
Pitkennedy. Ang 2J 67
Pitlessie. Fife 7G 67
Pitlochry. Per 2C 66
Pitmachie. Abers 3F 72
Pitmaduthy. High 6H 79
Pitmedden. Abers 3H 73
Pitminster. Som 4M 7
Pitnacree. Per 2C 66
Pitney. Som 3C 8
Pitroddie. Per 5F 66
Pitscottie. Fife 6H 67
Pitsea. Essx 5D 22
Pitsford. Nptn 5E 28
Pitsford Hill. Som 2L 7
Pitsmoor. S Yor 1A 36
Pitstone. Buck 2G 21
Pitt. Hants 3B 10
Pitt Court. Glos 4F 18
Pittentrail. High 3H 79
Pittenweem. Fife 7J 67
Pittington. Dur 7G 55
Pitton. Swan 8L 15
Pitton. Wilts 2L 9
Pittswood. Kent 1C 12
Pittulie. Abers 7J 81
Pittville. Glos 1H 19
Pitversie. Per 6E 66
Pity Me. Dur 7F 54
Pityme. Corn 4B 4
Pixey Green. Suff 4J 31
Pixley. Here 8E 26
Place Newton. N Yor 8F 48
Plaidy. Abers 8G 81
Plaidy. Corn 6E 4
Plain Dealings. Pemb 5G 15
Plains. N Lan 3F 58
Plainsfield. Som 2L 7
Plaish. Shrp 2D 26
Plaistow. Here 8E 26
Plaistow. W Sus 2H 11
Plaitford. Wilts 4L 9
Plastow Green. Hants 7C 20
Plas yn Cefn. Den 3K 33
The Platt. E Sus 2B 12
Platt Bridge. G Man 7E 40
Platt Lane. Shrp 6D 34
Platts Common. S Yor 7A 42
Platt's Heath. Kent 8E 22
Plawsworth. Dur 7F 54
Plaxtol. Kent 8C 22
Playden. E Sus 3F 12
Playford. Suff 7J 31
Play Hatch. Oxon 6E 20
Playing Place. Corn 4M 3
Playley Green. Glos 8F 26
Plealey. Shrp 1C 26
Plean. Stir 1G 59
Pleasington. Bkbn 5E 40
Pleasley. Derbs 3C 36
Pledgdon Green. Essx 1B 22
Plenmeller. Nmbd 5M 53
Pleshey. Essx 2C 22
Plockton. High 2K 69
Plocrapol. W Isl 4C 76
Ploughfield. Here 7B 26
Plowden. Shrp 3B 26
Ploxgreen. Shrp 1B 26
Pluckley. Kent 1F 12
Plucks Gutter. Kent 7J 23
Plumbland. Cumb 8F 52
Plumbridge. Derr 4D 92
Plumgarths. Cumb 6C 46
Plumley. Ches E 2F 34
Plummers Plain. W Sus 3K 11
Plumpton. Cumb 8J 53
Plumpton. E Sus 4L 11
Plumpton. Nptn 7C 28
Plumpton Foot. Cumb 8J 53
Plumpton Green. E Sus 4L 11
Plumpton Head. Cumb 8K 53
Plumstead. G Lon 6M 21
Plumstead. Norf 6H 39
Plumtree. Notts 6D 36
Plumtree Park. Notts 6D 36
Plungar. Leics 6E 36
Plush. Dors 5F 8
Plushabridge. Corn 8C 6
Plwmp. Cdgn 1K 15
Plymouth. Plym 115 (6G 5)
Plympton. Plym 6H 5
Plymstock. Plym 6H 5
Plymtree. Devn 5K 7
Pockley. N Yor 7D 48
Pocklington. E Yor 3F 42
Pode Hole. Linc 7K 37
Podimore. Som 3D 8
Podington. Bed 5G 29
Podmore. Staf 6F 34
Poffley End. Oxon 2A 20
Point Clear. Essx 2G 23
Pointon. Linc 6J 37
Pokesdown. Bour 6K 9
Polbae. Dum 4H 51
Polbain. High 3M 77
Polbathic. Corn 6F 4
Polbeth. W Lot 3J 59
Polbrock. Corn 5C 4
Polchar. High 5J 71
Polebrook. Nptn 3H 29
Pole Elm. Worc 7G 27
Polegate. E Sus 5B 12
Pole Moor. W Yor 6J 41
Poles. High 4H 79
Polesworth. Warw 1L 27
Polglass. High 3M 77
Polgooth. Corn 6B 4
Poling. W Sus 5H 11
Poling Corner. W Sus 5H 11
Polio. High 6H 79
Polkerris. Corn 6C 4
Polla. High 6F 84
Pollard Street. Norf 6K 39
Pollicott. Buck 2E 20
Pollington. E Yor 6D 42
Polloch. High 1B 64
Pollok. Glas 3D 58
Pollokshaws. Glas 3D 58
Pollokshields. Glas 3D 58
Polmaily. High 2E 70
Polmassick. Corn 7B 4
Polmont. Falk 2H 59
Polnessan. E Ayr 8C 58
Polnish. High 7J 69
Polperro. Corn 6E 4
Polruan. Corn 6D 4
Polscoe. Corn 5D 4
Polsham. Som 1D 8
Polskeoch. Dum 1A 52
Polstead. Suff 8F 30
Polstead Heath. Suff 7F 30
Poltesco. Corn 7L 3
Poltimore. Devn 6J 7
Polton. Midl 3L 59
Polwarth. Bord 4E 60
Polyphant. Corn 7B 6
Polzeath. Corn 4B 4
Pomeroy. M Ulst 5E 92
Ponde. Powy 1L 17
Pondersbridge. Cambs 2K 29
Ponders End. G Lon 4L 21
Pond Street. Essx 8A 30
Pondtail. Hants 8F 20
Ponsanooth. Corn 5L 3
Ponsongath. Corn 7L 3
Ponsworthy. Devn 8G 7
Pontamman. Carm 3F 16
Pontantwn. Carm 5L 15
Pontardawe. Neat 4G 17
Pontarddulais. Swan 4E 16
Pontarfynach. Cdgn 5G 25
Pont-ar-gothi. Carm 4M 15
Pont ar Hydfer. Powy 2H 17
Pontarllechau. Carm 2G 17
Pontarsais. Carm 4L 15
Pontblyddyn. Flin 3A 34
Pontbren Llwyd. Rhon 4J 17
Pont-Cyfyng. Cnwy 5G 33
Pontdolgoch. Powy 3K 25
Pontefract. W Yor 5B 42
Ponteland. Nmbd 4E 54
Ponterwyd. Cdgn 4G 25
Pontesbury. Shrp 1C 26
Pontesford. Shrp 1C 26
Pontfadog. Wrex 7M 33
Pont-Faen. Shrp 6A 34
Pont-faen. Powy 1J 17
Pontfaen. Pemb 3G 15
Pontgarreg. Cdgn 1K 15
Pont-Henri. Carm 6L 15
Ponthir. Torf 4B 18
Ponthirwaun. Cdgn 2J 15
Pont-iets. Carm 6L 15
Pontllanfraith. Cphy 5L 17
Pontlliw. Swan 4F 16
Pont Llogel. Powy 1K 25
Pontllyfni. Gwyn 5D 32
Pontlottyn. Cphy 4L 17
Pontneddfechan. Powy 4J 17
Pont-newydd. Carm 6L 15
Pont-newydd. Flin 4L 33
Pontnewydd. Torf 4A 18
Ponton. Shet 2D 90
Pont Pen-y-benglog. Gwyn 4F 32
Pontrhydfendigaid. Cdgn 6G 25
Pont Rhyd-y-cyff. B'end 6H 17
Pontrhydyfen. Neat 5G 17
Pont-rhyd-y-groes. Cdgn 5G 25
Pontrhydyrun. Torf 4A 18
Pont-Rhythallt. Gwyn 4E 32
Pontrilas. Here 1B 18
Pontrilas Road. Here 1B 18
Pontrobert. Powy 1L 25
Pont-rug. Gwyn 4E 32
Ponts Green. E Sus 4C 12
Pontshill. Here 1E 18
Pont-Sian. Cdgn 2L 15
Pontsticill. Mer T 3K 17
Pont-Walby. Neat 4H 17
Pontwelly. Carm 3L 15
Pontwgan. Cnwy 3G 33
Pontyates. Carm 6L 15
Pontyberem. Carm 5M 15
Pontybodkin. Flin 4A 34
Pontyclun. Rhon 6K 17
Pontycymer. B'end 5J 17
Pontyglazier. Pemb 3H 15
Pontygwaith. Rhon 5K 17
Pont-y-pant. Cnwy 5G 33
Pontypool. Torf 4A 18
Pontypridd. Rhon 6K 17
Pontypwl. Torf 4A 18
Pontywaun. Cphy 5M 17
Pooksgreen. Hants 4A 10
Pool. Corn 4K 3
Pool. W Yor 3L 41
Poole. N Yor 5B 42
Poole. Pool 118 (6J 9)
Poole. Som 3L 7
Poole Keynes. Glos 4H 19
Poolend. Staf 4H 35
Poolewe. High 5K 77
Pooley Bridge. Cumb 3C 46
Poolfold. Staf 4G 35
Pool Head. Here 6D 26
Pool Hey. Lanc 6B 40
Poolhill. Glos 1F 18
Poolmill. Here 1D 18
Pool o' Muckhart. Clac 7D 66
Pool Quay. Powy 8A 34
Poolsbrook. Derbs 2B 36
Pool Street. Essx 8D 30
Pootings. Kent 1A 12
Pope Hill. Pemb 5F 14
Pope's Hill. Glos 2E 18
Popeswood. Brac 7F 20
Popham. Hants 1C 10
Poplar. G Lon 5L 21
Popley. Hants 8D 20
Porchfield. IOW 6B 10
Porin. High 8D 78
Poringland. Norf 1J 31
Porkellis. Corn 5K 3
Porlock. Som 1H 7
Porlock Weir. Som 1H 7
Portachoillan. Arg 4G 57
Port Adhair Bheinn na Faoghla.
W Isl 8J 75
Port Adhair Thirlodh. Arg 3F 62
Portadown. Arm 6G 93
Portaferry. Ards 6J 93
Port Ann. Arg 1J 57
Port Appin. Arg 3D 64
Port Asgaig. Arg 3D 56
Port Askaig. Arg 3D 56
Portavadie. Arg 3J 57
Portavogie. Ards 5K 93
Portballintrae. Caus 1F 93
Port Bannatyne. Arg 3K 57
Portbury. N Som 6D 18
Port Carlisle. Cumb 5G 53
Port Charlotte. Arg 4B 56
Portchester. Hants 5D 10
Port Clarence. Stoc T 3B 48
Port Driseach. Arg 2J 57
Port Dundas. Glas 3D 58
Port Ellen. Arg 5C 56
Port Elphinstone. Abers 3G 73
Portencalzie. Dum 4F 50
Portencross. N Ayr 5L 57
Port Erin. IOM 8A 44
Port Erroll. Abers 2K 73
Porter's Fen Corner. Norf 1B 30
Portesham. Dors 7E 8
Portessie. Mor 7D 80
Port e Vullen. IOM 5D 44
Port-Eynon. Swan 8L 15
Portfield. Som 3C 8
Portfield Gate. Pemb 5F 14
Portgate. Devn 7D 6
Port Gaverne. Corn 3C 4
Port Glasgow. Inv 2B 58
Portglenone. ME Ant 3F 93
Portgordon. Mor 7C 80
Portgower. High 2L 79
Porth. Corn 2M 3
Porth. Rhon 5K 17
Porthaethwy. IOA 3E 32
Porthallow. Corn
nr. Looe 6E 4
nr. St Keverne 6L 3
Porthcawl. B'end 7H 17
Porthceri. V Glam 8K 17
Porthcothan. Corn 4A 4
Porthcurno. Corn 6G 3
Port Henderson. High 6J 77
Porthgain. Pemb 3E 14
Porthgwarra. Corn 6G 3
Porthill. Shrp 8C 34
Porthkerry. V Glam 8K 17
Porthleven. Corn 6K 3
Porthllechog. IOA 1D 32
Porthmadog. Gwyn 7E 32
Porthmeor. Corn 5H 3
Porth Navas. Corn 6L 3
Portholland. Corn 7B 4
Porthoustock. Corn 6M 3
Porthtowan. Corn 4K 3
Porth Tywyn. Carm 6L 15
Porth-y-felin. IOA 2B 32
Porthyrhyd. Carm
nr. Carmarthen 5M 15
nr. Llandovery 1G 17
Porth-y-waen. Shrp 7A 34
Portincaple. Arg 8G 65
Portington. E Yor 4E 42
Portinnisherrich. Arg 6D 64
Portinscale. Cumb 3A 46
Port Isaac. Corn 3B 4
Portishead. N Som 6C 18
Portknockie. Mor 7D 80
Port Lamont. Arg 2K 57
Portlethen. Abers 6J 73
Portlethen Village. Abers 6J 73
Portling. Dum 6C 52
Port Lion. Pemb 6F 14
Portloe. Corn 8B 4
Port Logan. Dum 7F 50
Portmahomack. High 5K 79
Portmead. Swan 5F 16
Portmeirion. Gwyn 7E 32
Portmellon. Corn 7C 4
Port Mholair. W Isl 8J 83
Port Mor. High 8F 68
Portmore. Hants 6M 9
Port Mulgrave. N Yor 4E 48
Portnacroish. Arg 3D 64
Portnahaven. Arg 4A 56
Portnalong. High 2E 68
Portnaluchaig. High 7H 69
Portnancon. High 5G 85
Port Nan Giuran. W Isl 8J 83
Port nan Long. W Isl 6K 75
Port Nis. W Isl 5J 83
Portobello. Edin 2M 59
Portobello. W Yor 6M 41
Port of Menteith. Stir 7K 65
Porton. Wilts 2K 9
Portormin. High 1A 80
Portpatrick. Dum 6F 50
Port Quin. Corn 3B 4
Port Ramsay. Arg 3C 64
Portreath. Corn 4K 3
Portree. High 1F 68
Port Righ. High 1F 68
Portrush. Caus 2F 93
Port St Mary. IOM 8B 44
Portscatho. Corn 8A 4
Portsea. Port 5D 10
Port Seton. E Lot 2B 60
Portskerra. High 5L 85
Portskewett. Mon 5D 18
Portslade-by-Sea. Brig 5K 11
Portsmouth. Port 115 (5D 10)
Portsmouth. W Yor 5H 41
Port Soderick. IOM 7C 44
Port Solent. Port 5D 10
Portsonachan. Arg 5E 64
Portsoy. Abers 7E 80
Portstewart. Caus 2F 93
Port Sunlight. Mers 1B 34
Portswood. Sotn 4B 10
Port Talbot. Neat 6G 17
Porttannachy. Mor 7C 80
Port Tennant. Swan 5F 16
Portuairk. High 1K 63
Portway. Here 7C 26
Portway. Worc 4J 27
Port Wemyss. Arg 4A 56
Port William. Dum 7J 51
Portwrinkle. Corn 6F 4
Poslingford. Suff 7D 30
Postbridge. Devn 8F 6
Postcombe. Oxon 4E 20
Post Green. Dors 6H 9
Postling. Kent 2H 13
Postlip. Glos 1J 19
Post-Mawr. Cdgn 1L 15
Postwick. Norf 1J 31
Potarch. Abers 6F 72
Potsgrove. C Beds 1G 21
Potten End. Herts 3H 21
Potter Brompton. N Yor 8G 49
Pottergate Street. Norf 2H 31
Potterhanworth. Linc 3H 37
Potterhanworth Booths.
Linc 3H 37
Potter Heigham. Norf 8L 39
Potter Hill. Leics 7E 36
The Potteries. Stoke 5G 35
Potterne. Wilts 8H 19
Potterne Wick. Wilts 8J 19
Potternewton. W Yor 4M 41
Potters Bar. Herts 3K 21
Potters Brook. Lanc 2C 40
Potter's Cross. Staf 3G 27
Potters Crouch. Herts 3J 21
Potter Somersal. Derbs 6K 35
Potterspury. Nptn 7E 28
Potter Street. Essx 3A 22
Potterton. Abers 4J 73
Potthorpe. Norf 7F 38
Pottle Street. Wilts 1G 9
Potto. N Yor 5B 48
Potton. C Beds 7K 29
Pott Row. Norf 7D 38
Pott Shrigley. Ches E 2H 35
Poughill. Corn 5B 6
Poughill. Devn 5H 7
Poulner. Hants 5K 9
Poulshot. Wilts 8H 19
Poulton. Glos 3K 19
Poulton-le-Fylde. Lanc 4B 40
Pound Bank. Worc 4F 26
Poundbury. Dors 6E 8
Poundfield. E Sus 2B 12
Poundgate. E Sus 3A 12
Pound Green. E Sus 3B 12
Pound Green. Suff 6D 30
Pound Hill. W Sus 2K 11
Poundland. S Ayr 3G 51

Poundon. Buck 1D 20
Poundsgate. Devn 8G 7
Poundstock. Corn 6B 6
Pound Street. Hants 7B 20
Pounsley. E Sus 3B 12
Powburn. Nmbd 8H 61
Powderham. Devn 7J 7
Powerstock. Dors 6D 8
Powfoot. Dum 5F 52
Powick. Worc 6G 27
Powmill. Per 8D 66
Poxwell. Dors 7F 8
Poyle. Slo 6H 21
Poynings. W Sus 4K 11
Poyntington. Dors 3E 8
Poynton. Ches E 1H 35
Poynton. Telf 8D 34
Poynton Green. Telf 8D 34
Poyntz Pass. Arm 7G 93
Poystreet Green. Suff 6F 30
Praa Sands. Corn 6J 3
Pratt's Bottom. G Lon 7A 22
Praze-an-Beeble. Corn 5K 3
Prees. Shrp 6D 34
Preesall. Lanc 3B 40
Preesall Park. Lanc 3B 40
Prees Green. Shrp 6D 34
Prees Higher Heath. Shrp 6D 34
Prendergast. Pemb 5F 14
Prendwick. Nmbd 8H 61
Pren-gwyn. Cdgn 2L 15
Prenteg. Gwyn 6E 32
Prenton. Mers 1B 34
Prescot. Mers 8C 40
Prescott. Devn 4K 7
Prescott. Shrp 7C 34
Preshute. Wilts 7K 19
Pressen. Nmbd 6F 60
Prestatyn. Den 2K 33
Prestbury. Ches E 2H 35
Prestbury. Glos 1H 19
Presteigne. Powy 5B 26
Presthope. Shrp 2D 26
Prestleigh. Som 1E 8
Preston. Brig 5L 11
Preston. Devn 8H 7
Preston. Dors 7F 8
Preston. E Lot
nr. East Linton 2C 60
nr. Prestonpans 2A 60
Preston. E Yor 4J 43
Preston. Glos 3J 19
Preston. Herts 1J 21
Preston. Kent
nr. Canterbury 7J 23
nr. Faversham 7G 23
Preston. Lanc 115 (5D 40)
Preston. Nmbd 7J 61
Preston. Rut 1F 28
Preston. Bord 4E 60
Preston. Shrp 8D 34
Preston. Suff 6F 30
Preston. Wilts
nr. Aldbourne 6L 19
nr. Lyneham 6J 19
Preston Bagot. Warw 5K 27
Preston Bissett. Buck 1D 20
Preston Bowyer. Som 3L 7
Preston Brockhurst. Shrp 7D 34
Preston Brook. Hal 1D 34
Preston Candover. Hants 1D 10
Preston Capes. Nptn 6C 28
Preston Cross. Glos 8E 26
Preston Gubbals. Shrp 8C 34
Preston-le-Skerne. Dur 3M 47
Preston Marsh. Here 7D 26
Prestonmill. Dum 6D 52
Preston on Stour. Warw 7L 27
Preston on the Hill. Hal 1D 34
Preston on Wye. Here 7B 26
Prestonpans. E Lot 2A 60
Preston Plucknett. Som 4D 8
Preston-under-Scar. N Yor 6J 47
Preston upon the Weald Moors.
Telf 8E 34
Preston Wynne. Here 7D 26
Prestwich. G Man 7G 41
Prestwick. Nmbd 4E 54
Prestwick. S Ayr 7B 58
Prestwold. Leics 7C 36
Prestwood. Buck 3F 20
Prestwood. Staf 5K 35
Price Town. B'end 5J 17
Prickwillow. Cambs 3B 30
Priddy. Som 8D 18
Priestcliffe. Derbs 2K 35
Priesthill. Glas 3D 58
Priest Hutton. Lanc 8D 46
Priestland. E Ayr 6D 58
Priest Weston. Shrp 2A 26
Priestwood. Brac 6F 20
Priestwood. Kent 7C 22
Primethorpe. Leics 2C 28
Primrose Green. Norf 8G 39
Primrose Hill. Glos 3E 18
Primrose Hill. Lanc 7B 40
Primrose Valley. N Yor 8J 49
Primsidemill. Bord 7F 60
Princes Gate. Pemb 5H 15
Princes Risborough. Buck 3F 20
Princethorpe. Warw 4B 28
Princetown. Devn 8E 6
Prinsted. W Sus 5E 10
Prion. Den 4K 33
Prior Muir. Fife 6J 67
Prior's Frome. Here 8D 26
Priors Halton. Shrp 4C 26
Priors Hardwick. Warw 6B 28
Priorslee. Telf 8F 34
Priors Marston. Warw 6B 28
Prior's Norton. Glos 1G 19
The Priory. W Ber 7M 19
Priory Wood. Here 7A 26
Priston. Bath 7E 18
Pristow Green. Norf 3H 31
Prittlewell. S'end 5E 22
Privett. Hants 3D 10
Prixford. Devn 2E 6
Probus. Corn 7A 4
Prospect. Cumb 7F 52
Prospect Village. Staf 8J 35
Provanmill. Glas 3E 58
Prudhoe. Nmbd 5D 54
Publow. Bath 7E 18
Puckeridge. Herts 1L 21
Puckington. Som 4B 8
Pucklechurch. S Glo 6E 18
Puckrup. Glos 8G 27
Puddinglake. Ches W 3F 34
Puddington. Ches W 2B 34
Puddington. Devn 4H 7
Puddlebrook. Glos 2E 18
Puddledock. Norf 2G 31
Puddletown. Dors 6F 8
Pudleston. Here 6D 26
Pudsey. W Yor 4L 41
Pulborough. W Sus 4H 11
Puleston. Telf 7F 34
Pulford. Ches W 4B 34
Pulham. Dors 5F 8
Pulham Market. Norf 3H 31
Pulham St Mary. Norf 3J 31
Pulley. Shrp 1C 26
Pulloxhill. C Beds 8H 29
Pulpit Hill. Arg 5C 64
Pulverbatch. Shrp 1C 26
Pumpherston. W Lot 3J 59
Pumsaint. Carm 8F 24
Puncheston. Pemb 4G 15
Puncknowle. Dors 7D 8
Punnett's Town. E Sus 3C 12
Purbrook. Hants 5D 10
Purfleet. Thur 6B 22
Puriton. Som 1B 8
Purleigh. Essx 3E 22
Purley. G Lon 7L 21
Purley on Thames. W Ber 6D 20
Purlogue. Shrp 4A 26
Purl's Bridge. Cambs 3A 30
Purse Caundle. Dors 4E 8
Purslow. Shrp 3B 26
Purston Jaglin. W Yor 6B 42
Purtington. Som 5B 8
Purton. Glos
nr. Lydney 3E 18
nr. Sharpness 3E 18
Purton. Wilts 5J 19
Purton Stoke. Wilts 4J 19
Pury End. Nptn 7E 28
Pusey. Oxon 4A 20
Putley. Here 8E 26
Putney. G Lon 6K 21
Putsborough. Devn 1D 6
Puttenham. Herts 2F 20
Puttenham. Surr 1G 11
Puttock End. Essx 7E 30
Puttock's End. Essx 2B 22
Puxey. Dors 4F 8
Puxton. N Som 7C 18
Pwll. Carm 6L 15
Pwll. Powy 2L 25
Pwllcrochan. Pemb 6F 14
Pwll-glas. Den 5L 33
Pwllgloyw. Powy 1K 17
Pwllheli. Gwyn 7C 32
Pwllmeyric. Mon 4D 18
Pwlltrap. Carm 5J 15
Pwll-y-glaw. Neat 5G 17
Pyecombe. W Sus 4K 11
Pye Corner. Herts 2M 21
Pye Corner. Newp 5B 18
Pye Green. Staf 8H 35
Pyewipe. NE Lin 6K 43
Pyle. B'end 6H 17
Pyle. IOW 8B 10
Pyle Hill. Surr 8G 21
Pylle. Som 2E 8
Pymoor. Cambs 3A 30
Pymore. Dors 6C 8
Pyrford. Surr 8H 21
Pyrford Village. Surr 8H 21
Pyrton. Oxon 4D 20
Pytchley. Nptn 4F 28
Pyworthy. Devn 5C 6

Q

Quabbs. Shrp 4M 25
Quadring. Linc 6K 37
Quadring Eaudike. Linc 6K 37
Quainton. Buck 1E 20
Quaking Houses. Dur 6E 54
Quarley. Hants 1L 9
Quarndon. Derbs 5M 35
Quarrendon. Buck 2F 20
Quarrier's Village. Inv 3B 58
Quarrington. Linc 5H 37
Quarrington Hill. Dur 8G 55
The Quarry. Glos 4F 18
Quarry Bank. W Mid 3H 27
Quarrywood. Mor 7A 80
Quartalehouse. Abers 1J 73
Quarter. N Ayr 3L 57
Quarter. S Lan 4F 58
Quatford. Shrp 2F 26
Quatt. Shrp 3F 26
Quebec. Dur 7E 54
Quedgeley. Glos 2G 19
Queen Adelaide. Cambs 3B 30
Queenborough. Kent 6F 22
Queen Camel. Som 3D 8
Queen Charlton. Bath 7E 18
Queen Dart. Devn 4H 7
Queenhill. Worc 8G 27
Queen Oak. Dors 2F 8
Queensbury. W Yor 4K 41
Queensferry. Flin 3B 34
Queensferry Crossing. Edin 2K 59
Queenstown. Bkpl 4B 40
Queen Street. Kent 1C 12
Queenzieburn. N Lan 2E 58
Quemerford. Wilts 7J 19
Quendale. Shet 6D 90
Quendon. Essx 8B 30
Queniborough. Leics 8D 36
Quenington. Glos 3K 19
Quernmore. Lanc 1D 40
Quethiock. Corn 5F 4
Quholm. Orkn 8B 88
Quick's Green. W Ber 6C 20
Quidenham. Norf 3G 31
Quidhampton. Hants 8C 20
Quidhampton. Wilts 2K 9
Quilquox. Abers 2J 73
Quina Brook. Shrp 6D 34
Quindry. Orkn 2F 86
Quine's Hill. IOM 7C 44
Quinton. Nptn 6E 28
Quinton. W Mid 3H 27
Quintrell Downs. Corn 2M 3
Quixhill. Staf 5K 35
Quoditch. Devn 6D 6
Quorn. Leics 8C 36
Quorndon. Leics 8C 36
Quothquan. S Lan 6H 59
Quoyloo. Orkn 7B 88
Quoyness. Orkn 1D 86
Quoys. Shet
on Mainland 1E 90
on Unst 2L 91

R

Rableyheath. Herts 2K 21
Raby. Cumb 6F 52
Raby. Mers 2B 34
Rachan Mill. Bord 6K 59
Rachub. Gwyn 4F 32
Rack End. Oxon 3B 20
Rackenford. Devn 4H 7
Rackham. W Sus 4H 11
Rackheath. Norf 8J 39
Racks. Dum 4E 52
Rackwick. Orkn
on Hoy 2D 86
on Westray 5D 88
Radbourne. Derbs 6L 35
Radcliffe. G Man 7F 40
Radcliffe. Nmbd 1F 54
Radcliffe on Trent. Notts 6D 36
Radclive. Buck 8D 28
Radernie. Fife 7H 67
Radfall. Kent 7H 23
Radford. Bath 8E 18
Radford. Nott 5C 36
Radford. Oxon 1B 20
Radford. W Mid 3M 27
Radford. Worc 6J 27
Radford Semele. Warw 5M 27
Radipole. Dors 7E 8
Radlett. Herts 4J 21
Radley. Oxon 4C 20
Radnage. Buck 4E 20
Radstock. Bath 8E 18
Radstone. Nptn 7C 28
Radway. Warw 7A 28
Radway Green. Ches E 4F 34
Radwell. Bed 6H 29
Radwell. Herts 8K 29
Radwinter. Essx 8C 30
Radyr. Card 6L 17
RAF Coltishall. Norf 7J 39
Rafford. Mor 8L 79
Raffrey. New M 6J 93
Ragdale. Leics 8D 36
Ragdon. Shrp 2C 26
Ragged Appleshaw. Hants 1M 9
Raggra. High 7E 86
Raglan. Mon 3C 18
Ragnall. Notts 2F 36
Raholp. New M 6J 93
Raigbeg. High 3J 71
Rainford. Mers 7C 40
Rainford Junction. Mers 7C 40
Rainham. G Lon 5B 22
Rainham. Medw 7E 22
Rainhill. Mers 8C 40
Rainow. Ches E 2H 35
Rainton. N Yor 8A 48
Rainworth. Notts 4C 36
Raisbeck. Cumb 5E 46
Raise. Cumb 7M 53
Rait. Per 5F 66
Raithby. Linc 1L 37
Raithby by Spilsby. Linc 3L 37
Raithwaite. N Yor 4F 48
Rake. W Sus 3F 10
Rake End. Staf 8J 35
Rakeway. Staf 5J 35
Rakewood. G Man 6H 41
Ralia. High 6H 71
Ram Alley. Wilts 7L 19
Ramasaig. High 1C 68
Rame. Corn
nr. Millbrook 7G 5
nr. Penryn 5L 3
Ram Lane. Kent 1F 12
Ramnageo. Shet 3L 91
Rampisham. Dors 5D 8
Rampside. Cumb 8M 45
Rampton. Cambs 5M 29
Rampton. Notts 2E 36
Ramsbottom. G Man 6F 40
Ramsburn. Mor 8E 80
Ramsbury. Wilts 6L 19
Ramscraigs. High 1M 79
Ramsdean. Hants 3E 10
Ramsdell. Hants 8C 20
Ramsden. Oxon 2A 20
Ramsden. Worc 7H 27
Ramsden Bellhouse. Essx 4D 22
Ramsden Heath. Essx 4D 22
Ramsey. Cambs 3K 29
Ramsey. Essx 8J 31
Ramsey. IOM 5D 44
Ramsey Forty Foot. Cambs 3L 29
Ramsey Heights. Cambs 3K 29
Ramsey Island. Essx 3F 22
Ramsey Mereside. Cambs 3K 29
Ramsey St Mary's. Cambs 3K 29
Ramsgate. Kent 7K 23
Ramsgill. N Yor 8K 47
Ramshaw. Dur 7C 54
Ramshorn. Staf 5J 35
Ramsley. Devn 6F 6
Ramsnest Common. Surr 2G 11
Ramstone. Abers 4F 72
Ranais. W Isl 1F 76
Ranby. Linc 2K 37
Ranby. Notts 1D 36
Rand. Linc 2J 37
Randalstown. Ant 4G 93
Randwick. Glos 3G 19
Ranfurly. Ren 3B 58
Rangag. High 7C 86
Rangemore. Staf 7K 35
Rangeworthy. S Glo 5E 18
Rankinston. E Ayr 8C 58
Rank's Green. Essx 2D 22
Ranmore Common. Surr 8J 21
Rannoch Station. Per 2J 65
Ranochan. High 7K 69
Ranskill. Notts 1D 36
Ranton. Staf 7G 35
Ranton Green. Staf 7G 35
Ranworth. Norf 8K 39
Raploch. Stir 8A 66
Rapness. Orkn 5E 88
Rapps. Som 4B 8
Rascal Moor. E Yor 4F 42
Rascarrel. Dum 7B 52
Rasharkin. Caus 3F 93
Rashfield. Arg 1L 57
Rashwood. Worc 5H 27
Raskelf. N Yor 8B 48
Rassau. Blae 3L 17
Rastrick. W Yor 5K 41
Ratagan. High 4L 69
Ratby. Leics 1C 28
Ratcliffe Culey. Leics 2M 27
Ratcliffe on Soar. Notts 7B 36
Ratcliffe on the Wreake.
Leics 8D 36
Rathen. Abers 7K 81
Rathfriland. Arm 7G 93
Rathillet. Fife 5G 67
Rathmell. N Yor 1G 41
Ratho. Edin 2K 59
Ratho Station. Edin 2K 59
Rathven. Mor 7D 80
Ratley. Hants 3M 9
Ratley. Warw 7A 28
Ratlinghope. Shrp 2C 26
Rattar. High 4D 86
Ratten Row. Cumb 7H 53
Ratten Row. Lanc 3C 40
Rattery. Devn 5K 5
Rattlesden. Suff 6F 30
Ratton Village. E Sus 5B 12
Rattray. Abers 8K 81
Rattray. Per 3E 66
Raughton. Cumb 7H 53
Raughton Head. Cumb 7H 53
Raunds. Nptn 4G 29
Ravenfield. S Yor 8B 42
Ravenfield Common. S Yor 8B 42
Ravenglass. Cumb 5K 45
Ravenhills Green. Worc 6F 26
Raveningham. Norf 2K 31
Ravenscar. N Yor 5G 49
Ravensdale. IOM 5C 44
Ravensden. Bed 6H 29
Ravenseat. N Yor 5G 47
Ravenshead. Notts 4C 36
Ravensmoor. Ches E 4E 34
Ravensthorpe. Nptn 4D 28
Ravensthorpe. W Yor 5L 41
Ravenstone. Leics 8B 36
Ravenstone. Mil 6F 28
Ravenstonedale. Cumb 5F 46
Ravenstown. Cumb 8B 46
Ravenstruther. S Lan 5H 59
Ravensworth. N Yor 5K 47
Ravernet. Lis 5H 93
Raw. N Yor 5G 49
Rawcliffe. E Yor 5D 42
Rawcliffe. York 2C 42
Rawcliffe Bridge. E Yor 5D 42
Rawdon. W Yor 4L 41
Rawgreen. Nmbd 6C 54
Rawmarsh. S Yor 8B 42
Rawnsley. Staf 8J 35
Rawreth. Essx 4D 22
Rawridge. Devn 5M 7
Rawson Green. Derbs 5A 36
Rawtenstall. Lanc 5G 41
Raydon. Suff 8G 31
Raylees. Nmbd 2C 54
Rayleigh. Essx 4E 22
Raymond's Hill. Devn 6B 8
Rayne. Essx 1D 22
Rayners Lane. G Lon 5J 21
Reach. Cambs 5B 30
Read. Lanc 4F 40
Reading. Read 115 (6E 20)
Reading Green. Suff 4H 31
Reading Street. Kent 2F 12
Readymoney. Corn 6D 4
Reagill. Cumb 4E 46
Rearquhar. High 4H 79
Rearsby. Leics 8D 36
Reasby. Linc 2H 37
Reaseheath. Ches E 4E 34
Reaster. High 5D 86
Reawick. Shet 3D 90
Reay. High 5A 86
Rechullin. High 8K 77
Reculver. Kent 7J 23
Redberth. Pemb 6G 15
Redbourn. Herts 2J 21
Redbourne. N Lin 7G 43
Redbrook. Glos 3D 18
Redbrook. Wrex 5D 34
Redburn. High 1K 71
Redburn. Nmbd 5A 54
Redcar. Red C 3D 48
Redcastle. High 1F 70
Redcliffe Bay. N Som 6C 18
Red Dial. Cumb 7G 53
Redding. Falk 2H 59
Reddingmuirhead. Falk 2H 59
The Reddings. Glos 1H 19
Reddish. G Man 8G 41
Redditch. Worc 5J 27
Rede. Suff 6E 30
Redenhall. Norf 3J 31
Redesdale Camp. Nmbd 2B 54
Redesmouth. Nmbd 3B 54
Redford. Ang 3J 67
Redford. Dur 8D 54
Redford. W Sus 3F 10
Redfordgreen. Bord 8A 60
Redgate. Corn 5E 4
Redgrave. Suff 4G 31
Red Hill. Warw 6K 27
Red Hill. W Yor 5B 42
Redhill. Abers 5G 73
Redhill. Herts 8K 29
Redhill. N Som 7D 18
Redhill. Shrp 8F 34
Redhill. Surr 8K 21
Redhouses. Arg 3C 56
Redisham. Suff 3L 31
Redland. Bris 6D 18
Redland. Orkn 7C 88
Redlingfield. Suff 4H 31
Red Lodge. Suff 4C 30
Redlynch. Som 2F 8
Redlynch. Wilts 3L 9
Redmain. Cumb 8F 52
Redmarley. Worc 5F 26
Redmarley D'Abitot. Glos 8F 26
Redmarshall. Stoc T 3A 48
Redmile. Leics 6E 36
Redmire. N Yor 6J 47
Rednal. Shrp 7B 34
Redpath. Bord 6C 60
Redpoint. High 7J 77
Red Post. Corn 5B 6
Red Rock. G Man 7D 40
Red Roses. Carm 5J 15
Red Row. Nmbd 2F 54
Redruth. Corn 4L 3
Red Street. Staf 4G 35
Redvales. G Man 7G 41
Red Wharf Bay. IOA 2E 32
Redwick. Newp 5C 18
Redwick. S Glo 5D 18
Redworth. Darl 3L 47
Reed. Herts 8L 29
Reed End. Herts 8L 29
Reedham. Linc 4K 37
Reedham. Norf 1L 31
Reedness. E Yor 5F 42
Reeds Beck. Linc 3K 37
Reemshill. Abers 1G 73
Reepham. Linc 2H 37
Reepham. Norf 7G 39
Reeth. N Yor 6J 47
Regaby. IOM 5D 44
Regil. N Som 7D 18
Regoul. High 8J 79
Reiff. High 2L 77
Reigate. Surr 8K 21
Reighton. N Yor 8J 49
Reilth. Shrp 3A 26
Reinigeadal. W Isl 3D 76
Reisque. Abers 4H 73
Reiss. High 6E 86
Rejerrah. Corn 3L 3
Releath. Corn 5K 3
Relubbus. Corn 5J 3
Relugas. Mor 1K 71
Remenham. Wok 5E 20
Remenham Hill. Wok 5E 20
Rempstone. Notts 7C 36
Rendcomb. Glos 3J 19
Rendham. Suff 5K 31
Rendlesham. Suff 6K 31
Renfrew. Ren 3D 58
Renhold. Bed 6H 29
Renishaw. Derbs 2B 36
Rennington. Nmbd 8K 61
Renton. W Dun 2B 58
Renwick. Cumb 7K 53
Repps. Norf 8L 39
Repton. Derbs 7M 35
Rescassa. Corn 7B 4
Rescobie. Ang 2J 67
Rescorla. Corn
nr. Penwithick 6C 4
nr. Sticker 7B 4
Resipole. High 1B 64
Resolfen. Neat 4H 17
Resolis. High 7G 79
Resolven. Neat 4H 17
Rest and be thankful. Arg 7G 65
Reston. Bord 3F 60
Restrop. Wilts 5J 19
Retford. Notts 1E 36
Retire. Corn 5C 4
Rettendon. Essx 4D 22
Revesby. Linc 3K 37
Rew. Devn 8K 5
Rewe. Devn 6J 7
Rew Street. IOW 6B 10
Rexon. Devn 7D 6
Reybridge. Wilts 7H 19
Reydon. Suff 4M 31
Reymerston. Norf 1G 31
Reynalton. Pemb 6G 15
Reynoldston. Swan 8L 15
Rezare. Corn 8C 6
Rhadyr. Mon 3B 18
Rhaeadr Gwy. Powy 6J 25
Rhandirmwyn. Carm 8G 25
Rhayader. Powy 6J 25
Rheindown. High 1F 70
Rhemore. High 2L 63
Rhenetra. High 8F 76
Rhewl. Den
nr. Llangollen 6L 33
nr. Ruthin 4L 33
Rhewl. Shrp 6B 34
Rhewl-Mostyn. Flin 2L 33
Rhian. High 2F 78
Rhian Breck. High 3F 78
Rhicarn. High 1A 78
Rhiconich. High 6E 84
Rhicullen. High 6G 79
Rhidorroch. High 4B 78
Rhifail. High 7K 85
Rhigos. Rhon 4J 17
Rhilochan. High 3H 79
Rhiroy. High 5B 78
Rhitongue. High 6J 85
Rhiw. Gwyn 8B 32
Rhiwabon. Wrex 5B 34
Rhiwbina. Card 6L 17
Rhiwbryfdir. Gwyn 6F 32
Rhiwderin. Newp 5A 18
Rhiwlas. Gwyn
nr. Bala 7J 33
nr. Bangor 4E 32
Rhiwlas. Powy 7L 33
Rhodes. G Man 7G 41
Rhodesia. Notts 1C 36
Rhodes Minnis. Kent 1H 13
Rhodiad-y-Brenin. Pemb 4D 14
Rhondda. Rhon 5J 17
Rhonehouse. Dum 6B 52
Rhoose. V Glam 8K 17
Rhos. Carm 3K 15
Rhos. Neat 4G 17
The Rhos. Pemb 5G 15
Rhosaman. Carm 3G 17
Rhoscefnhir. IOA 3E 32
Rhoscolyn. IOA 3B 32
Rhos Common. Powy 8A 34
Rhoscrowther. Pemb 6F 14
Rhos-ddu. Gwyn 7B 32
Rhosdylluan. Gwyn 8H 33
Rhosesmor. Flin 4M 33
Rhos-fawr. Gwyn 7C 32
Rhosgadfan. Gwyn 5E 32
Rhosgoch. IOA 2D 32
Rhosgoch. Powy 8L 25
Rhos Haminiog. Cdgn 6E 24
Rhos-hill. Pemb 2H 15
Rhoshirwaun. Gwyn 8A 32
Rhoslan. Gwyn 6D 32
Rhoslefain. Gwyn 2E 24
Rhosllanerchrugog. Wrex 5A 34
Rhôs Lligwy. IOA 2D 32
Rhosmaen. Carm 2F 16
Rhosmeirch. IOA 3D 32
Rhosneigr. IOA 3C 32
Rhôs-on-Sea. Cnwy 2H 33
Rhossili. Swan 8L 15
Rhosson. Pemb 4D 14
Rhostrenwfa. IOA 3D 32
Rhostryfan. Gwyn 5D 32
Rhostyllen. Wrex 5B 34
Rhoswiel. Shrp 6A 34
Rhosybol. IOA 2D 32
Rhos-y-brithdir. Powy 8L 33
Rhos-y-garth. Cdgn 5F 24
Rhos-y-gwaliau. Gwyn 7J 33
Rhos-y-llan. Gwyn 7B 32
Rhos-y-meirch. Powy 5A 26
Rhu. Arg 1A 58
Rhuallt. Den 3K 33
Rhubha Stoer. High 8C 84
Rhubodach. Arg 2K 57
Rhuddall Heath. Ches W 3D 34
Rhuddlan. Cdgn 2L 15
Rhuddlan. Den 3K 33
Rhue. High 4A 78
Rhulen. Powy 8L 25
Rhunahaorine. Arg 5G 57
Rhuthun. Den 5L 33
Rhuvoult. High 6E 84
Y Rhws. V Glam 8K 17
Rhyd. Gwyn 6F 32
Rhydaman. Carm 3F 16
Rhydargaeau. Carm 4L 15
Rhydcymerau. Carm 1E 16
Rhydd. Worc 7G 27
Rhyd-Ddu. Gwyn 5E 32
Rhydding. Neat 5G 17
Rhydfudr. Cdgn 6E 24
Rhydlanfair. Cnwy 5H 33
Rhydlewis. Cdgn 2K 15
Rhydlios. Gwyn 7A 32
Rhydlydan. Cnwy 5H 33
Rhyd-meirionydd. Cdgn 4F 24
Rhydowen. Cdgn 2L 15
Rhyd-Rosser. Cdgn 6E 24
Rhydspence. Here 8M 25
Rhydtalog. Flin 5M 33
Rhyd-uchaf. Gwyn 7J 33
Rhydwyn. IOA 2C 32
Rhyd-y-clafdy. Gwyn 7C 32
Rhydycroesau. Powy 7M 33
Rhydyfelin. Cdgn 5E 24
Rhydyfelin. Rhon 6K 17
Rhyd-y-foel. Cnwy 3J 33
Rhyd-y-fro. Neat 4G 17
Rhydymain. Gwyn 8H 33
Rhyd-y-meudwy. Den 5L 33
Rhydymwyn. Flin 4M 33
Rhyd-yr-onen. Gwyn 2F 24
Rhyd-y-sarn. Gwyn 6F 32
Rhyl. Den 2K 33
Rhymney. Cphy 4L 17
Rhymni. Cphy 4L 17
Rhynd. Per 5E 66
Rhynie. Abers 3D 72
Ribbesford. Worc 4F 26
Ribbleton. Lanc 4D 40
Ribby. Lanc 4C 40
Ribchester. Lanc 4E 40
Riber. Derbs 4M 35
Ribigill. High 6H 85
Riby. Linc 7J 43
Riccall. N Yor 4D 42
Riccarton. E Ayr 6C 58
Richards Castle. Here 5C 26
Richborough Port. Kent 7K 23
Richhill. Arm 6F 93
Richings Park. Buck 6H 21
Richmond. G Lon 6J 21
Richmond. N Yor 5K 47
Rickarton. Abers 7H 73
Rickerby. Cumb 6J 53
Rickerscote. Staf 7H 35
Rickford. N Som 8C 18
Rickham. Devn 8K 5
Rickinghall. Suff 4G 31
Rickleton. Tyne 6F 54
Rickling. Essx 8A 30
Rickling Green. Essx 1B 22
Rickmansworth. Herts 4H 21
Riddings. Derbs 4B 36
Riddlecombe. Devn 4F 6
Riddlesden. W Yor 3J 41
Ridge. Dors 7H 9
Ridge. Herts 3K 21
Ridge. Wilts 2H 9
Ridgebourne. Powy 6K 25
Ridge Lane. Warw 2L 27
Ridgeway. Derbs
nr. Alfreton 4A 36
nr. Sheffield 1B 36
Ridgeway. Staf 4G 35
Ridgeway Cross. Here 7F 26
Ridgeway Moor. Derbs 1B 36
Ridgewell. Essx 7D 30
Ridgewood. E Sus 3A 12
Ridgmont. C Beds 8G 29
Ridgwardine. Shrp 6E 34
Riding Mill. Nmbd 5D 54
Ridley. Kent 7C 22
Ridley. Nmbd 5A 54
Ridlington. Norf 6K 39
Ridlington. Rut 1F 28
Ridsdale. Nmbd 3C 54
Riemore Lodge. Per 3D 66
Rievaulx. N Yor 7C 48
Rift House. Hart 8H 55
Rigg. Dum 5G 53
Riggend. N Lan 2F 58
Rigsby. Linc 2M 37
Rigside. S Lan 6G 59
Riley Green. Lanc 5E 40
Rileyhill. Staf 8K 35
Rilla Mill. Corn 8B 6
Rillington. N Yor 8F 48
Rimington. Lanc 3G 41
Rimpton. Som 3E 8
Rimsdale. High 7K 85
Rimswell. E Yor 5L 43
Ringasta. Shet 6D 90
Ringford. Dum 6A 52
Ringing Hill. Leics 8B 36
Ringinglow. S Yor 1L 35
Ringland. Norf 8H 39
Ringlestone. Kent 8E 22
Ringmer. E Sus 4M 11
Ringmore. Devn
nr. Kingsbridge 7J 5
nr. Teignmouth 8J 7
Ring o' Bells. Lanc 6C 40
Ring's End. Cambs 1L 29
Ringsfield. Suff 3L 31
Ringsfield Corner. Suff 3L 31
Ringshall. Buck 2G 21
Ringshall. Suff 6G 31
Ringshall Stocks. Suff 6G 31
Ringstead. Norf 5D 38
Ringstead. Nptn 4G 29
Ringwood. Hants 5K 9
Ringwould. Kent 1K 13
Rinmore. Abers 4D 72
Rinnigill. Orkn 2E 86
Rinsey. Corn 6J 3
Riof. W Isl 8E 82
Ripe. E Sus 4B 12
Ripley. Derbs 4B 36
Ripley. Hants 6K 9
Ripley. N Yor 1L 41
Ripley. Surr 8H 21
Riplingham. E Yor 4G 43
Ripon. N Yor 8M 47
Rippingale. Linc 7H 37
Ripple. Kent 1K 13
Ripple. Worc 8G 27
Ripponden. W Yor 6J 41
Rireavach. High 4M 77
Risabus. Arg 5C 56
Risbury. Here 6D 26
Risby. E Yor 4H 43
Risby. N Lin 6G 43
Risby. Suff 5D 30
Risca. Cphy 5M 17
Rise. E Yor 3J 43
Riseden. E Sus 2C 12
Riseden. Kent 2D 12
Rise End. Derbs 4L 35
Risegate. Linc 7K 37
Riseholme. Linc 2G 37
Riseley. Bed 5H 29
Riseley. Wok 7E 20
Rishangles. Suff 5H 31
Rishton. Lanc 4F 40
Rishworth. W Yor 6J 41
Risley. Derbs 6B 36
Risley. Warr 8E 40
Risplith. N Yor 1L 41
Rispond. High 5G 85
Rivar. Wilts 7M 19
Rivenhall. Essx 2E 22
Rivenhall End. Essx 2E 22
River. Kent 1J 13
River. W Sus 3G 11
River Bank. Cambs 5B 30
Riverhead. Kent 8B 22
Rivington. Lanc 6E 40
Roach Bridge. Lanc 5D 40
Roachill. Devn 3H 7
Roade. Nptn 6E 28
Road Green. Norf 2J 31
Roadhead. Cumb 4K 53
Roadmeetings. S Lan 5G 59
Roadside. High 5C 86
Roadside of Catterline.
Abers 8H 73
Roadside of Kinneff. Abers 8H 73
Roadwater. Som 2K 7
Road Weedon. Nptn 6D 28
Roag. High 1D 68
Roa Island. Cumb 8M 45
Roath. Card 7L 17
Roberton. Bord 8B 60
Roberton. S Lan 7H 59
Robertsbridge. E Sus 3D 12
Robertstown. Mor 1B 72
Robertstown. Rhon 4J 17
Roberttown. W Yor 5K 41
Robeston Back. Pemb 5G 15
Robeston Wathen. Pemb 5G 15
Robeston West. Pemb 6E 14
Robin Hood. Lanc 6D 40
Robin Hood. W Yor 5M 41
Robinhood End. Essx 8D 30
Robin Hood's Bay. N Yor 5G 49
Roborough. Devn
nr. Great Torrington 4E 6
nr. Plymouth 5H 5
Rob Roy's House. Arg 6F 64
Roby Mill. Lanc 7D 40
Rocester. Staf 6K 35
Roch. Pemb 4E 14
Rochdale. G Man 6G 41
Roche. Corn 5B 4
Rochester. Medw
Medway Towns 111 (7D 22)
Rochester. Nmbd 2B 54
Rochford. Essx 4E 22
Rock. Corn 4B 4
Rock. Nmbd 7K 61
Rock. W Sus 4J 11
Rock. Worc 4F 26
The Rock. M Ulst 5E 92
Rockbeare. Devn 6K 7
Rockbourne. Hants 4K 9
Rockcliffe. Cumb 5H 53
Rockcliffe. Dum 6C 52
Rockcliffe Cross. Cumb 5H 53
Rock Ferry. Mers 1B 34
Rockfield. High 5K 79
Rockfield. Mon 2C 18
Rockford. Hants 5K 9
Rockgreen. Shrp 4D 26
Rockhampton. S Glo 4E 18
Rockhead. Corn 3C 4
Rockingham. Nptn 2F 28
Rockland All Saints. Norf 2F 30
Rockland St Mary. Norf 1K 31
Rockland St Peter. Norf 2F 30
Rockley. Wilts 6K 19
Rockwell End. Buck 5E 20
Rockwell Green. Som 4L 7
Rodborough. Glos 3G 19
Rodbourne. Wilts 5H 19
Rodd. Here 5B 26
Roddam. Nmbd 7H 61
Rodden. Dors 7E 8
Roddenloft. E Ayr 7C 58
Roddymoor. Dur 8E 54
Rode. Som 8G 19
Rode Heath. Ches E 4G 35
Rodeheath. Ches E 3G 35
Rodel. W Isl 5B 76
Roden. Telf 8D 34
Rodhuish. Som 2K 7
Rodington. Telf 8D 34
Rodington Heath. Telf 8D 34
Rodley. Glos 2F 18
Rodmarton. Glos 4H 19
Rodmell. E Sus 5M 11
Rodmersham. Kent 7F 22
Rodmersham Green. Kent 7F 22
Rodney Stoke. Som 1C 8
Rodsley. Derbs 5L 35
Rodway. Som 2A 8
Rodway. Telf 8E 34
Rodwell. Dors 8E 8
Roecliffe. N Yor 1A 42
Roe Green. Herts 8L 29
Roehampton. G Lon 6K 21
Roesound. Shet 1D 90
Roffey. W Sus 2J 11
Rogart. High 3H 79
Rogate. W Sus 3F 10
Roger Ground. Cumb 6B 46
Rogerstone. Newp 5A 18
Rogiet. Mon 5C 18
Rogue's Alley. Cambs 1L 29
Roke. Oxon 4D 20
Rokemarsh. Oxon 4D 20
Roker. Tyne 6H 55
Rollesby. Norf 8L 39
Rolleston. Leics 1E 28
Rolleston. Notts 4E 36
Rolleston on Dove. Staf 7L 35
Rolston. E Yor 3K 43
Rolvenden. Kent 2E 12
Rolvenden Layne. Kent 2E 12
Romaldkirk. Dur 3H 47
Roman Bank. Shrp 2D 26
Romanby. N Yor 6A 48
Romannobridge. Bord 5K 59
Romansleigh. Devn 3G 7
Romers Common. Worc 5D 26
Romesdal. High 8F 76
Romford. Dors 5J 9
Romford. G Lon 5B 22
Romiley. G Man 8H 41
Romsey. Hants 3A 10
Romsley. Shrp 3F 26
Romsley. Worc 4H 27
Ronague. IOM 7B 44
Ronaldsvoe. Orkn 2F 86
Rookby. Cumb 4G 47
Rookhope. Dur 7C 54
Rooking. Cumb 4C 46
Rookley. IOW 7C 10
Rooks Bridge. Som 8B 18
Rooksey Green. Suff 6F 30
Rook's Nest. Som 2K 7
Rookwood. W Sus 6E 10
Roos. E Yor 4K 43
Roosebeck. Cumb 8M 45
Roosecote. Cumb 8M 45
Rootfield. High 8F 78
Rootham's Green. Bed 6J 29
Rootpark. S Lan 4H 59
Ropley. Hants 2D 10
Ropley Dean. Hants 2D 10
Ropsley. Linc 6G 37
Rora. Abers 8K 81
Rorandle. Abers 4F 72
Rorrington. Shrp 1B 26
Rose. Corn 3L 3
Roseacre. Lanc 4C 40
Rose Ash. Devn 3G 7
Rosebank. S Lan 5G 59
Rosebush. Pemb 4G 15
Rosedale Abbey. N Yor 6E 48
Roseden. Nmbd 7H 61
Rose Green. Essx 1E 22
Rose Green. Suff 7F 30
Rosehall. High 3E 78
Rosehearty. Abers 7J 81
Rose Hill. E Sus 4A 12
Rose Hill. Lanc 4G 41
Rosehill. Shrp
nr. Market Drayton 6E 34
nr. Shrewsbury 8C 34
Roseisle. Mor 7M 79
Rosemarket. Pemb 6F 14
Rosemarkie. High 8H 79
Rosemary Lane. Devn 4L 7
Rosemount. Per 3E 66
Rosenannon. Corn 5B 4
Roser's Cross. E Sus 3B 12
Rosevean. Corn 6C 4
Rosewell. Midl 3L 59
Roseworth. Stoc T 3B 48
Roseworthy. Corn 5K 3
Rosgill. Cumb 4D 46
Roshven. High 8J 69
Roskhill. High 1D 68
Roskorwell. Corn 6L 3
Rosley. Cumb 7H 53
Roslin. Midl 3L 59
Rosliston. Derbs 8L 35
Rosneath. Arg 1A 58
Ross. Dum 7M 51
Ross. Nmbd 6J 61
Ross. Per 5A 66
Ross. Bord 3G 61
Rossendale. Lanc 5F 40
Rossett. Wrex 4B 34
Rossington. S Yor 8D 42
Rosskeen. High 7G 79
Rossland. Ren 2C 58
Rosslea. Ferm 7D 92
Ross-on-Wye. Here 1E 18
Roster. High 8D 86
Rostherne. Ches E 1F 34
Rostholme. S Yor 7C 42
Rosthwaite. Cumb 4A 46
Roston. Derbs 5K 35
Rostrevor. New M 7G 93
Rosudgeon. Corn 6J 3
Rosyth. Fife 1K 59
Rothbury. Nmbd 1D 54
Rotherby. Leics 8D 36
Rotherfield. E Sus 3B 12
Rotherfield Greys. Oxon 5E 20
Rotherfield Peppard. Oxon 5E 20
Rotherham. S Yor 8B 42
Rothersthorpe. Nptn 6E 28
Rotherwick. Hants 8E 20
Rothes. Mor 1B 72
Rothesay. Arg 3K 57
Rothienorman. Abers 2G 73
Rothiesholm. Orkn 7F 88
Rothley. Leics 8C 36
Rothley. Nmbd 3D 54
Rothwell. Linc 8J 43
Rothwell. Nptn 3F 28
Rothwell. W Yor 5M 41
Rotsea. E Yor 2H 43
Rottal. Ang 1G 67
Rotten End. Suff 5K 31
Rotten Row. Norf 8G 39
Rotten Row. W Ber 6C 20
Rotten Row. W Mid 4K 27
Rottingdean. Brig 5L 11
Rottington. Cumb 3J 45
Roud. IOW 7C 10
Rougham. Norf 7E 38
Rougham. Suff 5F 30
Rough Close. Staf 6H 35
Rough Common. Kent 8H 23
Roughcote. Staf 5H 35
Roughfort. Ant 4H 93
Rough Haugh. High 7K 85
Rough Hay. Staf 7L 35
Roughlee. Lanc 3G 41
Roughley. W Mid 2K 27
Roughsike. Cumb 4K 53
Roughton. Linc 3K 37
Roughton. Norf 6J 39
Roughton. Shrp 2F 26
Roundbush Green. Essx 2B 22
Roundham. Som 5C 8
Roundhay. W Yor 4M 41
Round Hill. Torb 5L 5
Roundhurst. W Sus 2G 11
Round Maple. Suff 7F 30
Round Oak. Shrp 3B 26
Roundstreet Common.
W Sus 3H 11
Roundthwaite. Cumb 5E 46
Roundway. Wilts 7J 19
Roundyhill. Ang 2G 67
Rousdon. Devn 6A 8
Rousham. Oxon 1B 20
Rousky. Ferm 4D 92
Rous Lench. Worc 6J 27
Routh. E Yor 3H 43
Rout's Green. Buck 4E 20
Row. Corn 4C 4
Row. Cumb
nr. Kendal 7C 46
nr. Penrith 8L 53
The Row. Lanc 8C 46
Rowanburn. Dum 4J 53
Rowanhill. Abers 8K 81
Rowardennan. Stir 8H 65
Rowarth. Derbs 1J 35
Row Ash. Hants 4C 10
Rowberrow. Som 8C 18
Rowde. Wilts 7H 19
Rowden. Devn 6F 6
Rowen. Cnwy 3G 33
Rowfoot. Nmbd 5L 53
Row Green. Essx 1D 22
Row Heath. Essx 2H 23
Rowhedge. Essx 1G 23
Rowhook. W Sus 2J 11
Rowington. Warw 5L 27
Rowland. Derbs 2L 35
Rowlands Castle. Hants 4E 10
Rowlands Gill. Tyne 6E 54
Rowledge. Hants 1F 10
Rowley. Dur 7D 54
Rowley. E Yor 4G 43
Rowley. Shrp 1B 26
Rowley Hill. W Yor 6K 41
Rowley Regis. W Mid 3H 27
Rowlstone. Here 1B 18
Rowly. Surr 1H 11
Rowner. Hants 5C 10
Rowney Green. Worc 4J 27
Rownhams. Hants 4A 10
Rowrah. Cumb 3K 45
Rowsham. Buck 2F 20
Rowsley. Derbs 3L 35
Rowstock. Oxon 5B 20
Rowston. Linc 4H 37
Rowthorne. Derbs 3B 36
Rowton. Ches W 3C 34
Rowton. Shrp
nr. Ludlow 3C 26
nr. Shrewsbury 8B 34
Rowton. Telf 8E 34
Row Town. Surr 7H 21
Roxburgh. Bord 6E 60
Roxby. N Lin 6G 43
Roxby. N Yor 4E 48
Roxhill. Ant 4G 93
Roxton. Bed 6J 29
Roxwell. Essx 3C 22
Royal Leamington Spa.
Warw 5M 27
Royal Oak. Darl 3L 47
Royal Oak. Lanc 7C 40
Royal Oak. N Yor 8J 49
Royal's Green. Ches E 5E 34
Royal Sutton Coldfield.
W Mid 2K 27
Royal Tunbridge Wells.
Kent 2B 12
Royal Wootton Bassett.
Wilts 5J 19
Roybridge. High 7C 70
Roydon. Essx 2M 21
Roydon. Norf
nr. Diss 3G 31
nr. King's Lynn 7D 38
Roydon Hamlet. Essx 3M 21
Royston. Herts 7L 29
Royston. S Yor 6A 42
Royston Water. Som 4M 7
Royton. G Man 7H 41
Ruabon. Wrex 5B 34
Ruaig. Arg 3F 62
Ruan High Lanes. Corn 8B 4
Ruan Lanihorne. Corn 7A 4
Ruan Major. Corn 7L 3
Ruan Minor. Corn 7L 3
Ruarach. High 3L 69
Ruardean. Glos 2E 18
Ruardean Hill. Glos 2E 18
Ruardean Woodside. Glos 2E 18
Rubane. Ards 5K 93
Rubery. Worc 4H 27
Ruchazie. Glas 3E 58
Ruckcroft. Cumb 7K 53
Ruckinge. Kent 2G 13
Ruckland. Linc 2L 37
Rucklers Lane. Herts 3H 21
Ruckley. Shrp 1D 26
Rudbaxton. Pemb 4F 14
Rudby. N Yor 5B 48
Ruddington. Notts 6C 36
Rudford. Glos 1F 18
Rudge. Shrp 2G 27
Rudge. Wilts 8G 19
Rudge Heath. Shrp 2F 26
Rudgeway. S Glo 5E 18
Rudgwick. W Sus 2H 11
Rudhall. Here 1E 18
Rudheath. Ches W 2E 34
Rudley Green. Essx 3E 22
Rudloe. Wilts 6G 19
Rudry. Cphy 6M 17
Rudston. E Yor 1H 43
Rudyard. Staf 4H 35
Rufford. Lanc 6C 40
Rufforth. York 2C 42
Rugby. Warw 4C 28
Rugeley. Staf 8J 35
Ruglen. S Ayr 1H 51
Ruilick. High 1F 70
Ruisaurie. High 1E 70
Ruishton. Som 3A 8
Ruisigearraidh. W Isl 5L 75
Ruislip. G Lon 5H 21
Ruislip Common. G Lon 5H 21
Rumbling Bridge. Per 8D 66
Rumburgh. Suff 3K 31
Rumford. Corn 4A 4
Rumford. Falk 2H 59
Rumney. Card 7M 17
Rumwell. Som 3L 7
Runcorn. Hal 1D 34
Runcton. W Sus 5F 10
Runcton Holme. Norf 1C 30
Rundlestone. Devn 8E 6
Runfold. Surr 1F 10
Runhall. Norf 1G 31
Runham. Norf 8L 39
Runnington. Som 3L 7
Runshaw Moor. Lanc 6D 40
Runswick. N Yor 4F 48
Runtaleave. Ang 1F 66
Runwell. Essx 4D 22
Ruscombe. Wok 6E 20
Rushall. Here 8E 26
Rushall. Norf 3H 31
Rushall. W Mid 1J 27
Rushall. Wilts 8K 19
Rushbrooke. Suff 5E 30
Rushbury. Shrp 2D 26
Rushden. Herts 8L 29
Rushden. Nptn 5G 29
Rushenden. Kent 6F 22
Rushford. Devn 8D 6
Rushford. Suff 3F 30
Rush Green. Herts 1K 21
Rushlake Green. E Sus 4C 12
Rushmere. Suff 3L 31
Rushmere St Andrew. Suff 7J 31
Rushmoor. Surr 1F 10
Rushock. Worc 4G 27
Rusholme. G Man 8G 41
Rushton. Ches W 3D 34
Rushton. Nptn 3F 28
Rushton. Shrp 1E 26
Rushton Spencer. Staf 3H 35
Rushwick. Worc 6G 27
Rushyford. Dur 3L 47
Ruskie. Stir 7L 65
Ruskington. Linc 4H 37
Rusland. Cumb 7B 46
Rusper. W Sus 2K 11
Ruspidge. Glos 2E 18
Russell's Water. Oxon 5E 20
Russel's Green. Suff 4J 31
Russ Hill. Surr 1K 11
Russland. Orkn 8C 88
Rusthall. Kent 2B 12
Rustington. W Sus 5H 11
Ruston. N Yor 7G 49
Ruston Parva. E Yor 1H 43
Ruswarp. N Yor 5F 48
Rutherglen. S Lan 3E 58
Ruthernbridge. Corn 5C 4
Ruthin. Den 5L 33
Ruthin. V Glam 7J 17
Ruthrieston. Aber 5J 73
Ruthven. Abers 1E 72
Ruthven. Ang 3F 66
Ruthven. High
nr. Inverness 2J 71
nr. Kingussie 6H 71
Ruthvoes. Corn 5B 4
Ruthwaite. Cumb 8G 53
Ruthwell. Dum 5F 52
Ruxton Green. Here 2D 18
Ruyton-XI-Towns. Shrp 7B 34
Ryal. Nmbd 4D 54
Ryall. Dors 6C 8
Ryall. Worc 7G 27
Ryarsh. Kent 8C 22
Rychraggan. High 2E 70
Rydal. Cumb 5B 46
Ryde. IOW 6C 10
Rye. E Sus 3F 12
Ryecroft Gate. Staf 3H 35
Ryeford. Here 1E 18
Rye Foreign. E Sus 3F 12
Rye Harbour. E Sus 4F 12
Ryehill. E Yor 5K 43
Rye Street. Worc 8F 26
Ryhall. Rut 8H 37
Ryhill. W Yor 6A 42
Ryhope. Tyne 6H 55
Ryhope Colliery. Tyne 6H 55
Rylands. Notts 6C 36
Rylstone. N Yor 2H 41
Ryme Intrinseca. Dors 4D 8
Ryther. N Yor 4C 42
Ryton. Glos 8F 26
Ryton. N Yor 8E 48
Ryton. Shrp 1F 26
Ryton. Tyne 5E 54
Ryton. Warw 3B 28
Ryton-on-Dunsmore. Warw 4A 28
Ryton Woodside. Tyne 5E 54

S

Saasaig. High 5H 69
Sabden. Lanc 4F 40
Sacombe. Herts 2L 21
Sacriston. Dur 7F 54
Sadberge. Darl 4M 47
Saddell. Arg 6G 57
Saddington. Leics 2D 28
Saddle Bow. Norf 8C 38
Saddlescombe. W Sus 4K 11
Saddleworth. G Man 7H 41
Sadgill. Cumb 5C 46
Saffron Walden. Essx 8B 30
Sageston. Pemb 6G 15
Saham Hills. Norf 1F 30
Saham Toney. Norf 1E 30
Saighdinis. W Isl 7K 75
Saighton. Ches W 3C 34
Sain Dunwyd. V Glam 8J 17
Sain Hilari. V Glam 7K 17
St Abbs. Bord 3G 61
St Agnes. Corn 3L 3
St Albans. Herts 3J 21

St Allen—Slaley

St Allen. *Corn* 3M 3
St Andrews. *Fife* 6J 67
St Andrews Major. *V Glam* 7L 17
St Anne's. *Lanc* 5B 40
St Ann's. *Dum* 2E 52
St Ann's Chapel. *Corn* 8D 6
St Ann's Chapel. *Devn* 7J 5
St Anthony. *Corn* 8A 4
St Anthony-in-Meneage.
Corn 6L 3
St Arvans. *Mon* 4D 18
St Asaph. *Den* 3K 33
Sain Tathan. *V Glam* 8K 17
St Athan. *V Glam* 8K 17
St Austell. *Corn* 6C 4
St Bartholomew's Hill. *Wilts* 3H 9
St Bees. *Cumb* 3J 45
St Blazey. *Corn* 6C 4
St Blazey Gate. *Corn* 6C 4
St Boswells. *Bord* 6C 60
St Breock. *Corn* 4B 4
St Breward. *Corn* 4C 4
St Briavels. *Glos* 3D 18
St Brides. *Pemb* 5D 14
St Brides Major. *V Glam* 7H 17
St Bride's Netherwent. *Mon* 5C 18
St Bride's-super-Ely.
V Glam 7K 17
St Brides Wentlooge. *Newp* 5A 18
St Budeaux. *Plym* 6G 5
Saintbury. *Glos* 8K 27
St Buryan. *Corn* 6H 3
St Catherine. *Bath* 6F 18
St Catherines. *Arg* 7F 64
St Clears. *Carm* 5J 15
St Cleer. *Corn* 5E 4
St Clement. *Corn* 7A 4
St Clether. *Corn* 7B 6
St Colmac. *Arg* 3K 57
St Columb Major. *Corn* 5B 4
St Columb Minor. *Corn* 2M 3
St Columb Road. *Corn* 6B 4
St Combs. *Abers* 7K 81
St Cross. *Hants* 3B 10
St Cross South Elmham.
Suff 3J 31
St Cyrus. *Abers* 1L 67
St David's. *Per* 5C 66
St Davids. *Pemb* 4D 14
St Day. *Corn* 4L 3
St Dennis. *Corn* 6B 4
St Dogmaels. *Pemb* 2H 15
St Dominick. *Corn* 5F 4
St Donat's. *V Glam* 8J 17
St Edith's Marsh. *Wilts* 7H 19
St Endellion. *Corn* 4B 4
St Enoder. *Corn* 6A 4
St Erme. *Corn* 4M 3
St Erney. *Corn* 6F 4
St Erth. *Corn* 5J 3
St Erth Praze. *Corn* 5J 3
St Ervan. *Corn* 4A 4
St Eval. *Corn* 5A 4
St Ewe. *Corn* 7B 4
St Fagans. *Card* 7L 17
St Fergus. *Abers* 8K 81
Saintfield. *New M* 6J 93
St Fillans. *Per* 5L 65
St Florence. *Pemb* 6G 15
St Gennys. *Corn* 6A 6
St George. *Cnwy* 3J 33
St George's. *N Som* 7B 18
St Georges. *V Glam* 7K 17
St George's Hill. *Surr* 7H 21
St Germans. *Corn* 6F 4
St Giles in the Wood. *Devn* 4E 6
St Giles on the Heath. *Devn* 6C 6
St Giles's Hill. *Hants* 3B 10
St Gluvias. *Corn* 5L 3
St Harmon. *Powy* 5J 25
St Helena. *Warw* 1L 27
St Helen Auckland. *Dur* 3K 47
St Helen's. *E Sus* 4E 12
St Helens. *Cumb* 8E 52
St Helens. *IOW* 7D 10
St Helens. *Mers* 8D 40
St Hilary. *Corn* 5J 3
St Hilary. *V Glam* 7K 17
Saint Hill. *Devn* 5K 7
Saint Hill. *W Sus* 2L 11
St Illtyd. *Blae* 4M 17
St Ippolyts. *Herts* 1J 21
St Ishmael. *Carm* 6K 15
St Ishmael's. *Pemb* 6E 14
St Issey. *Corn* 4B 4
St Ive. *Corn* 5F 4
St Ives. *Cambs* 4L 29
St Ives. *Corn* 4J 3
St Ives. *Dors* 5K 9
St James' End. *Nptn* 5E 28
St James South Elmham.
Suff 3K 31
St Jidgey. *Corn* 5B 4
St John. *Corn* 6G 5
St John's. *IOM* 6B 44
St John's. *Worc* 6G 27
St John's Chapel. *Devn* 3E 6
St John's Chapel. *Dur* 8B 54
St John's Fen End. *Norf* 8B 38
St John's Town of Dalry.
Dum 3M 51
St Judes. *IOM* 5C 44
St Just. *Corn* 5G 3
St Just in Roseland. *Corn* 8A 4
St Katherines. *Abers* 2G 73
St Keverne. *Corn* 6L 3
St Kew. *Corn* 4C 4
St Kew Highway. *Corn* 4C 4
St Keyne. *Corn* 5E 4
St Lawrence. *Corn* 5C 4
St Lawrence. *Essx* 3F 22
St Lawrence. *IOW* 8C 10
St Leonards. *Buck* 3G 21
St Leonards. *Dors* 5K 9
St Leonards. *E Sus* 5D 12
St Levan. *Corn* 6G 3
St Lythans. *V Glam* 7L 17
St Mabyn. *Corn* 4C 4
St Madoes. *Per* 5E 66
St Margaret's. *Herts* 2H 21
St Margaret's. *Wilts* 7L 19
St Margarets. *Here* 8B 26
St Margarets. *Herts* 2L 21
St Margaret's at Cliffe. *Kent* 1K 13
St Margaret's Hope. *Orkn* 2F 86
St Margaret South Elmham.
Suff 3K 31
St Mark's. *IOM* 7B 44
St Martin. *Corn*
nr. Helston 6L 3
nr. Looe 6E 4
St Martin's. *Shrp* 6B 34
St Martins. *Per* 4E 66
St Mary Bourne. *Hants* 8B 20
St Mary Church. *V Glam* 7K 17
St Marychurch. *Torb* 5M 5
St Mary Cray. *G Lon* 7A 22
St Mary Hill. *V Glam* 7J 17
St Mary Hoo. *Medw* 6E 22
St Mary in the Marsh. *Kent* 3G 13
St Mary's. *Orkn* 1F 86
St Mary's Airport. *IOS* 1H 3
St Mary's Bay. *Kent* 3G 13
St Marys Platt. *Kent* 8C 22
St Maughan's Green. *Mon* 2C 18
St Mawes. *Corn* 5M 3
St Mawgan. *Corn* 5A 4
St Mellion. *Corn* 5F 4
St Mellons. *Card* 6M 17
St Merryn. *Corn* 4A 4
St Mewan. *Corn* 6B 4
St Michael Caerhays. *Corn* 7B 4
St Michael Penkevil. *Corn* 7A 4
St Michaels. *Kent* 2E 12
St Michaels. *Torb* 6L 5
St Michaels. *Worc* 5D 26
St Michael's on Wyre. *Lanc* 3C 40
St Michael South Elmham.
Suff 3K 31
St Minver. *Corn* 4B 4
St Monans. *Fife* 7J 67
St Neot. *Corn* 5D 4
St Neots. *Cambs* 5J 29
St Newlyn East. *Corn* 3M 3
St Nicholas. *Pemb* 3E 14
St Nicholas. *V Glam* 7K 17
St Nicholas at Wade. *Kent* 7J 23
St Nicholas South Elmham.
Suff 3K 31
St Ninians. *Stir* 8A 66
St Olaves. *Norf* 2L 31
St Osyth. *Essx* 2H 23
St Osyth Heath. *Essx* 2H 23
St Owen's Cross. *Here* 1D 18
St Paul's Cray. *G Lon* 7A 22
St Paul's Walden. *Herts* 1J 21
St Peter's. *Kent* 7K 23
St Peter The Great. *Worc* 6G 27
St Petrox. *Pemb* 7F 14
St Pinnock. *Corn* 5E 4
St Quivox. *S Ayr* 7B 58
St Ruan. *Corn* 7L 3
St Stephen. *Corn* 6B 4
St Stephens. *Corn*
nr. Launceston 7C 6
nr. Saltash 6G 5
St Teath. *Corn* 3C 4
St Thomas. *Devn* 6J 7
St Thomas. *Swan* 5F 16
St Tudy. *Corn* 4C 4
St Twynnells. *Pemb* 7F 14
St Veep. *Corn* 6D 4
St Vigeans. *Ang* 3K 67
St Wenn. *Corn* 5B 4
St Weonards. *Here* 1C 18
St Winnolls. *Corn* 6F 4
St Winnow. *Corn* 6D 4
Salcombe. *Devn* 8K 5
Salcombe Regis. *Devn* 7L 7
Salcott. *Essx* 2F 22
Sale. *G Man* 8F 40
Saleby. *Linc* 2A 38
Sale Green. *Worc* 6H 27
Salehurst. *E Sus* 3D 12
Salem. *Carm* 2F 16
Salem. *Cdgn* 4F 24
Salen. *Arg* 3L 63
Salen. *High* 1A 64
Salesbury. *Lanc* 4E 40
Saleway. *Worc* 6H 27
Salford. *C Beds* 8G 29
Salford.
G Man
.....**Manchester 111** (8G 41)
Salford. *Oxon* 1L 19
Salford Priors. *Warw* 6J 27
Salfords. *Surr* 1K 11
Salhouse. *Norf* 8K 39
Saligo. *Arg* 3B 56
Saline. *Fife* 8D 66
Salisbury. *Wilts* **115** (2K 9)
Salkeld Dykes. *Cumb* 8K 53
Sallachan. *High* 1D 64
Sallachy. *High*
nr. Lairg 3F 78
nr. Stromeferry 2L 69
Salle. *Norf* 7H 39
Salmonby. *Linc* 2L 37
Salmond's Muir. *Ang* 4J 67
Salperton. *Glos* 1J 19
Salph End. *Bed* 6H 29
Salsburgh. *N Lan* 3G 59
Salt. *Staf* 7H 35
Salta. *Cumb* 7E 52
Saltaire. *W Yor* 4K 41
Saltash. *Corn* 6G 5
Saltburn. *High* 7H 79
Saltburn-by-the-Sea. *Red C* 3D 48
Saltby. *Leics* 7F 36
Saltcoats. *Cumb* 5K 45
Saltcoats. *N Ayr* 5M 57
Saltdean. *Brig* 5L 11
Salt End. *E Yor* 5J 43
Salter. *Lanc* 1E 40
Salterforth. *Lanc* 3G 41
Salters Lode. *Norf* 1B 30
Salterswall. *Ches W* 3E 34
Salterton. *Wilts* 2K 9
Saltfleet. *Linc* 8M 43
Saltfleetby All Saints. *Linc* 1A 38
Saltfleetby St Clements.
Linc 1A 38
Saltfleetby St Peter. *Linc* 1M 37
Saltford. *Bath* 7E 18
Salthouse. *Norf* 5G 39
Saltmarshe. *E Yor* 5E 42
Saltness. *Orkn* 3D 86
Saltness. *Shet* 3C 90
Saltney. *Flin* 3B 34
Salton. *N Yor* 8E 48
Saltrens. *Devn* 3D 6
Saltwick. *Nmbd* 4E 54
Saltwood. *Kent* 2H 13
Salum. *Arg* 3F 62
Salwarpe. *Worc* 5G 27
Salwayash. *Dors* 6C 8
Samalaman. *High* 8H 69
Sambourne. *Warw* 5J 27
Sambourne. *Wilts* 1G 9
Sambrook. *Telf* 7F 34
Samhia. *W Isl* 7J 75
Samlesbury. *Lanc* 4D 40
Samlesbury Bottoms. *Lanc* 5E 40
Sampford Arundel. *Som* 4L 7
Sampford Brett. *Som* 1K 7
Sampford Courtenay. *Devn* 5F 6
Sampford Peverell. *Devn* 4K 7
Sampford Spiney. *Devn* 8E 6
Samsonslane. *Orkn* 7F 88
Samuelston. *E Lot* 2B 60
Sanaigmore. *Arg* 2B 56
Sancreed. *Corn* 6H 3
Sancton. *E Yor* 4G 43
Sand. *High* 4L 77
Sand. *Shet* 3D 90
Sand. *Som* 1C 8
Sandaig. *Arg* 3E 62
Sandaig. *High* 5J 69
Sandale. *Cumb* 7G 53
Sandal Magna. *W Yor* 6M 41
Sandavore. *High* 7F 68
Sanday Airport. *Orkn* 5F 88
Sandbach. *Ches E* 3F 34
Sandbank. *Arg* 1L 57
Sandbanks. *Pool* 7J 9
Sandend. *Abers* 7E 80
Sanderstead. *G Lon* 7L 21
Sandfields. *Neat* 5G 17
Sandford. *Cumb* 4F 46
Sandford. *Devn* 5H 7
Sandford. *Dors* 7H 9
Sandford. *Hants* 5K 9
Sandford. *IOW* 7C 10
Sandford. *N Som* 8C 18
Sandford. *Shrp*
nr. Oswestry 7B 34
nr. Whitchurch 6D 34
Sandford. *S Lan* 5F 58
Sandfordhill. *Abers* 1L 73
Sandford-on-Thames.
Oxon 3C 20
Sandford Orcas. *Dors* 3E 8
Sandford St Martin. *Oxon* 1B 20
Sandgate. *Kent* 2H 13
Sandgreen. *Dum* 6L 51
Sandhaven. *Abers* 7J 81
Sandhead. *Dum* 6F 50
Sandhill. *Cambs* 3B 30
Sandhills. *Dors* 4E 8
Sandhills. *Oxon* 3C 20
Sandhills. *Surr* 2G 11
Sandhoe. *Nmbd* 5C 54
Sand Hole. *E Yor* 4F 42
Sandholes. *M Ulst* 5E 92
Sandholme. *E Yor* 4F 42
Sandholme. *Linc* 6L 37
Sandhurst. *Brac* 7F 20
Sandhurst. *Glos* 1G 19
Sandhurst. *Kent* 3D 12
Sandhurst Cross. *Kent* 3D 12
Sand Hutton. *N Yor* 2D 42
Sandhutton. *N Yor* 7A 48
Sandiacre. *Derbs* 6B 36
Sandilands. *Linc* 1B 38
Sandiway. *Ches W* 2E 34
Sandleheath. *Hants* 4K 9
Sandling. *Kent* 8D 22
Sandlow Green. *Ches E* 3F 34
Sandness. *Shet* 2B 90
Sandon. *Essx* 3D 22
Sandon. *Herts* 8L 29
Sandon. *Staf* 7H 35
Sandonbank. *Staf* 7H 35
Sandown. *IOW* 7C 10
Sandplace. *Corn* 6E 4
Sandridge. *Herts* 2J 21
Sandringham. *Norf* 7C 38
The Sands. *Surr* 1F 10
Sandsend. *N Yor* 4F 48
Sandside. *Cumb* 8B 46
Sandsound. *Shet* 3D 90
Sandtoft. *N Lin* 7E 42
Sandvoe. *Shet* 4H 91
Sandway. *Kent* 8E 22
Sandwich. *Kent* 8K 23
Sandwick. *Cumb* 4C 46
Sandwick. *Orkn*
on Mainland 8B 88
on South Ronaldsay 3F 86
Sandwick. *Shet*
on Mainland 5E 90
on Whalsay 1F 90
Sandwith. *Cumb* 3J 45
Sandy. *Carm* 6L 15
Sandy. *C Beds* 7J 29
Sandy Bank. *Linc* 4K 37
Sandycroft. *Flin* 3B 34
Sandy Cross. *Here* 6E 26
Sandygate. *Devn* 8H 7
Sandygate. *IOM* 5C 44
Sandy Haven. *Pemb* 6E 14
Sandyhills. *Dum* 6C 52
Sandylands. *Lanc* 1C 40
Sandy Lane. *Wilts* 7H 19
Sandylane. *Swan* 6E 16
Sandystones. *Bord* 7C 60
Sandyway. *Here* 1C 18
Sangobeg. *High* 5G 85
Sangomore. *High* 5G 85
Sankyn's Green. *Worc* 5F 26
Sanna. *High* 1K 63
Sanndabhaig. *W Isl*
on Isle of Lewis 8H 83
on South Uist 1E 74
Sannox. *N Ayr* 5K 57
Sanquhar. *Dum* 8F 58
Santon. *Cumb* 4K 45
Santon Bridge. *Cumb* 4L 45
Santon Downham. *Suff* 3E 30
Sapcote. *Leics* 2B 28
Sapey Common. *Here* 5F 26
Sapiston. *Suff* 4F 30
Sapley. *Cambs* 4K 29
Sapperton. *Derbs* 6K 35
Sapperton. *Glos* 3H 19
Sapperton. *Linc* 6H 37
Saracen's Head. *Linc* 7L 37
Sarclet. *High* 7E 86
Sardis. *Carm* 4E 16
Sardis. *Pemb*
nr. Milford Haven 6F 14
nr. Tenby 6H 15
Sarisbury Green. *Hants* 5C 10
Sarn. *B'end* 6J 17
Sarn. *Powy* 3M 25
Sarnau. *Carm* 4L 15
Sarnau. *Cdgn* 1K 15
Sarnau. *Gwyn* 7J 33
Sarnau. *Powy*
nr. Brecon 1K 17
nr. Welshpool 1M 25
Sarn Bach. *Gwyn* 8C 32
Sarnesfield. *Here* 6B 26
Sarn Meyllteyrn. *Gwyn* 7B 32
Saron. *Carm*
nr. Ammanford 3F 16
nr. Newcastle Emlyn 3K 15
Saron. *Gwyn*
nr. Bethel 4E 32
nr. Bontnewydd 5D 32
Sarratt. *Herts* 4H 21
Sarre. *Kent* 7J 23
Sarsden. *Oxon* 1L 19
Satley. *Dur* 7E 54
Satron. *N Yor* 6H 47
Satterleigh. *Devn* 3F 6
Satterthwaite. *Cumb* 6B 46
Satwell. *Oxon* 5E 20
Sauchen. *Abers* 4F 72
Saucher. *Per* 4E 66
Saughall. *Ches W* 2B 34
Saughtree. *Bord* 2K 53
Saul. *Glos* 3F 18
Saul. *New M* 6J 93
Saundby. *Notts* 1E 36
Saundersfoot. *Pemb* 6H 15
Saunderton. *Buck* 3E 20
Saunderton Lee. *Buck* 4F 20
Saunton. *Devn* 2D 6
Sausthorpe. *Linc* 3L 37
Saval. *High* 3F 78
Saverley Green. *Staf* 6H 35
Sawbridge. *Warw* 5C 28
Sawbridgeworth. *Herts* 2A 22
Sawdon. *N Yor* 7G 49
Sawley. *Derbs* 6B 36
Sawley. *Lanc* 3F 40
Sawley. *N Yor* 1L 41
Sawston. *Cambs* 7A 30
Sawtry. *Cambs* 3J 29
Saxby. *Leics* 7F 36
Saxby. *Linc* 1H 37
Saxby All Saints. *N Lin* 6G 43
Saxelby. *Leics* 7D 36
Saxelbye. *Leics* 7D 36
Saxham Street. *Suff* 5G 31
Saxilby. *Linc* 2F 36
Saxlingham. *Norf* 6G 39
Saxlingham Green. *Norf* 2J 31
Saxlingham Nethergate.
Norf 2J 31
Saxlingham Thorpe. *Norf* 2J 31
Saxmundham. *Suff* 5K 31
Saxondale. *Notts* 5D 36
Saxon Street. *Cambs* 6C 30
Saxtead. *Suff* 5J 31
Saxtead Green. *Suff* 5J 31
Saxthorpe. *Norf* 6H 39
Saxton. *N Yor* 4B 42
Sayers Common. *W Sus* 4K 11
Scackleton. *N Yor* 8D 48
Scadabhagh. *W Isl* 4C 76
Scaddy. *New M* 6J 93
Scaftworth. *Notts* 8D 42
Scagglethorpe. *N Yor* 8F 48
Scaitcliffe. *Lanc* 5F 40
Scaladal. *W Isl* 2C 76
Scalasaig. *Arg* 8J 63
Scalby. *E Yor* 5F 42
Scalby. *N Yor* 6H 49
Scalby Mills. *N Yor* 6H 49
Scaldwell. *Nptn* 4E 28
Scaleby. *Cumb* 5J 53
Scaleby Hill. *Cumb* 5J 53
Scale Houses. *Cumb* 7K 53
Scales. *Cumb*
nr. Barrow-in-Furness 8A 46
nr. Keswick 3B 46
Scalford. *Leics* 7E 36
Scaling. *N Yor* 4E 48
Scaling Dam. *Red C* 4E 48
Scalloway. *Shet* 4E 90
Scalpaigh. *W Isl* 4D 76
Scalpay House. *High* 3H 69
Scamblesby. *Linc* 2K 37
Scamodale. *High* 8K 69
Scampston. *N Yor* 8F 48
Scampton. *Linc* 2G 37
Scaniport. *High* 2G 71
Scapa. *Orkn* 1F 86
Scapegoat Hill. *W Yor* 6J 41
Scar. *Orkn* 5F 88
Scarasta. *W Isl* 4B 76
Scarborough. *N Yor* 7H 49
Scarcliffe. *Derbs* 3B 36
Scarcroft. *W Yor* 3A 42
Scardroy. *High* 8C 78
Scarfskerry. *High* 4D 86
Scargill. *Dur* 4J 47
Scarinish. *Arg* 3F 62
Scarisbrick. *Lanc* 6B 40
Scarning. *Norf* 8F 38
Scarrington. *Notts* 5E 36
Scarth Hill. *Lanc* 7C 40
Scartho. *NE Lin* 7K 43
Scarva. *Arm* 6G 93
Scarvister. *Shet* 3D 90
Scatness. *Shet* 7D 90
Scatwell. *High* 8D 78
Scaur. *Dum* 6C 52
Scawby. *N Lin* 7G 43
Scawby Brook. *N Lin* 7G 43
Scawsby. *S Yor* 7C 42
Scawton. *N Yor* 7C 48
Scaynes Hill. *W Sus* 3L 11
Scethrog. *Powy* 2L 17
Scholar Green. *Ches E* 4G 35
Scholes. *G Man* 7D 40
Scholes. *W Yor*
nr. Bradford 5K 41
nr. Holmfirth 7K 41
nr. Leeds 4A 42
Scholey Hill. *W Yor* 5A 42
School Aycliffe. *Darl* 3L 47
School Green. *Ches W* 3E 34
School Green. *Essx* 8D 30
Scissett. *W Yor* 6L 41
Scleddau. *Pemb* 3F 14
Scofton. *Notts* 1D 36
Scole. *Norf* 4H 31
Scollogstown. *New M* 7J 93
Scolpaig. *W Isl* 6J 75
Scolton. *Pemb* 4F 14
Scone. *Per* 5E 66
Sconser. *High* 2G 69
Scoonie. *Fife* 7G 67
Scopwick. *Linc* 4H 37
Scoraig. *High* 4M 77
Scorborough. *E Yor* 3H 43
Scorrier. *Corn* 4L 3
Scorriton. *Devn* 5K 5
Scorton. *Lanc* 3D 40
Scorton. *N Yor* 5L 47
Sco Ruston. *Norf* 7J 39
Scotbheinn. *W Isl* 8K 75
Scotby. *Cumb* 6J 53
Scotch Corner. *N Yor* 5L 47
Scotch Street. *Arm* 6F 93
Scotforth. *Lanc* 1C 40
Scot Hay. *Staf* 5G 35
Scothern. *Linc* 2H 37
Scotland End. *Oxon* 8A 28
Scotlandwell. *Per* 7E 66
Scot Lane End. *G Man* 7E 40
Scotsburn. *High* 6H 79
Scotsburn. *Mor* 7B 80
Scotsdike. *Cumb* 4H 53
Scot's Gap. *Nmbd* 3D 54
Scotstoun. *Glas* 3D 58
Scotstown. *High* 1C 64
Scotswood. *Tyne* 5F 54
Scottas. *High* 5J 69
Scotter. *Linc* 7F 42
Scotterthorpe. *Linc* 7F 42
Scottlethorpe. *Linc* 7H 37
Scotton. *Linc* 8F 42
Scotton. *N Yor*
nr. Catterick Garrison 6K 47
nr. Harrogate 2M 41
Scottow. *Norf* 7J 39
Scoulton. *Norf* 1F 30
Scounslow Green. *Staf* 7J 35
Scourie. *High* 7D 84
Scourie More. *High* 7D 84
Scousburgh. *Shet* 6D 90
Scout Green. *Cumb* 5D 46
Scouthead. *G Man* 7H 41
Scrabster. *High* 4B 86
Scrafield. *Linc* 3L 37
Scrainwood. *Nmbd* 1C 54
Scrane End. *Linc* 5L 37
Scraptoft. *Leics* 1D 28
Scratby. *Norf* 8M 39
Scrayingham. *N Yor* 1E 42
Scredington. *Linc* 5H 37
Scremby. *Linc* 3M 37
Scremerston. *Nmbd* 5H 61
Screveton. *Notts* 5E 36
Scrivelsby. *Linc* 3K 37
Scriven. *N Yor* 2A 42
Scronkey. *Lanc* 3C 40
Scrooby. *Notts* 8D 42
Scropton. *Derbs* 6K 35
Scrub Hill. *Linc* 4K 37
Scruton. *N Yor* 6L 47
Scuggate. *Cumb* 4J 53
Sculamus. *High* 3H 69
Sculcoates. *Hull* 4H 43
Sculthorpe. *Norf* 6F 38
Scunthorpe. *N Lin* 6F 42
Scurlage. *Swan* 8L 15
Sea. *Som* 4B 8
Seaborough. *Dors* 5C 8
Seabridge. *Staf* 5G 35
Seabrook. *Kent* 2H 13
Seaburn. *Tyne* 5H 55
Seacombe. *Mers* 8B 40
Seacroft. *Linc* 3B 38
Seacroft. *W Yor* 4M 41
Seadyke. *Linc* 6L 37
Seafield. *High* 5K 79
Seafield. *Midl* 3L 59
Seafield. *S Ayr* 7B 58
Seafield. *W Lot* 3J 59
Seaford. *E Sus* 6A 12
Seaforde. *New M* 6J 93
Seaforth. *Mers* 8B 40
Seagrave. *Leics* 8D 36
Seaham. *Dur* 7H 55
Seahouses. *Nmbd* 6K 61
Seal. *Kent* 8B 22
Sealand. *Flin* 3B 34
Seale. *Surr* 1F 10
Seamer. *N Yor*
nr. Scarborough 7H 49
nr. Stokesley 4B 48
Seamill. *N Ayr* 5M 57
Sea Mills. *Bris* 6D 18
Sea Palling. *Norf* 7L 39
Seapatrick. *Arm* 6G 93
Searby. *Linc* 7H 43
Seasalter. *Kent* 7G 23
Seascale. *Cumb* 4K 45
Seaside. *Per* 5F 66
Seater. *High* 4E 86
Seathorne. *Linc* 3B 38
Seathwaite. *Cumb*
nr. Buttermere 3M 45
nr. Ulpha 5M 45
Seatle. *Cumb* 7B 46
Seatoller. *Cumb* 3M 45
Seaton. *Corn* 6F 4
Seaton. *Cumb* 8E 52
Seaton. *Devn* 6M 7
Seaton. *Dur* 6G 55
Seaton. *E Yor* 3J 43
Seaton. *Nmbd* 4G 55
Seaton. *Rut* 2G 29
Seaton Burn. *Tyne* 4F 54
Seaton Carew. *Hart* 3C 48
Seaton Delaval. *Nmbd* 4G 55
Seaton Junction. *Devn* 6A 8
Seaton Ross. *E Yor* 3E 42
Seaton Sluice. *Nmbd* 4G 55
Seatown. *Abers* 7E 80
Seatown. *Dors* 6C 8
Seatown. *Mor*
nr. Cullen 7E 80
nr. Lossiemouth 6B 80
Seave Green. *N Yor* 5C 48
Seaview. *IOW* 6D 10
Seaville. *Cumb* 6F 52
Seavington St Mary. *Som* 4C 8
Seavington St Michael. *Som* 4C 8
Seawick. *Essx* 2H 23
Sebastopol. *Torf* 4A 18
Sebergham. *Cumb* 7H 53
Seckington. *Warw* 1L 27
Second Coast. *High* 4L 77
Sedbergh. *Cumb* 6E 46
Sedbury. *Glos* 4D 18
Sedbusk. *N Yor* 6G 47
Sedgeberrow. *Worc* 8J 27
Sedgebrook. *Linc* 6F 36
Sedgefield. *Dur* 3A 48
Sedgeford. *Norf* 6D 38
Sedgehill. *Wilts* 3G 9
Sedgley. *W Mid* 2H 27
Sedgwick. *Cumb* 7D 46
Sedlescombe. *E Sus* 4D 12
Seend. *Wilts* 7H 19
Seend Cleeve. *Wilts* 7H 19
Seer Green. *Buck* 4G 21
Seething. *Norf* 2K 31
Sefster. *Shet* 2D 90
Sefton. *Mers* 7B 40
Sefton Park. *Mers* 1B 34
Segensworth. *Hants* 5C 10
Seggat. *Abers* 1G 73
Seghill. *Nmbd* 4F 54
Seifton. *Shrp* 3C 26
Seighford. *Staf* 7G 35
Seilebost. *W Isl* 4B 76
Seisdon. *Staf* 2G 27
Seisiadar. *W Isl* 8J 83
Selattyn. *Shrp* 6A 34
Selborne. *Hants* 2E 10
Selby. *N Yor* 4D 42
Selham. *W Sus* 3G 11
Selkirk. *Bord* 7B 60
Sellack. *Here* 1D 18
Sellafirth. *Shet* 4K 91
Sellick's Green. *Som* 4M 7
Sellindge. *Kent* 2H 13
Selling. *Kent* 8G 23
Sells Green. *Wilts* 7H 19
Selly Oak. *W Mid* 3J 27
Selmeston. *E Sus* 5B 12
Selsdon. *G Lon* 7L 21
Selsey. *W Sus* 6F 10
Selsfield Common. *W Sus* 2L 11
Selside. *Cumb* 6D 46
Selside. *N Yor* 8F 46
Selsley. *Glos* 3G 19
Selsted. *Kent* 1J 13
Selston. *Notts* 4B 36
Selworthy. *Som* 1J 7
Semblister. *Shet* 2D 90
Semer. *Suff* 7G 31
Semington. *Wilts* 7G 19
Semley. *Wilts* 3G 9
Sempringham. *Linc* 6J 37
Send. *Surr* 8H 21
Send Marsh. *Surr* 8H 21
Senghenydd. *Cphy* 5L 17
Sennen. *Corn* 6G 3
Sennen Cove. *Corn* 6G 3
Sennybridge. *Powy* 2J 17
Serlby. *Notts* 1D 36
Seskinore. *Ferm* 5D 92
Sessay. *N Yor* 8B 48
Setchey. *Norf* 8C 38
Setley. *Hants* 5M 9
Setter. *Shet* 5J 91
Settiscarth. *Orkn* 8C 88
Settle. *N Yor* 1G 41
Settrington. *N Yor* 8F 48
Seven Ash. *Som* 2L 7
Sevenhampton. *Glos* 1J 19
Sevenhampton. *Swin* 4L 19
Sevenoaks. *Kent* 8B 22
Sevenoaks Weald. *Kent* 8B 22
Seven Sisters. *Neat* 4H 17
Seven Springs. *Glos* 2H 19
Severn Beach. *S Glo* 5D 18
Severn Stoke. *Worc* 7G 27
Sevington. *Kent* 1G 13
Sewards End. *Essx* 8B 30
Sewardstone. *Essx* 4L 21
Sewell. *C Beds* 1G 21
Sewerby. *E Yor* 1K 43
Seworgan. *Corn* 5L 3
Sewstern. *Leics* 7F 36
Sgallairidh. *W Isl* 6C 74
Sgarasta Mhor. *W Isl* 4B 76
Sgiogarstaigh. *W Isl* 5J 83
Sgreadan. *Arg* 8J 63
Shabbington. *Buck* 3D 20
Shackerley. *Shrp* 1G 27
Shackerstone. *Leics* 1A 28
Shackleford. *Surr* 1G 11
Shadforth. *Dur* 7G 55
Shadingfield. *Suff* 3L 31
Shadoxhurst. *Kent* 2F 12
Shadsworth. *Bkbn* 5F 40
Shadwell. *Norf* 3F 30
Shadwell. *W Yor* 4M 41
Shaftesbury. *Dors* 3G 9
Shafton. *S Yor* 6A 42
Shafton Two Gates. *S Yor* 6A 42
Shaggs. *Dors* 7G 9
Shakesfield. *Glos* 8E 26
Shalbourne. *Wilts* 7M 19
Shalcombe. *IOW* 7A 10
Shalden. *Hants* 1D 10
Shaldon. *Devn* 8J 7
Shalfleet. *IOW* 7B 10
Shalford. *Essx* 1D 22
Shalford. *Surr* 1H 11
Shalford Green. *Essx* 1D 22
Shallowford. *Devn* 1G 7
Shallowford. *Staf* 7G 35
Shalmsford Street. *Kent* 8G 23
Shalstone. *Buck* 8D 28
Shamley Green. *Surr* 1H 11
Shandon. *Arg* 1A 58
Shandwick. *High* 6J 79
Shangton. *Leics* 2E 28
Shankhouse. *Nmbd* 4F 54
Shanklin. *IOW* 7C 10
Shannochie. *N Ayr* 7J 57
Shap. *Cumb* 4D 46
Shapwick. *Dors* 5H 9
Shapwick. *Som* 2C 8
Sharcott. *Wilts* 8K 19
Shardlow. *Derbs* 6B 36
Shareshill. *Staf* 1H 27
Sharlston. *W Yor* 6A 42
Sharlston Common. *W Yor* 6A 42
Sharnal Street. *Medw* 6D 22
Sharnbrook. *Bed* 6G 29
Sharneyford. *Lanc* 5G 41
Sharnford. *Leics* 2B 28
Sharnhill Green. *Dors* 5F 8
Sharoe Green. *Lanc* 4D 40
Sharow. *N Yor* 8M 47
Sharpenhoe. *C Beds* 8H 29
Sharperton. *Nmbd* 1C 54
Sharpness. *Glos* 3E 18
Sharp Street. *Norf* 7K 39
Sharpthorne. *W Sus* 2L 11
Sharrington. *Norf* 6G 39
Shatterford. *Worc* 3F 26
Shatton. *Derbs* 1K 35
Shaugh Prior. *Devn* 5H 5
Shavington. *Ches E* 4F 34
Shaw. *G Man* 7H 41
Shaw. *W Ber* 7B 20
Shaw. *Wilts* 7G 19
Shawbirch. *Telf* 8E 34
Shawbury. *Shrp* 7D 34
Shawell. *Leics* 3C 28
Shawford. *Hants* 3B 10
Shawforth. *Lanc* 5G 41
Shaw Green. *Lanc* 6D 40
Shawhead. *Dum* 4C 52
Shaw Mills. *N Yor* 1L 41
Shawwood. *E Ayr* 7D 58
Shearington. *Dum* 5E 52
Shearsby. *Leics* 2D 28
Shearston. *Som* 2A 8
Shebbear. *Devn* 5D 6
Shebdon. *Staf* 7F 34
Shebster. *High* 5B 86
Sheddocksley. *Aber* 5H 73
Shedfield. *Hants* 4C 10
Shedog. *N Ayr* 6J 57
Sheen. *Staf* 3K 35
Sheepbridge. *Derbs* 2A 36
Sheep Hill. *Dur* 6E 54
Sheepscar. *W Yor* 4M 41
Sheepscombe. *Glos* 2G 19
Sheepstor. *Devn* 5H 5
Sheepwash. *Devn* 5D 6
Sheepwash. *Nmbd* 3F 54
Sheepway. *N Som* 6C 18
Sheepy Magna. *Leics* 1M 27
Sheepy Parva. *Leics* 1M 27
Sheering. *Essx* 2B 22
Sheerness. *Kent* 6F 22
Sheerwater. *Surr* 7H 21
Sheet. *Hants* 3E 10
Sheffield. *S Yor* **116** (1A 36)
Sheffield Bottom. *W Ber* 7D 20
Sheffield Green. *E Sus* 3M 11
Shefford. *C Beds* 8J 29
Shefford Woodlands.
W Ber 6A 20
Sheigra. *High* 5D 84
Sheinton. *Shrp* 1E 26
Shelderton. *Shrp* 4C 26
Sheldon. *Derbs* 3K 35
Sheldon. *Devn* 5L 7
Sheldon. *W Mid* 3K 27
Sheldwich. *Kent* 8G 23
Sheldwich Lees. *Kent* 8G 23
Shelf. *W Yor* 5K 41
Shelfanger. *Norf* 3H 31
Shelfield. *Warw* 5K 27
Shelfield. *W Mid* 1J 27
Shelford. *Notts* 5D 36
Shelford. *Warw* 3B 28
Shell. *Worc* 6H 27
Shelley. *Suff* 8G 31
Shelley. *W Yor* 6L 41
Shell Green. *Hal* 1D 34
Shellingford. *Oxon* 4M 19
Shellow Bowells. *Essx* 3C 22
Shelsley Beauchamp. *Worc* 5F 26
Shelsley Walsh. *Worc* 5F 26
Shelthorpe. *Leics* 8C 36
Shelton. *Bed* 5H 29
Shelton. *Norf* 2J 31
Shelton. *Notts* 5E 36
Shelton. *Shrp* 8C 34
Shelton Green. *Norf* 2J 31
Shelton Lock. *Derb* 6A 36
Shelve. *Shrp* 2B 26
Shelwick. *Here* 7D 26
Shelwick Green. *Here* 7D 26
Shenfield. *Essx* 4C 22
Shenington. *Oxon* 7A 28
Shenley. *Herts* 3J 21
Shenley Brook End. *Mil* 8F 28
Shenleybury. *Herts* 3J 21
Shenley Church End. *Mil* 8F 28
Shenmore. *Here* 8B 26
Shennanton. *Dum* 5J 51
Shenstone. *Staf* 1K 27
Shenstone. *Worc* 4G 27
Shenstone Woodend. *Staf* 1K 27
Shenton. *Leics* 1A 28
Shenval. *Mor* 3B 72
Shepeau Stow. *Linc* 8L 37
Shephall. *Herts* 1K 21
Shepherd's Bush. *G Lon* 5K 21
Shepherd's Gate. *Norf* 8B 38
Shepherd's Green. *Oxon* 5E 20
Shepherd's Port. *Norf* 6C 38
Shepherdswell. *Kent* 1J 13
Shepley. *W Yor* 7K 41
Sheppardstown. *High* 7C 86
Shepperdine. *S Glo* 4E 18
Shepperton. *Surr* 7H 21
Shepreth. *Cambs* 7L 29
Shepshed. *Leics* 8B 36
Shepton Beauchamp. *Som* 4C 8
Shepton Mallet. *Som* 1E 8
Shepton Montague. *Som* 2E 8
Shepway. *Kent* 8D 22
Sheraton. *Dur* 8H 55
Sherborne. *Dors* 4E 8
Sherborne. *Glos* 2K 19
Sherborne. *Som* 8D 18
Sherborne Causeway. *Dors* 3G 9
Sherborne St John. *Hants* 8D 20
Sherbourne. *Warw* 5L 27
Sherburn. *Dur* 7G 55
Sherburn. *N Yor* 8G 49
Sherburn Hill. *Dur* 7G 55
Sherburn in Elmet. *N Yor* 4B 42
Shere. *Surr* 1H 11
Shereford. *Norf* 7E 38
Sherfield English. *Hants* 3L 9
Sherfield on Loddon. *Hants* 8D 20
Sherford. *Devn* 7K 5
Sherford. *Dors* 6H 9
Sheriffhales. *Shrp* 8F 34
Sheriff Hutton. *N Yor* 1D 42
Sheriffston. *Mor* 7B 80
Sheringham. *Norf* 5H 39
Sherington. *Mil* 7F 28
Shermanbury. *W Sus* 4K 11
Shernal Green. *Worc* 5H 27
Shernborne. *Norf* 6D 38
Sherrington. *Wilts* 2H 9
Sherston. *Wilts* 5G 19
Sherwood. *Nott* 5C 36
Sherwood Green. *Devn* 3E 6
Shettleston. *Glas* 3E 58
Shevington. *G Man* 7D 40
Shevington Moor. *G Man* 6D 40
Shevington Vale. *G Man* 7D 40
Sheviock. *Corn* 6F 4
Shide. *IOW* 7B 10
Shiel Bridge. *High* 4L 69
Shieldaig. *High*
nr. Charlestown 6K 77
nr. Torridon 8K 77
Shieldhill. *Dum* 3E 52
Shieldhill. *Falk* 2G 59
Shieldhill. *S Lan* 5J 59
Shieldmuir. *N Lan* 4F 58
Shielfoot. *High* 8H 69
Shielhill. *Abers* 8K 81
Shielhill. *Ang* 2H 67
Shifnal. *Shrp* 1F 26
Shilbottle. *Nmbd* 1E 54
Shilbottle Grange. *Nmbd* 1F 54
Shildon. *Dur* 3L 47
Shillford. *E Ren* 4C 58
Shillingford. *Devn* 3J 7
Shillingford. *Oxon* 4C 20
Shillingford St George. *Devn* 7J 7
Shillingstone. *Dors* 4G 9
Shillington. *C Beds* 8J 29
Shillmoor. *Nmbd* 1B 54
Shilton. *Oxon* 3L 19
Shilton. *Warw* 3B 28
Shilvinghampton. *Dors* 7E 8
Shilvington. *Nmbd* 3E 54
Shimpling. *Norf* 3H 31
Shimpling. *Suff* 6E 30
Shimpling Street. *Suff* 6E 30
Shincliffe. *Dur* 7F 54
Shiney Row. *Tyne* 6G 55
Shinfield. *Wok* 7E 20
Shingay. *Cambs* 7L 29
Shingham. *Norf* 1D 30
Shingle Street. *Suff* 7K 31
Shinner's Bridge. *Devn* 5K 5
Shinness. *High* 2F 78
Shipbourne. *Kent* 8B 22
Shipdham. *Norf* 1F 30
Shipham. *Som* 8C 18
Shiphay. *Torb* 5L 5
Shiplake. *Oxon* 6E 20
Shipley. *Derbs* 5B 36
Shipley. *Nmbd* 8J 61
Shipley. *Shrp* 2G 27
Shipley. *W Sus* 3J 11
Shipley. *W Yor* 4K 41
Shipley Bridge. *Surr* 1L 11
Shipmeadow. *Suff* 3K 31
Shippon. *Oxon* 4B 20
Shipston-on-Stour. *Warw* 7L 27
Shipton. *Buck* 1E 20
Shipton. *Glos* 2J 19
Shipton. *N Yor* 2C 42
Shipton. *Shrp* 2D 26
Shipton Bellinger. *Hants* 1L 9
Shipton Gorge. *Dors* 6C 8
Shipton Green. *W Sus* 6F 10
Shipton Moyne. *Glos* 5G 19
Shipton-on-Cherwell. *Oxon* 2B 20
Shiptonthorpe. *E Yor* 3F 42
Shipton-under-Wychwood.
Oxon 2L 19
Shirburn. *Oxon* 4D 20
Shirdley Hill. *Lanc* 6B 40
Shire. *Cumb* 8L 53
Shirebrook. *Derbs* 3C 36
Shiregreen. *S Yor* 8A 42
Shirehampton. *Bris* 6D 18
Shiremoor. *Tyne* 4G 55
Shirenewton. *Mon* 4C 18
Shireoaks. *Notts* 1C 36
Shires Mill. *Fife* 1J 59
Shirkoak. *Kent* 2F 12
Shirland. *Derbs* 4A 36
Shirley. *Derbs* 5L 35
Shirley. *Sotn* 4A 10
Shirley. *W Mid* 4K 27
Shirleywich. *Staf* 7H 35
Shirl Heath. *Here* 6C 26
Shirrell Heath. *Hants* 4C 10
Shirwell. *Devn* 2E 6
Shiskine. *N Ayr* 7J 57
Shobdon. *Here* 5B 26
Shobnall. *Staf* 7L 35
Shobrooke. *Devn* 5H 7
Shoby. *Leics* 7D 36
Shocklach. *Ches W* 5C 34
Shoeburyness. *S'end* 5F 22
Sholden. *Kent* 8K 23
Sholing. *Sotn* 4B 10
Sholver. *G Man* 7H 41
Shoot Hill. *Shrp* 8C 34
Shop. *Corn*
nr. Bude 4B 6
nr. Padstow 4A 4
Shop. *Devn* 4C 6
Shopford. *Cumb* 4K 53
Shoreditch. *G Lon* 5L 21
Shoreditch. *Som* 3M 7
Shoregill. *Cumb* 5F 46
Shoreham. *Kent* 7B 22
Shoreham-by-Sea. *W Sus* 5K 11
Shoresdean. *Nmbd* 5G 61
Shoreswood. *Nmbd* 5G 61
Shorncote. *Glos* 4J 19
Shorne. *Kent* 6C 22
Shorne Ridgeway. *Kent* 6C 22
Shortacombe. *Devn* 7E 6
Shortbridge. *E Sus* 3A 12
Shortgate. *E Sus* 4A 12
Short Green. *Norf* 3G 31
Shorthampton. *Oxon* 1M 19
Short Heath. *Derbs* 8M 35
Short Heath. *W Mid*
nr. Erdington 2J 27
nr. Wednesfield 1H 27
Shortlanesend. *Corn* 4M 3
Shorton. *Torb* 5L 5
Shortstown. *Bed* 7H 29
Shortwood. *S Glo* 6E 18
Shorwell. *IOW* 7B 10
Shoscombe. *Bath* 8F 18
Shotesham. *Norf* 2J 31
Shotgate. *Essx* 4D 22
Shotley. *Suff* 8J 31
Shotley Bridge. *Dur* 6D 54
Shotleyfield. *Nmbd* 6D 54
Shotley Gate. *Suff* 8J 31
Shottenden. *Kent* 8G 23
Shottermill. *Surr* 2F 10
Shottery. *Warw* 6K 27
Shotteswell. *Warw* 7B 28
Shottisham. *Suff* 7K 31
Shottle. *Derbs* 5M 35
Shotton. *Dur*
nr. Peterlee 8H 55
nr. Sedgefield 3A 48
Shotton. *Flin* 3B 34
Shotton. *Nmbd*
nr. Morpeth 4F 54
nr. Town Yetholm 6F 60
Shotton Colliery. *Dur* 7G 55
Shotts. *N Lan* 3G 59
Shotwick. *Ches W* 2B 34
Shouldham. *Norf* 1C 30
Shouldham Thorpe. *Norf* 1C 30
Shoulton. *Worc* 6G 27
Shrawardine. *Shrp* 8C 34
Shrawley. *Worc* 5G 27
Shreding Green. *Buck* 5H 21
Shrewley. *Warw* 5L 27
Shrewsbury. *Shrp* **116** (8C 34)
Shrewton. *Wilts* 1J 9
Shrigley. *New M* 6J 93
Shripney. *W Sus* 5G 11
Shrivenham. *Oxon* 5L 19
Shropham. *Norf* 2F 30
Shroton. *Dors* 4G 9
Shrub End. *Essx* 1F 22
Shucknall. *Here* 7D 26
Shudy Camps. *Cambs* 7C 30
Shulishadermor. *High* 1F 68
Shulista. *High* 6F 76
Shurdington. *Glos* 2H 19
Shurlock Row. *Wind* 6F 20
Shurrery. *High* 6B 86
Shurton. *Som* 1M 7
Shustoke. *Warw* 2L 27
Shute. *Devn*
nr. Axminster 6A 8
nr. Crediton 5H 7
Shutford. *Oxon* 7A 28
Shut Heath. *Staf* 7G 35
Shuthonger. *Glos* 8G 27
Shutlanehead. *Staf* 5G 35
Shutlanger. *Nptn* 7E 28
Shutt Green. *Staf* 1G 27
Shuttington. *Warw* 1L 27
Shuttlewood. *Derbs* 2B 36
Shuttleworth. *G Man* 6G 41
Siabost. *W Isl* 7F 82
Siabost bho Dheas. *W Isl* 7F 82
Siabost bho Thuath. *W Isl* 7F 82
Siadar. *W Isl* 6G 83
Siadar Uarach. *W Isl* 6G 83
Sibbaldbie. *Dum* 3F 52
Sibbertoft. *Nptn* 3D 28
Sibdon Carwood. *Shrp* 3C 26
Sibertswold. *Kent* 1J 13
Sibford Ferris. *Oxon* 8A 28
Sibford Gower. *Oxon* 8A 28
Sible Hedingham. *Essx* 8D 30
Sibsey. *Linc* 4L 37
Sibsey Fen Side. *Linc* 4L 37
Sibson. *Cambs* 2H 29
Sibson. *Leics* 1A 28
Sibster. *High* 6E 86
Sibthorpe. *Notts* 5E 36
Sibton. *Suff* 5K 31
Sicklesmere. *Suff* 5E 30
Sicklinghall. *N Yor* 3A 42
Sid. *Devn* 7L 7
Sidbury. *Devn* 6L 7
Sidbury. *Shrp* 3E 26
Sidcot. *N Som* 8C 18
Sidcup. *G Lon* 6A 22
Siddick. *Cumb* 8E 52
Siddington. *Ches E* 2G 35
Siddington. *Glos* 4J 19
Side of the Moor. *G Man* 6F 40
Sidestrand. *Norf* 6J 39
Sidford. *Devn* 6L 7
Sidlesham. *W Sus* 6F 10
Sidley. *E Sus* 5D 12
Sidlow. *Surr* 1K 11
Sidmouth. *Devn* 7L 7
Sigford. *Devn* 8G 7
Sigglesthorne. *E Yor* 3J 43
Sighthill. *Edin* 2K 59
Sigingstone. *V Glam* 7J 17
Signet. *Oxon* 2L 19
Silchester. *Hants* 7D 20
Sildinis. *W Isl* 2D 76
Sileby. *Leics* 8D 36
Silecroft. *Cumb* 6L 45
Silfield. *Norf* 2H 31
Silian. *Cdgn* 7E 24
Silkstone. *S Yor* 7L 41
Silkstone Common. *S Yor* 7L 41
Silksworth. *Tyne* 6G 55
Silk Willoughby. *Linc* 5H 37
Silloth. *Cumb* 6F 52
Sills. *Nmbd* 1B 54
Sillyearn. *Mor* 8E 80
Silpho. *N Yor* 6G 49
Silsden. *W Yor* 3J 41
Silsoe. *C Beds* 8H 29
Silverbank. *Abers* 6G 73
Silverbridge. *New M* 7F 93
Silverburn. *Midl* 3L 59
Silverdale. *Lanc* 8C 46
Silverdale. *Staf* 5G 35
Silverdale Green. *Lanc* 8C 46
Silver End. *Essx* 2E 22
Silver End. *W Mid* 3H 27
Silvergate. *Norf* 7H 39
Silver Green. *Norf* 2J 31
Silverhillocks. *Abers* 7G 81
Silverley's Green. *Suff* 4J 31
Silverstone. *Nptn* 7D 28
Silverton. *Devn* 5J 7
Silverton. *W Dun* 2C 58
Silvington. *Shrp* 4E 26
Simm's Cross. *Hal* 1D 34
Simm's Lane End. *Mers* 7D 40
Simonburn. *Nmbd* 4B 54
Simonsbath. *Som* 2G 7
Simonstone. *Lanc* 4F 40
Simprim. *Bord* 5F 60
Simpson. *Pemb* 5E 14
Simpson Cross. *Pemb* 5E 14
Sinclairston. *E Ayr* 8C 58
Sinclairtown. *Fife* 8F 66
Sinderby. *N Yor* 7M 47
Sinderhope. *Nmbd* 6B 54
Sindlesham. *Wok* 7E 20
Sinfin. *Derb* 6M 35
Singleborough. *Buck* 8E 28
Singleton. *Kent* 1F 12
Singleton. *Lanc* 4B 40
Singleton. *W Sus* 4F 10
Singlewell. *Kent* 6C 22
Sinkhurst Green. *Kent* 1E 12
Sinnahard. *Abers* 4D 72
Sinnington. *N Yor* 7E 48
Sinton Green. *Worc* 5G 27
Sion Mills. *Derr* 4C 92
Sipson. *G Lon* 6H 21
Sirhowy. *Blae* 3L 17
Sisland. *Norf* 2K 31
Sissinghurst. *Kent* 2D 12
Siston. *S Glo* 6E 18
Sithney. *Corn* 6K 3
Sittingbourne. *Kent* 7F 22
Six Ashes. *Staf* 3F 26
Six Bells. *Blae* 4M 17
Six Hills. *Leics* 7D 36
Sixhills. *Linc* 1J 37
Six Mile Bottom. *Cambs* 6B 30
Sixmilecross. *Ferm* 5D 92
Sixpenny Handley. *Dors* 4H 9
Sizewell. *Suff* 5L 31
Skail. *High* 7K 85
Skaill. *Orkn* 8B 88
Skaills. *Orkn* 1G 87
Skares. *E Ayr* 8D 58
Skateraw. *E Lot* 2E 60
Skaw. *Shet* 1F 90
Skeabost. *High* 1F 68
Skeabrae. *Orkn* 7B 88
Skeeby. *N Yor* 5K 47
Skeffington. *Leics* 1E 28
Skeffling. *E Yor* 6L 43
Skegby. *Notts*
nr. Mansfield 3B 36
nr. Tuxford 2E 36
Skegness. *Linc* 3B 38
Skelberry. *Shet*
nr. Boddam 6D 90
nr. Housetter 5H 91
Skelbo. *High* 4H 79
Skelbo Street. *High* 4H 79
Skelbrooke. *S Yor* 6C 42
Skeldyke. *Linc* 6L 37
Skelfhill. *Bord* 1J 53
Skellingthorpe. *Linc* 2G 37
Skellister. *Shet* 2E 90
Skellorn Green. *Ches E* 1H 35
Skellow. *S Yor* 6C 42
Skelmanthorpe. *W Yor* 6L 41
Skelmersdale. *Lanc* 7C 40
Skelmorlie. *N Ayr* 3L 57
Skelpick. *High* 6K 85
Skelton. *Cumb* 8J 53
Skelton. *E Yor* 5E 42
Skelton. *N Yor*
nr. Richmond 5J 47
nr. Ripon 1A 42
Skelton. *Red C* 4D 48
Skelton. *York* 2C 42
Skelton Green. *Red C* 4D 48
Skelwick. *Orkn* 5D 88
Skelwith Bridge. *Cumb* 5B 46
Skendleby. *Linc* 3M 37
Skendleby Psalter. *Linc* 2M 37
Skenfrith. *Mon* 1C 18
Skerne. *E Yor* 2H 43
Skeroblingarry. *Arg* 7G 57
Skerray. *High* 5J 85
Skerricha. *High* 6E 84
Skerries Airport. *Shet* 6L 91
Skerton. *Lanc* 1C 40
Sketchley. *Leics* 2B 28
Sketty. *Swan* 5F 16
Skewen. *Neat* 5G 17
Skewsby. *N Yor* 8D 48
Skeyton. *Norf* 7J 39
Skeyton Corner. *Norf* 7J 39
Skiall. *High* 5B 86
Skidbrooke. *Linc* 8M 43
Skidbrooke North End.
Linc 8M 43
Skidby. *E Yor* 4H 43
Skilgate. *Som* 3J 7
Skillington. *Linc* 7F 36
Skinburness. *Cumb* 6F 52
Skinflats. *Falk* 1H 59
Skinidin. *High* 1D 68
Skinnet. *High* 5H 85
Skinningrove. *Red C* 4E 48
Skipness. *Arg* 4H 57
Skippool. *Lanc* 3B 40
Skiprigg. *Cumb* 7H 53
Skipsea. *E Yor* 2J 43
Skipsea Brough. *E Yor* 2J 43
Skipton. *N Yor* 2H 41
Skipton-on-Swale. *N Yor* 8A 48
Skipwith. *N Yor* 4D 42
Skirbeck. *Linc* 5L 37
Skirbeck Quarter. *Linc* 5L 37
Skirlaugh. *E Yor* 4J 43
Skirling. *Bord* 6J 59
Skirmett. *Buck* 4E 20
Skirpenbeck. *E Yor* 2E 42
Skirwith. *Cumb* 8L 53
Skirwith. *N Yor* 8F 46
Skirza. *High* 5E 86
Skitby. *Cumb* 5J 53
Skitham. *Lanc* 3C 40
Skittle Green. *Buck* 3E 20
Skroo. *Shet* 2M 89
Skulamus. *High* 3H 69
Skullomie. *High* 5J 85
Skyborry Green. *Shrp* 4A 26
Skye Green. *Essx* 1E 22
Skye of Curr. *High* 3K 71
Slack. *W Yor* 5H 41
The Slack. *Dur* 3K 47
Slackhall. *Derbs* 1J 35
Slack Head. *Cumb* 8C 46
Slackhead. *Mor* 7D 80
Slackholme End. *Linc* 2B 38
Slacks of Cairnbanno.
Abers 1H 73
Slad. *Glos* 3G 19
Slade. *Swan* 8L 15
The Slade. *W Ber* 7C 20
Slade End. *Oxon* 4C 20
Slade Field. *Cambs* 3L 29
Slade Green. *G Lon* 6B 22
Slade Heath. *Staf* 1H 27
Slade Hooton. *S Yor* 1C 36
Sladesbridge. *Corn* 4C 4
Slaggyford. *Nmbd* 6L 53
Slaidburn. *Lanc* 2F 40
Slaid Hill. *W Yor* 3M 41
Slaithwaite. *W Yor* 6J 41
Slaley. *Derbs* 4L 35

Slaley—Sudbrook

Slaley. Nmbd 6C 54
Slamannan. Falk 2G 59
Slapton. Buck 1G 21
Slapton. Devn 7L 5
Slapton. Nptn 7D 28
Slattocks. G Man 7G 41
Slaugham. W Sus 3K 11
Slaughterbridge. Corn 3D 4
Slaughterford. Wilts 6G 19
Slawston. Leics 2E 28
Sleaford. Hants 2F 10
Sleaford. Linc 5H 37
Sleagill. Cumb 4D 46
Sleap. Shrp 7C 34
Sledmere. E Yor 1G 43
Sleightholme. Dur 4H 47
Sleights. N Yor 5F 48
Slepe. Dors 6H 9
Slickly. High 5D 86
Sliddery. N Ayr 7J 57
Sligachan. High 3F 68
Slimbridge. Glos 3F 18
Slindon. Staf 6G 35
Slindon. W Sus 5G 11
Slinfold. W Sus 2J 11
Slingsby. N Yor 8D 48
Slip End. C Beds 2H 21
Slipton. Nptn 4G 29
Slitting Mill. Staf 8J 35
Slochd. High 3J 71
Slockavullin. Arg 8C 64
Sloley. Norf 7J 39
Sloncombe. Devn 7G 7
Sloothby. Linc 2A 38
Slough. Slo 6G 21
Slough Green. Som 3A 8
Slough Green. W Sus 3K 11
Sluggan. High 3J 71
Slyne. Lanc 1C 40
Smailholm. Bord 6D 60
Smallbridge. G Man 6H 41
Smallbrook. Devn 6H 7
Smallburgh. Norf 7K 39
Smallburn. E Ayr 7E 58
Smalldale. Derbs 2J 35
Small Dole. W Sus 4K 11
Smalley. Derbs 5B 36
Smallfield. Surr 1L 11
Small Heath. W Mid 3J 27
Smallholm. Dum 4F 52
Small Hythe. Kent 2E 12
Smallrice. Staf 6H 35
Smallridge. Devn 5B 8
Smallwood Hey. Lanc 3B 40
Smallworth. Norf 3G 31
Smannell. Hants 1A 10
Smardale. Cumb 5F 46
Smarden. Kent 1E 12
Smarden Bell. Kent 1E 12
Smart's Hill. Kent 1B 12
Smeatharpe. Devn 4M 7
Smeeth. Kent 2G 13
The Smeeth. Norf 8B 38
Smeeton Westerby. Leics 2D 28
Smeircleit. W Isl 4D 74
Smerral. High 8C 86
Smestow. Staf 2G 27
Smethwick. W Mid 3J 27
Smirisary. High 8H 69
Smisby. Derbs 8M 35
Smitham Hill. Bath 8D 18
Smith End Green. Worc 6F 26
Smithfield. Cumb 5J 53
Smith Green. Lanc 2C 40
The Smithies. Shrp 2E 26
Smithincott. Devn 4K 7
Smith's Green. Essx 1B 22
Smithstown. High 6J 77
Smithton. High 1H 71
Smithwood Green. Suff 6F 30
Smithy Bridge. G Man 6H 41
Smithy Green. Ches E 2F 34
Smithy Lane Ends. Lanc 6C 40
Smockington. Leics 3B 28
Smoogro. Orkn 1E 86
Smythe's Green. Essx 2F 22
Snaigow House. Per 3D 66
Snailbeach. Shrp 1B 26
Snailwell. Cambs 5C 30
Snainton. N Yor 7G 49
Snaith. E Yor 5D 42
Snape. N Yor 7L 47
Snape. Suff 6K 31
Snape Green. Lanc 6B 40
Snapper. Devn 2E 6
Snarestone. Leics 1M 27
Snarford. Linc 1H 37
Snargate. Kent 3F 12
Snave. Kent 3G 13
Sneachill. Worc 6H 27
Snead. Powy 2B 26
Snead Common. Worc 5F 26
Sneaton. N Yor 5F 48
Sneatonthorpe. N Yor 5G 49
Snelland. Linc 1H 37
Snelston. Derbs 5K 35
Snetterton. Norf 2F 30
Snettisham. Norf 6C 38
Snibston. Leics 8B 36
Sniseabhal. W Isl 2D 74
Snitter. Nmbd 1D 54
Snitterby. Linc 8G 43
Snitterfield. Warw 6L 27
Snitton. Shrp 4D 26
Snodhill. Here 7B 26
Snodland. Kent 7D 22
Snods Edge. Nmbd 6D 54
Snowshill. Glos 8J 27
Snow Street. Norf 3G 31
Snydale. W Yor 5B 42
Soake. Hants 4D 10
Soar. Carm 2F 16
Soar. Gwyn 7F 32
Soar. IOA 3C 32
Soar. Powy 1J 17
Soberton. Hants 4D 10
Soberton Heath. Hants 4D 10
Sockbridge. Cumb 3D 46
Sockburn. Darl 5M 47
Sodom. Den 3K 33
Sodom. Shet 1F 90
Soham. Cambs 4B 30
Soham Cotes. Cambs 4B 30
Solas. W Isl 6K 75
Soldon Cross. Devn 4C 6
Soldridge. Hants 2D 10
Solent Breezes. Hants 5C 10
Sole Street. Kent
nr. Meopham 7C 22
nr. Waltham 1G 13
Solihull. W Mid 3K 27
Sollers Dilwyn. Here 6C 26
Sollers Hope. Here 8E 26
Sollom. Lanc 6C 40
Solva. Pemb 4D 14
Somerby. Leics 8E 36
Somerby. Linc 7H 43
Somercotes. Derbs 4B 36
Somerford. Dors 6K 9
Somerford. Staf 1G 27
Somerford Keynes. Glos 4J 19
Somerley. W Sus 6F 10
Somerleyton. Suff 2L 31
Somersal Herbert. Derbs 6K 35
Somersby. Linc 2L 37
Somersham. Cambs 4L 29
Somersham. Suff 7G 31
Somerton. Oxon 1B 20
Somerton. Som 3C 8
Somerton. Suff 6E 30
Sompting. W Sus 5J 11
Sonning. Wok 6E 20
Sonning Common. Oxon 5E 20
Sonning Eye. Oxon 6E 20
Sookholme. Notts 3C 36
Sopley. Hants 6K 9
Sopworth. Wilts 5G 19
Sorbie. Dum 7K 51
Sordale. High 5C 86
Sorisdale. Arg 1H 63
Sorn. E Ayr 7D 58
Sornhill. E Ayr 6D 58
Sortat. High 5D 86
Sotby. Linc 2K 37
Sots Hole. Linc 3J 37
Sotterley. Suff 3L 31
Soudley. Shrp
nr. Church Stretton 2C 26
nr. Market Drayton 7F 34
Soughton. Flin 4M 33
Soulbury. Buck 1F 20
Soulby. Cumb
nr. Appleby 4F 46
nr. Penrith 3C 46
Souldern. Oxon 8C 28
Souldrop. Bed 5G 29
Sound. Ches E 5E 34
Sound. Shet
nr. Lerwick 3E 90
nr. Tresta 2D 90
Soundwell. S Glo 6E 18
Sourhope. Bord 7F 60
Sourin. Orkn 6D 88
Sour Nook. Cumb 7H 53
Sourton. Devn 6E 6
Soutergate. Cumb 6M 45
South Acre. Norf 8E 38
Southall. G Lon 6J 21
South Allington. Devn 8K 5
South Alloa. Falk 8B 66
Southam. Glos 1H 19
Southam. Warw 5B 28
South Ambersham. W Sus 3G 11
Southampton. Sotn 116 (4B 10)
Southampton Airport. Hants 4B 10
Southannan. N Ayr 4M 57
South Anston. S Yor 1C 36
South Ascot. Wind 7G 21
South Baddesley. Hants 6A 10
South Balfern. Dum 6K 51
South Ballachulish. High 2E 64
South Bank. Red C 3C 48
South Barrow. Som 3E 8
South Benfleet. Essx 5D 22
South Bents. Tyne 5H 55
South Bersted. W Sus 5G 11
Southborough. Kent 1B 12
Southbourne. Bour 6K 9
Southbourne. W Sus 5E 10
South Bowood. Dors 6C 8
South Brent. Devn 6J 5
South Brewham. Som 2F 8
South Broomage. Falk 1G 59
South Broomhill. Nmbd 2F 54
Southburgh. Norf 1F 30
South Burlingham. Norf 1K 31
Southburn. E Yor 2G 43
South Cadbury. Som 3E 8
South Carlton. Linc 2G 37
South Cave. E Yor 4G 43
South Cerney. Glos 4J 19
South Chailey. E Sus 4L 11
South Chard. Som 5B 8
South Charlton. Nmbd 7J 61
South Cheriton. Som 3E 8
South Church. Dur 3L 47
Southchurch. S'end 5F 22
South Cleatlam. Dur 4K 47
South Cliffe. E Yor 4F 42
South Clifton. Notts 2F 36
South Clunes. High 1F 70
South Cockerington. Linc 1L 37
South Common. Devn 5B 8
South Cornelly. B'end 6H 17
Southcott. Devn
nr. Great Torrington 4D 6
nr. Okehampton 6E 6
Southcott. Wilts 8K 19
Southcourt. Buck 2F 20
South Cove. Suff 3L 31
South Creagan. Arg 3D 64
South Creake. Norf 6E 38
South Crosland. W Yor 6K 41
South Croxton. Leics 8D 36
South Dalton. E Yor 3G 43
South Darenth. Kent 7B 22
Southdean. Bord 1L 53
Southdown. Bath 7F 18
South Duffield. N Yor 4D 42
Southease. E Sus 5M 11
South Elkington. Linc 1K 37
South Elmsall. W Yor 6B 42
South End. Cumb 8M 45
South End. N Lin 5J 43
Southend. Arg 1B 50
Southend. Glos 4F 18
Southend. W Ber 6C 20
Southend Airport. Essx 5E 22
Southend-on-Sea. S'end 5E 22
Southerfield. Cumb 7F 52
Southerhouse. Shet 4D 90
Southerly. Devn 7E 6
Southernden. Kent 1E 12
Southerndown. V Glam 7H 17
Southerness. Dum 6D 52
South Erradale. High 6J 77
Southerton. Devn 6K 7
Southery. Norf 2C 30
Southey Green. Essx 8D 30
South Fambridge. Essx 4E 22
South Fawley. W Ber 5A 20
South Feorline. N Ayr 7J 57
South Ferriby. N Lin 5G 43
South Field. E Yor 5H 43
Southfleet. Kent 6C 22
South Garvan. High 8L 69
Southgate. Cdgn 4E 24
Southgate. G Lon 4L 21
Southgate. Norf
nr. Aylsham 7H 39
nr. Fakenham 6E 38
Southgate. Swan 6E 16
South Gluss. Shet 6H 91
South Godstone. Surr 1L 11
South Gorley. Hants 4K 9
South Green. Essx
nr. Billericay 4C 22
nr. Colchester 2G 23
South Green. Kent 7E 22
South Hanningfield. Essx 4D 22
South Harting. W Sus 4E 10
South Hayling. Hants 6E 10
South Hazelrigg. Nmbd 6H 61
South Heath. Buck 3G 21
South Heath. Essx 2H 23
South Heighton. E Sus 5M 11
South Hetton. Dur 7G 55
South Hiendley. W Yor 6A 42
South Hill. Corn 8C 6
South Hill. Som 3C 8
South Hinksey. Oxon 3C 20
South Hole. Devn 3B 6
South Holme. N Yor 8E 48
South Holmwood. Surr 1J 11
South Hornchurch. G Lon 5B 22
South Huish. Devn 7J 5
South Hykeham. Linc 3G 37
South Hylton. Tyne 6G 55
Southill. C Beds 7J 29
Southington. Hants 1C 10
South Kelsey. Linc 8H 43
South Kessock. High 1G 71
South Killingholme. N Lin 6J 43
South Kilvington. N Yor 7B 48
South Kilworth. Leics 3D 28
South Kirkby. W Yor 6B 42
South Kirkton. Abers 5G 73
South Knighton. Devn 8H 7
South Kyme. Linc 5J 37
South Lancing. W Sus 5J 11
South Ledaig. Arg 4D 64
South Leigh. Oxon 3A 20
Southleigh. Devn 6M 7
South Leverton. Notts 1E 36
South Littleton. Worc 7J 27
South Lopham. Norf 3G 31
South Luffenham. Rut 1G 29
South Malling. E Sus 4M 11
South Marston. Swin 5K 19
South Middleton. Nmbd 7G 61
South Milford. N Yor 4B 42
South Milton. Devn 7K 5
South Mimms. Herts 3K 21
Southminster. Essx 4F 22
South Molton. Devn 3G 7
South Moor. Dur 6E 54
Southmoor. Oxon 4A 20
South Moreton. Oxon 5C 20
South Mundham. W Sus 5F 10
South Muskham. Notts 4E 36
South Newbald. E Yor 4G 43
South Newington. Oxon 8B 28
South Newsham. Nmbd 4G 55
South Newton. N Ayr 4J 57
South Newton. Wilts 2J 9
South Normanton. Derbs 4B 36
South Norwood. G Lon 7L 21
South Nutfield. Surr 1L 11
South Ockendon. Thur 5B 22
Southoe. Cambs 5J 29
Southolt. Suff 5H 31
South Ormsby. Linc 2L 37
Southorpe. Pet 1H 29
South Otterington. N Yor 7A 48
South Owersby. Linc 8H 43
Southowram. W Yor 5K 41
South Oxhey. Herts 4J 21
South Perrott. Dors 5C 8
South Petherton. Som 4C 8
South Petherwin. Corn 7C 6
South Pickenham. Norf 1E 30
South Pool. Devn 7K 5
South Poorton. Dors 6D 8
South Port. Arg 5E 64
Southport. Mers 6B 40
Southpunds. Shet 6E 90
South Queensferry. Edin 2K 59
South Radworthy. Devn 2G 7
South Rauceby. Linc 5H 37
South Raynham. Norf 7E 38
Southrepps. Norf 6J 39
South Reston. Linc 1M 37
Southrey. Linc 3J 37
Southrop. Glos 3K 19
Southrope. Hants 1D 10
South Runcton. Norf 1C 30
South Scarle. Notts 3F 36
Southsea. Port 6D 10
South Shields. Tyne 5G 55
South Shore. Bkpl 4B 40
Southside. Orkn 7E 88
South Somercotes. Linc 8M 43
South Stainley. N Yor 1M 41
South Stainmore. Cumb 4G 47
South Stifford. Thur 6B 22
South Stoke. Bath 7F 18
South Stoke. Oxon 5C 20
South Stoke. W Sus 5H 11
South Street. E Sus 4L 11
South Street. Kent
nr. Faversham 8G 23
nr. Whitstable 7H 23
South Tawton. Devn 6F 6
South Thoresby. Linc 2M 37
South Tidworth. Wilts 1L 9
South Town. Devn 7J 7
South Town. Hants 2D 10
Southtown. Norf 1M 31
Southtown. Orkn 2F 86
South View. Shet 3D 90
Southwaite. Cumb 7J 53
South Walsham. Norf 8K 39
South Warnborough. Hants 1E 10
Southwater. W Sus 3J 11
Southwater Street. W Sus 3J 11
Southway. Som 1D 8
South Weald. Essx 4B 22
South Weirs. Hants 5L 9
Southwell. Dors 8E 8
Southwell. Notts 4E 36
South Weston. Oxon 4E 20
South Wheatley. Corn 6B 6
South Wheatley. Notts 1E 36
Southwick. Hants 5D 10
Southwick. Nptn 2H 29
Southwick. Tyne 6G 55
Southwick. W Sus 5K 11
Southwick. Wilts 8G 19
South Widcombe. Bath 8D 18
South Wigston. Leics 2C 28
South Willingham. Linc 1J 37
South Wingfield. Derbs 4A 36
South Witham. Linc 8G 37
Southwold. Suff 4M 31
South Wonston. Hants 2B 10
Southwood. Norf 1K 31
Southwood. Som 2D 8
South Woodham Ferrers. Essx 4E 22
South Wootton. Norf 7C 38
South Wraxall. Wilts 7G 19
South Zeal. Devn 6F 6
Soval Lodge. W Isl 1E 76
Sowerby. N Yor 7B 48
Sowerby. W Yor 5J 41
Sowerby Bridge. W Yor 5J 41
Sowerby Row. Cumb 7H 53
Sower Carr. Lanc 3B 40
Sowley Green. Suff 6D 30
Sowood. W Yor 6J 41
Sowton. Devn 6J 7
Soyal. High 4F 78
Soyland Town. W Yor 5J 41
The Spa. New M 6H 93
Spacey Houses. N Yor 2M 41
Spa Common. Norf 6J 39
Spalding. Linc 7K 37
Spaldington. E Yor 4E 42
Spaldwick. Cambs 4J 29
Spalford. Notts 3F 36
Spamount. Derr 4C 92
Spanby. Linc 6H 37
Sparham. Norf 8G 39
Sparhamhill. Norf 8G 39
Spark Bridge. Cumb 7B 46
Sparket. Cumb 3C 46
Sparkford. Som 3E 8
Sparkwell. Devn 6H 5
Sparrow Green. Norf 8F 38
Sparrowpit. Derbs 1J 35
Sparrow's Green. E Sus 2C 12
Sparsholt. Hants 2B 10
Sparsholt. Oxon 5M 19
Spartylea. Nmbd 7B 54
Spath. Staf 6J 35
Spaunton. N Yor 7E 48
Spaxton. Som 2M 7
Spean Bridge. High 7C 70
Spear Hill. W Sus 4J 11
Speen. Buck 4F 20
Speen. W Ber 7B 20
Speeton. N Yor 8J 49
Speke. Mers 1C 34
Speldhurst. Kent 1B 12
Spellbrook. Herts 2A 22
Spelsbury. Oxon 1A 20
Spencers Wood. Wok 7E 20
Spennithorne. N Yor 7K 47
Spennymoor. Dur 8F 54
Spernall. Warw 5J 27
Sperrin. Derr 4E 92
Spetchley. Worc 6G 27
Spetisbury. Dors 5H 9
Spexhall. Suff 3K 31
Speybank. High 5J 71
Spey Bay. Mor 7C 80
Speybridge. High 3L 71
Speyview. Mor 1B 72
Spilsby. Linc 3M 37
Spindlestone. Nmbd 6J 61
Spinkhill. Derbs 2B 36
Spinney Hills. Leic 1D 28
Spinningdale. High 5G 79
Spital. Mers 1B 34
Spitalhill. Derbs 5K 35
Spital in the Street. Linc 8G 43
Spithurst. E Sus 4M 11
Spittal. Dum 6J 51
Spittal. E Lot 2B 60
Spittal. High 6C 86
Spittal. Nmbd 4H 61
Spittal. Pemb 4F 14
Spittalfield. Per 3E 66
Spittal of Glenmuick. Abers 7C 72
Spittal of Glenshee. Per 8M 71
Spittal-on-Rule. Bord 7C 60
Spixworth. Norf 8J 39
Splatt. Corn 7B 6
Spofforth. N Yor 2A 42
Spondon. Derb 6B 36
Spon End. W Mid 4M 27
Spooner Row. Norf 2G 31
Sporle. Norf 8E 38
Spott. E Lot 2D 60
Spratton. Nptn 4E 28
Spreakley. Surr 1F 10
Spreyton. Devn 6G 7
Spridlington. Linc 1H 37
Springburn. Glas 3E 58
Springfield. Dum 5H 53
Springfield. Ferm 6B 92
Springfield. Fife 6G 67
Springfield. High 7G 79
Springfield. W Mid 3J 27
Spring Hill. W Mid 2G 27
Springhill. Staf 1H 27
Springholm. Dum 5C 52
Springside. N Ayr 6B 58
Springthorpe. Linc 1F 36
Spring Vale. IOW 6D 10
Spring Valley. IOM 7C 44
Springwell. Tyne 6F 54
Sproatley. E Yor 4J 43
Sproston Green. Ches W 3F 34
Sprotbrough. S Yor 7C 42
Sproughton. Suff 7H 31
Sprouston. Bord 6E 60
Sprowston. Norf 8J 39
Sproxton. Leics 7F 36
Sproxton. N Yor 7D 48
Sprunston. Cumb 7J 53
Spurstow. Ches E 4D 34
Squires Gate. Bkpl 4B 40
Sraid Ruadh. Arg 3E 62
Srannda. W Isl 5B 76
Sron an t-Sithein. High 1C 64
Sronphadruig Lodge. Per 8H 71
Sruth Mor. W Isl 7L 75
Stableford. Shrp 2F 26
Stackhouse. N Yor 1G 41
Stackpole. Pemb 7F 14
Stackpole Elidor. Pemb 7F 14
Stacksford. Norf 2G 31
Stacksteads. Lanc 5G 41
Staddiscombe. Plym 6H 5
Staddlethorpe. E Yor 5F 42
Staddon. Devn 5C 6
Stadhampton. Oxon 4D 20
Stadhlaigearraidh. W Isl 2D 74
Stafainn. High 7F 76
Staffield. Cumb 7K 53
Staffin. High 7F 76
Stafford. Staf 7H 35
Stafford Park. Telf 1F 26
Stagden Cross. Essx 2C 22
Stagsden. Bed 7G 29
Stag's Head. Devn 3F 6
Stainburn. Cumb 2K 45
Stainburn. N Yor 3L 41
Stainby. Linc 7G 37
Staincliffe. W Yor 5L 41
Staincross. S Yor 6M 41
Staindrop. Dur 3K 47
Staines-upon-Thames. Surr 6H 21
Stainfield. Linc
nr. Bourne 7H 37
nr. Lincoln 2J 37
Stainforth. N Yor 1G 41
Stainforth. S Yor 6D 42
Staining. Lanc 4B 40
Stainland. W Yor 6J 41
Stainsacre. N Yor 5G 49
Stainton. Cumb
nr. Carlisle 6H 53
nr. Kendal 7D 46
nr. Penrith 3C 46
Stainton. Dur 4J 47
Stainton. Midd 4B 48
Stainton. N Yor 6K 47
Stainton. S Yor 8C 42
Stainton by Langworth. Linc 2H 37
Staintondale. N Yor 6G 49
Stainton le Vale. Linc 8J 43
Stainton with Adgarley. Cumb 8A 46
Stair. Cumb 2M 45
Stair. E Ayr 7C 58
Stairhaven. Dum 6H 51
Staithes. N Yor 4E 48
Stakeford. Nmbd 3F 54
Stake Pool. Lanc 3C 40
Stakes. Hants 5D 10
Stalbridge. Dors 4F 8
Stalbridge Weston. Dors 4F 8
Stalham. Norf 7K 39
Stalham Green. Norf 7K 39
Stalisfield Green. Kent 8F 22
Stallen. Dors 4E 8
Stallingborough. NE Lin 6K 43
Stalling Busk. N Yor 7H 47
Stallington. Staf 6H 35
Stalmine. Lanc 3B 40
Stalybridge. G Man 8H 41
Stambourne. Essx 8D 30
Stamford. Linc 1H 29
Stamford. Nmbd 8K 61
Stamford Bridge. Ches W 3C 34
Stamford Bridge. E Yor 2E 42
Stamfordham. Nmbd 4D 54
Stamperland. E Ren 4D 58
Stanah. Lanc 3B 40
Stanborough. Herts 2K 21
Stanbridge. C Beds 1G 21
Stanbridge. Dors 5J 9
Stanbury. W Yor 4J 41
Stand. N Lan 3F 58
Standburn. Falk 2H 59
Standeford. Staf 1H 27
Standen. Kent 1E 12
Standen Street. Kent 2E 12
Standerwick. Som 8G 19
Standford. Hants 2F 10
Standford Bridge. Telf 7F 34
Standingstone. Cumb 7G 53
Standish. Glos 3G 19
Standish. G Man 6D 40
Standish Lower Ground. G Man 7D 40
Standlake. Oxon 3A 20
Standon. Hants 3B 10
Standon. Herts 1L 21
Standon. Staf 6G 35
Standon Green End. Herts 2L 21
Stane. N Lan 4G 59
Stanecastle. N Ayr 6B 58
Stanfield. Norf 7F 38
Stanfield. Suff 6D 30
Stanford. C Beds 7J 29
Stanford. Kent 2H 13
Stanford Bishop. Here 6E 26
Stanford Bridge. Worc 5F 26
Stanford Dingley. W Ber 6C 20
Stanford in the Vale. Oxon 4M 19
Stanford-le-Hope. Thur 5C 22
Stanford on Avon. Nptn 4C 28
Stanford on Soar. Notts 7C 36
Stanford on Teme. Worc 5F 26
Stanford Rivers. Essx 3B 22
Stanfree. Derbs 2B 36
Stanghow. Red C 4D 48
Stanground. Pet 2K 29
Stanhoe. Norf 6E 38
Stanhope. Dur 8C 54
Stanhope. Bord 7K 59
Stanion. Nptn 3G 29
Stanley. Derbs 5B 36
Stanley. Dur 6E 54
Stanley. Per 4E 66
Stanley. Shrp 3F 26
Stanley. Staf 4H 35
Stanley. W Yor 5M 41
Stanley Common. Derbs 5B 36
Stanley Crook. Dur 8E 54
Stanley Hill. Here 7E 26
Stanlow. Ches W 2C 34
Stanmer. Brig 5L 11
Stanmore. G Lon 4J 21
Stanmore. Hants 3B 10
Stanmore. W Ber 6B 20
Stannersburn. Nmbd 3M 53
Stanningfield. Suff 6E 30
Stannington. Nmbd 4F 54
Stannington. S Yor 1M 35
Stansbatch. Here 5B 26
Stanshope. Staf 4K 35
Stanstead. Suff 7E 30
Stanstead Abbotts. Herts 2L 21
Stansted. Kent 7C 22
Stansted Airport. Essx 119 (1B 22)
Stansted Mountfitchet. Essx 1B 22
Stanthorne. Ches W 3E 34
Stanton. Derbs 8L 35
Stanton. Glos 8J 27
Stanton. Nmbd 2E 54
Stanton. Staf 5K 35
Stanton. Suff 4F 30
Stanton by Bridge. Derbs 7A 36
Stanton-by-Dale. Derbs 6B 36
Stanton Chare. Suff 4F 30
Stanton Drew. Bath 7D 18
Stanton Fitzwarren. Swin 4K 19
Stanton Harcourt. Oxon 3B 20
Stanton Hill. Notts 3B 36
Stanton in Peak. Derbs 3L 35
Stanton Lacy. Shrp 4C 26
Stanton Long. Shrp 2D 26
Stanton-on-the-Wolds. Notts 6D 36
Stanton Prior. Bath 7E 18
Stanton St Bernard. Wilts 7J 19
Stanton St John. Oxon 3C 20
Stanton St Quintin. Wilts 6H 19
Stanton Street. Suff 5F 30
Stanton under Bardon. Leics 8B 36
Stanton upon Hine Heath. Shrp 7D 34
Stanton Wick. Bath 7E 18
Stanwardine in the Fields. Shrp 7C 34
Stanwardine in the Wood. Shrp 7C 34
Stanway. Essx 1F 22
Stanway. Glos 8J 27
Stanwell. Surr 6H 21
Stanwell Green. Suff 4H 31
Stanwell Moor. Surr 6H 21
Stanwick. Nptn 4G 29
Stanydale. Shet 2C 90
Staoinebrig. W Isl 2D 74
Stape. N Yor 6E 48
Stapehill. Dors 5J 9
Stapeley. Ches E 5E 34
Stapenhill. Staf 7L 35
Staple. Kent 8J 23
Staple Cross. Devn 3K 7
Staplecross. E Sus 3D 12
Staplefield. W Sus 3K 11
Staple Fitzpaine. Som 4A 8
Stapleford. Cambs 6A 30
Stapleford. Herts 2L 21
Stapleford. Leics 8F 36
Stapleford. Linc 4F 36
Stapleford. Notts 6B 36
Stapleford. Wilts 2J 9
Stapleford Abbotts. Essx 4B 22
Stapleford Tawney. Essx 4B 22
Staplegrove. Som 3M 7
Staplehay. Som 3M 7
Staple Hill. S Glo 6E 18
Staplehurst. Kent 1D 12
Staplers. IOW 7C 10
Stapleton. Bris 6E 18
Stapleton. Cumb 4K 53
Stapleton. Here 5B 26
Stapleton. Leics 2B 28
Stapleton. N Yor 4L 47
Stapleton. Shrp 1C 26
Stapleton. Som 3C 8
Stapley. Som 4L 7
Staploe. Bed 5J 29
Staplow. Here 7E 26
Star. Fife 7G 67
Star. Pemb 3J 15
Starbeck. N Yor 2M 41
Starbotton. N Yor 8H 47
Starcross. Devn 7J 7
Stareton. Warw 4M 27
Starkholmes. Derbs 4M 35
Starling. G Man 6F 40
Starling's Green. Essx 8A 30
Starston. Norf 3J 31
Start. Devn 7L 5
Startforth. Dur 4J 47
Start Hill. Essx 1B 22
Startley. Wilts 5H 19
Stathe. Som 3B 8
Stathern. Leics 6E 36
Station Town. Dur 8H 55
Staughton Green. Cambs 5J 29
Staughton Highway. Cambs 5J 29
Staunton. Glos
nr. Cheltenham 1F 18
nr. Monmouth 2D 18
Staunton in the Vale. Notts 5F 36
Staunton on Arrow. Here 5B 26
Staunton on Wye. Here 7B 26
Staveley. Cumb 6C 46
Staveley. Derbs 2B 36
Staveley. N Yor 1A 42
Staveley-in-Cartmel. Cumb 7B 46
Staverton. Devn 5K 5
Staverton. Glos 1G 19
Staverton. Nptn 5C 28
Staverton. Wilts 7G 19
Stawell. Som 2B 8
Stawley. Som 3K 7
Staxigoe. High 6E 86
Staxton. N Yor 8H 49
Staylittle. Powy 3H 25
Staynall. Lanc 3B 40
Staythorpe. Notts 4E 36
Stean. N Yor 8J 47
Stearsby. N Yor 8D 48
Steart. Som 1A 8
Stebbing. Essx 1C 22
Stebbing Green. Essx 1C 22
Stedham. W Sus 3F 10
Steel. Nmbd 6C 54
Steel Cross. E Sus 2B 12
Steelend. Fife 8D 66
Steele Road. Bord 2K 53
Steel Heath. Shrp 6D 34
Steen's Bridge. Here 6D 26
Steep. Hants 3E 10
Steep Lane. W Yor 5J 41
Steeple. Dors 7H 9
Steeple. Essx 3F 22
Steeple Ashton. Wilts 8H 19
Steeple Aston. Oxon 1B 20
Steeple Barton. Oxon 1B 20
Steeple Bumpstead. Essx 7C 30
Steeple Claydon. Buck 1D 20
Steeple Gidding. Cambs 3J 29
Steeple Langford. Wilts 2J 9
Steeple Morden. Cambs 7K 29
Steeton. W Yor 3J 41
Stein. High 8D 76
Steinmanhill. Abers 1G 73
Stelling Minnis. Kent 1H 13
Stembridge. Som 3C 8
Stemster. High
nr. Halkirk 5C 86
nr. Westfield 5B 86
Stenalees. Corn 6C 4
Stenhill. Devn 4K 7
Stenhouse. Edin 2L 59
Stenhousemuir. Falk 1G 59
Stenigot. Linc 1K 37
Stenscholl. High 7F 76
Stenso. Orkn 7C 88
Stenson. Derbs 7M 35
Stenson Fields. Derbs 6M 35
Stenton. E Lot 2D 60
Stenwith. Linc 6F 36
Steòrnabhagh. W Isl 8H 83
Stepaside. Pemb 6H 15
Stepford. Dum 3C 52
Stepney. G Lon 5L 21
Steppingley. C Beds 8H 29
Stepps. N Lan 3E 58
Sterndale Moor. Derbs 3K 35
Sternfield. Suff 5K 31
Stert. Wilts 8J 19
Stetchworth. Cambs 6C 30
Stevenage. Herts 1K 21
Stevenston. N Ayr 5A 58
Stevenstone. Devn 4E 6
Steventon. Hants 1C 10
Steventon. Oxon 4B 20
Steventon End. Essx 7B 30
Stevington. Bed 6G 29
Stewartby. Bed 7H 29
Stewarton. Arg 8F 56
Stewarton. E Ayr 5C 58
Stewartstown. M Ulst 5F 93
Stewkley. Buck 1F 20
Stewkley Dean. Buck 1F 20
Stewley. Som 4B 8
Stewton. Linc 1L 37
Steyning. W Sus 4J 11
Steynton. Pemb 6F 14
Stibb. Corn 4B 6
Stibbard. Norf 7F 38
Stibb Cross. Devn 4D 6
Stibb Green. Wilts 7L 19
Stibbington. Cambs 2H 29
Stichill. Bord 6E 60
Sticker. Corn 6B 4
Stickford. Linc 3L 37
Sticklepath. Devn 6F 6
Sticklinch. Som 2D 8
Stickling Green. Essx 8A 30
Stickney. Linc 4L 37
Stiffkey. Norf 5F 38
Stifford's Bridge. Here 7F 26
Stileway. Som 1C 8
Stillingfleet. N Yor 3C 42
Stillington. N Yor 1C 42
Stillington. Stoc T 3A 48
Stilton. Cambs 3J 29
Stinchcombe. Glos 4F 18
Stinsford. Dors 6F 8
Stiperstones. Shrp 1B 26
Stirchley. Telf 1F 26
Stirchley. W Mid 3J 27
Stirling. Abers 1L 73
Stirling. Stir 116 (8A 66)
Stirton. N Yor 2H 41
Stisted. Essx 1D 22
Stitchcombe. Wilts 7L 19
Stithians. Corn 5L 3
Stittenham. High 6G 79
Stivichall. W Mid 4M 27
Stixwould. Linc 3J 37
Stoak. Ches W 2C 34
Stobo. Bord 6K 59
Stobo Castle. Bord 6K 59
Stoborough. Dors 7H 9
Stoborough Green. Dors 7H 9
Stobs Castle. Bord 1K 53
Stobswood. Nmbd 2F 54
Stock. Essx 4C 22
Stockbridge. Hants 2A 10
Stockbridge. W Yor 3J 41
Stockbury. Kent 7E 22
Stockcross. W Ber 7B 20
Stockdalewath. Cumb 7H 53
Stocker's Head. Kent 8F 22
Stockerston. Leics 2F 28
Stock Green. Worc 6H 27
Stocking. Here 8E 26
Stockingford. Warw 2M 27
Stocking Green. Essx 8B 30
Stocking Pelham. Herts 1A 22
Stockland. Devn 5M 7
Stockland Bristol. Som 1M 7
Stockleigh English. Devn 5H 7
Stockleigh Pomeroy. Devn 5H 7
Stockley. Wilts 7J 19
Stocklinch. Som 4B 8
Stockport. G Man 1G 35
The Stocks. Kent 3F 12
Stocksbridge. S Yor 8L 41
Stocksfield. Nmbd 5D 54
Stockstreet. Essx 1E 22
Stockton. Here 5D 26
Stockton. Norf 2K 31
Stockton. Shrp
nr. Bridgnorth 2F 26
nr. Chirbury 1A 26
Stockton. Telf 8F 34
Stockton. Warw 5B 28
Stockton. Wilts 2H 9
Stockton Brook. Staf 4H 35
Stockton Cross. Here 5D 26
Stockton Heath. Warr 1E 34
Stockton-on-Tees. Stoc T 4B 48
Stockton on Teme. Worc 5F 26
Stockton-on-the-Forest. York 2D 42
Stockwell Heath. Staf 7J 35
Stock Wood. Worc 6J 27
Stockwood. Bris 7E 18
Stodmarsh. Kent 7J 23
Stody. Norf 6G 39
Stoer. High 1M 77
Stoford. Som 4D 8
Stoford. Wilts 2J 9
Stogumber. Som 2K 7
Stogursey. Som 1M 7
Stoke. Devn 3B 6
Stoke. Hants
nr. Andover 8B 20
nr. South Hayling 5E 10
Stoke. Medw 6E 22
Stoke. W Mid 4A 28
Stoke Abbott. Dors 5C 8
Stoke Albany. Nptn 3F 28
Stoke Ash. Suff 4H 31
Stoke Bardolph. Notts 5D 36
Stoke Bliss. Worc 5E 26
Stoke Bruerne. Nptn 7E 28
Stoke by Clare. Suff 7D 30
Stoke-by-Nayland. Suff 8F 30
Stoke Canon. Devn 6J 7
Stoke Charity. Hants 2B 10
Stoke Climsland. Corn 8C 6
Stoke Cross. Here 6E 26
Stoke D'Abernon. Surr 8J 21
Stoke Doyle. Nptn 3H 29
Stoke Dry. Rut 2F 28
Stoke Edith. Here 7E 26
Stoke Farthing. Wilts 3J 9
Stoke Ferry. Norf 1D 30
Stoke Fleming. Devn 7L 5
Stokeford. Dors 7G 9
Stoke Gabriel. Devn 6L 5
Stoke Gifford. S Glo 6E 18
Stoke Golding. Leics 2A 28
Stoke Goldington. Mil 7F 28
Stokeham. Notts 2E 36
Stoke Hammond. Buck 1F 20
Stoke Heath. Shrp 7E 34
Stoke Holy Cross. Norf 1J 31
Stokeinteignhead. Devn 8J 7
Stoke Lacy. Here 7E 26
Stoke Lyne. Oxon 1C 20
Stoke Mandeville. Buck 2F 20
Stokenchurch. Buck 4E 20
Stoke Newington. G Lon 5L 21
Stokenham. Devn 7L 5
Stoke on Tern. Shrp 7E 34
Stoke-on-Trent. Stoke 116 (5G 35)
Stoke Orchard. Glos 1H 19
Stoke Pero. Som 1H 7
Stoke Poges. Buck 5G 21
Stoke Prior. Here 6D 26
Stoke Prior. Worc 5H 27
Stoke Rivers. Devn 2F 6
Stoke Rochford. Linc 7G 37
Stoke Row. Oxon 5D 20
Stoke St Gregory. Som 3B 8
Stoke St Mary. Som 3A 8
Stoke St Michael. Som 1E 8
Stoke St Milborough. Shrp 3D 26
Stokesay. Shrp 3C 26
Stokesby. Norf 8L 39
Stokesley. N Yor 5C 48
Stoke sub Hamdon. Som 4C 8
Stoke Talmage. Oxon 4D 20
Stoke Town. Stoke 116 (5G 35)
Stoke Trister. Som 3F 8
Stoke Wake. Dors 5F 8
Stolford. Som 1M 7
Stondon Massey. Essx 3B 22
Stone. Buck 2E 20
Stone. Glos 4E 18
Stone. Kent 6B 22
Stone. Som 2D 8
Stone. Staf 6H 35
Stone. Worc 4G 27
Stonea. Cambs 2A 30
Stoneacton. Shrp 2D 26
Stone Allerton. Som 8C 18
Ston Easton. Som 8E 18
Stonebridge. N Som 8B 18
Stonebridge. Surr 1J 11
Stone Bridge Corner. Pet 1K 29
Stonebroom. Derbs 4B 36
Stonebyres Holdings. S Lan 5G 59
Stone Chair. W Yor 5K 41
Stone Cross. E Sus 5C 12
Stone Cross. Kent 2B 12
Stone-edge Batch. N Som 6C 18
Stoneferry. Hull 4H 43
Stonefield. Arg 4D 64
Stonefield. S Lan 4E 58
Stonegate. E Sus 3C 12
Stonegate. N Yor 5E 48
Stonegrave. N Yor 8D 48
Stonehall. Worc 7G 27
Stonehaugh. Nmbd 4A 54
Stonehaven. Abers 7H 73
Stone Heath. Staf 6H 35
Stone Hill. Kent 2G 13
Stone House. Cumb 7F 46
Stonehouse. Glos 3G 19
Stonehouse. Nmbd 6L 53
Stonehouse. S Lan 5F 58
Stone in Oxney. Kent 3F 12
Stoneleigh. Warw 4M 27
Stoneley Green. Ches E 4E 34
Stonely. Cambs 5J 29
Stonepits. Worc 6J 27
Stoner Hill. Hants 3E 10
Stonesby. Leics 7F 36
Stonesfield. Oxon 2A 20
Stones Green. Essx 1H 23
Stone Street. Kent 8B 22
Stone Street. Suff
nr. Boxford 8F 30
nr. Halesworth 3K 31
Stonethwaite. Cumb 4A 46
Stoneyburn. W Lot 3H 59
Stoney Cross. Hants 4L 9
Stoneyford. Devn 5K 7
Stoneygate. Leic 1D 28
Stoneyhills. Essx 4F 22
Stoneykirk. Dum 6F 50
Stoney Middleton. Derbs 2L 35
Stoney Stanton. Leics 2B 28
Stoney Stoke. Som 2F 8
Stoney Stratton. Som 2E 8
Stoney Stretton. Shrp 1B 26
Stoneywood. Aber 4H 73
Stonham Aspal. Suff 6H 31
Stonnall. Staf 1J 27
Stonor. Oxon 5E 20
Stonton Wyville. Leics 2E 28
Stonybreck. Shet 2M 89
Stony Cross. Devn 3E 6
Stony Cross. Here
nr. Great Malvern 7F 26
nr. Leominster 5D 26
Stonyford. Lis 5H 93
Stony Houghton. Derbs 3B 36
Stony Stratford. Mil 7E 28
Stoodleigh. Devn
nr. Barnstaple 2F 6
nr. Tiverton 4J 7
Stopham. W Sus 4H 11
Stopsley. Lutn 1J 21
Stoptide. Corn 4B 4
Storeton. Mers 1B 34
Stormontfield. Per 5E 66
Stornoway. W Isl 8H 83
Stornoway Airport. W Isl 8H 83
Storridge. Here 7F 26
Storrington. W Sus 4H 11
Storrs. Cumb 6B 46
Storth. Cumb 7C 46
Storwood. E Yor 3E 42
Stotfield. Mor 6B 80
Stotfold. C Beds 8K 29
Stottesdon. Shrp 3E 26
Stoughton. Leics 1D 28
Stoughton. Surr 8G 21
Stoughton. W Sus 4F 10
Stoul. High 6J 69
Stoulton. Worc 7H 27
Stourbridge. W Mid 3G 27
Stourpaine. Dors 5G 9
Stourport-on-Severn. Worc 4G 27
Stour Provost. Dors 3F 8
Stour Row. Dors 3G 9
Stourton. Staf 3G 27
Stourton. Warw 8L 27
Stourton. W Yor 4M 41
Stourton. Wilts 2F 8
Stourton Caundle. Dors 4F 8
Stove. Orkn 6F 88
Stove. Shet 5E 90
Stoven. Suff 3L 31
Stow. Linc
nr. Billingborough 6H 37
nr. Gainsborough 1F 36
Stow. Bord 5B 60
Stow Bardolph. Norf 1C 30
Stow Bedon. Norf 2F 30
Stowbridge. Norf 1C 30
Stow cum Quy. Cambs 5B 30
Stowe. Glos 3D 18
Stowe. Shrp 4B 26
Stowe. Staf 8K 35
Stowe-by-Chartley. Staf 7J 35
Stowell. Som 3E 8
Stowey. Bath 8D 18
Stowford. Devn
nr. Colaton Raleigh 7K 7
nr. Combe Martin 1F 6
nr. Tavistock 7D 6
Stowlangtoft. Suff 5F 30
Stow Longa. Cambs 4J 29
Stow Maries. Essx 4E 22
Stowmarket. Suff 6G 31
Stow-on-the-Wold. Glos 1K 19
Stowting. Kent 1H 13
Stowupland. Suff 6G 31
Straad. Arg 3K 57
Strabane. Derr 4C 92
Strachan. Abers 6F 72
Stradbroke. Suff 4J 31
Stradishall. Suff 6D 30
Stradsett. Norf 1C 30
Stragglethorpe. Linc 4G 37
Stragglethorpe. Notts 6D 36
Straid. Ant 4H 93
Straid. ME Ant 4G 93
Straid. S Ayr 2G 51
Straight Soley. Wilts 6M 19
Straiton. Midl 3L 59
Straiton. S Ayr 1J 51
Straloch. Per 1D 66
Stramshall. Staf 6J 35
Strang. IOM 7C 44
Strangford. Here 1D 18
Strangford. New M 6J 93
Stranocum. Caus 2G 93
Stranraer. Dum 5F 50
Strata Florida. Cdgn 6G 25
Stratfield Mortimer. W Ber 7D 20
Stratfield Saye. Hants 7D 20
Stratfield Turgis. Hants 8D 20
Stratford. G Lon 5L 21
Stratford. Worc 8G 27
Stratford St Andrew. Suff 5K 31
Stratford St Mary. Suff 8G 31
Stratford sub Castle. Wilts 2K 9
Stratford Tony. Wilts 3J 9
Stratford-upon-Avon. Warw 116 (6L 27)
Strath. High
nr. Gairloch 6J 77
nr. Wick 6D 86
Strathan. High
nr. Fort William 6L 69
nr. Lochinver 1A 78
nr. Tongue 5H 85
Strathan Skerray. High 5J 85
Strathaven. S Lan 5F 58
Strathblane. Stir 2D 58
Strathcanaird. High 3B 78
Strathcarron. High 1L 69
Strathcoil. Arg 4A 64
Strathdon. Abers 4C 72
Strathkinness. Fife 6H 67
Strathmashie House. High 6F 70
Strathmiglo. Fife 6F 66
Strathmore Lodge. High 7C 86
Strathpeffer. High 8E 78
Strathrannoch. High 6D 78
Strathtay. Per 2C 66
Strathvaich Lodge. High 6D 78
Strathwhillan. N Ayr 6K 57
Strathy. High
nr. Invergordon 6G 79
nr. Melvich 5L 85
Strathyre. Stir 6K 65
Stratton. Corn 5B 6
Stratton. Dors 6E 8
Stratton. Glos 3J 19
Stratton Audley. Oxon 1D 20
Stratton-on-the-Fosse. Som 8E 18
Stratton St Margaret. Swin 5K 19
Stratton St Michael. Norf 2J 31
Stratton Strawless. Norf 7J 39
Stravithie. Fife 6J 67
Straw. M Ulst 4E 92
Stream. Som 2K 7
Streat. E Sus 4L 11
Streatham. G Lon 6L 21
Streatley. C Beds 1H 21
Streatley. W Ber 5C 20
Street. Corn 6B 6
Street. Lanc 2D 40
Street. N Yor 5E 48
Street. Som
nr. Chard 5B 8
Street. Som
nr. Glastonbury 2C 8
Street Ash. Som 4A 8
Street Dinas. Shrp 6B 34
Street End. Kent 8H 23
Street End. W Sus 6F 10
Streetgate. Tyne 6F 54
Streethay. Staf 8K 35
Streethouse. W Yor 5A 42
Streetlam. N Yor 6M 47
Street Lane. Derbs 5A 36
Streetly. W Mid 2J 27
Streetly End. Cambs 7C 30
Street on the Fosse. Som 2E 8
Strefford. Shrp 3C 26
Strelley. Notts 5C 36
Strensall. York 1D 42
Strensall Camp. York 2D 42
Stretcholt. Som 1A 8
Strete. Devn 7L 5
Stretford. G Man 8G 41
Stretford. Here 6D 26
Strethall. Essx 8A 30
Stretham. Cambs 4B 30
Stretton. Ches W 4C 34
Stretton. Derbs 3A 36
Stretton. Rut 8G 37
Stretton. Staf
nr. Brewood 8G 35
nr. Burton upon Trent 7L 35
Stretton. Warr 1E 34
Stretton en le Field. Leics 8M 35
Stretton Grandison. Here 7E 26
Stretton Heath. Shrp 8B 34
Stretton-on-Dunsmore. Warw 4B 28
Stretton-on-Fosse. Warw 8L 27
Stretton Sugwas. Here 7C 26
Stretton under Fosse. Warw 3B 28
Stretton Westwood. Shrp 2D 26
Strichen. Abers 8J 81
Strines. G Man 1H 35
Stringston. Som 1L 7
Strixton. Nptn 5G 29
Stroanfreggan. Dum 2M 51
Stroat. Glos 4D 18
Stromeferry. High 2K 69
Stromemore. High 2K 69
Stromness. Orkn 1D 86
Stronachie. Per 7D 66
Stronachlachar. Stir 6J 65
Stronchreggan. High 8A 70
Strone. Arg 1L 57
Strone. High
nr. Drumnadrochit 3F 70
nr. Kingussie 5H 71
Stronenaba. High 7C 70
Stronganess. Shet 3K 91
Stronmilchan. Arg 5F 64
Stronsay Airport. Orkn 7F 88
Strontian. High 1C 64
Strood. Kent 2E 12
Strood. Medw 7D 22
Strood Green. Surr 1K 11
Strood Green. W Sus
nr. Billingshurst 3H 11
nr. Horsham 2J 11
Strothers Dale. Nmbd 6C 54
Stroud. Glos 3G 19
Stroud. Hants 3E 10
Stroud Green. Essx 4E 22
Stroxton. Linc 6G 37
Struan. High 2E 68
Struan. Per 1B 66
Struanmore. High 2E 68
Strubby. Linc 1A 38
Strugg's Hill. Linc 6K 37
Strumpshaw. Norf 1K 31
Strutherhill. S Lan 4F 58
Struy. High 2E 70
Stryd. IOA 2B 32
Stryt-issa. Wrex 5A 34
Stuartfield. Abers 1J 73
Stubbington. Hants 5C 10
Stubbins. Lanc 6F 40
Stubble Green. Cumb 5K 45
Stubb's Cross. Kent 2F 12
Stubbs Green. Norf 2K 31
Stubhampton. Dors 4H 9
Stubton. Linc 5F 36
Stubwood. Staf 6J 35
Stuckton. Hants 4K 9
Studham. C Beds 2H 21
Studland. Dors 7J 9
Studley. Warw 5J 27
Studley. Wilts 6H 19
Studley Roger. N Yor 8L 47
Stuntney. Cambs 4B 30
Stunts Green. E Sus 4C 12
Sturbridge. Staf 6G 35
Sturgate. Linc 1F 36
Sturmer. Essx 7C 30
Sturminster Marshall. Dors 5H 9
Sturminster Newton. Dors 4F 8
Sturry. Kent 7H 23
Sturton. N Lin 7G 43
Sturton by Stow. Linc 1F 36
Sturton le Steeple. Notts 1E 36
Stuston. Suff 4H 31
Stutton. N Yor 3B 42
Stutton. Suff 8H 31
Styal. Ches E 1G 35
Stydd. Lanc 4E 40
Styrrup. Notts 8D 42
Suainebost. W Isl 5J 83
Suardail. W Isl 8H 83
Succoth. Abers 2D 72
Succoth. Arg 7G 65
Suckley. Worc 6F 26
Suckley Knowl. Worc 6F 26
Sudborough. Nptn 3G 29
Sudbourne. Suff 6L 31
Sudbrook. Linc 5G 37
Sudbrook. Mon 5D 18

Sudbrooke—Tregrehan Mills

Sudbrooke. Linc 2H 37
Sudbury. Derbs 6K 35
Sudbury. Suff 7E 30
Sudgrove. Glos 3H 19
Suffield. Norf 6J 39
Suffield. N Yor 6G 49
Sugnall. Staf 6F 34
Sugwas Pool. Here 7C 26
Suisnish. High 2G 69
Sulaisiadar. W Isl 8J 83
Sùlaisiadar Mòr. High 1F 68
Sulby. IOM 5C 44
Sulgrave. Nptn 7C 28
Sulham. W Ber 6D 20
Sulhamstead. W Ber 7D 20
Sullington. W Sus 4H 11
Sullom. Shet 6H 91
Sully. V Glam 8L 17
Sumburgh. Shet 7E 90
Sumburgh Airport. Shet 6D 90
Summer Bridge. N Yor 1L 41
Summercourt. Corn 6A 4
Summergangs. Hull 4J 43
Summer Hill. W Mid 2H 27
Summerhill. Aber 5J 73
Summerhill. Pemb 6H 15
Summerhouse. Darl 4L 47
Summersdale. W Sus 5F 10
Summerseat. G Man 6F 40
Summit. G Man 6H 41
Sunbury. Surr 7J 21
Sunderland. Cumb 8F 52
Sunderland. Lanc 2C 40
Sunderland. Tyne 116 (6G 55)
Sunderland Bridge. Dur 8F 54
Sundon Park. Lutn 1H 21
Sundridge. Kent 8A 22
Sunk Island. E Yor 6K 43
Sunningdale. Wind 7G 21
Sunninghill. Wind 7G 21
Sunningwell. Oxon 3B 20
Sunniside. Dur 8E 54
Sunniside. Tyne 6F 54
Sunny Bank. Cumb 6A 46
Sunny Hill. Derb 6M 35
Sunnyhurst. Bkbn 5E 40
Sunnylaw. Stir 8A 66
Sunnymead. Oxon 3C 20
Sunnyside. S Yor 8B 42
Sunnyside. W Sus 2L 11
Sunton. Wilts 8L 19
Surbiton. G Lon 7J 21
Surby. IOM 7B 44
Surfleet. Linc 7K 37
Surfleet Seas End. Linc 7K 37
Surlingham. Norf 1K 31
Surrex. Essx 1E 22
Sustead. Norf 6H 39
Susworth. Linc 7F 42
Sutcombe. Devn 4C 6
Suton. Norf 2G 31
Sutors of Cromarty. High 7J 79
Sutterby. Linc 2L 37
Sutterton. Linc 6K 37
Sutterton Dowdyke. Linc 6K 37
Sutton. Buck 6H 21
Sutton. Cambs 4M 29
Sutton. C Beds 7K 29
Sutton. E Sus 6A 12
Sutton. G Lon 7K 21
Sutton. Kent 1K 13
Sutton. Norf 7K 39
Sutton. Notts 6E 36
Sutton. Oxon 3B 20
Sutton. Pemb 5F 14
Sutton. Pet 2H 29
Sutton. Shrp
nr. Bridgnorth 3F 26
nr. Market Drayton 6E 34
nr. Oswestry 7B 34
nr. Shrewsbury 8D 34
Sutton. Som 2E 8
Sutton. S Yor 6C 42
Sutton. Staf 7F 34
Sutton. Suff 7K 31
Sutton. W Sus 4G 11
Sutton. Worc 5E 26
Sutton Abinger. Surr 1J 11
Sutton at Hone. Kent 6B 22
Sutton Bassett. Nptn 2E 28
Sutton Benger. Wilts 6H 19
Sutton Bingham. Som 4D 8
Sutton Bonington. Notts 7C 36
Sutton Bridge. Linc 7A 38
Sutton Cheney. Leics 1B 28
Sutton Coldfield, Royal. W Mid 2K 27
Sutton Corner. Linc 7M 37
Sutton Courtenay. Oxon 4C 20
Sutton Crosses. Linc 7M 37
Sutton cum Lound. Notts 1D 36
Sutton Gault. Cambs 4M 29
Sutton Grange. N Yor 8L 47
Sutton Green. Surr 8H 21
Sutton Howgrave. N Yor 8M 47
Sutton in Ashfield. Notts 4B 36
Sutton-in-Craven. N Yor 3J 41
Sutton Ings. Hull 4J 43
Sutton in the Elms. Leics 2C 28
Sutton Lane Ends. Ches E 2H 35
Sutton Leach. Mers 8D 40
Sutton Maddock. Shrp 1F 26
Sutton Mallet. Som 2B 8
Sutton Mandeville. Wilts 3H 9
Sutton Montis. Som 3E 8
Sutton on Hull. Hull 4J 43
Sutton on Sea. Linc 1B 38
Sutton-on-the-Forest. N Yor 1C 42
Sutton on the Hill. Derbs 6L 35
Sutton on Trent. Notts 3E 36
Sutton Poyntz. Dors 7F 8
Sutton St Edmund. Linc 8L 37
Sutton St Edmund's Common. Linc 1L 29
Sutton St James. Linc 8L 37
Sutton St Michael. Here 7D 26
Sutton St Nicholas. Here 7D 26
Sutton Scarsdale. Derbs 3B 36
Sutton Scotney. Hants 2B 10
Sutton-under-Brailes. Warw 8M 27
Sutton-under-Whitestonecliffe. N Yor 7B 48
Sutton upon Derwent. E Yor 3E 42
Sutton Valence. Kent 1E 12
Sutton Veny. Wilts 1H 9
Sutton Waldron. Dors 4G 9
Sutton Weaver. Ches W 2D 34
Swaby. Linc 2L 37
Swadlincote. Derbs 8L 35
Swaffham. Norf 1E 30
Swaffham Bulbeck. Cambs 5B 30
Swaffham Prior. Cambs 5B 30
Swafield. Norf 6J 39
Swainby. N Yor 5B 48
Swainshill. Here 7C 26
Swainsthorpe. Norf 1J 31
Swainswick. Bath 7F 18
Swalcliffe. Oxon 8A 28
Swalecliffe. Kent 7H 23
Swallow. Linc 7J 43
Swallow Beck. Linc 3G 37
Swallowcliffe. Wilts 3H 9
Swallowfield. Wok 7E 20
Swallownest. S Yor 1B 36
Swampton. Hants 8B 20
Swanage. Dors 8J 9
Swanbister. Orkn 1E 86
Swanbourne. Buck 1F 20
Swanbridge. V Glam 8L 17
Swan Green. Ches W 2F 34
Swanland. E Yor 5G 43
Swanley. Kent 7B 22
Swanmore. Hants 4C 10
Swannington. Leics 8B 36
Swannington. Norf 8H 39
Swanpool. Linc 3G 37
Swanscombe. Kent 6C 22
Swansea. Swan 117 (5F 16)
Swan Street. Essx 1E 22
Swanton Abbott. Norf 7J 39
Swanton Morley. Norf 8G 39
Swanton Novers. Norf 6G 39
Swanton Street. Kent 8E 22
Swanwick. Derbs 4B 36
Swanwick. Hants 5C 10
Swanwick Green. Ches E 5D 34
Swarby. Linc 5H 37
Swardeston. Norf 1J 31
Swarister. Shet 5K 91
Swarkestone. Derbs 7A 36
Swarland. Nmbd 1E 54
Swarraton. Hants 2C 10
Swartha. W Yor 3J 41
Swarthmoor. Cumb 8A 46
Swaton. Linc 6J 37
Swatragh. M Ulst 3F 93
Swavesey. Cambs 5L 29
Sway. Hants 6L 9
Swayfield. Linc 7G 37
Swaythling. Sotn 4B 10
Sweet Green. Worc 5E 26
Sweetham. Devn 6H 7
Sweetholme. Cumb 4D 46
Sweets. Corn 6A 6
Sweetshouse. Corn 5C 4
Swefling. Suff 5K 31
Swell. Som 3B 8
Swepstone. Leics 8A 36
Swerford. Oxon 8A 28
Swettenham. Ches E 3G 35
Swetton. N Yor 8K 47
Swffryd. Blae 5M 17
Swiftsden. E Sus 3D 12
Swilland. Suff 6H 31
Swillington. W Yor 4A 42
Swimbridge. Devn 3F 6
Swimbridge Newland. Devn 2F 6
Swinbrook. Oxon 2L 19
Swincliffe. N Yor 2L 41
Swincliffe. W Yor 5L 41
Swinderby. Linc 3F 36
Swindon. Glos 1H 19
Swindon. Nmbd 2C 54
Swindon. Staf 2G 27
Swindon. Swin 117 (5K 19)
Swine. E Yor 4J 43
Swinefleet. E Yor 5E 42
Swineford. S Glo 7E 18
Swineshead. Bed 5H 29
Swineshead. Linc 5K 37
Swineshead Bridge. Linc 5K 37
Swiney. High 8D 86
Swinford. Leics 4C 28
Swinford. Oxon 3B 20
Swingate. Notts 5C 36
Swingbrow. Cambs 3L 29
Swingfield Minnis. Kent 1J 13
Swingfield Street. Kent 1J 13
Swingleton Green. Suff 7F 30
Swinhill. S Lan 5F 58
Swinhoe. Nmbd 7K 61
Swinhope. Linc 8K 43
Swinister. Shet 5H 91
Swinithwaite. N Yor 7J 47
Swinmore Common. Here 7E 26
Swinscoe. Staf 5K 35
Swinside Hall. Bord 8E 60
Swinstead. Linc 7H 37
Swinton. G Man 7F 40
Swinton. N Yor
nr. Malton 8E 48
nr. Masham 8L 47
Swinton. Bord 5F 60
Swinton. S Yor 8B 42
Swithland. Leics 8C 36
Swordale. High 7F 78
Swordly. High 5K 85
Sworton Heath. Ches E 1E 34
Swyddffynnon. Cdgn 6F 24
Swynnerton. Staf 6G 35
Swyre. Dors 7D 8
Sycharth. Powy 8M 33
Sychdyn. Flin 4M 33
Sychnant. Powy 5J 25
Sychtyn. Powy 2J 25
Syde. Glos 2H 19
Sydenham. G Lon 6L 21
Sydenham. Oxon 3E 20
Sydenham. Som 2B 8
Sydenham Damerel. Devn 8D 6
Syderstone. Norf 6E 38
Sydling St Nicholas. Dors 6E 8
Sydmonton. Hants 8B 20
Sydney. Ches E 4F 34
Syerston. Notts 5E 36
Syke. G Man 6G 41
Sykehouse. S Yor 6D 42
Sykes. Lanc 2E 40
Syleham. Suff 4J 31
Sylen. Carm 6M 15
Sylfaen. Powy 2L 25
Symbister. Shet 1F 90
Symington. S Ayr 6B 58
Symington. S Lan 6H 59
Symondsbury. Dors 6C 8
Symonds Yat. Here 2D 18
Synod Inn. Cdgn 1L 15
Syre. High 7J 85
Syreford. Glos 1J 19
Syresham. Nptn 7D 28
Syston. Leics 8D 36
Syston. Linc 5G 37
Sytchampton. Worc 5G 27
Sywell. Nptn 5F 28

T

Tabost. W Isl
nr. Cearsiadar 2E 76
nr. Suainebost 5J 83
Tachbrook Mallory. Warw 5M 27
Tackley. Oxon 1B 20
Tacleit. W Isl 8E 82
Tacolneston. Norf 2H 31
Tadcaster. N Yor 3B 42
Taddington. Derbs 2K 35
Taddington. Glos 8J 27
Taddiport. Devn 4D 6
Tadley. Hants 7D 20
Tadlow. Cambs 7K 29
Tadmarton. Oxon 8A 28
Tadwick. Bath 6F 18
Tadworth. Surr 8K 21
Tafarnaubach. Blae 3L 17
Tafarn-y-bwlch. Pemb 3G 15
Tafarn-y-Gelyn. Den 4L 33
Taff's Well. Rhon 6L 17
Tafolwern. Powy 2H 25
Tai-bach. Powy 8L 33
Taibach. Neat 6G 17
Taigh a Ghearraidh. W Isl 6J 75
Taigh Bhuirgh. W Isl 4B 76
Tain. High
nr. Invergordon 5H 79
nr. Thurso 5D 86
Tai-Nant. Wrex 5A 34
Tai'n Lon. Gwyn 5D 32
Tairbeart. W Isl 4C 76
Tairgwaith. Neat 3G 17
Takeley. Essx 1B 22
Takeley Street. Essx 1B 22
Talachddu. Powy 1K 17
Talacre. Flin 2L 33
Talardd. Gwyn 8H 33
Talaton. Devn 6K 7
Talbenny. Pemb 5E 14
Talbot Green. Rhon 6K 17
Taleford. Devn 6K 7
Talerddig. Powy 2J 25
Talgarreg. Cdgn 1L 15
Talgarth. Powy 1L 17
Talisker. High 2E 68
Talke. Staf 4G 35
Talkin. Cumb 6K 53
Talladale. High 6L 77
Talla Linnfoots. Bord 7K 59
Tallaminnock. S Ayr 2J 51
Tallarn Green. Wrex 5C 34
Tallentire. Cumb 8F 52
Talley. Carm 1F 16
Tallington. Linc 1H 29
Talmine. High 5H 85
Talog. Carm 4K 15
Talsarn. Carm 2G 17
Talsarn. Cdgn 1M 15
Talsarnau. Gwyn 7F 32
Talskiddy. Corn 5B 4
Talwrn. IOA 3D 32
Talwrn. Wrex 5A 34
Tal-y-Bont. Cnwy 4G 33
Tal-y-bont. Cdgn 4F 24
Tal-y-bont. Gwyn
nr. Bangor 3F 32
nr. Barmouth 8E 32
Talybont-on-Usk. Powy 2L 17
Tal-y-cafn. Cnwy 3G 33
Tal-y-coed. Mon 2C 18
Tal-y-llyn. Gwyn 2G 25
Talyllyn. Powy 2L 17
Talysarn. Gwyn 5D 32
Tal-y-waenydd. Gwyn 6F 32
Talywain. Torf 3A 18
Tal-y-Wern. Powy 2H 25
Tamerton Foliot. Plym 5G 5
Tamlaght. Ferm 6C 92
Tamlaght O'Crilly. M Ulst 3F 93
Tamnamore. M Ulst 5F 93
Tamworth. Staf 1L 27
Tamworth Green. Linc 5L 37
Tandlehill. Ren 3C 58
Tandragee. Arm 6G 93
Tandridge. Surr 8L 21
Tanerdy. Carm 4L 15
Tanfield. Dur 6E 54
Tanfield Lea. Dur 6E 54
Tangasdal. W Isl 5C 74
Tang Hall. York 2D 42
Tangiers. Pemb 5F 14
Tangley. Hants 8M 19
Tangmere. W Sus 5G 11
Tangwick. Shet 6G 91
Tankerness. Orkn 1G 87
Tankersley. S Yor 8M 41
Tankerton. Kent 7H 23
Tan-lan. Cnwy 4G 33
Tan-lan. Gwyn 6F 32
Tannach. High 7E 86
Tannadice. Ang 2H 67
Tanner's Green. Worc 4J 27
Tannington. Suff 5J 31
Tannochside. N Lan 3F 58
Tan Office Green. Suff 6D 30
Tansley. Derbs 4M 35
Tansley Knoll. Derbs 3M 35
Tansor. Nptn 2H 29
Tantobie. Dur 6E 54
Tanton. N Yor 4C 48
Tanvats. Linc 3J 37
Tanworth-in-Arden. Warw 4K 27
Tan-y-bwlch. Gwyn 6F 32
Tan-y-fron. Cnwy 4J 33
Tanyfron. Wrex 4A 34
Tanygrisiau. Gwyn 6F 32
Tan-y-groes. Cdgn 2J 15
Tan-y-pistyll. Powy 8K 33
Tan-yr-allt. Den 2K 33
Taobh a Chaolais. W Isl 4D 74
Taobh a Deas Loch Aineort. W Isl 3D 74
Taobh a Ghlinne. W Isl 2E 76
Taobh a Tuath Loch Aineort. W Isl 3D 74
Taplow. Buck 5G 21
Tapton. Derbs 2A 36
Tarbert. Arg
on Jura 1F 56
on Kintyre 3H 57
Tarbert. W Isl 4C 76
Tarbet. Arg 7H 65
Tarbet. High
nr. Mallaig 6J 69
nr. Scourie 7D 84
Tarbock Green. Mers 1C 34
Tarbolton. S Ayr 7C 58
Tarbrax. S Lan 4J 59
Tardebigge. Worc 5H 27
Tarfside. Ang 8D 72
Tarland. Abers 5D 72
Tarleton. Lanc 5C 40
Tarlogie. High 5H 79
Tarlscough. Lanc 6C 40
Tarlton. Glos 4H 19
Tarnbrook. Lanc 2D 40
Tarnock. Som 8B 18
Tarns. Cumb 7F 52
Tarporley. Ches W 3D 34
Tarpots. Essx 5D 22
Tarr. Som 2L 7
Tarrant Crawford. Dors 5H 9
Tarrant Gunville. Dors 4H 9
Tarrant Hinton. Dors 4H 9
Tarrant Keyneston. Dors 5H 9
Tarrant Launceston. Dors 5H 9
Tarrant Monkton. Dors 5H 9
Tarrant Rawston. Dors 5H 9
Tarrant Rushton. Dors 5H 9
Tarrel. High 5J 79
Tarring Neville. E Sus 5M 11
Tarrington. Here 7E 26
Tarsappie. Per 5E 66
Tarscabhaig. High 5G 69
Tarskavaig. High 5G 69
Tarves. Abers 2H 73
Tarvie. High 8E 78
Tarvin. Ches W 3C 34
Tasburgh. Norf 2J 31
Tasley. Shrp 2E 26
Tassagh. Arm 7F 93
Taston. Oxon 1A 20
Tatenhill. Staf 7L 35
Tathall End. Mil 7F 28
Tatham. Lanc 1E 40
Tathwell. Linc 1L 37
Tatling End. Buck 5H 21
Tatsfield. Surr 8M 21
Tattenhall. Ches W 4C 34
Tatterford. Norf 7E 38
Tattersett. Norf 6E 38
Tattershall. Linc 4K 37
Tattershall Bridge. Linc 4J 37
Tattershall Thorpe. Linc 4K 37
Tattingstone. Suff 8H 31
Tattingstone White Horse. Suff 8H 31
Tattle Bank. Warw 5K 27
Tatworth. Som 5B 8
Taunton. Som 117 (3M 7)
Taverham. Norf 8H 39
Taverners Green. Essx 2B 22
Tavernspite. Pemb 5H 15
Tavistock. Devn 8D 6
Tavool House. Arg 5K 63
Taw Green. Devn 6F 6
Tawstock. Devn 3E 6
Taxal. Derbs 1J 35
Tayinloan. Arg 5F 56
Taynish. Arg 1G 57
Taynton. Glos 1F 18
Taynton. Oxon 2L 19
Taynuilt. Arg 4E 64
Tayport. Fife 5H 67
Tay Road Bridge. D'dee 5H 67
Tayvallich. Arg 1G 57
Tealby. Linc 8J 43
Tealing. Ang 4H 67
Teams. Tyne 5F 54
Teangue. High 5H 69
Teanna Mhachair. W Isl 7J 75
Tebay. Cumb 5E 46
Tebworth. C Beds 1G 21
Tedburn St Mary. Devn 6H 7
Teddington. Glos 8H 27
Teddington. G Lon 6J 21
Tedsmore. Shrp 7B 34
Tedstone Delamere. Here 6E 26
Tedstone Wafer. Here 6E 26
Teemore. Ferm 7C 92
Teesport. Red C 3C 48
Teesside. Stoc T 3C 48
Teeton. Nptn 4D 28
Teffont Evias. Wilts 2H 9
Teffont Magna. Wilts 2H 9
Tegryn. Pemb 3J 15
Teigh. Rut 8F 36
Teigncombe. Devn 7F 6
Teigngrace. Devn 8H 7
Teignmouth. Devn 8J 7
Telford. Telf 8E 34
Telham. E Sus 4D 12
Tellisford. Som 8G 19
Telscombe. E Sus 5M 11
Telscombe Cliffs. E Sus 5L 11
Tempar. Per 2L 65
Templand. Dum 3E 52
Temple. Corn 4D 4
Temple. Glas 3D 58
Temple. Midl 4M 59
Temple Balsall. W Mid 4L 27
Temple Bar. Carm 3E 16
Temple Bar. Cdgn 1M 15
Temple Cloud. Bath 8E 18
Templecombe. Som 3F 8
Temple Ewell. Kent 1J 13
Temple Grafton. Warw 6K 27
Temple Guiting. Glos 1J 19
Templehall. Fife 8F 66
Temple Hirst. N Yor 5D 42
Temple Normanton. Derbs 3B 36
Templepatrick. Ant 4H 93
Temple Sowerby. Cumb 3E 46
Templeton. Devn 4H 7
Templeton. Pemb 5H 15
Templeton. W Ber 7A 20
Templetown. Dur 7E 54
Tempo. Ferm 6C 92
Tempsford. C Beds 6J 29
Tenandry. Per 1C 66
Tenbury Wells. Worc 5D 26
Tenby. Pemb 6H 15
Tendring. Essx 1H 23
Tendring Green. Essx 1H 23
Tenga. Arg 3L 63
Ten Mile Bank. Norf 2C 30
Tenterden. Kent 2E 12
Terfyn. Cnwy 3J 33
Terhill. Som 2L 7
Terling. Essx 2D 22
Termon Rock. Ferm 5E 92
Ternhill. Shrp 6E 34
Terregles. Dum 4D 52
Terrick. Buck 3F 20
Terrington. N Yor 8D 48
Terrington St Clement. Norf 7B 38
Terrington St John. Norf 8B 38
Terry's Green. Warw 4K 27
Teston. Kent 8D 22
Testwood. Hants 4M 9
Tetbury. Glos 4G 19
Tetbury Upton. Glos 4G 19
Tetchill. Shrp 6B 34
Tetcott. Devn 6C 6
Tetford. Linc 2L 37
Tetney. Linc 7L 43
Tetney Lock. Linc 7L 43
Tetsworth. Oxon 3D 20
Tettenhall. W Mid 1G 27
Teversal. Notts 3B 36
Teversham. Cambs 6A 30
Teviothead. Bord 1J 53
Tewel. Abers 7H 73
Tewin. Herts 2K 21
Tewkesbury. Glos 8G 27
Teynham. Kent 7F 22
Teynham Street. Kent 7F 22
Thackthwaite. Cumb 3C 46
Thakeham. W Sus 4J 11
Thame. Oxon 3E 20
Thames Ditton. Surr 7J 21
Thames Haven. Thur 5D 22
Thamesmead. G Lon 5A 22
Thamesport. Medw 6E 22
Thanington Without. Kent 8H 23
Thankerton. S Lan 6H 59
Tharston. Norf 2H 31
Thatcham. W Ber 7C 20
Thatto Heath. Mers 8D 40
Thaxted. Essx 8C 30
Theakston. N Yor 7M 47
Thealby. N Lin 6F 42
Theale. Som 1C 8
Theale. W Ber 6D 20
Thearne. E Yor 4H 43
Theberton. Suff 5L 31
Theddingworth. Leics 3D 28
Theddlethorpe All Saints. Linc 1A 38
Theddlethorpe St Helen. Linc 1A 38
Thelbridge Barton. Devn 4G 7
Thelnetham. Suff 4G 31
Thelveton. Norf 3H 31
Thelwall. Warr 1E 34
Themelthorpe. Norf 7G 39
Thenford. Nptn 7C 28
Therfield. Herts 8L 29
Thetford. Linc 8J 37
Thetford. Norf 3E 30
Thethwaite. Cumb 7H 53
Theydon Bois. Essx 4M 21
Thick Hollins. W Yor 6K 41
Thickwood. Wilts 6G 19
Thimbleby. Linc 3K 37
Thimbleby. N Yor 6B 48
Thingwall. Mers 1A 34
Thirlby. N Yor 7B 48
Thirlestane. Bord 5C 60
Thirn. N Yor 7L 47
Thirsk. N Yor 7B 48
Thirtleby. E Yor 4J 43
Thistleton. Lanc 4C 40
Thistleton. Rut 8G 37
Thistley Green. Suff 4C 30
Thixendale. N Yor 1F 42
Thockrington. Nmbd 4C 54
Tholomas Drove. Cambs 1M 29
Tholthorpe. N Yor 1B 42
Thomas Chapel. Pemb 6H 15
Thomas Close. Cumb 7J 53
Thomastown. Abers 1G 73
Thomastown. Rhon 6K 17
Thompson. Norf 2F 30
Thomshill. Mor 8B 80
Thong. Kent 6C 22
Thongsbridge. W Yor 7K 41
Thoralby. N Yor 7J 47
Thoresby. Notts 2D 36
Thoresway. Linc 8J 43
Thorganby. Linc 8K 43
Thorganby. N Yor 3D 42
Thorgill. N Yor 6E 48
Thorington. Suff 4L 31
Thorington Street. Suff 8G 31
Thorlby. N Yor 2H 41
Thorley. Herts 2A 22
Thorley Street. Herts 2A 22
Thorley Street. IOW 7A 10
Thormanby. N Yor 8B 48
Thorn. Powy 5A 26
Thornaby-on-Tees. Stoc T 4B 48
Thornage. Norf 6G 39
Thornborough. Buck 8E 28
Thornborough. N Yor 8L 47
Thornbury. Devn 5D 6
Thornbury. Here 6E 26
Thornbury. S Glo 4E 18
Thornby. Cumb 6G 53
Thornby. Nptn 4D 28
Thorncliffe. Staf 4J 35
Thorncombe. Dors 5B 8
Thorncombe Street. Surr 1G 11
Thorncote Green. C Beds 7J 29
Thorndon. Suff 5H 31
Thorndon Cross. Devn 6E 6
Thorne. S Yor 6D 42
Thornehillhead. Devn 4D 6
Thorner. W Yor 3A 42
Thorne St Margaret. Som 3K 7
Thorney. Notts 2F 36
Thorney. Pet 1K 29
Thorney. Som 3C 8
Thorney Hill. Hants 6K 9
Thorney Toll. Cambs 1L 29
Thornfalcon. Som 3A 8
Thornford. Dors 4E 8
Thorngrafton. Nmbd 5A 54
Thorngrove. Som 2B 8
Thorngumbald. E Yor 5K 43
Thornham. Norf 5D 38
Thornham Magna. Suff 4H 31
Thornham Parva. Suff 4H 31
Thornhaugh. Pet 1H 29
Thornhill. Cphy 6L 17
Thornhill. Cumb 4K 45
Thornhill. Derbs 1K 35
Thornhill. Dum 2C 52
Thornhill. Sotn 4B 10
Thornhill. Stir 8L 65
Thornhill. W Yor 6L 41
Thornhill Lees. W Yor 6L 41
Thornhills. W Yor 5K 41
Thornholme. E Yor 1J 43
Thornicombe. Dors 5G 9
Thornington. Nmbd 6F 60
Thornley. Dur
nr. Durham 8G 55
nr. Tow Law 8E 54
Thornley Gate. Nmbd 6B 54
Thornliebank. E Ren 3D 58
Thornroan. Abers 2H 73
Thorns. Suff 6D 30
Thornsett. Derbs 1J 35
Thornthwaite. Cumb 2M 45
Thornthwaite. N Yor 2K 41
Thornton. Ang 3G 67
Thornton. Buck 8E 28
Thornton. E Yor 3E 42
Thornton. Fife 8F 66
Thornton. Lanc 3B 40
Thornton. Leics 1B 28
Thornton. Linc 3K 37
Thornton. Mers 7B 40
Thornton. Midd 4B 48
Thornton. Nmbd 5G 61
Thornton. Pemb 6F 14
Thornton. W Yor 4J 41
Thornton Curtis. N Lin 6H 43
Thorntonhall. S Lan 4D 58
Thornton Heath. G Lon 7L 21
Thornton Hough. Mers 1B 34
Thornton-in-Craven. N Yor 3H 41
Thornton in Lonsdale. N Yor 8E 46
Thornton-le-Beans. N Yor 6A 48
Thornton-le-Clay. N Yor 1D 42
Thornton-le-Dale. N Yor 7F 48
Thornton le Moor. Linc 8H 43
Thornton-le-Moor. N Yor 7A 48
Thornton-le-Moors. Ches W 2C 34
Thornton-le-Street. N Yor 7B 48
Thorntonloch. E Lot 2E 60
Thornton Rust. N Yor 7H 47
Thornton Steward. N Yor 7K 47
Thornton Watlass. N Yor 7L 47
Thornwood Common. Essx 3A 22
Thornythwaite. Cumb 3B 46
Thoroton. Notts 5E 36
Thorp Arch. W Yor 3B 42
Thorpe. Derbs 4K 35
Thorpe. E Yor 3G 43
Thorpe. Linc 1A 38
Thorpe. Norf 2L 31
Thorpe. N Yor 1J 41
Thorpe. Notts 5E 36
Thorpe. Surr 7H 21
Thorpe Abbotts. Norf 4H 31
Thorpe Acre. Leics 7C 36
Thorpe Arnold. Leics 7E 36
Thorpe Audlin. W Yor 6B 42
Thorpe Bassett. N Yor 8F 48
Thorpe Bay. S'end 5F 22
Thorpe by Water. Rut 2F 28
Thorpe Common. S Yor 8A 42
Thorpe Common. Suff 8J 31
Thorpe Constantine. Staf 1L 27
Thorpe End. Norf 8J 39
Thorpe Fendike. Linc 3A 38
Thorpe Green. Essx 1H 23
Thorpe Green. Suff 6F 30
Thorpe Hall. N Yor 8C 48
Thorpe Hamlet. Norf 1J 31
Thorpe Hesley. S Yor 8A 42
Thorpe in Balne. S Yor 6C 42
Thorpe in the Fallows. Linc 1G 37
Thorpe Langton. Leics 2E 28
Thorpe Larches. Dur 3A 48
Thorpe Latimer. Linc 5J 37
Thorpe-le-Soken. Essx 1H 23
Thorpe le Street. E Yor 3F 42
Thorpe Malsor. Nptn 4F 28
Thorpe Mandeville. Nptn 7C 28
Thorpe Market. Norf 6J 39
Thorpe Marriott. Norf 8H 39
Thorpe Morieux. Suff 6F 30
Thorpeness. Suff 6L 31
Thorpe on the Hill. Linc 3G 37
Thorpe on the Hill. W Yor 5M 41
Thorpe St Andrew. Norf 1J 31
Thorpe St Peter. Linc 3A 38
Thorpe Salvin. S Yor 1C 36
Thorpe Satchville. Leics 8E 36
Thorpe Thewles. Stoc T 3A 48
Thorpe Tilney. Linc 4J 37
Thorpe Underwood. N Yor 2B 42
Thorpe Waterville. Nptn 3H 29
Thorpe Willoughby. N Yor 4C 42
Thorpland. Norf 1C 30
Thorrington. Essx 1G 23
Thorverton. Devn 5J 7
Thrandeston. Suff 4H 31
Thrapston. Nptn 4G 29
Thrashbush. N Lan 3F 58
Threapland. Cumb 8F 52
Threapland. N Yor 1H 41
Threapwood. Ches W 5C 34
Threapwood. Staf 5J 35
Three Ashes. Here 1D 18
Three Bridges. Linc 1M 37
Three Bridges. W Sus 2K 11
Three Burrows. Corn 4L 3
Three Chimneys. Kent 2E 12
Three Cocks. Powy 1L 17
Three Crosses. Swan 5E 16
Three Cups Corner. E Sus 3C 12
Threehammer Common. Norf 7K 39
Three Holes. Norf 1B 30
Threekingham. Linc 6H 37
Three Leg Cross. E Sus 2C 12
Three Legged Cross. Dors 5J 9
Three Mile Cross. Wok 7E 20
Threemilestone. Corn 4L 3
Three Oaks. E Sus 4E 12
Threlkeld. Cumb 3B 46
Threshfield. N Yor 1H 41
Thrigby. Norf 8L 39
Thringarth. Dur 3H 47
Thringstone. Leics 8B 36
Thrintoft. N Yor 6M 47
Thriplow. Cambs 7M 29
Throckenholt. Linc 1L 29
Throcking. Herts 8L 29
Throckley. Tyne 5E 54
Throckmorton. Worc 7H 27
Throop. Bour 6K 9
Throphill. Nmbd 3E 54
Thropton. Nmbd 1D 54
Throsk. Stir 8B 66
Througham. Glos 3H 19
Throughgate. Dum 3C 52
Throwleigh. Devn 6F 6
Throwley. Kent 8F 22
Throwley Forstal. Kent 8F 22
Throxenby. N Yor 7H 49
Thrumpton. Notts 6C 36
Thrumster. High 7E 86
Thrunton. Nmbd 8H 61
Thrupp. Glos 3G 19
Thrupp. Oxon 2B 20
Thrushelton. Devn 7D 6
Thrushgill. Lanc 1E 40
Thrussington. Leics 8D 36
Thruxton. Hants 1L 9
Thruxton. Here 8C 26
Thrybergh. S Yor 8B 42
Thulston. Derbs 6B 36
Thundergay. N Ayr 5H 57
Thundersley. Essx 5D 22
Thundridge. Herts 2L 21
Thurcaston. Leics 8C 36
Thurcroft. S Yor 1B 36
Thurdon. Corn 4B 6
Thurgarton. Norf 6H 39
Thurgarton. Notts 5D 36
Thurgoland. S Yor 7L 41
Thurlaston. Leics 2C 28
Thurlaston. Warw 4B 28
Thurlbear. Som 3A 8
Thurlby. Linc
nr. Alford 2A 38
nr. Baston 8J 37
nr. Lincoln 3G 37
Thurleigh. Bed 6H 29
Thurlestone. Devn 7J 5
Thurloxton. Som 2A 8
Thurlstone. S Yor 7L 41
Thurlton. Norf 2L 31
Thurmaston. Leics 1D 28
Thurnby. Leics 1D 28
Thurne. Norf 8L 39
Thurnham. Kent 8E 22
Thurning. Norf 7G 39
Thurning. Nptn 3H 29
Thurnscoe. S Yor 7B 42
Thursby. Cumb 6H 53
Thursford. Norf 6F 38
Thursford Green. Norf 6F 38
Thursley. Surr 2G 11
Thurso. High 5C 86
Thurso East. High 5C 86
Thurstaston. Mers 2M 33
Thurston. Suff 5F 30
Thurston End. Suff 6D 30
Thurstonfield. Cumb 6H 53
Thurstonland. W Yor 6K 41
Thurton. Norf 1K 31
Thurvaston. Derbs
nr. Ashbourne 6K 35
nr. Derby 6L 35
Thuxton. Norf 1G 31
Thwaite. Dur 4J 47
Thwaite. N Yor 6G 47
Thwaite. Suff 5H 31
Thwaite Head. Cumb 6B 46
Thwaites. W Yor 3J 41
Thwaite St Mary. Norf 2K 31
Thwing. E Yor 8H 49
Tibbermore. Per 5D 66
Tibberton. Glos 1F 18
Tibberton. Telf 7E 34
Tibberton. Worc 6H 27
Tibenham. Norf 3H 31
Tibshelf. Derbs 3B 36
Tibthorpe. E Yor 2G 43
Ticehurst. E Sus 2C 12
Tichborne. Hants 2C 10
Tickencote. Rut 1G 29
Tickenham. N Som 6C 18
Tickhill. S Yor 8C 42
Ticklerton. Shrp 2C 26
Ticknall. Derbs 7A 36
Tickton. E Yor 3H 43
Tidbury Green. W Mid 4K 27
Tidcombe. Wilts 8L 19
Tiddington. Oxon 3D 20
Tiddington. Warw 6L 27
Tiddleywink. Wilts 6G 19
Tidebrook. E Sus 3C 12
Tideford. Corn 6F 4
Tideford Cross. Corn 5F 4
Tidenham. Glos 4D 18
Tideswell. Derbs 2K 35
Tidmarsh. W Ber 6D 20
Tidmington. Warw 8L 27
Tidpit. Hants 4J 9
Tidworth. Wilts 1L 9
Tidworth Camp. Wilts 1L 9
Tiers Cross. Pemb 5F 14
Tiffield. Nptn 6D 28
Tifty. Abers 1G 73
Tigerton. Ang 1J 67
Tighnabruaich. Arg 2J 57
Tigley. Devn 5K 5
Tilbrook. Cambs 5H 29
Tilbury. Thur 6C 22
Tilbury Green. Essx 7D 30
Tilbury Juxta Clare. Essx 7D 30
Tile Hill. W Mid 4L 27
Tilehurst. Read 6D 20
Tilford. Surr 1F 10
Tilgate Forest Row. W Sus 2K 11
Tillathrowie. Abers 2D 72
Tillers Green. Glos 8E 26
Tillery. Abers 3J 73
Tilley. Shrp 7D 34
Tillicoultry. Clac 8C 66
Tillingham. Essx 3F 22
Tillington. Here 7C 26
Tillington. W Sus 3G 11
Tillington Common. Here 7C 26
Tillybirloch. Abers 5F 72
Tillyfourie. Abers 4F 72
Tilmanstone. Kent 8K 23
Tilney All Saints. Norf 8B 38
Tilney Fen End. Norf 8B 38
Tilney High End. Norf 8B 38
Tilney St Lawrence. Norf 8B 38
Tilshead. Wilts 1J 9
Tilstock. Shrp 6D 34
Tilston. Ches W 4C 34
Tilstone Fearnall. Ches W 3D 34
Tilsworth. C Beds 1G 21
Tilton on the Hill. Leics 1E 28
Tiltups End. Glos 4G 19
Timberland. Linc 4J 37
Timbersbrook. Ches E 3G 35
Timberscombe. Som 1J 7
Timble. N Yor 2K 41
Timperley. G Man 1F 34
Timsbury. Bath 8E 18
Timsbury. Hants 3M 9
Timsgearraidh. W Isl 8D 82
Timworth Green. Suff 5E 30
Tincleton. Dors 6F 8
Tindale. Cumb 6L 53
Tindale Crescent. Dur 3L 47
Tingewick. Buck 8D 28
Tingrith. C Beds 8H 29
Tingwall. Orkn 7D 88
Tinhay. Devn 7C 6
Tinshill. W Yor 4L 41
Tinsley. S Yor 8B 42
Tinsley Green. W Sus 2K 11
Tintagel. Corn 3C 4
Tintern. Mon 3D 18
Tintinhull. Som 4C 8
Tintwistle. Derbs 8J 41
Tinwald. Dum 3E 52
Tinwell. Rut 1H 29
Tippacott. Devn 1G 7
Tipperty. Abers 3J 73
Tipps End. Cambs 2B 30
Tiptoe. Hants 6L 9
Tipton. W Mid 2H 27
Tipton St John. Devn 6K 7
Tiptree. Essx 2E 22
Tiptree Heath. Essx 2E 22
Tirabad. Powy 8H 25
Tircoed Forest Village. Swan 4F 16
Tiree Airport. Arg 3F 62
Tirinie. Per 1B 66
Tirley. Glos 1G 19
Tiroran. Arg 5K 63
Tir-Phil. Cphy 4L 17
Tirril. Cumb 3D 46
Tirryside. High 2F 78
Tir-y-dail. Carm 3F 16
Tisbury. Wilts 3H 9
Tisman's Common. W Sus 2H 11
Tissington. Derbs 4K 35
Titchberry. Devn 3B 6
Titchfield. Hants 5C 10
Titchmarsh. Nptn 4H 29
Titchwell. Norf 5D 38
Tithby. Notts 6D 36
Titley. Here 6B 26
Titlington. Nmbd 8H 61
Titsey. Surr 8M 21
Titson. Corn 5B 6
Tittensor. Staf 6G 35
Tittleshall. Norf 7E 38
Titton. Worc 5G 27
Tiverton. Ches W 3D 34
Tiverton. Devn 4J 7
Tivetshall St Margaret. Norf 3H 31
Tivetshall St Mary. Norf 3H 31
Tivington. Som 1J 7
Tixall. Staf 7H 35
Tixover. Rut 1G 29
Toab. Orkn 1G 87
Toab. Shet 6D 90
Toadmoor. Derbs 4A 36
Tobermore. M Ulst 4F 93
Tobermory. Arg 2L 63
Toberonochy. Arg 7B 64
Tobha Beag. W Isl 2D 74
Tobha-Beag. W Isl 6A 76
Tobha Mor. W Isl 2D 74
Tobhtarol. W Isl 8E 82
Tobson. W Isl 8E 82
Tocabhaig. High 4H 69
Tocher. Abers 2F 72
Tockenham. Wilts 6J 19
Tockenham Wick. Wilts 5J 19
Tockholes. Bkbn 5E 40
Tockington. S Glo 5E 18
Tockwith. N Yor 2B 42
Todber. Dors 3G 9
Todding. Here 4C 26
Toddington. C Beds 1H 21
Toddington. Glos 8J 27
Todenham. Glos 8L 27
Todhills. Cumb 5H 53
Todmorden. W Yor 5H 41
Todwick. S Yor 1B 36
Toft. Cambs 6L 29
Toft. Linc 8H 37
Toft Hill. Dur 3K 47
Toft Monks. Norf 2L 31
Toft next Newton. Linc 1H 37
Toftrees. Norf 7E 38
Tofts. High 5E 86
Toftwood. Norf 8F 38
Togston. Nmbd 1F 54
Tokavaig. High 4H 69
Tokers Green. Oxon 6E 20
Tolastadh a Chaolais. W Isl 8E 82
Tolladine. Worc 6G 27
Tolland. Som 2L 7
Tollard Farnham. Dors 4H 9
Tollard Royal. Wilts 4H 9
Toll Bar. S Yor 7C 42
Toller Fratrum. Dors 6D 8
Toller Porcorum. Dors 6D 8
Tollerton. N Yor 1C 42
Tollerton. Notts 6D 36
Toller Whelme. Dors 5D 8
Tollesbury. Essx 2F 22
Tolleshunt D'Arcy. Essx 2F 22
Tolleshunt Knights. Essx 2F 22
Tolleshunt Major. Essx 2F 22
Tollie. High 8F 78
Tollie Farm. High 6K 77
Tolm. W Isl 8H 83
Tolpuddle. Dors 6F 8
Tolstadh bho Thuath. W Isl 7J 83
Tolworth. G Lon 7J 21
Tomachlaggan. Mor 3A 72
Tomaknock. Per 5B 66
Tomatin. High 3J 71
Tombuidhe. Arg 7E 64
Tomdoun. High 5B 70
Tomich. High
nr. Cannich 3D 70
nr. Invergordon 6H 79
nr. Lairg 3G 79
Tomintoul. Mor 4A 72
Tomnavoulin. Mor 3B 72
Tomsléibhe. Arg 4M 63
Ton. Mon 4B 18
Tonbridge. Kent 1B 12
Tondu. B'end 6H 17
Tonedale. Som 3L 7
Tonfanau. Gwyn 2E 24
Tong. Shrp 1F 26
Tonge. Leics 7B 36
Tong Forge. Shrp 1F 26
Tongham. Surr 1F 10
Tongland. Dum 6A 52
Tong Norton. Shrp 1F 26
Tongue. High 6H 85
Tongue End. Linc 8J 37
Tongwynlais. Card 6L 17
Tonmawr. Neat 5H 17
Tonna. Neat 5G 17
Tonnau. Neat 5G 17
Ton Pentre. Rhon 5J 17
Ton-Teg. Rhon 6K 17
Tonwell. Herts 2L 21
Tonypandy. Rhon 5J 17
Tonyrefail. Rhon 6K 17
Toome. Ant 4F 93
Toot Baldon. Oxon 3C 20
Toot Hill. Essx 3B 22
Toothill. Hants 4A 10
Topcliffe. N Yor 8B 48
Topcliffe. W Yor 5L 41
Topcroft. Norf 2J 31
Topcroft Street. Norf 2J 31
Toppesfield. Essx 8D 30
Toppings. G Man 6F 40
Toprow. Norf 2H 31
Topsham. Devn 7J 7
Torbay. Torb 5M 5
Torbeg. N Ayr 7H 57
Torbothie. N Lan 4G 59
Torbryan. Devn 5L 5
Torcross. Devn 7L 5
Tore. High 8G 79
Torgyle. High 4D 70
Torinturk. Arg 3H 57
Torksey. Linc 2F 36
Torlum. W Isl 8J 75
Torlundy. High 8B 70
Tormarton. S Glo 6F 18
Tormitchell. S Ayr 2H 51
Tormore. High 5H 69
Tormore. N Ayr 6H 57
Tornagrain. High 1H 71
Tornaveen. Abers 5F 72
Torness. High 3F 70
Toronto. Dur 8E 54
Torpenhow. Cumb 8G 53
Torphichen. W Lot 2H 59
Torphins. Abers 5F 72
Torpoint. Corn 6G 5
Torquay. Torb 5M 5
Torr. Devn 6H 5
Torra. Arg 4C 56
Torran. High 1G 69
Torrance. E Dun 2E 58
Torrans. Arg 5K 63
Torranyard. N Ayr 5B 58
Torre. Som 2K 7
Torre. Torb 5M 5
Torridon. High 8L 77
Torrin. High 3G 69
Torrisdale. Arg 6G 57
Torrisdale. High 5J 85
Torrish. High 2K 79
Torrisholme. Lanc 1C 40
Torroble. High 3F 78
Torroy. High 4F 78
Torry. Aber 5J 73
Torryburn. Fife 1J 59
Torthorwald. Dum 4E 52
Tortington. W Sus 5H 11
Tortworth. S Glo 4F 18
Torvaig. High 1F 68
Torver. Cumb 6A 46
Torwood. Falk 1G 59
Torworth. Notts 1D 36
Toscaig. High 2J 69
Toseland. Cambs 5K 29
Tosside. N Yor 2F 40
Tostock. Suff 5F 30
Totaig. High 8C 76
Totardor. High 2E 68
Tote. High 1F 68
Totegan. High 5L 85
Tothill. Linc 1M 37
Totland. IOW 7M 9
Totley. S Yor 2M 35
Totnell. Dors 5E 8
Totnes. Devn 5L 5
Toton. Notts 6B 36
Totronald. Arg 2G 63
Totscore. High 7E 76
Tottenham. G Lon 4L 21
Tottenhill. Norf 8C 38
Tottenhill Row. Norf 8C 38
Totteridge. G Lon 4K 21
Totternhoe. C Beds 1G 21
Tottington. G Man 6F 40
Totton. Hants 4A 10
Touchen-end. Wind 6F 20
Toulvaddie. High 5J 79
The Towans. Corn 5J 3
Toward. Arg 3L 57
Towcester. Nptn 7D 28
Towednack. Corn 5H 3
Tower End. Norf 8C 38
Tower Hill. Mers 7C 40
Tower Hill. W Sus 3J 11
Towersey. Oxon 3E 20
Towie. Abers 4D 72
Towiemore. Mor 1C 72
Tow Law. Dur 8E 54
The Town. IOS 1G 3
Town End. Cambs 2M 29
Town End. Cumb
nr. Ambleside 5C 46
nr. Kirkby Thore 3E 46
nr. Lindale 7C 46
nr. Newby Bridge 7B 46
Town End. Mers 1C 34
Townend. W Dun 2C 58
Townfield. Dur 7C 54
Towngate. Cumb 7K 53
Towngate. Linc 8J 37
Town Green. Lanc 7C 40
Town Head. Cumb
nr. Grasmere 5B 46
nr. Great Asby 4E 46
Townhead. Cumb
nr. Lazonby 8K 53
nr. Maryport 8E 52
nr. Ousby 8L 53
Townhead. Dum 7A 52
Townhead of Greenlaw. Dum 5B 52
Townhill. Fife 1K 59
Townhill. Swan 5F 16
Townjoy. M Ulst 5F 93
Town Kelloe. Dur 8G 55
Town Littleworth. E Sus 4M 11
Town Row. E Sus 2B 12
Towns End. Hants 8C 20
Townsend. Herts 3J 21
Townshend. Corn 5J 3
Town Street. Suff 3D 30
Town Yetholm. Bord 7F 60
Towthorpe. E Yor 1G 43
Towthorpe. York 2D 42
Towton. N Yor 4B 42
Towyn. Cnwy 3J 33
Toxteth. Mers 1B 34
Toynton All Saints. Linc 3L 37
Toynton Fen Side. Linc 3L 37
Toynton St Peter. Linc 3M 37
Toy's Hill. Kent 8A 22
Trabboch. E Ayr 7C 58
Traboe. Corn 6L 3
Tradespark. High 8J 79
Tradespark. Orkn 1F 86
Trafford Park. G Man 8F 40
Trallong. Powy 2J 17
Y Trallwng. Powy 2M 25
Tranent. E Lot 2B 60
Tranmere. Mers 1B 34
Trantlebeg. High 6L 85
Trantlemore. High 6L 85
Tranwell. Nmbd 3E 54
Trapp. Carm 3F 16
Traquair. Bord 6M 59
Trash Green. W Ber 7D 20
Trawden. Lanc 4H 41
Trawscoed. Powy 1K 17
Trawsfynydd. Gwyn 7G 33
Trawsgoed. Cdgn 5F 24
Treaddow. Here 1D 18
Trealaw. Rhon 5K 17
Treales. Lanc 4C 40
Trearddur. IOA 3B 32
Treaslane. High 8E 76
Treator. Corn 4B 4
Trebanog. Rhon 5K 17
Trebanos. Neat 4G 17
Trebarber. Corn 5A 4
Trebartha. Corn 8B 6
Trebarwith. Corn 3C 4
Trebetherick. Corn 4B 4
Treborough. Som 2K 7
Trebudannon. Corn 5A 4
Trebullett. Corn 8C 6
Treburley. Corn 8C 6
Treburrick. Corn 4A 4
Trebyan. Corn 5C 4
Trecastle. Powy 2H 17
Trecenydd. Cphy 6L 17
Trecott. Devn 5F 6
Trecwn. Pemb 3F 14
Trecynon. Rhon 4J 17
Tredaule. Corn 7B 6
Tredavoe. Corn 6H 3
Tredegar. Blae 4L 17
Trederwen. Powy 8A 34
Tredington. Glos 1H 19
Tredington. Warw 7L 27
Tredinnick. Corn
nr. Bodmin 5D 4
nr. Looe 6E 4
nr. Padstow 4B 4
Tredogan. V Glam 8K 17
Tredomen. Powy 1L 17
Tredunnock. Mon 4B 18
Tredustan. Powy 1L 17
Treen. Corn
nr. Land's End 6G 3
nr. St Ives 5H 3
Treeton. S Yor 1B 36
Trefaldwyn. Powy 3M 25
Trefasser. Pemb 3E 14
Trefdraeth. IOA 3D 32
Trefdraeth. Pemb 3G 15
Trefecca. Powy 1L 17
Trefechan. Mer T 4K 17
Trefeglwys. Powy 3J 25
Trefenter. Cdgn 6F 24
Treffgarne. Pemb 4F 14
Treffynnon. Flin 3L 33
Treffynnon. Pemb 4E 14
Trefil. Blae 3L 17
Trefilan. Cdgn 1M 15
Trefin. Pemb 3E 14
Treflach. Shrp 7A 34
Trefnant. Den 3K 33
Trefonen. Shrp 7A 34
Trefor. Gwyn 6C 32
Trefor. IOA 2C 32
Treforest. Rhon 6K 17
Trefrew. Corn 3D 4
Trefriw. Cnwy 4G 33
Tref-y-Clawdd. Powy 4A 26
Trefynwy. Mon 2D 18
Tregada. Corn 7C 6
Tregadillett. Corn 7B 6
Tregare. Mon 2C 18
Tregarne. Corn 6L 3
Tregaron. Cdgn 7F 24
Tregarth. Gwyn 4F 32
Tregear. Corn 6A 4
Tregeare. Corn 7B 6
Tregeiriog. Wrex 7L 33
Tregele. IOA 1C 32
Tregeseal. Corn 5G 3
Tregiskey. Corn 7C 4
Tregole. Corn 6A 6
Tregolwyn. V Glam 7J 17
Tregonetha. Corn 5B 4
Tregonhawke. Corn 6G 5
Tregony. Corn 7B 4
Tregoodwell. Corn 3D 4
Tregorrick. Corn 6C 4
Tregoss. Corn 5B 4
Tregowris. Corn 6L 3
Tregoyd. Powy 1L 17
Tregrehan Mills. Corn 6C 4

Tre-groes—Welford-on-Avon

Tre-groes. Cdgn 2L 15
Tregullon. Corn 5C 4
Tregurrian. Corn 5A 4
Tregynon. Powy 3K 25
Trehafod. Rhon 5K 17
Trehan. Corn 6G 5
Treharris. Mer T 5K 17
Treherbert. Rhon 5J 17
Trehunist. Corn 5F 4
Trekenner. Corn 8C 6
Trekenning. Corn 5B 4
Treknow. Corn 3C 4
Trelales. B'end 6H 17
Trelan. Corn 7L 3
Trelash. Corn 6A 6
Trelassick. Corn 6A 4
Trelawnyd. Flin 3K 33
Trelech. Carm 3J 15
Treleddyd-fawr. Pemb 4D 14
Trelewis. Mer T 5L 17
Treligga. Corn 3C 4
Trelights. Corn 4B 4
Trelill. Corn 4C 4
Trelissick. Corn 5M 3
Trellech. Mon 3D 18
Trelleck Grange. Mon 3C 18
Trelogan. Flin 2L 33
Trelystan. Powy 1A 26
Tremadog. Gwyn 6E 32
Tremail. Corn 7A 6
Tremain. Cdgn 2J 15
Tremaine. Corn 7B 6
Tremar. Corn 5E 4
Trematon. Corn 6F 4
Tremeirchion. Den 3K 33
Tremore. Corn 5C 4
Tremorfa. Card 7M 17
Trenance. Corn
nr. Newquay 5A 4
nr. Padstow 4B 4
Trenarren. Corn 7C 4
Trench. Telf 8E 34
Trencreek. Corn 2M 3
Trendeal. Corn 6A 4
Trenear. Corn 5K 3
Treneglos. Corn 7B 6
Trenewan. Corn 6D 4
Trengune. Corn 6A 6
Trent. Dors 4D 8
Trentham. Stoke 5G 35
Trentishoe. Devn 1F 6
Trentlock. Derbs 6B 36
Treoes. V Glam 7J 17
Treorchy. Rhon 5J 17
Treorci. Rhon 5J 17
Tre'r-ddol. Cdgn 3F 24
Tre'r llai. Powy 2M 25
Trerulefoot. Corn 6F 4
Tresaith. Cdgn 1J 15
Trescott. Staf 2G 27
Trescowe. Corn 5J 3
Tresham. Glos 4F 18
Tresigin. V Glam 7J 17
Tresillian. Corn 7A 4
Tresimwn. V Glam 7K 17
Tresinney. Corn 3D 4
Treskillard. Corn 5K 3
Treskinnick Cross. Corn 6B 6
Tresmeer. Corn 7B 6
Tresparrett. Corn 2D 4
Tresparrett Posts. Corn 6A 6
Tressady. High 3G 79
Tressait. Per 1B 66
Tresta. Shet
on Fetlar 4L 91
on Mainland 2D 90
Treswell. Notts 2E 36
Treswithian. Corn 5K 3
Tre Taliesin. Cdgn 3F 24
Trethomas. Cphy 6L 17
Trethosa. Corn 6B 4
Trethurgy. Corn 6C 4
Tretio. Pemb 4D 14
Tretire. Here 1D 18
Tretower. Powy 2L 17
Treuddyn. Flin 4A 34
Trevadlock. Corn 8B 6
Trevalga. Corn 3C 4
Trevalyn. Wrex 4B 34
Trevance. Corn 4B 4
Trevanger. Corn 4B 4
Trevanson. Corn 4B 4
Trevarrack. Corn 5H 3
Trevarren. Corn 5B 4
Trevarrian. Corn 5A 4
Trevarrick. Corn 7B 4
Trevaughan. Carm
nr. Carmarthen 4L 15
nr. Whitland 5H 15
Treveighan. Corn 4C 4
Trevellas. Corn 3L 3
Trevelmond. Corn 5E 4
Treverva. Corn 5L 3
Trevescan. Corn 6G 3
Trevethin. Torf 3A 18
Trevia. Corn 3C 4
Trevigro. Corn 5F 4
Trevilley. Corn 6G 3
Treviscoe. Corn 6B 4
Trevivian. Corn 7A 6
Trevone. Corn 4A 4
Trevor. Wrex 5A 34
Trevor Uchaf. Den 6M 33
Trew. Corn 6K 3
Trewalder. Corn 3C 4
Trewarlett. Corn 7C 6
Trewarmett. Corn 3C 4
Trewassa. Corn 3D 4
Treween. Corn 7B 6
Trewellard. Corn 5G 3
Trewen. Corn 7B 6
Trewennack. Corn 6K 3
Trewern. Powy 8A 34
Trewetha. Corn 4C 4
Trewidland. Corn 6E 4
Trewint. Corn 6A 6
Trewithian. Corn 8A 4
Trewoofe. Corn 6H 3
Trewoon. Corn 6B 4
Treworthal. Corn 8A 4
Trewyddel. Pemb 2H 15
Treyarnon. Corn 4A 4
Treyford. W Sus 4F 10
Triangle. Staf 1J 27
Triangle. W Yor 5J 41
Trickett's Cross. Dors 5J 9
Trillick. Ferm 6C 92
Trimdon. Dur 8G 55
Trimdon Colliery. Dur 8G 55
Trimdon Grange. Dur 8G 55
Trimingham. Norf 6J 39
Trimley Lower Street. Suff 8J 31
Trimley St Martin. Suff 8J 31
Trimley St Mary. Suff 8J 31
Trimpley. Worc 4F 26
Trimsaran. Carm 6L 15
Trimstone. Devn 1E 6
Trinafour. Per 1M 65
Trinant. Cphy 5M 17
Tring. Herts 2G 21
Trinity. Ang 1K 67
Trinity. Edin 2L 59
Trisant. Cdgn 5G 25
Triscombe. Som 2L 7
Trislaig. High 8A 70
Trispen. Corn 3M 3
Tritlington. Nmbd 2F 54
Trochry. Per 3C 66
Troedrhiwdalar. Powy 7J 25
Troedrhiwfuwch. Cphy 4L 17
Troedrhiw-gwair. Blae 4L 17
Troedyraur. Cdgn 2K 15
Troedyrhiw. Mer T 4K 17
Trondavoe. Shet 6H 91
Troon. Corn 5K 3
Troon. S Ayr 6B 58
Troqueer. Dum 4D 52
Troston. Suff 4E 30
Trottiscliffe. Kent 7C 22
Trotton. W Sus 3F 10
Troutbeck. Cumb
nr. Ambleside 5C 46
nr. Penrith 3B 46
Troutbeck Bridge. Cumb 5C 46
Troway. Derbs 2A 36
Trowbridge. Wilts 8G 19
Trowell. Notts 6B 36
Trowle Common. Wilts 8G 19
Trowley Bottom. Herts 2H 21
Trowse Newton. Norf 1J 31
Trudoxhill. Som 1F 8
Trull. Som 3M 7
Trumaisgearraidh. W Isl 6K 75
Trumpan. High 7D 76
Trumpet. Here 8E 26
Trumpington. Cambs 6M 29
Trumps Green. Surr 7G 21
Trunch. Norf 6J 39
Trunnah. Lanc 3B 40
Truro. Corn 4M 3
Trusham. Devn 7H 7
Trusley. Derbs 6L 35
Trusthorpe. Linc 1B 38
Tryfil. IOA 2D 32
Trysull. Staf 2G 27
Tubney. Oxon 4B 20
Tuckenhay. Devn 6L 5
Tuckhill. Shrp 3F 26
Tuckingmill. Corn 4K 3
Tuckton. Bour 6K 9
Tuddenham. Suff 4D 30
Tuddenham St Martin.
Suff 7H 31
Tudeley. Kent 1C 12
Tudhoe. Dur 8F 54
Tudhoe Grange. Dur 8F 54
Tudorville. Here 1D 18
Tudweiliog. Gwyn 7B 32
Tuesley. Surr 1G 11
Tufton. Hants 1B 10
Tufton. Pemb 4G 15
Tugby. Leics 1E 28
Tugford. Shrp 3D 26
Tughall. Nmbd 7K 61
Tulchan. Per 5C 66
Tullibardine. Per 6C 66
Tullibody. Clac 8B 66
Tullich. Arg 6E 64
Tullich. High
nr. Lochcarron 1L 69
nr. Tain 6J 79
Tullich. Mor 1C 72
Tullich Muir. High 6H 79
Tulliemet. Per 2C 66
Tulloch. Abers 2H 73
Tulloch. High
nr. Bonar Bridge 4G 79
nr. Fort William 7D 70
nr. Grantown-on-Spey 4K 71
Tulloch. Per 5D 66
Tullochgorm. Arg 8D 64
Tullybeagles Lodge. Per 4D 66
Tullyhogue. M Ulst 5F 93
Tullymurdoch. Per 2F 66
Tullynessle. Abers 4E 72
Tumble. Carm 5M 15
Tumbler's Green. Essx 1E 22
Tumby. Linc 3K 37
Tumby Woodside. Linc 4K 37
Tummel Bridge. Per 2A 66
Tunbridge Wells, Royal.
Kent 2B 12
Tunga. W Isl 8H 83
Tungate. Norf 7J 39
Tunley. Bath 8E 18
Tunstall. E Yor 4L 43
Tunstall. Kent 7E 22
Tunstall. Lanc 8E 46
Tunstall. Norf 1L 31
Tunstall. N Yor 6L 47
Tunstall. Staf 7F 34
Tunstall. Stoke 4G 35
Tunstall. Suff 6K 31
Tunstall. Tyne 6G 55
Tunstead. Derbs 2K 35
Tunstead. Norf 7J 39
Tunstead Milton. Derbs 1J 35
Tunworth. Hants 1D 10
Tupsley. Here 7D 26
Tupton. Derbs 3A 36
Turfholm. S Lan 6G 59
Turfmoor. Devn 5A 8
Turgis Green. Hants 8D 20
Turkdean. Glos 2K 19
Turkey Island. Hants 4C 10
Tur Langton. Leics 2E 28
Turleigh. Wilts 7G 19
Turlin Moor. Pool 6H 9
Turnastone. Here 8B 26
Turnberry. S Ayr 1H 51
Turnchapel. Plym 6G 5
Turnditch. Derbs 5L 35
Turners Hill. W Sus 2L 11
Turners Puddle. Dors 6G 9
Turnford. Herts 3L 21
Turnhouse. Edin 2K 59
Turnworth. Dors 5G 9
Turriff. Abers 1G 73
Tursdale. Dur 8G 55
Turton Bottoms. Bkbn 6F 40
Turtory. Mor 1E 72
Turves Green. W Mid 4J 27
Turvey. Bed 6G 29
Turville. Buck 4E 20
Turville Heath. Buck 4E 20
Turweston. Buck 8D 28
Tushielaw. Bord 8M 59
Tutbury. Staf 7L 35
Tutnall. Worc 4H 27
Tutshill. Glos 4D 18
Tuttington. Norf 7J 39
Tutts Clump. W Ber 6C 20
Tutwell. Corn 8C 6
Tuxford. Notts 2E 36
Twatt. Orkn 7B 88
Twatt. Shet 2D 90
Twechar. E Dun 2E 58
Tweedale. Telf 1F 26
Tweedbank. Bord 6C 60
Tweedmouth. Nmbd 4G 61
Tweedsmuir. Bord 7J 59
Twelveheads. Corn 4L 3
Twemlow Green. Ches E 3F 34
Twenty. Linc 7J 37
Twerton. Bath 7F 18
Twickenham. G Lon 6J 21
Twigworth. Glos 1G 19
Twineham. W Sus 4K 11
Twinhoe. Bath 8F 18
Twinstead. Essx 8E 30
Twinstead Green. Essx 8E 30
Twiss Green. Warr 8E 40
Twiston. Lanc 3G 41
Twitchen. Devn 2G 7
Twitchen. Shrp 4B 26
Two Bridges. Devn 8F 6
Two Bridges. Glos 3E 18
Two Dales. Derbs 3L 35
Two Gates. Staf 1L 27
Two Mile Oak. Devn 5L 5
Twycross. Leics 1M 27
Twyford. Buck 1D 20
Twyford. Derbs 7M 35
Twyford. Dors 4G 9
Twyford. Hants 3B 10
Twyford. Leics 8E 36
Twyford. Norf 7G 39
Twyford. Wok 6E 20
Twyford Common. Here 8D 26
Twynholm. Dum 6A 52
Twyning. Glos 8G 27
Twyning Green. Glos 8H 27
Twynllanan. Carm 2G 17
Twyn-y-Sheriff. Mon 3C 18
Twywell. Nptn 4G 29
Tyberton. Here 8B 26
Tyburn. W Mid 2K 27
Tyby. Norf 7G 39
Tycroes. Carm 3F 16
Tycrwyn. Powy 1L 25
Tyddewi. Pemb 4D 14
Tydd Gote. Linc 8A 38
Tydd St Giles. Cambs 8M 37
Tydd St Mary. Linc 8M 37
Tye. Hants 5E 10
Tye Green. Essx
nr. Bishop's Stortford 1B 22
nr. Braintree 1D 22
nr. Saffron Walden 8B 30
Tyersal. W Yor 4K 41
Ty Issa. Powy 7L 33
Tyldesley. G Man 7E 40
Tyler Hill. Kent 7H 23
Tyler's Green. Essx 3B 22
Tylers Green. Buck 4F 20
Tylorstown. Rhon 5K 17
Tylwch. Powy 4J 25
Y Tymbl. Carm 5M 15
Tynan. Arm 6E 92
Ty-nant. Cnwy 6J 33
Tyndrum. Stir 4H 65
Tyneham. Dors 7G 9
Tynehead. Midl 4A 60
Tynemouth. Tyne 5G 55
Tyneside. Tyne 5F 54
Tyne Tunnel. Tyne 5G 55
Tynewydd. Rhon 5J 17
Tyninghame. E Lot 2D 60
Tynron. Dum 2C 52
Ty'n-y-bryn. Rhon 6K 17
Tyn-y-celyn. Wrex 7L 33
Tyn-y-cwm. Swan 4F 16
Tyn-y-ffridd. Powy 7L 33
Tynygongl. IOA 2E 32
Tynygraig. Cdgn 6F 24
Ty'n-y-groes. Cnwy 3G 33
Ty'n-yr-eithin. Cdgn 6F 24
Tyn-y-rhyd. Powy 1K 25
Tyn-y-wern. Powy 8K 33
Tyrie. Abers 7J 81
Tyringham. Mil 7F 28
Tythecott. Devn 4D 6
Tythegston. B'end 7H 17
Tytherington. Ches E 2H 35
Tytherington. Som 1F 8
Tytherington. S Glo 5E 18
Tytherington. Wilts 1H 9
Tytherleigh. Devn 5B 8
Tywardreath. Corn 6C 4
Tywardreath Highway. Corn 6C 4
Tywyn. Cnwy 3G 33
Tywyn. Gwyn 2E 24

U

Uachdar. W Isl 8K 75
Uags. High 2J 69
Ubbeston Green. Suff 4K 31
Ubley. Bath 8D 18
Uckerby. N Yor 5L 47
Uckfield. E Sus 3A 12
Uckinghall. Worc 8G 27
Uckington. Glos 1H 19
Uckington. Shrp 1D 26
Uddingston. S Lan 3E 58
Uddington. S Lan 6G 59
Udimore. E Sus 4E 12
Udny Green. Abers 3H 73
Udny Station. Abers 3J 73
Udston. S Lan 4E 58
Udstonhead. S Lan 5F 58
Uffcott. Wilts 6K 19
Uffculme. Devn 4K 7
Uffington. Linc 1H 29
Uffington. Oxon 5M 19
Uffington. Shrp 8D 34
Ufford. Pet 1H 29
Ufford. Suff 6J 31
Ufton. Warw 5A 28
Ufton Nervet. W Ber 7D 20
Ugadale. Arg 7G 57
Ugborough. Devn 6J 5
Ugford. Wilts 2J 9
Uggeshall. Suff 3L 31
Ugglebarnby. N Yor 5F 48
Ugley. Essx 1B 22
Ugley Green. Essx 1B 22
Ugthorpe. N Yor 4E 48
Uidh. W Isl 6C 74
Uig. Arg 2G 63
Uig. High
nr. Balgown 7E 76
nr. Dunvegan 8C 76
Uigshader. High 1F 68
Uisken. Arg 6J 63
Ulbster. High 7E 86
Ulcat Row. Cumb 3C 46
Ulceby. Linc 2M 37
Ulceby. N Lin 6J 43
Ulceby Skitter. N Lin 6J 43
Ulcombe. Kent 1E 12
Uldale. Cumb 8G 53
Uley. Glos 4F 18
Ulgham. Nmbd 2F 54
Ullapool. High 4B 78
Ullenhall. Warw 5K 27
Ulleskelf. N Yor 4C 42
Ullesthorpe. Leics 3C 28
Ulley. S Yor 1B 36
Ullingswick. Here 6D 26
Ullinish. High 2E 68
Ullock. Cumb 2K 45
Ulpha. Cumb 5L 45
Ulrome. E Yor 2J 43
Ulsta. Shet 5J 91
Ulting. Essx 3E 22
Ulva House. Arg 4K 63
Ulverston. Cumb 8A 46
Ulwell. Dors 7J 9
Umberleigh. Devn 3F 6
Unapool. High 8E 84
Underbarrow. Cumb 6C 46
Undercliffe. W Yor 4K 41
Underdale. Shrp 8D 34
Underhoull. Shet 3K 91
Underriver. Kent 8B 22
Under Tofts. S Yor 1M 35
Underton. Shrp 2E 26
Underwood. Newp 5B 18
Underwood. Notts 4B 36
Underwood. Plym 6H 5
Undley. Suff 3C 30
Undy. Mon 5C 18
Union Mills. IOM 7C 44
Union Street. E Sus 2D 12
Unstone. Derbs 2A 36
Unstone Green. Derbs 2A 36
Unthank. Cumb
nr. Carlisle 7H 53
nr. Gamblesby 7L 53
nr. Penrith 8J 53
Unthank End. Cumb 8J 53
Upavon. Wilts 8K 19
Up Cerne. Dors 5E 8
Upchurch. Kent 7E 22
Upcott. Devn 5E 6
Upcott. Here 6B 26
Upend. Cambs 6C 30
Up Exe. Devn 5J 7
Upgate. Norf 8H 39
Upgate Street. Norf 2G 31
Uphall. Dors 5D 8
Uphall. W Lot 2J 59
Uphall Station. W Lot 2J 59
Upham. Devn 5H 7
Upham. Hants 3C 10
Uphampton. Here 5B 26
Uphampton. Worc 5G 27
Up Hatherley. Glos 1H 19
Uphill. N Som 8B 18
Up Holland. Lanc 7D 40
Uplawmoor. E Ren 4C 58
Upleadon. Glos 1F 18
Upleatham. Red C 4D 48
Uplees. Kent 7F 22
Uploders. Dors 6D 8
Uplowman. Devn 4K 7
Uplyme. Devn 6B 8
Up Marden. W Sus 4E 10
Upminster. G Lon 5B 22
Up Nately. Hants 8D 20
Upottery. Devn 5M 7
Uppat. High 3J 79
Upper Affcot. Shrp 3C 26
Upper Arley. Worc 3F 26
Upper Armley. W Yor 4L 41
Upper Arncott. Oxon 2D 20
Upper Astrop. Nptn 8C 28
Upper Badcall. High 7D 84
Upper Ballinderry. Lis 5G 93
Upper Bangor. Gwyn 3E 32
Upper Basildon. W Ber 6C 20
Upper Batley. W Yor 5L 41
Upper Beeding. W Sus 4J 11
Upper Benefield. Nptn 3G 29
Upper Bentley. Worc 5H 27
Upper Bighouse. High 6L 85
Upper Boddam. Abers 2F 72
Upper Boddington. Nptn 6B 28
Upper Bogside. Mor 8B 80
Upper Booth. Derbs 1K 35
Upper Borth. Cdgn 4F 24
Upper Boyndlie. Abers 7J 81
Upper Brailes. Warw 7M 27
Upper Breinton. Here 7C 26
Upper Broughton. Notts 7D 36
Upper Brynamman. Carm 3G 17
Upper Bucklebury. W Ber 7C 20
Upper Bullington. Hants 1B 10
Upper Burgate. Hants 4K 9
Upper Caldecote. C Beds 7J 29
Upper Canterton. Hants 4L 9
Upper Catesby. Nptn 6C 28
Upper Chapel. Powy 8K 25
Upper Cheddon. Som 3M 7
Upper Chicksgrove. Wilts 3H 9
Upper Church Village.
Rhon 6K 17
Upper Chute. Wilts 8L 19
Upper Clatford. Hants 1A 10
Upper Coberley. Glos 2H 19
Upper Coedcae. Torf 3A 18
Upper Cound. Shrp 1D 26
Upper Cudworth. S Yor 7A 42
Upper Cumberworth.
W Yor 7L 41
Upper Cuttlehill. Abers 1D 72
Upper Cwmbran. Torf 4A 18
Upper Dallachy. Mor 7C 80
Upper Dean. Bed 5H 29
Upper Denby. W Yor 7L 41
Upper Derraid. High 2L 71
Upper Diabaig. High 7K 77
Upper Dicker. E Sus 5B 12
Upper Dinchope. Shrp 3C 26
Upper Dochcarty. High 7F 78
Upper Dounreay. High 5A 86
Upper Dovercourt. Essx 8J 31
Upper Dunsforth. N Yor 1B 42
Upper Dunsley. Herts 2G 21
Upper Eastern Green.
W Mid 3L 27
Upper Elkstone. Staf 4J 35
Upper Ellastone. Staf 5K 35
Upper End. Derbs 2J 35
Upper Enham. Hants 1A 10
Upper Farmcote. Shrp 2F 26
Upper Farringdon. Hants 2E 10
Upper Framilode. Glos 2F 18
Upper Froyle. Hants 1E 10
Upper Gills. High 4E 86
Upper Glenfintaig. High 7C 70
Upper Godney. Som 1C 8
Upper Gravenhurst. C Beds 8J 29
Upper Green. Essx 8M 29
Upper Green. W Ber 7A 20
Upper Green. W Yor 5L 41
Upper Grove Common.
Here 1D 18
Upper Hackney. Derbs 3L 35
Upper Hale. Surr 1F 10
Upper Halliford. Surr 7H 21
Upper Halling. Medw 7C 22
Upper Hambleton. Rut 1G 29
Upper Hardres Court.
Kent 8H 23
Upper Hardwick. Here 6C 26
Upper Hartfield. E Sus 2A 12
Upper Haugh. S Yor 8B 42
Upper Hayton. Shrp 3D 26
Upper Heath. Shrp 3D 26
Upper Hellesdon. Norf 8J 39
Upper Helmsley. N Yor 2D 42
Upper Hengoed. Shrp 6A 34
Upper Hergest. Here 6A 26
Upper Heyford. Nptn 6D 28
Upper Heyford. Oxon 1B 20
Upper Hill. Here 6C 26
Upper Hindhope. Bord 1A 54
Upper Hopton. W Yor 6K 41
Upper Howsell. Worc 7F 26
Upper Hulme. Staf 3J 35
Upper Inglesham. Swin 4L 19
Upper Kilcott. S Glo 5F 18
Upper Killay. Swan 5E 16
Upper Kirkton. Abers 2G 73
Upper Kirkton. N Ayr 4L 57
Upper Knockando. Mor 1A 72
Upper Knockchoilum.
High 4E 70
Upper Lambourn. W Ber 5M 19
Upperlands. M Ulst 3F 93
Upper Langford. N Som 8C 18
Upper Langwith. Derbs 3C 36
Upper Largo. Fife 7H 67
Upper Latheron. High 8C 86
Upper Layham. Suff 7G 31
Upper Leigh. Staf 6J 35
Upper Lenie. High 3F 70
Upper Lochton. Abers 6F 72
Upper Longdon. Staf 8J 35
Upper Longwood. Shrp 1E 26
Upper Lybster. High 8D 86
Upper Lydbrook. Glos 2E 18
Upper Lye. Here 5B 26
Upper Maes-coed. Here 8B 26
Upper Midway. Derbs 7L 35
Uppermill. G Man 7H 41
Upper Millichope. Shrp 3D 26
Upper Milovaig. High 1C 68
Upper Minety. Wilts 4J 19
Upper Mitton. Worc 4G 27
Upper Nash. Pemb 6G 15
Upper Neepaback. Shet 5K 91
Upper Netchwood. Shrp 2E 26
Upper Nobut. Staf 6J 35
Upper North Dean. Buck 4F 20
Upper Norwood. W Sus 4G 11
Upper Nyland. Dors 3F 8
Upper Oddington. Glos 1L 19
Upper Ollach. High 2G 69
Upper Outwoods. Staf 7L 35
Upper Padley. Derbs 2L 35
Upper Pennington. Hants 6M 9
Upper Poppleton. York 2C 42
Upper Quinton. Warw 7K 27
Upper Rissington. Glos 2L 19
Upper Rochford. Worc 5E 26
Upper Rusko. Dum 5L 51
Upper Sandaig. High 4J 69
Upper Sanday. Orkn 1G 87
Upper Sapey. Here 5E 26
Upper Seagry. Wilts 5H 19
Upper Shelton. C Beds 7G 29
Upper Sheringham. Norf 5H 39
Upper Skelmorlie. N Ayr 3L 57
Upper Slaughter. Glos 1K 19
Upper Sonachan. Arg 5E 64
Upper Soudley. Glos 2E 18
Upper Staploe. Bed 6J 29
Upper Stoke. Norf 1J 31
Upper Stondon. C Beds 8J 29
Upper Stowe. Nptn 6D 28
Upper Street. Hants 4K 9
Upper Street. Norf
nr. Horning 8K 39
nr. Hoveton 8K 39
Upper Street. Suff 8H 31
Upper Strensham. Worc 8H 27
Upper Studley. Wilts 8G 19
Upper Sundon. C Beds 1H 21
Upper Swell. Glos 1K 19
Upper Tankersley. S Yor 8M 41
Upper Tean. Staf 6J 35
Upperthong. W Yor 7K 41
Upperthorpe. N Lin 7E 42
Upper Thurnham. Lanc 2C 40
Upper Tillyrie. Per 7E 66
Upperton. W Sus 3G 11
Upper Tooting. G Lon 6K 21
Upper Town. Derbs
nr. Bonsall 4L 35
nr. Hognaston 4L 35
Upper Town. Here 7D 26
Upper Town. N Som 7D 18
Uppertown. Derbs 3M 35
Uppertown. High 4E 86
Uppertown. Nmbd 4B 54
Uppertown. Orkn 2F 86
Upper Tysoe. Warw 7M 27
Upper Upham. Wilts 6L 19
Upper Upnor. Medw 6D 22
Upper Urquhart. Fife 7E 66
Upper Wardington. Oxon 7B 28
Upper Weald. Mil 8E 28
Upper Weedon. Nptn 6D 28
Upper Wellingham. E Sus 4M 11
Upper Whiston. S Yor 1B 36
Upper Wield. Hants 2D 10
Upper Winchendon.
Buck 2E 20
Upperwood. Derbs 4L 35
Upper Woodford. Wilts 2K 9
Upper Wootton. Hants 8C 20
Upper Wraxall. Wilts 6G 19
Upper Wyche. Worc 7F 26
Uppincott. Devn 5H 7
Uppingham. Rut 2F 28
Uppington. Shrp 1E 26
Upsall. N Yor 7B 48
Upsettlington. Bord 5F 60
Upshire. Essx 3M 21
Up Somborne. Hants 2A 10
Upstreet. Kent 7J 23
Up Sydling. Dors 5E 8
Upthorpe. Suff 4F 30
Upton. Buck 2E 20
Upton. Cambs 4J 29
Upton. Ches W 3C 34
Upton. Corn
nr. Bude 5B 6
nr. Liskeard 8B 6
Upton. Cumb 8H 53
Upton. Devn
nr. Honiton 5K 7
nr. Kingsbridge 7K 5
Upton. Dors
nr. Poole 6H 9
nr. Weymouth 7F 8
Upton. E Yor 2J 43
Upton. Hants
nr. Andover 8A 20
nr. Southampton 4A 10
Upton. IOW 6C 10
Upton. Leics 2A 28
Upton. Linc 1F 36
Upton. Mers 1A 34
Upton. Norf 8K 39
Upton. Nptn 5E 28
Upton. Notts
nr. Retford 2E 36
nr. Southwell 4E 36
Upton. Oxon 5C 20
Upton. Pemb 6G 15
Upton. Pet 1J 29
Upton. Slo 6G 21
Upton. Som
nr. Somerton 3C 8
nr. Wiveliscombe 3J 7
Upton. Warw 6K 27
Upton. W Yor 6B 42
Upton. Wilts 2G 9
Upton Bishop. Here 1E 18
Upton Cheyney. S Glo 7E 18
Upton Cressett. Shrp 2E 26
Upton Crews. Here 1E 18
Upton Cross. Corn 8B 6
Upton End. C Beds 8J 29
Upton Grey. Hants 1D 10
Upton Heath. Ches W 3C 34
Upton Hellions. Devn 5H 7
Upton Lovell. Wilts 1H 9
Upton Magna. Shrp 8D 34
Upton Noble. Som 2F 8
Upton Pyne. Devn 6J 7
Upton St Leonards. Glos 2G 19
Upton Scudamore. Wilts 1G 9
Upton Snodsbury. Worc 6H 27
Upton upon Severn. Worc 7G 27
Upton Warren. Worc 5H 27
Upwaltham. W Sus 4G 11
Upware. Cambs 4B 30
Upwell. Norf 1B 30
Upwey. Dors 7E 8
Upwick Green. Herts 1A 22
Upwood. Cambs 3K 29
Urafirth. Shet 6H 91
Uragaig. Arg 8J 63
Urchany. High 1J 71
Urchfont. Wilts 8J 19
Urdimarsh. Here 7D 26
Ure. Shet 6G 91
Ure Bank. N Yor 8M 47
Urgha. W Isl 4C 76
Urlay Nook. Stoc T 4B 48
Urmston. G Man 8F 40
Urquhart. Mor 7B 80
Urra. N Yor 5C 48
Urray. High 8F 78
Usan. Ang 2L 67
Ushaw Moor. Dur 7F 54
Usk. Mon 3B 18
Usselby. Linc 8H 43
Usworth. Tyne 6G 55
Utkinton. Ches W 3D 34
Uton. Devn 6H 7
Utterby. Linc 8L 43
Uttoxeter. Staf 6J 35
Uwchmynydd. Gwyn 8A 32
Uxbridge. G Lon 5H 21
Uyeasound. Shet 3K 91
Uzmaston. Pemb 5F 14

V

Valley. IOA 3B 32
Valley End. Surr 7G 21
Valley Truckle. Corn 3D 4
Valsgarth. Shet 2L 91
Valtos. High 7G 77
Van. Powy 4J 25
Vange. Essx 5D 22
Varteg. Torf 3A 18
Vatsetter. Shet 5K 91
Vatten. High 1D 68
Vaul. Arg 3F 62
The Vauld. Here 7D 26
Vaynor. Mer T 3K 17
Veensgarth. Shet 3E 90
Velindre. Powy 1L 17
Vellow. Som 2K 7
Velly. Devn 3B 6
Veness. Orkn 7E 88
Venhay. Devn 4G 7
Venn. Devn 7K 5
Venngreen. Devn 4C 6
Vennington. Shrp 1B 26
Venn Ottery. Devn 6K 7
Venn's Green. Here 7D 26
Venny Tedburn. Devn 6H 7
Venterdon. Corn 8C 6
Ventnor. IOW 8C 10
Vernham Dean. Hants 8M 19
Vernham Street. Hants 8M 19
Vernolds Common. Shrp 3C 26
Verwood. Dors 5J 9
Veryan. Corn 8B 4
Veryan Green. Corn 8B 4
Vicarage. Devn 7M 7
Vickerstown. Cumb 8L 45
Victoria. Corn 5B 4
Victoria Bridge. Derr 4C 92
Vidlin. Shet 1E 90
Viewpark. N Lan 3F 58
Vigo. W Mid 1J 27
Vigo Village. Kent 7C 22
Vinehall Street. E Sus 3D 12
Vine's Cross. E Sus 4B 12
Viney Hill. Glos 3E 18
Virginia Water. Surr 7G 21
Virginstow. Devn 6C 6
Vobster. Som 1F 8
Voe. Shet
nr. Hillside 1E 90
nr. Swinister 5H 91
Vole. Som 1B 8
Vowchurch. Here 8B 26
Voxter. Shet 6H 91
Voy. Orkn 8B 88
Vulcan Village. Mers 8D 40

W

Waberthwaite. Cumb 5L 45
Wackerfield. Dur 3K 47
Wacton. Norf 2H 31
Wadbister. Shet 3E 90
Wadborough. Worc 7H 27
Wadbrook. Devn 5B 8
Waddesdon. Buck 2E 20
Waddeton. Devn 6L 5
Waddicar. Mers 8B 40
Waddingham. Linc 8G 43
Waddington. Lanc 3F 40
Waddington. Linc 3G 37
Waddon. Devn 8H 7
Wadebridge. Corn 4B 4
Wadeford. Som 4B 8
Wadenhoe. Nptn 3H 29
Wadesmill. Herts 2L 21
Wadhurst. E Sus 2C 12
Wadshelf. Derbs 2M 35
Wadsley. S Yor 8M 41
Wadsley Bridge. S Yor 8M 41
Wadswick. Wilts 7G 19
Wadwick. Hants 8B 20
Wadworth. S Yor 8C 42
Waen. Den
nr. Llandymog 4L 33
nr. Nantglyn 4J 33
Waen. Powy 3J 25
Waen Fach. Powy 1M 25
Waen Goleugoed. Den 3K 33
Wag. High 1L 79
Wainfleet All Saints. Linc 4A 38
Wainfleet Bank. Linc 4A 38
Wainfleet St Mary. Linc 4A 38
Wainhouse Corner. Corn 6A 6
Wainscott. Medw 6D 22
Wainstalls. W Yor 5J 41
Waitby. Cumb 5F 46
Waithe. Linc 7K 43
Wakefield. W Yor 5M 41
Wakerley. Nptn 2G 29
Wakes Colne. Essx 1E 22
Walberswick. Suff 4L 31
Walberton. W Sus 5G 11
Walbottle. Tyne 5E 54
Walby. Cumb 5J 53
Walcombe. Som 1D 8
Walcot. Linc 6H 37
Walcot. N Lin 5F 42
Walcot. Swin 5K 19
Walcot. Telf 8D 34
Walcot. Warw 6K 27
Walcote. Leics 3C 28
Walcot Green. Norf 3H 31
Walcott. Linc 4J 37
Walcott. Norf 6K 39
Walden. N Yor 7J 47
Walden Head. N Yor 7H 47
Walden Stubbs. N Yor 6C 42
Walderslade. Medw 7D 22
Walderton. W Sus 4E 10
Walditch. Dors 6C 8
Waldley. Derbs 6K 35
Waldridge. Dur 6F 54
Waldringfield. Suff 7J 31
Waldron. E Sus 4B 12
Wales. S Yor 1B 36
Walesby. Linc 8J 43
Walesby. Notts 2D 36
Walford. Here
nr. Leintwardine 4B 26
nr. Ross-on-Wye 1D 18
Walford. Shrp 7C 34
Walford. Staf 6G 35
Walford Heath. Shrp 8C 34
Walgherton. Ches E 5E 34
Walgrave. Nptn 4F 28
Walhampton. Hants 6M 9
Walkden. G Man 7F 40
Walker. Tyne 5F 54
Walkerburn. Bord 6A 60
Walker Fold. Lanc 3E 40
Walkeringham. Notts 8E 42
Walkerith. Linc 8E 42
Walkern. Herts 1K 21
Walker's Green. Here 7D 26
Walkerton. Fife 7F 66
Walkerville. N Yor 6L 47
Walkford. Dors 6L 9
Walkhampton. Devn 5H 5
Walkington. E Yor 4G 43
Walkley. S Yor 1M 35
Walk Mill. Lanc 4G 41
Wall. Corn 5K 3
Wall. Nmbd 5C 54
Wall. Staf 1K 27
Wallaceton. Dum 3C 52
Wallacetown. Shet 2D 90
Wallacetown. S Ayr
nr. Ayr 7B 58
nr. Dailly 1H 51
Wallands Park. E Sus 4M 11
Wallasey. Mers 8A 40
Wallaston Green. Pemb 6F 14
Wallbrook. W Mid 2H 27
Wallcrouch. E Sus 2C 12
Wall End. Cumb 6M 45
Wallend. Medw 6E 22
Wall Heath. W Mid 3G 27
Wallingford. Oxon 5D 20
Wallington. G Lon 7K 21
Wallington. Hants 5C 10
Wallington. Herts 8K 29
Wallis. Pemb 4G 15
Wallisdown. Bour 6J 9
Walliswood. Surr 2J 11
Wall Nook. Dur 7F 54
Walls. Shet 3C 90
Wallsend. Tyne 5G 55
Wallsworth. Glos 1G 19
Wall under Heywood. Shrp 2D 26
Wallyford. E Lot 2A 60
Walmer. Kent 8K 23
Walmer Bridge. Lanc 5C 40
Walmersley. G Man 6G 41
Walmley. W Mid 2K 27
Walnut Grove. Per 5E 66
Walpole. Suff 4K 31
Walpole Cross Keys. Norf 8B 38
Walpole Gate. Norf 8B 38
Walpole Highway. Norf 8B 38
Walpole Marsh. Norf 8A 38
Walpole St Andrew. Norf 8B 38
Walpole St Peter. Norf 8B 38
Walsall. W Mid 2J 27
Walsall Wood. W Mid 1J 27
Walsden. W Yor 5H 41
Walsgrave on Sowe.
W Mid 3A 28
Walsham le Willows. Suff 4G 31
Walshaw. G Man 6F 40
Walshford. N Yor 2B 42
Walsoken. Norf 8A 38
Walston. S Lan 5J 59
Walsworth. Herts 8J 29
Walter's Ash. Buck 4F 20
Walterston. V Glam 7K 17
Walterstone. Here 1B 18
Waltham. Kent 1H 13
Waltham. NE Lin 7K 43
Waltham Abbey. Essx 3L 21
Waltham Chase. Hants 4C 10
Waltham Cross. Herts 3L 21
Waltham on the Wolds.
Leics 7F 36
Waltham St Lawrence.
Wind 6F 20
Waltham's Cross. Essx 8C 30
Walthamstow. G Lon 5L 21
Walton. Cumb 5K 53
Walton. Derbs 3A 36
Walton. Leics 3C 28
Walton. Mers 8B 40
Walton. Mil 8F 28
Walton. Pet 1J 29
Walton. Powy 6A 26
Walton. Som 2C 8
Walton. Staf
nr. Eccleshall 7G 35
nr. Stone 6G 35
Walton. Suff 8J 31
Walton. Telf 8D 34
Walton. Warw 6L 27
Walton. W Yor
nr. Wakefield 6A 42
nr. Wetherby 3B 42
Walton Cardiff. Glos 8H 27
Walton East. Pemb 4G 15
Walton Elm. Dors 4F 8
Walton Highway. Norf 8A 38
Walton in Gordano. N Som 6C 18
Walton-le-Dale. Lanc 5D 40
Walton-on-Thames. Surr 7J 21
Walton on the Hill. Surr 8K 21
Walton-on-the-Hill. Staf 7H 35
Walton-on-the-Naze. Essx 1J 23
Walton on the Wolds. Leics 8C 36
Walton-on-Trent. Derbs 8L 35
Walton West. Pemb 5E 14
Walwick. Nmbd 4C 54
Walworth. Darl 4L 47
Walworth Gate. Darl 3L 47
Walwyn's Castle. Pemb 5E 14
Wambrook. Som 5A 8
Wampool. Cumb 6G 53
Wanborough. Surr 1G 11
Wanborough. Swin 5L 19
Wandel. S Lan 7H 59
Wandsworth. G Lon 6K 21
Wangford. Suff
nr. Lakenheath 3D 30
nr. Southwold 4L 31
Wanlip. Leics 8C 36
Wanlockhead. Dum 8G 59
Wannock. E Sus 5B 12
Wansford. E Yor 2H 43
Wansford. Pet 2H 29
Wanshurst Green. Kent 1D 12
Wanstead. G Lon 5M 21
Wanstrow. Som 1F 8
Wanswell. Glos 3E 18
Wantage. Oxon 5B 20
Wapley. S Glo 6F 18
Wappenbury. Warw 5A 28
Wappenham. Nptn 7D 28
Warbleton. E Sus 4C 12
Warblington. Hants 5E 10
Warborough. Oxon 4C 20
Warboys. Cambs 3L 29
Warbreck. Bkpl 4B 40
Warbstow. Corn 6B 6
Warburton. G Man 1F 34
Warcop. Cumb 4F 46
Warden. Kent 6G 23
Warden. Nmbd 5C 54
Ward End. W Mid 3K 27
Ward Green. Suff 5G 31
Ward Green Cross. Lanc 4E 40
Wardhedges. C Beds 8H 29
Wardhouse. Abers 2E 72
Wardington. Oxon 7B 28
Wardle. Ches E 4E 34
Wardle. G Man 6H 41
Wardley. Rut 1F 28
Wardley. W Sus 3F 10
Wardlow. Derbs 2K 35
Wardsend. Ches E 1H 35
Wardy Hill. Cambs 3A 30
Ware. Herts 2L 21
Ware. Kent 7J 23
Wareham. Dors 7H 9
Warehorne. Kent 2F 12
Warenford. Nmbd 7J 61
Waren Mill. Nmbd 6J 61
Warenton. Nmbd 6J 61
Wareside. Herts 2L 21
Waresley. Cambs 6K 29
Waresley. Worc 5G 27
Warfield. Brac 6F 20
Warfleet. Devn 6L 5
Wargate. Linc 6K 37
Wargrave. Wok 6E 20
Warham. Norf 5F 38
Waringsford. Arm 6H 93
Waringstown. Arm 6G 93
Wark. Nmbd
nr. Coldstream 6F 60
nr. Hexham 4B 54
Warkleigh. Devn 3F 6
Warkton. Nptn 4F 28
Warkworth. Nptn 7B 28
Warkworth. Nmbd 1F 54
Warlaby. N Yor 6M 47
Warland. W Yor 5H 41
Warleggan. Corn 5D 4
Warlingham. Surr 8L 21
Warmanbie. Dum 5F 52
Warmfield. W Yor 5A 42
Warmingham. Ches E 3F 34
Warminghurst. W Sus 4J 11
Warmington. Nptn 2H 29
Warmington. Warw 7B 28
Warminster. Wilts 1G 9
Warmley. S Glo 6E 18
Warmsworth. S Yor 7C 42
Warmwell. Dors 7F 8
Warndon. Worc 6G 27
Warners End. Herts 3H 21
Warnford. Hants 3D 10
Warnham. W Sus 2J 11
Warningcamp. W Sus 5H 11
Warninglid. W Sus 3K 11
Warren. Ches E 2G 35
Warren. Pemb 7F 14
Warrenby. Red C 3C 48
Warren Corner. Hants
nr. Aldershot 1F 10
nr. Petersfield 3E 10
Warrenpoint. New M 7G 93
Warren Row. Wind 5F 20
Warren Street. Kent 8F 22
Warrington. Mil 6F 28
Warrington. Warr 1E 34
Warsash. Hants 5B 10
Warse. High 4E 86
Warslow. Staf 4J 35
Warsop. Notts 3C 36
Warsop Vale. Notts 3C 36
Warter. E Yor 2F 42
Warthermarske. N Yor 8L 47
Warthill. N Yor 2D 42
Wartling. E Sus 5C 12
Wartnaby. Leics 7E 36
Warton. Lanc
nr. Carnforth 8C 46
nr. Freckleton 5C 40
Warton. Nmbd 1D 54
Warton. Warw 1L 27
Warwick. Warw 5L 27
Warwick Bridge. Cumb 6J 53
Warwick-on-Eden. Cumb 6J 53
Warwick Wold. Surr 8L 21
Wasbister. Orkn 6C 88
Wasdale Head. Cumb 4L 45
Wash. Derbs 1J 35
Washaway. Corn 5C 4
Washbourne. Devn 6K 5
Washbrook. Suff 7H 31
Wash Common. W Ber 7B 20
Washerwall. Staf 5H 35
Washfield. Devn 4J 7
Washfold. N Yor 5J 47
Washford. Som 1K 7
Washford Pyne. Devn 4H 7
Washingborough. Linc 2H 37
Washington. Tyne 6G 55
Washington. W Sus 4J 11
Washington Village. Tyne 6G 55
Waskerley. Dur 7D 54
Wasperton. Warw 6L 27
Wasp Green. Surr 1L 11
Wasps Nest. Linc 3H 37
Wass. N Yor 8C 48
Watchet. Som 1K 7
Watchfield. Oxon 4L 19
Watchgate. Cumb 6D 46
Watchhill. Cumb 7F 52
Watcombe. Torb 5M 5
Watendlath. Cumb 4A 46
Water. Devn 7G 7
Water. Lanc 5G 41
Waterbeach. Cambs 5A 30
Waterbeach. W Sus 5F 10
Waterbeck. Dum 4G 53
Waterditch. Hants 6K 9
Water End. C Beds 8H 29
Water End. E Yor 4E 42
Water End. Essx 7B 30
Water End. Herts
nr. Hatfield 3K 21
nr. Hemel Hempstead 2H 21
Waterfall. Staf 4J 35
Waterfoot. Caus 2H 93
Waterfoot. E Ren 4D 58
Waterfoot. Lanc 5G 41
Waterford. Herts 2L 21
Water Fryston. W Yor 5B 42
Waterhead. Cumb 5B 46
Waterhead. E Ayr 8D 58
Waterhead. S Ayr 2J 51
Waterheads. Bord 4L 59
Waterhouses. Dur 7E 54
Waterhouses. Staf 4J 35
Wateringbury. Kent 8C 22
Waterlane. Glos 3H 19
Waterlip. Som 1E 8
Waterloo. Cphy 6L 17
Waterloo. Corn 4D 4
Waterloo. Here 7B 26
Waterloo. High 3H 69
Waterloo. Mers 8B 40
Waterloo. Norf 8J 39
Waterloo. N Lan 4G 59
Waterloo. Pemb 6F 14
Waterloo. Per 4D 66
Waterloo. Pool 6J 9
Waterloo. Shrp 6C 34
Waterlooville. Hants 5D 10
Watermead. Buck 2F 20
Watermillock. Cumb 3C 46
Water Newton. Cambs 2J 29
Water Orton. Warw 2K 27
Waterperry. Oxon 3D 20
Waterrow. Som 3K 7
Watersfield. W Sus 4H 11
Waterside. Buck 3G 21
Waterside. Cambs 4C 30
Waterside. Cumb 7G 53
Waterside. E Ayr
nr. Ayr 1K 51
nr. Kilmarnock 5C 58
Waterside. E Dun 2E 58
Waterstein. High 1C 68
Waterstock. Oxon 3D 20
Waterston. Pemb 6F 14
Water Stratford. Buck 8D 28
Waters Upton. Telf 8E 34
Water Yeat. Cumb 7A 46
Watford. Herts 4J 21
Watford. Nptn 5D 28
Wath. Cumb 5E 46
Wath. N Yor
nr. Pateley Bridge 1K 41
nr. Ripon 8M 47
Wath Brow. Cumb 3K 45
Wath upon Dearne. S Yor 7B 42
Watlington. Norf 8C 38
Watlington. Oxon 4D 20
Watten. High 6D 86
Wattisfield. Suff 4G 31
Wattisham. Suff 6G 31
Wattlesborough Heath.
Shrp 8B 34
Watton. Dors 6C 8
Watton. E Yor 2H 43
Watton. Norf 1F 30
Watton at Stone. Herts 2K 21
Wattston. N Lan 2F 58
Wattstown. Rhon 5K 17
Wattsville. Cphy 5M 17
Wauldby. E Yor 5G 43
Waulkmill. Abers 6F 72
Waun. Powy 1M 25
Y Waun. Wrex 6A 34
Waunarlwydd. Swan 5F 16
Waun Fawr. Cdgn 4F 24
Waunfawr. Gwyn 5E 32
Waungilwen. Carm 3K 15
Waun-Lwyd. Blae 4L 17
Waun y Clyn. Carm 6L 15
Wavendon. Mil 8G 29
Waverbridge. Cumb 7G 53
Waverley. Surr 1F 10
Waverton. Ches W 3C 34
Waverton. Cumb 7G 53
Wavertree. Mers 1B 34
Wawne. E Yor 4H 43
Waxham. Norf 7L 39
Waxholme. E Yor 5L 43
Wayford. Som 5C 8
Way Head. Cambs 3A 30
Waytown. Dors 6C 8
Way Village. Devn 4H 7
Wdig. Pemb 3F 14
Wealdstone. G Lon 5J 21
Weardley. W Yor 3L 41
Weare. Som 8C 18
Weare Giffard. Devn 3D 6
Wearhead. Dur 8B 54
Wearne. Som 3C 8
Weasdale. Cumb 5E 46
Weasenham All Saints.
Norf 7E 38
Weasenham St Peter. Norf 7E 38
Weaverham. Ches W 2E 34
Weaverthorpe. N Yor 8G 49
Webheath. Worc 5J 27
Webton. Here 8C 26
Wedderlairs. Abers 2H 73
Weddington. Warw 2A 28
Wedhampton. Wilts 8J 19
Wedmore. Som 1C 8
Wednesbury. W Mid 2H 27
Wednesfield. W Mid 1H 27
Weecar. Notts 3F 36
Weedon. Buck 2F 20
Weedon Bec. Nptn 6D 28
Weedon Lois. Nptn 7D 28
Weeford. Staf 1K 27
Week. Devn
nr. Barnstaple 3E 6
nr. Okehampton 5F 6
nr. South Molton 4G 7
nr. Totnes 5K 5
Week. Som 2J 7
Weeke. Devn 5G 7
Weeke. Hants 2B 10
Week Green. Corn 6B 6
Weekley. Nptn 3F 28
Week St Mary. Corn 6B 6
Weel. E Yor 4H 43
Weeley. Essx 1H 23
Weeley Heath. Essx 1H 23
Weem. Per 3B 66
Weeping Cross. Staf 7H 35
Weethly. Warw 6J 27
Weeting. Norf 3D 30
Weeton. E Yor 5L 43
Weeton. Lanc 4B 40
Weeton. N Yor 3L 41
Weetwood Hall. Nmbd 7H 61
Weir. Lanc 5G 41
Welborne. Norf 8G 39
Welbourn. Linc 4G 37
Welburn. N Yor
nr. Kirkbymoorside 7D 48
nr. Malton 1E 42
Welbury. N Yor 5A 48
Welby. Linc 6G 37
Welches Dam. Cambs 3A 30
Welcombe. Devn 4B 6
Weld Bank. Lanc 6D 40
Weldon. Nptn 3G 29
Weldon. Nmbd 2E 54
Welford. Nptn 3D 28
Welford. W Ber 6B 20
Welford-on-Avon. Warw 6K 27

INDEX TO SELECTED PLACES OF INTEREST

(1) A strict alphabetical order is used e.g. Benmore Botanic Gdn. follows Ben Macdui but precedes Ben Nevis.

(2) Places of Interest which fall on City and Town Centre maps are referenced first to the detailed map page, followed by the main map page if appropriate. The name of the map is included if it is not clear from the index entry.
e.g. Ashmolean Mus. of Art & Archaeology (OX1 2PH) . . . . Oxford 114 (3C 20)

(3) Entries in italics are not named on the map but are shown with a symbol only.
e.g. Aberdour Castle (KY3 0XA) 1K 59

SAT NAV POSTCODES

Postcodes are shown to assist Sat Nav users and are included on this basis.
It should be noted that postcodes have been selected by their proximity to the Place of Interest and that they may not form part of the actual postal address. Drivers should follow the Tourist Brown Signs when available.

ABBREVIATIONS USED IN THIS INDEX

Centre : Cen.   Garden : Gdn.   Gardens : Gdns.   Museum : Mus.   National : Nat.   Park : Pk.